"For decades my ministry has been greatly impacted by the expository excellence, shepherding care, and gospel-centered teachings and writings of James Montgomery Boice. Written with a pastoral tone, *Foundations of the Christian Faith* is a beautiful and timeless systematic volume that provides a comprehensive education on biblical doctrines with clarity and practicality. This is a most helpful theological resource for all readers, as it elevates Christ and Scripture."

Doug Logan Jr., director of diversity and codirector of Church in Hard Places with Acts 29, author of *On the Block*

"Republication of *Foundations of the Christian Faith* by James Montgomery Boice, the superlative minister of Tenth Presbyterian Church, will surely be welcomed by scholars and serious students of the Bible. This classic overview of Christian faith is a masterful balance of often opposing qualities. It is simultaneously comprehensive yet readable. It is accessible for serious believers, seeking college students, and newcomers to the faith. It is warmly pastoral yet theologically rich. It is theologically Calvinistic and trinitarian but above all focused on Scripture. Herein, ancient truth illuminates contemporary life. This monumental harvest of Dr. Boice's ministry belongs in every serious Christian's study."

Peter A. Lillback, president, Westminster Theological Seminary, Philadelphia

"James Boice was the best preacher I've known, but he was also a major figure in the defense of the faith against liberalism. Widely educated, he was always consumed with a passion to proclaim God's word rather than flatter the academy. This is a learned but also pastoral theology, practical because it feeds the sheep with the rich pastures of Scripture. I'm so glad that this one-volume edition is being made available to a new audience! Read, mark, learn, and inwardly digest this feast of the soul."

Michael Horton, J. Gresham Machen Professor of Systematic Theology and Apologetics, Westminster Seminary California

"*Foundations of the Christian Faith* is one resource that every church and family should own. It's one of the best summaries of Christian doctrine—with a highly accessible format and pastoral tone—that modern Protestantism has ever produced. Dr. Boice left a theological legacy in this volume that will endure for generations to come as a deep dive into the theology of grace and one that encourages us all to remain committed to 'the faith that was once for all delivered to the saints.'"

Anthony B. Bradley, professor and chair of religious and theological studies, The King's College

"My original copy of James Montgomery Boice's *Foundations of the Christian Faith* is worn out. It was extremely helpful to me as a pastor not simply as a reference book but as a rich readable theology, the fruit of his own preaching ministry. I am delighted to see this volume reissued. It is Boice at his best."

Donald W. Sweeting, president, Colorado Christian University

"I miss his voice. As a pastor headed home from my own church service, I would many times have the privilege of listening to James Montgomery Boice on the radio. Through his wise and pastoral teaching, I knew that Dr. Boice desired to bring glory to God and also draw people to Christ. *Foundations of the Christian Faith* is a significant one-volume resource that weaves biblical material, orthodox theology, and pastoral insights for all those interested in rooting their faith in God's revelation. This revised and expanded edition of his classic work allows Dr. Boice's voice to be heard again and invites us into the conversation with a trusted friend by way of new study guides that will help individuals, groups, and churches deepen their understanding of God and this world that he so loves. Through this volume, you and I can still hear the voice of Dr. Boice and be blessed by this servant of God."

Jul Medenblik, president of Calvin Theological Seminary, Grand Rapids, Michigan

"The proper home of theology is not the classroom but the church, and theologians serve the church best when they help its members think and speak about God rightly. James Montgomery Boice understood the importance of theology, and this book bears witness to a life spent in service to the church. Boice presents complicated doctrines with clarity, and he always pays close attention both to Scripture and the Christian tradition. His writing is accessible and pastorally sensitive, and he displays a deep concern for the needs of everyday believers. This book should be in every pastor's study. It would make an excellent graduation gift, could serve as the basis for rich small group discussions, and would enrich the work of academics from a variety of disciplines. It has endured the test of time for good reason, and it will continue to enrich the church wherever it is read."

Keith L. Johnson, associate professor of theology, Wheaton College

FOUNDATIONS
of the
CHRISTIAN
FAITH

REVISED *&* EXPANDED

A Comprehensive & Readable Theology

James Montgomery Boice

FOREWORD BY **PHILIP RYKEN**

An imprint of InterVarsity Press
Downers Grove, Illinois

InterVarsity Press
P.O. Box 1400, Downers Grove, IL 60515-1426
ivpress.com
email@ivpress.com

Second edition ©2019 by InterVarsity Christian Fellowship/USA.
First edition ©1986 by InterVarsity Christian Fellowship/USA.
Original four-volume edition ©1978, 1979, 1981 by InterVarsity Christian Fellowship of the United States of America.

InterVarsity Press® is the book-publishing division of InterVarsity Christian Fellowship/USA®, a movement of students and faculty active on campus at hundreds of universities, colleges, and schools of nursing in the United States of America, and a member movement of the International Fellowship of Evangelical Students. For information about local and regional activities, visit intervarsity.org.

Scripture quotations, unless otherwise noted, are from the ESV® Bible (The Holy Bible, English Standard Version®), copyright 2001 by Crossway, a publishing ministry of Good News Publishers. Used by permission. All rights reserved.

Acknowledgment is made to the following for permission to reprint copyrighted material:
From Body Life by Ray C. Stedman. © 1972. Regal Books, Ventura, CA 93006.
From "Deacons, the Neglected Ministry." The Presbyterian Journal, 8 (November 1978): 9. Used by permission of the author, George C. Fuller.

Cover design: David Fassett
Interior design: Daniel van Loon
Images: Jesus' crucifixion: © Jesus: Crucifixion, miniature, France 13th-14th Century. / De Agostini Picture Library / G. Dagli Orti / Bridgeman Images
        blue grunge texture: © belterz / E+ / Getty Images

ISBN 978-0-8308-5214-7 (print)
ISBN 978-0-8308-7409-5 (digital)

Printed in the United States of America ∞

Library of Congress Cataloging-in-Publication Data
Names: Boice, James Montgomery, 1938-2000, author.
Title: Foundations of the Christian faith : a comprehensive & readable theology / James Montgomery Boice ; foreword by Philip Ryken.
Description: Revised and Expanded [edition]. | Westmont : InterVarsity Press, 2018. | Includes index.
Identifiers: LCCN 2018045277 (print) | LCCN 2018047011 (ebook) | ISBN 9780830874095 (eBook) | ISBN 9780830852147 (hardcover : alk. paper)
Subjects: LCSH: Theology, Doctrinal.
Classification: LCC BT75.3 (ebook) | LCC BT75.3 .B65 2018 (print) | DDC 230/.51—dc23
LC record available at https://lccn.loc.gov/2018045277

| P | 25 | 24 | 23 | 22 | 21 | 20 | 19 | 18 | 17 | 16 | 15 | 14 | 13 | 12 | 11 | 10 | 9 | 8 | 7 | 6 | 5 | 4 | 3 | 2 | 1 |
| Y | 37 | 36 | 35 | 34 | 33 | 32 | 31 | 30 | 29 | 28 | 27 | 26 | 25 | 24 | 23 | 22 | 21 | 20 | 19 | | | | | | |

To him whom to know is life eternal

CONTENTS

BOOK 4~GOD *and* HISTORY

FOREWORD
Philip Ryken

Over the course of the forty years or so since it was first published, this book by James Montgomery Boice has become something of a classic. Many Christians have come to a deeper understanding of biblical doctrine—and a closer relationship with Jesus Christ—by reading its pages and carefully studying its profound truths.

Dr. Boice served for thirty-two years (from 1968 until his death in 2000) as the senior minister of Tenth Presbyterian Church, a historic congregation near the heart of Center City, Philadelphia. As you will learn from the book's preface, each chapter was first preached to Tenth's large, multiethnic, multigenerational congregation. This context helps to explain the book's warmly personal and pastoral tone. Dr. Boice was trying to help the people under his spiritual care grow in the love and knowledge of Jesus Christ. But as he edited his sermons for publication, he also had college students in mind. He wanted to write a complete basic course in Christian theology that would serve as a foundation for a lifetime of service in the church and witness to the world.

The overall structure of *Foundations of the Christian Faith* is trinitarian. The first three major sections of the book (originally published separately and widely read by students in InterVarsity and other campus fellowships in the late 1970s and 1980s) offer basic teaching on God the Father, God the Son, and God the Holy Spirit, with the fourth and final section addressing the work of the church and the work of God throughout human history (and on into eternity). Most of the chapters are based on a particular Bible passage. By taking this approach,

Boice produced a book that is theologically comprehensive, addressing most major topics in Christian doctrine, and at the same time thoroughly biblical, helping readers understand and apply scriptural teaching to daily life.

The best way to get the most out of *Foundations of the Christian Faith* is to read it from start to finish. But the book's coherent structure and clear chapter titles also make it useful as a theological reference book whenever questions arise about particular points of Christian doctrine. It is not primarily for learned theologians but for ordinary people who are serious about their faith and want to become better theologians and better Christians.

Perhaps you would like to know more about what kind of person James Boice was and what kind of pastor he became. We served together in ministry for five years at Tenth Church, and although other people knew him much better than I, we worked closely enough for me to have a good sense of the man.

The first and most important thing to say is that Dr. Boice's life was squarely focused on God and what God said in his Word, especially about salvation in Jesus Christ. For that reason, you will not find many personal stories in this book. Dr. Boice was more interested in drawing worship to Christ than in calling attention to himself.

Dr. Boice was learned enough to be a serious scholar, but he also had a rare gift for taking complex topics and making them clear enough for most people to understand. He was definitely a Calvinist in the best sense of that word: he believed strongly in the sovereignty of God and the absolute graciousness of God in salvation, as John Calvin did. As a result, he was very joyful in public worship, often smiling as he preached or as he sang his favorite hymns in church. In fact, one of my clearest memories of Dr. Boice is seeing him smile broadly when he heard me preach—not because my sermons were especially good (or funny), but because he regarded them as faithful to God's Word, which was his primary passion. This passion fueled his popular radio broadcast, "The Bible Study Hour," which has attracted devoted listeners across the United States and beyond.

James Boice was deeply committed to the city—specifically, to God's work in the city of Philadelphia. Together with his wife, Linda, he not only raised three beautiful daughters in the city but also founded a Christian school there that is still thriving today. He was committed to racial reconciliation, and as a white pastor built strong relationships with leading black pastors in Philadelphia. He faithfully supported outreach to the poor and homeless, to people suffering and dying from AIDS, to people in bondage to sexual addiction, and to women with crisis pregnancies. In short, Dr. Boice believed that the gospel is powerful enough to address the most difficult problems we face in the world today.

Dr. Boice also believed in the power of the risen Christ to conquer death, including his own death. On Good Friday, in April 2000, he received an unexpected diagnosis of liver cancer. His case was terminal. Barely a week later he stood in his pulpit and addressed his beloved congregation for the very last time. As Dr. Boice encouraged his congregation to pray for him, he posed the question, "Pray for what?" Here was his answer:

> Above all, I would say pray for the glory of God. If you think of God glorifying himself in history and you say, Where in all of history has God most glorified himself? He did it at the cross of Jesus Christ, and it wasn't by delivering Jesus from the cross, though he could have. Jesus said, "Don't you think I could call down from my Father ten legions of angels for my defense?" But he didn't do that. And yet that's where God is most glorified.
>
> If I were to reflect on what goes on theologically here, there are two things I would stress. One is the sovereignty of God. That's not novel. We have talked about the sovereignty of God here forever. God is in charge. When things like this come into our lives, they are not accidental. It's not as if God somehow forgot what was going on, and something bad slipped by. God does everything according to his will. We've always said that.
>
> But what I've been impressed with mostly is something in addition to that. It's possible, isn't it, to conceive of God as sovereign and yet indifferent? God's in charge, but he doesn't care. But it's not that. God is not only the One who is in charge; God is also good. Everything he does is good. And what Romans 12 verses 1 and 2 says is that we have the opportunity by the renewal of our minds—that is, how we think about these things—actually to prove what God's will is. And then it says, "His good, pleasing, and perfect will." Is that good, pleasing, and perfect to God? Yes, of course, but the point of it is that it's good, pleasing, and perfect to us. If God does something in your life, would you change it? If you'd change it, you'd make it worse. It wouldn't be as good. So that's the way we want to accept it and move forward, and who knows what God will do?[1]

The goodness of God, the grace of God, and the glory of God in Jesus Christ— these were the foundations of James Boice's faith, and you will learn more about them on every page of this marvelous book.

---

[1]James Montgomery Boice, "Final Address at Tenth Presbyterian Church," in *The Life of Dr. James Montgomery Boice, 1938–2000* (Philadelphia: Tenth Presbyterian Church, 2001), 43-44.

PREFACE

Shortly after Harvard College was founded in 1636, the trustees of the school wrote, "Let every student be plainly instructed, and earnestly pressed to consider well [that the] maine end of his life and studies is to know God and Jesus Christ . . . and therefore to lay Christ in the bottome, as the only foundation of all sound knowledge and learning." In the 350 or so years since, Harvard (as well as most other schools, colleges, and universities) has moved far in a purely secular direction. But the words of those early trustees are still true, and many people still see their chief goal in life as knowing God better.

It is for such people that this book, originally published as four separate paperback volumes (InterVarsity Press, 1978–1981), has been written.

Not often do I, as an author, sense an area in which no book seems to exist and for which one should be written. But the area covered by this volume is an exception, in my judgment. For years I had looked for a work that could be given to a person (particularly a new Christian) who is alert and questioning and who could profit from a comprehensive but readable overview of the Christian faith, a basic theology from A to Z. But I could not find anything that was quite what I had in mind and, thus, determined that I should attempt to write it myself.

It is impossible for anyone to do something of this scope perfectly, of course. So I delayed the beginning of my work for several years. I could have delayed indefinitely. A time comes, however, when regardless of limitations one should simply go ahead and do the best one can. The result is this four-book, sixteen-part work, corresponding more or less to the ground covered by John Calvin in the four books of his monumental *Institutes of the Christian Religion.*

This volume is not a rehash of the *Institutes,* however, although I am greatly indebted to Calvin and although the theology of this work is Calvinistic. Rather, it is an attempt (a) to cover the same ground in highly readable language, yet at the same time (b) to introduce themes that Calvin did not treat but that call for treatment today, and (c) to seek to relate all doctrine to contemporary rather than ancient views and problems. Book one deals with the doctrine of God and how we know God, book two with sin and the redemptive work of Christ, book three with the Holy Spirit and the application of redemption to the individual, and book four with the church and the meaning of history.

I am indebted to a number of other writers and thinkers, as the footnotes indicate. Among them are men whom I have come to know and with whom I have worked as a result of the annual Philadelphia Conference on Reformed Theology, founded in 1974—John R. W. Stott, J. I. Packer, R. C. Sproul, John Gerstner, and Roger Nicole. I am also indebted to (and quote from) Thomas Watson, B. B. Warfield, R. A. Torrey, A. W. Tozer, A. W. Pink, C. S. Lewis, Emil Brunner, F. F. Bruce, John Warwick Montgomery, Jonathan Edwards, Francis A. Schaeffer, and others. In book three my biggest debt is to John Murray, who has dealt with the work of the Holy Spirit brilliantly and concisely in *Redemption Accomplished and Applied.* In my discussion of the doctrine of the church, I have been helped immeasurably by others who have explored the nature of the church and its ministry in recent days—Ray C. Stedman, Gene A. Getz, and Elton Trueblood. I have also been helped by older thinkers such as James Bannerman, a Scottish preacher and seminary lecturer of the nineteenth century. It has been harder to find good contemporary Christian works on history, but I have read and drawn on works by Reinhold Niebuhr, Oscar Cullmann, R. G. Collingwood, Herbert Butterfield, and others.

A portion of this material has already appeared in an article titled "New Vistas in Historical Jesus Research," *Christianity Today* (March 14, 1968). Other parts are similar to portions of my other writings, particularly the material on Scripture that appears in *The Gospel of John,* vol. 2, chapters 12–15. Some material has appeared in a shortened version in the June–August 1976 and June–August 1977 issues of *Bible Studies Magazine.* A discussion of "The Bondage of the Will" has appeared in similar form in *Tenth: An Evangelical Quarterly* (July 1983). "The Marks of the Church" is condensed from *The Gospel of John,* vol. 4, chapters 50–55, 58, and has been printed in Earl D. Radmacher, editor, *Can We Trust the Bible?*

The decision of the publishers to reissue this work in a new format has given me an opportunity to re-edit the whole and change portions in accord with what I think I have learned since the four separate volumes were issued. The most extensive changes are in book three, particularly in the discussion of the place of works in the Christian life. I have also made alterations to the discussion of the will in book two, based on the contribution of Jonathan Edwards. Books one and four have few changes.

I wish to express appreciation to Miss Caecilie M. Foelster, my editorial assistant, who helps in the production of all my books. She carries the heavy burden of typing, proofreading, and preparing the indexes. I am also thankful to the congregation of Tenth Presbyterian Church in Philadelphia, to whom these chapters were first preached in sermon form and who responded with many helpful comments and suggestions.

May God be honored in the distribution and use of this volume, and may it cause many to awake to him whose call is life eternal.

BOOK 1

The SOVEREIGN GOD

PART I

THE
KNOWLEDGE
OF GOD

The fear of the LORD *is the beginning of wisdom,*
and the knowledge of the Holy One is insight.

PROVERBS 9:10

And this is eternal life, that they know you the only true God,
and Jesus Christ whom you have sent.

JOHN 17:3

For the wrath of God is revealed from heaven against all ungodliness and
unrighteousness of men, who by their unrighteousness suppress the truth.
For what can be known about God is plain to them, because God has
shown it to them. For his invisible attributes, namely, his eternal power
and divine nature, have been clearly perceived, ever since the creation of the
world, in the things that have been made. So they are without excuse. For
although they knew God, they did not honor him as God or give thanks
to him, but they became futile in their thinking, and their foolish hearts
were darkened. Claiming to be wise, they became fools, and exchanged the
glory of the immortal God for images resembling mortal man and birds
and animals and creeping things.

ROMANS 1:18-23

CHAPTER 1

ON KNOWING GOD

One hot night in the early years of the Christian era a sophisticated and highly educated man named Nicodemus came to see a young rabbi, Jesus of Nazareth. The man wanted to discuss reality. So he began the conversation with a statement of where his own personal search for truth had taken him. He said, "Rabbi, we know that you are a teacher come from God, for no one can do these signs that you do unless God is with him" (Jn 3:2).

With the exception of the word *Rabbi*, which was merely a polite form of address, the first words were a claim to considerable knowledge. Nicodemus said, "We know." Then he began to rehearse the things he knew (or thought he knew) and with which he wanted to begin the discussion: (1) that Jesus was continuing to do many miracles; (2) that these miracles were intended to authenticate him as a teacher sent from God; and that, therefore, (3) Jesus was one to whom he should listen. Unfortunately for Nicodemus, Jesus replied that such an approach to knowledge was wrong and that Nicodemus could therefore know nothing until he had first experienced an inward, spiritual transformation. "You must be born again," Jesus told him (Jn 3:7).

Nicodemus's subsequent remarks showed at least an implicit recognition of his lack of knowledge in important things. For he began to ask questions: "How can a man be born when he is old? . . . How can these things be?" (Jn 3:4, 9). Jesus taught him that true knowledge begins with spiritual knowledge, knowledge of God, and that this is to be found in God's revelation of himself in the Bible and in Jesus' own life and work, the work of the Savior.

CONTEMPORARY CRISIS

This ancient conversation is relevant to our day. For the problems and frustrations that Nicodemus faced nearly two thousand years ago are with us in our time also. Nicodemus possessed knowledge, but he lacked the key to that knowledge, the element that would put it all together. He knew certain things, but his search for truth had brought him to the point of personal crisis. In the same way, much is also known in our time. In the sense of information or technical knowledge, more is known today than at any previous time in history. Yet the kind of knowledge that integrates information and thereby gives meaning to life is strangely absent.

The nature of the problem can be seen by examining the two almost exclusive approaches to knowledge today. On the one hand there is the idea that reality can be known *by reason alone.* That approach is not new, of course. It is the approach developed by Plato and therefore assumed by much of the Greek and Roman thought after him. In Plato's philosophy, true knowledge is knowledge of the eternal and unalterable essence of things, not merely knowledge of changeable phenomena. That is, it is a knowledge of forms, ideas, or ideals. Our nearest equivalent would be the so-called laws of science.

On the surface, this approach to knowledge through the exercise of supposedly impartial reason seems desirable, for it is productive—as the technical advances of our day often indicate. But it is not without problems. For one thing, it is highly impersonal knowledge and, as some would say, highly depersonalizing. In this approach reality becomes a thing (an equation, law, or, worse yet, mere data), and men and women become things also, with the inevitable result that they may therefore be manipulated like any other raw material for whatever ends.

An example is the manipulation of poorer nations by rich nations for the sake of the rich nations' expanding economy, that is, the injustice analyzed and rightly condemned by Karl Marx in *The Communist Manifesto, Capital,* and other writings. Another example is that of communism itself, which, in spite of its desire to better the lot of the masses, actually manipulates them for ideological ends. On the personal level there is the science of behavioral technology and the frightening teaching of a man like B. F. Skinner of Harvard University who claims that individuals must be conditioned scientifically for the good of society.

There is also another problem with the attempt to know reality through reason alone. The approach does not give an adequate basis for ethics. It can tell us what *is,* but it cannot tell us what ought to be. Consequently, the extraordinary technical advances of our time are accompanied by an extreme and debilitating moral permissiveness that promises in time to break down even the values and system that made both the advances and the permissiveness possible. Interestingly, the same thing was also true of the Greek philosophers, who, although they were men of great intellect, on occasion led depraved lives.

In recent years the failures of the rationalistic system have impressed themselves on a new generation, with the result that many in the Western world have abandoned reason in order to seek reality *through emotional experience*. In the ancient world, in reaction to the impersonality of Greek philosophy, this was done through intense participation in the rites of the mystery religions. These promised an emotional union with some god, induced by lighting, music, incense, or perhaps by drugs. In our time the same approach has surfaced through the drug cult, rediscovery of the Eastern religions, Transcendental Meditation, the human potential movement, and other supposedly "mind-expanding" practices.

This modern approach also has several problems. First, the experience does not last. It is transient. Each attempt to achieve reality through emotional experience promises some sort of "high." But the "high" is inevitably followed by a "low," with the additional problem that increasingly intense stimuli seem to be necessary to repeat the experience. Eventually this ends either in self-destruction or acute disillusionment. A second problem is that the approach to reality through emotion does not satisfy the mind. Promoters of these experiences, particularly drug experiences, speak of a more intense perception of reality that results from them. But their experience has no rational content. The part of the human being that wants to think about such things and understand them is unsatisfied.

The result of this situation is a crisis in the area of knowledge today, as in ancient times. Many thinking people quite honestly do not know where to turn. The rationalistic approach is impersonal and amoral. The emotionalistic approach is without content, transient and also often immoral. "Is this the end?" many are asking. "Are there no other possibilities? Is there not a third way?"

A THIRD WAY

At this point Christianity comes forward with the claim that there is a third way and that this way is strong at precisely those points where the other approaches are lacking. The basis of this third approach is that there is a God who has created all things and who himself gives his creation meaning. Further, we can know him. This is an exciting and satisfying possibility. It is exciting because it involves the possibility of contact between the individual and God, however insignificant the individual may appear in his or her own eyes or in the eyes of others. It is satisfying because it is knowledge not of an idea or thing but of a supremely personal Being, and because it issues in a profound change of conduct.

This is what the Bible means when it says, "The fear of the LORD is the beginning of knowledge" (Prov 1:7). And, "The fear of the LORD is the beginning of wisdom, and the knowledge of the Holy One is insight" (Prov 9:10).

Here, however, we must be clear about what we mean when we speak of "knowing God," for many common uses of the word *know* are inadequate to convey the biblical understanding. There is a use of the word *know* by which we mean "awareness." In this sense we say that we know where somebody lives or that we know that certain events are transpiring somewhere in the world. It is a kind of knowledge, but it does not involve us personally. It has little bearing on our lives. This is not what the Bible means when it speaks of knowing God.

Another use of the word *know* means "knowing about" something or someone. It is knowledge by description. For instance, we may say that we know New York City or London or Moscow. By that we mean that we are aware of the geographic layout of the city; we know the names of the streets, where the major stores are, and other facts. We may have gained our knowledge of the city by actually living there. But it is also possible that we may have gained our knowledge by reading books. In the religious realm, this type of knowledge would apply to theology that, although important, is not the whole or even the heart of religion. The Bible tells us much about God that we should know. (In fact, much of what follows in this book is directed to our need for such knowledge.) But this is not enough. Even the greatest theologians can be confused and can find life meaningless.

True knowledge of God is also more than *knowledge by experience*. To go back to the earlier example, it would be possible for someone who has lived in a particular city to say, "But my knowledge is *not* book knowledge. I have actually lived there. I have walked the streets, shopped in the stores, attended the theaters. I have experienced the city. I really know it." To this we would have to reply that the knowledge involved is certainly a step beyond anything we have talked about thus far, but still it is not the full idea of knowledge in the Christian sense.

Suppose, for instance, that a person should go out into a starlit field in the cool of a summer evening and gaze up into the twinkling heavens and come away with the claim that in that field he has come to know God. What do we say to such a person? The Christian does not have to deny the validity of that experience, up to a point. It is certainly a richer knowledge than mere awareness of God ("There is a God") or mere knowledge about him ("God is powerful and is the Creator of all that we see and know"). Still, the Christian insists, this is less than what the Bible means by true knowledge. For when the Bible speaks of knowing God it means being made alive by God in a new sense (being "born again"), conversing with God (so that he becomes more than some great "Something" out there, so that he becomes a friend), and being profoundly changed in the process.

All this is leading us, step by step, to a better understanding of the word *knowledge*. But still another qualification is needed. According to the Bible, even when the highest possible meaning is given to the word *know*, knowing God is still not merely knowing *God*. For it is never *knowing God in isolation*. It is always knowing God in his relationship to us. Consequently, according to the Bible, knowledge of God takes place only where there is also knowledge of ourselves in our deep spiritual need and where there is an accompanying acceptance of God's gracious provision for our need through the work of Christ and the application of that work to us by God's Spirit. Knowledge of God takes place in the context of Christian piety, worship, and devotion. The Bible teaches that this knowledge of God takes place (where it does take place), not so much because we search after God—because we do not—but because God reveals himself to us in Christ and in the Scriptures.

J. I. Packer writes of this knowledge,

> Knowing God involves, first, listening to God's word and receiving it as the Holy Spirit interprets it, in application to oneself; second, noting God's nature and character, as His word and works reveal it; third, accepting His invitations, and doing what He commands; fourth, recognising, and rejoicing in, the love that He has shown in thus approaching one and drawing one into this divine fellowship.[1]

WHY KNOW GOD?

"But just a minute," someone might argue. "All that sounds complicated and difficult. In fact, it seems too difficult. If that's what is involved, I want no part of it. Give me one good reason why I should bother." That is a fair objection, but there is an adequate answer to it. In fact, there are several.

First, knowledge of God is important, for only through the knowledge of God can an individual enter into what the Bible terms *eternal life*. Jesus indicated this

[1]J. I. Packer, *Knowing God* (Downers Grove, IL: InterVarsity Press, 1973), 32.

when he prayed, "And this is eternal life, that they know you the only true God, and Jesus Christ whom you have sent" (Jn 17:3). At first glance even this does not seem important enough to make people want to know God at all costs. But this is because, lacking eternal life, they cannot begin to understand what they are missing. They are like people who say that they do not appreciate good music. Their dislike does not make the music worthless; it simply indicates an inadequate grounds of appreciation in the listeners. So also those who do not appreciate God's offer of life indicate that they do not have the capability of understanding or valuing what they are lacking. The Bible says, "The natural person does not accept the things of the Spirit of God, for they are folly to him, and he is not able to understand them because they are spiritually discerned" (1 Cor 2:14).

It might help such a person to be told that the promise of eternal life is also the promise of being able to live life fully as an authentic human being. This is true, but it is also true that eternal life means more than this. It means coming alive, not only in a new but also in an eternal sense. It is what Jesus meant when he said, "I am the resurrection and the life. Whoever believes in me, though he die, yet shall he live, and everyone who lives and believes in me shall never die" (Jn 11:25-26).

Second, knowledge of God is important because, as pointed out earlier, it also involves *knowledge of ourselves*. Our day is the day of the psychiatrist and psychologist. Men and women spend billions of dollars annually in an attempt to know themselves, to sort out their psyches. Certainly there is need for psychiatry, particularly Christian psychiatry. But this alone is inadequate in the ultimate sense if it does not bring individuals into a knowledge of God against which their own worth and failures may be estimated.

On the one hand, knowledge of ourselves through the knowledge of God is humbling. We are not God, nor are we like him. He is holy; we are unholy. He is good; we are not good. He is wise; we are foolish. He is strong; we are weak. He is loving and gracious; we are filled with hate and with selfish affectations. Therefore, to know God is to see ourselves as Isaiah did: "Woe is me! For I am lost; for I am a man of unclean lips, and I dwell in the midst of a people of unclean lips; for my eyes have seen the King, the LORD of hosts!" (Is 6:5). Or as Peter did: "Depart from me, for I am a sinful man, O Lord" (Lk 5:8). On the other hand, such knowledge of ourselves through the knowledge of God is also reassuring and satisfying. For in spite of what we have become, we are still God's creation and are loved by him. No higher dignity has been given to women and men than the dignity the Bible gives them.

Third, the knowledge of God also gives us *knowledge of this world:* its good and its evil, its past and its future, its purpose and its impending judgment at the hand of God. In one sense, this is an extension of the point just made. If knowledge of God gives us knowledge of ourselves, it also inevitably gives us knowledge of the world; for the world is mostly the individuals who compose it written large. On the other hand, the world stands in a special relationship to God, in its sin and rebellion as well as in its value as a vehicle for his purposes. It is a confusing place until we know the God who made it and learn from him why he made it and what is to happen to it.

A fourth reason the knowledge of God is important is that it is the only way to *personal holiness.* This is a goal that the natural person hardly desires. But it is essential nonetheless. Our problems derive not only from the fact that we are ignorant of God but also from the fact that we are sinful. We do not want the good. At times we hate it, even when the good is to our benefit.

The knowledge of God leads to holiness. To know God as he is is to love him as he is and to want to be like him. This is the message of one of the Bible's most important verses about the knowledge of God. Jeremiah, the ancient prophet of Israel, wrote, "Let not the wise man boast in his wisdom, let not the mighty man boast in his might, let not the rich man boast in his riches, but let him who boasts boast in this, that he understands and knows me, that I am the LORD who practice steadfast love, justice, and righteousness in the earth. For in these things I delight, declares the LORD" (Jer 9:23-24). Jeremiah also wrote about a day when those who do not know God will come to know him. "And no longer shall each one teach his neighbor and each his brother, saying, 'Know the LORD,' for they shall all know me, from the least of them to the greatest, declares the LORD. For I will forgive their iniquity, and I will remember their sin no more" (Jer 31:34).

Finally, the knowledge of God is important in that it is only through a knowledge of God that *the church and those who compose it can become strong.* In ourselves we are weak, but as Daniel wrote, "The people who know their God shall stand firm and take action" (Dan 11:32).

We do not have a strong church today, nor do we have many strong Christians. We can trace the cause to an acute lack of sound spiritual knowledge. Why is the church weak? Why are individual Christians weak? It is because they have allowed their minds to become conformed to the "spirit of this age," with its mechanistic, godless thinking. They have forgotten what God is like and what he promises to do for those who trust him. Ask an average Christian to talk about God. After getting past the expected answers, you will find that their god is a little god of vacillating sentiments. He is a god who would like to save the world, but who cannot. He would like to restrain evil, but somehow he finds it beyond his power. So he has withdrawn into semiretirement, being willing to give good advice in a grandfatherly sort of way, but for the most part he has left his children to fend for themselves in a dangerous environment.

Such a god is not the God of the Bible. Those who know their God perceive the error in that kind of thinking and act accordingly. The God of the Bible is not weak; he is strong. He is all-mighty. Nothing happens without his permission or apart from his purposes—even evil. Nothing disturbs or puzzles him. His purposes are always accomplished. Therefore, those who know him rightly act with boldness, assured that God is with them to accomplish his own desirable purposes in their lives.

Do we need an example? We can find no better one than Daniel. Daniel and his friends were godly men in the godless environment of ancient Babylon. They were slaves, good slaves. They served the court. But difficulty arose when they refused to obey anything in opposition to the commands of the true God whom they knew and worshiped. When Nebuchadnezzar's great statue was set up and all were required to fall down and worship it, Daniel and his friends refused. When prayer to anyone but King Darius was banned for thirty days, Daniel did as he always did: he prayed to God three times a day before an open window.

What was wrong with these men? Had they fooled themselves about the consequences? Did they think that their failure to comply would go unseen? Not at all. They knew the consequences, but they also knew God. They were able to be strong, trusting God to have his way with them, whether it meant salvation or destruction in the lions' den or the furnace. These men said, "If this be so, our God whom we serve is able to deliver us from the burning fiery furnace, and he will deliver us out of your hand, O king. But if not, be it known to you, O king, that we will not serve your gods or worship the golden image that you have set up" (Dan 3:17-18).

A weak god produces no strong followers, nor does he deserve to be worshiped. A strong God, the God of the Bible, is a source of strength to those who know him.

THE HIGHEST SCIENCE

So let us learn about God and come to know God in the fullest, biblical sense. Jesus encouraged us to do this when he said, "Come to me, all who labor and are heavy laden, and I will give you rest. Take my yoke upon you, and learn from me, for I am gentle and lowly in heart, and you will find rest for your souls" (Mt 11:28-29). This is true wisdom for everyone. It is the special duty and privilege of the Christian.

What is the proper course of study for one who is a child of God? Is it not God himself? There are other worthwhile areas of learning, it is true. But the highest science, the most mind-expanding area of all, is the Godhead. Spurgeon once wrote,

> There is something exceedingly improving to the mind in a contemplation of the Divinity. It is a subject so vast, that all our thoughts are lost in its immensity; so deep, that our pride is drowned in its infinity. Other subjects we can comprehend and grapple with; in them we feel a kind of self-content, and go on our way with the thought, "Behold I am wise." But when we come to this master-science, finding that our plumb-line cannot sound its depth, and that our eagle eye cannot see its height, we turn away with the . . . solemn exclamation, "I am but of yesterday and know nothing." . . . But while the subject humbles the mind, it also expands it. . . . Nothing will so enlarge the intellect, nothing so magnify the whole soul of man, as a devout, earnest, continuing investigation of the great subject of the Deity.[2]

Every Christian should confidently pursue this goal. God has promised that those who seek him will find him. To those who knock, the door shall be opened.

---

[2]Charles Haddon Spurgeon, *The New Park Street Pulpit*, vol. 1, 1855 (Pasadena, TX: Pilgrim Publications, 1975), 1.

CHAPTER 2

THE UNKNOWN GOD

"Nearly all the wisdom we possess, that is to say, true and sound wisdom, consists of two parts: the knowledge of God and of ourselves."[1] These words from the opening paragraph of John Calvin's *Institutes of the Christian Religion* mark the point to which the preceding chapter has brought us, but they also introduce a new problem. If it is true that wisdom consists in the "knowledge of God and of ourselves," we are at once led to ask, "But who has such knowledge? Who truly knows God or knows themselves?" If we are honest, we must admit that as long as we are left to ourselves and our own abilities, the only possible answer is "No one." Left to ourselves, not one of us truly knows God. Nor do we know ourselves adequately.

What is the trouble? Clearly, we do not know ourselves because we have first failed to know God. But why don't we know God? Is he unknowable? Is the fault his, or is it ours? Obviously, it is more appealing to us to blame God. But before we jump to that conclusion, we should be conscious of what is involved. If the fault is ours, although that fact in itself may be uncomfortable, then at least it can be corrected, for God can do anything. He can intervene. On the other hand, if the fault is God's (or, as we might prefer to say, if the fault is in the very nature of things), then nothing at all can be done. The key to knowledge will inevitably elude us, and life is absurd.

In *The Dust of Death*, Os Guinness makes this point by describing a comedy skit performed by the German comedian Karl Vallentin. In this routine the comic

---

[1]John Calvin, *Institutes of the Christian Religion*, ed. John T. McNeill, trans. Ford Lewis Battles, 2 vols. (Philadelphia: Westminster, 1960), 35.

comes onto a stage illuminated only by one small circle of light. He paces around and around this circle with a worried face. He is searching for something. After a while a policeman joins him and asks what he has lost. "I've lost the key to my house," Vallentin answers. The policeman joins the hunt, but the search eventually appears useless.

"Are you sure you lost it here?" asks the policeman.

"Oh no!" says Vallentin, pointing to a dark corner. "It was over there."

"Then why are you looking here?"

"There's no light over there," answers the comic.[2]

If there is no God or if there is a God but the failure to know him is God's fault, then the search for knowledge is like the search of the German comedian. Where the search should be made, there is no light; and where there is light there is no point in searching. But is this the case? The Bible declares that the problem is not God's but ours. Therefore, the problem is solvable. It is solvable because God can take, and actually has taken, steps to reveal himself to us, thereby providing us with the missing key to knowledge.

AWARENESS OF GOD

We must begin with the problem, however: strange as it may sound, the person who does not know God, still in some lesser but valid sense, does know him yet represses that knowledge.

Here we must go back to the distinction between an "awareness" of God and truly "knowing God." Knowing God is entering into a knowledge of our deep spiritual need and of God's provision for that need, and then coming to trust and reverence God. Awareness of God is merely the sense that there is a God and that he deserves to be obeyed and worshiped. Men and women do not naturally know, obey, or worship God. But they do have an awareness of him.

This brings us to some of the most important words ever recorded for the benefit of humanity—from the apostle Paul's letter to the newly established church in Rome. They contain the apostle's first thesis in his greatest exposition of Christian doctrine.

> For the wrath of God is revealed from heaven against all ungodliness and un-righteousness of men, who by their unrighteousness suppress the truth. For what can be known about God is plain to them, because God has shown it to them. For his invisible attributes, namely, his eternal power and divine nature, have been

---

[2]Os Guinness, *The Dust of Death* (Downers Grove, IL: InterVarsity Press, 1973), 148.

clearly perceived, ever since the creation of the world, in the things that have been made. So they are without excuse. For although they knew God, they did not honor him as God or give thanks to him, but they became futile in their thinking, and their foolish hearts were darkened. Claiming to be wise, they became fools, and exchanged the glory of the immortal God for images resembling mortal man and birds and animals and creeping things. (Rom 1:18-23)

Here we see three important ideas. First, the wrath of God is displayed against the natural person. Second, humanity has willfully rejected God. Third, this rejection has taken place in spite of a natural awareness of God possessed by each person.

TWOFOLD REVELATION

The third point, the natural awareness of God possessed by every person, is the necessary place to begin. For here we see that, although no one naturally knows God, the failure we have in knowing God is not God's fault. God has given us a twofold revelation of himself, and we all have this revelation.

The first part is the *revelation of God in nature*. Paul's argument may be rephrased as saying that all that can be known about God by the natural person has been revealed in nature. Of course, we must acknowledge that this is limited knowledge. In fact, Paul defines it as just two things: God's eternal power and his deity. But although such knowledge is limited, it is sufficient to remove excuse if any person fails to move on from it to seek God fully. In contemporary speech the phrase "eternal power" could be reduced to the word *supremeness*, and "deity" could be changed to *being*. Paul is saying then that there is ample and entirely convincing evidence in nature of a Supreme Being. God exists, and human beings know it. That is the argument. When men and women subsequently refuse to acknowledge and worship God, as they do, the fault is not in a lack of evidence but in their irrational and resolute determination not to know him.

The Old Testament speaks of the clear revelation of God in nature.

The heavens declare the glory of God,
    and the sky above proclaims his handiwork.
Day to day pours out speech,
    and night to night reveals knowledge.
There is no speech, nor are there words,
    whose voice is not heard.
Their voice goes out through all the earth,
    and their words to the end of the world. (Ps 19:1-4)

The point is that the revelation of God in nature is sufficient to convince anyone of God's existence and power, if the individual will have it.

There is a second part to God's self-revelation. We might call it an *internal revelation* or, at least, the internal capacity for receiving one. No one in his or her natural state has actually come to know God in the full biblical sense. But each person has been given the capacity for receiving the natural revelation. Paul is talking about this capacity when he says that "what can be known about God is plain *to them*" (Rom 1:19).

Suppose that you are driving down the street and come to a sign that says, "Detour—Turn Left." But you ignore this and drive on. It happens that there is a police officer present, who then stops you and begins to write out a ticket. What excuse might you have? You can argue that you didn't see the sign. But that makes no difference. As long as you are driving the car, the responsibility for seeing the sign and obeying it is yours. Further, you are responsible if, having ignored the sign, you recklessly plunge on over a cliff and destroy both yourself and your passengers.

Paul is saying, first, there is a sign. It is the revelation of God in nature. Second, you have "vision." If you choose to ignore the sign, and so court disaster, the guilt is your own. In fact, the judgment of God (like that of the police officer) comes, not because you didn't or couldn't know God, but because being aware of God, you nevertheless refused to acknowledge him as God. Paul writes, "So they are without excuse. For although they knew God, they did not honor him as God or give thanks to him" (Rom 1:20-21).

Paul is not saying that there is enough evidence about God in nature so that the scientist, who carefully probes nature's mysteries, can be aware of him. He is not saying that the sign is there but hidden, that we are only able to find it if we look carefully. Paul is saying that the sign is plain. It is a billboard. No one, no matter how weak-minded or insignificant, can be excused for missing it. There is enough evidence of God in a flower to lead a child as well as a scientist to worship him. There is sufficient evidence in a tree, a pebble, a grain of sand, a fingerprint, to make us glorify God and thank him. This is the way to knowledge. But people will not do this. They substitute nature or parts of nature for God and find their hearts darkened.

Calvin gives this conclusion: "But although we lack the natural ability to mount up unto the pure and clear knowledge of God, all excuse is cut off because the fault of dullness is within us. And, indeed, we are not allowed thus to pretend ignorance without our conscience itself always convicting us of both baseness and ingratitude."[3]

REJECTION OF GOD

When Calvin speaks of baseness and ingratitude, he brings us to the second point of Paul's argument in Romans: the fact that all have rejected God in spite of God's revelation of himself in nature. However, in developing this point in Romans (Rom 1:18) Paul also shows the nature of our rejection and why it has taken place.

The key to this universal rejection of God is found in the phrase "who by their unrighteousness suppress the truth." In Greek the word translated "suppress" is *katechein*, which means "hold," "hold fast," "keep," "take," "hold back," "restrain," or "repress." In a positive sense, the word is used to mean holding to whatever is good. Paul speaks of "holding fast to the word of life" (Phil 2:16). In a negative sense it is used to mean wrongly suppressing something or holding it down. Thus other translations of the Bible speak in Romans 1:18 of those who "suppress the truth by their wickedness" (NIV), "suppress the truth in unrighteousness" (NASB), and "keep truth imprisoned in their wickedness" (JB). The New English Bible says that such people are "stifling" the truth. This, then, is the nature of the problem. The wrath of God is revealed from heaven against human beings, not because they have simply and perhaps carelessly overlooked the truth, but rather because they have deliberately and wickedly repressed whatever, deep in their hearts, they know about God.

R. C. Sproul has called this argument "the heart of Paul's psychology of atheism,"[4] pointing out it is here that human guilt lies. Sufficient knowledge has been given to all people to cause them to turn from themselves and their own way of life to God and so at least to begin to seek him. But this knowledge, like a great spring, has been pressed down. Now the spring threatens to leap up and demolish the views and lifestyle of the one repressing it. So that person holds it down, suppressing the truth.

Why do we do this? If it is true, as pointed out in the last chapter, that the knowledge of God leads to our chief good, and if, as we have just said, the beginning of that knowledge is already present to us, then why do we repress it?

---

[3]Calvin, *Institutes*, 68-69.
[4]R. C. Sproul, *The Psychology of Atheism* (Minneapolis: Bethany Fellowship, 1974), 59.

Would we not welcome such truth and seek to draw it out? Are people simply irrational at this point? Or is Paul's view faulty?

Paul is not wrong. Men and women do suppress truth. But their reason for doing so is that *they do not like the truth about God.* They do not like the God to which the truth leads them.

Notice that Paul begins these verses from Romans by saying that the wrath of God is revealed from heaven against all "ungodliness and unrighteousness of men." *Ungodliness* has a variety of meanings. Here the meaning is not so much that human beings are not like God (though that is true) but that in addition they are in a state of opposition to God in his godly nature. God is sovereign, but people do not like his sovereignty. They do not want to acknowledge that there is one who rightly exercises rule over them. God is holy, but men and women do not like his holiness. His holiness calls our own sinfulness into question. God is all-knowing, but we do not like his knowledge. We do not like a God who sees into the dark recesses of our hearts and knows us intimately. Nearly everything that can be known about God is repugnant to the natural person in one way or another. So we repress the evidence that would lead us in the direction of a true knowledge of God.

The second word is "unrighteousness." Everything about God is repugnant to the natural person, but the dominant cause of this repugnance is God's righteousness. God is holy, but people are unholy. People are unrighteous, and they like their unrighteousness. Consequently, they do not wish to know a God who would press moral claims on them. To know God would require change. In other words, the refusal to know God is based not so much on intellectual causes as on moral ones.

REJECTING KNOWLEDGE OF GOD

At this point we have come to the true source of the human problem. Men and women have rejected the beginnings of the knowledge of God for moral and psychological reasons. But they find it impossible to stop there. They have rejected God; but they are still God's creatures and have a need for God (or something like him) in their intellectual and moral make-up. Being unwilling to know the true God and being unable to do without him, they invent substitute gods to take his place. These gods may be the sophisticated scientific laws of our culture, the gods and goddesses of the Greek and Roman worlds, or the depraved, bestial images of paganism.

The universality of religion on this planet is not due to men and women being seekers after God, as some have argued. Rather it is because they will not have God, yet need something to take God's place.

The process of rejection is a three-stage process well known to contemporary psychologists: trauma, repression, and substitution. In his analysis of atheism, Sproul shows that confrontation with the true God shocks and injures people. It is traumatic. Consequently, we repress what we know. "There is no trauma if the eyes are forever closed so that no light penetrates. But the eyes close in reaction to the shock of the light—after the pain has been experienced."[5] The important point here is that the knowledge of God, though repressed, is not destroyed. It remains intact, though deeply buried in the subconscious. The lack is therefore felt, and substitution of "that which is not God" for the true God follows.

GOD'S WRATH

At last, then, we arrive at Paul's first statement, having taken the three main points of the passage in reverse order: the wrath of God is justly revealed against human beings because they suppressed the knowledge of God that was plain to them.

Some people are deeply disturbed by the teaching that the great God of the universe expresses wrath. They understand that God is a God of love, as indeed he is, and cannot see how God can possess the one characteristic as well as the other. In this, they fail either to understand or to know God. A God who does not have wrath against sin is a deformed or crippled God. He lacks something. God is perfect in his love. That is true. But God is also perfect in his wrath, which, as Paul tells us in Romans, is "revealed from heaven against all ungodliness and wickedness of men."

In any logical presentation of doctrine, the wrath of God is the first truth we have to learn about him. Why didn't Paul begin by saying that the love of God is revealed from heaven? It is not that God is not love, for he is, as Paul will show later. Rather, it is so we will recognize our deep spiritual need and be prepared to receive the knowledge of God in the Lord Jesus Christ, the Savior, where alone we can receive it. If men and women come to God boasting of their alleged spiritual knowledge, God will declare them to be ignorant. If they come to God boasting of their own achievements, God cannot and will not receive

---

[5]Ibid., 75.

them. But if they come humbly, recognizing that they indeed have rejected what has been clearly revealed about God in nature, that they are without excuse, that God's wrath justly hangs over them, then God will work in their lives. He will show that he has already made a way for removing the wrath due them, that Jesus has borne it, and that the way is now open for their growth in both the love and knowledge of God which is salvation.

PART II

THE WORD OF GOD

All Scripture is breathed out by God and profitable for teaching, for reproof, for correction, and for training in righteousness, that the man of God may be complete, equipped for every good work.

2 TIMOTHY 3:16-17

They said to each other, "Did not our hearts burn within us while he talked to us on the road, while he opened to us the Scriptures?"

LUKE 24:32

The law of the LORD is perfect, reviving the soul; the testimony of the LORD is sure, making wise the simple; the precepts of the LORD are right, rejoicing the heart; the commandment of the LORD is pure, enlightening the eyes.

PSALM 19:7-8

I say to you, until heaven and earth pass away, not an iota, not a dot, will pass from the Law until all is accomplished.

MATTHEW 5:18

For the time is coming when people will not endure sound teaching, but having itching ears they will accumulate for themselves teachers to suit their own passions, and will turn away from listening to the truth and wander off into myths.

2 TIMOTHY 4:3-4

Do your best to present yourself to God as one approved, a worker who has no need to be ashamed, rightly handling the word of truth.

2 TIMOTHY 2:15

CHAPTER 3

THE BIBLE

*O*ur study of Christian doctrine has brought us to three great truths: first, the knowledge of God is our chief good; second, God has revealed in nature certain truths about himself to everyone; but third, people have rejected this revelation and have substituted false gods in place of the Creator. Awareness of the true God is conveyed to us externally, in all that we see, and internally through the workings of our own minds and hearts. But we have denied our awareness of God, changing the knowledge we do have into superstition. As a result, the world, for all its wisdom, does not know God and so lacks knowledge of itself also.

What is to be done? It is obvious from what has already been said that men and women can do nothing themselves. But the good news of the Christian religion is that although we can do nothing, God has done something. He has done what needs to be done. He has communicated with us. In other words, in addition to the general but limited revelation of himself in nature, God has provided a special revelation designed to lead those who did not know God and did not want to know God to a saving knowledge of him. This special revelation has three stages. First, there is *redemption in history*. This centers in the work of the Lord Jesus Christ. He died in the place of sinners and rose as proof of their divine justification. Second, there is a *revelation in writing*. This is the Bible. God has provided interpretive records of what he has done for our redemption. Finally, there is the *application* of these truths to the mind and heart of the individual by the Holy Spirit. As a result the individual is born again, receives the Lord Jesus Christ as Savior, and is enabled to follow him faithfully until life's end.

It is evident, however, that in this three-stage special revelation the Bible is of critical importance. In the Bible alone we learn of God's redemption of sinners in Christ; through the Bible the Spirit speaks to individuals. Therefore, as Calvin says, "Our wisdom ought to be nothing else than to embrace with humble teachableness, and at least without finding fault, whatever is taught in Sacred Scripture."[1]

Without the Scriptures our imagined wisdom runs to foolishness. With the Scriptures and under the guidance of the Holy Spirit, we are able to learn who God is, what he has done for us, and how we can respond to him and live our lives in fellowship with him.

GOD HAS SPOKEN

The importance of the Bible lies in its being the Word of God written. And the first reason for believing the Bible to be this is the Bible's own teaching about itself. That is where all people and particularly Christians should start. Many appeal to the Scriptures in defense of basic doctrines: the doctrine of God, the deity of Christ, the atonement, the resurrection, the nature of the church, the work of the Holy Spirit, the final judgment, and many other points of theology. They do so rightly. But if the Bible is authoritative and accurate in these matters, there is no reason why it should not be authoritative and accurate when speaking about itself.

When we take this approach, the first verse to look at is 2 Timothy 3:16. Here the New Testament speaks of the Old Testament, noting that "all Scripture is breathed out by God." The English phrase "is breathed out by" (ESV) or "is given by inspiration of" (KJV) translates only one Greek word. This word, as B. B. Warfield pointed out at the beginning of this century, "very distinctly does not mean 'inspired of God.'"[2] That English phrase has come down to us from the Latin Vulgate (*divinitus inspirata*) through the translation of Wycliffe ("Al Scripture of God ynspyrid is . . .") and other early English versions. But the Greek word does not mean "inspired." It literally means "God-breathed." This word was never correctly translated by any

---

[1]John Calvin, *Institutes of the Christian Religion*, ed. John T. McNeill, trans. Ford Lewis Battles, 2 vols. (Philadelphia: Westminster, 1960), 237.

[2]Benjamin Breckinridge Warfield, *The Inspiration and Authority of the Bible*, ed. Samuel G. Craig (London: Marshall, Morgan & Scott, 1959), 132.

English version until publication in 1973 of the New International Version: New Testament.

The Greek word *theopneustos* combines the word for "God" (*theos*) and the word for "breath" or "spirit" (*pneustos*). In English we have the word for God preserved in the words *theology, theophany, monotheism,* and *atheist,* and in the names *Dorothy, Theodore,* and others. *Pneuma* is preserved in the words *pneumatic* and *pneumonia.* Together the words teach that the Scriptures are the direct result of the breathing out of God. Warfield writes,

> The Greek term has . . . nothing to say of inspiring or of inspiration: it speaks only of a "spiring" or "spiration." What it says of Scripture is, not that it is "breathed into by God" or that it is the product of the Divine "inbreathing" into its human authors, but that it is breathed out by God. . . . When Paul declares, then, that "every scripture," or "all scripture" is the product of the Divine breath, "is God-breathed," he asserts with as much energy as he could employ that Scripture is the product of a specifically Divine operation.[3]

Some things recorded in the Bible, of course, are merely the words of weak and erring men. But when that is the case, the words are identified as such, and the divine teaching in the passages involved are that such views are indeed weak and erring. To give one extreme example, in the early chapters of the book of Job we read, "Skin for skin! All that a man has he will give for his life" (Job 2:4). But that is not true, at least not in all cases. How is this to be explained? When we read the chapter carefully we see that the words were spoken by the devil, who is elsewhere described as the father of all falsehood (Jn 8:44). Similarly, in the rest of the book we find long chapters filled with the vain and sometimes faulty advice of Job's comforters. But their words are not fully true, and suddenly God breaks into the nonsense to ask, "Who is this that darkens counsel by words without knowledge?" (Job 38:2). Here God specifically exposes the false opinions of Job's counselors.

The Bible carries absolute authority as to the factualness of the narratives, and whenever God speaks either directly or through one of his prophets there is not only perfect accuracy but absolute authority as well. It has been noted that in the Pentateuch alone the words "the LORD said" occur almost eight hundred times and that the words "Thus saith the LORD" is a recurring refrain throughout the prophets.

---

[3]Ibid., 133.

"IT SAYS"/"GOD SAYS"

Next to the verse from 2 Timothy may be placed a double series of passages, collected by Warfield, showing clearly that the New Testament writers identified the Bible that they possessed, the Old Testament, with the living voice of God. "In one of these classes of passages," writes Warfield, "the Scriptures are spoken of as if they were God; in the other, God is spoken of as if he were the Scriptures: in the two together, God and the Scriptures are brought into such conjunction as to show that in point of directness of authority no distinction was made between them."[4] The sensitive reader of the Bible can only conclude that the unique and divine character of the sacred books was by no means an invented or abstract affirmation of the biblical writers, but rather a basic assumption behind all that they taught or wrote.

Examples of the first class of passages are such as these: Galatians 3:8, "The Scripture, foreseeing that God would justify the Gentiles through faith, preached the gospel beforehand to Abraham, saying, 'In you shall all the nations be blessed'" (Gen 12:1-3); Romans 9:17, "The Scripture says to Pharaoh, 'For this very purpose I have raised you up, that I might show my power in you'" (Ex 9:16). It was not, however, the Scripture (which did not exist at the time) that, foreseeing God's purposes of grace in the future, spoke these precious words to Abraham, but God himself in his own person: it was not the not yet existent Scripture that made this announcement to Pharaoh, but God himself through the mouth of his prophet Moses. These acts could be attributed to "Scripture" only as the result of such a habitual identification, in the mind of the writer, of the text of Scripture with God as speaking, that it became natural to use the term "Scripture says," when what was really intended was "God, as recorded in Scripture, said."

Examples of the other class of passages are such as these: Matthew 19:4-5, "He answered, 'Have you not read that he who created them from the beginning made them male and female, and said, "Therefore a man shall leave his father and his mother and hold fast to his wife, and the two shall become one flesh?"'" (Gen 2:24); Hebrews 3:7, "Therefore, as the Holy Spirit says, 'Today, if you hear his voice'" (Ps 95:7); Acts 4:24-25, "Sovereign Lord . . . who through the mouth of our father David, your servant, said by the Holy Spirit, 'Why did the Gentiles rage, and the peoples plot in vain?'" (Ps 2:1); Acts 13:34-35, "And as for the fact that he raised him from the dead, no more to return to corruption, he has spoken in this way, 'I will give you the holy and sure blessings of David'" (Is 55:3);

[4]Ibid., 299.

"Therefore he says also in another psalm, 'You will not let your Holy One see corruption" (Ps 16:10); Hebrews 1:6-8, 10, "And again, when he brings the firstborn into the world, he says, 'Let all God's angels worship him'" (Deut 32:43); "Of the angels he says, 'He makes his angels winds, and his ministers a flame of fire'" (Ps 104:4); "But of the Son he says, 'Your throne, O God, is for ever and ever'" (Ps. 45:6); and "You, Lord, laid the foundation of the earth in the beginning" (Ps 102:25). It is not God, however, in whose mouth these sayings are placed in the text of the Old Testament: they are the words of others, recorded in the text of Scripture as spoken to or of God. They could be attributed to God only through such habitual identification, in the minds of the writers, of the text of Scripture with the utterances of God that it had become natural to use the term "God says" when what was really intended was "Scripture, the Word of God, says."

The two sets of passages, together, thus show an absolute identification, in the minds of these writers, of "Scripture" with the speaking of God.[5]

MOVED BY GOD

None of the preceding discussion is meant to deny the genuine human element in Scripture. In 2 Peter 1:21, Peter writes, "No prophecy was ever produced by the will of man, but men spoke from God as they were carried along by the Holy Spirit." It can hardly be overemphasized in the light of some current misunderstandings that Peter does acknowledge that people had a part in writing Scripture. He says, "Men spoke." But what makes the Bible different from other books is that in their speaking (or writing) the biblical authors were moved on by God.

The biblical writers wrote out of their own experience. They used their own vocabulary. The literary polish of their writings varies. They sometimes use secular sources. They are selective. In many ways the books of the Bible bear evidence of having been written by people who were very human and very much people of their time.

Yet the books of the Old and New Testaments bear evidence of being something more than merely human. Peter says that these writers "spoke from God" and were "carried along by the Holy Spirit." The word translated "carried along" is significant. It is used by Luke to describe the coming of the Holy Spirit at Pentecost as a "sound like a mighty rushing wind" (Acts 2:2). Later, Luke once

---

[5]Ibid., 299-300.

again employs the word in the dramatic account of the Mediterranean storm that ultimately destroyed the ship taking Paul to Rome. Luke notes that the ship was *carried along* by the wind. "When the ship was caught and could not face the wind, we gave way to it and were *driven along*" (Acts 27:15); "they lowered the gear, and thus they were *driven along*" (Acts 27:17). Luke was saying that the ship was at the mercy of the storm. It did not cease to be a ship, but it did cease to have control over its course and destination.

Similarly, Peter teaches that the writers of the Bible were borne along in their writing to produce the words that God intended to be recorded. They wrote as people, but as people moved by the Holy Spirit. The result was the revelation of God.

The verse in 2 Peter does not imply anything about a particular method by which the biblical writers became aware of God's Word and transcribed it. The methods that God used to communicate his revelation to the biblical writers varied. Some apparently wrote as people might write today, collecting material and composing it to bring out the most significant events or emphases. Such were John, the author of the fourth Gospel, and Luke, the author of the third Gospel and of Acts (Jn 20:30; Lk 1:1-4; Acts 1:1-2). They did not receive their books from God by dictation. Moses received a revelation of the law on Mount Sinai in the midst of fire, smoke, and thunder (Ex 19:18-19). The Lord came to Daniel in a vision (Dan 2:19), as he did perhaps also to the apostle Paul on one occasion (Gal 1:11-12). Isaiah claimed to have heard the voice of the Lord as he would have heard the voice of another human being. "The LORD of hosts has revealed himself in my ears" (Is 22:14). The methods are clearly varied, but the result is the same. The product is the specific revelation of God.

Most of the texts mentioned thus far have had to do with the Old Testament. But there are also texts that indicate that the teaching of the New Testament about the Old Testament applies to the New Testament writings too. Thus, Paul writes of the gospel that he had preached, "We also thank God constantly for this, that when you received the word of God, which you heard from us, you accepted it not as the word of men but as what it really is, the word of God, which is at work in you believers" (1 Thess 2:13; compare Gal 1:11-12). Similarly, Peter places the Pauline letters in the same category as the Old Testament. "Our beloved brother Paul also wrote to you according to the wisdom given him, as he does in all his letters when he speaks in them of these matters. There are some things in them that are hard to understand, which the ignorant and unstable twist to their own destruction, as they do *the other Scriptures*" (2 Pet 3:15-16).

Of course, the New Testament does not speak of itself with the same frequency and in exactly the same manner as it speaks of the Old Testament, since the New Testament books had not been collected into an authoritative volume during the lifetime of the writers. Nevertheless, on several occasions the New Testament writers do speak of their writings as the words of God. In some cases, when a New Testament book was written late enough to know of other New Testament writings, the later book speaks of the earlier ones in the same terms that Christians and Jews used to refer to the Old Testament.

THE WITNESS OF JESUS CHRIST

The most important reason for believing the Bible to be the Word of God written and hence the sole authority for Christians in all matters of faith and conduct is the teaching of Jesus Christ. Today it is common for some to contrast the Bible's authority unfavorably with Christ's. But such a contrast is unjustifiable. Jesus so identified himself with Scripture and so interpreted his ministry in the light of Scripture that it is impossible to weaken the authority of one without at the same time weakening the authority of the other.

Christ's high regard for the Old Testament is first seen by the fact that he appealed to it as an infallible authority. When tempted by the devil in the wilderness, Jesus replied three times by quotations from Deuteronomy (Mt 4:1-11). He replied to the question of the Sadducees about the heavenly status of marriage and the reality of the resurrection (Lk 20:27-40), first by a rebuke that they did not know either the Scriptures or the power of God, and second, by a direct quotation from Exodus 3:6, "I am the God of your father, the God of Abraham, the God of Isaac, and the God of Jacob." On many occasions Jesus appealed to Scripture in support of his actions, as in defense of his cleansing of the temple (Mk 11:15-17) or in reference to his submission to the cross (Mt 26:53-54). He taught that the "Scripture cannot be broken" (Jn 10:35). He declared, "Until heaven and earth pass away, not an iota, not a dot, will pass from the Law until all is accomplished" (Mt 5:18).

Matthew 5:18 deserves some additional consideration. It is evident, even as we read the phrase after a space of some two thousand years, that the words "not an iota, not a dot" were a common expression referring to the most minute parts of the Mosaic law. The iota stands for the smallest letter of the Hebrew alphabet, the letter that we would transliterate by an *i* or *y*. In written Hebrew it resembled a comma, though it was written near the top of the letters rather than near the bottom. The dot (or tittle, KJV) was what we would call a serif, the tiny projection on letters that distinguishes a roman typeface from a more modern one. In many Bibles Psalm 119 is divided into twenty-two sections, each beginning with a different letter of the Hebrew alphabet. If one's Bible is well printed, the English reader can see what a dot is by comparing the Hebrew letter before Psalm 119:9 with the Hebrew letter before Psalm 119:81. The first letter is a *beth*. The second is a *kaph*. The only difference between them is the serif. The same feature distinguishes *daleth* from *resh* and *vau* from *zayin*. According to Jesus, then, not even an *i* or a *serif* of the law would be lost until the whole law was fulfilled.

What can give the law so permanent a character? Obviously nothing human, for all things human pass away. The only basis for the law's imperishable quality is that it is actually divine. The reason it will not pass away is that it is the Word of the true, living, and eternal God. That is the substance of Christ's teaching.

Second, Jesus saw his life as a fulfillment of Scripture. He consciously submitted himself to it. He began his ministry with a quotation from Isaiah 61:1-2.

The Spirit of the Lord is upon me,
    because he has anointed me
        to proclaim good news to the poor.
He has sent me to proclaim liberty to the captives
    and recovering of sight to the blind,
        to set at liberty those who are oppressed,
    to proclaim the year of the Lord's favor. (Lk 4:18-19)

When he had finished reading he put the scroll down and said, "Today this Scripture has been fulfilled in your hearing" (Lk 4:21). Jesus was claiming to be the Messiah, the one about whom Isaiah had written. He was identifying his forthcoming ministry with the lines set out for it in Scripture.

Later in his ministry we find disciples of John the Baptist coming to Jesus with John's question: "Are you the one who is to come, or shall we look for another?" (Mt 11:3). Jesus answered by a second reference to this section of Isaiah's prophecy. He said, in effect, "Don't take my word for who I am. Look at what Isaiah foretold about the Messiah. Then see if I'm fulfilling it." Jesus challenged people to evaluate his ministry in the light of God's Word.

The Gospel of John shows Jesus talking to the Jewish rulers about authority, and the climax of what he says has to do entirely with Scripture. He says that nobody would ever believe in him who had not first believed in the writings of Moses, for Moses wrote about him. "You search the Scriptures because you think that in them you have eternal life; and it is they that bear witness about me. . . . Do not think that I will accuse you to the Father. There is one who accuses you: Moses, on whom you have set your hope. For if you believed Moses, you would believe me; for he wrote of me. But if you do not believe his writings, how will you believe my words?" (Jn 5:39, 45-47).

At the end of Jesus' life, as he is hanging on the cross, he is again thinking of Scripture. He says, "My God, my God, why have you forsaken me?" (a quotation from Ps 22:1). He says that he thirsts. They give him a sponge filled with vinegar that Psalm 69:21 might be fulfilled. Three days later, after the resurrection, he is on the way to Emmaus with two of his disciples, chiding them because they have not used Scripture to understand the necessity of his suffering. He says, "O foolish ones, and slow of heart to believe all that the prophets have spoken! Was it not necessary that the Christ should suffer these things and enter into his glory?" Then, "beginning with Moses and all the Prophets, he interpreted to them in all the Scriptures the things concerning himself" (Lk 24:25-27).

On the basis of these and many other passages, it is beyond doubt that Jesus highly esteemed the Old Testament and constantly submitted to it as to an authoritative revelation. He taught that the Scriptures bore a witness to him, just as he bore a witness to them. Because they are the words of God, Jesus assumed their complete reliability, in whole and to the smallest part.

Jesus also endorsed the New Testament, though in a different form from his endorsement of the Old Testament (because, of course, the New Testament had not yet been written). He foresaw the writing of the New Testament. So he chose the apostles to be the recipients of the new revelation.

There were two qualifications of an apostle, as Acts 1:21-26 and other passages indicate. First, the apostle was to be one who had known Jesus during the days of his earthly ministry and had been a witness of his resurrection in particular (Acts 1:21-22). Paul's apostleship was undoubtedly challenged at this point because he became a Christian after the return of Christ to heaven and thus had not known him in the flesh. But Paul cited his vision of the resurrected Christ on the road to Damascus as having met this requirement. "Am I not an apostle? . . . Have I not seen Jesus our Lord?" (1 Cor 9:1).

The second requirement was that Jesus had chosen the apostle for his unique role and task. As part of this he promised a unique giving of the Holy Spirit so that they would remember, understand, and be able to record the truths concerning his ministry. "But the Helper, the Holy Spirit, whom the Father will send in my name, he will teach you all things and bring to your remembrance all that I have said to you" (Jn 14:26). Similarly, "I still have many things to say to you, but you cannot bear them now. When the Spirit of truth comes, he will guide you into all the truth, for he will not speak on his own authority, but whatever he hears he will speak, and he will declare to you the things that are to come. He will glorify me, for he will take what is mine and declare it to you" (Jn 16:12-14).

Did the apostles fulfill their commission? Yes, they did. The New Testament is the result. What is more, the early church recognized their role. For when it came time to declare officially what books were to be included in the canon of the New Testament, the decisive factor was perceived to be whether or not they were written by the apostles or bore apostolic endorsement. The church did not create the canon; if it had, it would place itself over Scripture. Rather the church submitted to Scripture as a higher authority.

BELIEVING THE BIBLE

I end this chapter with an obvious question. Do we believe these teachings? Do we believe that the Bible is indeed the written Word of God in accord with its own teaching and that of the Lord Jesus Christ?

It is popular today to doubt this teaching. This has caused much current confusion in theology and in the Christian church. But the doubt is not new. It is the most fundamental and original of all doubts. It is found on the lips of Satan in the earliest chapters of the Bible. "He [the serpent] said to the woman, 'Did God actually say, "You shall not eat of any tree in the garden"?'" (Gen 3:1). The question is, can God be trusted? Is the Bible truly his Word? Do we believe this without any mental reservations? If we do question the Word of God and if we have mental reservations about its authority, we will never be interested in true Bible study, nor will we come into the fullness of wisdom about God and ourselves that he desires for us. On the other hand, if we do accept these truths, we will want to study the Bible, and we will grow in knowledge and devotion. In fact, the study of Scripture will bless us. The text that began this chapter goes on to say, "All Scripture is breathed out by God and profitable for teaching, for reproof, for correction, and for training in righteousness, that the man of God may be complete, equipped for every good work" (2 Tim 3:16-17).

CHAPTER 4

THE AUTHORITY
OF THE SCRIPTURES

*A*primary cause of the confusion within the Christian church today is its lack of a valid authority. There have been attempts to supply this authority through the pronouncements of church councils, existential encounters with an intangible "word" of God, and other means. But none of these recent approaches can claim to be very successful. What is wrong? What is the source of the Christian's authority?

The classical Protestant answer is the revealed Word of God, the Bible. The Bible is authoritative because it is not the words of mere humans, though humans were the channels by which it came to us, but it is the direct result of the "breathing-out" of God. It is his product. But there is another level on which the question of authority may be raised. This relates to the way in which we become convinced of the Bible's authority. What is there about the Bible or the study of the Bible that should convince us that it is indeed God's Word?

The human aspect of the authority question takes us a bit further into what we mean when we say that the Bible is the Word of God, for the full meaning of that statement is not only that God has spoken to give us the Bible but also that he continues to speak through it to individuals. In other words, as individuals study the Bible, God speaks to them in their study and transforms them by the truths they find there. There is a direct encounter of the individual believer with God. It is what Luther meant when he declared at the Diet of Worms, "My conscience has been taken captive by the Word of God." It is what Calvin meant when he declared that "Scripture indeed is self-authenticated."[1]

Nothing but direct experience will ever ultimately convince anybody that the Bible's words are the authentic and authoritative words of God. As Calvin said, "The same spirit, therefore, who has spoken through the mouths of the prophets must penetrate into our hearts to persuade us that they faithfully proclaimed what has been divinely commanded."[2]

The Bible is something more than a body of revealed truths, a collection of books verbally inspired of God. It is also the living voice of God. The living God speaks through its pages. Therefore, it is not to be valued as a sacred object to be placed on a shelf and neglected, but as holy ground, where people's hearts and minds may come into vital contact with the living, gracious, and disturbing God. For a proper perspective on Scripture and for a valid understanding of revelation, there must be a constant interworking of these factors: an infallible and authoritative Word, the activity of the Holy Spirit in interpreting and applying that Word, and a receptive human heart. No true knowledge of God takes place without these elements.

SOLA SCRIPTURA

The assurance that God has spoken to them directly through his Holy Scriptures gave the Reformers their unique boldness. The formation of that truth theologically was the fundamentally new element in the Reformation.

The Reformation battle cry was *sola Scriptura*, "Scripture alone." But *sola Scriptura* meant more to the Reformers than that God has revealed himself in the propositions of the Bible. The new element was not that the Bible, being given by God, speaks with God's authority. The Roman Church held to that as well as the Reformers. The new element, as Packer points out,

> was the belief, borne in upon the Reformers by their own experience of Bible study, that Scripture can and does interpret itself to the faithful from within— Scripture is its own interpreter, *Scriptura sui ipsius interpres*, as Luther puts it—so that not only does it not need Popes or Councils to tell us, as from God, what it means; it can actually challenge Papal and conciliar pronouncements, convince

---

[1]John Calvin, *Institutes of the Christian Religion*, ed. John T. McNeill, trans. Ford Lewis Battles, 2 vols. (Philadelphia: Westminster, 1960), 80.
[2]Ibid., 79.

them of being ungodly and untrue, and require the faithful to part company with them. . . . As Scripture was the only *source* from which sinners might gain true knowledge of God and godliness, so Scripture was the only *judge* of what the church had in each age ventured to say in her Lord's name.[3]

In Luther's time the Roman Church had weakened the authority of the Bible by exalting human traditions to the stature of Scripture and by insisting that the teaching of the Bible could be communicated to Christian people only through the mediation of popes, councils, and priests. The Reformers restored biblical authority by holding that the living God speaks to his people directly and authoritatively through its pages.

The Reformers called the activity of God by which the truth of his Word is borne in on the mind and consciences of his people, "the internal witness of the Holy Spirit." They stressed that such activity was the subjective or internal counterpart of the objective or external revelation, and often referred to texts from John's writings. "The wind blows where it wishes, and you hear the its sound, but you do not know where it comes or where it goes. So it is with everyone who is born of the Spirit" (Jn 3:8). "But you have been anointed by the Holy One, and you all have knowledge. . . . But the anointing that you received from him abides in you, and you have no need that anyone should teach you. But as his anointing teaches you about everything, and is true, and is no lie—just as it has taught you, abide in him" (1 Jn 2:20, 27). "And the Spirit is the one who testifies, because the Spirit is the truth" (1 Jn 5:6).

The same idea is present in Paul's writings.

We have received not the spirit of the world, but the Spirit who is from God, that we might understand the things freely given us by God. And we impart this in words not taught by human wisdom but taught by the Spirit, interpreting spiritual truths to those who are spiritual. The natural person does not accept the things of the Spirit of God, for they are folly to him, and he is not able to understand them because they are spiritually discerned. The spiritual person judges all things, but is himself to be judged by no one. (1 Cor 2:12-15)

I do not cease to give thanks for you, remembering you in my prayers, that the God of our Lord Jesus Christ, the Father of glory, may give you a spirit of wisdom and of revelation in the knowledge of him, having the eyes of your hearts enlightened, that you may know what is the hope to which he has called you, what

[3]J. I. Packer, "'Sola Scriptura' in History and Today," in *God's Inerrant Word*, ed. John Warwick Montgomery (Minneapolis: Bethany Fellowship, 1975), 44-45.

are the riches of his glorious inheritance in the saints, and what is the immeasurable greatness of his power toward us who believe, according to the working of his great might that he worked in Christ when he raised him from the dead and seated him at his right hand in the heavenly places. (Eph 1:16-20)

Taken together, these texts teach that not only our rebirth but our entire growth in spiritual wisdom and the knowledge of God is the result of the working of the divine Spirit on our life and mind through the Scriptures, and that no spiritual understanding is possible apart from this activity. The witness of the Holy Spirit is, therefore, the effectual reason why the Bible is received as the final authority in all matters of faith and practice by those who are God's children.

THE BOOK THAT UNDERSTANDS ME

When we begin to read the Bible and are spoken to by the Holy Spirit as we read it, several things happen. First, the reading affects us as no other reading does.

Dr. Emile Cailliet was a French philosopher who eventually settled in America and became a professor at Princeton Theological Seminary in New Jersey. He had been brought up with a naturalistic education. He had never shown the slightest interest in spiritual things. He had never seen a Bible. But World War I came, and as he sat in the trenches he found himself reflecting on the inadequacy of his world-and-life view. He asked himself the same questions Levin had asked in Leo Tolstoy's *Anna Karenina*, while sitting beside the bed of his dying brother: Where did life come from? What did it all mean, if anything? What value are scientific laws or theories in the face of reality? Cailliet later wrote, "Like Levin, I too felt, not with my reason but with my whole being, that I was destined to perish miserably when the hour came."

During the long night watches, Cailliet began to long for what he came to call "a book that would understand me." He was highly educated, but he knew of no such book. Thus, when he was later wounded and released from the army and returned to his studies, he determined that he would prepare such a book secretly for his own use. As he read for his courses, he would file away passages that seemed to speak to his condition. Afterward he would copy them over in a leather-bound book. He hoped that the quotations, which he carefully indexed and numbered, would lead him from fear and anguish to release and jubilation.

At last the day came when he had put the finishing touches to his book, "the book that would understand me." He went out and sat down under a tree and opened the anthology. He began to read, but instead of release and jubilation, a growing disappointment began to come over him as he recognized that instead of speaking to his condition, the various passages only reminded him of their context and of his own work in searching them out and recording them. Then he knew that the whole undertaking simply would not work, for the book was a book of his own making. It carried no strength of persuasion. Dejected, he returned it to his pocket.

At that very moment his wife (who knew nothing of the project) came by with an interesting story. She had been walking in their tiny French village that afternoon and had stumbled on a small Huguenot chapel. She had never seen it before, but she had gone in and had asked for a Bible, much to her own surprise. The elderly pastor had given her one. She began apologizing to her husband, for she knew his feelings about the Christian faith. But he was not listening to her apology. "A Bible, you say? Where is it? Show me," he said. "I have never seen one before." When she produced it he rushed to his study and began to read. In his own words,

> I opened it and "chanced" upon the Beatitudes! I read, and read, and read—now aloud with an indescribable warmth surging within. . . . I could not find words to express my awe and wonder. And suddenly the realization dawned upon me: This *was* the Book that would understand me! I needed it so much, yet, unaware, I had attempted to write my own—in vain. I continued to read deeply into the night, mostly from the gospels. And lo and behold, as I looked through them, the One of whom they spoke, the One who spoke and acted in them, became alive to me. This vivid experience marked the beginning of my understanding of prayer. It also proved to be my initiation to the notion of Presence which later would prove so crucial in my theological thinking.
>
> The providential circumstances amid which the Book had found me now made it clear that while it seemed absurd to speak of a book understanding a man, this could be said of the Bible because its pages were animated by the Presence of the Living God and the Power of His mighty acts. To this God I prayed that night, and the God who answered *was the same God* of whom it was spoken in the Book.[4]

In all ages God's people have discovered the Reformation insight. Here is Calvin's expression of the same truth:

---

[4]Emile Cailliet, *Journey into Light* (Grand Rapids: Zondervan, 1968), 11-18.

Now this power which is peculiar to Scripture is clear from the fact that of human writings, however artfully polished, there is none capable of affecting us at all comparably. Read Demosthenes or Cicero; read Plato, Aristotle, and others of that tribe. They will, I admit, allure you, delight you, move you, enrapture you in wonderful measure. But betake yourself from them to this sacred reading. Then, in spite of yourself, so deeply will it affect you, so penetrate your heart, so fix itself in your very marrow, that compared with its deep impression, such vigor as the orators and philosophers have will nearly vanish. Consequently, it is easy to see that the Sacred Scriptures, which so far surpass all gifts and graces of human endeavor, breathe something divine.[5]

Another example is recorded toward the end of Luke's Gospel. Jesus had just risen from the dead and had begun to appear to the disciples. Two of these, Cleopas and possibly his wife, were returning to their hometown of Emmaus when Jesus drew close to them on the road. They did not recognize him. When he asked why they were downcast, they replied by telling him what had happened in Jerusalem at the time of the Passover. They told him about Jesus, "who was a prophet mighty in deed and word before God and all the people." They told him how the chief priests and rulers "delivered him up to be condemned to death, and crucified him" (Lk 24:19-20). They had been in Jerusalem that very morning and had heard tales from the women who had been to the tomb, reporting that the body was gone and that angels had appeared proclaiming that Jesus had been made alive. But they didn't believe in resurrections. They hadn't even bothered to go to the tomb to see for themselves, although they were within a short walk of it. The dream was over. Jesus was dead. They were going home.

But Jesus began to talk to them and explain the mission of the Christ, teaching them from the Scriptures. He said, "O foolish ones, and slow of heart to believe all that the prophets have spoken! Was it not necessary that the Christ should suffer these things and enter into his glory?" (Lk 24:25-26). Then beginning with Moses and going through all the prophets, he explained to them out of the Scriptures the things they said about himself.

At last they came to where the two disciples lived. They invited Jesus in, and he revealed himself to them as they ate together. He vanished, and they at once returned to Jerusalem to tell the other disciples what had happened. Their own testimony was this: "Did not our hearts burn within us while he talked to us on the road, while he opened to us the Scriptures?" (Lk 24:32). They were convicted

---

[5]Calvin, *Institutes*, 82.

by the Word of God. In this instance Jesus himself fulfilled the role of the Holy Spirit by interpreting the Bible to his disciples and by applying its truths to them.

The Bible also changes us. We become different men and women as a result of encountering it. A section of the thirteenth chapter of Romans changed the life of St. Augustine as he turned to the Bible in the garden of a friend's estate near Milan, Italy. Luther tells how in meditating on the Scriptures while secluded in the Wartburg Castle, he felt himself to be "reborn," and tells how Romans 1:17 became for him "a gate to heaven." John Wesley's meditation on Scripture led to his conversion in the little meeting in Aldersgate. J. B. Phillips writes,

> Some years before the publication of the New English Bible, I was invited by the BBC to discuss the problems of translation with Dr. E. V. Rieu, who had himself recently produced a translation of the four Gospels for Penguin Classics. Towards the end of the discussion Dr. Rieu was asked about his general approach to the task, and his reply was this:
>
> "My personal reason for doing this was my own intense desire to satisfy myself as to the authenticity and the spiritual content of the Gospels. And, if I received any new light by an intensive study of the Greek originals, to pass it on to others. I approached them in the same spirit as I would have approached them had they been presented to me as recently discovered Greek manuscripts."
>
> A few minutes later I asked him, "Did you get the feeling that the whole material is extraordinarily alive? . . . I got the feeling that the whole thing was alive even while one was translating. Even though one did a dozen versions of a particular passage, it was still living. Did you get that feeling?"
>
> Dr. Rieu replied, "I got the deepest feeling that I possibly could have experienced. It—changed me; my work changed me. And I came to the conclusion that these words bear the seal of—the Son of man and God. And they're the Magna Carta of the human spirit."

Phillips concludes, "I found it particularly thrilling to hear a man who is a scholar of the first rank as well as a man of wisdom and experience openly admitting that these words written long ago were alive with power. They bore to him, as to me, the ring of truth."[6]

ONE SUBJECT

Another result of reading the Bible is that the Holy Spirit who speaks in its pages will direct the student to Jesus. The Bible contains many varieties of material. It

---

[6]J. B. Phillips, *Ring of Truth: A Translator's Testimony* (New York: Macmillan, 1967), 74-75.

covers hundreds of years of history. Still, the object of the Bible in each of its parts is to point to Jesus, and this goal is carried out on the subjective level by Christ's Spirit. Jesus said, "But when the Helper comes, whom I will send to you from the Father, the Spirit of truth, who proceeds from the Father, he will bear witness about me" (Jn 15:26). Since the role of the Holy Spirit is to point to Jesus in the Scriptures, we can be sure that we are listening to the voice of the Holy Spirit when that happens.

"Isn't the Bible mostly history?" a person might ask. "How can Jesus be its subject in the Old Testament? And how can the Holy Spirit point us to him?" Jesus becomes the subject of the Old Testament in two ways: (1) by fitting in with its general themes and (2) by fulfilling specific prophecies found there.

One main theme of the Old Testament is *human sin* and our resultant need. The Bible begins with the story of the creation. But no sooner is this story told (in the first chapter of Genesis) than we are also told of the fall of the human race. Instead of being humbly and gratefully dependent on our Creator, as we should have been, we were soon in a state of rebellion against God. We went our own way instead of God's. So the consequences of sin (ultimately, death) came on us.

In the rest of the Old Testament we see these consequences unfolding: the murder of Abel, the corruption leading up to the flood, demonism, sexual perversions, eventually even tragedy for the chosen nation of Israel in spite of great blessings. The Old Testament is best summarized in David's psalm of repentance, which ought properly to be the psalm of the whole human race.

> Have mercy on me, O God,
>   according to your steadfast love;
> according to your abundant mercy
>   blot out my transgressions.
> Wash me thoroughly from my iniquity,
>   and cleanse me from my sin!
> For I know my transgressions,
>   and my sin is ever before me. . . .
> Behold, I was brought forth in iniquity,
>   and in sin did my mother conceive me. (Ps 51:1-3, 5)

Here is one important biblical doctrine. But if we understand it rightly, even this doctrine is not an end in itself. The truth of our sin and need is expounded in the Bible because the Bible is also able to point to Christ as the solution to the dilemma.

A second Old Testament theme is the existence of a *God who acts in love* to redeem sinners. God the Father did this throughout the Old Testament period. At the same time, as he did it, he pointed to the coming of his Son, who would redeem men and women perfectly and forever.

When Adam and Eve sinned, sin separated them from the Creator. They tried to hide. God, however, came to them in the cool of the evening, calling them. It is true that God spoke in judgment, as he had to do. He revealed the consequences of their sin. Still, he also killed animals, clothed the man and woman with skins, covering their shame, and began his teaching of the way of salvation through sacrifice. In the same story he spoke to Satan revealing the coming of one who would one day defeat him forever: "He shall bruise your head, and you shall bruise his heel" (Gen 3:15).

Nine chapters later we find another, somewhat veiled reference to the "seed" who shall crush Satan. It is God's first great promise to Abraham, stressing that in him all nations would be blessed (Gen 12:3; 22:18). The blessing referred to is certainly not a blessing to come to all people through Abraham personally. It is not a blessing to come through all Jews indiscriminately, for all Jews are not even theists. The foretold blessing was to come through the seed of Abraham, the promised seed, the Messiah. Thus, years later the apostle Paul, who knew this text, used it to show (1) that the seed was the Lord Jesus, (2) that the promise to Abraham was one of blessing through him, and (3) that the blessing was to come through Christ's work of redemption (Gal 3:13-16).

An interesting prophecy was spoken by the Lord through Balaam, a shifty, half-hearted prophet of Moses' day. Balak, a king who was hostile to Israel, had hired Balaam to curse the Jewish people. But every time Balaam opened his mouth, blessings on the people came out instead. On one occasion he said,

> A star shall come out of Jacob,
> > and a scepter shall rise out of Israel. . . .
> And one from Jacob shall exercise dominion. (Num 24:17, 19)]

As he was dying, the patriarch Jacob said,

> The scepter shall not depart from Judah,
> > nor the ruler's staff from between his feet,
> until tribute comes to him;
> > and to him shall be the obedience of the peoples. (Gen 49:10)

Moses also spoke of the one who would come: "The LORD your God will raise up for you a prophet like me from among you, from your brothers—it is to him you shall listen" (Deut 18:15). And again, with God speaking, "I will put my words in his mouth, and he shall speak to them all that I command him" (Deut 18:18).

The book of Psalms contains great prophecies. The second psalm tells of Christ's victory and rule over the nations of this earth. This psalm was a popular one with the early Christians (see Acts 4). Psalm 16:10 foretells the resurrection (see Acts 2:31). In Psalms 22; 23; 24 we have three portraits of the Lord Jesus: the suffering Savior, the compassionate Shepherd, and the King. Other psalms speak of other aspects of his life and ministry. Psalm 110 returns to the theme of his rule, looking for the day when Jesus shall take his seat at the right hand of the Father when all his enemies shall be made his "footstool."

Details of Christ's life, death and resurrection occur in the books of the prophets—in Isaiah, Daniel, Jeremiah, Ezekiel, Hosea, Zechariah, and others.

The Lord Jesus Christ and his work are the chief subjects of the Bible. It is the work of the Holy Spirit to reveal him. As the revelation takes place the Bible becomes understandable, Scripture bears witness to Scripture, and the power of the living God is sensed to be surging through its pages.

WORD AND SPIRIT

The combination of an objective, written revelation and its subjective interpretation to the individual by God's Spirit is the key to the Christian doctrine of the knowledge of God. This combination keeps us from two errors.

The first is the error of overspiritualizing revelation. This is the error that entangled the Anabaptist "enthusiasts" in Calvin's day and that has since entrapped many of their followers. The enthusiasts laid claim to private, Spirit-given revelations as justification for their decisions and conduct. But these were often contrary to the express teaching of the Word of God, as, for example, their occasional decision to stop working and gather for the anticipated return of the Lord. Without the objective Word there was no way to judge such "revelations" or to keep the individuals from error who were caught up in them. Calvin wrote in reference to this dilemma:

> The Holy Spirit so inheres in his truth, which he expresses in Scripture, that only when its proper reverence and dignity are given to the Word does the Holy Spirit show forth his power. . . . The children of God . . . see themselves, without the

Spirit of God, bereft of the whole light of truth, so are not unaware that the Word is the instrument by which the Lord dispenses the illumination of his Spirit to believers. For they know no other Spirit than him who dwelt and spoke in the apostles, and by whose oracles they are continually recalled to the hearing of the Word.[7]

On the other hand, the combination of an objective Word and a subjective application of that Word by God's Spirit also keeps us from the error of overintellectualizing God's truth. That error was evident in the diligent Bible study habits of the scribes and Pharisees in Jesus' time. The scribes and Pharisees were not slothful students. They were meticulous in their pursuit of Bible knowledge, even to the point of counting the individual letters of the Bible books. Yet Jesus rebuked them, saying, "You search the Scriptures because you think that in them you have eternal life; and it is they that bear witness about me" (Jn 5:39).

To know God we must be taught from the Bible by the Holy Spirit. It is only then that a full awareness of the nature of the Bible and its authority is borne home on our minds and hearts, and we find ourselves taking a firm stand on that cherished revelation.

[7]Calvin, Institutes, 95-96.

CHAPTER 5

THE PROOF OF
THE SCRIPTURES

*T*he chief evidence for the Bible's being the Word of God is the internal testimony of the Holy Spirit to that truth. Without such testimony the truthfulness of Scripture will never impress itself adequately on a reader. But that does not mean that there are no rational supports for one's conviction. The rational arguments should be known by the mature Christian, as well as by anyone who is just beginning to consider the claims of Christianity.

What are these arguments? Some have already been suggested. First, there are the claims of the Scriptures themselves. The books of the Bible claim to be the Word of God, and, while this in itself does not prove that they are, nevertheless it is a fact to be accounted for. We must ask how books that seem to be right in so many other respects could yet be in error at the crucial point of their self-awareness. Second, there is the testimony of Jesus. His testimony is the greatest argument of all. For even if Jesus were only a great teacher, his regard for the Bible as the ultimate authority in life could hardly be disregarded. Third, there is the doctrinal and ethical superiority of the Bible to all other books. The Bible's superiority has often been acknowledged even by unbelievers and is denied by few who have actually read and studied its pages. Fourth, there is the power of the Bible to affect us as we read it. What produces such results if the Bible is not divine both in its source and its operation on human lives?

Thomas Watson, one of the great English Puritans, wrote,

I wonder whence the Scriptures should come, if not from God. Bad men could not be the authors of it. Would their minds be employed in inditing such holy lines? Would they declare so fiercely against sin? Good men could not be the authors of it. Could they write in such a strain? or could it stand with their grace to counterfeit God's name, and put, *Thus saith the Lord*, to a book of their own devising?[1]

Here are four good reasons for regarding the Bible as the revealed Word of God, plus a fifth arising out of Watson's argument: the biblical writers would not have claimed divine origin for a book they knew to be purely their own. What follows are five more supports for the same conclusion.

THE UNITY IN DIVERSITY

A sixth reason for regarding the Bible as the revealed Word of God is the extraordinary unity of the book. This is an old argument, but it is a good one nonetheless. It is one that grows in force the more one studies the documents. The Bible is composed of sixty-six parts, or books, written over a period of approximately fifteen hundred years (from about 1450 BC to about AD 90) by over forty different people. These people were not alike. They came from various levels of society and from diverse backgrounds. Some were kings. Others were statesmen, priests, prophets, a tax collector, a physician, a tentmaker, fishermen. If asked about any subject at all, they would have had views as diverse as the opinions of people living today. Yet together they produced a volume that is a marvelous unity in its doctrine, historical viewpoints, ethics, and expectations. It is, in short, a single story of divine redemption begun in Israel, centered in Jesus Christ, and culminating at the end of history. The nature of this unity is important. To begin with, as R. A. Torrey notes,

> It is not a superficial unity, but a profound unity. On the surface, we often find apparent discrepancy and disagreement, but, as we study, the apparent discrepancy and disagreement disappear, and the deep underlying unity appears. The more deeply we study, the more complete do we find the unity to be. The unity is also an organic one—that is, it is not the unity of a dead thing, like a stone, but of a living thing, like a plant. In the early books of the Bible we have the germinant thought; as we go on we have the plant, and further on the bud, and then the blossom, and then the ripened fruit. In Revelation we find the ripened fruit of Genesis.[2]

---

[1] Thomas Watson, *A Body of Divinity: Contained in Sermons upon the Westminster Assembly's Catechism* (1692; reprint ed., London: The Banner of Truth Trust, 1970), 26.
[2] R. A. Torrey, *The Bible and Its Christ* (New York: Fleming H. Revell, 1904–1906), 26.

What can account for this unity? There is only one way of accounting for it: behind the efforts of the more than forty human authors is the one perfect, sovereign, and guiding mind of God.

UNCOMMON ACCURACY

A seventh reason for believing the Bible to be the Word of God is its uncommon accuracy. To be sure, its accuracy does not prove the Bible to be divine—human beings are also sometimes quite accurate—but it is what we should expect if the Bible is the result of God's effort. On the other hand, if the accuracy of the Bible extends to the point of inerrancy (which we will consider in the next chapter), that would be a direct proof of its divinity. For, although error is human, inerrancy is certainly divine.

At some points the accuracy of the Bible may be tested *externally*, as in the historical portions of the New Testament. We may take the Gospel of Luke and the book of Acts as an example. Luke–Acts is an attempt to write an "orderly account" of Jesus' life and of the rapid expansion of the early Christian church (Lk 1:1-4; Acts 1:1-2). That would be an enormous undertaking even in our day. It was especially so in ancient times, when there were no newspapers or reference books. In fact there were few written documents of any kind. Yet in spite of this, Luke charted the growth of what began as an insignificant religious movement in a far corner of the Roman Empire, a movement that progressed quietly and without official sanction so that within forty years of the death and resurrection of Jesus Christ there were Christian congregations in most of the major cities of the empire. Does Luke's work succeed? It does so remarkably and with what is apparently total accuracy.

For one thing, both books show amazing accuracy in handling official titles and corresponding spheres of influence. This has been documented by F. F. Bruce of the University of Manchester, England, in a small work entitled *The New Testament Documents: Are They Reliable?* Bruce writes:

> One of the most remarkable tokens of his [Luke's] accuracy is his sure familiarity with the proper titles of all the notable persons who are mentioned in his pages. This was by no means such an easy feat in his days as it is in ours, when it is so simple to consult convenient books of reference. The accuracy of Luke's use of the various titles in the Roman Empire has been compared to the easy and confident way in which an Oxford man in ordinary conversation will refer to the Heads of colleges by their proper titles—the *Provost* of Oriel, the *Master* of Balliol, the *Rector*

of Exeter, the *President* of Magdalen, and so on. A non-Oxonian like the present writer never feels quite at home with the multiplicity of these Oxford titles.[3]

Luke obviously feels at home with the Roman titles; he never gets them wrong.

Bruce adds that Luke had a further difficulty in that the titles often did not remain the same for any great length of time. For example, the administration of a province might pass from a direct representative of the emperor to a senatorial government, and would then be governed by a proconsul rather than an imperial legate (*legatus pro praetore*). Cyprus, an imperial province until 22 BC, became a senatorial province in that year and was therefore no longer governed by an imperial legate but by a proconsul. Thus when Paul and Barnabas arrived in Cyprus about AD 47, it was the proconsul Sergius Paulus who greeted them (Acts 13:7).

Similarly, Achaia was a senatorial province from 27 BC to AD 15, and again subsequent to AD 44. Hence, Luke refers to Gallio, the Roman ruler in Greece, as "the proconsul of Achaia" (Acts 18:12), the title of the Roman representative during the time of Paul's visit to Corinth but not during the twenty-nine years prior to AD 44.[4]

This kind of accuracy by only one of the biblical writers is a testimony that may be multiplied almost indefinitely. For example, in Acts 19:38, the town clerk of Ephesus tries to calm the rioting citizens by referring them to the Roman authorities. "There are proconsuls," he says, using the plural. At first glance the writer seems to have made a mistake, since there was only one Roman proconsul in a given area at a time. But an examination shows that shortly before the rioting at Ephesus, Junius Silanus, the proconsul, had been murdered by messengers from Agrippina, the mother of the adolescent Nero. Since the new proconsul had not arrived in Ephesus, the town clerk's vagueness may be intentional or may even refer to the two emissaries, Helius and Celer, who were the apparent successors to Silanus's power. Luke captures the tone of the city in a time of internal disturbance, just as elsewhere he captures the tones of Antioch, Jerusalem, Rome, and other cities, each of which had its own unique flavor.

Archaeology has also substantiated an extraordinary reliability for the writings of Luke and for other biblical documents. A plaque has been found in Delphi identifying Gallio as the proconsul in Corinth at the precise time of Paul's visit

---

[3]F. F. Bruce, *The New Testament Documents: Are They Reliable?* (Downers Grove, IL: InterVarsity Press, 1974), 82.
[4]Ibid., 82-83.

to the city. The pool of Bethesda, containing five porticoes, has been found approximately seventy feet below the present level of the city of Jerusalem. It is mentioned in John 5:2, but it had been lost to view from the destruction of the city by the armies of Titus in AD 70 until recent times. The Pavement of Judgment, *Gabbatha*, mentioned in John 19:13, has also been uncovered.

Ancient documents—from Dura, Ras Shamra, Egypt, and the Dead Sea—have thrown light on biblical reliability. Recently reports have been received of remarkable finds at Tell Mardikh in northwest Syria, the site of ancient Ebla. Thus far, fifteen thousand tablets dating from approximately 2300 BC (two to five hundred years before Abraham) have been discovered. In them are hundreds of names such as Abram, Israel, Esau, David, Yahweh, and Jerusalem, showing these to be common names prior to their appearance in the biblical accounts. As they are studied carefully, these tablets will undoubtedly throw much light on customs in the subsequent era of the Old Testament patriarchs, Moses, David, and others. Their very existence already tends to verify the Old Testament narratives.

Internal evidence of the Bible's accuracy is also available, particularly where there are parallel accounts of the same events. The Gospel accounts of the resurrection appearances of the Lord Jesus Christ are an example. They are clearly four separate and independent accounts; otherwise there would be no apparent discrepancies. Writers working in collaboration would have cleared up any difficulties. Yet the Gospels do not really contradict each other. They are mutually supportive. Moreover, an incidental detail in one sometimes clarifies what seems to be a contradiction between two of the others.

Matthew speaks of Mary Magdalene and the "other" Mary as having gone to Christ's tomb on the first Easter morning. Mark mentions Mary Magdalene, Mary the mother of James (thus identifying Matthew's "other" Mary), and Salome. Luke mentions the two Marys, Joanna, and "the other women with them." John mentions only Mary Magdalene. On the surface these reports are different, but when they are examined further they reveal a remarkable harmony. Clearly a group of women, including all those mentioned, set out for the tomb. Finding the stone moved, the older women dispatched Mary Magdalene to tell the apostles of the disturbance and ask their advice. While she was gone the remaining women saw the angels (as Matthew, Mark, and Luke report) but not the risen Lord, at least not until later. On the other hand, Mary, returning later and alone, did see him (as John discloses). In the same way, John's mention of "that other disciple" who accompanied Peter to the tomb throws light on Luke 24:24; that verse says that "some of those who were with us went to the tomb," after the women had been there, though Luke mentions only Peter (a singular individual) in his own narration.

These are little things, to be sure. But because they are little, they lend special weight to the impression of the Gospels' total accuracy.

PROPHECY

An eighth reason for believing the Bible to be the Word of God is fulfilled prophecy. Here again is an extremely large subject, one clearly beyond the scope of this chapter. Nevertheless, it is possible to show briefly the general impact of the argument.

First, there are explicit prophecies. These concern the future of the Jewish people (including things that have already occurred and some that have not yet occurred) and the future of the Gentile nations. Above all, many describe the coming of the Lord Jesus Christ, first to die and then afterward to return in power and great glory. Torrey cites five passages—Isaiah 53 (the entire chapter); Micah 5:2; Daniel 9:25-27; Jeremiah 23:5-6; and Psalm 16:8-11— and comments,

> In the passages cited we have predictions of a coming King of Israel. We are told the exact time of his manifestation to his people, the exact place of his birth, the family of which he should be born, the condition of the family at the time of his birth (a condition entirely different from that existing at the time the prophecy was written, and contrary to all the probabilities in the case), the manner of his reception by his people (a reception entirely different from that which would naturally be expected), the fact, method, and details regarding his death, with the specific circumstances regarding his burial, his resurrection subsequent to his burial, and his victory subsequent to his resurrection. These predictions were fulfilled with the most minute precision in Jesus of Nazareth.[5]

Another writer, E. Schuyler English, former chairman of the editorial committee of *The New Scofield Reference Bible* (1967) and editor-in-chief of *The Pilgrim Bible* (1948), observed that

> more than twenty Old Testament predictions relating to events that would sur-round the death of Christ, words written centuries before his first advent, were fulfilled with precision within a twenty-four-hour period at the time of his crucifixion [alone]. For example, in Matthew 27:35 it is written, "And they

---

[5]Torrey, *The Bible and Its Christ*, 19.

crucified him, and parted his garments, casting lots." This was in fulfillment of
Psalm 22:18, where it is stated, "They part my garments among them, and cast
lots upon my vesture."[6]

Many of these prophecies have been questioned, and attempts have been
made to redate the Old Testament books, bringing them nearer to the time of
Christ. But one can bring some prophecies to the very latest date imagined by
the most radical and destructive critics, and they are still hundreds of years
before the birth of Christ. Moreover, their cumulative witness is devastating.
These are facts. They demand an accounting. What will account for them? The
only fact that will account for such evidence is the existence of a sovereign God.
He revealed in advance what would happen when he sent Jesus for the redemption
of our race and then saw to it that such things actually took place.

Much more can be said in reference to prophecy. The preceding material
relates only to the coming of Christ. There are also prophecies concerning the
scattering and regathering of Israel, as well as general and specific prophecies
concerning the Gentile nations and the capitals of those nations, many of which
have been destroyed in precisely the way the Bible had indicated generations
and even centuries before. The institutions, ceremonies, offerings, and feasts of
Israel are also prophetic of the life and ministry of Jesus.[7]

THE BIBLE'S PRESERVATION

A ninth reason for believing the Bible to be the Word of God is its extraordinary
preservation down through the centuries of Old Testament and church history.
Today, after the Bible has been translated in part or whole into hundreds of
languages, some with multiple versions, and after millions of copies of the sacred
text have been printed and distributed, it would be a nearly impossible feat to
destroy the Bible. But these conditions did not always prevail.

---

[6]E. Schuyler English, *A Companion to the New Scofield Reference Bible* (New York: Oxford University
Press, 1972), 26. The author invites the reader also to compare the following: Mt 26:21-25 with
Ps 41:9. Mt 26:31, 56; Mk 14:50 with Zech 13:7. Mt 26:59 with Ps 35:11. Mt 26:63; 27:12, 14;
Mk 14:61 with Is 53:7. Mt 26:67 with Is 50:6; 52:14; Mic 5:1; Zech 13:7. Mt 27:9 with
Zech 11:12-13. Mt 27:27 with Is 53:8. Mt 27:34; Mk 15:36; Jn 19:29 with Ps 69:21. Mt 27:38;
Mk 15:27-28; Lk 22:37; 23:32 with Is 53:12. Mt 27:46; Mk 15:34 with Ps 22:1. Mt 27:60;
Mk 15:46; Lk 23:53; Jn 19:41 with Is 53:9. Lk 23:34 with Is 53:12. Jn 19:28 with Ps 69:21.
Jn 19:33, 36 with Ps 34:20. Jn 19:34, 37 with Zech 12:10.
[7]For a fuller discussion of this interesting area of Old Testament studies, see Victor Buksbazen,
The Gospel in the Feasts of Israel (Fort Washington, PA: Christian Literature Crusade, 1954), and
Norman L. Geisler, *Christ: The Theme of the Bible* (Chicago: Moody Press, 1968), 31-68.

Until the time of the Reformation, the biblical text was preserved by the laborious and time-consuming process of copying it over and over again by hand, at first onto papyrus sheets and then onto parchments. Throughout much of this time the Bible was an object of extreme hatred by many in authority. They tried to stamp it out. In the early days of the church, Celsus, Porphyry, and Lucian tried to destroy it by arguments. Later the emperors Diocletian and Julian tried to destroy it by force. At several points it was actually a capital offense to possess a copy of parts of Holy Writ. Yet the text survived.

If the Bible had been only the thoughts and work of human beings, it would have been eliminated long ago in the face of such opposition, as other books have been. But it has endured, fulfilling the words of Jesus, who said, "Heaven and earth will pass away, but my words will not pass away" (Mt 24:35).

CHANGED LIVES

A tenth reason for believing the Bible to be the Word of God is its demonstrated ability to transform even the worst men and women, making them a blessing to their families, friends, and community. The Bible speaks of this power:

> The law of the LORD is perfect,
>> reviving the soul;
> the testimony of the LORD is sure,
>> making wise the simple;
> the precepts of the LORD are right,
>> rejoicing the heart;
> the commandment of the LORD is pure,
>> enlightening the eyes;
> the fear of the LORD is clean,
>> enduring forever;
> the rules of the LORD are true,
>> and righteous altogether. (Ps 19:7-9)

As discussed in the last chapter, the transformation takes place by the power of the Holy Spirit who works through the Word.

Does the Bible actually transform men and women, turning them into godly persons? It does. Prostitutes have been reformed. Drunkards have become sober. Those filled with pride have become humble. Dishonest people have become people of integrity. Weak women and men have become strong, and all because of the transformation wrought in them by God as they have heard and studied the Scriptures.

A remarkable illustration comes from the life of Dr. Harry A. Ironside. Early in his ministry, the great evangelist and Bible teacher was living in the San Francisco Bay area working with a group of believers called the Brethren. One Sunday, as he was walking through the city, he came upon a group of Salvation Army workers holding a meeting on the corner of Market and Grant Avenues. There were probably sixty of them. When they recognized Ironside, they immediately asked him if he would give his testimony. So he did, giving a word about how God had saved him through faith in the bodily death and literal resurrection of Jesus.

As he was speaking, Ironside noticed that on the edge of the crowd a well-dressed man had taken a card from his pocket and had written something on it. As Ironside finished his talk, this man came forward, lifted his hat, and very politely handed him the card. On one side was his name, which Ironside immediately recognized. The man was one of the early socialists who had made a name for himself lecturing not only for socialism but also against Christianity. As Ironside turned the card over, he read, "Sir, I challenge you to debate with me the question 'Agnosticism versus Christianity' in the Academy of Science Hall next Sunday afternoon at four o'clock. I will pay all expenses."

Ironside reread the card aloud and then replied somewhat like this.

I am very much interested in this challenge. . . . Therefore I will be glad to agree to this debate on the following conditions: namely, that in order to prove that Mr.————has something worth fighting for and worth debating about, he will promise to bring with him to the Hall next Sunday two people, whose qualifications I will give in a moment, as proof that agnosticism is of real value in changing human lives and building true character. First, he must promise to bring with him one man who was for years what we commonly call a "down-and-outer." I am not particular as to the exact nature of the sins that had wrecked his life and made him an outcast from society—whether a drunkard, or a criminal of some kind, or a victim of his sensual appetite—but a man who for years was under the power of evil habits from which he could not deliver himself, but who on some occasion entered one of Mr.————'s meetings and heard his glorification of agnosticism and his denunciations of the Bible and Christianity, and whose heart and mind as he listened to such an address were so deeply stirred that he went away from that meeting saying, "Henceforth, I too am an agnostic!" and as a result of imbibing that particular philosophy found that a new power had come into his life. The sins he once loved he now hates, and righteousness and goodness are now the ideals of his life. He is now an entirely new man, a credit to himself and an asset to society—all because he is an agnostic.

Secondly, I would like Mr.————to promise to bring with him one woman— and I think he may have more difficulty in finding the woman than the man—who was once a poor, wrecked, characterless outcast, the slave of evil passions, and the victim of man's corrupt living . . . perhaps one who had lived for years in some evil resort, . . . utterly lost, ruined and wretched because of her life of sin. But this woman also entered a hall where Mr.————was loudly proclaiming his ag- nosticism and ridiculing the message of the Holy Scriptures. As she listened, hope was born in her heart, and she said, "This is just what I need to deliver me from the slavery of sin!" She followed the teaching and became an intelligent agnostic or infidel. As a result, her whole being revolted against the degradation of the life she had been living. She fled from the den of iniquity where she had been held captive so long; and today, rehabilitated, she has won her way back to an honored position in society and is living a clean, virtuous, happy life—all because she is an agnostic.

"Now," he said, addressing the man who had presented him with his card and the challenge,

if you will promise to bring these two people with you as examples of what ag- nosticism can do, I will promise to meet you at the Hall of Science at four o'clock next Sunday, and I will bring with me at the very least 100 men and women who for years lived in just such sinful degradation as I have tried to depict, but who have been gloriously saved through believing the gospel which you ridicule. I will have these men and women with me on the platform as witnesses to the miraculous saving power of Jesus Christ and as present-day proof of the truth of the Bible.

Dr. Ironside then turned to the Salvation Army captain and said, "Captain, have you any who could go with me to such a meeting?"

She exclaimed with enthusiasm, "We can give you forty at least just from this one corps, and we will give you a brass band to lead the procession!"

"Fine," Dr. Ironside answered.

Now, Mr.————, I will have no difficulty in picking up sixty others from the various missions, gospel halls, and evangelical churches of the city; and if you will promise faithfully to bring two such exhibits as I have described, I will come marching in at the head of such a procession, with the band playing "Onward, Christian Soldiers," and I will be ready for the debate.

Apparently the man who had made the challenge must have had some sense of humor, for he smiled wryly and waved his hand in a deprecating kind of way as if to say, "Nothing doing!" and then edged out of the crowd while the bystanders clapped for Ironside and the others.[8]

The power of the living Christ operating by means of the Holy Spirit through the written Word changes lives. This has been true throughout history. It is a powerful proof that the Bible is indeed the Word of God.

---

[8]H. A. Ironside, *Random Reminiscences from Fifty Years of Ministry* (New York: Loizeaux Brothers, 1939), 99-107. I have also told this story in *The Gospel of John*, vol. 1 (Grand Rapids: Zondervan, 1975), 226-28.

CHAPTER 6

HOW TRUE IS
THE BIBLE?

From the beginning of the Christian church until well into the eighteenth century, the vast majority of Christians of all denominations acknowledged that the Scriptures of the Old and New Testaments were uniquely the Word of God. In these books God speaks. And because God speaks in Scripture—as he does nowhere else in the same way—all who claimed to be Christians recognized the Bible as a divine authority binding on all, a body of objective truth that transcends subjective understanding. In these books, God's saving acts in history are told to human beings so that we might believe. And the events of that history are divinely interpreted that men and women might understand the gospel and respond to it intelligently both in thought and action. The Bible is the written Word of God. Because the Bible is the Word of God, the Scriptures of the Old and New Testaments are authoritative and inerrant.

THE VIEW OF THE FIRST SIXTEEN CENTURIES

There are many statements to substantiate the existence of this high view of Scripture in the documents of the early church. Irenaeus, who lived and wrote in Lyons in the early years of the second century, wrote that we should be "most properly assured that the Scriptures are indeed perfect, since they were spoken by the Word of God and His Spirit."[1] Cyril of Jerusalem, who lived in the fourth

---

[1]Irenaeus, *Against Heresies*, II, xxvii, 2. *The Ante-Nicene Fathers*, vol. 1, ed. Alexander Roberts and James Donaldson (1885; reprint ed., Grand Rapids: Eerdmans, n.d.), 399.

century, said, "Not even a casual statement must be delivered without the Holy Scriptures; nor must we be drawn aside by mere probability and artifices of speech. . . . For this salvation which we believe depends not on ingenious reasoning, but on demonstration of the Holy Scriptures."[2]

In a letter to Jerome, the translator of the Latin Vulgate, Augustine said, "I . . . believe most firmly that not one of those authors had erred in writing anything at all. If I do find anything in those books which seems contrary to truth, I decide that either the text is corrupt, or the translator did not follow what was really said, or that I failed to understand it. . . . The canonical books are entirely free of falsehood."[3] And in his treatise "On the Trinity" he warns, "Do not be willing to yield to my writings as to the canonical Scriptures; but in these, when thou hast discovered even what thou didst not previously believe, believe it unhesitatingly."[4]

The same position holds for Luther. Some hold that Luther's reference to the Bible as "the cradle of Christ" proves that he believed in a revelation within the Bible (not one that was identical with it) and that he held the Scriptures in less esteem than the Christ they speak of. For some this means that not all the Bible is the Word of God. But this is not right.

Luther's phrase, the "cradle of Christ," occurs at the end of the third paragraph of his "Preface to the Old Testament." And there, as the late Lutheran scholar J. Theodore Mueller has demonstrated, Luther is actually defending the value of the Old Testament for Christians. Far from deprecating Scripture, Luther is actually concerned "to express his most reverent esteem of Holy Scripture, which offers to man the supreme blessing of eternal salvation in Christ."[5] Luther himself says, "I beg and faithfully warn every pious Christian not to be offended by the simplicity of the language and the stories that will often meet him here [in the Old Testament]. Let him not doubt that, however simple they may seem, they are the very words, works, judgments, and deeds of the high majesty, power, and wisdom of God."[6]

---

[2]Cyril of Jerusalem, *Catechetical Lectures*, IV, 17. *The Nicene and Post-Nicene Fathers*, series 2, vol. 7, ed. Philip Schaff and Henry Wace (1893; reprint ed., Grand Rapids: Eerdmans, n.d.), 23.

[3]Augustine, *Epistles*, 82. *St. Augustine: Letters 1–82*, trans. Wilfrid Parsons, The Fathers of the Church, vol. 12 (Washington, D.C.: The Catholic University of America Press, 1951), 392, 409.

[4]Augustine, "On the Trinity." Preface to chap. 3, *The Nicene and Post-Nicene Fathers*, series 1, vol. 3, ed. Philip Schaff (Buffalo, NY: The Christian Literature Company, 1887), 56.

[5]J. Theodore Mueller, "Luther's 'Cradle of Christ,'" *Christianity Today*, October 24, 1960, 11.

[6]Martin Luther, "Preface to the Old Testament," in *What Luther Says: An Anthology*, ed. Ewald M. Plass, vol. 1 (St. Louis: Concordia, 1959), 71. The passage is quoted in a slightly different translation by Mueller, "Luther's 'Cradle of Christ.'"

In another place Luther says, "The Scriptures, although they also were written by men, are not of men nor from men, but from God."[7] Again, "We must make a great difference between God's Word and the word of man. A man's word is a little sound, that flies into the air, and soon vanishes; but the Word of God is greater than heaven and earth, yea, greater than death and hell, for it forms part of the power of God, and endures everlastingly."[8]

In some places Calvin is even more outspoken. Commenting on 2 Timothy 3:16, the Geneva reformer maintains,

> This is the principle that distinguishes our religion from all others, that we know that God hath spoken to us and are fully convinced that the prophets did not speak of themselves, but as organs of the Holy Spirit uttered only that which they had been commissioned from heaven to declare. All those who wish to profit from the Scriptures must first accept this as a settled principle, that the Law and the prophets are not teachings handed on at the pleasure of men, or produced by men's minds as their source, but are dictated by the Holy Spirit.

He concludes, "We owe to the Scripture the same reverence as we owe to God, since it has its only source in Him and has nothing of human origin mixed with it."[9] In his comments on the Psalms, he speaks of the Bible as that "certain and unerring rule" (Ps 5:11).

John Wesley says the same. "The Scripture, therefore, is a rule sufficient in itself, and was by men divinely inspired at once delivered to the world."[10] "If there be any mistakes in the Bible, there may well be a thousand. If there be one falsehood in that book, it did not come from the God of truth."[11]

It was the glory of the church that in the first sixteen or seventeen centuries all Christians in every place, despite their differences of opinion on theology or on questions of church order, exhibited at least a mental allegiance to the Bible as the supreme and inerrant authority for the Christian in all matters. It might be neglected. There might be disagreements about what it actually teaches. It

---

[7]Martin Luther, "That Doctrines of Men Are to Be Rejected," in Plass, *What Luther Says*, 63.

[8]Martin Luther, *Table Talk*, 44, in *A Compend of Luther's Theology*, ed. Hugh Thomson Kerr (Philadelphia: Westminster, 1943), 10.

[9]John Calvin, *Calvin's New Testament Commentaries*, vol. 10, *The Second Epistle of Paul the Apostle to the Corinthians and the Epistles to Timothy, Titus and Philemon*, trans. T. A. Small (Grand Rapids: Eerdmans, 1964), 330.

[10]John Wesley, *The Works of John Wesley*, vol. 10, *A Roman Catechism*, question 5 (1872; reprint ed., Grand Rapids: Zondervan, n.d.), 90.

[11]Wesley, *The Works of John Wesley*, 4:82.

might even be contradicted. Still it was the Word of God. It was the only infallible rule of faith and practice.

POST-REFORMATION VIEWS

In the post-Reformation period the orthodox view of Scripture came under increasingly devastating attacks. In the Roman Catholic Church the attacks came from the church's established traditions. Already weakened by centuries of appealing to the early church fathers rather than to the Scripture in defense of points of doctrine and in violent reaction to the Protestant Reformation, the Roman Catholic Church in 1546 took the step of officially placing the tradition of the church alongside Scripture as an equally valid source of revelation. The full significance of that decision was doubtlessly overlooked at the time of the Council of Trent, but it was monumental. The act had tragic consequences for the Roman Catholic Church, as the continuing development of debilitating doctrines, such as Mariology and the veneration of the saints, indicates. In theory, the Bible remains inerrant, at least for large sectors of Catholicism. But the deep human preference for traditions rather than an absolute and inerrant Word inevitably shifts the balance of authority away from God's Word.

In Protestantism the attack came from the so-called higher criticism. For a time, as the result of their heritage and sharp polemic against Catholicism, Protestant churches generally held to an infallible Bible. But in the eighteenth and particularly in the nineteenth century a critical appraisal of the Scriptures, backed by a naturalistic rationalism, succeeded in dislodging the Bible from the place it had held previously. For the church of the age of rationalism, the Bible became humanity's word about God and humanity rather than God's Word to humanity. Eventually, having rejected the unique, divine character of the Bible, many critics rejected its authority also.

The Catholic Church weakened the orthodox view of the Bible by exalting human traditions to the stature of Scripture. Protestants weakened the orthodox view of Scripture by lowering the Bible to the level of traditions. The differences are great, but the results were similar. Neither group entirely denied the revelational quality of Scripture. But in both cases, the unique character of Scripture was lost, its authority forfeited, and the function of the Bible as the reforming voice of God within the church forgotten.

The fact that neither of these two positions is tenable should be evident to everyone, and should push the church back toward its original position. But this does not seem to be happening. Instead, some evangelicals who have traditionally insisted on an inerrant Word seem to be moving in a more liberal direction, displaying an increasingly ambivalent attitude toward infallibility.

We must be extremely careful at this point. There is value in questioning what we should mean by "inerrancy," which differs from outright and dangerous rejection of it. For example, some very conservative scholars have asked whether *inerrancy* is really the best term to use in reference to the Bible, since it would seem to demand a precision of detail so exact as to include even a need for faultless grammar, which does not exist. They have preferred the word *infallibility* at this point. Others have faulted the term *inerrancy* for seeming to require modern, scientific standards of accuracy in expression which the ancient writers obviously did not have. Such scholars have preferred to speak of the Bible as *trustworthy* or *truthful*. But these are not the areas of real concern. In these areas there may well be movement, based on the knowledge that no one term—*inerrancy, infallibility, trustworthiness, reliability, truthfulness*, or others—perfectly describes what we mean. But there must not be movement in holding to the unique character and authority of the Bible, in whole and in part, as the Word of God. The word *inerrancy*, whatever its limitations, at least preserves this emphasis.

THE PHILOSOPHY OF MODERN CRITICISM

Modern biblical criticism is generally credited with bringing down the old inerrancy view. It is said that inerrancy was a possible option in days when men and women knew very little about the biblical texts or biblical history. But modern discoveries have changed all that. Today we know that the Bible contains errors, so we are told, and therefore the overthrow of biblical infallibility is a fait accompli. For example, Quirinius was apparently "not strictly" the governor of Syria at the time of Christ's birth (Lk 2:2). Moses "did not" write the Pentateuch. One scholar wrote, "The scientific development of the last century has rendered untenable the whole conception of the Bible as a verbally inspired book, to which we can appeal with absolute certainty for infallible guidance in all matters of faith and conduct."[12]

But does modern critical study demand radical change of our view of Scripture? Doubts emerge when we realize that most of the alleged errors in the Bible are not recent discoveries, due to scientific criticism, but are only

---

[12]W. L. Knox, *Essays Catholic and Critical* (London: Society for Promoting Christian Knowledge, 1931), 99.

difficulties known centuries ago to most serious biblical students. Origen, Augustine, Luther, Calvin, and countless others were aware of these problems. They knew that various biblical time periods are reported differently by different writers. (For example, Gen 15:13 says the duration of the bondage in Israel in Egypt was four hundred years, while Ex 12:41 says it was 430 years.) They knew details of parallel narrations sometimes vary (as in the number of angels at the tomb of Christ following the resurrection). But they understood these to result merely from the authors' varying perspectives or specific intent in writing. They did not feel compelled to jettison the orthodox conception of Scripture because of these problems.

The real problem with inerrancy therefore goes beyond the data produced by scientific criticism to the philosophy underlying the modern critical enterprise. That philosophy is naturalism. This worldview denies the supernatural, or it seeks to place it beyond scientific investigation. The supernatural therefore has no direct correlation with the specific words of the biblical text. It is, to use Francis Schaeffer's term, an "upper story" reality, beyond proof or contradiction. Thus, writes Pinnock,

> Negative criticism is now the tool of the new theology. It is no longer employed in a hit-and-run way to ferret out objectionable features of biblical teaching. It now serves to discredit the entire notion at the heart of Christianity that there is a body of revealed information, normative for Christian theology. In the modern interest in hermeneutics we see no revival of concern to take Scriptural truth seriously, but only an attempt to use the Bible in a new, non-literal, existential way.[13]

A prime example of this would be the theology of Rudolf Bultmann, who writes volumes of theological exposition but who denies that Christian revelation possesses propositional content at all.

If that is the real issue in the inerrancy debate, then the debate is obviously far more important than whether or not a few insignificant errors can be shown to exist in the Scriptures. What is at stake is the whole matter of revelation. Can God reveal himself to humanity? And, to be more specific, can he reveal himself in language, the specifics of which become normative for Christian faith and action? With an inerrant Bible these things are possible. Without it, theology inevitably enters a wasteland of human speculation. The church, which needs a sure Word of God, flounders. Without an inerrant revelation, theology is not

---

[13]Clark H. Pinnock, *A Defense of Biblical Infallibility* (Philadelphia: Presbyterian and Reformed, 1967), 4.

only adrift, it is meaningless. Having repudiated its right to speak of Scripture on the basis of Scripture, it forfeits its right to speak on any other issue as well.

THE CASE FOR INERRANCY

Divine truthfulness is the rock beneath a defense of Scripture as the authoritative and entirely trustworthy Word of God. The steps in the defense are as follows:

1. The Bible is a generally trustworthy document. Its reliability is established by treating it like any other historical record, like, for instance, the works of Josephus or the accounts of war by Julius Caesar.

2. On the basis of the history recorded by the Bible, we have sufficient reason for believing that the central character of the Bible, Jesus Christ, did what he is claimed to have done and therefore is who he claimed to be: the unique Son of God.

3. As the unique Son of God, the Lord Jesus Christ is an infallible authority.

4. Jesus Christ not only assumed the Bible's authority; he taught it, going so far as to teach that it is entirely without error and is eternal, being the Word of God. "For truly, I say to you, until heaven and earth pass away, not an iota, not a dot, will pass from the Law until all is accomplished" (Mt 5:18).

5. If the Bible is the Word of God, as Jesus taught, it must for this reason alone be entirely trustworthy and inerrant, for God is a God of truth.

6. Therefore, on the basis of the teaching of Jesus Christ, the infallible Son of God, the church believes the Bible also to be infallible.[14]

In other words, the case for inerrancy rests on and is an inevitable consequence of the type of material presented in chapters 3–4. The Bible as a historical document gives us reliable knowledge of an infallible Christ. Christ gives the highest regard to Scripture. Consequently, the doctrines of Christ should and must be the doctrines of his followers.

---

[14]This classical approach to the defense of Scripture is discussed at length by R. C. Sproul in his essay "The Case for Inerrancy: A Methodological Analysis," in *God's Inerrant Word*, ed. John Warwick Montgomery (Minneapolis: Bethany Fellowship, 1975), 248-60.

THE CASE AGAINST INERRANCY

Many who follow the logic of the traditional defense of the inerrancy of Scripture are nevertheless bothered by what seem to be insurmountable objections. Let us look at these objections and see whether they are as formidable as they appear.

The first objection is based on the *character of the biblical texts.* "Granted," someone might say, "that these are reliable historical documents; isn't it true, nevertheless, that this is precisely one of the problems? They are obviously historical and therefore human documents. They are selective in what they contain. They use the limited, sometimes figurative language of the age in which they were written. Parallel accounts reveal different points of view possessed by the different authors. The literary polish of the material varies. Is that what we are to expect of a divine revelation? Doesn't this in itself mean that we are dealing with a purely human book?"

It is not up to us, however, to say in what form a divine revelation must be given, nor to insist that the revelation cannot be divine because of certain characteristics. Obviously, nothing human is a fit vehicle for God's truth. But God is not prevented from stooping to use human language to convey his truth inerrantly. Calvin compared God's action to that of a mother who uses baby talk in communicating with a child. It is obviously a limited communication, for the child cannot converse on the mother's level. But it is true communication nonetheless. Therefore, the character of the documents in itself has nothing to do with the inerrancy question.

A second objection to inerrancy begins where the first objection leaves off. It deals not so much with the character of the biblical books but with the simple fact that they are *obviously human productions.* "To err is human," such critics maintain. "Consequently, the Bible, as a human book, must contain errors."

At first glance this argument may appear logical, but further examination shows that it is not necessarily so. While human beings do err, it is not true that a given individual will err all the time or in any case necessarily. For example, the development of a scientific equation is, for the purpose for which it is given, literally infallible. The same can be said for a correctly printed announcement of a meeting, instructions for operating a car, and other things. "To be sure," as John Warwick Montgomery notes in developing this argument, "the production over centuries of sixty-six inerrant and mutually consistent books by different authors is a tall order—and we cheerfully appeal to God's Spirit to achieve it—but the point remains that there is nothing metaphysically inhuman or against human nature in such a possibility."[15]

The analogy between the conception and birth of the Lord Jesus Christ and the giving of our Bible is instructive. We read that, when the Lord was conceived in the womb of the virgin Mary, the Holy Spirit overshadowed her so that the child that was born was called "the Son of God" (Lk 1:35). The divine and the human met in Christ's conception, and the result was also in its turn both human and divine. Christ was a real man. He was a particular person, a Jew. He had a certain measurable weight and a recognizable appearance. You could have taken a picture of him. Still he was also God Almighty and without sin.

Somewhat comparably, just as the Holy Spirit came on the virgin Mary so that she conceived the human Son of God in her womb, so also did the Holy Spirit come on the brain cells of Moses, David, the prophets, the evangelists, Paul, and the other biblical writers, so that they brought forth from their minds those books that constitute our Bible. Their writings bear the marks of human personality. They differ in style. Yet the ultimate source is divine, and the touch of the human does not stamp them with error any more than the womb of Mary imparted sin to the Savior.

A third objection to inerrancy is based on the fact that *inerrancy is claimed only for the original autographs*, not the copies that have been made from them on which our contemporary translations are based. Since no one living has ever seen the autographs and we are therefore unable either to verify or falsify the claim, is it not epistemological nonsense to appeal to them? "So what if there is an inerrant original?" someone might argue. "Since we don't have it, the appeal to an inerrant Bible is meaningless."

But is it? It would be if two things were true: (1) if the number of apparent errors remained constant as one moved back through the copies toward the original writing, and (2) if believers in infallibility appealed to an original that differed substantially from the best manuscript copies in existence. But neither is the case. On the contrary,

> the number of textual errors steadily diminishes as one moves back in the direction of the lost autographs, reasonably encouraging the supposition that could we entirely fill in the interval between the originals and our earliest texts and fragments (some New Testament papyri going back to the first century

itself), all apparent errors would disappear. . . . The conservative evangelical only appeals to the missing autographs over against existent best texts in those limited and specific instances (such as the recording of numerals) where independent evidence shows a very high probability of transcriptional errors from the very outset.[16]

The believer in infallibility handles textual problems in the same way that a secular scholar handles problems relating to any ancient document. However, due to the extraordinary number and variety of the biblical manuscripts, there is no reason to doubt that today's text is identical to the original text in all but a few places. And these few problem areas are clearly known to commentators.

A fourth major objection to the doctrine of inerrancy concerns the proper *function of language as a vehicle of truth.* Some scholars imply that truth transcends language, so that the truth of Scripture is to be found in the thoughts of Scripture rather than in its words. But does that make sense? "To accept the inspiration of the thoughts and not the words of the biblical writers runs counter not only to the Scriptural claims, but is intrinsically meaningless," as Pinnock observes. "What is an inspired thought expressed in uninspired language?"[17] If the Bible is inspired at all, it must be inspired verbally. And verbal inspiration means infallibility.

To be sure, there are parts of Scripture where the choice of a word may make very little difference in recording a fact or doctrine. The wording of some verses can be changed, as translators regularly do to convey the proper meaning to a particular culture. But there are other places where the words are crucial, and a doctrine will inevitably suffer if we fail to take them seriously. Certainly, if we are to have an authoritative Bible, we must also have a verbally inspired and therefore an infallible Bible, a Bible that is infallible at the point in question and at other points as well. This view agrees with the Bible's own teaching and with the nature of language.

THE QUESTION OF ERRORS

Finally, there are those who would follow the argument so far, and even agree with it in places, but who, nevertheless, feel that certain "errors" have been disclosed by the "assured results" of biblical scholarship. Are there errors that have really been proven to exist? There are difficulties in places. No one

---

[16]Ibid., 36.
[17]Pinnock, *Defense of Biblical Infallibility,* 8.

questions that. But has scholarship actually demonstrated that the books of the Bible are fallible and therefore written only by men after all?

There was a time not long ago when claims such as these were made by many influential people and were made quite openly. In past years almost every biblical theologian and scholar spoke of so-called certain results or assured findings that were imagined to have laid the orthodox conception of the Bible to rest forever. Today, however, as anyone who has had the opportunity to delve deeply into such questions knows, these phrases no longer occur with such frequency. In fact, they hardly occur at all. Why? Simply because, as a result of a continuing march of biblical and archaeological investigations, many so-called assured results have blown up in the faces of those who propounded them.

In 2 Kings 15:29, there is a reference to a king of Assyria named Tiglath-Pileser. He is spoken of as having conquered the Israelites of the northern kingdom and as having taken many of them into captivity. A generation ago scholars were saying—their books are still in our libraries—that this king never existed and that the account of the fall of Israel to Assyria is something akin to mythology. Now, however, archaeologists have excavated Tiglath-Pileser's capital city and can give his history. They have even found his name pressed into bricks, which read, "I, Tiglath-Pileser, king of the west lands, king of the earth, whose kingdom extends to the great sea . . ." The English reader can find accounts of his battles with Israel in James B. Pritchard's volume *Ancient Near Eastern Texts Relating to the Old Testament*. About the same time, some scholars were denying that Moses could have written the first five books of the Bible on the grounds, which seemed irrefutable enough, that writing had not been invented in his day. Since that time, however, archaeologists have unearthed thousands of tablets and inscriptions written many hundreds of years before Moses and even before Abraham. In fact, they now know of six different written languages from or before Moses' period.

In more recent days, many could be found who denied that the historical books of the New Testament were written close enough to the events they relate to be reliable. The Synoptic Gospels (Matthew, Mark, and Luke) in particular were dated late; and John, which seemed to have the greatest measure of Greek flavoring, was pushed back well into the second or, by some scholars, into the third Christian century. In time, however, a piece of papyrus was uncovered in Egypt that required scholars to date the Fourth Gospel no later than the year AD 125, and presumably much before that time.

The results of scholarship, far from discrediting the Bible, actually increasingly validate its claims. They do not prove infallibility—no amount of data alone can do that—but they do lead in the direction of reliability. They reveal nothing incompatible with the highest view of Scripture. In fact, as *Time* magazine acknowledged in a 1974 cover story on the Bible,

> The breadth, sophistication and diversity of all this biblical investigation are impressive, but it begs a question: Has it made the Bible more credible or less? Literalists who feel the ground move when a verse is challenged would have to say that credibility has suffered. Doubt has been sown, faith is in jeopardy. But believers who expect something else from the Bible may well conclude that its credibility has been enhanced. After more than two centuries of facing the heaviest scientific guns that could be brought to bear, the Bible has survived—and is perhaps the better for the siege. Even on the critics' own terms—historical fact—the Scriptures seem more acceptable now than they did when the rationalists began the attack.[18]

The Christian need never fear to stand on the Word of God, recognizing its full authority as the Lord Jesus Christ himself did. At times there will be critical theories that run against it. The arguments may seem unanswerable, so much so that the one who tries to stand against them may be dismissed as an obscurantist. The wise of this world will say, "You can believe that if you want to, but the results of scientific criticism teach us better." Such things have happened before and will happen again. But Christians who will stand on Scripture will find even within their lifetime that, as the so-called assured results begin to crumble around the scholars, the view of the Bible held by the Lord Jesus Christ, the historical view of the church, will prevail.

A number of years ago, a former leader of the Church of England, Bishop Ryle of Liverpool, wrote, "Give me the 'plenary verbal' theory, with all its difficulties, rather than this. I accept the difficulties of that theory, and humbly wait for their solution. But while I wait, I feel that I am standing on a rock."[19]

[18]"The Bible: The Believers Gain," *Time*, December 30, 1974, 41.
[19]John Charles Ryle, *Expository Thoughts on the Gospel* (New York: Robert Carter & Brothers, 1974), vii.

CHAPTER 7

MODERN BIBLICAL CRITICISM

*M*odern biblical criticism, more than anything else, has weakened and almost destroyed the high view of the Bible previously held throughout Christendom. Thus it is necessary to look at the main lines of this criticism as it has developed in the last two centuries and then reflect on it from an evangelical perspective.

THE ROOTS OF HIGHER CRITICISM

Higher criticism of the Old and New Testaments along literary lines is not in itself peculiar to the nineteenth and twentieth centuries. Theodore of Mopsuestia, one of the most noted theologians of the Antiochian school, relegated a number of the psalms (such as Ps 51; 65; 127) to the age of the exile. During the Middle Ages, Ibn Ezra, a Jewish scholar, claimed to have discovered a number of anachronisms in the Pentateuch. Even Martin Luther applied a form of literary criticism in his occasional pronouncements about the authenticity and relative value of the biblical books. Nevertheless, it was not until the middle of the eighteenth century, 1753, to be exact, that higher criticism was introduced on a scale and with a purpose comparable to our use of the phrase today.

In that year a scientist and physician in the French court, Jean Astruc, published a work on the literary sources of Genesis and set forth a method of biblical study that was to find widespread acceptance, first in Germany, then throughout Europe and the United States. Astruc observed that in the Hebrew text of Genesis, God is designated by two different names. The first is Elohim, for, while this name has other meanings in Hebrew, it is especially applied to the Supreme Being. The other is Jehovah . . . the great name of God, expressing his essence. Now one might suppose that the two names were used indiscriminately as synonymous terms, merely to lend variety to the style. This, however, would be in error. The names are never intermixed; there are whole chapters, or large parts of chapters, in which God is always called Elohim, and others, at least as numerous, in which he is always named Jehovah. If Moses were the author of Genesis, we should have to ascribe this strange and harsh variation to himself. But can we conceive such negligence in the composition of so short a book as Genesis? Shall we impute to Moses a fault such as no other writer has committed? Is it not more natural to explain this variation by supposing that Genesis was composed of two or three memoirs, the authors of which gave different names to God, one using Elohim, another that of Jehovah or Jehovah Elohim?[1]

Astruc's statement is a primitive expression of the critical spirit, exhibiting characteristics that were soon to become representative of literary criticism at large. First, it reveals a break with traditional views, according to which Moses was the author of the Pentateuch. Second, it discloses a shift in the object of study, from the simple meaning of the words themselves to questions of the authenticity and integrity of the biblical books. Third, it displays a new method of procedure. By laying aside the testimony of history and tradition, at least temporarily, this criticism focuses on the style, vocabulary, syntax, ideas, and features of the documents as the sole basis on which questions concerning authenticity and integrity may be answered.

At first Astruc's work received little notice. Yet within a few years, it was picked up by some German scholars and others and was expanded to include the whole Old Testament. Johann Eichhorn applied Astruc's approach to the entire Pentateuch. Wilhelm De Wette and Edward Reuss attempted to bring the results into line with Jewish history. Reuss concluded that in the correct historical sequence the Prophets are earlier than the Law, and the Psalms later than both. The most popular and, in some sense, the culminating work in this field was the *Prolegomena* of Julius Wellhausen published in 1878. This work widely disseminated the four-stage documentary hypothesis known as JEPD (*J* for the Jehovah source, *E* for the Elohim source, *P* for the Priestly Documents and Code, and

---

[1]*Encyclopedia of Religion and Ethics*, ed. James Hastings, vol. 4 (New York: Charles Scribner's Sons, 1912), 315.

D for the later editorial work of the Deuteronomist or Deuteronomic school). Wellhausen dated the writing of the law after the Babylonian exile and placed only the Book of the Covenant and the most ancient editing of the J and E narrative sections prior to the eighth century BC.

The profound change this involved is clear in the words of E. C. Blackman, who hails Wellhausen's achievement as making possible "the understanding of the Old Testament in terms of progressive revelation . . . a real liberation."[2] Emil G. Kraeling notes that it also "marked the beginning of a completely secular and evolutionistic study of the Old Testament sources."[3]

THE JESUS OF HISTORY

In New Testament studies, the energies of the higher critics have been directed in a slightly different direction: namely, to recover the "Jesus of history" through a study of the origins of the Gospel narratives and the development of New Testament theology as preserved in the epistles of Paul, the pastorals, the Johannine literature, and Revelation. But the same principles are involved, and they have been carried forward in New Testament studies in an even more radical way than in the nineteenth-century investigation of the Pentateuch.

The origin of higher critical principles in New Testament study is usually traced to Ferdinand Christian Baur (1792–1860), who tried to organize the material along historical lines. Hegel had developed the theory that historical development proceeds by thesis, antithesis, and synthesis. Baur applied Hegelian principles to biblical history, citing the supposed conflict of Petrine and Pauline theology as evidence of a doctrinal thesis and antithesis within the early church. In Baur's view, this led to the synthesis of early Catholicism. Today Baur's general thesis is rejected. Still he succeeded in shaking the traditional views concerning the authorship and composition of the New Testament books, and called the attention of the scholarly world to a rediscovery of the historical Christ as the primary New Testament problem.

The so-called quest for the historical Jesus dates from the death in 1768 of Hermann Samuel Reimarus, the historian with whom Albert Schweitzer begins his survey of nineteenth-century research. Reimarus was no New Testament scholar, but at his death he left behind a manuscript that was to have far-reaching implications. He argued that historians must distinguish between the "aim" of

---

[2]E. C. Blackman, *Biblical Interpretation* (Philadelphia: Westminster, 1957), 141.
[3]Emil G. Kraeling, *The Old Testament since the Reformation* (New York: Harper and Brothers, 1955), 94.

Jesus and the "aim" of his disciples, that is, between the Jesus of history and the Christ of early Christian preaching. Faced with a choice between what he believed to be mutually exclusive aims, Reimarus opted for the former, positing a non-supernatural Jesus. According to him, Jesus preached the coming of God's kingdom, but he died forsaken by God and disillusioned. Christianity was viewed as the product of early disciples who stole the corpse, proclaimed a bodily resurrection, and gathered followers.

Reimarus was extreme and his work polemical. But his views of Christian origins set the pattern for a century of historical-Jesus research. Reacting against the supernatural element in the Gospels and casting about for a Jesus made in their own image, idealists found Christ to be the ideal man; rationalists saw him as the great teacher of morality; socialists viewed him as a friend of the poor and a revolutionary. The most popular "lives of Jesus," the two by David Friedrich Strauss, rejected most of the Gospel material as mythology; and Bruno Bauer ended his quest by denying that there ever was a historical Jesus. Bauer explained all the stories about Jesus as the products of the imagination of the primitive Christian community.

One can hardly fail to be impressed even today at the immense energy and talent that German scholars poured into the old quest for the "original" Jesus, but the results were meager and the conclusions wrong, as Schweitzer found in his study. Scholarship had attempted to modernize Jesus, but the Jesus they produced was neither the historical Jesus nor the Christ of Scripture.

BULTMANN AND MYTHOLOGY

In more recent years, higher criticism of the New Testament has centered around the work of Rudolf Bultmann, former professor at the University of Marburg, Germany, the acknowledged father of form criticism. Much of Bultmann's energy was expended on stripping away what he felt to be the "mythology" of the New Testament writers: heaven, hell, miracles. But Bultmann's views are misunderstood if one imagines that the historically real Jesus lies beneath the mythological layer. According to Bultmann, what lies beneath the mythology is the church's deepest understanding of life created by its experience with the *risen* Lord. Consequently, nothing may be known about Jesus in terms of pure history except the fact that he existed. In Bultmann's work *Jesus and the Word*, he states, "We can know almost nothing concerning the life and personality of Jesus."[4]

---

[4]Rudolf Bultmann, *Jesus and the Word* (New York: Charles Scribner's Sons, 1934), 8.

Operating under the assumption that a period of oral transmission intervened between the years of Christ's earthly ministry and the transcribing of the traditions about him in the Gospels, Bultmann envisions a creative church, one that gradually superimposed its own world picture on what it had received of the times and teachings of Jesus. The church's creativity took place in an "oral stage" in the development of the tradition. During this period, much of the Gospel material circulated in the form of separate oral units, which may today be classified and arranged in a time sequence on the basis of their form. It is believed, by Bultmann and others of his school, that much may be inferred about the situation in the church from these Gospel "units." But virtually nothing may be learned about the actual, historical Jesus. The expressions of faith of the early church, preserved for us in the New Testament, must be reinterpreted in existential terms if they are to have meaning for the modern era.

In rejecting the supposed New Testament mythology, Bultmann rejects a literal preexistence of Christ, his virgin birth, his sinlessness and deity, the value of his atoning death, a literal resurrection and ascension of Christ, and the future judgment of all people. They speak rather of a new "possibility of existence," meaning the possibility of letting go of the past (dying with Christ) and opening oneself to the future (rising with Christ). To embrace this possibility brings inner release and overwhelming freedom (salvation).

Lutheran scholar Edgar Krentz writes of Bultmann's conclusions,

> On the one hand the Scriptures are, like any other book, the object of historical inquiry, which seeks the facts. But no absolute meaning is to be found in the facts. Meaning is to be found only as man personally confronts history and finds meaning for his own existence (existential interpretations). Only as man is not subjected to a strange world view is he set free to believe. It is this self-understanding that determines the work of interpretation, for interpretation must give free play for faith, God's creation.[5]

To summarize, according to the Bultmannian school: (1) the earliest Christian sources show no interest in the actual history or personality of Jesus, (2) the biblical documents are fragmentary and legendary, (3) there are no other sources against which the data provided by the biblical writers may be checked, and (4) preoccupation with the historical Jesus is actually destructive of Christianity, for

---

[5]Edgar Krentz, *Biblical Studies Today: A Guide to Current Issues and Trends* (St. Louis: Concordia, 1966), 16.

it leads, not to faith in Jesus as God, but to a Jesus cult, the effects of which can be clearly seen in Pietism.

The weaknesses of some of these perspectives are now being seen in some quarters. Consequently, theological leadership is passing into other hands.[6]

MAJOR CHARACTERISTICS

Brief as it has been, our review of higher criticism reveals great diversity. Viewpoints are constantly changing, and even in the same period, those working in similar areas often contradict each other. However, in spite of the diversity, there are certain characteristics that tie the various expressions of the higher criticism together.

First, there is its *humanism*. In most forms of the modern debate, the Scriptures of the Old and New Testaments are handled as if they are *humanity's word about God, rather than God's Word to humanity*. But this, as J. I. Packer points out, is simply the Romantic philosophy of religion set out by Friedrich Schleiermacher (1768–1834), "namely that the real subject matter of theology is not divinely revealed truths, but human religious experience."[7] Within this framework, the Bible is only a record of human reflection and action in the field of religion. The interpreter's task becomes the work of sifting that experience out and evaluating it for possible use in our age.

It must be recognized of course, as was pointed out in an earlier chapter, that the Bible does have a genuinely human element. On the other hand, we must object to any attempt to make it human at the expense of its being divine. Besides, as Packer adds,

> if one factor must be stressed at the expense of the other, far less is lost by treating the Scriptures simply as the written oracles of God than simply as a collection of Jewish ideas about God. For we have no reason to regard merely human words as inerrant and authoritative; what will be authoritative for us, if we take the liberal view, is our own judgment as to how far they may be trusted and how far not. Thus, we land, willynilly, in subjectivism.[8]

A clear example of such subjectivism is the section on "Scripture" from *The Common Catechism*, a widely advertised modern statement of faith by an

---

[6]Portions of the above material on the quest for the historical Jesus and on Bultmann have already appeared in an article by the author titled "New Vistas in Historical Jesus Research," *Christianity Today*, March 15, 1968, 3-6.

[7]J. I. Packer, *"Fundamentalism" and the Word of God* (Grand Rapids: Eerdmans, 1960), 148.

[8]Ibid.

impressive team of contemporary Catholic and Protestant theologians. It states,

> Everything we will have to discuss . . . is based on this now unquestioned assumption that the evidence of the Bible may and must be examined as evidence of the faith of a number of men and a number of generations. . . . For the future we can no longer say, "The Bible *is* the word of God." Even saying "The word of God is in the Bible" would be wrong, if it were taken to mean that one set of statements in the Bible were purely human words and the rest God's word. We must say something like: "The Bible *is* not God's word, but *becomes* God's word for anyone who believes in it as God's word." That sounds dangerous . . .[9]

At this point we must answer that indeed it does.

The second common characteristic of higher criticism is its *naturalism*, expressed in the belief that *the Bible is the result of an evolutionary process*. Evidence of this belief can be seen in Old Testament studies in the way the documentary theory of the Pentateuch developed. The belief is also evident in Bultmann's form criticism, for everything depends on the early church's gradually developing its understanding of reality and preserving it at various stages through the written traditions. Early and primitive understandings of God and reality are presumed to have given way to later, more developed conceptions. So-called primitive ideas may be rejected in favor of more modern ones. Thus, reports of miracles may be discounted. Also, according to this view, crude notions such as the wrath of God, sacrifice, and a visible second coming of the Lord may be excluded from the religion of the New Testament.

The third major characteristic of the higher criticism is based on the first two. If people and their ideas change as the evolutionary hypothesis speculates, then they will continue to change; they have changed since the last books of the Bible were written; consequently, *we must go beyond the Scriptures to understand both humanity and true religion*. There are many examples of this attitude, particularly in popular sermons in which the viewpoints of secular thinkers are often widely aired while the contrary views of the biblical writers are forgotten.

A RESPONSE TO HIGHER CRITICISM

What is to be said in reply to this widespread and popular approach? There are two perspectives. On the one hand, there is a neutral area in which anyone may

---

[9]Johannes Feiner and Lukas Vischer, eds., *The Common Catechism: A Book of Christian Faith* (New York: The Seabury Press, 1975), 101.

properly use at least some parts of the critical method. It may be used to illuminate the human element in the biblical writings. Attention may be given to
words and their varying uses, the historical situation out of which the writings
came, and the unique features of the various biblical books. Besides, there are
matters of archaeology and parallel secular history, both of which shed light on
the texts. Use of the method in these areas and in this way is valuable. On the
other hand, the best-known exponents of the critical method have proceeded
on assumptions unacceptable to true biblical theologians, and the method may
therefore be judged a failure in their hands.

First, users of the critical method demand the right to be scientific in their
examination of the biblical data. But they are vulnerable, not when they are
scientific but rather when *they fail to be scientific enough*. The negative literary
critics presuppose the right to examine the Bible in a manner identical to that
which they would use in studying any secular literature. But is it valid to approach
Scripture as nothing more than a collection of secular writings? Is it scientific
or wise to neglect the fact that the books claim to be the result of the "breathing-
out" of God? Can a decision on this matter really be postponed while an examination of the books goes forward? If the books really are from God, doesn't their
nature in itself limit the critical options?

It is futile as well as erroneous to deny the critics the right to examine the
biblical texts. They will do it whether they are asked to or not. Besides, if the
Scriptures are truth, they must stand up beneath the barrage of any valid
critical method; we must not make the mistake of the fundamentalists of
the nineteenth century in claiming a special exemption for the Bible. On the
other hand, it must be maintained that any critical method must also take
into consideration the nature of the material at its disposal. In the case of the
Bible, criticism must either accept its claims to be the Word of God or else offer
satisfactory reasons for rejecting them. If the Bible is the Word of God, as it
claims to be, then criticism must include an understanding of revelation in its
methodological procedure.

The failure of criticism to do this is nowhere more apparent than in its efforts
to divorce the Jesus of history from the Christ of faith. If Jesus were no more
than a human being and the Bible no more than a human book, this could be
done. But if Christ is divine and if the Bible is the Word of the Father about
him, then it is the obligation of criticism to recognize the nature of the Gospels
as a divine and binding interpretation of the life, death, and resurrection of Jesus
of Nazareth, the Son of God. With a firm appreciation of the Bible as revelation,

literary criticism would be free, on the one hand, from all charges of irreverence and abuse, and, on the other, from an easy and unfounded optimism that would place the solution to all biblical problems within easy grasp.

The same failure is evident in the critics' treatment of the Bible as the result of a human evolutionary process, according to which one part of Scripture may easily contradict another. If the Bible is really from God, these will not be contradictions but rather complementary or progressive disclosures of one truth.

Second, having failed to accept the Bible for what it truly is, negative critics inevitably fall into error as they proceed on other premises. Thus, they eventually display *their own inherent weaknesses.* One clear example of this is the old quest for the historical Jesus, which, as was pointed out earlier, simply molded the historical Christ into the interpreter's own image. Another example is Bultmann who, although he once enjoyed almost legendary renown, is today increasingly deserted by his followers.

They ask, if, as Bultmann says, virtually all we need to know of the historicity of the Christian faith is the mere "thatness" of Jesus Christ, his existence, then why even that? Why was the incarnation necessary? And if it was *not* really necessary or if it is impossible to show *why* it was necessary, what is to keep the Christian faith from degenerating into the realm of abstract ideas? And what in that case is to distinguish its view of the incarnation from Docetism or from a gnostic redeemer myth?

Ernst Käsemann of Marburg, Bultmann's old stomping ground, raised these questions in a now famous address to the reunion of old Marburg students in 1953. He argued, "We cannot do away with the identity between the exalted and the earthly Lord without falling into Docetism and depriving ourselves of the possibility of drawing a line between the Easter faith of the community and myth."[10] A few years later Joachim Jeremias voiced a similar warning. "We are in danger of surrendering the affirmation 'the Word became flesh' and of abandoning the salvation-history, God's activity in the Man Jesus of Nazareth and in His message; we are in danger of approaching Docetism, where Christ becomes an idea."[11]

Even Bultmann's supporters must find it a bit incongruous that his *Theology of the New Testament* gives only thirty pages to the teachings of Jesus, while

---

[10]Ernst Käsemann, *Essays on New Testament Themes* (London: SCM Press, 1964), 34.
[11]Joachim Jeremias, "The Present Position in the Controversy concerning the Problem of the Historical Jesus," *The Expository Times* 69 (1957–1958): 335.

devoting more than one hundred pages to an imaginary account of the theology of the so-called Hellenistic communities, of which we know nothing.

Bultmann has minimized both the early church's concern for the facts of Jesus' life and its dependence on him as teacher. While it is true, as Bultmann argues, that the biblical documents are concerned primarily with Jesus' identity as the Messiah and with the revelation he brings of the Father, it is no less significant that their understanding of him is embodied, not in theological tracts or cosmic mythologies (as in Gnosticism), but in Gospels. Their structure is historical. Moreover, every verse of the Gospels seems to cry out that the origin of the Christian faith lies, not in the sudden enlightenment of the early Christians or in an evolving religious experience, but in the facts concerning Jesus Christ: his life, death, and particularly his resurrection. Even the kerygma proclaims the historical event, for it was Jesus of Nazareth who died for our sins according to the Scriptures, was buried and who rose again on the third day, according to the Scriptures (1 Cor 15:3-4).[12]

A third objection to this type of higher criticism is the most important one. Such critics have *a very small god*. They don't deny the existence of God entirely, but they do minimize his ability and his presence. He can speak to the individual, but he cannot guarantee the content of that revelation or preserve it in a reliable, written form. He can act in history, but he cannot act miraculously. Can miracles occur? If they can, then much of what the higher critics dismiss as mythological has a very good claim to being historical. If they can, the God of miracles is capable of giving us an authoritative and infallible revelation.

For all its alleged objectivity, in the ultimate analysis modern criticism is unable to escape the great questions: Is there a God? Is the God of the Bible the true God? Has God revealed himself in the Bible and in Jesus of Nazareth as the focal point of the written revelation? If, as has been suggested, it is necessary for criticism to deal with the full nature of the material, in particular with the claims of the Bible to be the Word of God as well as words written by particular people, then it must deal with a question that involves either denial or the response of faith.

When criticism faces the fact that the portrait of Jesus appearing in the Gospels makes the humble man from Nazareth the Son of God, then it must ask whether or not this interpretation is the right one, and if so, it must accept his teachings.

---

[12]Parts of this critique of Bultmann also appeared in Boice, "New Vistas in Historical Jesus Research," 3-6.

When it confronts the Bible's claims regarding its own nature, it must ask and answer whether the Bible is indeed God's express revelation. If the answer to these questions is yes, then a new kind of criticism will emerge. This new criticism will treat the biblical statements as being true rather than errant, it will look for complementary statements rather than contradictions, and it will perceive the voice of God (as well as the voices of people) throughout. Such a criticism will be judged by the Scriptures rather than the other way around.

CHAPTER 8

HOW TO INTERPRET THE BIBLE

"Some books are to be tasted, others to be swallowed, and some few to be chewed and digested; that is, some are to be read only in parts; others to be read, but not curiously; and some few to be read wholly, and with diligence and attention."[1]

The seventeenth-century English essayist Sir Francis Bacon was not thinking exclusively of the Bible as he wrote these words. But there is little doubt that if the admonition "to be read wholly and with diligence and attention" is to be applied to any book, it is certainly to be applied to the Scriptures of the Old and New Testaments, which are the Word of God. The Bible is one form of God's gracious revelation of himself to men and women. It should be highly cherished. Love for God, plus a desire to know him better, as well as to obey his express commands, should compel us to study it diligently.

But here a problem develops. If the Bible is God's book, given to us over a period of approximately fifteen hundred years by more than forty human authors, obviously it is unlike any other book we have encountered. The principles of study would therefore seem to be different. Are they? If so, what should they be? Should the Bible be considered spiritually—that is, in a mystical or magical sense? Those who take that approach seem to be led into strange and irrational persuasions. Or should it be read in a purely natural manner—that is, as we

---

[1]Francis Bacon, "Of Studies," in *Essays or Counsels Civil and Moral* in *Selected Writings of Francis Bacon*, ed. Hugh G. Dick (New York: Modern Library, 1955), 129.

would read any other book? The latter course seems proper, but this is the avowed purpose of the naturalistic higher criticism, which we have criticized strongly. What should the approach of the Christian reader or the Christian scholar be?

The answers are found in the four most important truths about the Bible, all of which have been covered in the previous chapters: (1) the Bible has one true author, who is God; (2) the Bible is given to us through human channels; (3) the Bible has a unifying purpose, namely, to lead us to an obedient and worshipful knowledge of the true God; and (4) understanding the Bible requires the supernatural activity of the Holy Spirit, whose work it is to interpret the Scriptures to us. The essential principles for study of God's Word are implied in these four propositions.

ONE BOOK, ONE AUTHOR, ONE THEME

First, the Scriptures have but one author and that is God. True, the Bible has also come by means of human channels, but far more important is the fact that the Bible as a whole and in all its parts is from God. Superficially, a person may see the Bible as a miscellaneous collection of writings tied together more or less by the accidents of history. But the Bible is not just a collection. It is, as J. I. Packer states, "a single book with a single author—God the Spirit—and a single theme— God the Son, and the Father's saving purposes, which all revolve around him."[2]

The Bible's authorship leads to two principles of interpretation: the principle of *unity* and the principle of *noncontradiction*. Taken together they mean that, if the Bible is truly from God, and if God is a God of truth (as he is), then (1) the parts of the book must go together to tell one story, and (2) if two parts seem to be in opposition or in contradiction to each other, our interpretation of one or both of these parts must be in error. It might even be said that if a scholar is expending effort to highlight contradictions in the biblical text and is not going beyond that to indicate how they may be resolved, then what is being demonstrated is not wisdom or honesty so much as failure as an interpreter of the Word of God.

Many will claim that an attempt to find unity where they say there is none is dishonesty. But the problem is actually one of interpretation and presuppositions.

We may take the matter of sacrifices as an example. Everyone recognizes that sacrifices play a large role in the Old Testament, and that they are not emphasized

---

[2]J. I. Packer, *"Fundamentalism" and the Word of God* (Grand Rapids: Eerdmans, 1960), 84.

in the New Testament. Why is this? How are we to regard them? Here one person brings in the idea of an evolving religious conscience. This person supposes that sacrifices are important in the most primitive forms of religion. They are to be explained by the individual's fear of the gods or God. God is imagined to be a capricious, vengeful deity, so worshipers try to appease him by sacrifice. This seems to be the general idea of sacrifice in the pagan religions of antiquity. It is assumed for the religion of the ancient Semite peoples too.

In time, however, such a primitive view of God is imagined to give way to a more elevated conception of him. God is then seen not so much as a God of capricious whim and wrath, but rather a God of justice. So law begins to take a more prominent place, eventually replacing sacrifice as the center of the religion. Finally, the worshipers rise to the conception of God as a God of love, and at that point sacrifice disappears entirely. The one who thinks this way might fix the turning point at the coming of Jesus Christ and his teachings. Therefore, today we would disregard both sacrifices and the idea of the wrath of God as outmoded concepts.

By contrast, another person (an evangelical might fall in this category) would approach the material with entirely different presuppositions and would therefore produce an entirely different interpretation. This person would begin by noting that the Old Testament does indeed tell a great deal about the wrath of God. But he or she would note that this element is hardly eliminated as one goes on through the Bible, most certainly not through the New Testament. It is, for instance, one of Paul's important themes. It emerges strongly in the book of Revelation, where we read about God's just wrath eventually being poured out against the sins of a rebellious and ungodly race. So far as sacrifices are concerned, it is true that the detailed sacrifices of the Old Testament system are no longer performed in the New Testament churches. But their disappearance is not because a supposed primitive conception of God has given way to a more advanced one, but rather because the great sacrifice of Jesus Christ has completed and superseded them all, as the book of Hebrews clearly maintains.

For such a person the solution is not to be found in an evolving conception of God; for this person, God is always the same—a God of wrath toward sin, a God of love toward the sinner. Rather it is to be found in God's progressive revelation of himself to humankind, a revelation in which the sacrifices (for which God gives explicit instructions) are intended to teach both the serious nature of sin and the way in which God had always determined to save sinners. The Old Testament sacrifices point to Christ. John the Baptist is able to say, referring to part of the sacrificial system in ancient Jewish life that all would understand, "Behold, the Lamb of God, who takes away the sin of the world!" (Jn 1:29). And Peter can write about "knowing that you were ransomed from the futile ways inherited from your forefathers, not with perishable things such as silver or gold, but with the precious blood of Christ, like that of a lamb without blemish or spot" (1 Pet 1:18-19).

In this example, as in all cases of biblical interpretation, the data are the same. The only difference is that one approaches Scripture looking for contradiction and development. The other approaches Scripture as if God has written it and therefore looks for unity, allowing one passage to throw light on another. The Westminster Confession states, "The infallible rule of interpretation of Scripture is the Scripture itself: and therefore, when there is a question about the true and full sense of any Scripture (which is not manifold, but one), it must be searched and known by other places that speak more clearly" (I, ix).

THE HUMAN COMPONENT

A second truth about the Bible is that it has been given to us through human channels, even though God is the ultimate source of the Scriptures. Its human component does not mean that the Bible is therefore subject to error, as all merely human books are. But it does mean that all sound principles of interpretation must be used in studying the Bible, precisely as they would be used in the study of any other ancient document. The way into the mind of God is through the mind of the human author, whom he used as a channel. Consequently, the only proper way to interpret the Bible is to discover what God's human speakers were concerned to express.

One necessary part of interpretation is to consider each biblical statement in *context*: that is, within the context of the chapter, the book, and eventually the entire Word of God. Understanding the context is an obvious need in the interpretation of any document. Taking a statement out of context is almost always misleading. But it is to be guarded against in interpreting the Bible especially, since Bible-believing people have such regard for the words of Scripture that they sometimes elevate them at the expense of the context. Frank E. Gaebelein, author of a valuable book on interpreting the Bible, says,

> Realizing that the Bible is God's inspired Word, the devout reader attaches peculiar
> importance to every statement it contains. This reverence is commendable, but
> when it descends to the practice of picking out single verses as proofs of all sorts

of things, it becomes positively dangerous. Were this a sound method of interpretation, one could find biblical support for nearly all the crimes on the calendar,
from drunkenness and murder to lying and deceit.[3]

The Bible itself speaks of the need for proper interpretation: "Do your best
to present yourself to God as one approved, a worker who has no need to
be ashamed, rightly handling the word of truth" (2 Tim 2:15). In this verse,
the word translated "rightly handling" literally means "to cut straight" or
"handle correctly."

A second need is to consider the *style* of the material and then to interpret it
within that framework. Consideration of style is obviously important in dealing
with poetical literature such as the books of Psalms, Proverbs, Job, and even
parts of prophetic material. The poetic books frequently employ symbols or
images; they are misinterpreted if metaphors are taken literally. The book of
Revelation is not to be taken literally in all its parts, as, for example, the vision
of Jesus found in the opening verses. The result of a literal interpretation is a
monstrosity, giving us a figure who is entirely white, having hair like wool, eyes
like fire, feet like heated and glowing bronze, a sword going out of his mouth,
with seven stars in his right hand. On the other hand, when each of these items
is discovered to be an image associated with God in the Old Testament, then
the vision yields us a portrait of Jesus who is thereby shown to be one with God
the Father in all his attributes: holy, eternal, omniscient, omnipresent, revealing,
and sovereign.

The matter of style also has its bearing on the New Testament parables. The
use of parables was a special method of teaching and must be recognized as such.
Usually a parable makes one or, at best, a few main points. Consequently, it is
an error to fix an application to each detail of the story. For example, an attempt
to assign a meaning to the husks, pigs, and other details of the story of the
prodigal son is ludicrous.

A third need is to consider the *purpose* for which a particular passage was
written. In other words, we must consider its scope. Gaebelein writes,

> The Bible has a single great purpose. It was given to reveal the love of God as
> manifested in the divine provision of salvation through our Lord Jesus Christ.
> This is its aim, and sound interpretation must never lose sight of this aim.
> Consequently, it is a serious and misleading error to regard the Bible as a

---

[3]Frank E. Gaebelein, *Exploring the Bible: A Study of Background and Principles* (Wheaton, IL: Van Kampen
Press, 1950), 134.

source-book on science, philosophy, or any subject other than its central theme of the Deity in relation to humanity. After all, there is a proper scope of Scripture, a scope determined not by individual writers, inspired though they were, but by the divine Author of it all. One cannot hold the Bible accountable for fields of knowledge outside the scope delineated by the divine purpose of the book.[4]

One obvious application is to those references that seem to have bothered Rudolf Bultmann so much, in which heaven is assumed to be "up there" and hell "below" our feet. Again, a consideration of purpose or scope applies to passages about bones crying out, bowels yearning, kidneys instructing, and ears judging. It is often said that such references reveal a mistaken notion of the universe and of human physiology, but this is absurd. All they show is that the biblical writers wrote in the language of their day, so that they would be understood. Their use of such phrases is no more scientific than our use of phrases like "walking on air," a "gut feeling," "deep in my heart," and so on.

It is not always easy to determine whether a passage is using literal or figurative language, of course, so we must be careful. Most important is to be aware of the problem and consciously to seek for the true scope of the passage. In seeking its purpose we may ask such questions as the following: To whom is it written? Who has written it? When was it written? What does it say?

A fourth need is to give full attention to the *meaning of the individual words.* It is possible that God can think without words or other symbols, but it is certain that we cannot. Consequently, the meaning of words and an individual's use of them are of great importance. When we fail to take them into consideration, we inevitably misinterpret.

Obviously Bible students must not fail to give close attention to the precise meaning of the biblical words. Word studies themselves can be extremely rewarding; words like *faith, salvation, righteousness, love, spirit, glory, church,* and many others are fascinating.

The summary of these points is contained in what has come to be called the historical-literal method of biblical interpretation. The method simply means, as Packer puts it, that "the proper, natural sense of each passage (i.e., the intended sense of the writer) is to be taken as fundamental." The intended meaning of the words in their own context and in the speech of the original writer or spokesman is the starting point.

---

[4]Ibid., 138-39.

In other words, Scripture statements must be interpreted in the light of the rules of grammar and discourse on the one hand, and of their own place in history on the other. This is what we should expect in the nature of the case, seeing that the biblical books originated as occasional documents addressed to contemporary audiences; and it is exemplified in the New Testament exposition of the Old, from which the fanciful allegorizing practiced by Philo and the rabbis is strikingly absent.[5]

The principle is based on the fact that the Bible is God's Word in human language. It means that Scripture is to be interpreted in its natural sense, and that theological or cultural preferences must not be allowed to obscure the fundamental meaning.

RESPONDING TO THE WORD

Third, the Bible is given by God in order to provoke a personal response in us. If we don't allow that to happen, we inevitably misuse the Bible (even in studying it) and misinterpret it. Once Christ told the Jewish leaders of his day,

> You search the Scriptures because you think that in them you have eternal life; and it is they that bear witness about me, yet you refuse to come to me that you may have life. I do not receive glory from people. But I know that you do not have the love of God within you. . . . How can you believe, when you receive glory from one another and do not seek the glory that comes from the only God? (Jn 5:39-42, 44)

No one could charge the Jews of Christ's day with having a low opinion of the Scriptures, for they actually had the highest regard for them. Nor could they be faulted for a lack of meticulous study. The Jews did study the Scriptures. They prized them. Yet in their high regard for the Bible they passed over its intention: their lives were not changed. Although they gained human acclaim for their detailed knowledge of the Bible, they did not gain salvation.

In John's Gospel we are told of the healing of a man who had been born blind. The meat of the story lies in the fact that, like everyone, he was also spiritually blind before Christ touched him. Afterward he came to spiritual sight.

When the man was healed, he came into conflict with the Jewish rulers. They knew about Jesus, but they did not believe in him. In fact, they did not believe in him precisely because of their attitude to the Scriptures. For them the revelation

---

[5]Packer, *"Fundamentalism" and the Word of God*, 102-3.

recorded in the Old Testament was an end in itself. Nothing could be added and nothing was required. They said, "We know that God has spoken to Moses, but as for this man, we do not know where he comes from" (Jn 9:29). The man who had been born blind did not try to compete with them in their mastery of the Old Testament, but he pointed to the unquestionable fact of his healing. He concluded, "If this man were not from God, he could do nothing" (Jn 9:33). In treating the Old Testament as an end in itself, the Jews, therefore, actually perverted it and missed its true meaning. They failed to see that it is precisely to Jesus that the Old Testament law (which came through Moses) testified.

The same thing happens when a person buys a beautiful Bible to place in an important position in his or her home but does not read it. Why do people do such a thing? In their minds the Bible is something special. They have a reverence for it. But their belief does not go beyond superstition. As a result, they never read it and never come into contact with its Author.

Jesus said that we will know the truth about himself only if we are willing to do his will, that is, if we allow ourselves to be changed by the truths we find in Scripture. He said, "If anyone's will is to do God's will [that is, if the person determines to do it], he will know whether the teaching is from God or whether I am speaking on my own authority" (Jn 7:17). We must not assume that we will be able fully to understand any passage of Scripture unless we are willing to be changed by it.

THE INTERNAL WITNESS OF THE SPIRIT

A final point lies in the internal witness of the Spirit to the truth of the Word of God. Here Scripture speaks succinctly. Not only was the Holy Spirit active in the writing of the biblical books, he is also active in conveying the truth of the Bible to the minds of those who read it. Paul writes, "We have received not the spirit of the world, but the Spirit who is from God, that we might understand the things freely given us by God. And we impart this in words not taught by human wisdom but taught by the Spirit, interpreting spiritual truths to those who are spiritual" (1 Cor 2:12-13). The Bible deals with spiritual themes, and therefore it requires the activity of the Holy Spirit for us to understand them. The Holy Spirit is the teacher of Christians. It is he who brings forth new life in those who hear the gospel.

So we must pray as we study the Scriptures, and we must ask the Holy Spirit to do his work of enlightenment in our hearts. The Spirit's presence is not given to us to make a careful and diligent study of the Word of God unnecessary. He is given to make our study effective.

God speaks in the Bible. We must allow him to speak, and we must listen to what he will say to us. One day at the height of the Reformation, Martin Luther was asked to autograph the flyleaf of a Bible, as often happened after his own translation was published. He took the Bible and wrote down John 8:25: "Who are you? . . . Just what I have been telling you from the beginning." Then Luther added,

> They . . . desire to know who he is and not to regard what he says, while he desires them first to listen; then they will know who he is. The rule is: Listen and allow the Word to make the beginning; then the knowing will nicely follow. If, however, you do not listen, then you will never know anything. For it is decreed: God will not be seen, known, or comprehended except through his Word alone. Whatever, therefore, one undertakes for salvation apart from the Word is in vain. God will not respond to that. He will not have it. He will not tolerate it any other way. Therefore, let his Book, in which he speaks with you, be commended to you; for he did not cause it to be written for no purpose. He did not want us to let it lie there in neglect, as if he were speaking with mice under the bench or with flies on the pulpit. We are to read it, to think and speak about it, and to study it, certain that he himself (not an angel or a creature) is speaking with us in it.[6]

The one who reads the Bible prayerfully, thoughtfully, and receptively will discover that it is indeed the Word of God and that it is "profitable for teaching, for reproof, for correction, and for training in righteousness, that the man of God may be complete, equipped for every good work" (2 Tim 3:16-17).

---

[6]Martin Luther, *What Luther Says: An Anthology*, ed. Ewald M. Plass, vol. 1 (St. Louis: Concordia, 1959), 81.

PART III

THE ATTRIBUTES OF GOD

God said to Moses, "I AM WHO I AM." And he said, "Say this to the people of Israel: 'I AM has sent me to you.'"

EXODUS 3:14

Go therefore and make disciples of all nations, baptizing them in the name of the Father and of the Son and of the Holy Spirit.

MATTHEW 28:19

Yours, O LORD, is the greatness and the power and the glory and the victory and the majesty, for all that is in the heavens and in the earth is yours. Yours is the kingdom, O LORD, and you are exalted as head above all.

1 CHRONICLES 29:11

And the four living creatures, each of them with six wings, are full of eyes all around and within, and day and night they never cease to say, "Holy, holy, holy, is the Lord God Almighty, who was and is and is to come!"

REVELATION 4:8

Oh, the depth of the riches and wisdom and knowledge of God! How unsearchable are his judgments and how inscrutable his ways! "For who has known the mind of the Lord, or who has been his counselor?"

ROMANS 11:33-34

CHAPTER 9

THE TRUE GOD

*I*t is evident that we need more than a theoretical knowledge of God. Yet we can know God only as he reveals himself to us in the Scriptures, and we cannot know the Scriptures until we are willing to be changed by them. Knowledge of God occurs only when we also know our deep spiritual need and when we are receptive to God's gracious provision for our need through the work of Christ and the application of that work to us by God's Spirit.

Having established this base, we nevertheless come back to the question of God himself and we ask, "But who is God? Who is this one who reveals himself in Scripture, in the person of Jesus Christ and through the Holy Spirit?" We may admit that a true knowledge of God must change us. We may be willing to be changed. But where do we begin?

SELF-EXISTENT

Since the Bible is a unity, we could answer these questions by starting at any point in the biblical revelation. We could begin with Revelation 22:21 as well as with Genesis 1:1. But there is no better starting point than God's revelation of himself to Moses at the burning bush. Moses, the great leader of Israel, had long been aware of the true God, for he had been born into a godly family. Still, when God said that he would send him to Egypt and through him deliver the people of Israel, Moses responded, "If I come to the people of Israel and say to them, 'The God of your fathers has sent me to you,' and they ask me, 'What is his name?' what shall I say to them?" We are told that God then answered Moses by saying, "I AM WHO I AM. . . . Say this to the people of Israel: 'I AM has sent me to you'" (Ex 3:13-14).

"I AM WHO I AM." The name is linked with the ancient name for God, Jehovah. But it is more than a name. It is a descriptive name, pointing to all that God is in himself. In particular, it shows him to be the one who is entirely self-existent, self-sufficient, and eternal.

These are abstract concepts, of course. But they are important, for these attributes more than any others set God apart from his creation and reveal him as being what he is in himself. God is perfect in all his attributes. But there are some attributes that we, his creatures, share. For instance, God is perfect in his love; yet by his grace we also love. He is all wise; but we also possess a measure of wisdom. He is all powerful; and we exercise a limited power. It is not like that in regard to God's self-existence, self-sufficiency, and eternity, however. He alone possesses those characteristics. He exists in and of himself; we do not. He is entirely self-sufficient; we are not. He is eternal; we are newcomers on the scene.

Self-existence means that God has no origins and consequently is answerable to no one. Matthew Henry says, "The greatest and best man in the world must say, By the grace of God *I am what I am*; but God says absolutely—and it is more than any creature, man or angel, can say—*I am that I am*."[1] So God has no origins; his existence does not depend on anybody.

Self-existence is a hard concept for us to grapple with, for it means that God as he is in himself is *unknowable*. Everything that we see, smell, hear, taste, or touch has origins. We can hardly think in any other category. Anything we observe must have a cause adequate to explain it. We seek for such causes. Cause and effect is even the basis for the belief in God possessed by those who, nevertheless, do not truly know him. Such individuals believe in God, not because they have had a personal experience of him or because they have discovered God in Scripture, but only because they infer his existence. "Everything comes from something; consequently, there must be a great something that stands behind everything." Cause and effect point to God, but—and this is the issue—they point to a God who is beyond understanding, indeed to one who is beyond us in every way. They indicate that God cannot be known and evaluated as other things can.

A. W. Tozer has noted that this is one reason why philosophy and science have not always been friendly toward the idea of God. These disciplines are

---

[1] Matthew Henry, *Commentary on the Whole Bible*, vol. 1 (New York: Fleming H. Revell, n.d.), 284.

dedicated to the task of accounting for things as we know them and are therefore impatient with anything that refuses to give an account of itself. Philosophers and scientists will admit that there is much they don't know. But it is another thing to admit that there is something they can never know completely and which, in fact, they don't even have techniques for discovering. To discover God, scientists may attempt to bring God down to their level, defining him as natural law, evolution, or some such principle. But still God eludes them. There is more to God than any such concepts can delineate.

Perhaps, too, this is why even Bible-believing people seem to spend so little time thinking about God's person and character. Tozer writes,

> Few of us have let our hearts gaze in wonder at the I AM, the self-existent Self back of which no creature can think. Such thoughts are too painful for us. We prefer to think where it will do more good—about how to build a better mousetrap, for instance, or how to make two blades of grass grow where one grew before. And for this we are now paying a too heavy price in the secularization of our religion and the decay of our inner lives.[2]

God's self-existence means that *he is not answerable to us or to anybody*, and we do not like that. We want God to give an account of himself, to defend his actions. Although he sometimes explains things to us, he does not have to and often he does not. God does not have to explain himself to anybody.

SELF-SUFFICIENT

The second quality of God communicated to us in the name "I AM WHO I AM" is self-sufficiency. Again it is possible to have at least a sense of the meaning of this abstract term. Self-sufficiency means God has no needs and therefore depends on no one.

Here we run counter to a widespread and popular idea: God cooperates with human beings, each thereby supplying something lacking in the other. It is imagined, for example, that God lacks glory and therefore creates men and women to supply it. He takes care of them as a reward. Or again, it is imagined that God needs love and therefore creates men and women to love him. Some talk about the creation as if God were lonely and therefore created us to keep him company. On a practical level we see the same thing in those who imagine that women and men are necessary to carry out God's work of salvation as witnesses

---

[2]A. W. Tozer, *The Knowledge of the Holy* (New York: Harper & Row, 1961), 34.

or as defenders of the faith, forgetting that Jesus himself declared that "God is able from these stones to raise up children for Abraham" (Lk 3:8).

God does not need *worshipers*. Arthur W. Pink, who writes on this theme in *The Attributes of God*, says,

> God was under no constraint, no obligation, no necessity to create. That he chose to do so was purely a sovereign act on his part, caused by nothing outside himself, determined by nothing but his own mere good pleasure; for he "worketh all things after the counsel of his own will" (Eph 1:11). That he did create was simply for his manifestative glory. . . . God is no gainer even from our worship. He was in no need of that external glory of his grace which arises from his redeemed, for he is glorious enough in himself without that. What was it moved him to predestinate his elect to the praise of the glory of his grace? It was, as Ephesians 1:5 tells us, "according to the good pleasure of his will." . . . The force of this is [that] it is impossible to bring the Almighty under obligations to the creature; God gains nothing from us.[3]

Tozer makes the same point:

> Were all human beings suddenly to become blind, still the sun would shine by day and the stars by night, for these owe nothing to the millions who benefit from their light. So, were every man on earth to become atheist, it could not affect God in any way. He is what he is in himself without regard to any other. To believe in him adds nothing to his perfections; to doubt him takes nothing away.[4]

Nor does God need *helpers*. This truth is probably harder for us to accept than almost any other. For we imagine God as a friendly, but almost pathetic, grandfather figure bustling about to see whom he can find to help him in managing the world and saving the world's race. What a travesty! To be sure, God has entrusted a work of management to us. He said to the original pair in Eden, "Be fruitful and multiply and fill the earth and subdue it, and have dominion over the fish of the sea and over the birds of the heavens and over every living thing that moves on the earth" (Gen 1:28). God also has given those who believe in him a commission to "go into all the world and proclaim the gospel to the whole creation" (Mk 16:15). True, but no aspect of God's ordering of his creation has a necessary grounding in himself. God has chosen to do things thus. He didn't need to do them. Indeed, he could have done them in any one of a million

---

[3]Arthur W. Pink, *The Attributes of God* (Grand Rapids: Baker Book House, n.d.), 2-3.
[4]Tozer, *The Knowledge of the Holy*, 40.

other ways. That he did choose to do things thus is therefore solely dependent on the free and sovereign exercise of his will and so does not give us any inherent value to him.

To say that God is self-sufficient also means that God does not need *defenders*. Clearly, we have opportunities to speak for God before those who would dishonor his name and malign his character. We ought to do so. But even if we should fail, we must not think that God is deprived thereby. God does not need to be defended, for he is as he is and will remain so regardless of the sinful and arrogant attacks of evil individuals. A God who needs to be defended is no God. Rather, the God of the Bible is the self-existent one who is the true defender of his people.

When we realize that God is the only truly self-sufficient one, we begin to understand why the Bible has so much to say about the need for faith in God alone and why unbelief in God is such sin. Tozer writes, "Among all created beings, not one dare trust in itself. God alone trusts in himself; all other beings must trust in him. Unbelief is actually perverted faith, for it puts its trust not in the living God but in dying men."[5] If we refuse to trust God, what we are actually saying is that either we or some other person or thing is more trustworthy. That is a slander against the character of God, and it is folly. Nothing else is all-sufficient. On the other hand, if we begin by trusting God (by believing in him), we have a solid foundation for all life. God is sufficient, and his Word to his creatures can be trusted.

Because God is sufficient, we may begin by resting in that sufficiency and so work effectively for him. God does not need us. But the joy of coming to know him is in learning that he nevertheless stoops to work in and through those who are his believing and obedient children.

ETERNAL

A third quality inherent in the name of God given to Moses ("I AM WHO I AM") is everlastingness, perpetuity, or eternity. The quality is difficult to put in one word, but it is simply that God is, has always been, and will always be, and that he is ever the same in his eternal being. We find this attribute of God everywhere in the Bible. Abraham called Jehovah "the Everlasting God" (Gen 21:33). Moses wrote,

> Lord, you have been our dwelling place
>   in all generations.

[5]Ibid., 42.

Before the mountains were brought forth,

    or ever you had formed the earth and the world,

    from everlasting to everlasting you are God. (Ps 90:1-2)

The book of Revelation describes God as the "Alpha and the Omega, the beginning and the end" (Rev 21:6; see Rev 1:8; 22:13). The creatures before the throne cry, "Holy, holy, holy, is the Lord God Almighty, who was and is and is to come!" (Rev 4:8).

The fact that God is eternal has two major consequences for us. The first is that *he can be trusted* to remain as he reveals himself to be. The word usually used to describe this quality is *immutability*, which means unchangeableness. "Every good gift and every perfect gift is from above, coming down from the Father of lights with whom there is no variation or shadow due to change" (Jas 1:17).

God is unchangeable in his attributes. So we need not fear, for example, that the God who once loved us in Christ will somehow change his mind and cease to love us in the future. God is always love toward his people. Similarly, we must not think that perhaps he will change his attitude toward sin, so that he will begin to classify as "permissible" something that was formerly prohibited. Sin will always be sin because it is defined as any transgression of or lack of conformity to the law of God, who is unchangeable. God will always be holy, wise, gracious, just, and everything else that he reveals himself to be. Nothing that we do will ever change the eternal God.

God is also unchangeable in his counsels or will. He does what he has determined beforehand to do and his will never varies. Some will point out that certain verses in the Bible tell us that God repented of some act—as in Genesis 6:6, "The LORD regretted that he had made man." In this example, a human word is being used to indicate God's severe displeasure with human activities. It is countered by such verses as Numbers 23:19 ("God is not man, that he should lie, or a son of man, that he should change his mind. Has he said, and will he not do it? Or has he spoken, and will he not fulfill it?"); 1 Samuel 15:29 ("The Glory of Israel will not lie or have regret, for he is not a man, that he should have regret"); Romans 11:29 ("The gifts and calling of God are irrevocable"); and Psalm 33:11 ("The counsel of the LORD stands forever, the plans of his heart to all generations").

Such statements are a source of great comfort to God's people. If God were like us, he could not be relied on. He would change, and as a result of that his will and his promises would change. We could not depend on him. But God is not like us. He does not change. Consequently, his purposes remain fixed from generation to generation. Pink says, "Here then is a rock on which we may fix our feet, while the mighty torrent is sweeping away everything around us. The permanence of God's character guarantees the fulfillment of his promises."[6]

The second major consequence for us of God's unchangeableness is that he is *inescapable*. If he were a mere human and if we did not like either him or what he was doing, we might ignore him, knowing that he might always change his mind, move away from us, or die. But God does not change his mind. He does not move away. He will not die. Consequently, we cannot escape him. Even if we ignore him now, we must reckon with him in the life to come. If we reject him now, we must eventually face the one we have rejected and experience his eternal rejection of us.

NO OTHER GODS

We are led to a natural conclusion, namely, that we should seek and worship the true God. This chapter has been based for the most part on Exodus 3:14, in which God reveals to Moses the name by which he desires to be known. That revelation came on the verge of the deliverance of the people of Israel from Egypt. After the exodus, God gave a revelation on Mount Sinai that applies the earlier disclosure of himself as the true God to the religious life and worship of the delivered nation.

God said,

> I am the LORD your God, who brought you out of the land of Egypt, out of the house of slavery.
>
> You shall have no other gods before me.
>
> You shall not make yourself a carved image, or any likeness of anything that is in heaven above, or that is in the earth beneath, or that is in the water under the earth. You shall not bow down to them or serve them, for I the LORD your God am a jealous God, visiting the iniquity of the fathers on the children to the third and the fourth generation of those who hate me, but showing steadfast love to thousands of those who love me and keep my commandments. (Ex 20:2-6)

These verses make three points, all based on the premise that the God who reveals himself in the Bible is the true God:

---

[6]Pink, *The Attributes of God*, 41.

1. We are to worship God and obey him.

2. We are to reject the worship of any other god.

3. We are to reject the worship of the true God by any means that are unworthy of him, such as the use of pictures or images.

At first glance it seems quite strange that a prohibition against the use of images in worship should have a place at the very start of the ten basic principles of biblical religion, the Ten Commandments. But it is not strange when we remember that the characteristics of a religion flow from the nature of the religion's god. If the god is unworthy, the religion will be unworthy too. If the concept of God is of the highest order, the religion will be of a high order also. So God tells us in these verses that any physical representation of him is dishonoring to him. Why? For two reasons. First, it obscures his glory, for nothing visible can ever adequately represent it. Second, it misleads those who would worship him.

Both of these errors are represented by Aaron's manufacture of the golden calf, as J. I. Packer indicates in his discussion of idolatry. In Aaron's mind, at least, though probably not in the minds of the people, the calf was intended to represent Jehovah. He thought, no doubt, that a figure of a bull (even a small one) communicated the thought of God's strength. But, of course, it did not do so adequately. And it did not at all communicate his other great attributes: his sovereignty, righteousness, mercy, love, and justice. Rather, it obscured them.

Moreover, the figure of the bull misled the worshipers. They readily associated it with the fertility gods and goddesses of Egypt, and the result of their worship was an orgy. Packer concludes,

> It is certain that if you habitually focus your thoughts on an image or picture of the One to whom you are going to pray, you will come to think of him, and pray to him, as the image represents him. Thus you will in this sense "bow down" and "worship" your image; and to the extent to which the image fails to tell the truth about God, to that extent you will fail to worship God in truth. That is why God forbids you and me to make use of images and pictures in our worship.[7]

THE WORSHIP OF GOD

To avoid the worship of images or even the use of images in the worship of the true God is not in itself worship, however. We are to recognize that the true God is the eternal, self-existent, and self-sufficient one, the one immeasurably

---

[7]J. I. Packer, *Knowing God* (Downers Grove, IL: InterVarsity Press, 1973), 41.

beyond our highest thoughts. We are to humble ourselves and learn from him, allowing him to teach us what he is like and what he has done for our salvation. Do we do what he commands? Are we sure that in our worship we are actually worshiping the true God who has revealed himself in the Bible?

There is only one way to answer that question truthfully. It is to ask, do I really know the Bible, and do I worship God on the basis of the truth I find there? That truth is centered in the Lord Jesus Christ, as seen in the Bible. There the invisible God is made visible, the inscrutable knowable, the eternal God disclosed in space and time. Do I look to Jesus in order to know God? Do I think of God's attributes by what Jesus shows me of them? If not, I am worshiping an image of God, albeit an image of my own devising. If I look to Jesus, then I can know that I am worshiping the true God, as he has revealed himself. Paul says that although some knew God, they nevertheless "did not honor him as God or give thanks to him" (Rom 1:21). Let us determine that this shall not be true of us.

CHAPTER 10

GOD IN THREE PERSONS

*I*n chapter nine, I distinguished between those attributes of God that we partially share—love, wisdom, power, and so on—and those that we do not share. The first we can understand. The second we cannot. To a degree, we can understand what is meant by God's self-existence, his self-sufficiency, and his eternity. We can express them negatively, saying that God has no origins, needs nothing, will never cease to exist, and does not change. But we do not understand what they mean in and of themselves. Therefore, the first answers to who God is and what he is like are humbling.

Chapter eleven looks at those attributes that we can better understand. But first, let us look at one more problem area: the Trinity—God, although one, nevertheless exists in three persons, God the Father, God the Son, and God the Holy Spirit. The word *Trinity* is not in the Bible. It comes from the Latin word *trinitas*, which means "threeness." But even though the word is not in the Bible, the trinitarian idea is there, and it is most important. It is important because there can be no real blessing either on ourselves or our work if we neglect any one of the persons of the Godhead.

In the minds of some, the difficulty of understanding how God can be both one and three is reason enough to reject the doctrine outright. Such people cannot understand the Trinity and therefore deny it. Often they complain that theology should be "simple," because simplicity is beautiful, God is beautiful, and must therefore be simple and so on. But this is a misunderstanding of reality as well as of the nature of the God revealed to us in the Bible.

Why should reality be simple? Actually, as C. S. Lewis has pointed out in *Mere Christianity*, it is usually the case that reality is odd. "It is not neat, not obvious, not what you expect. . . . Reality, in fact, is usually something you would not have guessed."[1] This is true for very common things—a table and chair, for example. They seem simple, but if we are to speak of their construction from atoms and of the forces that hold these atoms together, even these supposedly "simple" things go beyond our minds' comprehension. More complex things are even more beyond us. Thus, the maker of the table and chair is more complicated than the things the maker has made, and God, who made the maker, should be the most complicated and incomprehensible of all.

THREE PERSONS

God has revealed some of his complexity to us in the doctrine of the Trinity. What we know about the Trinity we know only because of God's revelation of it in the Bible, and even then we don't know it well. In fact, so prone are we to make mistakes in dealing with this subject that we must be specially careful lest we go beyond or misrepresent what we find in Scripture.

The first thing we must say is that Christians believe, just as much as Jews believe, that God is one. Because Christians also believe in the Trinity, they have been inaccurately accused of believing in three gods, a form of polytheism. It is true that Christians see a plurality within the Godhead, because God himself reveals that it is there. But that is not polytheism. Christians, like believing Jews, are monotheists. That is, we believe in one God. We will recite with the Jew,

> Hear, O Israel: The LORD our God, the LORD is one. You shall love the LORD your God with all your heart and with all your soul and with all your might. And these words that I command you today shall be on your heart. You shall teach them diligently to your children, and shall talk of them when you sit in your house, and when you walk by the way, and when you lie down, and when you rise. You shall bind them as a sign on your hand, and they shall be as frontlets between your eyes. You shall write them on the doorposts of your house and on your gates. (Deut 6:4-9)

Here in the clearest language is the teaching that God is one and that this teaching should be known by God's people, talked about by them and taught to their children.

---

[1] C. S. Lewis, *Mere Christianity* (New York: The Macmillan Company, 1958), 33.

The same truth is in the New Testament, which is uniquely Christian. We read that "an idol has no real existence" and that "there is no God but one" (1 Cor 8:4). We are reminded of the fact that there is but "one God and Father of us all, who is over all and through all and in all" (Eph 4:6). James says, "You believe that God is one; you do well" (Jas 2:19).

It has been argued that because the verses that we have quoted from Deuteronomy begin "Hear, O Israel: The LORD our God, the LORD is one" that the Trinity is excluded. But in this very verse the word for "one" is *echad*, which means not one in isolation but one in unity. In fact, the word is never used in the Hebrew Bible of a stark singular entity. It is the word used in speaking of one bunch of grapes, for example, or in saying that the people of Israel responded as one people.

> After God has brought his wife to him, Adam says,
> This at last is bone of my bones
>   and flesh of my flesh;
> she shall be called Woman,
>   because she was taken out of Man.

The text adds, "Therefore a man shall leave his father and his mother and hold fast to his wife, and they shall become one flesh" (Gen 2:23-24). Again the word is *echad*. It is not suggested that the man and woman were to become one person, but rather that in a divine way they do become one. In a similar but not identical way, God is one God but also existent in three "persons."

One of our difficulties at this point is that we do not have an adequate word in English, or any other language, to express the nature of the different existences within the Godhead. The best word we have is *person*, which comes from the Latin word *persona*—meaning the mask that an actor used when representing some character in a Greek drama. But when we talk of a mask, we are already off the track. For we must not think of the persons in God being merely a way in which God from time to time represents himself to human beings. This particular error is known as modalism or Sabellianism, from the name of the man who first popularized it in church history (about the middle of the third century).

The word most often used in the Greek language was *homoousios*, which literally means "one being." But again, this is misleading if we begin to think that there are therefore three distinct beings with different natures within the Godhead. Calvin liked none of these words. He preferred the word *subsistence*. But, while probably quite accurate, nevertheless this word hardly conveys much meaning to most readers in our century.

Actually, the word *person* is all right, as long as we understand what we mean by a person. In common speech the word normally denotes a human being, and therefore one who is uniquely an individual. We have that concept in mind when we speak of depersonalizing someone. But that is not the meaning of the word as used in theology. It is possible to be a person entirely apart from our bodily existence. We may, for example, lose an arm or leg in some accident, yet we will still be a person with all the marks of personality. Moreover, at least according to Christian teaching, even when we die and our bodies decay to ruin we will still be persons. What we are really talking about, then, is a sense of existence expressing itself in knowledge, feelings, and a will.

So there are three persons or subsistences within God, each with knowledge, feelings, and a will. And yet, even here we are getting off the track. For in the case of God, the knowledge, feelings, and will of each person within the Godhead—Father, Son, and Holy Spirit—are identical.

LIGHT, HEAT, AIR

How can we illustrate that God is one God but that he exists in three persons? It is almost impossible to find a good illustration, though many have been suggested. Some have suggested the idea of a cake that can at the same time be layers, slices, and ingredients. The Father could be compared to the ingredients, the Son to the layers (by which God comes down to us), and the Holy Spirit to the slices (by which he is passed around). Another illustration is that of a man who may at the same time be a father, a son, and a husband. But the problem with that illustration is that he can only be one of these things to one individual (or, in the case of being a father, to a small number of individuals), while in God's case he is Father, Son, and Holy Spirit to all.

Perhaps a better illustration of the Trinity is the illustration of light, heat, and air. If you hold your hand out and look at it, each of these three things is present. There is light, because it is only by light that you can see your hand. In fact, even if the darkness of night should descend, there would still be light. There would be infrared light. Although you couldn't see it, it could be picked up by special equipment. There is also heat between your head and your hand. You may prove it by holding out a thermometer. It will vary as you go from a cold room to a warm room or from the outside to indoors. Finally, there is air. You can blow on your hand and feel it. You can wave your hand and thus fan your face.

The point is that each of these three—light, heat, and air—is distinct. Each obeys its own laws and may be studied separately. And yet, at the same time it is (at least in a normal earthly setting) impossible to have any one without the others. They are three and yet they are one. Together they make up the environment in which we have our being.

The interesting thing about this illustration is that the Bible speaks of each of these elements in relation to God.

Light: "This is the message we have heard from him and proclaim to you, that God is light, and in him is no darkness at all" (1 Jn 1:5).

Heat: "For our God is a consuming fire" (Heb 12:29).

Air, breath, or wind (the root meaning of the word *Spirit*): "The wind blows where it wishes, and you hear its sound, but you do not know where it comes or where it goes. So it is with everyone who is born of the Spirit" (Jn 3:8).[2]

THE BIBLE'S TEACHING

The important point is not whether we can understand the Trinity, even with the help of illustrations, but whether we will believe what the Bible has to say about the Father, Son, and Holy Spirit, and about their relationship to each other. What the Bible says may be summarized in the following five propositions:

1. There is but one living and true God who exists in three persons: God the Father, God the Son, and God the Holy Spirit. We have already looked at this truth in general. We will see it more fully when I talk about the full deity of the Son and Holy Spirit in books two and three in this volume. Here we note a plurality within the Godhead that is suggested even in the pages of the Old Testament, before the incarnation of the Lord Jesus Christ or the coming of the Holy Spirit on all God's people. The plurality may be seen, in the first instance, in those passages in which God speaks about himself in the plural. One example is Genesis 1:26. "Then God said, 'Let us make man in our image, after our likeness.'" Another is Genesis 11:7. "Come, let us go down and there confuse their language." A third is Isaiah 6:8. "And I heard the voice of the Lord saying, 'Whom shall I send, and who will go for us?'" In other passages a heavenly being termed "the angel of the Lord" is, on the one hand, identified with God, and yet, on the other hand, is also distinguished from him. Thus, we read, "The angel of the LORD found her [Hagar] by a spring of water in the wilderness. . . . The

---

[2]The illustration of the Trinity by light, heat, and air is an old one, but I have borrowed this particular expression of it from Donald Grey Barnhouse, *Man's Ruin* (Grand Rapids: Eerdmans, 1952), 64-65.

angel of the LORD also said to her, 'I will surely multiply your offspring so that they cannot be numbered for multitude.' . . . So she called the name of the LORD who spoke to her, 'You are a God of seeing'" (Gen 16:7, 10, 13). An even stranger case is the appearance of the three angels to Abraham and Lot. The angels are sometimes spoken of as three and sometimes as one. Moreover, when they speak, it is the Lord who, we are told, speaks to Lot and Abraham (Gen 18).

A final, startling passage is Proverbs 30:4. The prophet Agur is speaking about the nature of Almighty God, confessing his ignorance of him.

> Who has ascended to heaven and come down?
>   Who has gathered the wind in his fists?
> Who has wrapped up the waters in a garment?
>   Who has established all the ends of the earth?

Then comes, "What is his name, and what is his son's name? Surely you know!" In that day the prophet knew only the Father's name, the name Jehovah. Today we know that his Son's name is the Lord Jesus Christ.

2. The Lord Jesus Christ is fully divine, being the second person of the Godhead who became man. This, of course, is where the crux of debate on the Trinity is to be found; those who dislike the doctrine dislike it primarily because they are unwilling to give such an exalted position to "the man" Jesus.

Such reluctance is seen first in the teachings of Arius of Alexandria (died AD 336). Sabellius, mentioned earlier, tended to merge the persons of the Trinity, so that Father, Son, and Holy Spirit were only temporary manifestations of the one God, assumed for the purposes of our redemption. Arius, whose main work was done just after Sabellius, went to the other extreme. He divided the persons of the Trinity so the Son and the Spirit became less than God the Father. According to Arius, the Son and Spirit were beings willed into existence by God for the purpose of acting as his agents in redemption. Thus, they were not eternal (as God is), and they were not fully divine. Arius used the word *divine* to describe them in some lesser sense than when applying it to the Father. In more recent centuries the same error has been espoused by Unitarians and by some modern cults.

But it is a great error. For if Christ is not fully divine, then our salvation is neither accomplished nor assured. No being less than God himself, however exalted, is able to bear the full punishment of the world's sin.

The deity of the Lord Jesus Christ is taught in many crucial passages. We read, "In the beginning was the Word, and the Word was with God, and the Word was God. He was in the beginning with God" (Jn 1:1-2). That John 1:1-2 speaks of the Lord Jesus Christ is clear from John 1:14, in which we are told that the "Word" of John 1:1 "became flesh and dwelt among us." Similarly, Paul writes, "Have this mind among yourselves, which is yours in Christ Jesus, who, though he was in the form of God, did not count equality with God a thing to be grasped, but emptied himself, taking the form of a servant, being born in the likeness of men. And being found in human form, he humbled himself and became obedient to the point of death, even death on a cross" (Phil 2:5-8). The words "did not count equality with God a thing to be grasped, but emptied himself" do not mean that Jesus ceased to be fully God in the incarnation, as some have maintained, but only that he temporarily laid aside his divine glory and dignity in order to live among us. We remember that it was during the days of his life here that Jesus said, "I and the Father are one" (Jn 10:30), and "Whoever has seen me has seen the Father" (Jn 14:9).[3]

3. *The Holy Spirit is fully divine.* It is the Lord Jesus Christ who most clearly teaches the nature of the Holy Spirit. In the Gospel of John, Jesus compares the ministry of the coming Holy Spirit to his own ministry. "And I will ask the Father, and he will give you another Helper, to be with you forever, even the Spirit of truth, whom the world cannot receive, because it neither sees him nor knows him" (Jn 14:16-17). This understanding of the Holy Spirit is supported by the fact that distinctly divine attributes are ascribed to him: everlastingness (Heb 9:14), omnipresence (Ps 139:7-10), omniscience (1 Cor 2:10-11), omnipotence (Lk 1:35), and others.

4. *While each is fully divine, the three persons of the Godhead are related to each other in a way that implies some differences.* Thus, it is usually said in Scripture that the Father (not the Spirit) sent the Son into the world (Mt 10:40; Mk 9:37; Gal 4:4), but that both the Father and the Son send the Spirit (Jn 14:26; 15:26; 16:7). We don't know fully what such a description of relationships within the Trinity means. But usually it is said that the Son is subject to the Father, for the Father sent him, and that the Spirit is subject to both the Father and the Son, for he is sent into the world by both the Son and Father. However, we must remember that when we speak of subjection we do not mean inequality. Although related to each other in these ways, the members of the Godhead are nevertheless "the same in substance, equal in power and glory," as the Westminster Shorter Catechism says (Q. 6).

---

[3]The way in which Jesus may be said to have "emptied himself" is discussed at greater length by J. I. Packer, *Knowing God* (Downers Grove, IL: InterVarsity Press, 1973), 51-55.

5. *In the work of God, the members of the Godhead work together.* It is common among Christians to divide the work of God among the three persons, applying the work of creation to the Father, the work of redemption to the Son, and the work of sanctification to the Holy Spirit. A more correct way of speaking is to say that each member of the Trinity cooperates in each work.

One example is the work of *creation.* It is said of God the Father, "Of old you laid the foundation of the earth, and the heavens are the work of your hands" (Ps 102:25); and "In the beginning, God created the heavens and the earth" (Gen 1:1). It is written of the Son, "For by him all things were created, in heaven and on earth, visible and invisible" (Col 1:16); and "All things were made through him, and without him was not any thing made that was made" (Jn 1:3). It is written of the Holy Spirit, "The Spirit of God has made me" (Job 33:4). In the same way, the *incarnation* is shown to have been accomplished by the three persons of the Godhead working in unity, though only the Son became flesh (Lk 1:35). At *the baptism of the Lord* all three were also present: the Son came up out of the water, the Spirit descended in the appearance of a dove, and the voice of the Father was heard from heaven declaring, "This is my beloved Son, with whom I am well pleased" (Mt 3:16-17). All three persons were present in the *atonement,* as Hebrews 9:14 declares. "Christ . . . through the eternal Spirit offered himself without blemish to God." The *resurrection* of Christ is likewise attributed sometimes to the Father (Acts 2:32), sometimes to the Son (Jn 10:17-18), and sometimes to the Holy Spirit (Rom 1:4).

We are not surprised, therefore, that our salvation as a whole is also attributed to each of the three persons: "according to the foreknowledge of God the Father, in the sanctification of the Spirit, for obedience to Jesus Christ and for sprinkling with his blood" (1 Pet 1:2). Nor are we surprised that we are sent forth into all the world to "make disciples of all nations, baptizing them in the name of the Father and of the Son and of the Holy Spirit" (Mt 28:19).

THREEFOLD REDEMPTION

Again let me note, although we can say meaningful things about the Trinity (on the basis of God's revelation of them), the Trinity is still unfathomable. We should be humble before the Trinity. Someone once asked Daniel Webster, the orator, how a man of his intellect could believe in the Trinity. "How can a man of your mental caliber believe that three equals one?" his assailant chided. Webster replied, "I do not pretend fully to understand the arithmetic of heaven now." The doctrine of the Trinity does not mean that three equals one, of course, and

Webster knew that. It means rather that God is three in one sense and one in another. But Webster's reply nevertheless showed a proper degree of creature humility. We believe the doctrine of the Trinity, not because we understand it, but because the Bible teaches it and because the Spirit himself witnesses within our heart that it is so.

CHAPTER 11

OUR SOVEREIGN GOD

There are qualities in God we will never fully understand. We can speak of God's self-existence, self-sufficiency, eternity, and triune nature. Nevertheless, we must always recognize that we do not understand them completely, for we are not like God in any of these qualities. We must simply confess that he is God and that we are his creatures. The infinite is beyond our understanding. On the other hand, there are qualities of God that we can understand, because to a limited degree we share in them. This is true of most of God's attributes: wisdom, truthfulness, mercy, grace, justice, wrath, goodness, faithfulness, and others. It is this category that will occupy us now.

Let me begin with God's sovereignty. He has absolute authority and rule over his creation. In order to be sovereign, God must also be all-knowing, all-powerful, and absolutely free. If he were limited in any one of these areas, he would not be entirely sovereign. Yet the sovereignty of God is greater than any one of the attributes that it contains. Others may seem more important to us—love, for instance. But a little thought will show that the exercise of any of these attributes is made possible only by the sovereignty of God. God might love, for example, but if he were not sovereign, circumstances could thwart his love, making it useless to us. It is the same with God's justice. God may desire to establish justice among human beings, but if he were not sovereign, justice could be frustrated and injustice prevail.

So the doctrine of the sovereignty of God is no mere philosophical dogma devoid of practical value. Rather, it is the doctrine that gives meaning and substance to all other doctrines. It is, as Arthur Pink observes, "the foundation of Christian theology . . . the center of gravity in the system of Christian truth—the sun around which all the lesser orbs are grouped."[1] It is also, as we will see, the Christian's strength and comfort amid the storms of this life.

Intellectual Questions

Of course there are problems in asserting God's rule in relation to a world that has obviously gone its own way. We may grant that God rules heaven. But the earth is an ungodly place. Here God's authority is flouted and sin often prevails. Can we really say that God is sovereign in the midst of such a world? The answer is that if we look at the world alone, obviously not. But if we begin with the Scriptures, as we must do if we would know God, then we can affirm it; for the Bible everywhere declares that God is sovereign. We may not understand that doctrine. We may still wonder why God tolerates sin. But still we won't doubt the doctrine nor retreat from its consequences.

In Scripture the sovereignty of God is so pervasive and important a concept that it is impossible to treat it comprehensively. A few texts, however, will make the doctrine plain. "Yours, O LORD, is the greatness and the power and the glory and the victory, and the majesty, for all that is in the heavens and in the earth is yours. Yours is the kingdom, O LORD, and you are exalted as head above all . . . you rule over all" (1 Chron 29:11-12). The Psalms contain the same teaching.

> The earth is the LORD's and the fullness thereof,
>   the world and those who dwell therein. (Ps 24:1)

> Be still, and know that I am God.
>   I will be exalted among the nations,
>   I will be exalted in the earth! (Ps 46:10)

> God is the king of all the earth. (Ps 47:7)

The doctrine of the sovereignty of God lies at the root of all admonitions to trust in, praise, and commit one's way to him.

In addition to these texts and many others like them, there are also examples of God's rule over the material order. The world of objects and matter obeys those rules which God has set over it. They are the laws of nature or science.

---

[1] Arthur W. Pink, *The Sovereignty of God* (Grand Rapids: Baker Book House, 1969), 263.

We must not think, however, that the so-called laws are absolute and that God is somehow controlled or limited by them; for on some occasions God acts in an unpredictable way to do what we term a miracle.

God showed his sovereignty over nature in dividing the Red Sea so the children of Israel could pass over from Egypt into the wilderness, and then by returning the waters to destroy the pursuing Egyptian soldiers. He showed his sovereignty in sending manna to feed the people while they were in the wilderness. On another occasion he sent quails into the camp for meat. God divided the waters of the Jordan River so the people could pass over into Canaan. He caused the walls of Jericho to fall. He stopped the sun in the days of Joshua at Gibeon so that Israel might gain a full victory over her fleeing enemies. In the days of Jesus, God's sovereignty was seen in the feeding of the four and five thousand from a few small loaves and fish, in acts of healing the sick and raising the dead. Eventually, it was seen in the events connected with the crucifixion of Christ and the resurrection.

Other texts show that God's sovereignty extends to the human will and therefore also to human actions. Thus, God hardened Pharaoh's heart so that he refused to let the people of Israel go. On the other hand, he melts some individuals' hearts so that they respond to his love and obey him.

It may be objected, as we noted above, that some men and women nevertheless defy God and disobey him. But this observation cannot overthrow the teaching of the Bible concerning God's rule over his creation, unless the Bible is allowed to be self-contradictory. The explanation of the seeming contradiction is that human rebellion, while it is in opposition to God's express command, falls within his eternal or hidden purpose. That is, God permits sin for his own reasons, knowing in advance that he will bring sin to judgment in the day of his wrath, and that in the meantime it will not go beyond the bounds that he has fixed for it. Many things work against the sovereignty of God—from our perspective. But from God's perspective, his decrees are always established. They are, in fact, as the Westminster Shorter Catechism describes them, "his eternal purpose, according to the counsel of his will, whereby, for his own glory, he hath foreordained whatsoever comes to pass."

HUMAN QUESTIONS

The real problem with the sovereignty of God, from a human perspective, is not that the doctrine seems untrue, though there are problems in sorting it out intellectually, but rather that men and women basically do not like this disturbing and humbling aspect of God's character. We might think, if we were to look at the matter superficially, that men and women living in the midst of a chaotic culture would welcome sovereignty. "For what could be better," we might argue, "than knowing that things are really under control, in spite of appearances, and that God is able to work all events out for good eventually?" But this opinion fails to reckon with humanity's basic rebellion against God seen in our human quest for autonomy.

Rebellion has been characteristic of humankind since the earliest moments in the history of our race. But it is particularly visible in contemporary culture, as R. C. Sproul points out in *The Psychology of Atheism*. Our democratic system, for example, rejects all monarchical authority. "We serve no sovereign here" was a slogan of the American War of Independence. Today, though over two hundred years have gone by, the motif is still with us. So "government of the people" really means "government by myself" or at least by those who are basically like me and agree with me. God, the rightful Lord over all nations as well as over all individuals, is carefully excluded from the decision-making institutions of our national life.

Nor is the church much better, as Sproul also indicates. We often hear the "Savior" characteristics of God stressed—his love, mercy, goodness, and so on— but the matter of his lordship is absent. The distortion is particularly clear in evangelism. In modern practice the call to repentance is usually called an "invitation," which one can obviously accept or refuse. It is offered politely. Seldom do we hear presented God's sovereign demand to repent or his demand for total submission to the authority of his appointed king, Christ Jesus.

Today, even in theology, the emphasis in the church's proclamation is on liberation. But sometimes the liberation is from God as well as from "oppressive social structures," as the proponents of liberation theology term it. "In a word," says Sproul, "modern 'liberation' involves a revolt against the sovereign authority of God as members of Church and State join forces in a mutual act of cosmic treason."[2]

The basic reason why women and men do not like the doctrine of God's sovereignty is that they do not want a sovereign God. They wish to be autonomous. So they either deny God's existence entirely, deny this attribute of his existence, or else simply ignore him for all practical purposes.

The immediate factor in the current breakdown in respect for authority is the impact of European existentialism through the works of such men as Friedrich

---

[2]R. C. Sproul, *The Psychology of Atheism* (Minneapolis: Bethany Fellowship, 1974), 139.

Nietzsche, Jean-Paul Sartre, Albert Camus, and Martin Heidegger. In their works, the autonomy of the individual is a dominant philosophical ideal before which all other concepts, including the existence of God, must be eliminated. We find ourselves only when all external restraints are cast off. Only when God is eliminated can we be truly human. But does this work? In Nietzsche's work the ideal figure is the "superman" or *Uebermensch*, the one who creates his own values and who is answerable to no one but himself. But Nietzsche, the inventor of this philosophy, died not as a free person but as a prisoner of his own mind through insanity. The philosophy of existential autonomy is a dead end—worse than that, a disaster. But still it is the dominant philosophy of our age. God is restricting, so he must be cast off—that is the viewpoint. Questions must therefore be answered, not on the basis of a divinely revealed principle of right versus wrong, but on the basis of what the individual or a majority of individuals desire. Sometimes the majority within one particular segment of society stands in opposition to those in other segments.

The problem did not begin with existentialism, however. It began long before that—when Satan confronted the first woman in the garden of Eden by asking her the diabolical question, "Did God say?" and then by suggesting that in disobeying what God said, she and her husband would become "as God, knowing good and evil." *As God* is the crucial phrase, for it means to become autonomous. It was the temptation to attempt to replace God in the matter of his sovereignty, as Satan had himself tried to do earlier.

Did the results promised by the serpent follow? Not at all. It is true that the man and woman did learn the difference between good and evil, in a perverted way. They learned by doing evil. But they did not gain the freedom they wished. Instead they gained bondage to sin, from which only the Lord Jesus Christ through his obedience to the Father was able to deliver both them and us. Human autonomy led to the crucifixion of Christ.

> The kings of the earth set themselves,
>> and the rulers take counsel together,
>> against the LORD and his Anointed, saying,
> "Let us burst their bonds apart
>> and cast away their cords from us." (Ps 2:2-3)

True freedom comes by crucifixion *with* Christ, as the apostle Paul indicates: "I have been crucified with Christ. It is no longer I who live, but Christ who lives in me. And the life I now live in the flesh I live by faith in the Son of God, who loved me and gave himself for me" (Gal 2:20).

This is a paradox, of course, as Augustine, Luther, Edwards, Pascal, and others have pointed out. When individuals rebel against God, they don't achieve freedom. They fall into bondage, because rebellion is sin, and sin is a tyrant. On the other hand, when men and women submit to God, becoming his slaves, they become truly free. They achieve the ability fully to become the special, unique beings that God created them to be.

BLESSINGS OF SOVEREIGNTY

We find true freedom when we are willing to accept reality as it is (including God's rightful and effective sovereignty over all his creation) and when we allow him to make us into all that he would have us be. The matter of God's sovereignty, far from continuing to be an offense to us, can become a wonderful doctrine from which we derive great blessings.

What are these blessings? First, a realization of God's sovereignty inevitably *deepens our veneration of the living and true God.* Without an understanding and appreciation of these truths, it is questionable whether we know the God of the Old and New Testaments at all. For what is a God whose power is constantly being thwarted by the designs of people and Satan? What kind of a God is he whose sovereignty must be increasingly restricted, lest he be imagined to be invading the citadel of our "free will"? Who can worship such a truncated and pitiable deity? Pink says, "A 'god' whose will is resisted, whose designs are frustrated, whose purpose is checkmated, possesses no title to Deity, and so far from being a fit object of worship, merits nought but contempt."[3] On the other hand, a God who truly rules his universe is a God to be joyfully sought after, worshiped and obeyed.

Such is the God whom Isaiah saw:

> I saw the Lord sitting upon a throne, high and lifted up; and the train of his robe filled the temple. Above him stood the seraphim. Each had six wings: with two he covered his face, and with two he covered his feet, and with two he flew. And one called to another and said:
>
> "Holy, holy, holy is the LORD of hosts;
>   the whole earth is full of his glory!" (Is 6:1-3)

---

[3]Arthur W. Pink, *The Attributes of God* (Grand Rapids: Baker Book House, n.d.), 28.

Such is the God of the Scriptures. It was a vision of him, not of a lesser god, that transformed Isaiah's ministry.

Second, a knowledge of God in his sovereignty *gives comfort in the midst of trials, temptation, or sorrow.* Temptations and sorrows come to Christians and non-Christians alike. The question is, how shall we meet them? Clearly, if we must face them with no clear certainty that they are controlled by God and are permitted for his good purposes, then they are meaningless and life is a tragedy. That is precisely what many existentialists say. But if God is still in control, then such circumstances are known to him and have their purpose.

We do not know all God's purposes, of course. To know that, we would have to be God. Nevertheless, we can know some of them because God reveals them to us. For example, the aged apostle Peter writes to some who had endured great trials, reminding them that the end is not yet—Jesus will return—and that in the meantime God is strengthening and purifying them through their struggles. "In this you rejoice, though now for a little while, if necessary, you have been grieved by various trials, so that the tested genuineness of your faith—more precious than gold that perishes though is tested by fire—may be found to result in praise and glory and honor at the revelation of Jesus Christ" (1 Pet 1:6-7). Similarly, Paul writes to those at Thessalonica who had lost loved ones through death, reminding them that the Lord Jesus Christ will return and will at that time reunite all who are living then with their loved ones. He concludes, "Therefore encourage one another with these words" (1 Thess 4:18).

Third, an understanding of the sovereignty of God will *provide encouragement and joy in evangelism.* How can one evangelize without such confidence? How can one propose to take a message that is so obviously unpalatable to the natural man or woman and have any hope of moving him or her to accept it, unless God is able to take rebellious sinners and turn them in spite of their own inclinations to faith in Jesus? If God cannot do that, how can any sane human being hope to do it? That person would have to be either oblivious to the problem or else ridiculously self-confident. But if God is sovereign in this as in all other matters—if God calls whom he wills and calls "effectively"—then we can be bold in evangelism, knowing that God by grace may use us as channels of his blessing. Indeed, we can know that he will use us. For it is by human testimony that he has determined to bring others to him.

Finally, a knowledge of the sovereignty of God will *afford a deep sense of se-curity.* If we look to ourselves, we have no security at all. The lust of the flesh and eyes, the pride of life, are stronger than we are. Yet, when we look to the strength of our God, we can be confident. Paul writes,

> What then shall we say to these things? If God is for us, who can be against us? . . . Who shall separate us from the love of Christ? Shall tribulation, or distress, or persecution, or famine, or nakedness, or danger, or sword? . . . No, in all these things we are more than conquerors through him who loved us. For I am sure that neither death nor life, nor angels nor rulers, nor things present nor things to come, nor powers, nor height nor depth, nor anything else in all creation, will be able to separate us from the love of God in Christ Jesus our Lord. (Rom 8:31, 35, 37-39)

GOD IS ABLE

The Bible is filled from beginning to end with statements of what God is able to do and will do for those who are his people. Here are seven verses that, when put together, cover almost all the fundamental doctrines of Christianity.

1. Hebrews 7:25 in one sense includes all the rest. It tells us that Jesus Christ "is able to save to the uttermost those who draw near to God through him, since he always lives to make intercession for them." Mel Trotter, an evangelist of an earlier generation whom God had called from a life of alcoholism, said that this was his verse; it told of God's ability to save a person "to the uttermost." That is our story also. It covers the past, present, and future of salvation.

2. In 2 Timothy 1:12 Paul writes, "For I know whom I have believed, and I am convinced that he is able to guard until that Day what has been entrusted to me." The metaphor is that of banking, and the verse literally means, "God has the power to keep my spiritual deposits." He will not disappoint us.

3. Next, 2 Corinthians 9:8 says, "God is able to make all grace abound to you, so that having all sufficiency in all things at all times, you may abound in every good work." Some Christians think that the salvation of a man or woman by God is for the future only, more or less a "pie in the sky by and by" philosophy. Not so. The Bible tells us that God's grace is available to help us in every good work now. It is in this life that we are to abound in his sufficiency.

4. We are also told that God is able to help us in times of temptation. The Bible says of Jesus, "Because he himself has suffered when tempted, he is able to help those who are being tempted" (Heb 2:18). The best commentary on this verse is found in Scripture; we are told elsewhere that although temptation is the common human lot, God does not allow us to be tempted above our capacity to resist it, and, what is more, has provided a means of escape even before the temptation comes on us (1 Cor 10:13).

5. Ephesians 3:20-21 tells us that God is able to help us grow spiritually. It is in the form of a benediction. "Now to him who is able to do far more abundantly than all that we ask or think, according to the power at work within us, to him be glory in the church and in Christ Jesus throughout all generations, forever and ever. Amen."

6. God's ability to save also extends to our bodies. The Lord Jesus Christ "will transform our lowly body to be like his glorious body, by the power that enables him even to subject all things to himself" (Phil 3:21).

7. Finally, in another verse that is also a great benediction, Jude says, "Now to him who is able to keep you from stumbling and to present you blameless before the presence of his glory with great joy, to the only God, our Savior, through Jesus Christ our Lord, be glory, majesty, dominion, and authority, before all time and now and forever. Amen" (Jude 24-25).

Taken together, these verses declare that God is able to save us for this life and for eternity, to keep us from falling into sin and temptation, to lead us to the best in human experience and to satisfy us completely. Are these things true? Yes . . . but for one reason only. They are true because they are the eternal and immutable counsel of the God who is sovereign.

CHAPTER 12

HOLY, HOLY, HOLY

*F*rom the standpoint of revelation the first thing that has to be said about God is his sovereignty. But this first point is intimately connected with a second—so closely indeed that we might even ask whether it ought not to have come first: God is the Holy One."[1]

These words by the noted Swiss theologian Emil Brunner reflect the importance of God's holiness. The Bible itself readily confirms Brunner's view, since it calls God *holy* more than anything else. *Holy* is the epithet most often affixed to his name. Also we read that God alone is holy. "Who will not fear, O Lord, and glorify your name? For you alone are holy" (Rev 15:4).

God is said to be glorious in holiness. "Who is like you, O LORD, among the gods? Who is like you, majestic in holiness, awesome in glorious deeds, doing wonders?" (Ex 15:11). God's holiness is celebrated without ceasing by the seraphim before his throne. Isaiah heard them sing, "Holy, holy, holy is the LORD of hosts; the whole earth is full of his glory!" (Is 6:3). The apostle John heard the seraphim declare, "Holy, holy, holy, is the Lord God Almighty, who was and is and is to come!" (Rev 4:8). God's people are called on to join in these praises. We read, "Sing praises to the LORD, O you his saints, and give thanks to his holy name" (Ps 30:4). Because of this emphasis the Christian church prays in the words of the Lord's Prayer, "Hallowed be thy name" (Mt 6:9 KJV).

---

[1]Emil Brunner, *The Christian Doctrine of God: Dogmatics*, trans. Olive Wyon, vol. 1 (Philadelphia: Westminster, 1950), 157.

SET APART

To say that the attribute of holiness is important is not to say that we understand it. Of all the attributes of God, in fact, this one is most misconstrued.

One misconception is to think of God's holiness largely in human terms. It is imagined that holiness or righteousness is something that can be graded, more or less. That is, as we look about us we see men and women who come very low on the scale: criminals, perverts, and so on. If a perfect score of righteousness is to be considered as, say, one hundred, we might conclude that such persons score in the low teens. Above them are the average individuals of our society. They score in the thirties or forties. Next are the very good people, the judges, philanthropists, and other humanitarians; they are imagined to score possibly in the sixties or seventies—not one hundred, of course, for even they are not as good as they could be. Then, if you push the total on up to one hundred (or beyond, if that is possible), one arrives at the goodness of God.

Most people imagine something like that when they think of God's holiness, if they think of it at all. It is only a perfection of the good in people. But according to the Bible, the holiness of God cannot be placed in the same category as human goodness.

We see the truth of the biblical concept when we study a text such as Romans 10:3, in which the apostle Paul writes of two kinds of righteousness. He says, speaking of the Israel of his day, "For, being ignorant of the righteousness that comes from God, and seeking to establish their own, they did not submit to God's righteousness." This verse distinguishes very clearly between God's righteousness and our righteousness. So even if we were to take all the righteousness of which human beings are capable and heap it all up so that it made a great mountain, it still would not begin to approach the righteousness of God; that is in a different category entirely.

What do we mean when we talk about the holiness of God? To answer that question we must *not* begin with ethics. Ethics is involved, as we will see. But in its original and most fundamental sense, *holy* is not an ethical concept at all. Rather it means that which is of the very nature of God and that therefore distinguishes him from everything else. It is what sets God apart from his creation. It has to do with his transcendence.

The fundamental meaning of the word *holy* is preserved in the meaning of the words *saint* and *sanctify*, which are nearly identical to it. *Holy* comes from the Germanic languages. *Saint* comes from the Romance languages. But the root meaning of both is identical. In the biblical sense, a saint is not a person who has achieved a certain level of goodness (as most people think), but rather one who has been "set apart" by God. Saints are the "called-out ones" who make up God's church. The same idea is also present when, as in Exodus 40, the Bible refers to the sanctification of objects. In that chapter Moses is instructed to sanctify the altar and basin in the middle of the tabernacle. The chapter does not refer to any intrinsic change in the nature of the stones; they are not made righteous. It merely indicates that they were to be set apart for a special use. Similarly, Jesus prays, saying, "I consecrate [or sanctify] myself, that they also may be sanctified in truth" (Jn 17:19). The verse does not mean that Jesus makes himself more righteous, for he already was righteous. It means that he separated himself to a special task, the task of providing salvation for all people by his death.

Holiness, then, is the characteristic of God that sets him apart from his creation. In this, holiness has at least four elements.

The first is *majesty*. Majesty is "dignity," "authority of sovereign power," "stateliness," or "grandeur." It is the proper characteristic of monarchs and is, of course, supremely the attribute of that one who is Monarch over all. Majesty is the dominant element in the visions of God in his glory seen both in the Old Testament and the New. The element of majesty links the idea of holiness to sovereignty.

A second element in the idea of holiness is *will*, the will of a personality. Apart from it, the idea of holiness becomes abstract, impersonal, and static, rather than concrete, personal, and active. Moreover, if we ask what God's will is predominantly set on, the answer is that it is set on proclaiming himself as the "Wholly Other," whose glory must on no account be diminished because of human arrogance and willful rebellion. In the element of will, the idea of holiness comes quite close to the "jealousy" of God, which modern people find so repugnant.

"I the LORD your God am a jealous God" (Ex 20:5). Rightly understood, the idea of jealousy is central to any true concept of God. It is, as Brunner points out, analogous to a proper jealousy within marriage. A married person ought not to allow any third person to enter into the inner relationship. Similarly, God rejects every attack on his sole rights as Lord of his creation. "The holiness of God is therefore not only an absolute difference of nature, but it is an active self-differentiation, the willed energy with which God asserts and maintains the fact that He is Wholly Other against all else. The absoluteness of this difference becomes the absoluteness of his holy will, which is supreme and unique."[2]

---

[2]Ibid., 160.

In simpler terms, the holiness of God means that God is not indifferent to how men and women regard him. He does not go his solitary way heedless of their rejection of him. Rather, he wills and acts to see that his glory is recognized. Recognition will come now, in each individual case, or it will become true for each in the day of God's judgment.

A third element in the idea of holiness is the element of *wrath*. Wrath is an essential part of God's holiness, but we must not compare it to an emotional, human reaction to something, a reaction that we normally think of as anger. The wrath of God is not at all like any emotion we know in human experience. It is, rather, that necessary and proper stance of the holy God to all that opposes him. It means that he takes the matter of being God seriously, so seriously that he will not allow any thing or personality to aspire to his place. When Satan sought to do that, Satan was judged (and will yet be judged). When men and women refuse to take the place that God has given to them, they will be judged also.

A final element in the idea of holiness is one we mentioned earlier: *righteousness*. Righteousness is involved in holiness, not because it is the best category by which holiness may be understood, but because, having spoken of the will of God, we immediately go on to see that what God wills is righteousness or holiness in its ethical sense. In other words, when we ask, "What is right? What is moral?" we answer the questions not by appealing to some independent moral standard, as if there could be a standard for anything apart from God, but rather by appealing to the will and nature of God himself. The right is what God is and reveals to us.

The nature of God is an essential foundation for any true or lasting morality. Consequently, where God is not acknowledged, morality (however much talked about) inevitably declines, just as it is doing in contemporary Western civilization. It is the desire to obey God that ultimately makes ethical behavior possible.

THE TABERNACLE

We have a dramatization of the holiness of God in the laws given for the building of the Jewish tabernacle. On one level, the tabernacle was constructed to teach the immanence of God, the truth that God is always present with his people. But on the other hand, it also taught that God is separated from his people because of his holiness and their sin, and can therefore be approached only in the way he determines.

We must not think that the Jewish people had any more understanding of the holiness of God than we naturally do, for they did not. It was necessary for

God to teach them about it. The point of the tabernacle was that a sinful man or woman could not simply "barge in" on the Holy One. God was understood to have dwelt symbolically within the innermost chamber of the tabernacle, known as the "Holy of Holies." People could not go in there. A Greek could enter any of the temples of Greece and pray before the statue of the pagan god or goddess. A Roman could enter any of the temples of Rome. But a Jew could not enter the Holy of Holies. In fact, only one person could ever go in; that was the high priest of Israel; and even he could go in only once a year and that only after having first made sacrifices for himself and the people in the outer courtyard. The Holy of Holies (the innermost chamber of the tabernacle) was separated from the Holy Place (the outer chamber of the tabernacle) by a thick veil.

Nor was that all. Just as there was a veil between the Holy of Holies and the Holy Place, that is, dividing these two chambers within the tabernacle, so there was another thick veil separating the Holy Place from the outer courtyard. And then there was a third veil closing off the entrance of the courtyard from the surrounding camp of the Israelites.

The meaning of the word *veil* is to "separate" or (later) to "hide." So the meaning of the veils was that God, even though he chose to dwell with his people, was nevertheless separated from them or hidden from them because of his holiness and their sin. Communion with God was to be only within the Holy of Holies. But in order to enter, three curtains had to be passed, each of which added to the sense of the enormous gulf that exists between God and humanity: first, the curtain between the outer camp and the courtyard; second, the covering of the entrance to the Holy Place; third, the curtain separating the Holy Place from the innermost chamber. Likewise, in order to enter the Holy of Holies, the high priest had to perform a sacrifice at the brazen altar in the courtyard, wash at the basin in the courtyard, and then pass through the Holy Place in the light of the seven-branched golden candlestick and through the incense that was always burning on an altar within that room.

What would happen if a person should ignore these barriers? The answer is that he or she would immediately be consumed, as some who entered were. The wrath of God would flame out against that sin that sought thus to intrude on or compromise God's holiness. As we recognize his holiness, we begin to understand something of human sinfulness and the necessity for Christ's atoning death on the cross.

ATTRACTION AND TERROR

The holiness of God is another attribute that makes God undesirable and even threatening. We have already pointed out that men and women do not like the sovereignty of God because it is a threat to their desire for sovereignty. They do not find a sovereign God desirable. Negative reaction is even more apparent in regard to God's holiness.

Here we are greatly assisted by a careful analysis of the idea of the *holy* by the German theologian Rudolf Otto. Otto has written a book, called in German *Das Heilige* and in English *The Idea of the Holy*, in which he seeks to understand the specific nonrational or superrational nature of religious experience from a phenomenological perspective. The superrational element Otto calls the "numinous" or the "holy." There is a great deal of difference between the numinous or holy (as an abstract conception) in the non-Christian religions and the Holy One (as personal) within Judaism and Christianity. But as far as it goes, the analysis is quite helpful, for it shows that men and women find the true God threatening.

In his analysis, Otto distinguishes three elements in the Holy. The first is *awefulness*, by which he means "that which is profoundly awe-inspiring." We use the word *awful* to mean "extremely bad" or "terrible," but this is a different idea. The awefulness of the holy is that which is so awe-inspiring that it produces fear or trembling in the worshiper. The second element is *overpoweringness*. Supreme and majestic power inevitably engenders a sense of impotence and general worthlessness in the worshiper. The final element is *energy*, by which Otto speaks of the dynamic element present in the encounter.

The point is that the experience of confronting the Holy is supremely threatening. The worshiper is drawn to the Holy, but at the same time is terrified by it. The awe-inspiring, overpowering energy of the Holy threatens to destroy the worshiper.

We should notice that we find the same phenomenon in the Bible also, although the Bible goes on to explain it, as non-Christians do not. The account of Job is an example. Job had suffered the loss of his possessions, family, and health. When his friends came to convince him that his loss was because of some sin, either recognized or hidden, Job stoutly defended himself against their accusations. He was right to do so, for Job was suffering as an upright man. "Have you considered my servant Job, that there is none like him on the earth, a blameless and upright man, who fears God and turns away from evil?" (Job 1:8).

Obviously, if anyone could have stood before the holiness of God, it was Job. Yet, toward the end of the book, after God came to Job with a series of questions and statements designed to teach something of his true majesty to this suffering servant, Job was left nearly speechless and in a state of collapse. He replied to God, "Behold, I am of small account; what shall I answer you? . . . Therefore I despise myself, and repent in dust and ashes" (Job 40:4; 42:6).

We see the same phenomenon in Isaiah, who received a vision of the Lord "sitting upon a throne, high and lifted up" (Is 6:1). He heard the praise of the seraphim. But the effect on Isaiah, far from being a cause for self-satisfaction or pride that such a vision had been granted to him, was actually devastating. He responded, "Woe is me! For I am lost; for I am a man of unclean lips, and I dwell in the midst of a people of unclean lips; for my eyes have seen the King, the LORD of hosts!" (Is 6:5). Isaiah saw himself as ruined or undone. Only when a coal was taken from the altar and used to purge his lips was he able to stand upright again and respond affirmatively to God's call to him for service.

Habakkuk also had a vision of God. He had been distressed with the un-godliness in the world around him and had wondered how the ungodly could rightly triumph over the person who was more righteous. The prophet then entered into his watchtower and waited for God's answer. When God answered, Habakkuk was overcome with dread.

> I hear, and my body trembles;
> > my lips quiver at the sound;
> rottenness enters into my bones,
> > my legs tremble beneath me. (Hab 3:16)

Habakkuk was a prophet. But even so, a confrontation with God was shattering.

Similarly, although the glory of God was veiled in the person of Jesus Christ, from time to time those who were Christ's disciples perceived who he was, ever so slightly, and had a similar reaction. Thus, after Peter had recognized the glory of God in Christ's miracle in granting a great catch of fish in Galilee, Peter responded, "Depart from me, for I am a sinful man, O Lord" (Lk 5:8).

When the apostle John received a revelation of Christ's glory, seeing the risen Lord standing in the midst of the seven golden candlesticks, he "fell at his feet as though dead" and rose only after the Lord had touched him and given him a commission to write the book of Revelation (Rev 1:17). John could stand before the Lord only after he had experienced something like a resurrection.

That is what it means to come face to face with the Holy. It is not a pleasant experience. It is profoundly threatening, for the Holy cannot coexist in the same space with the unholy. God must destroy the unholy or else purge out the sin. Moreover, if this is true for the best people, for those whom God has chosen to be his prophets and whom even he calls "righteous," how much truer is it of those who are antagonistic to God? To them the experience is totally overwhelming. As a result they resist, try to make light of or run away from God. Tozer has written, "The moral shock suffered by us through our mighty break with the high will of heaven has left us all with a permanent trauma affecting every part of our nature."[3] He is right. Consequently, men and women will not come to God, and that which should be their great joy is abhorrent to them.

A HOLY PEOPLE

So what do we do, we who are sinful and yet are confronted with the holy God? Do we simply go our own way? Do the best we can? Turn our backs on the Holy? If it were not for the fact that God has chosen to do something about our predicament, that would be all we could do. But the glory of Christianity is its message that the holy God has done something. He has done what was needed. He has made for us a way into his presence through the Lord Jesus Christ, as a result of which the unholy becomes holy and is enabled to dwell with him.

Here we may go back to the illustration provided by the wilderness tabernacle. The tabernacle was intended to teach the great gulf that lay between God in his holiness and human beings in their sin. But it also taught the way by which that gulf could be bridged. In Old Testament times that way was symbolic. It was by the sacrifice of animals in which the sin of the people was symbolically transferred to the innocent victim, which then died in the worshipers' place. That was why the high priest was required to perform a sacrifice first for himself and then for the people before he could enter into the Holy of Holies on the Day of Atonement. But although the symbolism was important and vivid, it was not the death of the animals, however many, that actually purged away sin. The true and only atonement was to be provided by the Lord Jesus Christ who, as the perfect Lamb of God, died in place of sinners. Moreover, it was not only the sacrifices that prefigured his work. It was each part of the tabernacle, the altar, the basin, the candlesticks, the incense, the showbread within the Holy Place, and everything else. In other words, he is the one through whom we are washed from sin;

---

[3]A. W. Tozer, *The Knowledge of the Holy* (New York: Harper & Row, 1961), 110.

he is the light of the world; he is the bread of life; he is the basis of worship through prayer, as well as our once-and-for-all sufficient sacrifice.

And Christ is truly sufficient. At the moment when he bore our sin and was therefore judicially separated from the presence of the Father in our place—in that moment God himself tore the veil of the temple in two from top to bottom, thereby indicating that the way into his presence, into the Holy of Holies, is now open for all who will come to him through faith in Christ, as he requires. To those who will come, God then grants a measure of his own holiness in two senses. We will never be holy in the sense of the "Wholly Other," as he is. But we are first separated to him through Christ, as his holy ones, and then made righteous practically and increasingly as his nature gradually transforms our being.

There will be several consequences for those who come to the knowledge of the Holy. First, they will learn to hate sin. We do not naturally hate sin. In fact, the opposite is true. We generally love sin and are loath to part with it. But we must learn to hate sin, or else we will learn to hate God, who requires a holy life from those who are Christ's followers. We see a great tension during the lifetime of the Lord Jesus Christ. Some saw his holiness, came to hate sin and became his followers. Others saw him, came to hate him, and eventually crucified him.

Second, those who have come to the knowledge of the Holy One through faith in the Lord Jesus Christ will learn to love righteousness and strive for it. Such individuals often need urging. The apostle Peter wrote to those in his day saying, "But as he who called you is holy, you also be holy in all your conduct, since it is written, 'You shall be holy, for I am holy'" (1 Pet 1:15-16). It does not say "Be holy, *as* I am holy." None of us could do that. We cannot be holy in the same sense that God is holy. But we can be holy in the area of a righteous and upright walk before him.

Third, we must look to the day when God will be fully known in his holiness by all men and women, and we can rejoice in anticipation of that day. If we had not come to God through faith in Christ, that day would be terrible. It would mean the exposure of our sin and judgment. Having come, it means rather the completion of our salvation, in that we shall be made like Jesus. We shall be like him, in holiness and in every other way, "because we shall see him as he is" (1 Jn 3:2).

CHAPTER 13

THE GOD WHO KNOWS

The unique quality of God's knowledge is its totality or perfection: his *omniscience* is the proper theological term. Omniscience involves not only God's knowledge of us, but also his knowledge of nature, the past, present, and future. It involves everything that we can possibly imagine and much more besides. It is a knowledge that God has always had and will always have. There is no need for him to learn. In fact, if we are to take the scope of his knowledge at full value, it is necessary to say that God has never learned and cannot learn, for he already knows and has always known everything.

God's omniscience is seen in Isaiah's questionings of a rebellious nation.

Who has measured the Spirit of the LORD,
   or what man shows him his counsel?
Whom did he consult,
   and who made him understand?
Who taught him in the path of justice,
   and taught him knowledge,
   and showed him the way of understanding? (Is 40:13-14)

The answer clearly is no one. God is infinitely above his creation in all knowledge and understanding. Similarly, the Lord himself speaks to Job out of the whirlwind.

Who is this that darkens counsel by words without knowledge?
Dress for action like a man;
   I will question you, and you make it known to me.

Where were you when I laid the foundation of the earth?

Tell me, if you have understanding.

Who determined its measurements—surely you know!

Or who stretched the line upon it?

On what were its bases sunk,

or who laid its cornerstone,

when the morning stars sang together

and all the sons of God shouted for joy? (Job 38:2-7)

Once again, the answer is that next to the knowledge of God, which is perfect, human knowledge is near zero. The knowledge of God extends to the most intimate knowledge of the individual. "I know their works and their thoughts," said God to Isaiah, referring to the Jewish people (Is 66:18). David declared,

O LORD, you have searched me and known me!

You know when I sit down and when I rise up;

you discern my thoughts from afar.

You search out my path and my lying down

and are acquainted with all my ways.

Even before a word is on my tongue,

behold, O LORD, you know it altogether. (Ps 139:1-4)

The author of Hebrews writes, "No creature is hidden from his sight, but all are naked and exposed to the eyes of him to whom we must give account" (Heb 4:13).

It is impossible to overstate the qualities of God's knowledge. As Thomas Watson observed years ago, God's knowledge is *primary*, for he is the pattern and source of all knowledge from which others merely borrow; his knowledge is *pure*, for it is not contaminated by either the object or its sin; his knowledge is *facile*, for it is without any difficulty; it is *infallible*; it is *instantaneous*; it is entirely *retentive*. God is perfect in his knowledge.

THE THREAT OF OMNISCIENCE

We might think that God's omniscience would be comforting to us in our natural state, for the belief that perfect knowledge exists (even though we do not possess it ourselves) should make the world less threatening. Actually, the opposite is true. To acknowledge that there is a God who knows everything about everything is also to acknowledge that such a God knows us. And because we don't want some things about us to be known, we hide it—not only from others but also from ourselves as much as possible. A God who thoroughly knows us is unsettling.

Arthur W. Pink notes that the thought of divine omniscience "fills us with uneasiness."[1] A. W. Tozer observes, "In the divine omniscience we see set forth against each other the terror and fascination of the Godhead. That God knows each person through and through can be a cause of shaking fear to the man that has something to hide—some unforsaken sin, some secret crime committed against man or God."[2] But it is not just some other person about whom Tozer is speaking. It is descriptive of the entire race, and therefore of us. All have rebelled against God and thus fear exposure.

No one has documented our fear of being exposed more carefully in recent years than R. C. Sproul in *The Psychology of Atheism*. Sproul devotes a chapter to the theme of "God and Nakedness" and analyzes the fear modern people have of being exposed, first to others and then also to God. The first object of his analysis is the work of Jean-Paul Sartre. Sartre has spoken of the fear of being beneath the gaze of someone else. We don't mind staring at another, for instance. But the moment we become aware that another is staring at us we become embarrassed, confused, and fearful, and our behavior alters. We hate the experience and do whatever we can to avoid it. If we can't avoid it, the experience becomes intolerable.

In what is perhaps Sartre's best-known work, the play *No Exit*, four characters are confined in a room with nothing to do but talk to and stare at each other. It is a symbol of hell. In the closing lines of the play this becomes quite clear, as Garcin stands at the mantelpiece stroking a bronze bust. He says,

> Yes, now's the moment: I'm looking at this thing on the mantelpiece, and I understand that I'm in hell. I tell you, everything's been thought out beforehand. They knew I'd stand at the fireplace stroking this thing of bronze, with all those eyes intent on me. Devouring me. (*He swings round abruptly.*) What? Only two of you? I thought there were more; many more. (*Laughs.*) So this is hell. I'd never have believed it. You remember all we were told about the torture chambers, the fire and brimstone, the "burning marl." Old wives' tales! There's no need for red-hot pokers. Hell is—other people![3]

The final stage direction says that the characters slump down onto their respective sofas, the laughter dies away, and they "gaze" at each other.

---

[1] Arthur W. Pink, *The Attributes of God* (Grand Rapids: Baker Book House, n.d.), 13.
[2] A. W. Tozer, *The Knowledge of the Holy* (New York: Harper & Row, 1961), 63.
[3] Jean-Paul Sartre, *No Exit and Three Other Plays* (New York: Vintage Books, 1949), 47.

In Sartre's philosophy this fear of being under the gaze of another is reason for doing away with God; for beneath God's gaze we are reduced to objects and have our humanity destroyed. The point of interest here, however, is the fear of exposure. Where does it come from if not from a real and merited guilt arising from our rebellion against the only sovereign and holy God of the universe?

Sproul next analyzes Julius Fast's book *Body Language*. This book is a study of how human beings communicate nonverbally by various body positions, gestures, tilts of the head, liftings of the eyebrow, and so forth. Fast points out that one can stare at an object for very long periods. One can stare at animals. But to stare at another person is unacceptable behavior because, if a glance is held too long, it provokes either embarrassment or hostility or both. The fact that we have doors, window shades, clothes, and shower curtains demonstrates our desire and need for privacy.

Third, Sproul deals with Desmond Morris's *The Naked Ape*, another popular work. The "naked ape" is, of course, the human being. The title of the book as well as its content highlight the uniqueness of humans in their nakedness. We are naked animals, having no hair for a covering, but we are ashamed in our nakedness and seek to hide ourselves from the gaze of other persons.

Fourth, Sproul mentions the Danish philosopher and writer Søren Kierkegaard, noting that he "is sharply critical of the person who lives merely on the 'aesthetic' or 'spectator' plane of life, operating within the context of the concealment of a masquerade," while he himself "preserved an island of hiddenness for himself and for all men." He knew that "solitude affords a place of hiddenness that is necessary for the human subject."[4]

What emerges from these modern expressions is a strange ambivalence. On the one hand, women and men long to be known. The modern proof is in the popularity of encounter sessions, psychiatry, talk shows, and X-rated movies. But in a far deeper way, people fear such exposure, for they are ashamed of what is there to be seen—by other people and by God. With others there are always ways to achieve a covering. We wear clothes, for example. On the psychological level, we carefully guard what we say so that only those things about us that we wish to be known are known. Sometimes we put on a false front entirely. But what are we to do in regard to God before whom "all hearts are open, all desires known"? There is nothing to be done. Nothing can be done. Consequently, it is

[4]R. C. Sproul, *The Psychology of Atheism* (Minneapolis: Bethany Fellowship, 1974), 114-16. The entire analysis of nakedness in modern culture is found on 107-18.

an awareness of the knowledge of God, as well as his sovereignty and holiness, that produces anxiety and even dread in fallen women and men.

COVERED WITH ROBES OF RIGHTEOUSNESS

Dread of God's knowledge is not a normal experience for Christians. But before we see what it does mean to them, we must determine why it has ceased to be fearful. Here the experience of Adam and Eve is enlightening. Adam and Eve had sinned, and when they sinned they recognized that they were naked. They had been naked beforehand in a purely physical sense. But they had not yet sinned and so "were not ashamed" (Gen 2:25). After they became sinners, their nakedness became something more than merely physical. It had become a psychological nakedness connected to their moral guilt. They were guilty, before one another and also before God.

What happened? God came "walking in the garden" to confront them in their nakedness. He exposed their sin, for sin cannot be hidden in his presence. But then he did something tremendous. He clothed them, using skins from animals that he himself sacrificed.

This is the message of Christianity: we can be known and yet clothed at the same time. Yet being clothed is not accomplished ultimately with the skins of animals. The clothing of Adam and Eve was only a symbol, an acted parable, of what was to come for all when God sent Jesus Christ to die for our sin so that guilt might be removed. On the basis of his perfect and atoning sacrifice, God would then clothe all who believe in Christ with the Lord's own righteousness. Because of Christ's work, God no longer looks on us as sinners but as those who have become righteous in Christ. Now we can stand before him rather than hide—not because God has been ignorant of our sin or has refused to care about it, but because he has known about it and has dealt with it perfectly. Now we can cry with Isaiah,

I will greatly rejoice in the LORD;
> my soul shall exult in my God,
for he has clothed me with the garments of salvation,
> he has covered me with the robe of righteousness,
as a bridegroom decks himself like a priest with a beautiful headdress,
> and as a bride adorns herself with her jewels. (Is 61:10)

REASONS FOR JOY

The omniscience of God is a cause of uneasiness and even dread for those who do not have their sin covered with the righteousness of Christ. But for three reasons this omniscience is a great blessing and a cause for joy among Christians.

First, because God knows all things, he knows the *worst about us* and yet has loved us and saved us. In human relationships we often fear that something in us might come to light to break the relationship. Otherwise why would we be so careful to put on our best face with other people? But God already knows the worst about us and nevertheless continues to demonstrate his love. He "knows our frame" and "remembers that we are dust" (Ps 103:14). We needn't fear that something within us will rise up to startle God, that some forgotten skeleton will come tumbling out of our closet to expose our shameful past or that some informer will speak out against us to bring shame. Nothing can happen that isn't already known to God.

One writer links this sense of security to the ministry of the Holy Spirit within us.

> Let us take comfort that the Holy Spirit is not dwelling within us as a spy to discover our infirmities and to report them to God for condemnation. The Holy Spirit knows that Christ has been condemned in our place, and he has come within us as the bookkeeper and paying teller of God, to remind us ever of our credit balance, and to give us the fruits of our inheritance in order that we may live in the triumph purchased for us.[5]

Second, not only does God know the worst about us, he also knows *the best about us*, even though that best may be unknown to any other person. There are times in our lives when we do very well at something and yet find that we go unnoticed. Or we do as well as we possibly can but we fail. What we have done is therefore totally misinterpreted. Perhaps things go in a way we did not intend. Then people say—even our friends—"How could so-and-so do a thing like that? I would have thought better of him." They do not know the situation, nor do they know our hearts. They are critical, and nothing we can do or say seems to change their opinion. What then? There is comfort in knowing that God, who knows all things, also knows us and knows that we really did do the best of which we were capable. And he does not judge us. He does not condemn us.

---

[5]Donald Grey Barnhouse, *God's Heirs* (Grand Rapids: Eerdmans, 1963), 145-46.

A father is teaching his one-year-old daughter to walk. She is trying but she falls down. He puts her back on her feet and she falls down again. So he gets angry. He screams and shouts, "You're a dumb child. I'm a good teacher but you're not learning." When she falls the third time, he spanks her for it. Obviously we would think very poorly of that kind of father. On the other hand, we would think well of a father who says, "Don't worry about it. You fell down, but you'll walk someday. I know you're doing the very best you can." Our God is like the second of the two. He knows our weaknesses and sin, but he also knows when we are trying, and he is patient.

Third, God knows *what he is going to make of us*. That is, he knows the end we have been made for and he is most certainly going to bring us to it in his own proper time. That end is spelled out in Romans 8:29. Most Christians know the verse that comes immediately before, Romans 8:28. It is a reassuring promise: "We know that for those who love God all things work together for good, for those who are called according to his purpose." But it is a pity that very few have gone on to learn the next verse, because it tells what the "purpose" mentioned in Romans 8:28 is. "For those whom he foreknew he also predestined to be conformed to the image of his Son, in order that he might be the firstborn among many brethren." God is determined to make us like Jesus Christ. That is his purpose in redemption, and it is in this context that Romans 8:28 was written. Redemption begins with God's electing foreknowledge of his own people, his predestination of them to be conformed to Christ's image—his choice of material and the blueprint. Redemption further includes his call of these elected ones to salvation, their justification through the work of Christ, and their glorification, as a result of which God's purposes with them are finally and totally achieved.

We get discouraged in the Christian life, and with good cause. We take a step forward and fall half a step back. We succeed once, but then we fail twice. We overcome temptation, but we also fall in temptation, sometimes over and over again. We say, "Oh, I'm not making progress at all. I'm doing worse this year than last year. God must be discouraged with me." But God is not discouraged with us. That is the point. God knows everything. So while it is true that he is fully aware of our failures and victories, few as the victories may be, he is also aware of far more than that. He is aware of what we will one day be when by his grace we are fully conformed to the image of Jesus Christ. It is a sure thing. So we should take confidence in that, even though the discouragements are many and real. We have a great destiny; in its light all the vaunted achievements of our age and our personal achievements fade into virtual insignificance.

There are other areas in which God's omniscience affects our lives. First, if God is the God of all knowledge, then we should learn the importance of knowledge. We are made in the image of God. One of the things that means is that we can learn to think God's thoughts after him and share his knowledge. We can possess true knowledge in the same sense, although not to the same degree that God possesses knowledge. There is value in studying and learning.

Second, hypocrisy is foolishness. We may try to fool other people about what we're really like, and even succeed up to a point. But we cannot fool God. Therefore, when we stand before him exposed in our sin but covered by Christ's righteousness, then we can stand before anybody, never fearing that they might come to know us as we really are. And we can be bold to do the right thing, whether or not it is misunderstood or ridiculed. We can be women and men of our word. We can let our yes be yes and our no be no, because God knows us. We do not have to pretend to be something we are not.

Finally, we can be encouraged in difficulties. Job went through great difficulties, but still he said, "He knows the way that I take; when he has tried me, I shall come out as gold" (Job 23:10). Because God knows, believers can rest. We can pray, for we can be assured that no prayer, no cry for help, not even a sigh or a tear escapes the notice of him who sees deep into our hearts. Sometimes we may even fail to pray. But "before they call I will answer; while they are yet speaking I will hear" (Is 65:24). All that is needed is that we take these truths down off the high shelf of theology and put them to work as we live our daily lives.

CHAPTER 14

GOD WHO CHANGES NOT

*T*he unchangeableness of God is linked to his eternity (which was considered briefly in chapter nine), but they are not identical. The eternity of God means that God has always existed and always will exist; nothing comes before him, nothing after. The unchangeableness of God (immutability) means that God is always the same in his eternal being.

We can readily understand this. Yet this quality is one that separates the Creator from even the highest of his creatures. God is unchangeable, while no other part of his creation is. All that we know changes. The material world changes, and not merely in a circular sense, as the Greeks envisioned it—so that all things eventually return to what they were—but rather in the sense of running down, as science indicates. For example, although its decay is spread over a long period of time and is hard to notice, the sun constantly dissipates its energy and will eventually cool. The earth also runs down. Highly complex and active elements such as radioactive materials decay to less active ones. The varied and abundant resources of this earth are exhaustible. Species of life can become extinct and many have. On the individual level, men and women are born, grow, age, and eventually die. Nothing that we know lasts forever.

In human terms, mutability is due to the fact that we are fallen creatures and are separated from God. The Bible speaks of the wicked as being "like the tossing sea; for it cannot be quiet" (Is 57:20). Jude speaks of them as "waterless clouds, swept along by winds" and as "wandering stars," without a sure orbit (Jude 12-13). Surely the moral dimension of the variableness of humanity is nowhere better indicated than in the reaction of the masses to the Lord Jesus Christ. One week they were crying out, "Hosanna! Blessed be he who comes in the name of the Lord, even the King of Israel!" The next week they were shouting, "Away with him, crucify him!"

Human nature cannot be relied on, but God can be relied on. He is unchangeable. His nature is always the same. His will is invariable. His purposes are sure. God is the fixed point in a churning and decaying universe for those who truly know him. After James has spoken of human sin and error he adds that "every good gift and every perfect gift is from above, coming down from the Father of lights with whom there is no variation or shadow due to change" (Jas 1:17). The same perspective is shared by the prophet Malachi, who observes in a verse that comes toward the very end of the Old Testament, "I the LORD do not change; therefore you, O children of Jacob, are not consumed" (Mal 3:6).

NO CHANGE

Each of the above verses speaks of the immutability of God in his essential being. That is, being perfect, he never differs from himself. For a moral being to change, it would be necessary to change in one of two directions. Either the change is from something worse to something better, or else it is from something better to something worse. It should be evident that God can move in neither of these directions. God cannot change for the better, for that would mean that he had been imperfect beforehand. If we are talking about righteousness, for example, it would mean that he had been less than righteous and therefore sinful. If we are talking about knowledge, it would mean that he had not known everything and was therefore ignorant. On the other hand, God cannot change for the worse. In that case he would become less than he once was, becoming sinful or imperfect.

The immutability of God as presented in Scripture, however, is not the same thing as the immutability of "god" talked about by the Greek philosophers. In Greek thought, immutability meant not only unchangeability but also the inability to be affected by anything in any way. The Greek word for this, the primary characteristic of "god," was *apatheia*, from which we get our word "apathy." Apathy means indifference, but the Greek term goes beyond that idea. It means a total inability to feel any emotion whatever. The Greeks believed "god" possessed this quality because we would otherwise have power over him to the degree that we could move him to anger or joy or grief. He would cease to be absolute and sovereign. So the "god" of the philosophers (though not of the more popular mythologies) was lonely, isolated, and compassionless.

That makes good philosophy, of course. It is logical. But it is not what God reveals about himself in the Scriptures, and so we must reject it, however logical it may seem. The biblical perspective tells us that God is indeed immutable, but that he nevertheless notices and is affected by the obedience, plight, or sin of his creatures.

Brunner writes,

> If it be true that there really is such a fact as the Mercy of God and the Wrath of God, then God, too, is "affected" by what happens to his creatures. He is not like that divinity of Platonism who is unconcerned, and therefore unmoved, by all that happens upon the earth, but goes his way in heaven without looking around, without taking into consideration what is happening on earth. God does "look around"—he does care what happens to men and women—he is concerned about the changes on earth.[1]

A primary example is seen in the Lord Jesus Christ, who, though he was God, nevertheless wept over the city of Jerusalem and at the tomb of Lazarus.

A DISTURBING AND COMFORTING TRUTH

God's immutability also applies to his attributes. The Westminster Shorter Catechism defines God as "a Spirit, infinite, eternal and unchangeable in his being, wisdom, power, holiness, justice, goodness and truth." God is the possessor of all knowledge and wisdom, and he will always possess all wisdom. He is sovereign and will always be sovereign. He is holy and will always be holy. He is just and will always be just, good and will always be good, truthful and will always be truthful. Nothing that happens will ever diminish God in these or any of his attributes.

This truth has two faces: it is disturbing to those who are in rebellion against God, and it is comforting to those who have come to know him through Christ. The first is evident from what we have been saying in the last three chapters. If it is true that the sovereignty, holiness, and omniscience of God are unlikable concepts to the natural person, then it is clear that the fact that God will not change in any of these areas is even more disturbing. The unsaved would not be so troubled by God's sovereignty if they could think that one day God would

---

[1] Emil Brunner, *The Christian Doctrine of God: Dogmatics*, trans. Olive Wyon, vol. 1 (Philadelphia: Westminster, 1950), 268.

become less sovereign and the individual more autonomous. It would be conceivable that the human race could replace God one day. Again, they would not be so bothered by thoughts of God's holiness if it could be imagined that in time God might become less holy, calling what he now regards as sin, not sin, and ignoring the guilty. Or, if God could forget, then the evil we do would not be so troublesome; given time, it might fade from God's memory. But the immutability of God means that God will always be sovereign, always be holy, always be omniscient. Consequently all things must be brought to light and be judged before him.

Another side of this doctrine faces the believer. To us it is a great comfort. In this world people forget us, even when we have worked hard and been a service to them. They change their attitudes toward us as their own needs and circumstances dictate. Often they are unjust (as we are also). But God is not like that. Rather, his attitude toward us now is the same as it was in the farthest reaches of eternity past and will be in the farthest reaches of eternity to come. The Father loves us to the end, as it was said of Jesus: "When Jesus knew that his hour had come to depart out of this world to the Father, having loved his own who were in the world, he loved them *to the end*" (Jn 13:1).

Tozer writes of the comfort found in God's immutability.

> What peace it brings to the Christian's heart to realize that our heavenly Father never differs from himself. In coming to him at any time we need not wonder whether we shall find him in a receptive mood. He is always receptive to misery and need, as well as to love and faith. He does not keep office hours nor set aside periods when he will see no one. Neither does he change his mind about anything. Today, this moment, he feels toward his creatures, toward babies, toward the sick, the fallen, the sinful, exactly as he did when he sent his only-begotten Son into the world to die for mankind. God never changes his moods or cools off in his affections or loses his enthusiasm.[2]

So here is great comfort. If God varied as his creatures do, if he willed one thing today and another thing tomorrow, who could confide in him or be encouraged by him? No one. But God is always the same. We shall always find him as he has disclosed himself to be in Christ Jesus.

---

[2]A. W. Tozer, *The Knowledge of the Holy* (New York: Harper & Row, 1961), 59.

UNCHANGEABLE PLANS

God is also immutable in his purposes or plans. We often change plans. Usually we have lacked foresight to anticipate everything that might happen, or we have lacked power to execute what we purposed. God is not like us in that respect. "Infinite in wisdom, there can be no error in [his plans'] conception; infinite in power, there can be no failure in their accomplishment."[3]

> God is not man, that he should lie,
>> or a son of man, that he should change his mind [or repent].
> Has he said, and will he not do it?
>> Or has he spoken, and will he not fulfill it? (Num 23:19)

Repenting means to revise one's plan of action, but God never does so. His plans are made on the basis of perfect knowledge, and his perfect power sees to their accomplishment.

> The counsel of the LORD stands forever,
>> the plans of his heart to all generations. (Ps 33:11)
> The LORD of hosts has sworn:
> "As I have planned,
>> so shall it be,
> and as I have purposed,
>> so shall it stand." (Is. 14:24)
> Remember the former things of old;
> for I am God, and there is no other;
>> I am God, and there is none like me,
> declaring the end from the beginning
>> and from ancient times things not yet done,
> saying, "My counsel shall stand,
>> and I will accomplish all my purpose." (Is 46:9-10)

Solomon wrote, "Many are the plans in the mind of a man, but it is the purpose of the LORD that will stand" (Prov 19:21).

What are the consequences of God's immutability? First, if God's purposes do not change, then *God's purposes for Christ will not change*. His purpose is to glorify him. "Therefore God has highly exalted him and bestowed on him the name that is above every name, so that at the name of Jesus every knee should

---

[3]Charles Hodge, *Systematic Theology*, vol. 1 (London: James Clarke & Co., 1960), 390.

bow, in heaven and on earth and under the earth, and every tongue confess that Jesus Christ is Lord, to the glory of God the Father" (Phil 2:9-11).

It is foolish then to resist Christ's glory. We may do so now, as many do, but the day is coming when Jesus must be confessed as Lord even by those who would not have him as Lord in this life. In these verses the word that is translated "confess" (*exhomologeō*) more often means "to acknowledge" than it means "to confess with thanksgiving." For example, it is used of an acknowledgement or confession of sin and of Judas's agreeing with the chief priests to betray his master. It is in the sense of acknowledgement that the word is used of those who have rebelled against Christ's authority and glory in this life. They have rejected him here, but they will acknowledge him there. They will not confess that "Jesus Christ is Lord" with gladness, but they will confess it as they are banished from his presence forever.

Second, *God's purposes for his redeemed people will not change*. He intends to make them into the image of Jesus Christ (as we saw in chapter thirteen) and to bring them safely into his presence at the end of their earthly pilgrimage. In the epistle to the Hebrews, God's promises to Abraham are said to disclose the nature of his promises to us.

> For when God made a promise to Abraham, since he had no one greater by whom to swear, he swore by himself, saying, "Surely I will bless you and multiply you." And thus Abraham, having patiently waited, obtained the promise. For people swear by something greater than themselves, and in all their disputes an oath is final for confirmation. So when God desired to show more convincingly to the heirs of the promise the unchangeable character of his purpose, he guaranteed it with an oath, so that by two unchangeable things, in which it is impossible for God to lie, we who have fled for refuge might have strong encouragement to hold fast to the hope set before us. (Heb 6:13-18)

God's purpose is to bring his own into full enjoyment of their promised inheritance, into their hope. So they can know it and be assured of it, he confirms it by an immutable oath. In that purpose every redeemed child of God should take courage.

Finally, *God's purposes for the wicked will not change*. It is his purpose to judge them, and that he will do. God "will by no means clear the guilty" (Ex 34:7). Many other passages speak, often in vivid terms, of the judgment itself. The immutability of God's judgments should be a warning to any who have not yet turned to the Lord Jesus Christ as Savior, and should impel them toward him while there is yet hope.

The unchangeableness of God also means that God's truth does not change.

> Men sometimes say things that they do not really mean, simply because they do not know their own mind; also, because their views change, they frequently find that they can no longer stand to things that they said in the past. All of us sometimes have to recall our words, because hard facts refute them. The words of men are unstable things. But not so the words of God. They stand forever, as abidingly valid expressions of his mind and thought. No circumstances prompt him to recall them; no changes in his own thinking require him to amend them. Isaiah writes, "All flesh is grass . . . the grass withereth . . . but the word of our God shall stand forever" (Is. 40:6-8).[4]

Christians should stand on the word and promises of our immutable God. God's promises are not "relics of a bygone age," as Packer notes, but rather the eternally valid disclosure of the mind and will of our heavenly Father. His promises will not alter. A wise man or woman builds on this truth.

---

[4]J. I. Packer, *Knowing God* (Downers Grove, IL: InterVarsity Press, 1973), 70.

PART IV

GOD'S CREATION

Then God said, "Let us make man in our image, after our likeness. And let them have dominion over the fish of the sea and over the birds of the heavens and over the livestock and over all the earth and over every creeping thing that creeps on the earth."

So God created man in his own image in the image of God he created him; male and female he created them.

GENESIS 1:26-27

In the beginning, God created the heavens and the earth.

GENESIS 1:1

Then I looked, and I heard around the throne and the living creatures and the elders the voice of many angels, numbering myriads of myriads and thousands of thousands, saying with a loud voice, "Worthy is the Lamb who was slain, to receive power and wealth and wisdom and might and honor and glory and blessing!"

REVELATION 5:11-12

Many are the plans in the mind of a man, but it is the purpose of the Lord that will stand.

PROVERBS 19:21

CHAPTER 15

THE CREATION
OF HUMANITY

*T*here are three reasons why the creation of humanity must be studied when dealing with the knowledge of God: one general, one specific, and one theological. The general reason is that creation as a whole reveals something of its Creator so that, as was seen in chapter two, even though a man or woman will not worship and serve God, nevertheless what is revealed about God in nature will rise up to confound and condemn that person. The specific reason is that humanity as a unique part of that creation is made in the image of God, according to the Bible's testimony. Humankind reveals aspects of God's being that are not seen in the rest of the created order but must be seen if we are to understand God. The theological reason is that since we cannot have a genuine knowledge of God unless it is accompanied by a corresponding knowledge of ourselves, we must at least know ourselves—made in God's image, fallen and yet redeemed—if we would truly know and reverence our Creator.

The place to begin in a study of God's creation is with humankind in general, for men and women are the most important part of creation. To say that humanity is the most important part of creation might be thought to be a provincial or chauvinistic statement (that is, as if we were fish, we would undoubtedly say that fish were most important). But men and women actually are, and sense themselves to be, higher than forms of the creation around them. They rule over creation, for one thing, and not by brute force either, for many animals are stronger. Rather, they rule by the power of their minds and personality. For another thing, men and women have "God-consciousness," which animals do not have. God-consciousness causes people to become guilty in God's sight for refusing to worship him. No animal is guilty of moral or spiritual sin. On the other hand, God-consciousness is also our glory. For no other creature can in the same sense truly "glorify God, and enjoy him forever."

The Bible stresses our high position when it says toward the end of the first creation account,

> Then God said, "Let us make man in our image, after our likeness. And let them have dominion over the fish of the sea and over the birds of the heavens and over the livestock and over all the earth and over every creeping thing that creeps on the earth."
>
> > So God created man in his own image,
> > > in the image of God he created him;
> > > male and female he created them. (Gen 1:26-27)

In these verses our uniqueness and superiority to the rest of creation are expressed in three ways. First, we are said to have been made in God's image, which is not said of either objects or animals. Second, we are given dominion over the fish, birds, animals, and even the earth itself. Third, there is a repetition of the word *created*. The same word is used at only three points in the creation narrative: first, when God created matter from nothing (Gen 1:1); second, when God created conscious life (Gen 1:21); and third, when God created humankind (Gen 1:27). The progression is from the body (or matter) to soul (or personality) to spirit (or life with God-consciousness). Thus, humanity stands at the pinnacle of creation. As Francis Schaeffer writes, by repeating the word *created*, "it is as though God put exclamation points here to indicate that there is something special about the creation of man."[1]

IN GOD'S IMAGE

Let's look more closely at what it means to be created in the image of God. One thing it means is that women and men possess those attributes of *personality* that God himself possesses, but that animals, plants, and matter do not. To have personality one must possess knowledge, feelings (including religious feelings), and a will. God has personality, and so do we. To say that an animal possesses something akin to human personality is meaningful only to a point. Personality,

---

[1]Francis A. Schaeffer, *Genesis in Space and Time* (Downers Grove, IL: InterVarsity Press, 1972), 33.

in the sense that we are speaking of it here, is something that links humanity to God but does not link either humanity or God to the rest of creation.

A second element in being created in the image of God is *morality*. Morality includes the two further elements of freedom and responsibility. To be sure, the freedom that men and women possess is not absolute. Even in the beginning the first man, Adam, and the first woman, Eve, were not autonomous. They were creatures and were responsible for acknowledging their status by their obedience. Since the fall that freedom has been further restricted so that, as Augustine said, the original *posse non peccare* ("able not to sin") has become a *non posse non peccare* ("not able not to sin"). Still, there is a limited freedom for women and men, even in their fallen state, and with that comes moral responsibility. In brief, we do not need to sin always as we do, or as often as we do. And even when we sin under compulsion (as may sometimes be the case), we still know that it is wrong—and thus we inadvertently confess our likeness to God (though fallen) in morality as in other areas.

The third element in being made in God's image is *spirituality*. Humanity exists for communion with God, who is Spirit (Jn 4:24). This communion is intended to be eternal as God is eternal. Here we might say that although we have physical bodies, as do plants, and souls, as do animals, only human beings possess spirits. It is on the level of the spirit alone that we are aware of God and commune with him.

There is an ongoing debate between those who believe in a three-part construction of our being and those who believe that humanity can properly be considered on two levels only. The debate need not overly concern us. All parties to the debate recognize that human beings consist at least of the physical part that dies and needs to be resurrected, and of an immaterial part that lives beyond death, the part we call the person themselves. The only question is whether the immaterial part can be further distinguished as containing that which men and women share with animals—personality in the limited sense—and spirit, which relates them to God.

Here the linguistic data should be determinative, but they are not as clear as one could wish. Sometimes, particularly in the earlier parts of the Old Testament, soul (*nephesh*) and spirit (*ruach*) are used interchangeably, which has introduced confusion. Still, as time went on, *ruach* increasingly came to designate that element by which men and women relate to God, in distinction from *nephesh*, which then meant merely the life-principle. In conformity to that distinction, "soul" is often used in reference to animals, but "spirit" is not. Conversely, the prophets, who heard the voice of God and communed with him in a special sense, are always said to be animated by the "spirit" (but not the "soul") of God. In the New Testament, the linguistic data are similar. Thus, while soul (*psychē*) and spirit (*pneuma*) are sometimes freely exchanged for one another as in the Old Testament, *pneuma* nevertheless also expresses that particular capacity for relating to God that is the redeemed person's glory, as opposed to *psyche*, which even the unsaved and unresponsive possess (1 Cor 2:9-16). It is possible, though not certain, that in the Pauline writings the spirit of a person is considered as being lost or dead as a result of the fall and as being restored only in those who are regenerate.[2]

Yet we must not get off the track here. For whether we speak of two parts or three parts to the human being, an individual is nevertheless a unity. His or her salvation consists in the redemption of the whole, not merely of the soul or spirit, just as (in a parallel but contrary way) each part is affected by sin.

In this area, the particular words used are less important than the truths they are meant to convey. Even those who would insist most strongly on the unity of humanity nevertheless believe that we are more than matter. Or, if they adhere to a two-part scheme, they nevertheless recognize that there is something about humans that sets them off from animals. That is all that the distinction between spirit and soul in the three-part system means. Spirit, soul, and body are simply good terms to use to talk about what it really means to be a human being.

The *body*, then, is the part of the person we see, the part that possesses physical life. At first glance we tend to think that this is what differentiates us from God, and it does in a sense. We have a body; he does not. But on further consideration this distinction is not so obvious as it might seem. What about the incarnation of the Lord Jesus Christ, for instance? Or again, which came first in the mind of God, the body of Christ or Adam's body? Did Christ become like us by means of the incarnation or did we become like him by means of God's creative act? Calvin, who discusses this question briefly in the *Institutes*, does not believe that Adam was fashioned on the pattern of the Messiah to come. Calvin dismisses the idea that Christ would have come even if Adam had not sinned.[3] But the two ideas are not necessarily in conflict. One might even speculate that when

---

[2]Reinhold Niebuhr, *The Nature and Destiny of Man*, vol. 1, *Human Nature* (New York: Charles Scribner's Sons, 1941), 151-52.

[3]John Calvin, *Institutes of the Christian Religion*, ed. John T. McNeill, trans. Ford Lewis Battles, 2 vols. (Philadelphia: Westminster, 1960), 186-89; 470-74.

God walked in the garden with Adam and Eve before the fall, he did so as the second person of the Trinity, in a preincarnate but nevertheless corporeal form.

The point of the discussion is that our bodies are of great value and should be honored in the way we treat them. As redeemed men and women, we should see that our bodies are God's "temple" (1 Cor 6:19).

The soul is the human part that we call "personality." It is also not a simple matter to talk about. The soul is certainly related to the body through the brain, and is a part of the body. It is also difficult to think of it without the qualities we associate with spirit. Nevertheless, in general terms, soul refers at least to what makes the individual a unique individual. We might say that the soul centers in the mind and includes all likes and dislikes, special abilities or weaknesses, emotions, aspirations, and anything else that makes the individual different from all others of the species. Because we have souls, we are able to have fellowship, love, and communication with one another.

But we do not have fellowship, love, and communication only with others of our species. We also have love and communion with God, for which we need a *spirit*. The spirit is, therefore, that part of human nature that communes with God and partakes in some measure of God's own essence. God is nowhere said to be body or soul, though he may possess each of these aspects in the senses indicated earlier. But God *is* defined as spirit. "God is spirit," said Jesus. Therefore, "those who worship him must worship in spirit and truth" (Jn 4:24). Because a human being is spirit (or comes to possess a spirit once more by means of new birth), that person can have fellowship with God and love him.

Herein lies our true worth. We are made in God's image and are therefore valuable to God and to others. God loves men and women, far beyond his love for animals, plants, or inanimate matter. Moreover, he feels for men and women, identifies with them in Christ, grieves for them, and intervenes in history to make each of us into all he has determined we should be. We get some idea of the special nature of this relationship when we remember that in a similar way the woman, Eve, was made in the image of man. Therefore, though different, Adam saw himself in her and loved her as his companion and corresponding member in the universe. It is not wrong to say that men and women are to God somewhat as a woman is to a man. They are God's unique and valued companions. In support of this idea, we need only to think of the New Testament teaching concerning Christ as the bridegroom and the church as his bride.

MORAL AGENTS

Another part of being made in the image of God is that we are responsible moral agents in God's universe. Moral responsibility is implied in the attributes of our being (knowledge, feelings, will, God-consciousness) and in the test of obedience to God given later (Gen 2:16-17). Yet the concept is present even in the creation account. The same verse that tells of God's decision to make humanity in his own image also tells us that humans are to "have dominion over the fish of the sea and over the birds of the heavens and over the livestock and over all the earth and over every creeping thing that creeps on the earth" (Gen 1:26). Dominion of any kind, but particularly of this scope, clearly involves the ability to act responsibly.

Today in the Western world there is a strong tendency to deny human moral responsibility on the basis of some kind of determinism. The Bible does not allow such a possibility. Today's determinism usually takes one of two forms. It may be a physical, mechanical determinism ("human beings are the product of their genes and body chemistry") or it may be a psychological determinism ("human beings are the product of their environment and past history"). In either case, the individual is excused from responsibility for what he or she does. Thus, we have gone through a period in which criminal behavior was increasingly termed a sickness, and the criminal was regarded more as a victim of environment than as the victimizer. (Recently there has been a tendency at least to reconsider this matter.) Less blatant but nevertheless morally reprehensible acts are still excused with statements like "I suppose he just couldn't help it."

The biblical view could hardly be more different. Schaeffer notes, "Since God has made man in his own image, man is not caught in the wheels of determinism. Rather man is so great that he can influence history for himself and for others, for this life and the life to come."[4] We are fallen, but even in our fallen state we are responsible. We can do great things, or we can do terrible things, things for which we must give an accounting before God.

There are four areas in which our responsibility should be exercised. First, it should be exercised *toward God*. God is the One who created man and woman and gave them dominion over the created order. Consequently, they were responsible to him for what they did with it. When humans sin, as the Genesis account goes on to show they do, it is God who comes to require a reckoning: "Where are you? . . . Who told you that you were naked? . . . What is this that you have done?" (Gen 3:9, 11, 13). In the thousands of years since Eden, many have convinced

---

[4]Francis A. Schaeffer, *Death in the City* (Downers Grove, IL: InterVarsity Press, 1969), 80.

themselves that they are responsible to no one. But the testimony of Scripture is that this area of responsibility still stands and that all will one day answer to God at the judgment of the great white throne. "And the dead were judged by what was written in the books, according to what they had done" (Rev 20:12).

Second, people are responsible for their acts *toward other people*. That is the reason for those biblical statements instituting capital punishment as a proper response to murder; for instance, "Whoever sheds the blood of man, by man shall his blood be shed" (Gen 9:6). Such verses are not in the Bible as relics of a more barbarous age or because in the biblical outlook people are not valuable. Rather, they are there for the opposite reason. They are there because people are too valuable to be wantonly destroyed, and thus the harshest penalties are reserved for those who commit such destruction.

In a related way, James 3:9-10 forbids the use of the tongue in cursing others for the simple reason that all others are also made in God's image. "With it we bless our Lord and Father, and with it we curse people who are made in the likeness of God. . . . My brothers, these things ought not to be so." In these texts, murder of another or cursing of another is forbidden on the grounds that the other person (even after the fall) retains something of God's image and is therefore to be valued by us, as God also values him or her.

Third, we have a responsibility *toward nature* (to be discussed in more detail in the next chapter). We need to see that how we behave toward nature, whether we cultivate and advance it or whether we use and destroy it, is not without moral dimensions. Nor is it a matter of indifference to God. The depth of this responsibility is seen in the way in which God himself speaks of nature, noting that "the creation was subjected to futility" by reason of humanity's sin, but that it shall yet "be set free from its bondage to corruption and obtain the freedom of the glory of the children of God" at the time of the final resurrection and consummation of all things (Rom 8:20-21).

The fourth area of an individual's responsibility is *toward himself or herself*. As the Bible describes them, the man and the woman were made "a little lower than the angels" (Ps 8:5 KJV); that is, they were placed between the highest and lowest beings, between angels and beasts.[5] But it is significant that we are

---

[5]The reference to being made "a little lower than the angels" applies in the first instance to the person of the coming Messiah, the Lord Jesus Christ. But it is in reference to his incarnation alone that this is said. Therefore, the phrase and, indeed, the entire psalm is also rightly understood as having reference to men and women in general. The following verses refer back to the role of dominion given to Adam and Eve in Genesis: "You have given him dominion over the works of your hands; you have put all things under his feet" (Ps 8:6).

described as being slightly lower than the angels rather than being slightly higher than the beasts. Our place and privilege is to be a mediating figure, but to be one who looks up rather than down. When we sever the tie that binds us to God and try to cast off God's rule, we do not rise up to take God's place, as we desire to do, but rather sink to a more bestial level. In fact, we come to think of ourselves as beasts ("the naked ape") or, even worse, as machines.

In contrast, the redeemed person (who has the God-tie restored) is to look up and exercise full responsibility toward himself or herself on each level of his or her being. We each have a body, and we must use it as what it really is, "the temple of God's spirit." We must not allow it to be corrupted by physical laziness, overeating, habit-forming drugs, alcohol, or any other physically debilitating practice. We each have a soul, and we must use it fully—allowing our minds and personalities to develop as God blesses and instructs us. We each have a spirit, which we must exercise in worshiping and serving the true God.

Christians particularly need to use and develop their minds. Today there is a strong tendency toward a mindless or anti-intellectual form of Christianity, as John R. W. Stott points out in *Your Mind Matters*. This anti-intellectualism is unfortunate, because it is through the mind that God primarily speaks to us (as we study his Word and think about it), causes us to grow in grace ("by the renewal of your mind," Rom 12:2), and allows us to win others (by giving a "defense" for our Christian hope, 1 Pet 3:15).

> The current mood (cultivated in some Christian groups) of anti-intellectualism . . . is not true piety at all but part of the fashion of the world and therefore a form of worldliness. To denigrate the mind is to undermine foundational Christian doctrines. Has God created us rational beings, and shall we deny our humanity which he has given to us? Has God spoken to us, and shall we not listen to his words? Has God renewed our mind through Christ, and shall we not think with it? Is God going to judge us by his Word, and shall we not be wise and build our house upon this rock?[6]

Clearly, Christians should allow God to develop them intellectually to the fullest extent, thereby becoming known as thinking men and women. As Stott goes on to show, without respect for the mind there is no true worship, faith, holiness, guidance, evangelism, or Christian ministry.

---

[6]John R. W. Stott, *Your Mind Matters: The Place of the Mind in the Christian Life* (Downers Grove, IL: InterVarsity Press, 1972), 26.

SHATTERED IMAGE

In this chapter, we have been looking at humanity as God made them and intends them to be—that is, before the fall, or as they will eventually become in Christ. Nevertheless, it would not be right to ignore the fact that, although men and women were made in the image of God, that image has nevertheless been greatly marred or shattered as a result of their sin. True, vestiges of the image remain. But we are today not what God intended. We are fallen beings, and the effects of the fall are seen on each level of our being: body, soul, and spirit.

When God gave Adam and Eve the test of the forbidden tree, which was to be a measure of their obedience and responsibility toward the one who had created them, God said, "You may surely eat of every tree of the garden, but of the tree of the knowledge of good and evil you shall not eat, for in the day that you eat of it you shall surely die" (Gen 2:16-17). Adam and Eve did eat of the forbidden tree, and they did die. Their spirits, that part of them that had communion with God, died instantly. Their spiritual death is clear from the fact that they ran from God when God came to them in the garden. Men and women have been running and hiding ever since. Further, the soul, the seat of intellect, feelings, and identity, began to die. So men and women began to lose a sense of their own identity, to give vent to bad feelings, and to suffer the decay of their intellect. Describing this type of decay, Paul says that, having rejected God, people inevitably "became futile in their thinking, and their foolish hearts were darkened. Claiming to be wise, they became fools, and exchanged the glory of the immortal God for images resembling mortal man and birds and animals and creeping things" (Rom 1:21-23). Eventually even the body dies. So it is said of us all, "You are dust, and to dust you shall return" (Gen 3:19).

Donald Grey Barnhouse has compared the result to a three-story house that has been bombed in wartime and severely damaged. The bomb has destroyed the top floor entirely. Debris has fallen down into the second floor, severely damaging it. The weight of the two ruined floors plus the shock have produced cracks in the walls of the first floor, so that it is doomed to collapse eventually. Thus it was with Adam. His body was the dwelling of the soul and his spirit was above that. When he fell, the spirit was entirely destroyed, the soul ruined, and the body destined to final collapse and ruin.[7]

---

[7] Donald Grey Barnhouse, *Let Me Illustrate* (Westwood, NJ: Fleming H. Revell, 1967), 32; *Teaching the Word of Truth* (Grand Rapids: Eerdmans, 1966), 36-37.

However, the glory and fullness of the Christian gospel are seen at precisely this point. For when God saves an individual, he saves the whole person, beginning with the spirit, continuing with the soul, and finishing with the body. The salvation of the spirit comes first; God establishes contact with the one who has rebelled against him. That is regeneration or the new birth. Second, God begins to work with the soul, renewing it after the image of the perfect human, the Lord Jesus Christ. That work is sanctification. Finally, there is the resurrection, in which even the body is redeemed from destruction.

Moreover, God makes of the redeemed person a new creation, as Paul suggests in 2 Corinthians 5:17. He does not merely patch up the old spirit, the old soul, and the old body, as if the collapsing house were just being buttressed up and given a new coat of paint. Rather, he creates a new spirit, a new soul (known as the new man), and a new body. That body is on the same order as the resurrection body of the Lord Jesus Christ. Today we are saved as Christians, but we are also in the process of salvation, which means that the present matters. Moreover, we have an eye on the future, for it is only at the future moment of the resurrection that the redemption begun in this life will be complete and we will stand perfected before our great God and Savior, even Jesus Christ.

CHAPTER 16

NATURE

*I*t is not enough to study human nature to learn about God through creation, for humanity does not make up the whole of the created order. Nor, for that matter, is it first, except in importance. Actually, the man and woman were the last of God's creation, having been made on the last of the six days. When the man and woman were created, there already was a beautiful and varied universe established by God to receive them. So we conclude that nature should be studied if for no other reason than because it is there, was there first, and is our inescapable environment.

But there are more important reasons. For one thing, nature too reveals God, even by itself. It is a limited revelation, as has been pointed out several times already. But it is still a revelation, and it becomes a fuller revelation for those who are redeemed. This thought is the basis of the nineteenth psalm. "The heavens declare the glory of God, and the sky above proclaims his handiwork" (Ps 19:1). Further, men and women are not only in nature in the sense of nature being their environment. They are linked to nature as also being finite and created. True, there is a distinction between humanity and the rest of nature. Men and women alone are made in the image of God. But the purposes of God on a human level will therefore unfold fully only when God's purposes with nature are also included in the picture.

THE ORIGIN OF THE UNIVERSE

The big question in reference to nature is this: Where did the universe come from? Something is there—an immense, intricate, and orderly something. It was there before we were. We cannot even imagine our existence without it. But how did it get there? And how did it get to be as we detect it?

As with all big questions, only a few answers are possible. One view is that the universe had no origin. That is, there is no origin to the universe because in some form the universe always existed; matter existed. Second, everything came from a personal something and that personal something was good (which corresponds to the Christian view). Third, everything came from a personal something and that something was bad. Fourth, there is and always has been a dualism. The last view takes several forms, depending on whether one is thinking of a personal or impersonal, moral or amoral dualism, but the views are related.

The four possibilities may be narrowed down. Number three, which gives a personal but evil origin to the universe, does not need to be pursued at great length, for, although it is a philosophical possibility, hardly anybody seriously upholds it. While it is possible to think of evil as a corruption of the good, it is not really possible to think of good as having emerged out of evil. Evil can be a misuse of otherwise good traits or abilities. But there is nothing for the good to come from if only evil exists.

The fourth possibility is unsatisfying too, although its deficiencies are not readily apparent. Belief in a dualism has often been popular and has endured for long periods of history, but it does not stand up under close analysis. For, having stated a dualism, we immediately want to pass behind it to some type of unity that includes the dualism. Or else we choose one part of the dualism and make it prominent over the other, in which case we are really easing into one of the other possibilities.

C. S. Lewis has pointed to the catch in this system. According to dualism, the two powers (spirits or gods), one good and one evil, are supposed to be independent and eternal. Neither is responsible for the other, and each has an equal right to call itself God. Each presumably thinks that it is good and the other bad. But what do we mean when we say that the one power is good and the other bad? Do we mean merely that we prefer the one to the other? If that is all we mean, then we must give up any real talk about good or evil. And if we do that, then the moral dimension of the universe vanishes entirely, and we are left with nothing more than matter operating in certain ways. We cannot mean that and still hold to the dualism.

If, on the contrary, we mean that one power really is good and the other really is bad, then we are actually introducing some third thing into the universe, "some law or standard or rule of good which one of the powers conforms to and the other fails to conform to." And this standard, rather than the others, will turn out to be God. Lewis concludes, "Since the two powers are judged by this standard, then this standard, or the Being who made this standard, is farther back and higher up than either of them, and he will be the real God. In fact, what we meant by calling them good and bad turns out to be that one of them is in a right relation to the real ultimate God and the other in a wrong relation to him."[1]

Again, we may say that for the evil power to be evil, he must possess the attributes of intelligence and will. But since these attributes are in themselves good, he must be getting them from the good power and is thus dependent on him.

Neither an evil origin for the universe, from which good arose, nor a dualism adequately accounts for reality as we know it. So the real alternative is between the view that posits an eternity of matter and the view that sees everything as having come into existence through the will of an eternal, personal, and moral God.

The first view is the dominant philosophy of current Western civilization. That view usually does not deny that there is such a thing as personality in the world today, but it conceives of it as having arisen out of impersonal substance. It does not deny the complexity of the universe, but it supposes that the complexity came from what was less complex, and that in turn from something still less complex, until eventually one arrives back at what is ultimately simple, that is, to matter. Matter, it is supposed, always existed—because there is no further explanation. That view is the philosophical basis of most modern science, and it is what lies beneath most ideas of evolution.

But such a description of the origin of the universe has already introduced problems that the theory itself apparently has no means of solving. First, we have spoken of a form to matter and then of more complex forms. But where does form come from? Form means organization and perhaps purpose. But how can organization and purpose come from matter? Some would insist that organization and purpose were in the matter inherently, like genes in an egg or spermatozoon. But in addition to making nonsense of the theory—such matter

---

[1]C. S. Lewis, *Mere Christianity* (New York: The Macmillan Company, 1958), 34.

is no longer *mere* matter—the basic question still remains unanswered, for the problem is how the organization and purpose got there. At some level, then, either early or late, we have to account for the form; we soon find ourselves looking for the Former, Organizer, or Purposer.

Moreover, we also have introduced the idea of the personal; if we begin with an impersonal universe, we have no real explanation for the emergence of personality. Francis Schaeffer writes, "The assumption of an impersonal beginning can never adequately explain the personal beings we see around us, and when men try to explain man on the basis of an original impersonal, man soon disappears."[2]

Christianity begins with the remaining answer. Christianity maintains that the universe exists with form and personality, as we know it does, because it has been brought into being by a personal and orderly God. In other words, God was there before the universe came into existence, and he was and is personal. He created all we know, including ourselves. Consequently, the universe quite naturally bears these marks.

IN THE BEGINNING

What do we find when we turn to the opening chapter of Genesis? Here the Christian view is stated for the first time and in definitive form. It is a theological statement, however, and we must acknowledge this because if we do not, we will inevitably find ourselves looking for a scientific explanation of things and will be misled. Not that the Genesis record will be opposed to any established scientific data; truth in one area, if it really is truth, will never contradict truth in another area. Still, Genesis 1 is not a description from which we can expect to find answers to purely scientific questions. Rather, it is a statement of origins in the area of meanings, purpose, and the relationship of all things to God.

The chapter makes three main points. First and most obvious, it teaches that *God stands at the beginning* of all things, and is himself the One through whom all things came into existence. The chapter captures this eloquently in the first four words: "In the beginning, God . . ." At the very beginning, then, our thought is directed to the existence and nature of this God.

In the Hebrew language, the name for God in this verse is *Elohim*, a plural form. That it is plural suggests that there are plural dimensions to his being. In chapter ten, I discussed how this and other biblical evidence suggest the three

---

[2]Francis A. Schaeffer, *Genesis in Space and Time* (Downers Grove, IL: InterVarsity Press, 1972), 21.

members of the Trinity being present at the beginning, having existed before anything else. The elements that we associate with the Trinity—love, personality, and communication—are therefore eternal and have value. This is the Christian answer to the human fear of being lost in an impersonal and loveless universe.

The second major point of Genesis 1 is that the creation was according to *an orderly unfolding of the mind and purposes of God*. That is, it was a step-by-step progression, marked by a sequence of six significant days. We read this account, and immediately we think of questions along a scientific line that we would like to have answered: Is the sequence of the Genesis days to be compared with the sequence of the so-called geological periods? Do the fossils substantiate this narrative? How long are the "days"—twenty-four-hour periods or indefinite ages? And, perhaps most importantly, does the Genesis account leave room for evolutionary development (guided by God) or does it require a divine intervention and instantaneous creation in each case? The chapter does not answer our questions. I noted a moment ago that the Genesis account is a theological rather than a scientific statement, and we need to keep that in mind here. It is true that it provides us with grounds for constructive speculation, and at some point it is even rather explicit. But it is not written primarily to answer such questions; we must remember that.

Actually, there is no firm biblical reason for rejecting some forms of evolutionary theory, so long as they are carefully qualified at key points. There is, for example, no reason to deny that one form of fish may have evolved from another form, or even that one form of land animal may have evolved from a sea creature. The Hebrew term translated by our word *let*, which occurs throughout the creation account, would permit such a possibility.

There are, however, three significant points at which a unique action of God to create in a special sense seems to be marked off by the powerful Hebrew word *bara*, rendered "created." *Bara* generally means to create out of nothing, which means that the activity it describes is therefore a prerogative of God. And, as I pointed out in chapter fifteen, it is used in Genesis 1 to mark the creation of matter, of personality, and of God-consciousness. This means that although there may have been something like an evolutionary development taking place in the periods between the use of the word *bara*, this was not the case at least at those three points. Besides, the chapter teaches that the whole creation was not a random development but rather a result of the direct guidance of God.

It should be noted that today's scientific world may be witnessing the beginnings of a movement away from some forms of naturalistic evolution, particularly

Darwinism, as an explanation of the universe. To give one example, the February 1976 issue of *Harper's Magazine* carried an important article by Thomas Bethell, editor of *The Washington Monthly*, titled "Darwin's Mistake." It was essentially a review of recent writing on the evolution question, and its point was that scientists are in the process of quietly abandoning Darwin's theory. Why? Because, according to Bethell, Darwin's theory fails to account for the very thing that evolution is supposed to account for, namely, the varieties of plants, fish, animals, and other forms of life.

In Darwin's approach, the key element was natural selection, which was supposed to explain how the various forms came about. But as scientists look back on his theory, they see natural selection as explaining only how some organisms had more offspring than others and therefore survived, but not how there came to be the various organisms (some of which survived and some of which did not survive) in the first place. Bethell observes, "There is, then, no 'selection' by nature at all. Nor does nature 'act,' as it is so often said to do in biology books. One organism may indeed be 'fitter' than another from an evolutionary point of view, but the only event that determines this fitness is death (or infertility). This, of course, is not something which helps *create* the organism, but is something that terminates it."

The author concludes, "Darwin, I suggest, is in the process of being discarded, but perhaps in deference to the venerable old gentleman, resting comfortably in Westminster Abbey next to Sir Isaac Newton, it is being done as discreetly and gently as possible, with a minimum of publicity."[3]

The third point of the Genesis account of creation is *God's moral pronouncement* on what he has done. It appears in the repeated phrase, "And God saw that it was good." This pronouncement is not made in reference to some object, because we in a pragmatic way can point to it and say, "That thing is useful to me." God's pronouncement on the goodness of the rest of creation came before we were even made. And that means that a tree, to give an example, is not good only because we can cut it down and make a house out of it, or because we can burn it in order to get heat. It is good because God made it and pronounced it good. It is good because, like everything else in creation, it conforms to God's nature. Schaeffer writes of the divine benediction, "This is not a relative judgment, but a judgment of the holy God who has a character and whose character is the law of the universe. His conclusion: Every step and every sphere of creation, and

---

[3]Thomas Bethell, "Darwin's Mistake," *Harper's Magazine*, February 1976, 70-75.

the whole thing put together—man himself and his total environment, the heavens and the earth—conforms to myself."⁴

God's evaluation in Genesis 1 is confirmed by God's covenant with the human race and the earth given at the time of Noah—after the fall. There God says, "Behold, I establish my covenant with you and your offspring after you, and with every living creature that is with you, the birds, the livestock, and every beast of the earth with you, as many as came out of the ark. . . . I have set my bow in the cloud, and it shall be a sign of the covenant between me and the earth" (Gen 9:9-10, 13). Here God's concern is expressed, not just for Noah and those human beings who were with him in the ark, but for the birds and cattle and even the earth itself. His whole creation is "good."

Similarly, Romans 8 expresses the value of all God has made. He intends to redeem the whole earth afflicted by the fall.

> The creation itself will be set free from its bondage to corruption and obtain the freedom of the glory of the children of God. For we know that the whole creation has been groaning together in the pains of childbirth until now. And not only the creation, but we ourselves, who have the firstfruits of the Spirit, groan inwardly as we wait for adoption as sons, the redemption of our bodies. (Rom 8:21-23)

RESPONSE TO NATURE

The value of creation brings us to a natural conclusion: if God finds the universe good in its parts and as a whole, then we must find it good also. That does not mean that we will refuse to see that nature has been marred by sin. Indeed, the verses from Genesis 9 and Romans 8 are inexplicable apart from the realization that nature has suffered as a result of the fall of humankind. It is marred by thorns, weeds, disease, and death. But even in its marred state it has value, just as fallen humanity has value.

Therefore we must be *thankful* for the world God has made and praise him for it. In some expressions of Christian thought and piety, only the soul has value. That view is neither correct nor Christian. Actually, the elevation of the value of the soul and the debasement of the body and other material things is a pagan, Greek idea based on a false understanding of creation. If God had made the soul (or spirit) alone and if the material world had come from some lesser or even evil source, then the Greeks would have been right. But the Christian

---

⁴Schaeffer, *Genesis in Space and Time*, 55.

view is that God has made all that is and that it therefore has value and should be valued by us because of its origin.

Second, we should *delight* in creation. To delight is closely related to being thankful, but it is a step beyond it. It is a step that many Christians have never taken. Frequently Christians look on nature only as one of the classic proofs of God's existence. Instead, they should really enjoy what they see. We should appreciate natural beauty. Moreover, we should exult in it more than non-Christians because of its revelation of the God who stands behind nature.

Third, Christians should demonstrate a *responsibility* toward nature. We should not destroy it simply for the sake of destroying it but rather seek to elevate it to its fullest potential. There is a parallel here between the responsibility of men and women toward the creation and the responsibility of a husband toward his wife in marriage. In each case the responsibility is based on a God-given dominion (though the two are not identical). "Husbands, love your wives, as Christ loved the church and gave himself up for her, that he might sanctify her, having cleansed her by the washing of water with the word, so that he might present the church to himself in splendor, without spot or wrinkle or any such thing, that she might be holy and without blemish" (Eph 5:25-27). In a similar way, men and women together should properly seek to sanctify and cleanse the earth in order that it might be more as God created it, in anticipation of its ultimate redemption.

Certainly the universe is to be used by people in a proper way. Where trees are abundant, some can be cut down to make wood for a home. But they should not be cut down simply for the pleasure of cutting them down or because that is the easiest way to increase the value of the ground. In every area, careful thought must be given to the value and purpose of each object, and there must be a Christian rather than a purely utilitarian approach to it.

Finally, after they have contemplated nature and come to value it, Christians should turn once again to the God who made it and sustains it moment by moment and should learn to *trust* him. God cares for nature, in spite of its abuse through our sins. But if he cares for nature, then we may trust him to care for each of us also. Such an argument occurs in the midst of Christ's sermon on the mount, in which he draws our attention to God's care of the birds (animal life) and lilies (plant life) and then asks, "Are you not of more value than they? . . . But if God so clothes the grass of the field, which today is alive and tomorrow is thrown into the oven, will he not much more clothe you, O you of little faith?" (Mt 6:26, 30).

CHAPTER 17

THE SPIRIT WORLD

*B*efore men and women were created, God had already made a beautiful and varied universe to receive them, as we saw in the last chapter. But if Job 38:7 is to be taken as referring to angels, as there is every reason for it to be, then even before the creation of the material universe there was a vast world of spirit beings. We don't know when these were created. In fact we know very little about them at all. But we know that they existed before all we can see was created and that they exist today. As God said to Job,

> Where were you when I laid the foundation of the earth?
>   Tell me, if you have understanding.
> Who determined its measurements—surely you know!
>   Or who stretched the line upon it?
> On what were its bases sunk,
>   or who laid its cornerstone,
> when the morning stars sang together,
>   and all the *sons of God* shouted for joy? (Job 38:4-7)

It is interesting in view of the Bible's testimony to the existence of spirits that the mythologies of ancient civilizations also claim their existence. Babylonian mythology portrayed the spirits as gods who brought messages from the world of the gods above to earth beneath. Greek and Roman mythology had gods and demigods visiting the earth. So it is with virtually all ancient civilizations. Critics of the Bible sometimes see its references to a spirit world as evidence that the Bible is also mythology, that is, as having no factual basis, at least in that area.

But it is equally possible that the mythologies actually preserve a distorted memory of an early experience of the race. That possibility is enhanced, even for non-Christians, by the striking current renewal of interest in the spirit world.

Are there such beings? Do angels or demons really exist? Do they visit earth? The Bible gives trustworthy answers to such questions. Though it is true that the Bible does not tell us all that we might like to know—much about the origin and function of the spirit world is shrouded in mystery—it does tell us what needs to be known and tells us truly.

ANGELS

Angels are mentioned over one hundred times in the Old Testament and more than 160 times in the New Testament. We are told that they are God's messengers—that is what the word *angel* means. They are immortal; that is, they do not die, though they have been created and therefore are not eternal. They exist in vast numbers. "Then I looked, and I heard around the throne and the living creatures and the elders the voice of many angels, numbering myriads of myriads and thousands of thousands" (Rev 5:11). Angels possess the elements of personality; they render intelligent worship to God: "saying with a loud voice, 'Worthy is the Lamb who was slain, to receive power and wealth and wisdom and might and honor and glory and blessing!'" (Rev 5:12).

Some of these qualities are also indicated by the terms used to refer to them in Scripture. They are called the "heavenly host," for example (Lk 2:13). That suggests that as the troops of an emperor surround his person and serve him, so these beings serve God and make his glory visible. They are called "rules," "powers," "dominions," "authorities," and "thrones" (Eph 1:21; Col 1:16) because they are those through whom God administers his authority in the world.

The Bible also reveals something of an angelic hierarchy; certain classes or orders of angels are mentioned. In the first class is the angel most mentioned in the Bible: Michael (the names of only two angels are recorded). He is described as being "the archangel," that is, the head of all the holy angels. His name means "he who is like God" (Dan 10:21; 12:1; 1 Thess 4:16; Jude 9; Rev 12:7-10).

A second category contains those who are God's special messengers. The second angel mentioned by name, Gabriel, would be in this category, for he was entrusted with a special revelation for Daniel, the message to Zacharias about the birth of John the Baptist, and the announcement of the birth of Jesus to the virgin Mary (Dan 8:16; 9:21; Lk 1:18-19, 26-38).

A third category contains those angels called "cherubim." They are depicted as magnificent creatures who surround God's throne and defend his holiness from any contamination by sin (Gen 3:24; Ex 25:18, 20; Ezek 1:1-18). God instructed that gold figures of these beings be placed on the mercy seat of the ark of the covenant within the holy of holies of the Jewish tabernacle. The cherubim may be identical with the "seraphim" described by Isaiah in 6:2-7.

Finally, there are vast numbers of angelic hosts to whom no special names are given. They are described merely as the "elect angels" to distinguish them from those angels that sinned with Satan and so fell from their first estate (see 1 Tim 5:21).

The grandeur and complexity of the angelic world are enough to pique us to study it. But in addition, such study enhances our sense of God's glory. Calvin observes, "If we desire to recognize God from his works, we ought by no means to overlook such an illustrious and noble example" as his angels.[1]

THE MINISTRY OF ANGELS

The first and most obvious work of angels is the *worship and praise of God*, which we see at many places in the Bible. For example, Isaiah writes that the seraphim, who stood above the throne of Jehovah, called one "to another and said: 'Holy, holy, holy, is the LORD of hosts; the whole earth is full of his glory!'" (Is 6:3). Daniel describes the scene as involving even greater numbers.

> As I looked,
> > thrones were placed
> > > and the Ancient of Days took his seat;
> > his clothing was white as snow,
> > > and the hair of his head like pure wool;
> > his throne was fiery flames,
> > > its wheels were burning fire.
> A stream of fire issued
> > and came out from before him;
> a thousand thousands served him,
> > and ten thousand times ten thousand stood before him. (Dan 7:9-10)

In Revelation the angels—described as the four living creatures, the four and twenty elders (who may be redeemed human beings), and the thousands upon thousands of spirit beings—

---

[1] John Calvin, *Institutes of the Christian Religion*, ed. John T. McNeill, trans. Ford Lewis Battles, 2 vols. (Philadelphia: Westminster, 1960), 162.

never cease to say,

    "Holy, holy, holy, is the Lord God Almighty,

        who was and is and is to come!" (Rev 4:8; see 5:9-12)

The fact that the angels worship God in such numbers should both humble us and encourage us in our worship. It should humble us because God would not be deprived of worship even if we should fail to honor him. Angels are doing that already. On the other hand, it should encourage us, because our voices shall one day be joined to those of the great angelic choir (Rev 7:9-12; 19:1-6).

Second, angels *serve God* as agents of his many works. We read that angels were present at creation (Job 38:7) and at the giving of the law; the law is said to have been given "delivered by angels" (Acts 7:53; see Gal 3:19; Heb 2:2 KJV). An angel was the vehicle of God's revelation to Daniel; several were used to reveal future events to the apostle John (Dan 10:10-15; Rev 17:1; 21:9; 22:16). Gabriel announced the births of both John the Baptist and of Jesus Christ (Lk 1:11-38; 2:9-12; Mt 1:19-23). Many more sang of the event in the presence of the shepherds (Lk 2:13-14). Similarly, at the time of Christ's temptation angels were present to minister to him (Mt 4:11), as well as in the garden of Gethsemane (Lk 22:43), at the resurrection to announce Christ's victory over death to the women who had come to the tomb (Mt 28:2-7), and at the ascension (Acts 1:10-11). They will appear again in large numbers at Christ's second coming (Mt 24:31; 25:31; 2 Thess 1:7).

Third, angels are ministering spirits sent to *assist and defend God's people.* Thus, we read, first in reference to Christ but then also to ourselves as his people,

    For he will command his angels concerning you
        to guard you in all your ways.
    On their hands they will bear you up,
        lest you strike your foot against a stone. (Ps 91:11-12)

And,

    The angel of the LORD encamps
        around those who fear him, and delivers them. (Ps 34:7)

From a practical standpoint, if Christian people thought more often of this angelic protection, they would be less fearful of circumstances and enemies. At the same time, our forgetfulness is understandable, for generally angels are not visible to us.

We are like Elisha's servant at Dothan before his vision of God's hosts. Elisha had been revealing the counsels of Israel's enemy Ben-hadad of Syria to Israel's king, and Ben-hadad had reacted by trying to capture Elisha. Thus, by night he had surrounded Dothan, where Elisha and his servant were staying. He was present in full force when Elisha's servant went out of the city to draw water the next morning. The account says that the servant discovered an "army" encompassing the city, "with horses and chariots." He was terrified! He ran to Elisha saying, "Alas, my master! What shall we do?"

Elisha replied, "Do not be afraid, for those who are with us are more than those who are with them." Then he prayed that the young man's eyes might be opened to see the Lord's angels. "So the LORD opened the eyes of the young man, and he saw, and behold, the mountain was full of horses and chariots of fire all around Elisha" (2 Kings 6:15-17). Angels then struck the hosts of Ben-hadad with blindness so that Elisha was able to lead them captive into the Israelite capital of Samaria.

In a similar way we read that one angel of God killed 185,000 soldiers of Assyria in order to deliver Jerusalem from Sennacherib's armies in the days of King Hezekiah.

A fourth special ministry of angels is in *service to God's people at the time of their death*. There are not many texts from which to argue this point, but it should be noticed that, according to Jesus, angels carried Lazarus to Abraham's bosom (Lk 16:22).

Finally, angels are to be God's *agents in the final judgments* prophesied for men and women, the devils and this world. The extent of these judgments is more fully described in the book of Revelation than anywhere else. There is, first, a series of partial judgments against the earth released through the seals that are broken (Rev 6:1–8:1), the trumpets that are blown (Rev 8:2–11:19), and the seven bowls of wrath that are poured out (Rev 15:1–16:21). These judgments fill the main part of the book, and angels are associated with each one. Second, there is a judgment against the great city of Babylon (perhaps a symbol of Rome) and of those associated with her in her sins. Angels are also part of that judgment (Rev 17:1–18:24). Third, there are judgments against the beast, who is probably antichrist, and against Satan and the false prophet (Rev 19:17–20:3, 10). At last, there is the judgment of the great white throne at which the dead are judged according to their works (Rev. 20:11-15).

FALLEN ANGELS

Mention of judgment, including the judgment against Satan, leads to a second aspect of this subject. According to the Bible, there are legions of fallen angels who, under the malevolent rule of Satan, are bent on opposing God's rule and doing his people harm. They comprise a great and terrifying force, as the Bible describes them. But they are described for us not to induce terror, but to warn us of danger so that we might draw near to God as the One who alone can protect us. The number of fallen angels can be gauged somewhat from the fact that Mary Magdalene alone is said to have been delivered from seven of them (Mk 16:9; Lk 8:2) and from knowing that many, calling themselves Legion, had possessed the man Christ encountered in the territory of the Gerasenes opposite Galilee (Lk 8:26-33).

What is God's purpose in telling us of this vast host?

We have been forewarned that an enemy relentlessly threatens us, an enemy who is the very embodiment of rash boldness, of military prowess, of crafty wiles, of untiring zeal and haste, of every conceivable weapon, and of skill in the science of warfare. We must, then, bend our every effort to this goal: that we should not let ourselves be overwhelmed by carelessness or faintheartedness, but on the contrary, with courage rekindled stand our ground in combat.[2]

The place to begin in preparing to stand against Satan and his hosts is with a knowledge of Satan himself, in both his strengths and weaknesses. And the place to begin knowing about Satan is with the fact that he is both real and personal. He is real in that he is not a figment of the human imagination. He is personal in that he is not merely some vague embodiment of evil. Jesus bore witness to these truths when he referred to the devil by name (Mt 4:10; 16:23; Lk 22:31) and when he overcame him at the time of his temptation in the wilderness (Mt 4:1-11).

The idea of a personal devil has been denied by large segments of the Christian church, and to some has become almost a laughing matter. Because of the revival of witchcraft and Satanism in recent years, it is perhaps not so much a laughing matter as before. Still, many would regard thoughts about the existence of a real devil as hardly serious. To the popular mind the devil is a funny creature in red underwear with horns and a tail. That is not at all the image of Satan portrayed in the Bible.

The apostle Paul noted that we are not ignorant of Satan's "devices" (2 Cor 2:11 KJV). The word *device* means "a trick, plot, scheme, contrivance, or stratagem." So the point is that Christians know, or should know, about Satan's tricks for seeking to blind people's minds and secure them for himself. One of

---

[2]Ibid., 173.

these, which he uses at some points of history, is to make people believe that he does not exist.

The picture of a funny little being with horns has had an interesting development, which at one point was connected (wrongly) with the Bible. In the Middle Ages, when most of the people were illiterate and the church used miracle plays to teach basic Bible stories, there was a need to make whatever character represented the devil immediately recognizable on the stage. The convention chosen was based on a pagan idea in vogue, according to which Satan was somewhat of a monster with horns. That caricature was assumed to be supported by the Bible.

In Isaiah, in a prophecy against Babylon, there is mention of a creature that would one day, it is said, roam about over the fallen and deserted city. The Hebrew word for this animal or creature is *sair*—meaning a wild goat—but few knew what it meant. So in some early translations of the Bible it was called a "satyr," which was one of the half-human, half-bestial figures of mythology. The Bible was thereby assumed to have described a creature like the then-popular Satan figure, and the medieval practice seemed vindicated. In modern times, with an equal lack of support, the devil has been conceived of as the sophisticated tempter of the Faust legend or of the popular American stage play and movie *Damn Yankees*.

Since the devil of fiction is so unbelievable, it is no wonder that millions discount him. But that is a mistake. According to Jesus, there is a devil and there are those who follow him. In fact, he warned his disciples to pray, "And lead us not into temptation, but deliver us from [the evil one]" (Mt 6:13).

A FALLEN BEING

The devil is also a fallen being, as Jesus taught in John 8:44. Jesus showed the height from which Satan fell ("he does not stand in the truth") and the depths to which he descended ("he is a liar and the father of lies" and "he was a murderer from the beginning"). Jesus also said, "I saw Satan fall like lightning from heaven" (Lk 10:18).

This point too is often rejected by men and women, even if they believe in a devil. Thus, rather than believing that Satan is a depraved form of what he once was, they prefer to think of him as heroic and, more or less, as the champion of fallen humanity. John Milton, though he did not glorify Satan, nevertheless contributed to that idea. Although it is true that in the opening pages of his great epic, *Paradise Lost*, Milton does describe the fall of Satan from heaven and later

anticipates his final judgment, it is also true that the greater part of the first book
of the epic describes Lucifer's heroic efforts to rise from the depths of hell and
make something of his supposed new kingdom. Milton does this so brilliantly
that it is possible to sympathize with Satan. We receive quite a different impression
from Scripture.

To begin with, Satan has never been in hell and does not control hell. The
Bible tells us that God has created hell, preparing it in part for the devil and his
angels, and that Satan will one day end up there.

The Bible also describes Satan as at one time being "full of wisdom and perfect
in beauty." It says that he was once "in Eden, the garden of God," that he was
"blameless" in all his ways from the day he was created, until "unrighteousness"
was found in him (Ezek 28:12-15).

In Isaiah we are told of Satan's fall through pride, which expressed itself in
an arrogant desire to replace God. Satan says,

> I will ascend to heaven;
> above the stars of God
>   I will set my throne on high;
> I will sit on the mount of assembly
>   in the far reaches of the north;
> I will ascend above the heights of the clouds,
>   I will make myself like the Most High.
>
> God replies that as a result of his sin he will actually be
>   brought down to Sheol,
>   to the far reaches of the pit. (Is 14:13-15)

This is not the portrait of a heroic being but of a fallen being. It is a being from
whom a person should turn in horror.

Satan has wrought havoc on the human race. He is a murderer and the author
of murder, as Jesus told his listeners. The first crime following the fall of Adam
and Eve was a murder; as a result of the fall, Cain murdered his brother. We
also read that Satan entered into Judas to betray Christ into the hands of his
enemies so that they might kill him (Jn 13:2). Satan's history is written in blood.

It is also written in deceit, for he is a liar, as Christ said. Satan lied to Eve—
"You will not surely die" (Gen 3:4). But she did die. In 1 Kings we read that
lying spirits (presumably demons) went forth into the prophets of Ahab so that
he would go into battle against the Syrians and fall at Ramoth-gilead
(1 Kings 22:21-23). In Acts we are told that Satan entered into Ananias to cause

him to lie about the price of his property, as a result of which he died (Acts 5:3). Satan lies today. Consequently we are to regard him as dangerous, deceitful, and malicious, but above all as a sinner and as a failure. He sinned when he failed to remain in his high calling.

A LIMITED BEING

Finally, Satan is a limited being. That is, he is not omniscient, as God is; he is not omnipotent, as God is; he is not omnipresent, as God is. If Satan is a murderer from the beginning, he is limited in the area of the ethical life. If he is to face judgment, he is obviously limited in power. Although we should be aware of Satan and warned about him, we should not get into the habit of thinking of the tempter as anything like an evil equivalent of God.

Satan is not omniscient. God knows all things but Satan does not. Above all, he does not know the future. No doubt Satan can make shrewd guesses, for he knows human nature and the tendencies of history. The so-called revelations of mediums and fortunetellers—when they are not outright deceits—fall in this category. But they do not give true knowledge of what is to come. Thus, the predictions are vague and generally do not hold water. At one point God stated this in the form of a challenge to all false gods, saying,

> Set forth your case, says the LORD;
>> bring your proofs, says the King of Jacob.
> Let them bring them, and tell us
>> what is to happen. . . .
> Tell us what is to come hereafter,
>> that we may know that you are gods;
> do good, or do harm,
>> that we may be dismayed and terrified.
> Behold, you are nothing,
>> and your work is less than nothing;
>> an abomination is he who chooses you. (Is 41:21-24)

Neither is Satan omnipotent. Thus, he cannot do everything he wants to do, and, in the case of believers especially, he can do only what God will permit. The best-known example is Job, who was safe until God had first lowered the hedge that he had thrown up about him. Even so, God had his own worthwhile purposes and kept Job from sinning.

Satan is not omnipresent, which means that he cannot be everywhere at the same time tempting everybody. God is omnipresent. He can help all who call on him, all at one time. But Satan must tempt one individual at a time, or else operate through one or more of those angels, now demons, who fell with him. The interesting consequence of this fact is that Satan has probably never tempted you or anyone you know. Even in the Bible we find very few who were tempted by Satan directly. There was Eve, of course. Christ was tempted. Peter was tempted. The devil entered into Ananias to cause him to lie about the price of his land. But that is about all. On one occasion Paul may have been hindered in his plans by Satan (1 Thess 2:18); but on another it was only a *messenger* of Satan who buffeted him (2 Cor 12:7). Similarly, lesser demons opposed an angel bringing a revelation to Daniel (Dan 10:13, 20). And, although there may have been a great host of devils that surrounded Elisha at Dothan—outnumbered by the Lord's host, however—Satan himself is not said to have been among them (2 Kings 6:16-17).

Although Christians must never ignore or underestimate Satan and his stratagems, neither must they overestimate him. Above all, they must never concentrate on Satan to the point of taking their eyes away from God. God is our strength and our tower. He limits Satan. God will never permit Christians to be tempted above what we are able to bear, and he will always provide the way of escape that we may be able to bear it (1 Cor 10:13). As for Satan, his end is the lake of fire (Mt 25:41).[3]

---

[3]The material on Satan is borrowed in part from chapter 52 ("That Other Family," Jn 8:41-50) of my book *The Gospel of John*, vol. 2 (Grand Rapids: Zondervan, 1976).

CHAPTER 18

GOD'S PROVIDENCE

*T*here is probably no point at which the Christian doctrine of God comes more into conflict with contemporary worldviews than in the matter of God's providence. Providence means that God has not abandoned the world that he created, but rather works within that creation to manage all things according to the "immutable counsel of His own will" (Westminster Confession of Faith, V, i). By contrast, the world at large, even if it will on occasion acknowledge God to have been the world's Creator, is at least certain that he does not now intervene in human affairs. Many think that miracles do not happen, that prayer is not answered, and that most things "fall out" according to the functioning of impersonal and unchangeable laws.

The world argues that evil abounds. How can evil be compatible with the concept of a good God who is actively ruling this world? There are natural disasters: fires, earthquakes, floods. In the past these have been called "acts of God." Should we blame God for them? Isn't it better to imagine that he simply has left the world to pursue its own course?

Such speculation can be answered on two levels. First, even from the secular perspective, such thinking is not as obvious as it seems. Second, it is not the teaching of the Bible.

GOD'S RULE OF NATURE

The idea of an absentee God is certainly not obvious in reference to nature, the first of the three major areas of God's creation discussed earlier. The great question about nature, raised by even the earliest Greek philosophers as well as by contemporary scientists, is why there is a pattern to nature's operations even though nature is constantly changing. Nothing is ever the same. Rivers flow, mountains rise and fall, flowers grow and die, the sea is in constant motion. Yet in a sense everything remains the same. The experience of one generation with nature is akin to the experience of generations that have gone before.

Science tends to explain this uniformity by the laws of averages or by laws of random motion. But that is not a full explanation. For example, by the very laws of averages it is quite possible that at some time all molecules of a gas or solid (or the great preponderance of them) might be moving in the same direction instead of in random directions, and if that were the case, then the substance would cease to be as we know it and the laws of science regarding it would be inoperable.

Where does uniformity come from if not from God? The Bible says that uniformity comes from God when it speaks of how Christ "upholds the universe by the word of his power" (Heb 1:3) and argues that "in him all things hold together" (Col 1:17). The point is that the providence of God lies behind the orderly world that we know. That was the primary thought in the minds of the authors of the Heidelberg Catechism when they defined *providence* as "the almighty and ever-present power of God whereby he still upholds, as it were by his own hand, heaven and earth together with all creatures, and rules in such a way that leaves and grass, rain and drought, fruitful and unfruitful years, food and drink, health and sickness, riches and poverty, and everything else, come to us not by chance but by his fatherly hand" (Question 27). Remove the providence of God over nature, and—not only is all sense of security gone—the world is gone; meaningless change would soon replace its order.

The same thing is true of human society. Once again, there is great diversity and change. But there are also patterns to human life and limits beyond which, for example, evil does not seem permitted to go. Pink argues along such lines in his study of God's sovereignty:

> For the sake of argument we will say that every man enters this world endowed with a will that is absolutely free, and that it is impossible to compel or even coerce him without destroying his freedom. Let us say that every man possesses a knowledge of right and wrong, that he has the power to choose between them, and that he is left entirely free to make his own choice and go his own way. Then

what? Then it follows that man is sovereign, for he does as he pleases and is the architect of his own future. But in such a case we can have no assurance that ere long every man will reject the good and choose the evil. In such a case we have no guaranty against the entire human race committing moral suicide. Let all divine restraints be removed and man be left absolutely free, and all ethical distinctions would immediately disappear, the spirit of barbarism would prevail universally, and pandemonium would reign supreme.[1]

But that does not happen. And the reason it does not happen is that God does not leave his creatures to the exercise of an absolute autonomy. They are free, yet within limits. Moreover, God in his perfect freedom also intervenes directly, as he chooses, to order their wills and actions.

The book of Proverbs contains many verses on this theme. Proverbs 16:1 says that although an individual may debate with himself about what he will say, it is the Lord who determines what he actually speaks: "The plans of the heart belong to man, but the answer of the tongue is from the LORD." Proverbs 21:1 applies the same principle to human affections, using the dispositions of the king as an example. "The king's heart is a stream of water in the hand of the LORD; he turns it wherever he will." Actions are also under the sphere of God's providence. "The heart of man plans his way, but the LORD establishes his steps" (Prov 16:9). So is the outcome. "Many are the plans in the mind of a man, but it is the purpose of the LORD that will stand" (Prov 19:21). Proverbs 21:30 sums up by saying, "No wisdom, no understanding, no counsel, can avail against the LORD."

In the same way, God also exercises his rule over the spirit world. The angels are subject to his express command and rejoice to do his bidding. The demons, while in rebellion against him, are still subject to God's decrees and restraining hand. Satan was unable to touch God's servant Job until God gave his permission, and even then certain bounds were set: "Behold, all that he has is in your hand. Only against him do not stretch out your hand" (Job 1:12); "Behold, he is in your hand; only spare his life" (Job 2:6).

GOD'S RULE OVER PEOPLE

The point of major interest for us is not in the area of God's rule over nature or the angels, however. It is how God's providence operates with human beings, particularly when we decide to disobey him.

---

[1]Arthur W. Pink, *The Attributes of God* (Grand Rapids: Baker Book House, n.d.), 42-43.

There is, of course, no problem at all with the providence of God in human affairs if we obey him. God simply declares what he wants done, and it is done—willingly. But what about those times when we disobey? And what about the great number of unregenerate people who apparently never obey God willingly? Does God say, "Well, I love you in spite of your disobedience, and I certainly don't want to insist on anything unpleasant; we'll just forget about my desires"? God does not operate in that fashion. If he did, he would not be sovereign. On the other hand, God does not always say, "You *are* going to do it; therefore, I will smash you down so you have to!" What does happen when we decide we do not want to do what he wants us to do?

The basic answer is that God has established laws to govern disobedience and sin, just as he has established laws to govern the physical world. When people sin, they usually think that they are going to do so on their own terms. But God says, in effect, "When you disobey, it is going to be according to my laws rather than your own."

We see a broadly stated example in the first chapter of Romans. After having described how the natural person will not acknowledge God as the true God or worship him and be thankful to him as the Creator, Paul shows that such people are thereby launched on a path that leads away from God, which causes them to suffer grim consequences, including the debasement of their own being. "Claiming to be wise, they became fools, and exchanged the glory of the immortal God for images resembling mortal man and birds and animals and creeping things" (Rom 1:22-23).

Then comes a most interesting part of the chapter. Three times in the verses that follow we read that because of their rebellion, "God gave them up." Terrible words. But when it says that God gave them up, it does not say that God gave them up to nothing, as if he merely removed his hand from them and allowed them to drift away. In each case it says that God gave them up *to* something: in the first case, "to impurity, to the dishonoring of their bodies" (Rom 1:24); in the second case, "to dishonorable passions" (Rom 1:26); and in the third case, "to a debased mind and to what ought not to be done" (Rom 1:28). In other words, God will permit the ungodly to go their own way, but he has determined in his wisdom that when they go, it will be according to his rules rather than their own.

If anger and tension go unchecked, they produce ulcers or high blood pressure. Profligacy is a path to broken lives and venereal disease. Pride will be self-destructive. These spiritual laws are the equivalent of the laws of science in the physical creation.

The principle is true for unbelievers, but it is also true for believers. The Old Testament story of Jonah teaches that believers can disobey God, in fact, with such determination that it takes a direct intervention by God in history to turn them around. But when believers do so, they suffer the consequences that God has previously established to govern disobedience. Jonah had been given a commission to take a message of judgment to Nineveh. It was similar to the Great Commission that has been given to all Christians, for he was told to "Arise, go to Nineveh, that great city, and call out against it, for their evil has come up before me" (Jon 1:2). But Jonah did not want to do God's bidding, as Christians today often don't. So he went in the other direction, taking a ship from Joppa, on the coast of Palestine, to Tarshish, which was probably on the coast of Spain. Did Jonah succeed? Not at all. We know what happened to him. He ran into trouble as God took drastic measures to turn him around. After God let him sit in the belly of a great fish for three days, Jonah decided he would obey God and be his missionary.

THE FLOW OF HISTORY

Thus far, our study has revealed several uniquely Christian attitudes toward providence. First, the Christian doctrine is personal and moral rather than abstract and amoral. That makes it entirely different from the pagan idea of fate. Second, providence is a specific operation. In Jonah's case it dealt with a particular man, ship, fish, and revelation of the divine will in the call to Nineveh.

There is something else that must be said about the providence of God. It is *purposive*; that is, it is directed to an end. There is such a thing as real history. The flow of human events is going somewhere, as opposed to being merely static or without meaning. In Jonah's case, the flow of history led to his own eventual, though reluctant, missionary work and then to the conversion of the people of Nineveh. In the larger picture, history flows on to the glorification of God in all his attributes, primarily in the person of his Son, the Lord Jesus Christ. That idea is captured in the definition of providence found in the Westminster Confession of Faith, which reads, "God the great Creator of all things doth uphold, direct, dispose, and govern all creatures, actions, and things, from the greatest even to the least by His most wise and holy providence, according to His infallible fore-knowledge, and the free and immutable counsel of His own will, *to the praise of the glory of His wisdom, power, justice, goodness, and mercy*" (V, i).

The flow of history leading to the glorification of God is to our good also. For "we know that for those who love God all things work together for good, for those who are called according to his purpose" (Rom 8:28). What is our good? Obviously, there are many "goods" to be enjoyed now, and this verse includes them. But in its fullest sense our good is to enter into the destiny we were created for: to be conformed to the image of Jesus Christ and thus "to glorify God, and to enjoy him forever." The providence of God will surely bring us there.

To speak of the "good" introduces the subject of the "bad." And since the verse in Romans says that "all things work together for good" for those who are the called ones of God, the question immediately arises as to whether or not this includes the evil. Is evil under God's direction? It would be possible to interpret Romans 8:28 as meaning that all things *consistent with righteousness* work for good for those who love God, but in the light of Scripture as a whole that would be an unjustified watering down of the text. It is *all* things, including evil, that God uses in accomplishing his good purposes in the world.

There are two areas in which God's use of evil for good must be considered. First, there is the evil of *others*. Does this work for the believer's good? The Bible answers yes by many examples. When Naomi's son, an Israelite, married Ruth, a Moabitess, the marriage was contrary to the revealed will of God and hence was sin. Jews were not to marry Gentiles. Still the marriage made Ruth a daughter-in-law of Naomi, and thus enabled her to be exposed to the true God and eventually come to the place where she made a choice to serve him. "Your people shall be my people, and your God my God" (Ruth 1:16). After Ruth's husband died, she married Boaz. Through her new husband, Ruth entered into the line of descent of the Lord Jesus Christ, the Messiah (Mt 1:5).

David was a person who undoubtedly suffered greatly through the sins of others against him, including even the sins of his sons. But as God worked in him through these experiences, he grew to see the hand of God in his suffering and expressed his faith in great psalms. The psalms have been an immeasurable blessing to millions.

Hosea suffered through the unfaithfulness of his wife Gomer. But God used his experience to bring forth one of the most beautiful, moving, and instructive books of the Old Testament.

By far the greatest example of the sin of others working for the good of God's people is the sin that poured itself out against the Lord Jesus Christ. The leaders of Christ's day hated him for his holiness and wished to eliminate his presence from their lives. Satan worked through their hatred to strike back at God by encouraging merciless treatment of the incarnate Christ. But God turned this to good, working through the crucifixion of the Lord for our salvation. In none of this was God responsible for evil, though human sin and the sin of Satan were involved. In none of this was God made a partner in sin. Jesus himself said, in reference to Judas, "The Son of Man goes as it is written of him, but woe to that man by whom the Son of man is betrayed!" (Mt 26:24). Earlier he had said, "It is necessary that temptations come, but woe to the one by whom the temptation comes!" (Mt 18:7). Nevertheless, without himself being a party to sin, God worked through it to bring forth good in line with his own eternal purposes.

The other area in which God's use of evil for his own purposes must be considered is *our own sin*. This point is somewhat harder to see, for sin also works to our own unhappiness and blinds our eyes to God's dealing. But there is good involved anyway. For example, Joseph's brothers were jealous of him because he was their father's favorite. So they conspired and sold him to a group of Midianite traders, who took him to Egypt. There Joseph worked as a slave. In time, he was thrown into prison through the unjust accusations of a rejected woman. Later he was brought to power as second only to Pharaoh, and became the means by which grain was stored during seven years of prosperity for the subsequent seven years of famine and widespread starvation. During that period his brothers, who were starving along with everyone else, came to Egypt and were helped by Joseph.

They were helped by the one they had rejected! And the outcome was in God's control, as Joseph later explained to them.

> I am your brother, Joseph, whom you sold into Egypt. And now do not be distressed or angry with yourselves because you sold me here, for God sent me before you to preserve life. For the famine has been in the land these two years, and there are yet five years in which there will be neither plowing nor harvest. And God sent me before you to preserve for you a remnant on earth, and to keep alive for you many survivors. So it was not you who sent me here, but God. (Gen 45:4-8)

After the death of their father, the brothers thought that Joseph would then take vengeance on them. But he again calmed their fears saying, "Do not fear, for am I in the place of God? As for you, you meant evil against me; but God meant it for good, to bring it about that many people should be kept alive, as they are today" (Gen 50:19-20). There had been great evil in the hearts of the brothers.

But God used their evil, not only to save others, but even to save their own lives and those of their wives and children.

HUMAN RESPONSIBILITY

There will always be some who hear such a truth and immediately cry out that it teaches that Christians may sin with impunity. This accusation was made against Paul (Rom 3:8). But it teaches nothing of the kind. Sin is still sin; it has consequences. Evil is still evil, but God is greater than the evil. That is the point. And he is determined to and will accomplish his purposes in spite of it.

The providence of God does not relieve us of responsibility. God works through means (the integrity, hard work, obedience, and faithfulness of Christian people, for example). The providence of God does not relieve us of the need to make wise judgments or to be prudent. On the other hand, it does relieve us of anxiety in God's service. "If God so clothes the grass of the field, which today is alive and tomorrow is thrown into the oven, will he not much more clothe you, O you of little faith?" (Mt 6:30). Rather than being a cause for self-indulgence, compromise, rebellion or any other sin, the doctrine of providence is actually a sure ground for trust and a spur to faithfulness.

Calvin has left us with wise advice on this subject.

> Gratitude of mind for the favorable outcome of things, patience in adversity, and also incredible freedom from worry about the future all necessarily follow upon this knowledge. Therefore whatever shall happen prosperously and according to the desire of his heart, God's servant will attribute wholly to God, whether he feels God's beneficence through the ministry of men, or has been helped by inanimate creatures. For thus he will reason in his mind: surely it is the Lord who has inclined their hearts to me, who has so bound them to me that they should become the instruments of his kindness.[2]

In such a frame of mind, the Christian will cease to fret in circumstances and will grow in the love and knowledge of Jesus Christ and of his Father, who has made us and who has planned and accomplished our salvation.

---

[2]John Calvin, *Institutes of the Christian Religion*, ed. John T. McNeill, trans. Ford Lewis Battles, 2 vols. (Philadelphia: Westminster, 1960), 219-20.

GOD *the* REDEEMER

PART I

THE FALL
OF THE RACE

And the Lord *God commanded the man, saying, "You may surely eat of every tree of the garden, but of the tree of the knowledge of good and evil you shall not eat, for in the day that you eat of it you shall surely die."*

Genesis 2:16-17

As it is written: "None is righteous, no, not one; no one understands, no one seeks for God. All have turned aside; together they have become worthless; no one does good, not even one."

Romans 3:10-12

No one can come to me unless the Father who sent me draws him.

John 6:44

CHAPTER 1

THE FALL

On the temple to Apollo at Delphi, nestled against a rugged mountain in one of the remote areas of Greece, an inscription summed up the wisdom of the ancient world: *gnōthi seauton* ("know thyself"). Those two words embody the deeply held conviction that, as Alexander Pope later phrased it, "the proper study of mankind is man." That is, our wisdom consists in the accuracy and depth of self-knowledge.

On one level Christianity has no quarrel with that analysis, so long as it is remembered that knowledge of oneself always involves a corresponding and personal knowledge of the God who made us. And knowledge of God will always involve knowledge of our personal need and of the salvation that he alone brings. What Christianity does deny is that we can know ourselves apart from God, that is, apart from God's own revelation of himself to our minds and consciences. True, we can know much *about* humanity, both male and female. We can study our chemical and emotional make-up. We can observe how we function. But we cannot know human beings as we are in ourselves. We cannot determine what we were meant to be or why we repeatedly fail to achieve that goal, apart from revelation. That is why, as Reinhold Niebuhr says in the opening line of *The Nature and Destiny of Man*, "Man has always been his own most vexing problem."[1]

---

[1]Reinhold Niebuhr, *The Nature and Destiny of Man*, one-volume edition of the Gifford Lectures on "Human Nature" and "Human Destiny" (New York: Charles Scribner's Sons, 1949), part 1, 1.

The biblical perspective on the human race is what must chiefly concern us in this chapter. It is best understood when contrasted with the two major non-Christian views that dominate our culture.

VIEWS OF HUMANITY

The first of these competing views of humankind is the outlook of classical antiquity, that is, the dominant perspective of the Greco-Roman world. Classical views of humanity, though varying in points from thinker to thinker, nevertheless had one idea in common: since the highest element in the human being was the *nous* or reasoning faculty, a person was to be understood primarily from the standpoint of that characteristic. A human being thinks or reasons; and that, according to Plato, Aristotle, and other Greek thinkers, sets the human being apart from the rest of the visible world. In Aristotle the *nous* is something that comes to us primarily from without. In Plato the *nous* is the highest element of the soul. But in both of these thinkers *reason* is the crucial element in which women and men find their uniqueness.

The consequences of giving such unique value to reason are well known. First, that emphasis tends to deify reason, making it the God-element in a human being. The justification for such deification is in the essential characteristics of reason, namely, its ability to rise above what it sees, to evaluate, to criticize, to form, to create. Each can be thought of as a "godlike" characteristic. A second consequence of the classical elevation of reason is a resulting dualism in which the body becomes something evil. If mind is good, matter is bad. Hence arises that eternal conflict between spirit and mind on the one hand, and flesh and matter on the other, that gives substance to the most characteristic expressions of Greek art, drama, and philosophy.

Another strain in Greek thought, seen most clearly in the mystery religions, viewed human nature in mechanical or materialistic terms—but that was not the dominant view of antiquity.

Two more facts may be noted about the classical view, as Niebuhr points out in his analysis. First, there is a basic optimism in the classical outlook. If reason is good and humanity is essentially reason, then humanity is essentially good. Humans are linked to the divine at the most fundamental level of their personality, and they have no defect there. On the other hand, there is a strange but unmistakably tragic note in the classical perspective. Thus, in the *Iliad* of Homer, Zeus is quoted as saying, "There is nothing, methinks, more piteous than a man, of all things that creep and breathe upon earth." Or as Aristotle comments, "Not to be born is the best thing, and death is better than life."[2] That pervasive pessimism is particularly marked in the Greek tragedies. They portray human beings as the victims of circumstances or of their own tragic flaws, neither of which they can change. The classical world saw no meaning to history.

A variation of the classical outlook is one of the competing views of humanity in modern culture: simple rationalism. In harmony with the major Greek thinkers, modern exponents of this view emphasize the supremacy of our reason as setting us apart from the remainder of creation, and assume that we are essentially good at the core of our beings. But the tragic element, perceived so clearly by the Greeks and Romans, is missing. Its lack does not mean that modern rationalists regard humans as actually better than the ancients perceived them, or that humans have become better over the intervening centuries, but rather that modern thinkers are strangely unwilling to face all reality. Georg Friedrich Hegel's theory of historical development through thesis, antithesis, and synthesis leaves no room for any real stalemate or regression due to human sin. The same is true of Karl Marx's dialectical materialism and Charles Darwin's biological evolution. Each assumes unending and inevitable progression. In recent years, as an aftermath of two world wars and current international unrest, there is enormous difficulty in maintaining an unlimited optimism. War, hatred, starvation, sickness, and turmoil must be reckoned with. Nevertheless, the dominant contemporary view is that such problems can all be handled, granted the opportunity for us fully to employ our reason.

Only a few perceptive thinkers seem aware that the root problems of this and every age are not in circumstances alone or in lack of education, but rather in the very make-up of the human being. The rational faculty is important, as the Greeks saw it to be, but it is neither divine nor perfect. And the body, like the mind, is of inestimable worth, though fallen. Such thinkers see that in all parts of our being, we are simply less than we were intended to be.

In the modern world, however, another perspective on humanity is competing, with increasing success, with the classical view. It is linked to the minority view of the ancients mentioned earlier, reflected in the mystery religions and in such thinkers as Heraclitus, Pythagoras, and Epicurus. In this view we are essentially flesh or matter, rather than mind or spirit. That is to say that the entire universe, including us, is mechanistic. There is nothing apart from matter. There is no universal mind or higher reason with which we are linked and that gives form

---

[2]Quoted in ibid., 9-10.

and direction to human life. Consequently, life is the inevitable working out of basic but impersonal laws.

The modern world has various expressions of the mechanistic view. One is the deterministic stance of Charles Darwin, according to which evolution proceeds by the laws of natural selection. Another example is communism, which views history as the outworking of the fixed laws of economics and class struggle. The behavioral psychology of B. F. Skinner of Harvard University also fits this category. Obviously, as in the ancient world, there are many variations among those who hold to a materialistic nature of things, but they are united in their commitment to an essential and amoral naturalism. The human being is an animal—that is the argument—and an animal is only an exceedingly complex machine.

Most people cannot be content with that kind of naturalism, just as they cannot be content with the modern version of the classical perspective. In fact, they are caught in a dilemma leading to deep perplexity. Niebuhr analyzes it, saying,

> If man insists that he is a child of nature and that he ought not to pretend to be more than the animal, which he obviously is, he tacitly admits that he is, at any rate, a curious kind of animal who has both the inclination and the capacity to make such pretensions. If on the other hand he insists upon his unique and distinctive place in nature and points to his rational faculties as proof of his special eminence, there is usually an anxious note in his avowals of uniqueness which betrays his unconscious sense of kinship with the brutes.[3]

Nothing in modern life explains our nature except the truths of Christianity, for both the greatness and tragedy of humankind exceed the comprehensions of our culture. We sense that we are more than matter. We sense that we are made in God's image, to be his companions. But we are also aware that we have lost that image and that the bond that should exist between ourselves and the Creator has been broken. Hence, "Under the perpetual smile of modernity there is a grimace of disillusion and cynicism."[4]

Where should one begin in one's effort to achieve self-understanding? Formally, we must begin with the Bible, for there God reveals our true condition to us (at least according to the convictions of Christianity). More specifically, we must begin with the Bible's analysis of the fall of humanity, for there, above all, we

---

[3]Ibid., 1.
[4]Ibid., 121.

see not only what we were intended to be, but also what we have unfortunately become because of sin.

UNFAITHFULNESS

According to the opening chapters of Genesis, when God placed the man and the woman in Eden to be his vice regents on earth, he gave them the maximum freedom, authority, and dominion possible for created beings. They were to rule the earth for him. And there were no apparent restrictions on how they were to do it, except in the matter of the tree of the knowledge of good and evil, of which they were not to eat—as a symbol of their dependence on God. Many foolish things have been imagined about that tree. It has been called an apple tree and an apple, the forbidden fruit, with no biblical justification. One writer has conjectured that the fruit was the grape and the sin that of making wine. That is ludicrous. Others perceive the fruit to be sex, a viewpoint that throws light on the barely suppressed guilt with which many of our contemporaries consider that subject, but that does not at all illuminate the book of Genesis. We know that such was not the meaning of the tree, because God instructed the first couple to be fruitful and multiply even before warning them about the fruit of the knowledge of good and evil (Gen 1:28). In fact, the command to multiply was part of the original gift to man and woman of dominion over the entire earth.

What, then, does the fruit symbolize? The answer is not difficult. The fruit was a tangible symbol of the fact that the man and woman, even with great freedom and dominion on the earth, were nevertheless God's creatures; they enjoyed their freedom and exercised their dominion as a result of God's free gift. The fruit was a restraint on them, to remind them that they were not God but were responsible to him. What kind of fruit it was makes no difference.

We do not know how long Adam and Eve lived in the Garden of Eden in an unfallen state, though Genesis gives the impression that the assault on them by Satan came quite early, before they had been well confirmed in any good pattern of obedience. Certainly Satan had heard God's warning, "You may surely eat of every tree of the garden, but of the tree of the knowledge of good and evil you shall not eat, for in the day that you eat of it you shall surely die" (Gen 2:16-17). Now Satan comes—immediately it seems—to suggest that God is not benevolent and that his word cannot be trusted.

The word of God is the issue in Satan's temptation of Eve. Satan's first words end in a question mark designed to cast doubt on God's veracity: "Did God actually say . . . ?" (Gen 3:1). That is the first question mark in the Bible. Of course, in the original Hebrew there are no punctuation marks of any kind, but the question in the thought makes the question mark appropriate in our English Bibles. "Did God actually say . . . ? Has God really said . . . ?" The essence of sin is in that speculation.

The exact words of Satan are of interest, for the sentence goes on to specify the matter that Satan is questioning. "Did God actually say, 'You shall not eat of any tree in the garden'?" But, of course, that is *not* what God said. God had said, "You may surely eat of every tree of the garden; but [here is the exception] of the tree of the knowledge of good and evil you shall not eat, for in the day that you eat of it you shall surely die" (Gen 2:16-17). Satan changes God's positive invitation to eat of every tree (with one exception) into a negative prohibition designed to cast doubt on God's goodness. Can we see what is happening here? God gives the man and the woman all creation to enjoy, with one exception—and even that prohibition is explained by means of the penalty attached to it. Satan suggests that God is essentially prohibitive, that he is not good, and that he does not wish the very best for his creatures.

The woman does not initially agree with the force of that argument. But Satan's skillful question puts her on the defensive, and she replies with a correct (or essentially correct) reiteration of what God had said, ending with the warning, "You shall not eat of the fruit of the tree that is in the midst of the garden, neither shall you touch it, lest you die" (Gen 3:3).

At that point Satan replies with an outright denial: "You will not surely die. For God knows that when you eat of it your eyes will be opened, and you will be like God, knowing good and evil" (Gen 3:4-5). What is at stake in his denial? Is it food? Apples? Inebriation? Sex? Freedom? It is none of those things. The issue in this first part of the temptation is simply the integrity of the word of God. Having begun to cast doubt on the benevolence of God, which the first pair had no reason for doubting, Satan now blatantly contradicts God's veracity. The issue is simply this: Does God speak truth? Then we are told that the woman looked at the fruit, saw that it was "a delight to the eyes, and that the tree was to be desired to make one wise," and ate of it (Gen 3:6). Moreover, she gave it to her husband, and he ate also.

Here, then, is the first revelation of sin's nature and of what is basically wrong with humankind. Sin is unfaithfulness. It is doubt of God's good will and truthfulness, leading inevitably to an act of outright rejection. In our day we see this most clearly in two ways: first, in the myriad of outright denials of the record of God's word in the Bible, even by theologians and pastors, and second, by the almost instinctive attempt by men and women to blame God for human tragedy.

In one episode of *All in the Family*, Archie Bunker is arguing about Christianity with his atheistic son-in-law, Michael, because Archie wants to have Michael's son baptized and Michael wants none of it. They argue about a number of unessential things. At last Michael asks Archie, "Tell me this, Archie. If there is a God, why is the world such a mess?"

Archie is dumbfounded. He stands stock-still for a moment, and then tries to bluff his way through. He turns to his wife Edith and says, "Why do I always have to give the answers, Edith? Tell this dumb Polack why, if God has created the world, the world is in such a mess."

Edith answers, "Well, I suppose it's to make us appreciate heaven better when we get there."

Any honest thinker will admit that the problem of evil is a great one and that it raises questions we will probably never be able fully to answer in this world. How evil could even enter a good world created by a good God is puzzling. Why God permits evil to exist even temporarily as he obviously does is also beyond our full comprehension. But one thing we can say is that evil is our fault, whatever reasons God may have for tolerating it. In the incident from *All in the Family* it never seems to occur to Michael, Archie, or Edith (or any of the writers) that this is so.

Rather than acknowledge that simple but unpleasant truth, people say, as did H. G. Wells, that faced with the world's evil, we must conclude that either God has the power but does not care, or cares but does not have the power. Or else he does not exist. Such expressions fail to recognize that the cause of the problem is in us and blind us to God's solution to sin through the Lord Jesus Christ.

REBELLION

Nothing we have yet said, however, gets to the most important fact about sin. The most important thing about sin is to be seen in the fall of the man, Adam, in which it is nowhere suggested that he fell through the deception of Satan. The woman did fall as a result of Satan's arguments. In fact, she fell with good will; she had come to believe that the tree of the knowledge of good and evil would make one wise, and she wanted both herself and her husband to enjoy that blessing. Eve erred and sinned in her error. But her error, serious as it was, was not duplicated in the case of Adam, nor was it as reprehensible. Adam sinned out of an attitude of rebellion against God. The distinction is noted in the apostle

Paul's interpretation of the fall. "And Adam was not deceived, but the woman was deceived and became a transgressor" (1 Tim 2:14).

God had placed Adam amd Eve in the garden to have dominion over creation (Gen 1:28) and had given them the fruit of all the trees of the garden to eat except one. If they ate of it, they would die. Adam, however, in full knowledge of what he was doing, looked at that one tree and said in effect, "I don't care if I am allowed to eat of all the trees north of here, east of here, south of here and west of here. So long as that one tree stands in the garden as a symbol of my creaturehood, so long as it is there to remind me that I am not God, that I am not perfectly autonomous—so long as it is there, I hate it! So I will eat of it and die, whatever that means." If Adam was not deceived, as 1 Timothy 2:14 clearly states, then he must have sinned in full knowledge of what he was doing. That is, he chose to eat in deliberate disobedience of God. And death, first the death of his spirit but then also the death of his soul and body, passed on to the human race.

The Bible never places the blame for the fall of the race on the woman. Our jokes and much of our popular literature blame Eve for getting us into sin—another example of male chauvinism—but there is never a word of blame placed on Eve in Scripture. Instead we read, "For as by a man came death . . . in Adam all die" (1 Cor 15:21-22); and "As sin came into the world through one man [Adam], and death through sin . . . because of one man's trespass, death reigned. . . . By one man's disobedience the many were made sinners" (Rom 5:12, 17, 19).

The nature of Adam's fall says something else important. Sin is apostasy, that is, a falling away from something that existed formerly and was good. It is the reversal of God's intentions for the race. We see this in nearly all the synonyms for sin found in the Scriptures: *pesha* ("transgression"), *chata* ("to miss the mark"), *shagah* ("to go astray"), *hamartia* ("shortcoming"), and *paraptōma* ("offense"). Each concept depicts a departure from a higher standard or from a state enjoyed originally.

As we suggested earlier, in the Greek view the essence of evil is to be found in matter or, more fully stated, in the life of the senses. That is, Emil Brunner points out, "The conception of sin in Greek philosophy . . . is based upon the fact that the sense instincts paralyze the will, or at least hinder or suppress it. Evil is thus due to the dual nature of man."[5] The reason is not entirely without

---

[5]Emil Brunner, *The Christian Doctrine of Creation and Redemption: Dogmatics*, trans. Olive Wyon, vol. 2 (Philadelphia: Westminster, 1952), 91.

fault, being unable to master the sense instincts quickly. But evil is in the lower element. "If this evil is to be brought into relation to time," says Brunner, "it has to be described as that which is 'not yet good,' or has 'not yet reached the plane of spirit,' or is 'not yet' dominated by spirit."[6] The biblical view reverses the matter, replacing the "not yet" by "no longer." Human beings were without sin, as was all creation. God created all things perfect. But they rebelled against God and perfection, falling away from that sublime nature and destiny God had for them.

This is the essential biblical note regarding sin, says Brunner:

> Whenever the Prophets reproach Israel for its sin, this is the decisive conception: "You have fallen away, you have strayed, you have been unfaithful. You have forsaken God; you have broken the Covenant, you have left Him for other gods. You have turned your backs upon Him!" Similarly, the Parables of Jesus speak of sin as rebellion, as leaving God. The Prodigal Son leaves home, goes away from the Father, turns his back upon him. The Wicked Husbandmen usurp the master's rights and wrongly seize the land which they only held on a rental. They are actually rebels, usurpers. The Lost Sheep has strayed away from the flock and from the Shepherd; it has gone astray.[7]

Sin is rebellion because it is not the primary element. It is only a secondary element. The primary element is that "good and acceptable and perfect" will of God from which we have strayed and to which we are restored only by the awe-inspiring power of the grace of God in Jesus Christ.

PRIDE

In our analysis of Genesis 3, we have taken time to isolate the sin of the woman and the sin of the man, contrasting them in order to define the two root elements of sin as "faithlessness" and "rebellion." When we compare the woman's sin and the man's for similarities, we soon discover a third root element in sin's nature: pride.

What lay at the root of the woman's determination to eat the forbidden fruit and give some to her husband Adam, if not pride? And what lay at the root of Adam's determination to go his own way rather than follow the path God placed before him, if not pride? In the woman's case, it was the conviction that she knew what was better for herself and her husband than God did. God had said

---

[6]Ibid.
[7]Ibid.

that eating the fruit of the tree of the knowledge of good and evil would bring dire consequences. It would bring death. But Eve was convinced by her own empirical observation—after Satan had raised the doubt—that the tree would actually be good for her and that God was mistaken. What arrogance! In the man's case, the same element was present. In his pride, he recapitulated the original sin of Satan, saying in effect, "I will cast off God's rule. I am too great to be bound by it. I shall declare myself autonomous. I will be like the Most High" (compare Is 14:14).

How terrible such pride is. And how pervasive—for it did not vanish in the death of the first man and woman. Pride lies at the heart of the sin of the human race. It is the "center" of immorality, "the utmost evil"; it "leads to every other vice," as C. S. Lewis warns us.[8] It makes us all want to be more than we are or can be and, consequently, causes us to fall short of the great destiny for which we were created.

Thus, we are fallen. We are not on the way up, as today's optimistic exponents of the classical view would indicate. We are not sinful by the very nature of things, as the ancient Greeks would argue. We are not mere machines, as if we could be excused on the grounds of such an analysis. We are fallen. We are faithless, rebellious, filled with pride. As a result, our only hope is in that grace of God by which he sends a redeemer, who instead of being faithless was faithful, instead of being rebellious was obedient, instead of being filled with pride was one who actually humbled himself to "even death on a cross" (Phil 2:8).

---

[8]C. S. Lewis, *Mere Christianity* (New York: The Macmillan Company, 1958), 94.

CHAPTER 2

THE RESULTS
OF THE FALL

As soon as we begin to talk about sin, we run into a problem. A dislike of the subject of sin and a desire to see ourselves in a better light than the Bible presents us causes us immediately to seek ways to excuse ourselves and our conduct. On the personal level, if we are criticized for doing something, we instinctively present a defense, even when clearly in the wrong. We say, "You have no right to say that," or "It's not my fault." Probably many persons never admit that they are in the wrong about anything.

We must stop here and grapple with this tendency in our nature. We must overcome it if we are to know ourselves and God. Without a knowledge of our unfaithfulness and rebellion, we will never come to know God as the God of truth and grace. Without a knowledge of our pride, we will never know him in his greatness. Nor will we come to him for the healing we need. When we are sick physically and know that we are sick, we seek out a doctor and follow his or her prescription for a cure. But if we did not know we were sick, we would not seek help and might well perish from the illness. It is the same spiritually. If we think we are well, we will never accept God's cure; we think we do not need it. Instead, if by God's grace we become aware of our sickness—actually, of something worse than sickness, of spiritual death so far as any meaningful response to God is concerned—then we have a basis for understanding the meaning of Christ's work on our behalf, and can embrace him as Savior and be transformed by him.

THE DEGREE AND EXTENT OF SIN

In facing this tendency of human nature and in attempting to understand sin, we must be on guard against two types of argument. They pertain to the degree and extent of sin. That is, how bad is sin, really? And, who is affected? We often hear the view—perhaps we raise it ourselves—that, although something is obviously wrong, surely human nature is not so bad as the Bible imagines it to be. After all, we are told, the biblical writers were melancholy prophets living in a grim age; they were naturally pessimistic. Their world was filled with wars, starvation, disease, and many forms of economic hardship. But this is not the year 2000 BC. We now have reason to be more optimistic. We are not perfect; we will grant that. But are not the imperfections just that, imperfections, to be considered merely as the flaws, shortcomings, or peccadilloes of the race?

One answer is that if human nature is only slightly flawed, as that argument supposes, then it should have been perfected by now. A more serious answer is that the "slightly flawed" view is totally unrealistic. The Bible points out that our state is desperate, and we can see it to be so. Sin is linked to death in the biblical perspective, and death is the ultimate enemy and inevitable victor over all. We must escape death if we sense that immortality is our rightful destiny. Again, even apart from that consideration, the tragedy of human existence is overwhelmingly visible to anyone who will honestly view the mounting starvation, suffering, hatred, selfishness, and indifference on our planet. The Christian faith is not insensitive to those things, although many Christians seem to be. In its emphasis on the permeation of every aspect of our being by sin, only Christianity gives a realistic appraisal.

The uniqueness of the biblical position can be seen by noting that in the long history of the race, there have been only three basic views of human nature. They may be summarized as the views that humanity is well, that humanity is sick, and that humanity is dead. (There are variations in the first two views, of course. Optimists unite in saying that humankind is well, but some may admit that we are perhaps not so well as we possibly could be. More realistic observers differ over how sick we are: acutely, gravely, critically, mortally.)

Proponents of the first view, that human beings are well, agree that all we need, if we need anything, is a little exercise, some vitamins, checkups once a year, and so on. "I'm all right, Jack" is the optimists' cry. Those who hold the second view are agreed that human nature is sick. We may even be mortally sick, some would say, but the situation is still not hopeless; with proper care, drugs, the miracles of modern spiritual medicine, and the will to live, who can tell what might happen? What we need is to work hard to cure our ills. After all, we are told, even if some diseases are beyond our ability to cure now, not all are, and even the remaining problems may be solved eventually. The situation may be bad, but—well, "where there's life, there's hope." There is no need to call the mortician yet.

The biblical view is that humankind is not well nor merely sick. Actually, we are already dead—so far as our relationship to God is concerned. We are "dead in the trespasses and sins" (Eph 2:1), as God warned we would be when God predicted the consequences of sin before the fall. "But of the tree of the knowledge of good and evil you shall not eat, for in the day that you eat of it you shall surely die" (Gen 2:17).

THE DEATH OF SPIRIT, SOUL, AND BODY

What is the degree of our sin? In considering this question it will be helpful to remember the threefold nature of our being discussed in book one, chapter fifteen.[1] There I pointed out that one thing the Bible means when it says that we are created in the image of God is that we are each created a trinity, analogous to the way in which God is a Trinity. God exists in three persons: God the Father, God the Son, and God the Holy Spirit. Yet God is One. In the same manner each of us is a trinity, created as a body, soul, and spirit. Yet each is one.

The human being that God created was perfect in regard to his spirit, soul, and body, the apex of creation. But the fall affected each part of this magnificent threefold nature. Specifically, the spirit died, for fellowship with God was broken; the soul began to die, for humans began to lie and cheat and kill; the body died eventually, for, as God said, "You are dust, and to dust you shall return" (Gen 3:19).

In the area of the spirit, the effect of Adam's sin was instantaneous and total. When the spirit died, communication with God was broken. Adam proved it by running away when God came to him in the garden. In contemporary language this is described as *alienation*, alienation from God, and it is the first result of that spiritual death that came to us as the result of sin. John Stott calls it "the most dreadful of all sin's consequences." "Man's highest destiny is to know God and to be in personal relationship with God. Man's chief claim to nobility is that he was made in the image of God and is therefore capable of knowing Him.

---

[1]See the section titled "In God's Image."

But this God whom we are meant to know and whom we ought to know is a moral Being," and we are sinners. Consequently, "our sins blot out God's face from us as effectively as the clouds do the sun. . . . We have no communication with God. We are 'dead through the trespasses and sins' (Eph 2:1) which we have committed."[2]

Alienation from God is total in its effect. It has plunged us into a state in which it is not possible for us to find our way back to God unless aided by his Holy Spirit. That is the meaning of Romans 3:10-12. The apostle Paul writes,

> As it is written:
> "None is righteous, no, not one;
> > no one understands;
> > no one seeks for God.
> All have turned aside; together they have become worthless;
> > no one does good,
> > not even one."

It is important to understand that each of the three main terms of Romans 3:10-12—righteousness, understanding, and seeking—is defined in terms of relationship to God. Otherwise, we distort the teaching of Scripture and affirm something that is not true. For example, if we fail to define righteousness in relation to God and his righteousness, we end by saying that there is no good in us at all. That is not true when we consider the matter from a human point of view. Not all persons are as bad as they possibly could be, and even the worst have what we might call some spark of goodness. At times there is "honor even among thieves." But that is not what the Romans passage is talking about. It is talking about righteousness as God sees righteousness. From that perspective it is true that "none is righteous, no, not one." The death of the spirit has affected us deeply and permanently in our moral nature.

Sin has also affected us in the area of intellect. Again, we must not make the mistake of explaining the phrase "no one understands" on a human level, although even on that level sin has had bad consequences. Human beings do have understanding in many areas, and some excel here. We have philosophers, scientists, and diplomats. Paul's words do not deny that. What they deny is that we have understanding in spiritual things apart from the working of the Spirit of God, who alone gives understanding. That is expressed in 1 Corinthians as "the natural

---

[2]John R. W. Stott, *Basic Christianity* (Grand Rapids: Eerdmans, 1958), 72, 75.

person does not accept the things of the Spirit of God, for they are folly to him, and he is not able to understand them because they are spiritually discerned" (1 Cor 2:14).

The third area affected by the death of the spirit is our will, to be discussed more fully in the next chapter. It is referred to in the sentence "no one seeks for God." The meaning is that not only are we incapable of coming to God because of our sin and his righteousness, and incapable of understanding him because his way can be discerned only by the aid of the Spirit of God, but in addition, we don't even want to come to God. Again, nearly all women and men do seek "a god," a god of their own making who they hope will fill the spiritual vacuum of their lives. But they do not seek the true God who reveals himself to us in the Scriptures and in the person of Christ. Jesus said, "No one can come to me unless the Father who sent me draws him" (Jn 6:44).

In medicine, there is a condition known as *myasthenia gravis*, in which the muscles of the body cannot respond to the signals being sent to them by the brain. In a normal patient, the brain signals the muscles to contract by sending electrical impulses along the nerves to the muscles, where they are received by a special apparatus known as the motor-end-plate. The motor-end-plate receives the signal and passes it along to the muscle. In those afflicted by *myasthenia gravis*, the end-plates are missing. Consequently, although the brain sends the signal, it is never received by the muscle. Because it is not received, the muscle does not respond and eventually shrivels up.

That is an analogy of what has happened in the human personality because of the death of the spirit. In the human system the spirit was meant to play the part of the motor-end-plates. It was meant to receive signals sent to it from God. When human beings sinned, however, the motor-end-plate died. Thus, although the signals are still there, although God is still speaking, the signal is not received and the spiritual life withers.

The illustration of *myasthenia gravis* also suggests a second result of the fall as it affects the individual. That the muscle cannot receive the brain's signals does not mean that the muscle merely fails to respond as the brain wishes. No, the muscle itself suffers, for it withers in its inactive state and dies. Death of the spirit also affects the soul, with the result that men and women become depraved in that area also.

We see this in Adam and Eve. After the fall and the subsequent appearance of God in the garden, we are told that the man and woman hid, attempting to escape the encounter. It was an example of their alienation from God, the first

visible effect of their sin. But God calls them forth to meet him and begins to
interrogate them about what they have done. "Adam," says God, "have you eaten
of the tree of which I commanded you not to eat?" (Gen 3:11).

Adam replies, "The woman whom you gave to be with me, she gave me fruit
of the tree, and I ate" (Gen 3:12).

On the surface, Adam's reply is simply a statement, and a true one at that.
The woman had given him the fruit. God had given him the woman. But that is
not the real meaning of the fallen man's reply. Adam is attempting to shift the
blame away from himself, where it primarily belongs, onto someone else. Most
obviously, he is trying to blame the woman—hardly a chivalrous thing to do,
not to mention the more basic virtue of honesty. Beyond that he is also trying
to blame God. What he is really saying is that the fall would not have taken
place if God had not been so mistaken in his judgment as to have provided him
with Eve.

In a similar way Eve also shifts the blame. When God asks, "'What is it that
you have done?' The woman said, 'The serpent deceived me, and I ate'" (Gen 3:13).

The point is that shifting the blame is typical of the sinful nature and illustrates
what happens once the connection with God has been broken. God is the source
of all good (Jas 1:17). When the connection with God is broken, irresponsibility,
cowardice, lying, jealousy, hatred, and every other evil descend on the race. To
put the situation into contemporary terminology as we did when we spoke of
alienation, we could say that we are dealing with moral and psychological *decay.*

But there is more. Personal decay inevitably has social implications. Thus a
further result of the fall is *conflict.* Was the relationship between Adam and Eve
as harmonious after Adam had tried to blame his wife for the Fall as beforehand?
Of course not. That was the beginning of marital conflict. Similarly, the wish to
blame others, self-interest, and desire for self-advancement produce conflict
between individuals, races, social stratifications, institutions, and nations.

Finally, the deaths of the spirit and soul, which have such dire effects, are
accompanied by death of the body also. When Adam sinned, the spirit died
instantly, with the result that all men and women since are born with what we
may call dead spirits. The soul began to die. In that area, the contagion may be
said to be spreading, with the result that we are increasingly captivated by sin.
The remaining part of human nature, the body, dies last. Death is universal. Paul
used this fact to show the extent of sin: "Death spread to all men because all
sinned" (Rom 5:12).

ORIGINAL SIN

Sad and overwhelming as it is, the death of the individual is only half of the sin problem. The extent of sin as well as its degree must be considered. Are only Adam and Eve involved, plus those who choose to follow them in their rebellion? Or is everyone involved? We might think that the universality of human misery clearly answers the question. But those who object to the biblical conception of the nature of sin ("It's not as bad as the Bible pictures it") might object again. They might argue that corruption due to sin is not universally true of the race; further, if all people *have* been affected by sin, that is because of external circumstances rather than because of anything basically and universally wrong within. The modern attempt is to locate sin in the injustice of society's structures.

So the question is this: Are all human beings affected by sin in the sense that they are inevitably involved in Adam and Eve's transgression? The biblical answer is clear. Paul writes, "Many died through one man's trespass." "Death reigned through that one man." "One trespass led to condemnation for all men." "By one man's disobedience the many were made sinners" (Rom 5:15, 17, 18, 19). "In Adam all die" (1 Cor 15:22). "All have sinned and fall short of the glory of God" (Rom 3:23).

Careful reading of the passages from which these verses are taken, however, shows that they are referring to something more than the universality of human sin. That all people sin might be affirmed by any honest secular writer. What a secular writer is not likely to say, however, but what the Bible says plainly, is that there is a necessary connection between all individual occurrences of sin. In other words, the point is not merely that all people sin and are therefore sinners, though that is true. The point is that all sin because they are sinners. The original sin of Adam and the guilt of sin in some inevitable way passed on to the entire human race. The biblical view is that God holds the entire race to be guilty because of Adam's transgression.

Is anything harder for the natural person to accept than this doctrine? Guilt by imputation? It is difficult to imagine anything more offensive to ideas of human justice and fair play. Hence the doctrine has often been assailed in particularly abusive language. It is thought to be unworthy of God, outrageous, revolting, a valid reason for despising such a God forever if it should be shown that this is in fact the way he operates. It is thought by some to be so unjust that no possible defense of it could be given. But is that so? Before the doctrine of original sin is rejected outright, it would be good to see if it might not represent the true state of affairs.

The truth or falsity of original sin may be settled by the answer given to a simple question: Where does sin come from, if it does not come to us as the Bible declares? We see the results of sin in the various forms of human misery and eventually in death. We may agree that in many cases, the misery is the direct result of our own sin or failings. Chain smokers cannot really blame anyone but themselves for their lung cancer. Overeaters are to blame for the weakened condition of their hearts. But it is not only the chain smoker who develops cancer or the overeater who has a weak heart. Those who do nothing to bring such things on themselves are also affected. Children, even infants, suffer. How can birth defects, colic, cancer in the newborn, and other forms of suffering by the innocent be explained, if not by the biblical teaching?

To my knowledge, in the whole history of ideas only two other answers have been given. One is not really an answer at all, and the other is inadequate. The first answer is the eternity of evil. That is, evil has existed from the very beginning of things, just as good has existed from the beginning; therefore all life is characterized by their mixture. But it is no real answer simply to affirm that sin or evil always existed. Moreover, it has always proved unsatisfactory as an explanation of reality because, whatever a person's philosophical position might be, he or she nevertheless inevitably comes down on one side or the other, usually on the side that explains evil as a derivation or corruption of the good. But that does not explain the universality of sin.

The other explanation has been known popularly as reincarnation, transmigration, or metapsychosis of souls. It is the idea that each of us has had a previous existence and, presumably, an existence before that and another before that and so on. The evil we inherit in this life is supposed to come to us because of what we have done in those previous incarnations. It should be said in defense of this view that it is at least a serious attempt to account for our present state on the basis of specific individual actions. It thereby attempts to satisfy the basic idea of justice that we all share, namely, that each must suffer for their own sins and not those of another. But as an ultimate solution it is clearly unsatisfactory. We immediately want to ask, how did individuals get to be wrongdoers in their previous existence? Reincarnation merely pushes the question back and back without resolving the difficulty.

What other answer is there? None, except the biblical answer: The universality of sin is the result of God's judgment on the race because of Adam's transgression.

Adam was the representative of the race. He stood before God for us so that, as Paul says, when he fell, we fell and were caught up inevitably in the results of his rebellion.

REPRESENTATIVE CONDEMNATION AND JUSTIFICATION

It is conceivable that a person might follow the Christian argument up to this point, agreeing that the doctrine of original sin is the only possible explanation of the universality of sin as we know it. But that person might still be angry at a God who could act so unjustly. Is the objector right? Even if the biblical picture is true, should we not hate a God who is so arbitrary as to visit the judgment of sin on all because of one man's transgression?

Actually, the fact that Adam was made a representative of the race is proof of God's grace.

In the first place, it was an example of his grace toward Adam. For what could be better calculated to bring forth an exalted sense of responsibility and obedience in Adam than the knowledge that what he would do in regard to God's commandment would affect untold billions of his descendants. We know this even in the more limited area of one human family. For what father is there, and what mother is there, who is not influenced for good by the thought that what he or she does for good or evil inevitably affects the offspring? Parents who are inclined to drink may hold back at least somewhat if they know that their children will be hurt by their drinking. Parents who have a chance to steal might not steal if they realize that being caught would inevitably injure their family. Likewise, the knowledge of the effect of his sin on the entire race should have acted as a restraining factor on Adam. That must have been a powerful incentive for good. If Adam fell, it was in spite of the grace of God toward him and not as a justifiable reaction to an arbitrary decree.

Even more important, the representative nature of Adam's sin is an example of God's grace toward us, for it is on the basis of that representation that God is able to save us. Paul says, "For as by one man's disobedience the many were made sinners, so by the one man's [Jesus'] obedience the many will be made righteous" (Rom 5:19). If you and I and all human beings were as the angels, who have no family or representative relationships, and if we were judged as the angels were judged when they fell—immediately, individually, and for their own sin (which is how most men and women think they would like to be judged)— there would be no hope of salvation, just as there is none for the fallen angels. But because we are beings who live in relationships and because God has chosen to deal with us in that way, both in regard to Adam and his sin and to Jesus and his righteousness, there can be salvation. For in Jesus, we who are sinners can be made righteous. We who are "dead through the trespasses and sins" can be made alive spiritually.

The blessings of salvation come, not by fighting against God's ways or by hating him for what we consider to be an injustice, but rather by accepting his verdict on our true nature as fallen beings and turning to Christ in faith for salvation.

CHAPTER 3

THE BONDAGE
OF THE WILL

After having described the nature of sin and its radical and pervasive effects on the race, it is still necessary to discuss the bondage of the will. At that point the sharpest disagreements come and the results of sin are most clearly exposed.

Luther recognized the importance of the issue. At the end of his monumental defense of the will's bondage, after demolishing the arguments of the humanist Desiderius Erasmus of Rotterdam, Luther turned to Erasmus and complimented his writings for at least focusing on the crucial issue. Luther wrote, "I give you hearty praise and commendation on this further account—that you alone, in contrast with all others, have attacked the real thing, that is, the essential issue."[1] Similarly, Emil Brunner speaks of the understanding of freedom and "unfreedom" as "the decisive point" for understanding humankind and sin.[2]

How far did humanity fall when we sinned? Did we merely stumble? Did we fall part way, but nevertheless not so far as to render ourselves hopeless? Or did we fall totally, so far that we cannot even will to seek God or obey him? What does the Bible mean when it says that we are "dead in trespasses and sins"? Does it mean that we really are dead so far as any ability to respond to God or to

---

[1]Martin Luther, *The Bondage of the Will*, trans. J. I. Packer and O. R. Johnston (Westwood, NJ: Fleming H. Revell, 1957), 319.

[2]Emil Brunner, *The Christian Doctrine of Creation and Redemption: Dogmatics*, trans. Olive Wyon, vol. 2 (Philadelphia: Westminster, 1952), 121.

choose God is concerned? Or do we still have the ability at least to respond to God when the offer of salvation is made to us? If we can respond, what does Paul mean when he says that "no one seeks for God" (Rom 3:11)? What does Jesus mean when he says that "no one can come to me unless the Father who sent me draws him" (Jn 6:44)? On the other hand, if we cannot respond, what is the meaning of those many passages in which the gospel is offered to fallen men and women? How is a person to be held responsible for failing to believe in Jesus if he or she is unable to do it?

Such questions suggest the importance of the will's bondage. They indicate how the doctrines of sin and depravity, election, grace, and human responsibility flow from it.

THE HISTORY OF THE DEBATE

The importance of determining whether the will is bound or free is also forced on us by the history of Christian dogma. Significant theological debates in the history of the church have centered on the issue. In the early years of the church, the majority of theologians seemed to endorse free will; they were concerned to overcome the entrenched determinism of the Greek and Roman world. On one level they were right. Determinism is not the Christian view, nor does it excuse human responsibility for sin. The early fathers—Chrysostom, Origen, Jerome, and others—were right to oppose it. In opposing determinism, however, they slipped by varying degrees into a kind of unbiblical exaltation of human ability that prevented them from seeing the true depths of human sin and guilt. Augustine of Hippo rose to challenge that position and to argue fiercely for the bondage of the will, at that time largely against Pelagius, his most outspoken opponent.

It was not the intention of Pelagius to deny the universality of sin, at least at the beginning. In that, he wished to remain orthodox. But he was unable to see how responsibility could reside in us without free will. Ability must be present if there is to be obligation, he argued. If I ought to do something, I can. Pelagius argued that the will, rather than being bound over to sin, is actually neutral—so that at any given moment or in any situation it is free to choose the good and do it.

In his approach, sin became only those deliberate and unrelated acts in which the will chooses to do evil, and any necessary connection between sins or any hereditary principle of sin within the race was forgotten. Pelagius further stated the following: first, the sin of Adam affected no one but himself; second, those who have been born since Adam have been born into the condition Adam possessed before his fall, that is, into a position of neutrality, so far as sin is concerned; and third, human beings are able to live free from sin if they desire to do so, and they can do so even without an awareness of the work of Christ and the supernatural working of the Holy Spirit.

Pelagius's position greatly limited the true scope of sin, and inevitably led to a denial of the absolute need for the unmerited grace of God in salvation. Moreover, according to Pelagius, even where the gospel of grace is freely preached to the sinner, what ultimately determines whether he or she will be saved is not the supernatural working of the Holy Spirit within, but the person's will, which either receives or rejects the Savior.

Early in his life, Augustine had thought along similar lines. But he had come to see that the view did not do justice either to the biblical doctrine of sin, always portrayed as far more than mere individual and isolated acts, or to the grace of God, ultimately the only fully determining element in salvation. Augustine argued that there is an inherited depravity, as the result of which it is simply not possible for the individual to stop sinning. His key phrase was *non posse non peccare*. It means that a person is not able to choose God. Augustine said that humankind, having used its free will badly in the fall, lost both itself and his its. He said that the will has been so enslaved that it can have no power for righteousness. He said that the will is indeed free—of righteousness—but enslaved to sin. He said that the will is free to turn from God, but not to come to him.

Augustine was concerned to stress that grace is an absolute necessity; apart from it no one can be saved. Moreover, it is a matter of grace from beginning to end, not just of "prevenient" grace, or partial grace to which the sinner adds his own efforts. Otherwise, salvation would not be entirely of God, God's honor would be diminished, and people would have room for boasting in heaven. In defending such views Augustine won the day, and the church supported him. But the church increasingly drifted back toward Pelagianism during the Middle Ages.

Later, at the time of the Reformation, the same battle erupted again on several fronts. One direct confrontation was the exchange between Erasmus and Luther. Erasmus had been sympathetic to the Reformation in its early stages, for he saw the corruptions of the medieval church and longed for their correction. But Erasmus, without Luther's deep spiritual undergirdings, was eventually prevailed on to challenge him. Erasmus said that the will must be free, for reasons much like those given by Pelagius. It was not a subject for which Erasmus had great interest, however, so he counseled moderation, even though he opposed Luther.

It was no small matter to Luther. Luther plunged into the subject zealously, viewing it as an issue on which the very truth of God depended. Luther, of course, did acknowledge the psychological fact that men and women make choices. That is so obvious that no one can really deny it. But in the specific area of an individual's choice of God or failure to choose God, Luther denied the freedom of the will as much as Erasmus affirmed it. We are wholly given over to sin, said Luther. Therefore, our only proper role is humbly to acknowledge that sin, confess our blindness, and acknowledge that we can no more choose God by our enslaved wills than we can please him by our sullied moral acts. Our sole role is to admit our sin and call on the eternal God for mercy, knowing even as we seek to do so that we cannot do it unless God is first of all active in us to convict us of sin and lead our wills to embrace the Lord Jesus Christ for salvation.

John Calvin, Ulrich Zwingli, Martin Bucer, and all the other leading Protestant Reformers were one with Luther in these convictions. In reaction to the Reformation, however, the Roman Catholic Church at the Council of Trent took a semi-Pelagian position, in which the human will cooperates with unmerited divine assistance in believing. Later, in Holland, Jacob Arminius and the more radical Remonstrant Arminians revived the concerns of Pelagius in different forms. Today, probably the majority of Christians from all denominations and many theological traditions are Pelagian, though they would not recognize their beliefs by that word. Are they right? Or are Augustine and the leaders of the Reformation right? Is humanity totally ruined by its fall into sin? Or did it fall only part way?

EDWARDS'S "FREEDOM OF THE WILL"

Before we answer those questions directly, it is important to look at one other theological contribution to this debate, perhaps the most significant of all. It is that of the American theologian and preacher Jonathan Edwards. So far as his main thrust was concerned, Edwards wanted to say the same things as Augustine, Luther, and Calvin. But it is an interesting feature of his treatise that it does not have the title of Martin Luther's great study, *The Bondage of the Will*, but rather what seems to be at a first glance the exact opposite: "The Freedom of the Will."[3]

---

[3]Jonathan Edwards, "A Careful and Strict Inquiry into the Prevailing Notions of the Freedom of the Will," in *The Works of Jonathan Edwards*, vol. 1, revised by Edward Hickman with a memoir by Sereno E. Dwight (Edinburgh: Banner of Truth Trust, 1976), 3-93.

That requires some explanation. It is to be found in Edwards's unique contributions to the subject. The first significant thing Edwards did was to define the will, which nobody had done previously. Everybody had operated on the assumption that we all know what the will is. We call the will that thing in us that makes choices. Edwards defined the will as "that by which *the mind* chooses any thing." In other words, what we choose is determined (according to Edwards) not by the will itself but by the mind. Our choices are determined by what we think is the most desirable course of action.

Edwards's second contribution concerned "motives." He asked, why is it that the mind chooses any one thing and not another? He answered that "the mind chooses as it does because of motives." That is, the mind chooses what it thinks is best. Edwards makes this point over many pages, and it is hard to condense his arguments. But I can make his point quickly by quoting from a small primer on free will by John Gerstner. Gerstner addresses the reader:

> Your choices, as a rational person, are always based on various considerations or motives that are before you at the time. Those motives have a certain weight with you, and the motives for and against reading a book [for example] are weighed in the balance of your mind; the motives which outweigh all others are what you, indeed, choose to follow. You, being a rational person, will always choose what seems to you to be the right thing, the wise thing, the advisable thing to do. If you choose not to do the right thing, the advisable thing, the thing that you are inclined to do, you would, of course, be insane. You would be choosing something which you didn't choose. You would find something preferable which you didn't prefer. But you, being a rational and sane person, choose something because it seems to you the right, proper, good, advantageous thing to do.[4]

I can put the matter negatively. Suppose that when you are confronted by a certain choice no motive whatever enters into the choice. It would then follow, would it not, that the choice would be impossible for you and a decision would not be made? Suppose there is a donkey standing in the middle of the room. To the right of the donkey there is a bunch of carrots precisely matched (in the mind of the donkey) with a bunch of carrots placed on the left. How can the donkey choose between those bunches? If one bunch of carrots is exactly the same as the other and no motives whatever for choosing one rather than the other enter into the picture, what is going to happen to the donkey? The donkey is going

---

[4]John H. Gerstner, *A Primer on Free Will* (Phillipsburg, NJ: Presbyterian and Reformed Publishing Company, 1982), 4-5.

to starve standing between the two bunches of carrots! There is nothing to incline it one way or the other. So if it does go one way or the other, it is because for some reason (unknown to us but certainly clear in the mind of the donkey), one choice or the other is preferable. When you and I make a choice it is on that same basis. For whatever reason, one thing seems good to us, and because it seems good it is the thing we choose.

The third thing Edwards dealt with was the matter of responsibility, the issue that had troubled Pelagius so profoundly. What Edwards did here, and did very wisely, was to distinguish between what he called "natural" and what he called "moral" inability. Let me give three illustrations of this distinction; first, my own; second, one from the writings of Arthur W. Pink; and third, one from Edwards himself.

In the animal world there are animals that eat nothing but meat: carnivores. There are other animals that eat nothing but grass or plants: herbivores. Imagine then that we have a lion, who is a carnivore, and place a beautiful bundle of hay or a trough of oats before him. It will not eat the hay or the oats. Why not? Is it because it is physically unable? No. Physically, it could easily begin to munch on this food and swallow it. Then why does it not eat it? The answer is that it is not in its nature to do so. Moreover, if it were possible to ask the lion why it will not eat the herbivore's meal, and if it could answer, it would say, "I can't eat this food; I hate it; I will eat nothing but meat." We are speaking in a similar way when we say that the natural person cannot respond to or choose God in salvation. Physically the person is able, but spiritually they are not. The natural person cannot come because they will not come. They will not because they really hate God.

Arthur W. Pink turns to Scripture to illustrate the distinction. In 1 Kings 14:4 ("Now Ahijah could not see, for his eyes were dim because of his age") and Jonah 1:13 ("The men rowed hard to get back to dry land, but they could not, for the sea grew more and more tempestuous"), it is natural inability that is in view. No guilt is attached to it. On the other hand, in Genesis 37:4 we read, "When his brothers saw that their father loved him [Joseph] more than all his brothers, they hated him and could not speak peacefully to him." This is a spiritual or moral inability. For this they were guilty, which the passage indicates by explaining their inability to speak kindly to Joseph by their hatred of him.[5]

---

[5]Arthur W. Pink, *The Sovereignty of God* (Grand Rapids: Baker Book House, 1969), 187-88.

Now I come to Edwards's illustration. He is talking about Arminians who claim that the Calvinistic position is unreasonable. No, he says, they are the unreasonable ones.

> Let common sense determine whether there be not a great difference between these two cases: the one, that of a man who has offended his prince, and is cast into prison; and after he has lain there a while, the king comes to him, calls him to come forth; and tells him, that if he will do so, and will fall down before him and humbly beg his pardon, he shall be forgiven, and set at liberty, and also be greatly enriched, and advanced to honour: the prisoner heartily repents of the folly and wickedness of his offence against his prince, is thoroughly disposed to abase himself, and accept of the king's offer; but is confined by strong walls, with gates of brass, and bars of iron. The other case is, that of a man who is of a very unreasonable spirit, of a haughty, ungrateful, willful disposition; and moreover, has been brought up in traitorous principles; and has his heart possessed with an extreme and inveterate enmity to his lawful sovereign; and for his rebellion is cast into prison, and lies long there, loaded with heavy chains, and in miserable circumstances. At length the compassionate prince comes to the prison, orders his chains to be knocked off, and his prison doors to be set wide open; calls to him and tells him, if he will come forth to him, and fall down before him, acknowledge that he has treated him unworthily, and ask his forgiveness; he shall be forgiven, set at liberty, and set in a place of great dignity and profit in his court. But he is so stout, and full of haughty malignity, that he cannot be willing to accept the offer; his rooted strong pride and malice have perfect power over him, and as it were bind him, by binding his heart: the opposition of his heart has the mastery over him, having an influence on his mind far superior to the king's grace and condescension, and to all his kind offers and promises. Now, is it agreeable to common sense, to assert and stand to it, that there is no difference between these two cases, as to any worthiness of blame in the prisoners?[6]

When we read an illustration like that, our first instinct is to claim that while the doctrine of depravity may be true in that particular example, it is not true of us because, so we say, we are not that haughty or prideful or set against the majesty of God. But, of course, that is precisely what the Bible tells us we are like. We are so set against God that when the offer of the gospel is presented to us, we do not receive it—not because in a natural sense we cannot receive it—but because the motives that operate in us are hostile to God.

---

[6]Edwards, "The Freedom of the Will," 66.

As we judge the matter, coming to a God like the one presented in the Bible is the very thing we do not want to do. That God is a sovereign God; if we come to him, we must acknowledge his sovereignty over our lives. We do not want to do that. Coming to a God like the one presented in the Bible means coming to one who is holy; if we come to a holy God, we must acknowledge his holiness and confess our sin. We do not want to do that either. Again, if we come to God, we must admit his omniscience, and we do not want to do that. If we would come to God, we must acknowledge his immutability, because any God worthy of the name does not change in any of his attributes. God is sovereign, and he will always be sovereign. God is holy, and he will always be holy. God is omniscient, and he will always be omniscient. That is the very God we do not want. So we will not come. Indeed, we cannot come until God by grace does what can only properly be described as a miracle in our sinful lives.

Someone who does not hold to Reformed doctrine might say, "But surely the Bible teaches that anyone who will come to Christ may come to him? Jesus himself said that if we come he will not cast us out." The answer is that, of course, this is true. But it is not the point. Certainly, anyone who wills may come. It is this that makes our refusal to come so unreasonable and increases our guilt. But who wills to come? The answer is no one, except those in whom the Holy Spirit has already performed the entirely irresistible work of the new birth so that, as the result of this miracle, the spiritually blind eyes of the natural self are opened to see God's truth and the totally depraved mind of the sinner is renewed to embrace Jesus Christ as Savior.

NO NEW DOCTRINE

Is this new teaching? Not at all. It is merely the purest and most basic form of that doctrine of humanity embraced by most Protestants and even (privately) by some Catholics. The Thirty-Nine Articles of the Church of England say,

> The condition of man after the fall of Adam is such, that he cannot turn and prepare himself by his own natural strength and good works to faith, and calling upon God; wherefore we have no power to do good works, pleasant and acceptable to God, without the grace of God by Christ preventing us [that is, being with us beforehand to motivate us], that we may have a good will, and working with us when we have that will. (Article 10)

The Westminster Larger Catechism declares, "The sinfulness of that state whereinto man fell, consisteth in the guilt of Adam's first sin, the wont of that righteousness wherein he was created, and the corruption of his nature, whereby he is utterly indisposed, disabled, and made opposite to all that is spiritually good, and wholly inclined to all evil, and that continually" (Answer to Question 25).

An understanding of the will's bondage is important for every person, for it is only in such understanding that sinful human beings learn how desperate their situation is and how absolutely essential is God's grace. If we are hanging onto some confidence in our own spiritual ability, no matter how small, then we will never worry seriously about our condition. We may know that we need to believe in Jesus Christ as our Savior, but there will be no sense of urgency. Life is long. There will be time to believe later. We can bring ourselves to believe when we want to, perhaps on our deathbed after we have done what we wish with our lives. At least we can take a chance on that possibility. On the other hand, if we are truly dead in our sin, as the Bible indicates, and if that involves our will as well as all other parts of our physical and psychological make-up, then we will find ourselves in despair. We will see our state as hopeless apart from the supernatural and totally unmerited workings of the grace of God.

That is what God requires if we would be saved from our sin and come to him. He will not have us boasting even of the smallest human contribution in the matter of salvation. But if we will renounce all thoughts of such ability, he will show us the way of salvation through Christ and lead us to him.

PART II

LAW AND GRACE

Now we know that whatever the law says it speaks to those who are under the law, so that every mouth may be stopped, and the whole world may be held accountable to God. For by works of the law no human being will be justified in his sight, since through the law comes knowledge of sin.

ROMANS 3:19-20

And one of them, a lawyer, asked him a question, to test him. "Teacher, which is the great commandment in the Law?" And he said to him, "You shall love the Lord your God with all your heart and with all your soul and with all your mind. This is the great and first commandment. And a second is like it: You shall love your neighbor as yourself."

MATTHEW 22:35-39

For the wrath of God is revealed from heaven against all ungodliness and unrighteousness of men, who by their unrighteousness suppress the truth.

ROMANS 1:18

The LORD God said to the serpent, "Because you have done this, cursed are you above all livestock, and above all beasts of the field; on your belly you shall go, and dust you shall eat all the days of your life. I will put enmity between you and the woman, and between your offspring and her offspring; he shall bruise your head, and you shall bruise his heel.

GENESIS 3:14-15

CHAPTER 4

THE PURPOSE OF GOD'S LAW

*I*t is one thing to state a doctrine, quite another to be convinced by it and to change one's life accordingly. That is true for any biblical teaching, but particularly true for the doctrine of the fall and human sin. Those are unpalatable teachings that we do not readily accept. Therefore, God seems to go to great lengths to convince us of them.

The primary means by which God reveals sin to be sin and the sinner to be a sinner is the law of God contained in the Scriptures, and that revelation is the primary purpose of the law. A typical view of the law is that its purpose is to teach us how to be good. That is not the Bible's emphasis. It is true that the law does instruct the wicked in order to restrain evil, and it instructs even believers as one expression of the will and character of God by which they may be urged on in living the Christian life. But its main purpose is to convince us that we are sinners and that we need a Savior. It is to point us to him.

Someone has said that we are sinners in God's sight in three ways. We are sinners by birth (we inherit sin and its guilt from Adam), by choice (we willingly recapitulate our forefathers' sin), and by divine verdict. It is by the law that the decree is passed against us. The law is God's standard before which we all fall short. Thus we are either condemned by it or are driven to the Savior.

DEFINING THE LAW

What is God's law? That question is not so easy to answer as we might at first suppose. The concept of law is complex and difficult to grasp. We get a sense of the problem even from our English dictionaries. For example, the comprehensive *Oxford English Dictionary* lists twenty-three definitions of the word *law*. The more limited *Webster's New Collegiate Dictionary* lists nine meanings, plus a lengthy paragraph of synonyms. Under biblical meanings it suggests, "The Jewish or Mosaic law contained in the Hexateuch (Pentateuch and Joshua) and in Ezekiel 40–48" and, in Christian usage, "the Old Testament."

The biblical meaning is what concerns us in this study, but even so the matter is not simple. There is variety both in Old Testament usage and in distinctly New Testament ideas. In the Old Testament, the simplest and most limited use of the word *law* is for the "book of the law," to be identified either as the book of Deuteronomy or, more specifically, as the Decalogue or Ten Commandments that form the heart of that book. That law is said to have been written on a stone memorial set up in Israel after the people had passed over the Jordan River at the beginning of their conquest (Deut 27:2-3) and to have been kept within the ark of the covenant within the tabernacle. Later the word referred in a broader sense to the first five books of the Old Testament, the Pentateuch, also called the Torah. That would be the meaning of *law* in the historical books in which the earlier written law is referred to (compare 1 Chron 16:40; 22:12). Evidently the concept broadened continually. The phrase "the law and the prophets," which appears frequently in the New Testament but which was in use before that time, suggests that the law is the whole of the Old Testament with the exception of the prophetic books. In fact, in the Psalms the word seems to go beyond even that to denote the divine revelation in general (Ps 1:2; 19:7-9; 94:12).[1]

In the uniquely New Testament references, particularly in the writings of Paul, those four Old Testament meanings are both broadened and narrowed. Thus on the one hand, *law* can refer merely to a single statute of the law, as in Romans 7:3—"But if her husband dies, she is free from that law." On the other hand, it can refer to a principle of law so broad that even the Gentiles can be conscious of it. Thus, "When Gentiles, who have not the law, by nature do what the law requires, they are a law to themselves, even though they do not have the

---

[1]Compare the article on *nomos* ("law") in the *Theological Dictionary of the New Testament*, ed. Gerhard Kittel and trans. Geoffrey W. Bromiley, vol. 4 (Grand Rapids: Eerdmans, 1967), 1022-85, particularly 1044-46.

law" (Rom 2:14). In Paul's polemic writings *law* can even refer to the law principle by which no one can be justified (Gal 2:15-16; 3:2, 5).

What does it mean that we have such a variety of definition in the Bible's use of the word *law*? If the various definitions were inherently contradictory, it could mean that the Bible provides no universally accepted definition of what the law is. But there is no contradiction. Rather, careful study reveals that each writer is aware of an important and formative concept of divine law in the broadest sense, a concept out of which all lesser definitions come and that gives the specific definitions meaning. In other words, the important idea is that *law* is an expression of the character of God and is therefore a unity, as he is a unity, despite the various particular expressions of law. This understanding of the biblical outlook is supported by the fact that *law* is never used of the oral Torah or of any other form of merely human traditions.

RESTRAINING EVIL

Why was the written law given? Already we have suggested two answers to that question, namely, to convict us of sin and to point us to the Lord Jesus Christ as Savior. We need to look at these more closely.

It might be thought at first glance that the law of the Old Testament has no relationship at all to those who are not God's elect people. We might argue that the law was given to Israel, not to all nations generally. That would be a mistake for two reasons. First, it would overlook the fact that not all within Israel were saved; it was always a matter of the remnant rather than the people as a whole. Yet whether saved or not, they were under what was to them at least a civil law, which prohibited certain things and affixed certain penalties. Second, it would overlook the similarity between the law of Israel and the best laws of the ancient Gentile nations. The similarity indicates that although the Old Testament law is the purest expression of the holy character of God, nevertheless God's character also has been expressed in the general moral consciousness (though in a debased form). Thus there is something like a universal awareness of moral law and a sense of need for it. So there is some value to the law for non-Christians, apart from the working of the Spirit by which they are brought to repentance from sin and to faith in Christ.

In that respect the purpose of the law is *to restrain evil*. As Calvin says, one "function of the law is . . . by fear of punishment to restrain certain men who are untouched by any care for what is just and right unless compelled by hearing the dire threats in the law," adding that "this constrained and forced righteousness is necessary for the public community of men, for whose tranquility the Lord herein provided when he took care that everything be not tumultuously confounded."[2] Paul seems to be talking about this function of law in writing to Timothy: "Understanding this, that the law is not laid down for the just but for the lawless and disobedient, for the ungodly and sinners, for the unholy and profane, for those who strike their fathers and mothers, for murderers, the sexually immoral, men who practice homosexuality, enslavers, liars, perjurers, and whatever else is contrary to sound doctrine" (1 Tim 1:9-10).

Those verses and others indicate that the law is something like a tether to restrain the otherwise wild and destructive ragings of our sinful nature. But if so, something else follows: the law is not the primary thing in God's revelation of himself to humanity. The law comes in because of sin, as Paul says (Rom 5:20; Gal 3:19). The law is good, for it is an expression of the character of God. But it is not the basis for the relationship between his creatures and himself that God desires. It is an interim thing. Thus there was a time when the written law was not given, and there will be a time when it will no longer need to function.

REVEALING EVIL

A second function of the law is *to reveal sin as sin* and the sinner as a sinner. The law is given to strip away the hypocrisy of the human heart, which constantly imagines that it is right before God, and to show its depravity. Paul writes, "If it had not been for the law, I would not have known sin. For I would not have known what it is to covet if the law had not said, 'You shall not covet'" (Rom 7:7). And "Sin . . . through the commandment [has] become sinful beyond measure" (Rom 7:13).

Brief summations of law occur throughout the Bible. A person asked Jesus which of all the commandments in the law was greatest. Jesus replied, "You shall love the Lord your God with all your heart and with all your soul and with all your mind" (Mt 22:37, a reference to Deut 6:5). He then added, "And a second is like it" You shall love your neighbor as yourself" (Mt 22:39, a reference to Lev 19:18). That summation of the law places it high above ceremonies or regulations and instead fixes it to a proper relationship between an individual and God, and between an individual and all other individuals. Both relationships are to be characterized by love. That is where our duty lies. But we do

---

[2]John Calvin, *Institutes of the Christian Religion*, ed. John T. McNeill, trans. Ford Lewis Battles, 2 vols. (Philadelphia: Westminster, 1960), 358-59.

not love God with all our heart and soul and mind, nor do we love our neighbor as ourselves.

The great summation of law in the Old Testament, the Decalogue, is contained in Exodus 20:1-17 and Deuteronomy 5:6-21. We will study those laws in detail in the next chapter, noting here only that no one has ever kept them perfectly. We may come to them intending to keep them. But if we are serious and really examine our hearts in the light of what we find in those laws, we are undone. Half of the Decalogue deals with our relationship to God, just as Christ's choice of the first commandment does. It tells us that we are to worship only him, that we are to have no idols (either physical or mental), that we are to keep his name holy, that we are to keep his sabbath. But we do not obey, nor did the Jews to whom that law was particularly and solemnly given. The second half of the Decalogue speaks of the relationship we should have to others, as Christ's choice of the second greatest commandment also does. It tells us that we are to honor our parents, refrain from killing, adultery, stealing, and lying, and that we are not even to wish for anything that belongs to another. But we do not behave that way. Consequently, the law exposes our sin and reduces us to helplessness before God.

The law's function in exposing sin was demonstrated historically at the time of the giving of the law. At the very moment when Moses was on Mount Sinai receiving the commandments, the people who were to receive them were down in the valley practicing the very things that God was forbidding. It was a poignant demonstration that God's righteousness cannot be achieved by human beings.

Some might object at this point that God's expecting us to live up to his standards of righteousness is unjust. Therefore, it might be argued, we should be talking not about the first and greatest commandment or the second commandment or even the first ten commandments, but rather something more like the Golden Rule: "So whatever you wish that others would do to you, do also to them" (Mt 7:12). Didn't Jesus himself say, "This is the Law and the Prophets"? In answer, we must say that if the intention of that objection is to whittle down God's standards, it is improper, impossible, and foolish. God has a right to the highest standards—in fact, no other standards are possible for him—and it is by those standards that we will be judged, whether we consider it just or not. But apart from that consideration, we answer that it does not really matter in one sense which standard we wish to be judged by; we are condemned by the Golden Rule as well, because we do not in fact do to others everything we wish they would do to us.

What about even lesser standards? What about the rock-bottom standard of "fair play"? Why not just treat the other person fairly? Do we do that? Do we always treat other persons by the same measure of fairness that we would apply if we were thinking of their relationship to us? To ask that question is to answer it. Everyone knows that they do not behave that way, at least not all the time. Consequently, we conclude that the law, in whatever form it appears, from the highest expressions to the lowest, exposes sin and brings its just condemnation on the sinner. The law is, in fact, a mirror, as Calvin notes, in which "we contemplate our weakness, then the iniquity arising from this, and finally the curse coming from both—just as a mirror shows us the spots on our face."[3]

Paul says, "Now we know that whatever the law says it speaks to those who are under the law, so that every mouth may be stopped, and the whole world may be held accountable to God. For by works of the law no human being will be justified in his sight, since through the law comes knowledge of sin" (Rom 3:19-20). The law has several functions, but the one thing it cannot do is make a woman or man righteous before God. Instead, it reveals us to be guilty.

THE GOSPEL IN THE LAW

Although the primary function of the law is to expose sin, it is not as if God gave it to bring himself delight when his rebellious creatures find themselves to be sinful and are repulsed by it. God does not rub his hands together and say, "Well, at least they know how sinful they are. I hope they like it." No, even in the disclosure of sin a further purpose is evident: that having discovered their sin, people might *turn to Christ* for cleansing from it. The mirror is provided so that having seen the dirt on their faces, people will turn from the mirror to the soap and water with which the dirt may be washed away.

The fault in that illustration is the suggestion that the law has nothing to say about the solution to the problem. Here the broadest of our earlier definitions of the law, the whole of the biblical revelation, must be brought in. The law in that sense includes not merely the prohibitions before which we are condemned, but also the promise of a perfect salvation. When God gave the law, he also gave instructions concerning the sacrifices. When God chose Moses as the lawgiver, he also chose Aaron to be the high priest. It is as though God, in the moment in which he thundered out in the Decalogue, "You shall not . . . ," also went on to say quietly, "But I know you will, and so this is the way to get out of it."

---

[3]Ibid., 355.

All the Old Testament sacrifices point in one way or another to the coming of the Lord Jesus Christ. But the meaning of Christ's sacrifice was made particularly clear in the instructions for the two sacrifices to be performed in Israel on the Day of Atonement. In the first sacrifice, a goat was driven away into the wilderness to die there. That goat was first brought to Aaron or to a priest who succeeded him. The priest placed his hands on the goat's head, thereby identifying himself and the people whom he represented with the goat. He confessed the sins of the people in prayer, thereby in a symbolic fashion transferring them to the goat. Then the goat was driven out into the wilderness. The description of that ceremony states, "The goat shall bear all their iniquities on itself" (Lev 16:22). The sacrifice points to Jesus, who, like that goat, "suffered outside the gate" in order to carry our iniquities away from us (compare Heb 13:12).

The other sacrifice was made in the courtyard of the temple, from which blood was then carried into the holy of holies to be sprinkled on the ark of the covenant. The place where the blood was to be put was symbolic, as was the whole ritual. It was called the mercy seat. Being on the lid of the ark, the mercy seat was between the stone tablets of the law of Moses (within the ark) and the space between the outstretched wings of the cherubim over the ark (symbolizing the place of God's dwelling).

Without the blood, the ark with its law and cherubim paints a terrible picture. There is the law, which we have broken. There is God, whom we have offended. Moreover, as God looks down, it is the law broken by us that he sees. It is a picture of judgment, of our hopelessness apart from grace. But then the sacrifice is performed, and the high priest enters the holy of holies and places the blood of the innocent victim on the mercy seat, which thus comes between God in his holiness and ourselves in our sin. There has been substitution. An innocent has died in the place of those who should have died, and the blood is proof. Wrath is averted. Now God looks in grace on the sinner.

Who is that sacrifice? He is Jesus. We cannot say how much those who lived before the time of Christ understood about salvation. Some, like the prophets, undoubtedly understood much. Others understood little. But whatever the level of understanding, the purpose of the law was plain. It was to reveal the sin and then to point to the coming of the Lord Jesus Christ as the Savior. Before God can give us the gospel, he must slay us with the law. But as he does so, he shows us that the law contains the gospel and points us to it.

CHAPTER 5

THE TEN COMMANDMENTS: LOVE OF GOD

*I*t is unrealistic, even wrong, to focus on the Ten Commandments as if they were the whole or even the most important part of the law. The law is a unity, and nothing in either the Old or New Testaments justifies the kind of isolating of the Decalogue that has taken place in some of the writings of the church. The Ten Commandments have assumed such great importance largely because of their value for catechetical instruction.

Still the Ten Commandments should be carefully discussed for several reasons. First, such a discussion brings the law down from the abstract position it often seems to have (perhaps even in the last chapter) to specific issues. For the law to fulfill its primary role in convicting us of sin, it must convict us of particular sins of which we each are guilty. To admit "I am a sinner" may mean little more than "I'm not perfect"—but it is quite another thing to admit "I am an idolater, a murderer, an adulterer, a thief, and so on." It is at that level that the law must be applied. Second, the Ten Commandments are of particular value because they are comprehensive. In most Protestant enumerations, the first four range over the area Christ covered by his "great and first commandment": "You shall love the Lord your God with all your heart and with all your soul and with all your mind" (Mt 22:37). The remaining six deal with the second area of responsibility: "You shall love your neighbor as yourself" (Mt 22:39). In medieval

Catholicism, followed by Luther, the list was arranged to give three commandments to the first category and seven to the second.

As we turn to the specific commandments of the Decalogue, we must not
forget their broader context. In fact, we must be careful to interpret each in light
of the full biblical revelation. The following guidelines apply:

1. *The commandments are not restricted to outward actions, but apply also to
   the dispositions of the mind and heart.* Human law concerns itself with
   outward actions alone, because human beings cannot see into the hearts
   of others. But God, who can see within, also deals with attitudes. In the
   Sermon on the Mount, Christ taught that the sixth commandment is
   concerned with anger and hate as well as with the act of murder
   (Mt 5:21-22), and that the seventh commandment is concerned with lust
   as well as with the act of adultery (Mt 5:27-30). The apostle John reflects
   this view in his first letter, arguing that "everyone who hates his brother
   is a murderer" (1 Jn 3:15).

2. *The commandments always contain more than a minimum interpretation of
   the words.* Thus the command to honor our father and mother could be
   interpreted as meaning only that we are to show them proper respect and
   not speak badly of them. But that would be too little, for Jesus himself
   taught that it includes our obligation to provide for them financially in
   their old age (Mt 15:3-6). In other words, the commandment refers to
   everything that could possibly be done for one's parents under the guidelines of Christ's second greatest commandment.

3. *A commandment expressed in positive language also involves the negative, and
   a negative commandment also involves the positive.* Thus, when we are told
   not to take the name of God in vain, we are to understand that the contrary
   duty, to reverence his name, is commanded (Deut 28:58; Ps 34:3; Mt 6:9).
   The commandment not to kill means not only am I not to kill or even
   hate my neighbor, but also that I am to do all I can for his or her betterment
   (Lev 19:18).

4. *The law is a whole in that each commandment is related to the others.* We
   cannot perform some of the duties enumerated in the commandments,
   thinking we are thereby relieved of performing others. "Whoever keeps
   the whole law but fails in one point has become guilty of all of it" (Jas 2:10;
   compare Deut 27:26).

THE FIRST COMMANDMENT: NO OTHER GODS

The first commandment begins where by now we should expect it to begin, in the area of our relationship to God. It is a demand for our exclusive and zealous worship. "I am the LORD your God, who brought you out of the land of Egypt, out of the house of slavery. You shall have no other gods before me" (Ex 20:2-3). To worship any god but the biblical Lord is to break this commandment. But to break it one need not worship a clearly defined god—Zeus, Minerva, a Roman emperor, or one of the countless modern idols. We break it whenever we give some person or some thing the first place in our affections, which belongs to God alone. Quite often, the substitute god is ourselves or our opinion of ourselves. It can be such things as success, material possessions, fame, or dominance over others.

How do we keep this commandment? John Stott writes,

> For us to keep this first commandment would be, as Jesus said, to love the Lord our God with all our heart and with all our soul and with all our mind (Mt 22:37); to see all things from his point of view and do nothing without reference to him; to make his will our guide and his glory our goal; to put him first in thought, word and deed; in business and leisure; in friendships and career; in the use of our money, time and talents; at work and at home. . . . No man has ever kept this commandment except Jesus of Nazareth.[1]

But why should we have no other gods? The answer is in the preface to the commandment, which also serves as a preface to the whole Decalogue. The answer is in two parts: first, because of who God is; second, because of what he has done.

Who the true God is, is expressed in the words, "I am the LORD your God." In Hebrew the words are *Yahweh Eloheka.* The reason we should obey these commandments is that the God who is speaking in the commandments is the true God, the God who is without a beginning and without an end. "I AM WHO I AM" (Ex 3:14). He is self-existent. No one created him, and he is therefore responsible to no one. He is self-sufficient. He needs no one, and therefore he does not depend on anyone for anything. Any god less than this is not God, and all so-called gods are less than this. It is because of who God is that he can demand such worship.

What God has done is indicated in the words "who brought you out of the land of Egypt, out of the house of slavery." In their primary frame of reference,

---

[1]John R. W. Stott, *Basic Christianity* (Grand Rapids: Eerdmans, 1958), 65.

the words apply exclusively to Israel, the nation delivered out of slavery in Egypt, and to whom these commandments were particularly given. Even if God were only a limited tribal god, the Israelites would owe him reverence for their deliverance. But the literal reference does not exhaust the statement. It applies to anyone who has experienced deliverance, whether from death or slavery or poverty or disease. There is no one who has not been blessed by God in some area, even though one may be unaware of it and not acknowledge God as the source. In addition, the deliverance applies to spiritual as well as material matters. Israel's deliverance was not merely physical, but included deliverance from Egyptian idolatry as well, a deliverance from false gods. Similarly, Abraham's call to leave Ur was a call to serve the Lord rather than the unworthy gods of Mesopotamia (Josh 24:2-3, 14).

From such a perspective, the reasoning behind the first commandment applies to every human being. All have experienced the Lord's deliverance. All have benefited from the progressive advance of truth over superstition through the revelation conveyed to the world through Judaism and Christianity. But do we worship God wholly and exclusively as a result? No, we do not. Consequently, the first commandment virtually shouts to us that we are ungrateful, disobedient, rebellious, and ruled by sin.

THE SECOND COMMANDMENT: NO GRAVEN IMAGE

The first commandment deals with the object of our worship, forbidding the worship of any false god. The second commandment deals with the manner of our worship, forbidding us to worship even the true God unworthily. It is a demand for spiritual worship.

> You shall not make for yourself a carved image, or any likeness of anything that is in heaven above, or that is in the earth beneath, or that is in the water under the earth. You shall not bow down to them or serve them, for I the LORD your God am a jealous God, visiting the iniquity of the fathers on the children to the third and the fourth generation of those who hate me, but showing steadfast love to thousands of those who love me and keep my commandments. (Ex 20:4-6)

If this commandment is looked at apart from the first commandment, it seems to be merely forbidding the worship of idols. But when the first commandment is taken with it, such an interpretation is seen to be inadequate; it would be merely a repetition of the first in different words. We have already outlined the progression: first God forbids the worship of all other gods; then he forbids the worship even of himself by images.

The worship of God by images or the lesser use of images as an enhancement of worship does not seem so serious. We might argue that worship is a pragmatic question as much as a theological one. What is wrong with using images in worship if they are helpful? Some people claim that images help to focus their attention. But even if they are wrong in this, what damage can it do? The puzzle becomes greater when we note the severe warning attached to this commandment. "For I the LORD your God am a jealous God, visiting the iniquity of the fathers on the children to the third and the fourth generation of those who hate me." Why is this so serious?

There are two answers to that question. The first is simply that *images dishonor God*, as J. I. Packer points out.[2] They dishonor God because they obscure God's glory. That is not what the worshiper thinks, of course—he or she thinks that the image represents some valuable aspect of God's glory—but nothing material can adequately represent God's attributes.

We have an example in the book of Exodus. Not long after Moses had gone up on Mount Sinai to receive the law, the Israelites who were waiting below grew restless and asked Aaron, Moses' brother, to make an idol for them. They argued that they did not know what had become of Moses and they needed a god to go before them on their journey. Aaron complied, taking their gold and silver to make a calf, probably a miniature version of the bull gods worshiped in Egypt. The interesting thing about Aaron's attitude, however, is that he at least did not consider the calf to represent another god. Rather, he saw it as the Lord in visible form, as is clear from the wording of the account. He identified the idol with the God who had brought the people out of Egypt (Ex 32:4) and announced its dedication with the words, "Tomorrow shall be a feast to the LORD" (Ex 32:5). Aaron would probably have said that the choice of a calf (or bull) was to suggest the great strength of the Lord. But that is precisely what was wrong. A calf, even a great bull, could not possibly have represented the Lord's true strength. The Israelites were really lowering their truly great God to the category of the impotent bull gods of Egypt.

One point of the plagues on Egypt had been to show God's superiority over all the gods of Egypt. By turning the water of the Nile to blood, God showed his power over the Nile gods Osiris, Hapimon, and Tauret. By producing an

---

[2]J. I. Packer, *Knowing God* (Downers Grove, IL: InterVarsity Press, 1973), 40.

overabundance of frogs, God showed his power over the goddess Hekt, who was always pictured with the head and body of a frog. The judgments on the land showed God's power over Geb, the earth god. And so on throughout all the plagues, right up to the judgment against the sun god Ra, when the sun was blotted out by darkness, and the judgment against the firstborn of all Egypt, including Pharaoh's firstborn, who was to be the next "supreme god." Israel's God was not to be placed in such a category, but that is what Aaron did by making a representation of him.

The second reason why we are forbidden to worship even the true God by images is that *images mislead the worshiper*, as Packer also comments. Thus, in the example of Aaron's calf, the result of the "feast" was hardly the kind of holy Sabbath God was describing to Moses on Mount Sinai at the time. It became an orgy in which most, if not all, of the other commandments were also violated.[3]

The positive side of the second commandment is important. If the worship of God by unworthy means is forbidden, we should take the utmost care to discover what he is truly like, and thus increasingly worship him as the only great, transcendent, spiritual, and inscrutable God of the universe. Do we worship him that way? We do not. Rather than seeking him out, striving to know him and to worship him properly, we still turn from him to make gods of our own devising. Paul says, "For although they knew God, they did not honor him as God or give thanks to him, but they became futile in their thinking, and their foolish hearts were darkened. Claiming to be wise, they became fools, and exchanged the glory of the immortal God for images resembling mortal man and birds and animals and creeping things" (Rom 1:21-23).

That is the reason for the terrible warning that closes the second commandment. God is not jealous in the way we define jealousy and thus piqued when we disregard him. Rather our disregard is such base ingratitude, vanity, and sin, that it merits God's judgment. At the same time, as he speaks of judgment, God also speaks of having mercy on the many generations of those who love him and keep his commandments.

THE THIRD COMMANDMENT: KEEP MY NAME HOLY

"You shall not take the name of the LORD your God in vain, for the LORD will not hold him guiltless who takes his name in vain" (Ex 20:7). The third commandment

---

[3]Ibid., 41. See this volume, ch. 9, "No Other Gods."

is to be taken with the sentence in the Lord's Prayer in which Jesus admonished his disciples to pray, "Hallowed be your name" (Mt 6:9). That petition adds a positive dimension to the negative cast of the Old Testament commandment. The name of God represents the nature of God. Consequently, to dishonor that name is to dishonor God, and hallowing the name means honoring him. Since the various names of God represent his many praiseworthy attributes, we hallow his name when we honor some aspect of his character. Calvin says,

> We must, in my opinion, diligently observe the three following points: first, whatever our mind conceives of God, whatever our tongue utters, should savor of his excellence, match the loftiness of his sacred name, and lastly, serve to glorify his greatness. Secondly, we should not rashly or perversely abuse his Holy Word and worship mysteries either for the sake of our own ambition, or greed, or amusement; but, as they bear the dignity of his name imprinted upon them, they should ever be honored and prized among us. Finally, we should not defame or detract from his works, as miserable men are wont abusively to cry out against him; but whatever we recognize as done by him we should speak of with praise of his wisdom, righteousness, and goodness. That is what it means to hallow God's name.[4]

The various names of God have specific meanings. *Elohim* is his most common biblical name. *Elohim* acknowledges God to be the Creator of all that is. It is the name used in the opening verse of the Bible: "In the beginning, God created the heavens and the earth" (Gen 1:1). *Elohim* formed the sun, moon, and planets. He formed the earth, covering it with plants, fish, and animals. He made men and women. He made you. Do you honor him as your Creator? If not, you dishonor his name and break the third commandment.

Another name of God is *El Elyon*, which means "God the Most High." It occurs first in the account of Abraham's meeting with Melchizedek after his battle with the kings of the plains and his rescue of Lot. Melchizedek was "priest of God Most High" (Gen 14:18). *El Elyon* also occurs in Isaiah's description of the rebellion of Satan: "I will make myself like the Most High" (Is 14:14). This name emphasizes God's rule and sovereignty. Do you honor him as the sovereign God? Not if you complain about circumstances or doubt his ability to care for you and keep his promises.

Yahweh means "I AM THAT I AM." It speaks of God's self-existence, self-sufficiency, and eternity; it is also characteristically used in God's revelations of

---

[4]John Calvin, *Institutes of the Christian Religion*, ed. John T. McNeill, trans. Ford Lewis Battles, 2 vols. (Philadelphia: Westminster, 1960), 388.

himself as redeemer, for example, to Moses before God's deliverance of the people of Israel from Egypt. Do we honor him as our redeemer? Do we praise him for the fullness of his redemption in Jesus Christ?

All God's names reveal something about him, and he should be honored by us in regard to all of them. We have looked at the names *Elohim, El Elyon*, and *Yahweh* particularly. But he is also *Yahweh Jireh*, the God who provides. He is the Lord of hosts. He is the Father, Son, and Holy Spirit. He is the Alpha and Omega. He is the Ancient of Days, seated on the throne of heaven. He is our Wonderful Counselor, the Mighty God, the Everlasting Father, the Prince of Peace. He is our rock and our high tower into which we run and are safe. He is the way, the truth, and the life. He is the light of the world. He is the bread of life. He is the resurrection and the life. He is the good shepherd, the great shepherd, the chief shepherd. He is the God of Abraham, Isaac, and Jacob. He is the God of Joseph, Moses, David. He is the God of Deborah, Hannah, Esther. He is the God of the New Testament writers and of all the apostles. He is the Lord of lords and King of kings. If we do not honor him in respect to these names, we dishonor him and break his commandment.

Moreover, our actions matter as much as our words. Whenever our conduct is inconsistent with our profession of Christian faith, even if it is a thoroughly orthodox profession, we dishonor God. Those who belong to God have taken his name, so to speak, and must hallow it by their actions. If they "commit adultery" with the world, they transgress against his great love; they dishonor the name Christian (which means "a Christ one"). Such dishonor is worse than the ravings of the ungodly.

THE FOURTH COMMANDMENT: KEEP MY DAY HOLY

At no point in their handling of the Old Testament law have Christians had more difficulty than in their interpretation of the fourth commandment. The fourth commandment prescribes the seventh day of the week, Saturday, as a day of Sabbath rest, but the great majority of Christians do not observe it. Instead, as everyone knows, they worship on Sunday. What is more, they do not even observe Sunday according to the rules given for the Sabbath. Is that right? Can Sunday observance be justified?

What cannot be done is to treat the matter lightly. Of all the commandments, this one dealing with the Sabbath is the longest and perhaps the most solemn. It says,

Remember the Sabbath day, to keep it holy. Six days you shall labor, and do all your work, but the seventh day is a Sabbath to the LORD your God. On it you shall not do any work, you, or your son, or your daughter, your male servant, or your female servant, or your livestock, or the sojourner who is within your gates. For in six days the LORD made heaven and earth, the sea, and all that is in them, and rested on the seventh day. Therefore the LORD blessed the Sabbath day and made it holy. (Ex 20:8-11)

In general there have been three approaches to the sabbath-Sunday question. First, it has been taught by some that Christians should worship on Saturday. This is the view of the Seventh-Day Adventists, for example, and of others also. Second, there is the view that Sunday is merely the New Testament equivalent of the Old Testament Sabbath and is to be observed in a similar way. The Westminster Confession of Faith calls the Lord's Day "the Christian sabbath," adding that "this sabbath is then kept holy unto the Lord, when men, after a due preparing of their hearts, and ordering of their common affairs beforehand, do not only observe an holy rest all the day from their own works, words, and thoughts, about their worldly enjoyments and rec-reations; but also are taken up the whole time in the public and private exercises of his worship, and in the duties of necessity and mercy" (XXI, 7, 8). Later, reformed and Puritan theology strongly upheld this position. Third, there is the view that the Sabbath has been abolished by the death and resur-rection of Christ and that a new day, the Lord's Day, which has its own characteristics, has replaced it. That was the view of John Calvin, who said clearly that "the day sacred to the Jews was set aside" and that "another was appointed" for it.[5]

What is the solution? We are helped by noting several important things. First, the Sabbath was a uniquely Jewish institution and was neither given to nor fully observed by any other race or nation, either ancient or modern. This is not true of the other commandments; they are generally paralleled in other ancient law codes. Sabbatarians generally appeal to Genesis 2:2-3 (referred to in the fourth commandment) as showing the contrary. Those verses say, "And on the seventh day God finished his work that he had done, and he rested on the seventh day from all his work that he had done. So God blessed the seventh day and made it holy, because on it God rested from all his work that he had done in creation." Strictly speaking, however, those verses do not say that God instituted the Sabbath

---

[5]Ibid., 399.

at the time of creation; indeed, there are other verses that seem to teach that he did it later.

Two such verses are Nehemiah 9:13-14. Nehemiah, who had been instrumental in furthering a great revival among the Jews who had returned to Jerusalem after the captivity in Babylon, had arranged a special service of worship and rededication. In that service the priests led the people in their worship, saying in relation to God, "You came down on Mount Sinai and spoke with them from heaven and gave them right rules and true laws, good statutes and commandments, and you made known to them your holy Sabbath and commanded them commandments and statutes and a law by Moses your servant." Those verses link the giving of the law concerning the Sabbath to Mount Sinai and imply that the Sabbath was not known or observed before that time.

Another important passage is in Exodus.

> And the LORD said to Moses, "You are to speak to the people of Israel and say, 'Above all you shall keep my Sabbaths, for this is a sign between me and you throughout your generations, that you may know that I, the LORD, sanctify you. You shall keep the Sabbath, because it is holy for you. Everyone who profanes it shall be put to death. Whoever does any work on it, that soul shall be cut off from among his people. Six days shall work be done, but the seventh day is a Sabbath of solemn rest, holy to the LORD. Whoever does any work on the Sabbath day shall be put to death. Therefore the people of Israel shall keep the Sabbath, observing the Sabbath throughout their generations, as a covenant forever. It is a sign forever between me and the people of Israel that in six days the LORD made heaven and earth, and on the seventh day he rested and was refreshed.'" (Ex 31:12-17)

Those verses portray the Sabbath as a covenant sign between God and Israel; that is important, for it is repeated twice. It is hard to see, therefore, how the observance of the Sabbath can legitimately be said to be applied to other nations. On the contrary, it was the observance of the Sabbath that was to distinguish Israel from the nations, much as circumcision also set them apart.

But what about Sunday? Sunday is another day established by God, but for the church rather than for Israel, and with quite different characteristics. The Sabbath was a time of rest and inactivity. In fact, failure to rest had strict penalties attached to it. By contrast, the Christian Sunday is a day of joy, activity, and expectation, the character of which is set by the events of the first Lord's Day, on which Christ arose. The Lord regathered the disciples, taught them, imparted the Holy Spirit (Jn 20:22), and commissioned his own to world evangelism. The fact that Sunday was established and the Sabbath abolished is seen in the speed and totality with which Sunday replaced the Sabbath in the worship of the early church. In the Old Testament the word *sabbath* is mentioned frequently. In Acts, by contrast, the word is found only nine times, and not once is it said to be a day observed by Christians. The first chapter speaks of it in the phrase "a Sabbath day's journey" (Acts 1:12). In chapter 13 it occurs four times in describing how Paul used the Sabbath day for his evangelistic ends, going into the synagogue to preach to the Jews who were assembled there (Acts 13:14, 27, 42, 44). Later chapters give a few more similar references (Acts 15:21; 17:2; 18:4). Nowhere is it suggested that the church met on the Sabbath day or even regarded it with any special affection or attention.

However, we must not think that the fourth commandment or the Christian celebration of the Lord's Day has nothing to say about human sin or our need of a Savior. The Sabbath was a day of remembrance of God as Creator and deliverer of his people. The Christian Sunday is a day of celebration of Christ's resurrection. But do we observe either naturally? Does the human heart naturally set aside time, any time, to worship and serve God and to rejoice in his manifold favors? It does not. It is neither responsive nor grateful. Consequently, we stand condemned by this area of the law also.

CHAPTER 6

THE TEN COMMANDMENTS: LOVE OF OTHERS

*A*t one point in his writings, the great Puritan divine, Thomas Watson, compares the Ten Commandments of Exodus 20 to Jacob's ladder. "The first table respects God," he says, "and is the top of the ladder that reaches to heaven; the second respects superiors and inferiors, and is the foot of the ladder that rests on the earth. By the first table we walk religiously towards God; by the second, we walk religiously towards man. He cannot be good in the first table that is bad in the second."[1] The truth of Watson's last sentence should be evident. Just as we cannot know ourselves or others adequately without knowing God, neither can we act properly toward others without acting properly toward God, and vice versa. To serve God we must serve others. To be "heavenly minded" is, contrary to the popular saying, to be of "earthly use."

THE FIFTH COMMANDMENT: HONOR YOUR PARENTS

The second table of the law begins with a person's relationship toward his or her parents. This is deliberate, for in dealing with parents the commandment focuses on the smallest unit of society, the family, fundamental to all other social

---

[1]Thomas Watson, *The Ten Commandments* (1692; reprint ed., London: The Banner of Truth Trust, 1970), 122.

relationships and structures. Other kinds of "fathers" or "mothers" are included in the intent of the commandment. Commentators have pointed out that there are political fathers (those in secular positions of authority), spiritual fathers (pastors and other Christian ministers), and those who are called father by virtue of their old age and experience. Yet the fifth commandment has the home and natural parents particularly in mind. The commandment is "Honor your father and your mother, that your days may be long in the land that the LORD your God is giving you" (Ex 20:12). It means we should look up to those whom God has placed over us and treat them with "honor, obedience and gratefulness."[2]

The dark background of this commandment is to be found in the natural human dislike for authority. That is why the family is so important in God's economy. If children are not taught to respect their parents but allowed to get away with disobeying and dishonoring them, later in life they will rebel against other valid forms of authority. If they disobey their parents, they will disobey the laws of the state. If they do not respect their parents, they will not respect teachers, those who possess unusual wisdom, elected officials, and others. If they do not honor their parents, they will not honor God.

In this commandment is found the need to discipline children, a responsibility about which the Bible is explicit. The Bible says, "Train up a child in the way he should go; even when he is old he will not depart from it" (Prov 22:6). It says, "Discipline your son, for there is hope; do not set your heart on putting him to death" (Prov 19:18).

On the other hand, when the Bible admonishes children to honor their parents, it says an equally serious word to parents. They must be the kind of parents their children can honor. In one sense, children must always honor their parents: in giving them due respect and consideration, despite deficiencies. But in another sense, they cannot fully honor one who is dishonorable, as, for example, a drunken, irresponsible profligate. Since they can fully honor and obey one who is devout, honest, hard-working, faithful, compassionate, and wise, the fifth commandment encourages all who are parents to be like that. Moreover, it enjoins such standards on all who are in positions of authority: politicians, leaders in industry and labor, educators, and all who exercise any kind of leadership or influence.

---

[2]John Calvin, *Institutes of the Christian Religion*, ed. John T. McNeill, trans. Ford Lewis Battles, 2 vols. (Philadelphia: Westminster, 1960), 401.

THE SIXTH COMMANDMENT:
YOU SHALL NOT KILL

The sixth commandment has been misleading to many because of the faulty translation of *ratsach* as "kill" in most English Bibles. The word actually means "murder," "slay," "assassinate"; the noun forms of the word mean "manslayer." This brief commandment should be translated "You shall not murder." Failure to understand that has led some to cite biblical authority against all forms of killing. That position fails to see that the Bible recognizes the necessity of killing animals for food and sacrifice, enemies in battle, and those guilty of capital offenses by judicial process. Other parts of the law prescribe the death penalty for some of the offenses listed in the Decalogue.

To say that the word means "murder" rather than "kill" should be of comfort to no one, however. For in the biblical perspective, murder is considered broadly, and thus contains elements of which all are guilty. Here the teaching of the Lord Jesus Christ in the Sermon on the Mount is particularly important. In Jesus' day and for many years before that, murder had been defined by the leaders of Israel (and others also) as merely the external act, and they had taught that the commandment refers to nothing more than such an act.

"But is that all that murder is?" asked Jesus. "Is murder nothing more than the act of killing unjustly? What about attitudes? What about the person who has planned to kill another but who is prevented from doing it by some external circumstance? Or what about the one who wishes to kill but does not, because he is afraid of getting caught? What about the person who kills by look or words?" Human beings do make distinctions along such lines, and rightly so, from the perspective of human law. But God looks on the heart, and is therefore concerned with attitudes also. Jesus said, "You have heard that it was said to those of old, 'You shall not murder; and whoever murders will be liable to judgment.' But I say to you that everyone who is angry with his brother will be liable to judgment" (Mt 5:21-22).

Nor is it anger alone that the sixth commandment forbids. According to Jesus, God will not excuse even expressions of contempt. "Whoever insults his brother shall be liable to the council; and whoever says, 'You fool!' will be liable to the hell of fire" (Mt 5:22). In the Greek text, this verse contains two key words: *raca* and *mōros*. *Raca* is a pejorative term meaning "empty," but the insult is more in the sound than the meaning. It could be translated "a nothing" or "a nobody." *Mōros* means "fool" (we get our term *moron* from it), but one who is a fool morally. It is one who "plays the fool." Consequently the word has the effect of being a slur on someone's reputation. By those words, Jesus taught that by God's standards the utterance of slurs and other such comments constitutes a breaking of the sixth commandment.

Obviously this interpretation searches to the depth of our beings. It does not help much to remember that there is such a thing as righteous anger, or that there is a valid distinction between being angry against sin and against the sinner. Of course there is righteous anger. But our anger is not often like that; we are often improperly angry at some real or imagined wrong against ourselves. Do we commit murder? Yes, we do, according to Jesus' definition. We harbor grudges. We gossip and slander. We lose our temper. We kill by neglect, spite, and jealousy. And we doubtless do even worse things, which we would recognize if we could see into our hearts as God does.[3]

THE SEVENTH COMMANDMENT:
YOU SHALL NOT COMMIT ADULTERY

The seventh commandment is also very brief: "You shall not commit adultery" (Ex 20:14). In the Sermon on the Mount, the Lord amplifies this commandment also, explaining that it has to do with the thoughts and intents of the heart as well as with outward acts. Moreover, he joins it to a proper regard for marriage by his accompanying condemnation of divorce. He says,

> You have heard that it was said, "You shall not commit adultery." But I say to you that every one who looks at a woman with lustful intent has already committed adultery with her in his heart. . . . It was also said, "Whoever divorces his wife, let him give her a certificate of divorce." But I say to you that everyone who divorces his wife, except on the ground of sexual immorality, makes her commit adultery, and whoever marries a divorced woman commits adultery. (Mt 5:27-28, 31-32)

According to Jesus' view of the law, lust is the equivalent of adultery, just as hate is the equivalent of murder. God's standard is purity before marriage and fidelity afterward.

At no other point is contemporary morality in more obvious conflict with biblical standards. The mass media uses the lure of sex to push materialism and glamorize the pursuit of pleasure. Television fills our living rooms with sex-filled advertisements. Movies are worse; even the best areas of our cities feature

---

[3]I have discussed this same theme at greater length in *The Sermon on the Mount* (Grand Rapids: Zondervan, 1972), 105-11.

X-rated movies or titillating horror films. Newspapers advertise such films with pictures that would have been considered outrageous even a few years ago, and report sexual crimes in a details that were formerly avoided by at least the best papers. Twentieth-century hedonism is symbolized by the so-called playboy philosophy. The dubious achievement of *Playboy* magazine was to take the exploitation of sex out of the gutter, print it on glossy paper, and sell it to millions by a philosophy that makes pleasure the chief goal in life—in sex as in all other areas. Hedonism makes personal pleasure the number-one objective; it is seen in the pursuit of a second home, a third car, and the right kind of friends, just as much as in so-called sexual freedom and experimentation. *Playboy* and dozens of even worse magazines preach the importance of choosing the best wine or stereo as well as the right kind of sexual playmate.

The problem is not *Playboy* itself, but the "pleasure first" philosophy on which the *Playboy* empire has capitalized: what contributes to my own pleasure comes first, and in the pursuit of that pleasure no norms apply.

The mention of norms leads us to another challenge to the biblical ethic, the so-called New Morality, initially popularized by such well-known churchmen as Bishop J. A. T. Robinson of England, Joseph Fletcher, Harvey Cox, the late James Pike, and others. Since the early publication of their views, some of these writers have changed direction. But they once advanced an approach to morality based on two convictions: first, that the proper course of action in any given set of circumstances is to be determined by the situation itself and not by any predetermined ethical norm (even a biblical one); and second, that the only absolute in any ethical situation is the demand for love. Anything is right if it does not hurt the other person, and whether it hurts that person or not is a conclusion to be reached in the context of the situation only. It follows according to those rules that fornication and adultery are not necessarily wrong. Their rightness or wrongness depends on whether the act "helps" or "hurts" the other person. Similarly, lying, stealing, lawlessness, and other things formerly thought to be wrong are not necessarily to be avoided.

We must say in response to the New Morality that love would be an adequate guide to right action were we able to love as God loves and with full knowledge of the situation and the total consequences of our actions. But we do not love like that. We love selfishly. Besides, we do not know what the full consequences of our supposed "selfless" and "loving" action might be. A couple may decide that intercourse before marriage will be good for them and that no one will be hurt. But they do not know that for sure, and many, if not all, who have thought this way have been wrong. There is too much guilt, too many deeply entrenched patterns of unfaithfulness, and even too many unwanted children to make the New Morality a valid option.

Under the impact of the drift of the mass media, popular hedonism, and the New Morality, the cry, "If it feels good, do it," has become the watchword of our age. Should that new standard be accepted? In the light of God's commandments in the Decalogue and the Sermon on the Mount, the Christian must answer no. But at the same time we must acknowledge honestly, as C. S. Lewis says, that the Christian standard "is so difficult and so contrary to our instincts" that obviously something is wrong both with us personally and with our society.[4]

We must acknowledge that all are sinners and that even Christians are not automatically victorious over sexual sins and perversions.[5]

Like all negative commandments in the Decalogue, this one also implies the positive. The positive statement, as mentioned earlier, is purity before marriage and fidelity afterward. We are not pure before marriage nor faithful afterward if thoughts are to be taken into consideration, and many individuals sin not only in thought. How far we come short of God's standards! How much misery we bring on ourselves and others as a consequence!

THE EIGHTH COMMANDMENT:
YOU SHALL NOT STEAL

The view that one should not steal is a generally accepted standard of the human race, but only biblical religion shows why it is wrong. What the other person rightly possesses has been imparted to him or her by God. "Every good gift and every perfect gift is from above, coming down from the Father" (Jas 1:17). Therefore, to steal from another is to sin against God. Of course, theft is also an offense against others. It may harm them if they cannot afford the loss. It always diminishes them, for it treats them as no longer worthy of our respect or love. But even in this we sin against God, since it is he who has given value to the other person. We see an example of this perspective in David's great psalm of confession. Although he had stolen Bathsheba's good name from her and even taken her husband's life, David said in reference to God, "Against you, you only, have I sinned" (Ps 51:4).

---

[4]C. S. Lewis, *Mere Christianity* (New York: The Macmillan Company, 1958), 75.
[5]The material on contemporary sexual morality also occurs in my book *The Sermon on the Mount*, 112-15. A full discussion of Christ's interpretation of the seventh commandment and the divorce question occupies 112-48.

We are not to think that we have kept this commandment just because we have not broken into a home and walked off with someone else's possessions. There are different subjects from whom we can steal: God, others, or ourselves. There are many ways to steal: by stealth, violence, or deceit. There are many objects we can steal: money, time, or even a person's reputation.

We steal from God when we fail to worship as we ought or when we set our own concerns ahead of his. We steal from him when we spend our time in personal self-indulgence and do not tell others of his grace. We steal from an employer when we do not give the best work of which we are capable, or when we overextend our coffee breaks or leave work early. We steal if we waste the raw products with which we are working, or if we use the telephone for prolonged personal conversations rather than for the business we are assigned. We steal if, as a merchant, we charge too much for our product or try to make a "killing" in a lucrative field. We steal if we sell an inferior product, pretending that it is better than it is. We steal from our employees if their work environment harms their health or if we do not pay them enough to guarantee a healthy, adequate level of living. We steal by mismanaging others' money. We steal when we borrow but do not repay a loan on time or at all. We steal from ourselves if we waste our resources, whether time, talents, or money. We steal when we indulge ourselves in material goods while others go without the necessities of existence: food, clothing, shelter, or medical care. We steal if we become so zealous in saving or accumulating money that we rob even ourselves of necessities.

The positive side of this commandment is obvious. If we are to refrain from taking what belongs to another, we are also to do everything in our power to prosper others, helping them to attain their full potential. The Lord captures this duty in the Golden Rule: "So whatever you wish that others would do to you, do also to them, for this is the Law and the Prophets" (Mt 7:12).

We cannot miss seeing that this commandment indirectly establishes the right to private property. If we are not to take from another, the basis of the prohibition is quite obviously that what others have rightly belongs to them and is recognized to be theirs by God. Some teach that Christians should hold all things in common, at least if they are sufficiently spiritual, but that is not biblical. It is true that for various historical and social reasons a group of people may choose to place their possessions in common ownership, as the early Christians did for a time in Jerusalem following the day of Pentecost (Acts 2:44-45). Some may be specifically called to that, either as a testimony before the world that an individual's life does not consist in the abundance of the things he or she possesses, or because that person is particularly bound by possessions and must be free of them in order to grow spiritually. The rich young ruler was told by Jesus to divest himself of his goods and give the proceeds to the poor. Nevertheless, in spite of such special situations, neither the Old nor the New Testament forbids private ownership of goods, but rather endorses it.

The case of Ananias and Sapphira is sometimes cited in support of the communal theory, for they were struck dead for holding back from the church a portion of the proceeds from the sale of some property (Acts 5:1-11). Their sin, however, was not the possession of the property, but rather that they lied to the members of the church and to the Holy Spirit. They pretended to be giving all when actually they were keeping back some. In that connection, the apostle Peter even endorsed their right to such possessions. "Ananias," he said, "why has Satan filled your heart to lie to the Holy Spirit and to keep back for yourself part of the proceeds of the land? *While it remained unsold, did it not remain your own? And after it was sold, was it not at your disposal?* Why is it that you have contrived this deed in your heart? You have not lied to man but to God" (Acts 5:3-4).

The fact that the Bible establishes the right of private property does not make it easier for us to keep the eighth commandment. It makes it harder. There is no escaping the fact that we often rob others of what is their due and so become thieves in God's judgment.

THE NINTH COMMANDMENT: YOU SHALL NOT LIE

In speaking of the theft of one's reputation in the last section, we anticipated the ninth commandment, "You shall not bear false witness against your neighbor" (Ex 20:16).

This is the last of a sequence of commandments having to do with concern for the rights of another as a proper expression of the command to love. If we slander people, we rob them of their good name and social standing.

> This commandment is not only applicable to the lawcourts. It does include perjury. But it also includes all forms of scandal and slander, all idle talk and tittle-tattle, all lies and deliberate exaggerations or distortions of the truth. We can bear false witness by listening to unkind rumors as well as by passing them on, by making jokes at somebody else's expense, by creating false impressions, by not correcting untrue statements, and by our silence as well as by our speech.[6]

---

[6]John R. W. Stott, *Basic Christianity* (Grand Rapids: Eerdmans, 1958), 69.

Our duty toward the other person is only half the picture. It is not only that we harm another individual by false witness or swearing. We also dishonor God by our untruthfulness. He is the God of truth and he hates lying (Is 65:16; Jn 14:6). The Bible tells us, "Behold, you [God] delight in truth in the inward being" (Ps 51:6). It tells us that the one who is obedient to God "does not rejoice at wrongdoing, but rejoices with the truth" (1 Cor 13:6). It says, "Let each one of you speak the truth with his neighbor" (Eph 4:25).

That is not easy to do, as anyone concerned about personal integrity is aware. In some situations telling a lie or at least shading the truth seems almost to be demanded. In other situations telling the truth seems impossible. Well, with us it may be impossible; but with God all things are possible (Lk 18:27). How do we begin to grow in this area? We do so when we begin to realize that "out of the abundance of the heart the mouth speaks" (Mt 12:34) and that the heart can be changed only when it is possessed by the Lord Jesus Christ. If our hearts are filled with self, then we will inevitably shade the truth to our own advantage. But if truth fills the heart, which it will do if Christ controls it, then what we say will increasingly be true and edifying.

THE TENTH COMMANDMENT: YOU SHALL NOT COVET

The tenth commandment is perhaps the most revealing and devastating of all the commandments, for it deals explicitly with the inward nature of the law. Covetousness is an attitude of the inward nature that may or may not express itself in an outward acquisitive act. Moreover, it can be directed to almost anything. The text says, "You shall not covet your neighbor's house; you shall not covet your neighbor's wife, or his male servant, or his female servant, or his ox, or his donkey, or anything that is your neighbor's" (Ex 20:17).

How modern this is, and how keenly it strikes at the roots of our materialistic Western culture. One offensive element of our materialism is insensitivity to the needs of others that it so often breeds, insensitivity to the poor in our own cities and to the deprived around the world. But even more offensive than this is our unreasonable dissatisfaction with our abundance of wealth and opportunity. True, not all in the West are wealthy, and it is not inherently wrong to attempt to improve our lot in reasonable measure, especially when we are low on the economic scale. That in itself is not covetousness. But it is wrong to want something simply because we see another enjoying it. It is wrong constantly to seek to possess more when there is no need for it. It is wrong to be unhappy with our limited resources. Unfortunately, covetousness is what the media seems determined to instill in us so that our extravagant and wasteful economy will continue to grow, even if this means harming the economies of less developed nations.

There is another way in which we see our covetousness. Many, particularly Christian people, really are content with what God has given them. They are not overly materialistic. But they are covetous for their children. They want them to have the best, and in many cases would be hurt and even feel rejected were the children to sense God's call to renounce the life of materialistic abundance for missionary or other Christian service.

SIN'S WAGES AND GOD'S GIFT

We must not close this study of God's law as expressed in the Ten Commandments without applying it personally. We have looked at ten areas in which God requires certain standards of conduct from men and women. As we have looked at them we have found ourselves judged. We have not worshiped God as we ought. We have worshiped idols. We have not fully honored God's name. We have not rejoiced in the Lord's Day nor served him in it. We are delinquent in regard to our earthly parents. We have killed, by anger and looks, if not literally. We have committed adultery by thoughts and perhaps by acts as well. We have not been consistently truthful. We have wished for and plotted to get things that are our neighbor's.

God sees us in our sin. "All [things] are naked and exposed to the eyes of him to whom we must give account" (Heb 4:13). What is God's reaction? Not to excuse us certainly, for he cannot condone sin, however much we might wish it. On the contrary, he tells us that he will by no means clear the guilty. He teaches that "the wages of sin is death" (Rom 6:23). The judgment is soon to be executed.

What can we do? Left to ourselves, we can do nothing. But the glory of the gospel is that we are not left to ourselves. Rather, God has intervened to do what we cannot. We are judged by the law and found wanting. But God has sent Jesus, judged by the law and found perfect. He has died in our place to bear our just judgment in order that the way might be clear for God to clothe us in his righteousness. The Bible goes beyond "the wages of sin is death" to insist that "the free gift of God is eternal life in Christ Jesus our Lord" (Rom 6:23). If the law does its proper work in us, it will not make us self-righteous. It will make us Christ-righteous, as it turns us from our own corrupt works to the Savior who is our only hope.

CHAPTER 7

THE WRATH OF GOD

*A*t one point in *The Nature and Destiny of Man*, Reinhold Niebuhr speaks of three elements in the confrontation of God by the individual. First, there is "the sense of reverence for a majesty and of dependence upon an ultimate source of being." Second, "the sense of moral obligation laid upon one from beyond oneself and of moral unworthiness before a judge." Third, "the longing for forgiveness."[1] These three elements correspond to our knowledge of God as Creator, Judge, and Redeemer. But what is most important about them is their order. They are in that order because we obviously cannot adequately know God as Judge until we know something of our obligation to him as Creator. Nor can we know him as Redeemer until we are aware of how dreadfully we have sinned against him and how we have thereby fallen under the shadow of his judicial wrath.

That means, of course, that we must study the wrath of God before we can properly appreciate the doctrines of redemption. But here a problem develops. In the thinking of most of our contemporaries, including many Christians, the wrath of God is looked on almost as an embarrassment, as being something basically unworthy of God. So it is not often spoken of, at least publicly. We hear many sermons about the love of God. Scores of books deal with the power of God to help us in temptation, discouragement, sorrow, and many other things. Evangelists often stress God's grace and his plan for our lives. But we hear little

---

[1]Reinhold Niebuhr, *The Nature and Destiny of Man*, vol. 1, *Human Nature* (New York: Charles Scribner's Sons, 1941), 131.

about God's wrath or God's judgment. What is wrong? The biblical writers had no such reticence. They spoke of God's wrath, obviously considering it one of God's "perfections." It led them to present the gospel as God's "command" to repentance (Acts 17:30). Have modern Christians missed something that the biblical writers knew and appreciated? Have they neglected a doctrine without which the other doctrines are inevitably distorted? Or is the modern viewpoint more correct?

One problem is that English words fail to capture the essence of God's wrath. *Wrath* generally means "anger," and anger (at least human anger) is not much like what we mean when we speak of God's wrath in judging sin. But language is not the greatest problem. The greatest problem is the broken relationship between the entire race and God, due to sin. Sin has produced a state in which we stand condemned as sinners but in which, because of the very sin, we fail to admit our culpability and thus consider the wrath of God toward us to be unworthy of him and unjust. Why have Christians tended to accept this contemporary but nonbiblical judgment? The idea of God's wrath has never been popular, yet the prophets, apostles, theologians, and teachers of old did not fail to talk of it. It is biblical. In fact, "one of the most striking things about the Bible is the vigor with which both Testaments emphasize the reality and terror of God's wrath."[2] The way to overcome our reluctance is to seek to rediscover the importance of God's wrath by careful study of the entire teaching of the Bible about it.

WRATH IN THE OLD TESTAMENT

In the Old Testament, more than twenty words are used to express wrath as it relates to God himself; many other words relate only to human anger. There are nearly six hundred important passages. Moreover, they are not isolated and unrelated passages, as if they were all the work of one gloomy author edited into the text of the Old Testament later by one equally gloomy redactor. No, they are connected with the most basic themes of the Old Testament: the giving of the law, life in the land, disobedience on the part of God's people, and eschatology.

The earliest mentions of the wrath of God are in connection with the giving of the law at Mount Sinai. In fact, the earliest reference occurs just two chapters after the account of the giving of the Ten Commandments. "You shall not

---

[2]J. I. Packer, *Knowing God* (Downers Grove, IL: InterVarsity Press, 1973), 134-35.

mistreat any widow or fatherless child. If you do mistreat them, and they cry out to me, I will surely hear their cry, and my wrath will burn, and I will kill you with the sword, and your wives shall become widows and your children fatherless" (Ex 22:22-24). Ten chapters later, in a passage about the sin of the people in making and worshiping the golden calf, God and Moses discuss wrath. God says, "Now therefore let me alone, that my wrath may burn hot against them and I may consume them." And Moses pleads, "O LORD, why does your wrath burn hot against your people, whom you have brought out of the land of Egypt with great power and with a mighty hand? Why should the Egyptians say, 'With evil intent did he bring them out, to slay them in the mountains and to consume them from the face of the earth'? Turn from your burning anger and relent from this disaster against your people" (Ex 32:10-12).

It is evident in this passage that Moses' appeal to God is not based either on imagined innocence of the people (they were not innocent, and Moses knew it), nor on the thought that wrath was unworthy of God. Moses appeals only on the basis of God's name and how his acts would be misconstrued by the heathen. No doubt is expressed that wrath is a proper reaction of God's holy character against sin.

The first uniquely biblical characteristic of the divine wrath is a characteristic that immediately sets it off from the wrath displayed by heathen deities: its *consistency*. God's wrath is not arbitrary, as if God for some minor matter or according to his own caprice simply turns against those whom he had formerly loved and favored. On the contrary, wrath is God's consistent and unyielding resistance to sin and evil. In the first passage it is wrath brought on by sin against others, widows and orphans. In the second passage it is wrath brought on by sins against God.

Other examples may be given. In the last chapter of the book of Job, God's wrath is provoked against Job's friends because of their foolish and arrogant counsel (Job 42:7). Deuteronomy 29:23-28 speaks of the outpouring of God's wrath against Sodom and Gomorrah and other cities because of their idolatry. In Deuteronomy 11:16-17, the sin is likewise described as serving "other gods" and worshiping them. Ezra speaks of the wrath of God being against "all who forsake him" (Ezra 8:22).

Something else is evident in these passages. Because the sin that calls forth the wrath of God is essentially a turning away from him or rejecting him, wrath is something human beings *choose for themselves*. We may say that the wrath of God is that perfection of the divine nature into which we throw ourselves by our rebellion. That does not mean, of course, that the wrath of God is passive, for it works actively now and will do so in perfect measure at the final judgment. But it does mean that wrath is a side of the divine nature that we need not have discovered; having once discovered it, we find it as real as all other sides of God's nature. We are not able to shut God out, even by sin. All we do is exchange one relationship to God for another. If we will not have God's love and grace, we will have God's wrath. For God cannot look tolerantly on evil.

The wrath of God always has *a judicial element* to it. Thus, since it is evident that justice is never fully attained in this world (for whatever reason), the Old Testament writers tend to look toward the future day of the perfect outpouring of God's wrath against sin, when all accounts will be settled. We find repeated reference to "the day of God's wrath" or judgment. The first chapter of Nahum is an example.

> The LORD is a jealous and avenging God;
>> the LORD is avenging and wrathful;
> the LORD takes vengeance on his adversaries
>> and keeps wrath for his enemies.
> The LORD is slow to anger and great in power,
>> and the LORD will by no means clear the guilty. . . .
> Who can stand before his indignation?
>> Who can endure the heat of his anger?
> His wrath is poured out like fire,
>> and the rocks are broken into pieces by him.
> The LORD is good,
>> a stronghold in the day of trouble;
> he knows those who take refuge in him.
>> But with an overflowing flood
> he will make a complete end of the adversaries. (Nahum 1:2-3, 6-8)

The second psalm speaks of God's wrath being directed against the pagan nations in that day.

> [The Lord] will speak to them in his wrath,
>> and terrify them in his fury, saying,
> "As for me, I have set my King
>> on Zion, my holy hill."
> I will tell of the decree:
> the LORD said to me, "You are my son;

today I have begotten you.
Ask of me, and I will make the nations your heritage,
and the ends of the earth your possession.
You shall break them with a rod of iron,
and dash them in pieces like a potter's vessel." (Ps 2:5-9)

Amos directs God's warning against those who are nominally religious, who think wrongly that the day of God's wrath will be a day of their own vindication.

Woe to you who desire the day of the LORD!
Why would you have the day of the LORD?
It is darkness, and not light;
as if a man fled from a lion,
and a bear met him;
or went into the house and leaned with his hand against the wall,
and a serpent bit him.
Is not the day of the LORD darkness, and not light,
and gloom with no brightness in it? (Amos 5:18-20)

Because of the accumulation of sin and the increasing need for a final and retributive justice, there is increasing emphasis on the future day of God's wrath in the later books of the Old Testament.

WRATH IN THE NEW TESTAMENT

Examination of the smaller number of passages in the New Testament dealing with the wrath of God shows that it was as real for Jesus and the New Testament writers as for the writers of the Old Testament.

The Greek New Testament has only two main words for *wrath*. One word is *thymos*, from a root (*thyō*) that means "to rush along fiercely," "to be in a heat of violence," or "to breathe violently." Its unique meaning would be "a panting rage." The other word is *orgē*, which comes from a quite different root. Its root (*orgaō*) means "to grow ripe for something"; the noun form denotes wrath that has been slowly building over a long period of time. In many usages the two words have apparently lost those early distinctions and are used interchangeably. But where there is a distinction, *orgē* is best suited to denote God's wrath, in that it depicts a gradually building and intensifying opposition to sin. Leon Morris notes that, outside the book of Revelation, *thymos* is used only once of God's anger. He concludes, "The biblical writers habitually use for the divine wrath a word which denotes not so much a sudden flaring up of passion which is soon over, as a strong and settled opposition to all that is evil arising out of God's very nature."[3]

The New Testament writers speak of "the wrath to come." There is widespread recognition in the New Testament that we live in a day of God's grace, a day characterized by the free offer of the gospel of salvation through faith in Jesus Christ. Yet that does not mean that God has ceased to be wrathful toward sin or that he will not yet show forth wrath in the future day of his judgment. Rather, one's apprehension of that day is intensified. Jesus frequently spoke of hell. He warned of the consequences of sin and of God's just and certain punishment of ungodly persons. The author of Hebrews wrote,

> Anyone who has set aside the law of Moses dies without mercy on the evidence of two or three witnesses. How much worse punishment, do you think, will be deserved by the one who has trampled underfoot the Son of God, and has profaned the blood of the covenant by which he was sanctified, and has outraged the Spirit of grace? For we know him who said, "Vengeance is mine; I will repay." And again, "The Lord will judge his people." It is a fearful thing to fall into the hands of the living God. (Heb 10:28-31)

But the New Testament revelation of the wrath of God also pertains to the present, just as it did in the Old Testament. Romans 1:18 uses the present tense: "For the wrath of God is revealed from heaven against all ungodliness and unrighteousness of men, who by their unrighteousness suppress the truth." If the tense of the verb were future, that too would make sense. It would refer to the future day of God's final judgment. But in the present tense, the verse seems to refer to a continuing disclosure of the wrath of God against wickedness at all periods of history and in all places—in other words, to the kind of outworking of the effects of sin discussed in the remainder of the chapter. The effects include a darkening of the understanding wherever the truth about God is rejected (Rom 1:21). They include the debasement of one's religious awareness and a corresponding debasement of one's person (Rom 1:23), sexual perversions, lies, envies, hatred, murder, strife, deceit, disobedience to parents, and other consequences (Rom 1:24-31). Nothing in these lists suggests that the apostle Paul was substituting a present, mechanical outworking of the effects of sin for a personal, direct manifestation of the wrath of God at some future day, as some

---

[3]Leon Morris, *The Apostolic Preaching of the Cross* (Grand Rapids: Eerdmans, 1956), 162-63.

contemporary theologians have taught.[4] Paul, too, speaks of a future day of wrath (Rom 2:5; 1 Thess 1:10; 2:16; 5:9). However, Paul sees the evidence of that future wrath in sin's present effects.

We can say that God has warned us of judgment to come: first, by our own awareness of right and wrong, of justice and injustice; and second, by the evidences of an inevitable outworking of God's justice even now. Paul described that process as he witnessed it in paganism. There are parallel evidences today. For when men and women give up God, God gives them up to "impurity . . . dishonorable passions . . . [and] a debased mind" (Rom 1:24, 26, 28). We see it in the progressive moral decline of Western civilization, the breakup of families, insanity, and other forms of psychological disintegration. We see it in our own lives in such supposedly minor things as restlessness, insomnia, a feeling of being unfulfilled, and unhappiness.

To sum up these matters, on the one hand we have the basic and almost universal reaction of the human race against the idea of God's wrath. It is considered ignoble of God, perhaps even vindictive and cruel. On the other hand we have the whole of the biblical revelation, in which the wrath of God is portrayed as one of his perfections. His wrath is portrayed as being consistent in its opposition to evil, as being judicial, as being an aspect of God that human beings choose for themselves and (no less important) as being something about which we have been clearly warned.

The wrath of God is not ignoble. Rather, it is too noble, too just, too perfect—it is this that bothers us. In human affairs we rightly value justice and the "wrath" of the judicial system, for they protect us. If by chance we ourselves run afoul of the law, there is always the chance that we can cop a plea, escape on a technicality, or plead guilty to some lesser offense and be excused for it. But we cannot do that with God. With him, we deal not with the imperfections of human justice but with the perfections of divine justice. We deal with the one to whom not only actions but also thoughts and intentions are visible. Who can escape such justice? Who can stand before such an unyielding judge? No one. Sensing this truth, we therefore resent God's justice and deny its reality in every way we can.

Yet we must not deny it. If we do, we will never see our spiritual need, as we must if we are to turn to the Lord Jesus Christ as our Savior. If we do not

---

[4]The best example here is C. H. Dodd (*The Epistle of Paul to the Romans* [London: Hodder and Stoughton, 1932], 20ff., and other writings), but he is only one of many.

turn to him, we will never truly know God, nor come to see ourselves adequately. It is only when we know God as Creator that we can discern him as Judge. And it is only as we acknowledge him as Judge that we can discover him to be our Redeemer.

SATISFYING GOD'S WRATH

We must go on to consider the revelation of God as Redeemer in the Old and New Testaments. This will occupy us in the next chapter (for the Old Testament) and then in chapters nine through eighteen (for the New Testament) as we deal with the person and work of Jesus Christ. Before that, however, we must again look at that exchange between God and Moses over the sin of Israel. In a sense, that passage comes between the declaration of the wrath of God against sin and the subsequent revelation of God's way of salvation.

Moses had been up in the mountain for forty days receiving the law. As the days had stretched into weeks, the restless people waiting below had eventually prevailed on Moses' brother Aaron to make a substitute god for them. Now, knowing what was going on in the valley, God interrupted his giving of the law to tell Moses what the people were doing and to send Moses back down to them.

It was an ironic situation. God had just given Moses the Ten Commandments. They had begun,

I am the LORD your God, who brought you out of the land of Egypt, out of the house of slavery.

You shall have no other gods before me.

You shall not make yourself a carved image, or any likeness of anything that is in heaven above, or that is in the earth beneath, or that is in the water under the earth. You shall not bow down to them or serve them, for I the LORD your God am a jealous God, visiting the iniquity of the fathers on the children to the third and the fourth generation of those who hate me, but showing steadfast love to thousands of those who love me and keep my commandments. (Ex 20:2-6)

While God was giving these words, the people whom he had saved from slavery in Egypt were doing precisely what he was prohibiting. Not only that, they were also committing adultery, lying, coveting, dishonoring their parents, and no doubt breaking all the other commandments. At that point, when God declared his intention to judge the people immediately and totally, Moses interceded for them in the words referred to earlier.

At last Moses started down the mountain to deal with the people. Even on a human level and quite apart from any thought of God's grace, sin must be judged. So Moses began to deal with it in the best way he knew. First, he rebuked Aaron publicly. Then he called for any who still remained on the side of the Lord to separate themselves from the others and stand beside him. The tribe of Levi responded. At Moses' command they were sent forth into the camp to execute those who had led the rebellion. The chapter says that three thousand men died, approximately 0.5 percent of the six hundred thousand who left Egypt at the exodus (Ex 12:37; 32:28; with women and children, the total number in the exodus may have been two million). At the same time Moses also destroyed the golden calf. He ground it up, mixed it with water, and made the people drink it.

From a human point of view Moses had dealt with the sin. The leaders were punished. Aaron was rebuked. The allegiance of the people was at least temporarily reclaimed. All seemed to be well. But Moses stood in a special relationship to God as well as in a special relationship to the people. God still waited in wrath on the mountain. What was Moses to do? For theologians sitting in a library somewhere, the idea of the wrath of God may seem to be no more than speculation. But Moses was no armchair theologian. He had been talking with that God. He had heard his voice. By that time not all of the law had been given, but Moses had received enough of it to know something of the horror of sin and of the uncompromising nature of God's righteousness. Had not God said, "You shall have no other gods before me"? Had not he promised to visit the iniquity of the fathers upon the children to the third and fourth generations? Who was Moses to think that the limited judgment he had begun would satisfy the holiness of such a God?

The night passed, and the morning came when Moses was to reascend the mountain. He had been thinking. Sometime during the night, a way that might possibly divert the wrath of God against the people had come to him. He remembered the sacrifices of the Hebrew patriarchs and the newly instituted sacrifice of the Passover. Certainly God had shown by such sacrifices that he was prepared to accept an innocent substitute in place of the just death of the sinner. His wrath could sometimes fall on the substitute. Perhaps God would accept. . . . When morning came, Moses ascended the mountain with great determination.

Reaching the top, he began to speak to God. It must have been in great anguish, for the Hebrew text is uneven and Moses' second sentence breaks off without ending, indicated by a dash in the middle of Exodus 32:32. It is a strangled cry, a sob welling up from the heart of a man who is asking to be damned if that could mean the salvation of the people he had come to love. "So Moses returned to the LORD and said, 'Alas, this people has sinned a great sin. They have made for themselves gods of gold. But now, if you will forgive their sin—but if not, please blot me out of your book that you have written'" (Ex 32:31-32).

Moses was offering to take the place of his people as a recipient of God's judgment, to be separated from God for them. On the preceding day, before Moses had come down the mountain, God had said something that could have been a great temptation. If Moses would agree, God would destroy the people for their sin and would begin again to make a new Jewish nation from Moses (Ex 32:10). Even then Moses had rejected the offer. But after having been with his people and being reminded of his love for them, his answer, again negative, rises to even greater heights. God had said, "I will destroy them and make a great nation of you." Moses says, "No, rather destroy me and save them."

Moses lived in the early years of God's revelation to his people, and at that point probably understood very little. Certainly he did not know, as we know, that what he had prayed for could not be. Moses offered to give himself for his people to save them. But Moses could not save even himself, let alone them; for he too was a sinner. He had once even committed murder, thus breaking the sixth commandment. He could not substitute for his people. He could not die for them.

But there is one who could. Thus, "When the fullness of time had come, God sent forth his Son, born of woman, born under the law, to redeem those who were under the law, so that we might receive adoption as sons" (Gal 4:4-5). Jesus' death was not just for those who believed in Old Testament times, for those who sinned in the wilderness and for their successors. It was also for us who live today, both Jews and Gentiles. On the basis of Christ's death, in which he himself received the full judicial outpouring of God's wrath against sin, those who believe now come to experience not wrath (though we richly deserve it) but grace abounding.

Grace does not eliminate wrath; wrath is still stored up against the unrepentant. But grace does eliminate the necessity for everyone to experience it.

CHAPTER 8

SALVATION IN THE OLD TESTAMENT

*I*t should be evident from comments made in the preceding study of the law that a person was saved in the Old Testament period in the same way in which a person is saved today. That is, the person who lived before Christ's time was saved by grace through faith in a Redeemer who was to come, just as today a person is saved by grace through faith in the Redeemer who has already come. The Old Testament women and men looked forward to Christ. We look back. Beyond that, the grounds of salvation are identical. The Old Testament sacrifices pointed forward to Jesus.

However, if an average Christian (not to mention a non-Christian) were asked how any one of the Old Testament figures was saved, it is likely that a wrong answer would be given. For example, some think that the Old Testament figures were saved by being Jews. They base this view on their understanding that God's promises to Israel were given to Israel collectively, that is, as including each and every descendant of Abraham. They would find support in such texts as John 4:22, in which Jesus told the woman of Samaria, "Salvation is from the Jews." That view was shared by the majority of Jews in Paul's day, as evidenced by his treatment of the subject in Romans 9. It is shared by most Jews and even by a significant number of Christians today. But are all Jews saved? Or to put it in a more limited way, were all Jews saved before Christ's day? Both the Old and the New Testaments deny that.

A second erroneous view, perhaps more common, is that the Old Testament figures were saved by keeping the law. That, of course, does not explain how Adam and Eve or Abraham and Sarah or any others who lived before the giving of the law were saved, but it does fit in with the fundamental human desire to achieve one's own salvation. Men and women earnestly want to be saved by doing something for themselves. Actually, the law condemns them.

Finally, some would say that the Old Testament figures were saved by keeping the sacraments, that is, by performing the sacrifices and other rites specified in the Levitical code. That gets closer to the real issue, for salvation did consist in what the sacrifices signified. Still, salvation was not by the sacrifices any more than it is by baptism or the Lord's Supper today.

THE CASE OF ABRAHAM

How were the Old Testament figures saved? The apostle Paul was faced by those who thought that Jews were saved by birth, keeping the law, observing the sacrifices, or by some combination of the three. He answered such views by teaching that salvation is always by grace, not through works of any kind; hence salvation is always ultimately a matter of God's sovereign choice or election.

In Romans 4 Paul devotes an entire chapter to showing that Abraham, the father of the Jewish nation, was saved by faith apart from the law. But even if this does show God's way of salvation, it leaves unanswered the question why Israel as a whole was not responding to God's offer in Christ. Israel had received promises of Christ's coming and had the sacrifices, which pointed forward to him. Israel should have believed. Yet when the early preachers of the gospel went forth with their message, it seemed that Israel was largely rejecting the Savior, while the Gentiles, by contrast, were believing. Why? Was God casting off his people? Had the way of salvation changed? Paul answers such questions in Romans 9, first by denying that Jews were ever saved by birth. Always, he shows, some were not saved and others were. "For," he says, speaking spiritually, "not all who are descended from Israel belong to Israel, and not all are children of Abraham [that is, spiritual children] because they are his offspring" (Rom 9:6-7). Second, he shows that those who are Abraham's true spiritual seed become so only by God's sovereign election. "It is not the children of the flesh who are the children of God, but the children of the promise" (Rom 9:8). Therefore, Jews were saved during the Old Testament period and are saved today precisely as Gentiles are saved, that is, by God's electing grace focused in the work of Christ on Calvary.

What was Abraham when God called him? He was not a Jew in the later nationalistic sense, although he was to become the first of the Jewish nation. When God called Abraham, he was merely one member of a very large number of Semitic people who occupied the ancient Near East at that time, most of whom worshiped idols. Abraham himself came from such a family. Thus, he was saved, not because of any supposed merit in him (as if he had sought God, for he had not), but because God elected him to salvation.

God's election of Abraham is stated at several places in the Bible. Joshua, for example, delivered a final charge to the people in which he reminded them of their pagan past, God's deliverance of them from that past, and their resulting obligation to serve him. At one point he deals with Abraham, saying,

> Thus says the LORD, the God of Israel, "Long ago, your fathers lived beyond the Euphrates, Terah, the father of Abraham and of Nahor; and they served other gods. Then I took your father Abraham from beyond the River and led him through all the land of Canaan, and made his offspring many. I gave him Isaac. And to Isaac I gave Jacob and Esau. And I gave Esau the hill country of Seir to possess, but Jacob and his children went down to Egypt. And I sent Moses and Aaron, and I plagued Egypt with what I did in the midst of it; and afterward I brought you out. . . . Now therefore fear the LORD and serve him in sincerity and in faithfulness. Put away the gods that your fathers served beyond the River and in Egypt, and serve the LORD." (Josh 24:2-5, 14)

Those verses say clearly that Abraham was chosen by God from out of a pagan ancestry and that he, Terah, and Nahor once worshiped false gods.

> Isaiah says the same thing.
>> Listen to me, you who pursue righteousness,
>>> you who seek the LORD;
>> look to the rock from which you were hewn,
>>> and to the quarry from which you were dug.
>> Look to Abraham your father
>>> and to Sarah who bore you. (Is 51:1-2)

Nothing in their ancestry could possibly commend Israel to God. Salvation is always of grace.

At other points in his writing, Paul denies that Abraham was saved either by keeping the law or observing the sacraments. He shows that Abraham lived 430 years before the law was even given (Gal 3:17), and that he was declared righteous by God through faith before receiving the rite of circumcision (Rom 4:9-11).

One might argue that although God's call of Abraham was according to grace ("After all, God had to start somewhere"), after that salvation was by physical descent. One might conclude that all Abraham's descendants were therefore saved. But that is precisely the opinion against which Paul writes in Romans and that he answers specifically in the ninth chapter. The Jews of Paul's day were arguing that they had a special relationship with God because of their physical descent from Abraham, but in doing so they had overlooked the fact that Abraham had more than one son. There had been Isaac, the child of God's promise. But before Isaac there had been Ishmael. What about Ishmael? Clearly God had chosen Isaac rather than Ishmael, though Isaac was younger, thereby demonstrating that salvation is the result of God's free choice and that (whatever we may think of the matter) he obviously does not grant the same privileges to everyone.

There were undoubtedly some who argued that the case of Isaac did not prove Paul's position. Isaac had been born of Abraham and Sarah, thus of two good Jewish parents, but Ishmael had been born of Abraham and Hagar, Sarah's Egyptian slave girl. Ishmael was of mixed blood, they would hold; so Paul's denial of salvation by birth was unproven. Paul answers by passing on to the next generation. In that generation, in the case of Isaac's two sons, Jacob and Esau, God made his choice between sons of the same Jewish mother. Moreover, lest anyone try to introduce the matter of age as a factor, the two boys are twins. And, in order that no one could argue that the choice was made on the basis of the character or moral choices of the sons, God announced his decision while the children were still in Rebecca's womb, that is, before either had a chance to do or choose anything. Paul writes of that generation, "When Rebekah had conceived children by one man, our forefather Isaac, though they were not yet born and had done nothing either good or bad—in order that God's purpose of election might continue, not because of works but because of him who calls—she was told, 'The older will serve the younger.' As it is written, 'Jacob I loved, but Esau I hated'" (Rom 9:10-13).

The point of the argument is that the choice of who would receive the blessing of salvation lay with God entirely, then as now. God gives life to whom he chooses.

LOOKING AHEAD TO THE REDEEMER

To say that the Jews of the Old Testament period were saved by the electing grace of God, as Gentiles are saved today, is only one part of the picture, however. Although election is the initiating cause of salvation, it is nevertheless only that. We are left with these questions: On what grounds does God save the ungodly? How can God forgive sin? Can God justify the ungodly and still be just? The importance of these questions leads to the importance of Christ's death even for the Old Testament figures.

The apostle Paul deals with this issue in at least two places. In his first full statement of the gospel, Paul speaks of the revelation of the righteousness of God through Christ. First, righteousness is "unto all and upon all them that believe" (Rom 3:22 KJV). The words suggest being clothed with that righteousness or having it deposited to our account, as in a bank.

Second, Paul's argument is that God is shown to be righteous by the death of Christ. Before the time of Christ, God had been saving numerous Old Testament figures by election. But they were still sinners, so it appeared as if God were simply forgetting about their sin, which was not right. We may sympathize with God's decision to forgive, but that does not make it right. What about justice? What about the sin? Those questions are resolved by the revelation of God's righteousness in Jesus Christ. It was on the basis of Christ's death that God had been forgiving sin all along, though that death had not yet occurred. When it occurred, the mystery was explained—and God was seen to be just.

Paul expresses this by writing about those who had been

> justified by his grace as a gift, through the redemption that is in Christ Jesus, whom God put forward as a *propitiation* by his blood, to be received by faith. This was to show God's righteousness, because in his divine forbearance he had passed over former sins. It was to show his righteousness at the present time, so that he might be just and the justifier of the one who has faith in Jesus. (Rom 3:24-26)

The initiating cause in salvation is God's free grace, but the formal cause is, and has always been, the death of the mediator.

The second important passage from Paul's writing on these themes is Galatians 3, in which Paul bases on Abraham his argument for salvation by grace through faith in the Lord Jesus Christ. There Paul says three things: Abraham was saved by believing God (Gal 3:6); the essence of his belief was that God was going to send a Savior, who was Jesus Christ (Gal 3:16); and the work of Christ was to be a work of redemption (Gal 3:13-14).

Some may say, "Do you really mean that the Old Testament figures looked forward to Christ's coming and were saved by faith in him, just as we look back to Christ and are saved by believing in him as our Savior? How could they believe in him? He had not yet come. The prophecies of his coming were vague. And if even Christ's disciples had a wrong idea of his ministry—thinking he was to be a political Messiah (Acts 1:6)—how could ordinary people have a correct view? How could anyone really be saved through faith in a coming redeemer?"

One answer is that many obviously did not look forward to Christ and so were not saved. Certainly, of the many who actually encountered Christ later on, most were not saved. The masses could be attracted by his teaching one day and praise him, but cry out for his crucifixion the next. In Christ's day, as in every period of Old Testament history, those who were saved were a remnant.

A second answer is that there were obviously different degrees of understanding. The essence of faith in all who had any understanding was that they recognized themselves to be sinners in need and turned to God for salvation. Each one who came honestly to present a sacrifice for sin confessed that much.

A full answer to the question goes beyond either of these, however. We must say on the basis of the fullest biblical evidence that many did believe. Further, they undoubtedly understood more than we often give them credit for.

We find the evidence throughout the Scriptures. When Adam and Eve sinned in Eden, God came to them to convict them of sin and lead them to repentance. When he clothed them with skins taken from animals he himself had undoubtedly slain, he already pictured the future death of Christ, who would be slain by the Father in order that we who are sinners might be clothed with his righteousness. God promised a redeemer, saying to Satan,

> I will put enmity between you and the woman,
>   and between your offspring and her offspring;
> he shall bruise your head,
>   and you shall bruise his heel. (Gen 3:15)

Clearly, these words do not refer simply to a general human fear of snakes, as some modern theologians would interpret them, but rather to the coming of the Messiah, who would defeat Satan and destroy his power. That is where salvation from the curse of sin was to lie. That is what Adam and Eve understood. When their first child was born, they called him Cain, which means "Here he is" or "Acquisition," thereby testifying to their faith (however mistaken) that the promised one had now come.

We have already looked at Abraham with reference to his election by God to salvation, and his own personal faith in the Redeemer who was to come. But we have not looked at what is probably the most important verse on the subject. In John 8:56, Jesus says, "Your father Abraham rejoiced that he would see my day. He saw it and was glad."

One way of interpreting that difficult verse is to assume that Jesus meant that Abraham was alive in heaven (or paradise) at the time, rejoicing in Christ's ministry. The difficulty with such a view is that the subject of dispute in John 8 is not Abraham's continued consciousness beyond the grave, but rather Christ's preexistence. John 8:58 says, "Before Abraham was, I am." If Christ had wanted to say that Abraham was still living and rejoiced in Christ's birth and ministry, it would have been more natural to use present tenses for the verbs ("Abraham is rejoicing to see my day; he sees it, and is glad"). It seems proper to refer the saying to Abraham's understanding in his own day rather than to something contemporary with Christ's ministry.

To place the vision in Abraham's time does not in itself solve the problem. For most of the rabbis did this—that is, they spoke of a vision of the messiah that Abraham was supposed to have had—yet disagreed on how it happened.

Abraham's vision of Christ's day may well be found in the story of the near sacrifice of Isaac on Mount Moriah. Here Abraham learned in a new way that "the Lord will provide." God came to Abraham and told him to take his son, the heir of the promise, and sacrifice him on a mountain three days' journey away. It must have been a terrible struggle for Abraham as he wrestled with God's command. He knew that he must obey God, but he also knew that God was a God of his word and that he had committed himself to produce a nation through Isaac. Isaac had no children at this point. So if God was telling Abraham to kill Isaac, then the God who had done a miracle in Isaac's birth would have to do a miracle in his death. There would have to be a resurrection.

The narrative indicates that Abraham expected to bring Isaac back down the mountain with him after the sacrifice took place (Gen 22:5). And the author of Hebrews states explicitly, "By faith Abraham, when he was tested, offered up Isaac, and he who had received the promises was in the act of offering up his only son, of whom it was said, 'Through Isaac shall your offspring be named.' He considered that God was able even to raise him from the dead, from which, figuratively speaking, he did receive him back" (Heb 11:17-19).

Abraham believed that God was going to do a miracle in bringing Isaac back from the dead, precisely the miracle that God the Father did with Jesus Christ the Son, as the special language of those verses from Hebrews indicates. But even this is not all. For when the trial was over and God had intervened to save Isaac and provide a ram for the sacrifice in place of the boy, Abraham rejoiced and called the name of the place Jehovah-jireh, which means "The LORD will provide" (Gen 22:14). Earlier this could have meant, "The Lord will provide a resurrection of Isaac." Now it could only mean that the same God who provided a ram in substitution for Isaac would one day provide his own Son as the perfect substitute and sacrifice for our salvation. Thus Abraham saw the coming of Jesus, including the meaning of his death and resurrection and rejoiced in that coming.

Suppose we should ask Abraham, "Abraham, why are you in heaven today? Was it because you left your home in Ur of the Chaldees and went to Canaan? Was it because of your faith or your character or your obedience?"

"No," Abraham would say. "Haven't you read my story? God promised me a great inheritance. I believed his promises about it. And the greatest promise was that he would send a Savior through my line through whom he would bring blessing to all nations. I am in heaven because I believed that God would do that."

"How about you, Jacob? Why are you in heaven? Are you in heaven because of your faith or because you were born in the line of your grandfather Abraham?"

"No," Jacob answers. "I am in heaven because I looked for a Redeemer. Remember how I spoke about him to my son Judah as I lay dying? I didn't know his name then. But I said, 'The scepter shall not depart from Judah, nor the ruler's staff from between his feet, until he comes to whom it belongs; and to him shall be the obedience of the peoples' (Gen 49:10). I am in heaven because I looked for his coming."

"Why are you in heaven, David? It must be because of your character. You were called 'a man after God's own heart.' "

"My character!" says David. "Are you forgetting that I committed adultery with Bathsheba and then tried to cover it up by having her husband killed? I am in heaven because I looked for the one who was promised as my Redeemer and the Redeemer of my people. I knew that God had promised him a kingdom that would endure forever."

"What about you, Isaiah? Did you expect the Redeemer?"

"Of course, I did," Isaiah answers. "I spoke of him as the one who 'has borne our griefs, and carried our sorrows,' who was 'wounded for our transgressions' and 'bruised for our iniquities.' I knew that the Lord would lay on him the iniquity of us all."

We come to the time of Christ and find the same kind of response, only now those who believe are not from the so-called important levels of society, from the palace of Herod or from among the priests. They are common people. They are people like Simeon to whom "it had been revealed . . . by the Holy Spirit that he would not see death before he had seen the Lord's Christ" (Lk 2:26), or Anna, a prophetess, who when Simeon was blessing the infant Christ, "began to give thanks to God and to speak of him to all who were waiting for the redemption of Jerusalem" (Lk 2:38). Such has always been the faith of God's children. In announcing the birth of Christ the angel said, "You shall call his name Jesus, for he will save his people from their sins" (Mt 1:21). In every age, God has always had those who looked to that Savior for their salvation. In ancient times there were Abraham, Jacob, David, Isaiah, Malachi, and many more, both women and men. In Christ's time there were Elizabeth, Zechariah, John the Baptist, Joseph, Mary, and many others. There are many today.

There is only one way of salvation. "For there is one God, and there is one mediator between God and men, the man Christ Jesus, who gave himself as a ransom for all, which is the testimony given at the proper time" (1 Tim 2:5-6). It is to the person and work of this mediator that we must turn in the following chapters.

PART III

THE PERSON OF CHRIST

In the beginning was the Word, and the Word was with God,
and the Word was God. He was in the beginning with God.

JOHN 1:1-2

And the Word became flesh and dwelt among us, . . .
full of grace and truth.

JOHN 1:14

For there is one God, and there is one mediator between God and men,
the man Christ Jesus, who gave himself as a ransom for all,
which is the testimony given at the proper time.

1 TIMOTHY 2:5-6

CHAPTER 9

THE DEITY
OF JESUS CHRIST

*I*f you have been following the thoughts of the preceding chapters but are not yet a Christian, perhaps you are thinking we have placed all our eggs in too fragile a basket. We have obviously placed our entire hope for salvation from our own and this world's ills on the shoulders of a promised Redeemer, whom Christians identify as Jesus Christ of Nazareth. You may be wondering if any one person, however extraordinary, is equal to that task. How could any one man, a mere man, do so much?

That is the issue. Is it a man whom we are talking about? Or is he God? Christians readily admit that if Jesus were no more than a man, however remarkable he might be, he clearly could not be our Savior, nor is it likely that he did the many supernatural things attributed to him. On the other hand, if he is not only a man but is also God, then nothing is impossible to him and he did achieve our salvation. God cannot lie, so what he has promised he will necessarily perform. The question of Christ's deity is, therefore, *the* question about Jesus Christ. The question does not mean that Jesus must be approached in some mystical way. On the contrary, we must approach him as a true man within the context of history, a man who actually said and did certain things. But we will not understand him even in that context until we recognize that he is also God and that his divinity alone gives meaning to his speech and actions.

That was the experience of the first disciples and apostles. Brunner writes that "only when they understand him as this absolute Lord, to whom the full divine sovereignty belongs, did Easter as victory, and Good Friday as a saving Fact, become intelligible. Only when they knew Jesus as the present Heavenly Lord, did they know themselves to be sharers in the Messianic Kingdom as men of the new, the Messianic era."[1] In considering the person of Jesus Christ, we therefore want to begin with the teaching of those men, that is, with the Bible's own teaching.

PAUL'S TEACHING

We begin with the writings of the apostle Paul, for, aside from Jesus himself, Paul was unquestionably the major teacher and theologian of the early church. Moreover, Paul was not one of Christ's original disciples, whose opinion we might suspect to be colored by personal affection. Rather, Paul began as an enemy of Christ and the church, which in his youth he even tried to destroy. Further, his was a carefully thought-out opposition. Paul, a serious-minded and pious Jew, approached religion on the premise of the unity of God. He was a monotheist. He thought that the Christians' claims to divinity for Jesus were nothing short of blasphemy. Clearly, if such a man as Paul was converted, it must have been on the grounds of a profound religious experience and sound evidence.

A key passage in which Paul reveals his understanding of Jesus is Philippians 2:5-11. In that brief section, Paul traces Christ's life from eternity past, when he was in the form of God and equal to God, through the events of his earthly life to eternity future, where he once again is glorified with the Father. It has been described as a parabola, for it begins in an infinite past, descends to the point of Christ's death on the cross, and then ascends to an infinite future again.

> Have this mind among yourselves, which is yours in Christ Jesus, who, though he was in the form of God, did not count equality with God a thing to be grasped, but emptied himself, taking the form of a servant, being born in the likeness of men. And being found in human form, he humbled himself by becoming obedient to the point of death, even death on a cross. Therefore God has highly exalted him and bestowed on him the name that is above every name, so that at the name of Jesus every knee should bow, in heaven and on earth and under the

---

[1]Emil Brunner, *The Christian Doctrine of Creation and Redemption: Dogmatics*, trans. Olive Wyon, vol. 2 (Philadelphia: Westminster, 1952), 339.

earth, and every tongue confess that Jesus Christ is Lord, to the glory of God the Father.

In speaking of the position that Jesus enjoyed with the Father in eternity past, Paul uses two words that deserve close study. The first is the Greek word *morphē*, found in the phrase "the form of God." In English the word *form* usually refers to the outward shape of an object, that is, to something external. In the Bible that is one meaning—it occurs in Paul's description of those who have "a form of religion" but deny the power of it (2 Tim 3:5 RSV)—but it is a less common meaning. Another use of the English word suggests the dominant biblical idea. Sometimes we say, "I'm in good form today," by which we mean not merely external appearance but internal fitness as well. That is what Paul has in mind primarily as he writes about Jesus in his preincarnate state. He means, as one commentator has phrased it, that "he possessed inwardly and displayed outwardly the very nature of God himself."[2]

The second word is even more important. It is *isos*, meaning "equal." We have it in English in the scientific terms *isomer*, *isomorph*, *isometric*, and in *isosceles triangle*. An isomer is a molecule having a slightly different structure from another molecule (as, for example, being a mirror image of it), but identical to it in chemical composition. An isomorph is something that has the same form as something else. Isometric means "in equal measure." An isosceles triangle has two equal sides. Paul's use of this word in reference to Jesus teaches that Jesus is God's equal.

Moreover, that is the way the passage moves as a whole. Having described how Jesus laid aside his former glory in order to become man and die for us, Paul goes on to show how he received that glory back, noting that he is now to be confessed as Lord by every intelligent creature in God's universe. In the last section, "the name that is above every name" is the name of God, "the Lord." No other name than Lord can rightly be called "the name that is above every name." The passage flows on to his confession, for that is what the affirmation "Jesus is Lord" means. It means "Jesus is God." Paul's phrasing of the homage of the universe to Jesus is a fairly direct allusion to Isaiah 45:23, in which God declares that he himself will be the object of universal adoration: "To me every knee shall bow, every tongue shall swear allegiance."

These verses in Philippians are remarkable for their high theology concerning the Lord Jesus Christ. They cut across all lesser confessions of Christ's person,

---

[2]J. A. Motyer, *Philippian Studies: The Richness of Christ* (Chicago: InterVarsity Press, 1966), 74.

showing that any view that would make him merely a great teacher or a great prophet is inadequate. They are also remarkable because their doctrine of Christ is indirect. That is, it is brought forward, not for its own sake, but in support of another point entirely. Paul's major point is not that Jesus is who he is, but rather that we should be like him. Bishop Handley C. G. Moule, an English commentator, has written of this section of Paul's letter:

> We have here a chain of assertions about our Lord Jesus Christ, made within some thirty years of his death at Jerusalem; made in the open day of public Christian intercourse, and made (every reader must feel this) not in the least manner of controversy, of assertion against difficulties and denials, but in the tone of a settled, common, and most living certainty. These assertions give us on the one hand the fullest possible assurance that he is man, man in nature, in circumstances and experience, and particularly in the sphere of relation to God the Father. But they also assure us, in precisely the same tone, and in a way which is equally vital to the argument in hand, that he is as genuinely divine as he is genuinely human.[3]

The various parts of Paul's doctrine of the Lord Jesus Christ are stated in that passage with unusual fullness, and therefore we have looked at it at some length. But one must not conclude that the letter to the Philippians is the only place in which such high themes are presented. On the contrary, they occur in much the same way, though less elaborately developed, throughout Paul's writings.

Two passages with the same scope (from eternity past to eternity future) are 2 Corinthians 8:9 and Galatians 4:4-5. In the former, Paul speaks of the Lord Jesus Christ who "though . . . rich, yet for your sake he became poor," that we "by his poverty might become rich." In the second passage, he writes that "when the fullness of time had come, God sent forth his Son, born of woman, born under the law, to redeem those who were under the law, so that we might receive adoption as sons." In both cases, Paul is thinking of a former glory of Christ temporarily laid aside in order that he might accomplish our redemption. All passages that speak of God "sending his own Son" are also in this framework (compare Rom 8:3; 1 Cor 15:47; Eph 4:8-10). In Colossians 1:19, we are told that "in him all the fullness of God was pleased to dwell." In Colossians 2:9, "In him the whole fullness of deity dwells bodily." In other places Paul speaks of Jesus as God "manifested in the flesh" (1 Tim 3:16), of his appearance on earth

---

[3]Handley C. G. Moule, *Philippian Studies: Lessons in Faith and Love* (London: Pickering and Inglis, n.d.), 97.

as an "epiphany" (2 Tim 1:10, Greek text) and, most dramatically of all, of "our great God and Savior Jesus Christ" (Titus 2:13).[4]

"The conception of the person of Christ which underlies and finds expression in the epistle to the Hebrews is indistinguishable from that which governs all the allusions to our Lord in the epistles of Paul,"[5] wrote B. B. Warfield, professor of theology at Princeton Theological Seminary until his death in 1921. Hebrews 2, like Philippians 2:5-11, is based on the premise of the preexistence and full divinity of Christ. Its major point is that Christ moved from his prior position of glory to the incarnation in order to achieve our salvation and is now fully glorified once again. "You made him for a little while lower than the angels; you have crowned him with glory and honor, putting everything in subjection under his feet" (Heb 2:7-8). "We see him who for a little while was made lower than the angels [that is, was made human], namely Jesus, crowned with glory and honor because of the suffering of death" (Heb 2:9). Elsewhere in Hebrews, Jesus is described as reflecting "the glory of God" and bearing "the exact imprint of his nature" (Heb 1:3), "holy, innocent, unstained, separated from sinners" (Heb 7:26), and one to whom shall be given "glory forever and ever" (Heb 13:21).

JOHN'S TEACHING

In the books traditionally ascribed to the apostle John, particularly the fourth Gospel, the deity of Christ is the overriding theme. The purpose of Mark's Gospel, if it may be so narrowed down, is to reveal the Lord Jesus Christ as God's servant. Matthew portrays him as the Jewish Messiah. Luke stresses Christ's humanity. But in John, Jesus is revealed as the eternal, preexisting Son of God, who became human in order to reveal the Father and bring eternal life through his death and resurrection. In fact, toward the end of the Gospel, John tells us explicitly that this is his purpose: "Now Jesus did many other signs in the presence of the disciples, which are not written in this book; but these are written that you may believe that Jesus is the Christ, the Son of God, and that by believing you may have life in his name" (Jn 20:30-31).

Since that is John's purpose in writing, we are not surprised to find this great thesis—Jesus is God—at the very beginning. There he writes, "In the beginning was the Word, and the Word was with God, and the Word was God. He was in

---

[4]For a full discussion of these and other texts, see Benjamin Breckinridge Warfield, "The Person of Christ According to the New Testament," in *The Person and Work of Christ* (Philadelphia: Presbyterian and Reformed, 1970), 38-47.
[5]Ibid., 47.

the beginning with God" (Jn 1:1-2). We know from John 1:14, which says that "the Word became flesh," that this key term, *Word*, refers to Jesus. Hence, the opening verses of the Gospel are telling us that Jesus was with God from the very beginning, that is, from eternity past, and was in fact himself fully God. The opening sentences of the Gospel are a categorical statement of Christ's divinity. There are three distinct statements in these verses, one of them being repeated again in slightly different language.

The first statement, the one repeated, is that Jesus existed with God "in the beginning." This phrase is used in several different ways in the Bible. In 1 John it is used of the beginning of Christ's earthly ministry: "That which was from the beginning, which we have heard, which we have seen with our eyes, which we have looked upon and touched with our hands, concerning the word of life . . . we proclaim also to you" (1 Jn 1:1, 3). In Genesis, it is used of the beginning of creation: "In the beginning, God created the heavens and the earth" (Gen 1:1). But in John's Gospel, the reference in the phrase goes back even beyond that. John is referring to eternity past, saying in effect that when a person begins to talk about Jesus Christ, he or she can do so properly only by going back beyond his earthly life, beyond even the beginning of creation, into eternity. That is where Jesus was. In that perspective John is clearly at one with the teaching of Paul in Philippians and with the teaching of the book of Hebrews.

The second statement in John 1 is that Jesus Christ was "with" God. This is an affirmation of Christ's separate personality in the sense that it has come to be expressed in the doctrine of the division of persons within the Trinity. But it is subtle. John wishes to say that Jesus is fully God. Later he will report Jesus as saying, "Whoever has seen me has seen the Father" (Jn 14:9). But John is also aware that there is diversity within the Godhead, and he expresses that by this statement.

The final statement is the declaration that Jesus is fully divine. The Greek text says literally, "And God was the Word," which means "And fully divine in all respects was Jesus." Everything that can be said about the Father can be said of the Son as well. Is the Father sovereign? So is Jesus. Is the Father omniscient? So is Jesus. Is he omnipresent? So is Jesus. In fact, in Jesus may be found all the wisdom, glory, power, love, holiness, justice, goodness, and truth of God.

In a sense, everything that follows in John's Gospel illustrates that Jesus is God. John organizes the Gospel as a student might organize a term paper, first telling what he is going to prove, then proving it, and finally summarizing it, as if to say to the reader, "See, I have done what I said I would do." Because of that, everything in the Gospel could be considered at this point of our study: the miracles, the discourses, the reaction of Christ's enemies and friends, even John's own comments.

Instead of doing that in full, however, it may be worth taking a single text as indicative of John's overall orientation. This text shows without question that John's conception of Christ was the highest that can possibly be imagined. The text is John 12:41, in which, after John has referred to Isaiah's vision of God (Is 6), he says, "Isaiah said these things because he saw his [Jesus'] glory and spoke of him."

To people living today, particularly Christians, the reference may seem natural, for we are used to theological statements giving full deity to Christ. But that was hardly natural for John, a monotheistic Jew, or for his contemporaries. For a Jew of John's time, God was almost inaccessible in his transcendence. He was the holy One of Israel. He dwelt in glory unapproachable. None actually saw him. And when on some unusual occasion some remarkably privileged person, such as Moses or Isaiah, had received a vision of God in his glory, it was not believed even then to be an actual vision of God as he is in himself, but rather only an image or reflection of him. Yet such a vision filled one with awe and wonder.

What Isaiah saw was the closest thing in all Jewish writings or tradition to an actual "portrait" of the living and holy God. Yet that vision, with all its breathtaking splendor, John applies to Jesus. Without questioning, it would seem, John takes the most exalted vision of God in the Old Testament and says that it was a portrait of a carpenter from Nazareth who was about to be crucified—so great is John's opinion of him.

CHRIST'S CLAIMS

Where did these men, who were obviously impressed with Christ but who were not fools, get such an opinion of him? Why did they believe that he is God? The answer to those questions is on two levels. First, because that is what Jesus himself taught. Second, because their observation of his life left no other explanation.

Christ's own claims occur throughout the Gospels, both directly and indirectly. Practically everything Jesus said was an indirect claim to divinity. His first preaching is an example. When John the Baptist had come declaring the imminent arrival of God's kingdom, he pointed to one who would himself embody that kingdom. When Jesus came, his own first preaching was an announcement of the kingdom's arrival. "The time is fulfilled, and the kingdom of God is at hand; repent and believe in the gospel" (Mk 1:15). Later he said of himself in speaking to the Pharisees, "The kingdom of God is in the midst of you" (Lk 17:21). He was claiming that the prophecies of the Old Testament were about him and were fulfilled in him.

All Christ's words about the Old Testament fall into that category. The sum of his teaching was this: "Do not think that I have come to abolish the Law or the Prophets; I have come not to abolish them but to fulfill them" (Mt 5:17). When he invited men to follow him—"Follow me, and I will make you fishers of men" (Mt 4:19)—he implied that he was of sufficient stature to be worth following. When he forgave sins, he did it knowing he was doing what only God can do (Mk 2:1-12). Toward the end of his life he promised to send God's Holy Spirit to be with the disciples after his departure, which again implies divinity.

Very remarkable among his claims was his unique reference to God as his Father. That was by no means a common form of expression in Judaism (as it is in the English language). No Jew ever spoke of God directly as "my Father." Yet that was the form of address Jesus used, particularly in his prayers. In fact, it was his only mode of addressing God. It referred to his relationship to the Father exclusively. Jesus said, "I and the Father are one" (Jn 10:30). He said, "Father, the hour has come; glorify thy Son that the Son may glorify you. . . . O righteous Father, even though the world does not know you, I know you" (Jn 17:1, 25). Eventually he taught his disciples to address God as Father also, as a result of their relationship to himself. But even in that case his relationship to God as Father and their relationship to God as Father were different. Thus he spoke to Mary Magdalene, saying, "Go to my brothers and say to them, 'I am ascending to my Father and your Father, to my God and your God'" (Jn 20:17). He did not say "to *our* Father" or "to *our* God." "So close was his connection with God that he equated a man's attitude to himself with his attitude to God. Thus, to know him was to know God (Jn 8:19; 14:7); to see him was to see God (Jn 12:45; 14:9); to believe in him was to believe in God (Jn 12:44; 14:1); to receive him was to receive God (Mk 9:37); to hate him was to hate God (Jn 15:23); and to honor him was to honor God (Jn 5:23)."[6]

Jesus' "I am" sayings are worthy of special notice, for he claimed to be all that human beings need for a full spiritual life. Only God can rightly make such claims. "I am the bread of life" (Jn 6:35). "I am the light of the world" (Jn 8:12; 9:5).

---

[6]John R. W. Stott, *Basic Christianity* (Grand Rapids: Eerdmans, 1958), 26.

"I am the door" (Jn 10:7, 9). "I am the good shepherd" (Jn 10:11, 14). "I am the resurrection and the life" (Jn 11:25). "I am the way, and the truth, and the life" (Jn 14:6). "I am the true vine" (Jn 15:1, 5).

In addition to these indirect statements, a number of statements claim divinity directly. Such claims were considered blasphemous in Christ's day and were punishable by death. To avoid a hasty and premature death, Jesus had to be careful in what he said and to whom. Nevertheless, he made a number of direct claims. In John 8, for example, the leaders of the people had been challenging everything Jesus said, and now challenged his statement that Abraham had rejoiced that he was to see the day of Christ and had seen it and was glad. They said, "You are not yet fifty years old, and have you seen Abraham?" He replied, using his most solemn form of introducing a saying, "Truly, truly, I say to you, before Abraham was, I am" (Jn 8:57-58). That so infuriated the leaders that they immediately took up stones to stone him.

To our way of thinking it is a bit hard to see why that particular saying would have provoked such a violent response. Stoning was the penalty for blasphemy, for making oneself out to be God. But how does one get blasphemy from Jesus' words? It is obvious from the saying itself that Jesus was claiming to have existed before Abraham was born. It is also obvious from the tense of the verb—"before Abraham was, I *am*"—that he was claiming an eternal preexistence. But that alone would not be sufficient cause for stoning. The real reason for their violent reaction is that when Jesus said "I am," he was using the divine name by which God had revealed himself to Moses at the burning bush. When Moses had asked, "If I come to the people of Israel and say to them, 'The God of your fathers has sent me to you,' and they ask me, 'What is his name?' what shall I say to them?" God said to Moses, "'I AM WHO I AM.' . . . Say this to the people of Israel: 'I AM has sent me to you'" (Ex 3:13-14). That is the name that Jesus took to himself. Because of that, the Jews, who immediately recognized his claim for what it was, reached out to kill him.

A final example of Christ's unique conception of himself occurred shortly after the resurrection on the day that Jesus appeared among the disciples, Thomas being present. Jesus had appeared to the disciples earlier when Thomas was absent. But when Thomas was told about the appearance, Thomas had replied, "Unless I see in his hands the mark of the nails, and place my finger into the mark of the nails, and place my hand into his side, I will never believe" (Jn 20:25). Then the Lord appeared to them once more and asked Thomas to make the test he had wanted to make. "Put your finger here, and see my hands; and put out your hand, and place it in my side" (Jn 20:27). Overcome by Christ's presence, Thomas immediately fell to the ground and worshiped him, saying, "My Lord and my God!" (Jn 20:28). Lord and God! *Adonai! Elohim!* And Jesus accepted that designation. He did not deny it.

GOOD MAN, MADMAN, CON MAN, OR SON OF MAN?

We have traced the claims of Christ's divinity through the writings of the apostle Paul, the book of Hebrews, and John's Gospel to the teachings of Jesus himself. "Is it possible to believe this?" someone might ask. "Is it possible to believe that a carpenter from Nazareth, however extraordinary, was actually God?" Well, what are the possibilities?

One truly impossible answer was first given by the people of Jerusalem. They said on one occasion, "He is a good man" (Jn 7:12). Whatever else he may be, he certainly cannot be merely a good man. No good man can honestly make the claims he made. He put himself forward as the Savior of the human race, claiming to be God and therefore being able to save. Is he? If so, he is obviously much more than a man. If not, then he is at best mistaken (consequently, not "good"), and at worst a deceiver. What are we to do with his claims? We cannot escape them. John R. W. Stott has written, "The claims are there. They do not in themselves constitute evidence of deity. The claims may have been false. But some explanation of them must be found. We cannot any longer regard Jesus as simply a great Teacher, if he was so grievously mistaken in one of the chief subjects of his teaching, namely himself."[7] C. S. Lewis wrote similarly, "You must make your choice. Either this man was, and is, the Son of God: or else a madman or something worse. You can shut him up for a fool; you can spit at him and kill him for a demon; or you can fall at his feet and call him Lord and God. But let us not come with any patronising nonsense about his being a great human teacher. He has not left that open to us. He did not intend to."[8]

The one impossible explanation of the person of Christ is, then, that he was a good man, a good and outstanding teacher to whom we should listen and from whom we should all learn. The quotation from C. S. Lewis has already suggested the remaining possibilities. There are three of them.

First, Jesus may have been *mad*. Or he was suffering from megalomania. That was the view of some in his own day who said, "You have a demon" (Jn 7:20).

---

[7]Ibid., 32.
[8]C. S. Lewis, *Mere Christianity* (New York: The Macmillan Company, 1958), 41.

Hitler suffered from megalomania. So also, probably, did Napoleon. Perhaps Jesus was like them. Was he? Before we jump too quickly at that explanation, we need to ask whether the total character of Jesus (as we know it) bears out this speculation. Did he act like one who was crazy? Did he speak like one suffering from megalomania? It is hard to read the Gospels and be satisfied with this explanation. Rather, as we read the Gospels the conclusion seems to be forced on us that, rather than being mad, Jesus was actually the sanest man who ever lived. He spoke with quiet authority. He always seemed to be in control of the situation. He was never surprised or rattled. He will not fit that easy classification.

Charles Lamb reportedly said, "If Shakespeare were to come into this room we should all rise up to meet him, but if that Person [Jesus] were to come into it, we should all fall down and try to kiss the hem of his garment."

Another reason why Jesus could not have been crazy is the reaction of others to him. People did not merely tolerate him; they either were for him or else were violently against him. That is not the way we react to those who are crazy. We may be irritated by a madman's irrational behavior. We may ignore him. We may lock him up if his delusions are dangerous. But we do not kill him. Yet that is what people did to Jesus.

A second possibility is that Jesus was a *deceiver*, the view of some others (Jn 7:12). That is, he deliberately set out to fool people. Before we settle on that answer, however, we need to be clear about what is involved in it. In the first place, if Jesus really was a deceiver he was certainly the best deceiver who ever lived. Jesus claimed to be God, but that claim was not made in a Greek or Roman environment where the idea of many gods or even half-gods was acceptable. It was made at the heart of monotheistic Judaism. The Jews were ridiculed, at times persecuted, for their strict belief in one God. Nevertheless, they stuck to that doctrine and were fanatical in its defense. In that theological climate Christ made his claims—and what happened? The remarkable thing is that he got people to believe in him. Lots of people—men and women, peasants and sophisticates, priests, eventually even members of his own family.

On the other hand, if Jesus was a deceiver, if he was not God, he could be termed a devil. Think it through clearly. Jesus did not merely say "I am God" and let it go at that. He said, "I am God come to save fallen humanity; I am the means of salvation; trust me with your life and your future." Jesus taught that God is holy and that we are barred from him because we are not holy. Our sin is a barrier between ourselves and God. Moreover, he taught that he had come to do something about our problem. He would die for our sin; he would bear its punishment. All who would trust in him would be saved. That is good news, even great news—but only if it is true. If it is not true, then his followers are of all human beings the most miserable, and Jesus Christ should be hated as a fiend from hell. If it is not true, Jesus has sent generations of gullible followers to a hopeless eternity.

But is he a deceiver? Is that the only explanation we can give for one who was known for being "meek and lowly," who became a poor itinerant evangelist in order to help the poor and teach those whom others despised, who said, "Come to me, all who labor and are heavy laden, and I will give you rest" (Mt 11:28)? Somehow the facts do not fit. We cannot face the facts of his life and teaching and still call this man a deceiver. What then? If he was not a deceiver and he was not mad, only one possibility is left. Jesus is who he said he is. He is God, and we should follow him.

CHAPTER 10

THE HUMANITY
OF JESUS CHRIST

*A*lthough there are those today, as in every age, who deny Christ's divinity, there are also those who affirm his divinity but stop with that description of him. This is also an error. A second, equally important fact is that he is also fully human. He is not human from eternity past, as is true of his Godhead. He became human at a particular point in time through the incarnation. But now, having become human, he is the God-man to whom alone we look for salvation.

In the Bible this truth is everywhere apparent, even in the Old Testament. For example, in that prophecy from Isaiah so often read at Christmas time, the twofold nature of the coming Christ is described.

> For to us a child is born,
>   to us a son is given;
> and the government shall be upon his shoulder,
>   and his name shall be called
> Wonderful Counselor, Mighty God,
>   Everlasting Father, Prince of Peace. (Is 9:6)

Here two important verbs are used of Christ's coming: "is born" and "is given." As a child he is *born*, but as a Son he is *given*.

The same distinction occurs in Paul's writings. We read, "Concerning his Son, who was descended from David according to the flesh and was declared to be the Son of God in power according to the Spirit of holiness by his resurrection from the dead, Jesus Christ our Lord" (Rom 1:3-4). Jesus was descended from David according to the flesh, but he was also designated God's Son. We read, "But when the fullness of time had come, God sent forth his Son, born of woman, born under the law, to redeem those who were under the law, so that we might receive adoption as sons" (Gal 4:4-5). As a Son, Jesus Christ was *sent*, because he was always God's Son. Nevertheless, he was *born* of woman under the law, and thus became human. The Bible is never hesitant to put the twin truths of the full deity and true humanity of Christ together.

These truths are also illustrated through various events in Christ's ministry. For instance, in the second chapter of John's Gospel, the Lord is at a wedding (Jn 2:1-11). Few things could be more human than that. Yet when the wine is exhausted and the host about to be embarrassed, Jesus makes new and better wine from the water in the great stone waterpots used for the Jewish purifications.

On another occasion, the disciples were crossing the Sea of Galilee from Capernaum to the land of the Gadarenes. Jesus, exhausted from the day's activities, was asleep in the boat. A storm arose that was so intense it frightened even those seasoned fishermen. They awoke him saying, "Save us, Lord; we are perishing," and Jesus stilled the storm (Mt 8:25). What could be more human than our Lord's total exhaustion in the boat? What could be more divine than his stilling of the winds and waves? The disciples exclaimed, "What sort of man is this, that even winds and sea obey him?" (Mt 8:27).

Nothing could be more human than Jesus' death by crucifixion. Nothing could be more divine than the darkening of the sky, the tearing of the veil of the temple, the opening of the graves of the saints buried near Jerusalem, and the triumphant rending of the tomb on that first Easter morning.

THE GNOSTIC HERESY

These twin truths have not always been acknowledged by everyone in all periods of church history. There is hardly a doctrine of Christianity that has not been denied by someone sometime. The heresy of denial of Christ's divinity usually goes by the name of Arianism (after Arius of Alexandria; died 335). Arius taught that the Son of God and the Holy Spirit were beings willed into existence by God for the purposes of redemption. Thus they were not eternal, as God is. There was a time "before which they were not."

The error on the other side, the heresy of denying Christ's true humanity, goes by the name of Docetism. Docetism grew out of a movement known as

Gnosticism, which was more or less contemporary with the early years of Christianity. It had two major characteristics. First, there was a principle that one
commentator calls "the supremacy of the intellect and the superiority of mental
enlightenment to faith and conduct."[1] The Gnostics thought of themselves as
"the knowing ones," which is what the word *gnostic* means, believing that salvation
is primarily by knowledge, that is, by initiation into the mystical and allegedly
superior knowledge that they possessed. Of course in such a system, the literal
incarnation of the Son of God was meaningless. What was important was the
"Christ idea" or the truths that Christ announced.

A second characteristic of the Gnostic system was its belief in the radical and
unbridgeable gulf between spirit and matter, coupled with the conviction that
matter is inherently evil and spirit alone is good. This view was held in common
by most other systems of thought in that period. On the one hand, it led to a
denial of the importance of the moral life; salvation was in the realm of the mind
or spirit, which alone is good, and therefore what the body did could not matter.
On the other hand, it produced a type of philosophical religion that was divorced
from concrete history. Obviously, Gnosticism came into conflict with authentic
Christianity. Given its system, any real incarnation of the Son of God was impossible. If matter is evil, then God could not have taken a human body upon himself.
And if that is so, then the incarnation of God in Christ must have been in appearance only. The word *Docetism* comes from the Greek verb *dokeō*, which
means "to appear." In some forms of supposedly Christian Gnosticism, the incarnation was therefore expressed by saying that the Spirit of God merely came
on the man Jesus at the time of his baptism, remained with him during the years
of his ministry, and then deserted him just before his crucifixion. In other forms,
it was said that Jesus only seemed to be a man, but actually was not one. Therefore,
he did not really possess a material body, did not really die, and so on.

Docetism was anathema to Christianity, of course, so it was forcefully rejected.
The first written reply to such views is that of the apostle John, preserved in his
epistles primarily. He insists on the true incarnation of the Son of God. Thus,
his first epistle begins by stressing the apostles' own physical experience of Jesus:

> That which was from the beginning, which we have heard, which we have seen
> with our eyes, which we have looked upon and touched with our hands, concerning
> the word of life—the life was made manifest, and we have seen it, and testify to

---

[1]Alexander Ross, *The Epistles of James and John*, New International Commentary on the New Testament (Grand Rapids: Eerdmans, 1954), 115.

it and proclaim to you the eternal life, which was with the Father and was made manifest to us—that which we have seen and heard we proclaim also to you, so that you too may have fellowship with us. (1 Jn 1:1-3)

These verses refer to three of the five physical senses. Later John gives this test of true Christianity: "Every spirit that confesses that Jesus Christ has come in the flesh is from God, and every spirit that does not confess Jesus is not from God. This is the spirit of antichrist, which you heard was coming and now is in the world already" (1 Jn 4:2-3).

Sometime later, Marcion of Pontus, who taught in Rome about the middle of the second century, also popularized Docetist views. He is known mostly for his rejection of the Old Testament, as well as parts of the New. But he was also a threat to the church through his rejection of the materiality of Christ's body. Another early heresy was Manichaeanism, which had a strong influence on Augustine's early years. It included the belief that Christ's body was composed of "heavenly" but not true material flesh. These errors were rejected soundly in a series of early church councils. The Creed of Chalcedon (AD 451) declares that the Lord Jesus Christ is

truly God and truly man, of a reasonable [rational] soul and body; consubstantial [coessential] with the Father according to the Godhead, and consubstantial with us according to the manhood; in all things like unto us without sin; begotten before all ages of the Father according to the Godhead, and in these latter days, for us and for our salvation, born of the Virgin Mary, the Mother of God, according to the manhood; one and the same Christ, Son, Lord, Only-begotten, to be acknowledged in two natures inconfusedly, unchangeably, indivisibly, inseparably; the distinction of natures being by no means taken away by the union, but rather the property of each nature being preserved, and concurring in one Person and one Subsistence, not parted or divided into two persons, but one and the same Son, Only-begotten, God, the Word, the Lord Jesus Christ.

The Athanasian Creed, attributed to Athanasius, a great third-century defender of orthodoxy, but more likely composed after Chalcedon, says more simply, "Our Lord Jesus Christ, the Son of God, is God and man . . . perfect God, and perfect man . . . who although he be [is] God and man; yet he is not two, but one Christ; one, not by conversion of the Godhead into flesh: but by taking [assumption] of the manhood into God." These creeds and the Scriptures they are based on teach that Jesus, the Son of God, became like us in every respect (except for sin) so that we might become like him.

CHRIST'S EMOTIONS

One area in which Jesus became like us through the incarnation is the emotional life, as B. B. Warfield pointed out in an essay on that subject in the early years of this century.[2] Some in the church have wanted to separate Christ from all emotions, as if emotions are not quite appropriate to him. Others have exaggerated his emotions to the point at which he hardly commands our reverence. The true picture, as presented in the New Testament, is somewhat between the two.

The emotion most frequently attributed to Christ is *compassion* or *pity*. It is his expression of deep love when confronted by the desperate need of fallen men and women. Sometimes it is occasioned by physical need. Thus on one occasion, when confronted by the hunger of a large crowd that had been following him, Jesus said, "I have compassion on the crowd, because they have been with me now three days and have nothing to eat. And if I send them away hungry to their homes, they will faint on the way. And some of them have come from far away" (Mk 8:2-3). We are told that he was "moved with pity" at the sight of a leper, and healed him (Mk 1:41), that he responded "in pity" to the appeal for healing by two blind men (Mt 20:34), that "compassion" caused him to raise the dead son of the widow of Nain (Lk 7:13). Spiritual need also drew forth his compassion. We are told again and again that he had compassion on the multitudes because "they were like sheep without a shepherd" (Mk 6:34; see also Mt 9:36; 14:14). At other times, he actually wept aloud over the stubborn unbelief of the city of Jerusalem (Lk 19:41) and at the tomb of Lazarus (Jn 11:35).

Mention of Christ's tears leads to another area of Christ's emotional life, the area of *grief*, leading even to *indignation* and *anger*. One important example of his grief, though difficult to interpret, is his weeping at the tomb of Lazarus. An unusual word, *embrimaomai*, is used either to say that Jesus was "angry" at what was taking place or else that he was "deeply moved." In the New Testament it is found in only three other passages (Mt 9:30; Mk 1:43; 14:5), in two of them meaning "sternly charged" and in the third "reproached." Neither of these meanings seems to fit the context of Christ's response at the tomb of Lazarus. However, William Barclay believes each of them seems to contain "a certain sternness, almost anger." Thus some commentators have placed the idea of

---

[2]Benjamin Breckenridge Warfield, "On the Emotional Life of Our Lord," in *The Person and Work of Christ* (Philadelphia: Presbyterian and Reformed, 1970), 93-145.

indignation or even anger in John's passage. They would translate the verse, "Jesus was moved to anger in his spirit." If we ask why Jesus should be angry, they answer either that he was angry with the supposed unbelief or hypocrisy of those who were weeping over Lazarus, or else he was angry with death, which he would have viewed as a tool of Satan and a great enemy. Insincerity is not mentioned or implied in the passage, however, and whatever may have been true of the crowd, Mary and Martha were certainly not faking their grief.

The other possibility, translating the word to suggest deep emotion, rests on the fact that one other known use of the word *embrimaomai* in the Greek language is to describe the snorting of a horse, as in the excitement of battle or under a heavy load. Thus Jesus may be said to have groaned with the sisters in deep emotion, emotion out of which an involuntary cry was wrung from his heart. That is the view of J. B. Phillips, who rendered the phrase, "He was deeply moved and visibly distressed," and by the translators of the New International Version, who say, "He was deeply moved and troubled."

Some Christians have found this unacceptable, for they imagine that it is not proper for Jesus to have been moved to such a degree, particularly by the grief of others. But how can we read the passage without seeing that Jesus wept with the sisters in their grief? "The expression used . . . implies that he now voluntarily and deliberately accepts and makes his own the emotion and the experience from which it is his purpose to deliver men."[3] "He . . . gathered up into his own personality all the misery resulting from sin, represented in a dead man and broken-hearted people round him."[4]

At times, however, the grief displayed by Jesus went on to anger, as in his stern denunciations of the religious leaders of his day. He calls them "hypocrites" (Mt 15:7), "whitewashed tombs" (Mt 23:27), "serpents" (Mt 23:33), "blind guides" (Mt 15:14), and "of [their] father the devil" (Jn 8:44). At times he could even be moved with anger against his own disciples. On the occasion when the disciples in a fit of self-importance tried to keep the children from coming to Jesus, we read, "But when Jesus saw it, he was indignant and said to them, 'Let the children come to me; do not hinder them, for to such belongs the kingdom of God'" (Mk 10:14).

It is not an impassible, insensitive, unmovable Christ that is presented to us in the New Testament. Rather it is one who has entered into our griefs and

---

[3]R. H. Lightfoot, *St. John's Gospel: A Commentary* (Oxford: The University Press, 1963), 229.
[4]G. Campbell Morgan, *The Gospel According to John* (Westwood, NJ: Fleming H. Revell, n.d.), 197.

understands our sorrows, one who was on occasion moved to righteous indignation and angered by sin.

A third area of Christ's emotional life is that of *joy* or *gladness*. Warfield wrote,

> We call our Lord "the Man of Sorrows," and the designation is obviously appropriate for one who came into the world to bear the sins of men and to give his life a ransom for many. It is, however, not a designation which is applied to Christ in the New Testament, and even in the Prophet (Isa. 53:3) it may very well refer rather to the objective afflictions of the righteous servant than to his subjective distresses. In any event we must bear in mind that our Lord did not come into the world to be broken by the power of sin and death, but to break it. He came as a conqueror with the gladness of the imminent victory in his heart; for the joy set before him he was able to endure the cross, despising the shame (Heb 12:2). And as he did not prosecute his work in doubt of the issue, neither did he prosecute it hesitantly as to its methods. He rather (so we are told, Luke 10:21) "exulted in the Holy Spirit" as he contemplated the ways of God in bringing many sons to glory.[5]

Sometimes Jesus spoke of his own joy and of his desire that it also be possessed by his followers. "These things I have spoken to you, that my joy may be in you, and that your joy may be full" (Jn 15:11). Again, in his high priestly prayer of John 17, "Now I am coming to you, and these things I speak in the world, that they may have my joy fulfilled in themselves" (Jn 17:13).

LIKE US IN TEMPTATION AND SUFFERING

Two more areas in which Jesus clearly became like us by means of his incarnation are important in relating to him as our guide in living the Christian life.

The first is that he became subject to *temptation*. "For we do not have a high priest who is unable to sympathize with our weaknesses, but one who in every respect has been tempted as we are, yet without sin" (Heb 4:15). We have a dramatic illustration of what this means in the story of Christ's temptation by Satan, recorded in Matthew 4:1-11 (parallel, Lk 4:1-13). After his baptism by John, Jesus was driven into the wilderness to be tempted by the devil. He spent forty days in fasting, and then the temptations began. The first was physical, the temptation to turn stones to bread. We learn the significance of it from Jesus' reply to Satan: "Man shall not live by bread alone, but by every word that comes

---

[5]Warfield, "On the Emotional Life of Our Lord," 122-23.

from the mouth of God" (Mt 4:4). It was the temptation to put physical needs over spiritual ones.

The second temptation was spiritual. The devil took Jesus to a pinnacle of the temple in Jerusalem and challenged him to throw himself down, presuming on God to rescue him. The devil said, "If you are the Son of God, throw yourself down; for it is written, 'He will give his angels charge of you,' and 'On their hands they will bear you up, lest you strike your foot against a stone'" (Mt 4:6). Jesus answered that it would be wrong to do that, because it is also written that we shall not put God to the test.

Finally, the devil produced a vocational temptation. He knew that Jesus was to receive the kingdoms of this world for his glory; it had been prophesied in the Old Testament. "Ask of me, and I will make the nations your heritage, and the ends of the earth your possession" (Ps 2:8). But the way to that inheritance was the cross, and Satan now argued that Jesus could obtain it without suffering. He would help. He said, "All these I will give you, if you will fall down and worship me" (Mt 4:9). Jesus rejected Satan's offer and instead set his face to go in the way that God had set before him.

A final area in which Jesus became like us in order that we might become like him is in *suffering*. Some of it was emotional and spiritual suffering. Some was physical. We read that Christ experienced hunger. That was true many times, no doubt, but we are told so explicitly in connection with his wilderness temptation (Mt 4:2). He also experienced thirst. On one occasion, weary with his journey, he sat on Jacob's well and asked a woman of Samaria for a drink. On the cross he cried, "I thirst," and they gave him vinegar (Jn 19:28). Once, when he fell asleep in a wildly rocking boat, he was so tired that even the wind and waves failed to rouse him. The greatest example of his suffering was the anguish of soul and body endured on the cross, before which even his soul shrank (Lk 22:39-46; compare Mt 26:36-46; Mk 14:32-42).

Jesus, by means of the incarnation, came to know all the vicissitudes of life: trials, joys, sufferings, losses, gains, temptations, griefs. He entered into them, understood them, and thus became a pattern for us, that we should go through these experiences as he did, and also an encouragement to us to come to him in prayer, knowing that he understands what we are going through. Peter speaks of the value of Christ as a pattern when he encouraged those of his day to endure suffering as Christ did. "For to this you have been called, because Christ also suffered for you, leaving you an example, so that you might follow in his steps" (1 Pet 2:21). The author of Hebrews refers to our encouragement in prayer, saying,

> For surely it is not angels that he [Christ] helps, but he helps the offspring of Abraham. Therefore he had to be made like his brothers in every respect, so that he might become a merciful and faithful high priest in the service of God, to make propitiation for the sins of the people. For because he himself has suffered and been tempted, he is able to help those who are being tempted. (Heb 2:16-18)

CHAPTER 11

WHY CHRIST BECAME HUMAN

*I*t has been said that "Christianity is Christ," and that Christian theology is therefore an explanation of who Christ is and what it means to have faith in him. That is not so simple as it might seem, however. For one thing, the most important statement to be made about Jesus is mind-boggling: he is both God and man. For another, the doctrines of Christ's person pass quickly and inevitably into the area of Christ's work. So it is impossible to talk meaningfully about who Jesus is without also talking about what he did and about the importance of that for us.

Why did Jesus become human? The answer to that question, as we will see, is that Jesus became human in order to die for those who were to believe in him. Such an answer deals with the work of Christ and could therefore properly be considered later, in the section on Christ's work. But it belongs here also, for the work of Christ relates closely to who he is, and the question "What did he do?" inevitably requires an explanation of his unique nature as the God-man. We might say that the nature of Christ gives meaning to his work. And his work, centered in the atonement, is the only proper foundation for a doctrine of his person.

James Denney, a professor at the United Free Church College in Glasgow, Scotland, around the turn of the century, discusses the matter. We need an atonement. But, as Denney writes, Christ is the only person who can do this work for us.

This is the deepest and most decisive thing we can know about him, and in answering the questions which it prompts we are starting from a basis in experience. There is a sense in which Christ confronts us as the reconciler. He is doing the will of God on our behalf, and we can only look on. We see in him the judgment and the mercy of God in relation to our sins. His presence and work on earth are a divine gift, a divine visitation. He is the gift of God to men, not the offering of men to God, and God gives himself to us in and with him. We owe to him all that we call divine life. On the other hand, this divine visitation is made, and this divine life is imparted, through a life and work which are truly human. The presence and work of Jesus in the world, even the work of bearing sin, does not prompt us to define human and divine by contrast with each other: there is no suggestion of incongruity between them. Nevertheless, they are both there, and the fact that they are both there justifies us in raising the question as to Jesus' relation to God on the one hand, and to men on the other.[1]

So the work of Christ, particularly as an explanation of the incarnation, must occupy us here. Only after that will we be free to survey Christ's work more comprehensively.

THE REASON FOR THE INCARNATION

A classic statement of the question why Jesus Christ became human and its answer is found in the works of Anselm of Canterbury (died 1109). Anselm's theological masterpiece, *Cur Deus Homo?* (literally "Why God Man?" or more colloquially, "Why Did God Become Man?") deals with the question of the incarnation. The answer is a carefully thought-out statement of the atonement. Anselm answered that God became human in Christ because only one who was both God and man could achieve our salvation. In approaching the subject from Anselm's perspective, we do not want to say that there are no other reasons for the incarnation. We have already noted that it reveals the value set by God on human life. Life is declared to be valuable by the creation alone, but sin has cheapened life. The incarnation, coming in the midst of a history of human sin, indicates that God has not abandoned us but loves us and values us even in our fallen state. The incarnation does two further things. It shows us that God is able to understand us and sympathize with us, which is an inducement to come to him in prayer (as suggested in the last chapter). Also, the incarnation gives an example of how a person ought to live in this world. Peter refers even to the

---

[1]James Denney, *The Death of Christ*, ed. R. V. G. Tasker (Chicago: InterVarsity Press, 1964), 175.

crucifixion in such terms: "Christ also suffered for you, leaving you an example, so that you might follow in his steps" (1 Pet 2:21).

But the atonement is the real reason for the incarnation. The author of Hebrews affirms this clearly.

> It is impossible for the blood of bulls and goats to take away sins.
>
> Consequently, when Christ came into the world, he said,
>
> "Sacrifices and offerings you have not desired,
>
> but a body you have prepared for me;
>
> in burnt offerings and sin offerings
>
> you have taken no pleasure.
>
> Then I said, "Behold, I have come to do your will, O God,"
>
> as it is written of me in the scroll of the book." (Heb 10:4-7)

The writer then adds that when Jesus says he is coming to do God's will, that will must be understood as the providing of a better sacrifice. "And by that will we have been sanctified through the offering of the body of Jesus Christ once for all" (Heb 10:10).

We find the same emphasis elsewhere. In its derivation the name Jesus ("Jehovah saves") looks forward to the atonement: "You shall call his name Jesus, for he will save his people from their sins" (Mt 1:21). Jesus himself spoke of his coming suffering (Mk 8:31; 9:31), linking the success of his mission to the crucifixion: "And I, when I am lifted up from the earth, will draw all people to myself" (Jn 12:32). At several places in John's Gospel the crucifixion is spoken of as that vital "hour" for which Christ came (Jn 2:4; 7:30; 8:20; 12:23, 27; 13:1; 17:1).

Moreover, the death of Jesus is the theme of the Old Testament also, first in regard to the full meaning of the sacrifices (the meaning at the heart of the law) and then in regard to the prophecies, which focused increasingly on the promise of a coming Redeemer. Isaiah 53 and other Old Testament texts speak of the suffering of the deliverer to come. In Galatians, the apostle Paul teaches that even Abraham, who lived before both the law and prophets, was saved by faith in Jesus (Gal 3:8, 16). Jesus taught the downcast Emmaus disciples that the Old Testament foretold his death and resurrection: "He said to them, 'O foolish ones, and slow of heart to believe all that the prophets have spoken! Was it not necessary that the Christ should suffer these things and enter into his glory?' And beginning with Moses and all the Prophets, he interpreted to them in all the Scriptures the things concerning himself" (Lk 24:25-27). In the light of these texts and many others, it is necessary to say that the atonement of Christ is *the* reason for the incarnation. It is the explanation of his twofold nature and the focal point of world and biblical history.

SALVATION THROUGH THE GOD-MAN

Why must the doctrine of the atonement be central to the Scriptures? Why must there even be a sacrifice? Or, granting that an atonement is needed, why must Jesus, the God-man, be the one to provide it? One answer, which Calvin gives in the *Institutes of the Christian Religion*, is that this is how God has chosen to do it and that it is therefore impertinent of us to ask if there could not be some other way. But that is not a full answer, as both Calvin and Anselm recognized. It is possible to ask without impertinence, in an effort to seek understanding why salvation had to be achieved in this way.[2]

Anselm (and Calvin after him) gave two answers. The first is that salvation had to be achieved by God, for no one else could achieve it. Certainly men and women could not achieve it, for we are the ones who have gotten ourselves into trouble in the first place. We have done so by our rebellion against God's just law and decrees. Moreover, we have suffered from the effects of sin to such a degree that our will is bound, and therefore we cannot even choose to please God, let alone actually please him. If we are to be saved, only God, who has both the will and power to save, must save us. Anselm's second answer is that, in apparent contradiction, salvation must also be achieved by humanity. Humanity is the one who has wronged God and must therefore make the wrong right. Granted this state of affairs, salvation can be achieved only by one who is both God and human, namely, by Christ.

> It would not have been right for the restoration of human nature to be left undone, and . . . it could not have been done unless man paid what was owing to God for sin. But the debt was so great that, while man alone owed it, only God could pay it, so that the same person must be both man and God. Thus it was necessary for God to take manhood into the unity of his Person, so that he who in his own nature ought to pay and could not should be in a person who could. . . . The life of this man was so sublime, so precious, that

---

[2]One of the most important themes of Anselm's work is in this area, in justification of inquiry into the reason for certain revealed truths. His phrase for this is *fides quaerens intellectum* ("faith in search of understanding"). It is the subject of a valuable study by Karl Barth, *Anselm: Fides Quaerens Intellectum* (Richmond, VA: John Knox Press, 1958).

it can suffice to pay what is owing for the sins of the whole world, and infinitely more.[3]

Three points must be remembered if Anselm's explanation of the incarnation is not to be misunderstood. First, it is God who initiates and carries out the action. If that is forgotten, it is easy to think of God as being somehow remote from the atonement and therefore merely requiring it as some abstract price paid to satisfy his justice. In that view, God appears disinterested, legalistic, and cruel. Actually, God's nature is characterized by love, and it is out of love that he planned and carried out the atonement. In Christ God himself was satisfying his own justice. So it is easy to see why the incarnation and the atonement must be considered together if each is not to be distorted.

Second, in Anselm's explanation there is no suggestion whatever of human beings somehow placating the wrath of an angry God. Propitiation does refer to the placating of wrath, as will be seen in the study of that concept in chapter thirteen. But it is not humanity who placates God. Rather, it is God placating his own wrath so that his love might go out to embrace and fully save the sinner.

Third, it is not a matter of substitution in the bald sense in which an innocent victim takes the place of another person who should be punished. Rather, it is substitution in a deeper sense. The one who takes the place of humankind in order to satisfy God's justice is actually one who had himself become human and is therefore what we might term our representative.

A proper recognition of the connection between the incarnation and the atonement makes the incarnation understandable. At the same time, it eliminates the most common misunderstandings of, and objections to, Christ's sacrifice of himself as the means of our salvation. One writer summarizes the matter like this:

> God is not only perfectly holy, but the source and pattern of holiness: He is the origin and the upholder of the moral order of the universe. He *must* be just. The Judge of all the earth *must* do right. Therefore it was impossible by the necessities of his own being that he should deal lightly with sin, and compromise the claims of holiness. If sin could be forgiven at all, it must be on some basis which would vindicate the holy law of God, which is not a mere code, but the moral order of the whole creation. But such vindication must be supremely costly. Costly to whom? Not to the forgiven sinner, for there could be no price asked from him for his forgiveness; both because the cost is far beyond his reach, and because

---

[3]Eugene R. Fairweather, ed. and trans., *A Scholastic Miscellany: Anselm to Ockham*, The Library of Christian Classics, X (Philadelphia: The Westminster Press, 1956), 176.

God loves to give and not to sell. Therefore God himself undertook to pay a cost, to offer a sacrifice, so tremendous that the gravity of his condemnation of sin should be absolutely beyond question even as he forgave it, while at the same time the Love which impelled him to pay the price would be the wonder of angels, and would call forth the worshipping gratitude of the redeemed sinner.

On Calvary this price was paid, paid by *God:* the Son giving himself, bearing our sin and its curse; the Father giving the Son, his only Son whom he loved. But it was paid by God become man, who not only took the place of guilty man, but also was his representative. . . .

The divine Son, one of the three persons of the one God, he through whom, from the beginning of the creation, the Father has revealed himself to man (John 1:18), took man's nature upon him, and so became our representative. He offered himself as a sacrifice in our stead, bearing our sin in his own body on the tree. He suffered, not only awful physical anguish, but also the unthinkable spiritual horror of becoming identified with the sin to which he was infinitely opposed. He thereby came under the curse of sin, so that for a time even his perfect fellowship with his Father was broken. Thus God proclaimed his infinite abhorrence of sin by being willing himself to suffer all that, in place of the guilty ones, in order that he might justly forgive. Thus the love of God found its perfect fulfillment, because he did not hold back from even that uttermost sacrifice, in order that we might be saved from eternal death through what he endured. Thus it was possible for him to be just, and to justify the believer, because as Lawgiver and as Substitute for the rebel race of man, he himself had suffered the penalty of the broken law.[4]

THE CENTRALITY OF THE CROSS

Several conclusions flow from this explanation of the incarnation. First, according to the Scriptures Calvary and not Bethlehem is the center of Christianity. An idea popular in some theological circles has been that the incarnation is the most important thing, that is, God identifying himself with humanity, and that the atonement was something like an afterthought. But according to the biblical teaching, the reason for the God-man is that it required a God-man to die for our salvation. Therefore, "The crucial significance of the cradle at Bethlehem lies in its place in the sequence of steps down that led the Son of God to the cross of Calvary, and we do not understand it till we see it in this context."[5] To focus

---

[4]H. E. Guillebaud, *Why the Cross?* (Chicago: InterVarsity Christian Fellowship, 1947), 130, 185.
[5]J. I. Packer, *Knowing God* (Downers Grove, IL: InterVarsity Press, 1973), 51.

on the incarnation apart from the cross leads to false sentimentality and neglect of the horror and magnitude of human sin.

Second, if the death of Christ on the cross is the true meaning of the incarnation, then there is no gospel without the cross. Christmas by itself is no gospel. The life of Christ is no gospel. Even the resurrection, important as it is in the total scheme of things, is no gospel by itself. For the good news is not just that God became human, nor that God has spoken to reveal a proper way of life to us, or even that death, the great enemy, is conquered. Rather, the good news is that sin has been dealt with (of which the resurrection is a proof); that Jesus has suffered its penalty for us as our representative, so that we might never have to suffer it; and that therefore all who believe in him can look forward to heaven. Moreover, the other biblical themes must be seen in that context, as we have already seen of the incarnation. Emulation of Christ's life and teaching is possible only to those who enter into a new relationship with God through faith in Jesus as their substitute. The resurrection is not merely a victory over death (though it is that), but a proof that the atonement was a satisfactory atonement in the sight of the Father (Rom 4:25); and that death, the result of sin, is abolished on that basis.

Any gospel that talks merely of the Christ-event, meaning the incarnation without the atonement, is a false gospel. Any gospel that talks about the love of God without pointing out that his love led him to pay the ultimate price for sin in the person of his Son on the cross is a false gospel. The only true gospel is of the "one mediator" (1 Tim 2:5-6), who gave himself for us.

Finally, just as there can be no gospel without the atonement as the reason for the incarnation, so also there can be no Christian life without it. Without the atonement, the incarnation theme easily becomes a kind of deification of the human and leads to arrogance and self-advancement. With the atonement, the true message of the life of Christ, and therefore also of the life of the Christian man or woman, is humility and self-sacrifice for the obvious needs of others. The Christian life is not indifference to those who are hungry or sick or suffering from some other lack. It is not contentment with our own abundance, neither the abundance of middle-class living with homes and cars and clothes and vacations, nor the abundance of education, nor even the spiritual abundance of good churches, Bibles, Bible teaching, or Christian friends and acquaintances. Rather, it is the awareness that others lack these things and that we must therefore sacrifice many of our own interests in order to identify with them and thus bring them increasingly into the abundance we enjoy.

Paul wrote of the incarnation, "For you know the grace of our Lord Jesus Christ, that though he was rich, yet for your sake he became poor, so that you by his poverty might become rich" (2 Cor 8:9). That is also a statement of the atonement and of the Christian life. In fact, it occurs in a chapter in which Paul is speaking about the duty of the Christians at Corinth to give money for the relief of those less fortunate who lived in Judea. We will live for Christ fully only when we are willing to be impoverished, if necessary, in order that others might be helped.

PART IV

THE WORK
OF CHRIST

Jesus of Nazareth, a man who was a prophet mighty in deed and word.

LUKE 24:19

Therefore he had to be made like his brothers in every respect, so that he might become a merciful and faithful high priest in the service of God, to make propitiation for the sins of the people.

HEBREWS 2:17

King of kings and Lord of lords.

REVELATION 19:16

They are justified by his grace as a gift, through the redemption that is in Christ Jesus, whom God put forward as a propitiation by his blood, to be received by faith.

ROMANS 3:24-25

For God so loved the world, that he gave his only Son, that whoever believes in him should not perish but have eternal life.

JOHN 3:16

For I delivered to you as of first importance what I also received: that Christ died for our sins in accordance with the Scriptures, that he was buried, that he was raised on the third day in accordance with the Scriptures, and that he appeared to Cephas, then to the twelve. Then he appeared to more than five hundred brethren at one time. . . . Then he appeared to James, then to all the apostles. Last of all, as to one untimely born, he appeared also to me.

1 CORINTHIANS 15:3-8

CHAPTER 12

PROPHET, PRIEST, AND KING

*I*t has been common in Protestant circles since the Reformation to speak of the work of Christ under three general heads: prophet, priest, and king. These refer to his roles as teacher, Savior, and ruler over the universe and the church. It has been objected by some that these roles are not always that distinct, either in Christ's own ministry or in the Old Testament offices on which they are built. Priests as well as prophets are found to be teachers. Several kings were recipients of God's inspired revelation, as were the prophets. Nevertheless, the usual threefold division of Christ's work has good scriptural support.

Christ is acknowledged to be a prophet in Luke 24:19. In that passage, Jesus is interrogating the Emmaus disciples, asking what had happened during the last tumultuous days in Jerusalem. They reply that those events concern "Jesus of Nazareth, a man who was a prophet mighty in deed and word before God and all the people."

Jesus is declared to be a priest throughout the book of Hebrews as, for example, in Hebrews 2:17. "Therefore he had to be made like his brothers in every respect, so that he might become a merciful and faithful high priest in the service of God, to make propitiation for the sins of the people."

Similarly, Revelation 19:16 declares, "On his robe and on his thigh he has a name written, King of kings and Lord of lords."

The notion of the threefold office of Christ also applies well to human spiritual need. One such need is for knowledge; we do not know God naturally, nor do we understand spiritual things apart from special divine illumination of our minds. Jesus meets our need by revealing God to us. He is our prophet-teacher. He does this through his own person, in whom the Father is fully revealed; through the gift to us of the written Word of God; and by the particular illumination of our minds by the Holy Spirit.

We also have need of salvation. We are not merely ignorant of God and of spiritual things; we are also sinful. We have rebelled against God and like sheep have all gone our own way. Jesus meets this need as our priest. He functions as priest on two levels: first, he offers himself up as a sacrifice, thereby providing the perfect atonement for our sin; second, he intercedes for us at the right hand of his Father in heaven, thereby guaranteeing our right to be heard.

Finally, we need spiritual discipline, guidance, and rule. We are not autonomous, even after our conversion. We do not have the right to rule ourselves, nor can we rule ourselves successfully. Christ meets our need by his proper and loving rule over us within the church. He is our master, our king. He is also the proper ruler of this world. Hence the future triumph and rule of Christ over all the world is also an aspect of this subject. Summing the matter up, Charles Hodge has said,

> We are enlightened in the knowledge of the truth; we are reconciled unto God by the sacrificial death of his Son; and we are delivered from the power of Satan and introduced into the kingdom of God; all of which supposes that our Redeemer is to us at once prophet, priest, and king. This is not, therefore, simply a convenient classification of the contents of his mission and work, but it enters into its very nature, and must be retained in our theology if we would take the truth as it is revealed in the Word of God.[1]

---

[1] Charles Hodge, *Systematic Theology*, vol. 2 (London: James Clarke & Co., 1960), 461. Martin Luther was probably the first to teach explicitly that Christ was a prophet, priest, and king, but he never spoke of this as a "threefold office." That distinction belongs to John Calvin, who, with his greater gift for systematization, develops it fully in book 2 of the *Institutes of the Christian Religion* (ch. 15). From this point it is seen often in Protestant writings, particularly those of the English and American Puritans. The Westminster Confession of Faith mentions the three offices in the chapter "Of Christ the Mediator." The Shorter Catechism asks in which way Christ "doth . . . execute" these offices, and replies, "Christ executeth the office of a prophet in revealing to us, by his Word and Spirit, the will of God for our salvation. . . . Christ executeth the office of a priest in his once offering up of himself a sacrifice to satisfy divine justice and reconcile us to God, and in making continual intercession for us . . . Christ executeth the office of a king in subduing us to himself, in ruling and defending us, and in restraining and conquering all his and our enemies" (Q. 24, 25, 26).

Therefore, although our discussion of the work of Christ will necessarily go beyond what these three categories suggest, it will nevertheless be of value to keep them in mind as we develop it.

THE LOGOS OF GOD: PROPHET

When we talk about Christ's prophetic office, we go back to a particularly rich lode of thought in the Old Testament. Abraham, the father of the Jewish people, was called a prophet (Gen 20:7). Moses was a prophet, even the greatest of all prophets (Deut 34:10). Saul prophesied (1 Sam 10:11; 19:20). David and Solomon were prophets in the sense that they received parts of God's inspired revelation and have thus contributed to our Old Testament. Beginning with Elijah and Elisha, the great prophetic movement was launched, bringing into view such names as Isaiah, Jeremiah, Ezekiel, Daniel, and the so-called minor prophets. On one occasion Moses is reported as saying, "Would that all the LORD's people were prophets!" (Num 11:29).

In the midst of this focus on the role of the prophet, there is, however, an increasing awareness that no human prophet is adequate for human need. Therefore, there is a sharpening expectation of one "great prophet" who should come.

The first clear statement of that expectation is in Deuteronomy 18, which contains a prophecy of a future prophetic figure like Moses, one to whom the people should hearken. Moses himself makes the announcement: "The LORD your God will raise up for you a prophet like me from among you, from your brothers—it is to him you shall listen" (Deut 18:15). Then the announcement is preserved in God's own words: "I will raise up for them a prophet like you from among their brothers. And I will put my words in his mouth, and he shall speak to them all that I command him" (Deut 18:18). It is possible on a superficial reading to take this as referring to some subsequent human figure, such as Isaiah or one of the other great prophets. It might even be applied to that special prophet who was to be the forerunner of the Messiah (Mal 4:5; Jn 1:25). However, in the New Testament the Deuteronomy reference is particularly applied to Jesus, as in one of Peter's sermons (Acts 3:22) and Stephen's address before the Sanhedrin (Acts 7:37).

Other passages develop the same theme. On several occasions the people who witnessed a striking work of Christ responded by identifying him as a prophet or *the* prophet to be expected in the last times (Mt 21:46; Lk 7:16; Jn 6:14). The Emmaus disciples identified him as such (Lk 24:19). On one occasion Jesus said in reference to himself, "A prophet is not without honor, except in his own hometown and among his relatives and in his own household" (Mk 6:4). From a theological standpoint, the major passage is probably the introduction to the book of Hebrews. "Long ago, at many times and in many ways, God spoke to our fathers by the prophets, but in these last days he has spoken to us by his Son" (Heb 1:1-2).

A prophet is one who speaks for another. In these verses Jesus is set forth as one who, like the Old Testament prophets, speaks for God. He is thus one who speaks authoritatively.

The matter of *authority* was particularly evident to Christ's hearers. At the end of the Sermon on the Mount, we are told that when Jesus had finished speaking, the people were "astonished at his teaching, for he was teaching them as one who had authority, and not as their scribes" (Mt 7:28-29). We might think that they should have been impressed with the content of his words, or with the need for repentance, or some such thing. But we are told that the people contrasted Christ with the scribes, who were the major teachers of the time, and concluded that he was teaching with an authority they did not possess.

A second major feature of Christ's teaching is what we might call its *egocentric* character. It is about himself. As early as his words about persecution in the Sermon on the Mount, Jesus assumes that his hearers would experience suffering not merely for the sake of truth or for some other good cause but "on my account" (Mt 5:11). Later in the sermon he says, "Do not think that I have come to abolish the Law or the Prophets; I have come not to abolish them but to fulfill them" (Mt 5:17). In other words, he identified himself as the Messiah about whom the Old Testament was written. In the final section he warns against anything that might turn attention from himself and thus lead the person involved into judgment. He concludes, "Everyone then who hears these words of mine and does them will be like a wise man who built his house on the rock. And the rain fell, and the floods came, and the winds blew and beat on that house, but it did not fall, because it had been founded on the rock" (Mt 7:24-25).

These statements, and others like them throughout the Gospels, immediately distinguish Jesus from all other religious teachers. As John R. W. Stott observes, "They are self-effacing; he is self-advancing. They point away from themselves and say, 'That is the truth as far as I perceive it; follow that.' Jesus says, 'I am the truth; follow me.'"[2]

---

[2]John R. W. Stott, *Basic Christianity* (Grand Rapids: Eerdmans, 1958), 22.

The fourth evangelist, John, was apparently very conscious of this aspect of Christ's teaching as he began to write his Gospel. In the opening pages he uses a word in reference to Christ that suggested both to Jews and Greeks that Christ himself was the focal point of God's revelation to humankind. The word is *logos*, which means "word," though in a fuller sense than is true of that term in English. It occurs in John 1:1, where John says, "In the beginning was the Word, and the Word was with God, and the Word was God," and in John 1:14, "And the Word became flesh and dwelt among us, . . . full of grace and truth."

What would that term have meant to a contemporary Jewish reader of John's Gospel? The first verses of his book, including the term *logos*, would have made a Jew think back to the first words of the Old Testament, where we are told that in the beginning God spoke and that as a result, all things came into being. In other words, Jesus would immediately be associated with the creative power of God and with the self-disclosure of God in creation. We can get a feeling for how this might operate by imagining ourselves to be reading a book that began with a reference to "the course of human events" and contained in the first few paragraphs the words "self-evident" and "inalienable rights." Clearly the author would be trying to remind us of the Declaration of Independence and of the founding principles of the American republic.

But that is not all these words would do for a Jewish reader. To a Jewish mind, the idea of a "word" would mean more than it does to us today. The reason is that to the Jewish way of thinking, a word was something concrete, something much closer to what we would call an event or a deed. We say, "Words are cheap." Children chant, "Sticks and stones may break my bones, but words will never hurt me!" But words do hurt, and the Jews were undoubtedly closer to the truth when they regarded a word spoken as a deed done. To their way of thinking, words were not to be used lightly. Moreover, there are theological implications. What happens when God speaks? The thing is accomplished instantly. "God said, 'Let there be light,' and there was light" (Gen 1:3). God said,

> So shall my word be that goes out from my mouth;
>> it shall not return to me empty,
> but it shall accomplish that which I purpose,
>> and shall succeed in the thing for which I sent it. (Is 55:11)

Because of this, the Jews would be more prepared than we are for the thought that the "Word" of God could somehow be seen and touched, and it would not be entirely strange for them to learn, as the author of Hebrews said in writing to largely Jewish readers, "In these last days [God] has spoken to us by his Son" (Heb 1:2).

What would the word *logos* have meant to a Greek or other Gentile reader? For the Greeks the answer is found, not in religion, but in philosophy. Almost twenty-six hundred years ago, in the sixth century BC, a philosopher named Heraclitus lived in Ephesus. He was the man who said that it is impossible to step into the same river twice. He meant that all life is in flux. Thus, although you step into the river once, step out, and then step in a second time, by the time you have taken the second step the river has flowed on and is a different river. To Heraclitus and to the philosophers who followed him, all life seemed like that. But they asked, if that is so, how is it that everything that exists is not in a state of perpetual chaos? Heraclitus answered that life is not chaos because the change that we see is not random change. It is ordered change. That means that there must be a divine "reason" or "word" that controls it. That is the *logos*, the word that John uses in the opening verse of his Gospel.

However, the *logos* also meant more than that to Heraclitus. Once he had discovered that the controlling principle of matter was God's *logos*, then it was only a small step for him to apply that concept also to all the events of history and to the mental order that rules in the minds of human beings. For Heraclitus, the *logos* became nothing less than the mind of God controlling everything.

By the time John came to write his Gospel, the age of Heraclitus lay nearly seven hundred years in the past. But Heraclitus's ideas had been so formative for Greek thought that they had survived not only in his philosophy but also in the philosophy of Plato and Socrates, the Stoics, and others who had built on it. Further, they were discussed by many ordinary persons. The Greek knew all about the *logos*: it was the creative and controlling mind of God; it kept the universe going. It was therefore with a stroke of divine genius that John seized on this word, one that was as meaningful to Greeks as to the Jewish people. "Listen, you Greeks, the very thing that has most occupied your philosophical thought and about which you have all been writing for centuries—the Logos of God, this word, this controlling power of the universe and the human mind—this has now come to earth as a man, and we have beheld him, full of grace and truth."

Plato, we are told, once turned to that little group of philosophers and students that had gathered around him during the Golden Age in Athens and said, "It may be that some day there will come forth from God a Word, a Logos, who will reveal all mysteries and make everything plain." Now John is saying, "Yes, Plato, the Logos has come; now God is revealed to us perfectly."[3]

This is the prophetic ministry of Jesus Christ. It is authoritative, and it is wrapped up in his own person in such a way that when we look to Jesus we see, not merely a man, but the God-man who thereby reveals God to us. In our day Jesus performs this ministry through his Holy Spirit, who communicates the person of Christ to our minds and hearts through the Scriptures and thus provides for our salvation and sanctification.

THE MEDIATOR OF GOD: PRIEST

The second of the three major divisions of Christ's work is his priesthood, a theme carefully prepared for in the Old Testament and developed in considerable detail in the book of Hebrews. A priest is a person appointed to act for others in things pertaining to God. That is, he is a mediator. In Christ this priestly or mediatorial function is fulfilled in two ways: first, by offering up himself as a sacrifice for sin (which the Old Testament priests could not do) and, second, by interceding for his people in heaven. The New Testament represents this last activity as Christ urging the sufficiency of his sacrifice as grounds on which his prayers and ours should be answered.

The fact that Jesus is himself the sacrifice for sins should make it clear that his priesthood is different from and superior to the Old Testament priestly functions. But not only in this regard is Christ superior. To begin with, under the Old Testament system the priests of Israel were required to offer a sacrifice not only for those whom they represented but also for themselves, since they were sinful. For example, before the high priest could go into the holy of holies on the Day of Atonement, which he did once a year, he first had to offer a bullock as a burnt offering for his own sin and that of his household (Lev 16:6). Only after that was he able to proceed with the ceremonies of the scapegoat and the offering whose blood was to be sprinkled on the mercy seat within the holy of holies. Again, the sacrifices that the priests of Israel offered were inadequate. They taught the way of salvation through the death of an innocent victim. But the blood of sheep and goats could not take away sins, as both the Old Testament and the New Testament recognize (Mic 6:6-7; Heb 10:4-7). Finally, the sacrifices of the earthly priests were incomplete, which is attested to by the fact that they

---

[3]I have discussed the Logos concept at greater length both in *The Gospel of John*, vol. 1 (Grand Rapids: Zondervan, 1975), 37-42, and in *Witness and Revelation in the Gospel of John* (Grand Rapids: Zondervan, 1970), 159-63.

were offered again and again. In Jerusalem, for example, the fire on the great altar of sacrifice never went out; and on a great Sabbath, such as the Passover, literally hundreds of thousands of lambs would be offered.

In contrast to that earthly priesthood, *the sacrifice of Jesus was by one who is himself perfect* and who therefore had no need that atonement be made for him. As the author of Hebrews says, "It was indeed fitting that we should have such a high priest, holy, innocent, unstained, separated from sinners, and exalted above the heavens. He has no need, like those high priests, to offer sacrifices daily, first for his own sins and then for those of the people" (Heb 7:26-27).

Second, being himself perfect and at the same time the sacrifice, it follows that *the sacrifice made by Jesus was itself perfect.* Hence, it could actually pay the price for sin and remove it, as the sacrifices in Israel could not. They were a shadow of things to come, but they were not the reality. Christ's death was the actual atonement on the basis of which alone God declares the sinner righteous. The author of Hebrews makes this point.

> But when Christ appeared as a high priest of the good things that have come . . . he entered once for all into the holy places, not by means of the blood of goats and calves but by the means of his own blood, thus securing an eternal redemption. For if the blood of goats and bulls, and the sprinkling of defiled persons with the ashes of a heifer, sanctify for the purification of the flesh, how much more will the blood of Christ, who through the eternal Spirit offered himself without blemish to God, purify our conscience from dead works to serve the living God. (Heb 9:11-14)

Finally, unlike the sacrifices of the Old Testament priests, which had to be repeated daily, *the sacrifice of Jesus was complete and eternal*—as evidence for which he is now seated at the right hand of God. In the Jewish temple there were no chairs, signifying that the work of the priests was never done. "But when Christ had offered for all time a single sacrifice for sins, he sat down at the right hand of God, waiting from that time until his enemies should be made a footstool for his feet. For by a single offering he has perfected for all time those who are being sanctified" (Heb 10:12-14).

Any teaching about priests and sacrifices today is hard for most people to understand, for we do not have sacrifice in most of the civilized world and do not understand its terminology. It was not so easy to understand in antiquity either. The author of Hebrews, in fact, acknowledges that in a parenthetical remark: "About this we have much to say, and it is hard to explain, since you have become dull of hearing" (Heb 5:11).

On the other hand, the elaborate instructions for the performances of sacrifices were given to teach both the serious nature of sin and the way God would provide for sin to be dealt with. The sacrifices taught two lessons. First, sin means death. It is a lesson of God's judgment. It means that sin is serious. "The soul who sins shall die" (Ezek 18:4). Second, there is the message of grace. The significance of the sacrifice is that by the grace of God an innocent substitute could be offered in the sinner's place. The goat or lamb was not that substitute, but could only point forward to it. Jesus was and is, for all who will have him as Savior. He is the only, perfect, all-sufficient sacrifice for sin on the basis of which God counts the sinner justified. This aspect of Christ's work is to be considered more fully in the chapters on propitiation and redemption.

A second way in which Jesus fulfills his priestly or mediatorial function is by interceding for us now. This is not a supplemental work adding to his sacrifice of himself on the cross, but rather a consequential work based on it. We have several examples of Christ's intercession for others in the New Testament.

One interesting example is his intercession for Peter, told after the fact. The story is that Satan came to God on one occasion and gave his opinion of Peter, saying in effect, "I don't know what your Son ever expects to accomplish with that bag of wind named Peter. If you would just give me permission to blow on him, he'd fly away like chaff at threshing time." At that point God gave Satan permission to blow, just as he had given Satan permission to blow on Job (Job 1:12; 2:6). But Jesus prayed for Peter, asking that the experience might prove strengthening rather than devastating. He asked that the chaff might be blown away so that more of the true grain, which he had put there, might be visible. His own words to Peter were, "Simon, Simon, behold, Satan demanded to have you, that he might sift you like wheat, but I have prayed for you that your faith may not fail. And when you have turned again, strengthen your brothers" (Lk 22:31-32).

We know from the outworking of the story that Christ's intercession for Peter prevailed. Later that evening, although Peter denied the Lord on three separate occasions, the last time with oaths and cursing, his faith did not fail. Rather, when what he had done became clear to him through the crowing of the cock, remorse overcame him and he went out and wept bitterly. It was to a greatly humbled Peter that the Lord later came with a recommissioning to service (Jn 21:15-19).

Another New Testament example of Christ's intercession is his prayer for his church (Jn 17). Jesus does not pray that the disciples might be made rich, or be brought to positions of respect and power in the Roman Empire, or even be spared persecution and suffering for the sake of their witness. Rather, his prayer is that they might be made the kind of men and women he would have them be—that is, men and women in whom the marks of the church are evident: joy, holiness, truth, mission, unity, and love. His concerns for them (and us) are spiritual.

A wonderful word is used for this mediatorial function of the Lord Jesus Christ, doubly wonderful because it is also used of the earthly ministry of the Holy Spirit on our behalf. In the Greek language the word is *paraklētos*. In English it is translated "Comforter" (though that is not the best translation), "Counselor," or "Advocate." It is used of the Holy Spirit in Christ's final discourses, in which he speaks of "another Helper" (Jn 14:16; compare Jn 14:26; 15:26; 16:7). It is used of Jesus himself (1 Jn 2:1). The real sense of the word comes from its legal or forensic overtones. Literally, *paraklētos* comes from two separate Greek words: *para*, meaning "alongside of" (we have it in the words *parable, paradox, parallel*, and others), and *klētos*, meaning "called" (it is also used in the Greek word for church, *ekklēsia*, meaning "the called out ones"). A paraclete is therefore one called alongside another to help him, in other words, a lawyer. Interestingly enough, that is the meaning of the word *advocate*. *Advocate* is composed of the two words, *ad*, meaning "to" or "towards," and *vocare*, "to call." So an advocate is one called to help another.

The picture, then, is of something we might call a heavenly law firm with us as clients. It has a heavenly branch presided over by the Lord Jesus Christ and an earthly branch directed by the Holy Spirit. Each of them pleads for us. It is the Spirit's role to move us to pray and to intensify that prayer to a point of which we ourselves are not capable. Paul writes, "Likewise the Spirit helps us in our weakness. For we do not know what to pray for as we ought, but the Spirit himself intercedes for us with groanings too deep for words" (Rom 8:26). Similarly, it is the ministry of the Lord in heaven to interpret our prayers aright and plead the efficacy of his sacrifice as the basis of our coming to God.

The consequence of this is that we can have great boldness in prayer. How could we ever have boldness if the answering of our prayers depended either on the strength with which we pray or on the correctness of the petitions themselves? Our prayers are weak, as Paul confesses, and we often pray wrongly. But we are bold, nevertheless, for we have the Holy Spirit to strengthen the requests, and the Lord Jesus Christ to interpret them rightly.

THE REIGN OF GOD: KING

The third aspect of Christ's work is kingship. Unlike the two other offices, which have a limited, explicit, textual basis, there is voluminous biblical material on Christ's kingship.

First, there is the strong theme of the sovereignty of God over his creation. Since Jesus is himself God, that clearly has bearing on his own rule or sovereignty. There are the particular messianic prophecies about the Messiah's kingly reign, as God promised King David. "Your house and your kingdom shall be made sure forever before me. Your throne shall be established forever" (2 Sam 7:16). Later, when the house of David was in evident decline, the prophet Isaiah intensified the promises and pointed to the Messiah yet to come.

> The government shall be upon his shoulder,
>> and his name shall be called
> Wonderful Counselor, Mighty God,
>> Everlasting Father, Prince of Peace.
> Of the increase of his government and of peace
>> there will be no end,
> on the throne of David and over his kingdom,
>> to establish it and to uphold it
> with justice and with righteousness
>> from this time forth and forevermore.
> The zeal of the LORD of hosts will do this. (Is 9:6-7)

Many psalms are given over to the theme (for example, Ps 45; 72; 110). Micah 5:2 speaks of the birthplace of this future king:

> But you, O Bethlehem Ephrathah,
>> who are little to be among the clans of Judah,
> from you shall come forth for me
>> one who is to be ruler in Israel,
> whose coming forth is from of old,
>> from ancient days.

Daniel contains a vision of one to whom

> was given dominion
>> and glory and a kingdom,
> that all peoples, nations, and languages
>> should serve him;

his dominion is an everlasting dominion,

which shall not pass away,

and his kingdom one

that shall not be destroyed. (Dan 7:13-14)

When Jesus was born, his birth was announced in these categories, and when he began his earthly ministry he himself played on these themes. The angel who announced his birth to Mary said, "He will be great and will be called the Son of the Most High. And the Lord God will give to him the throne of his father David, and he will reign over the house of Jacob forever, and of his kingdom there will be no end" (Lk 1:32-33). Later, John the Baptist spoke of the imminence of God's kingdom in the coming of Christ. Still later, Jesus himself began his ministry with the startling proclamation, "Repent, for the kingdom of heaven is at hand" (Mt 4:17).

At the end of the New Testament we find the culmination of this theme: the Lord seated on a throne, his enemies being made subject to him and a new name given. "On his robe and on his thigh he has a name written, King of kings and Lord of lords" (Rev 19:16).

Yet there is a problem here. If this theme is as dominant as it seems, and if Jesus really is the King of kings and Lord of lords, how is it that the world is so little changed and that his kingdom is so little acknowledged? Is it future? That would be one way to handle the problem, but how do we then deal with Christ's own statement that the kingdom of God is "in the midst of you" (Lk 17:21)? Is it spiritual? If so, how are we to think of the explicit prophecies of the continuation of the throne of David, or even the promises of utopian justice and peace to attend Messiah's reign? We note, for instance, that the lack of justice and peace in the world is one reason given by today's Jewish community for their refusal to believe that Jesus of Nazareth is their true Messiah. Can we eliminate these elements from our understanding of Christ's rule? Or are we to limit the kingship of Jesus to the church alone? The answers to each of these questions are complex, but it is only as we ask them and begin to search for answers in the Bible that we come by degrees actually to understand the concept of Christ's kingship.

I was once asked a question about whether the kingdom of God is past, present, or future. The questioner had in mind the debate on that subject going on in scholarly theological circles for some years, involving such names as T. W. Manson and C. H. Dodd of England, Rudolf Bultmann and Martin Dibelius of Germany, and Albert Schweitzer. I replied with a summary of that debate and then with the statement that the biblical view could not be expressed adequately even in those three terms. In one sense, the kingdom is certainly past, for God has always ruled over people and history. But at the same time it is also present and future. Thus God rules today and will continue to rule. The more one looks at the statements in the Bible about the kingdom, the more one feels that it transcends any of these temporal concepts.

Perhaps the most important thing to be said about the kingdom of God is that it is *God's* kingdom. That means it is far above human kingdoms and is infinitely superior to them.

We look into the pages of history and we see the kingdoms of this world rising and falling across the centuries. Historians tell us that the world has known twenty-one great civilizations, all of which have endured only for a time and then passed away unceremoniously. Once Egypt was a mighty world power, but today it is weak. It is unable to contend even with the tiny state of Israel. Babylon was mighty. Today it is gone, its territory divided. Syria, once strong, has become an archaeological curiosity. Greece and Rome have fallen. Moreover, we know that even the United States of America and Russia, although now at the pinnacle of world power, will not be able to escape that inexorable law of God for history: "Righteousness exalts a nation, but sin is a reproach to any people" (Prov 14:34). Pride can bring each of them down.

The normal course of the kingdoms of this world is described in a striking way in the book of Daniel. Belshazzar, king of Babylon, had given a party, in the course of which he had defiled the vessels taken from the temple of God at Jerusalem. In the midst of that party, handwriting had appeared on the wall of the palace, and Belshazzar was frightened. The writing said, "MENE, MENE, TEKEL, and PARSIN. This is the interpretation of the matter: MENE, God has numbered the days of your kingdom and brought it to an end; TEKEL, you have been weighed in the balances and found wanting; PERES, your kingdom is divided and given to the Medes and Persians" (Dan 5:25-28). Daniel said to the king,

> The Most High God gave Nebuchadnezzar your father kingship and greatness and
> glory and majesty. . . . But when his heart was lifted up and his spirit was hardened
> so that he dealt proudly, he was brought down from his kingly throne, and his
> glory was taken from him. He was driven from among the children of mankind,
> and his mind was made like that of a beast, and his dwelling was with the wild
> donkeys. He was fed grass like an ox, and his body was wet with the dew of heaven,
> until he knew that the Most High God rules the kingdom of mankind and sets

over it whom he will. And you his son, Belshazzar, have not humbled your heart, though you knew all this. (Dan 5:18, 20-22)

That night Belshazzar was killed, and Darius reigned in his stead.

That is the course of human kingdoms. God allows an individual or group to rise above their peers in power, their triumph brings pride and God removes them. Human powers rise and fall, but over all this seething about in human history, God reigns. God is sovereign over human history, even over realms that are in rebellion against him. This aspect of the kingdom of God brings comfort to those who would otherwise be in turmoil about upsetting world events. Jesus said, "Do not be anxious about your life" (Mt 6:25), adding that although there would always be "wars and rumors of wars," his followers were not to be troubled (Mt 24:6).

A second important fact about Christ's rule is that it has a present dimension. Jesus first exercises his rule of an individual soul by drawing it to faith in himself and directing it thereafter, and, second, by governing and directing his church so that the principles of the kingdom might be seen in the church and then move out from it to have bearing on the unbelieving world. When we pray "Thy kingdom come," as we do in the Lord's Prayer, it is this present rule (and not merely a future coming) that we have in mind. Paul defines the kingdom of God as a present-tense reality: "righteousness and peace and joy in the Holy Spirit" (Rom 14:17).

Unfortunately, some have gone on from an awareness of Christ's expanding rule over his church and the world to make the erroneous assumption that because the kingdom of God comes wherever individuals believe in Christ and respond to the gospel, the kingdom will therefore inevitably go on expanding until all or nearly all the world believes. That view was popular in the nineteenth century. Today the reality of two world wars, a cold war, and the acknowledged decline of the influence of Christianity in the Western world have taken enthusiasm for that sort of reasoning out of most Christians.

It is surprising that such a line of thought was followed at all. The Lord warned against it in the parables of the kingdom (Mt 13), teaching that large portions of the world would never be converted, that the devil's children would be present until the end even in the church, that his rule would come in totality only at the close of time, and that even then it would be established only by his power and in spite of continuing and bitter animosity. There are seven parables in that chapter, beginning with the sower who went forth to sow and ending with the story of the dragnet. They are designed to preview the last nineteen centuries of church history.

The first parable is the parable of the sower. Jesus said that a man went out to sow seed. Some of it fell on a hard surface where it was devoured by birds; some of it fell on shallow ground and sprang up quickly, only to be scorched by the sun; some fell among thorns and was choked by them; some fell on good ground, where it produced in some cases a hundred handfuls of grain for one handful, in others sixty for one, and in still others thirty for one. He then explained the parable, showing that the seed was the word of his kingdom and that the word was to have different effects in the lives of those who heard it. Some hearts would be so hard they would not receive it at all, and the devil's cohorts would soon snatch it away. Others would receive it as a novelty as did the Athenians in Paul's day, but they would soon lose interest, particularly in face of persecution. The third class would consist of those who allow the word to be choked out by worldly concerns and their delight in riches. Only the fourth class was to be made up of those in whom the gospel would take root.

The parable means that only part of the preaching of the kingdom of God will bear fruit. The parable does away with the idea that the preaching of the gospel will be more and more effective and will inevitably bring a total triumph for the church as history progresses.

The second parable makes the point even more clearly. It is the story of the wheat and tares. Jesus said that a man went out to sow grain, but that after he had done it an enemy came and sowed tares. The two kinds of plants grew up together, the one true wheat, the other plants that looked like wheat but were useless as food. In the story, the servants wanted to pull up the tares, but the owner told them not to do that lest they uproot some of the wheat also. Instead they were to let both grow together until the harvest, when the grain would be gathered into the barns and the tares burned.

When Jesus was alone with his disciples, he explained that the field was the world, the wheat represented those who belonged to him, and the tares were the children of the devil. This means that the world would always contain within it those who were God's true children and those who were children of the devil. That would be true throughout church history. Moreover, since some of his children would look so much like those whom the devil counterfeited, no one was to try to separate the two on this earth lest some Christians should perish with the others. The point of the parable is that these unsatisfactory conditions will remain until the end of this age.

The other parables make similar points; that is, the extension of the kingdom of God will be accompanied by the devil's influence and will always be imperfect. It should be evident from the imperfect nature of the kingdom of God, as we see it today, that there is yet to be a kingdom in which the rule of the Lord Jesus Christ will be fully recognized. This is the third important point that must be stated about Christ's rule.

Christ told his disciples that there was to be a spiritual kingdom throughout the "church age." But he taught that there was to be a literal, future kingdom as well. In one parable, he compared himself to a nobleman who went into a far country to receive a kingdom and then return. In the meantime, he left gifts in the hands of his servants, charging them to be faithful and ready to give a good accounting at his return (Lk 19:11-27). On another occasion, after the resurrection, the disciples asked Jesus, "Lord, will you at this time restore the kingdom to Israel?" (Acts 1:6). He answered, "It is not for you to know times or seasons that the Father has fixed by his own authority [in other words, you are right about the fact of the kingdom; but it is none of your business to know when]. But you will receive power when the Holy Spirit has come upon you, and you will be my witnesses in Jerusalem and in all Judea and Samaria, and to the end of the earth" (Acts 1:7-8).[4]

IMITATORS OF CHRIST

For us, the work of the kingdom of God falls in the last of those statements. We are Christ's witnesses. We are to bear the message of his rule throughout our cities, states, nations, and the world.

As we do this, we are to know that by the same exercise of Christ's authority in the church we are uniquely equipped for our task. He is our prophet, priest, and king—and in a lesser way we too are prophets, priests, and kings. We are prophets in the sense that we too are spokespersons for God in this world. In Moses' day that was a fond wish only: "Would that all the LORD's people were prophets!" (Num 11:29). But in our day, as a result of the outpouring of the Holy Spirit on the church at Pentecost, it has come true. Now, as Peter maintained, the words of the prophet Joel concerning the latter days have been fulfilled.

This is what was uttered through the prophet Joel:
"And in the last days it shall be, God declares,

---

[4]Some material on the kingdom of God has been borrowed from my work *The Sermon on the Mount* (Grand Rapids: Zondervan, 1972), 205-11.

> that I will pour out my Spirit on all flesh,
> and your sons and your daughters shall prophesy
>   and your young men shall see visions,
>   and your old men shall dream dreams;
> even on my male servants and my female servants
>   in those days I will pour out my Spirit,
>   and they shall prophesy." (Acts 2:16-18)

As prophets, we speak the Word of God to our contemporaries.

We are also priests. True, there will never be another priesthood like the Old Testament priesthood; Christ has perfected that forever. Yet there is a sense in which all God's people are priests. They all have access to God equally on the basis of Christ's sacrifice, and are called on to offer themselves to God in self-consecration, praise, and service. Peter speaks of this explicitly, reminding us that we are "a holy priesthood, to offer spiritual sacrifices acceptable to God through Jesus Christ" (1 Pet 2:5). Paul has the same idea in mind as he writes to the Romans. "I appeal to you therefore, brothers, by the mercies of God, to present your bodies as a living sacrifice, holy and acceptable to God, which is your spiritual worship" (Rom 12:1). We are also to exercise our priesthood in intercessory prayer for one another and for the world.

Finally, there is a sense in which we are also kings with Christ. The book of Revelation says of the saints of God, "You . . . have made them a kingdom and priests to our God, and they shall reign on the earth" (Rev 5:10). How shall we reign? Not by lording it over one another, for that is not how Jesus exerts his reign among us. Rather, as the hymn says,

> For not with swords' loud clashing,
> Nor roll of stirring drums,
> But deeds of love and mercy,
> The heavenly kingdom comes.
> Our kingship is expressed, not in privilege, but in responsibility.

CHAPTER 13

QUENCHING GOD'S WRATH

*T*o treat the work of the Lord Jesus Christ as prophet, priest, and king has the advantage of appearing to cover his work in one manageable chapter. The disadvantage is that it does not adequately show how the various offices relate to one another, nor indicate which office is most important. According to the Bible, Jesus' purpose was to die (Mk 10:45).

That leads us to a further discussion of the meaning of his death. When we focus on his death, the problem of accepting it as the central aspect of his work is aggravated rather than decreased for contemporary people. The central biblical concepts for understanding the meaning of Christ's death are propitiation and redemption, but each is difficult, if not offensive, to many. Propitiation deals with the idea of sacrifice, by which the wrath of God against sin is averted. Redemption refers to redeeming a slave from slavery. Neither of these seems compatible with the modern conception of what God does or should do. Can we believe that salvation is achieved by God's paying a price for our redemption? Doesn't that lead to those bizarre medieval ideas of Christ's becoming God's ransom price to the devil? As for propitiation, isn't the whole web of thought in which that idea operates outmoded? Can we really believe that wrath enters into the matter of salvation at all? Or if we can, how can it be that one man's death, however significant, can avert it?

Those are questions we must keep in mind as we begin to explore the matter of Christ's death. But we also want to ask, what exactly did the death of Christ accomplish? And how did it accomplish it? In answering these questions, we want to look at the idea of propitiation in this chapter and at redemption in the next.

Propitiation: God Pacifying His Own Wrath

Propitiation is a little-understood concept in the biblical interpretation of Christ's death. It has to do with sacrifices, and it refers to what Jesus accomplished in relation to God by his death. Redemption has to do with what he accomplished in relation to *us*. By redeeming us, Jesus freed *us* from the bondage of sin. In contrast, propitiation relates to *God*, so we can say that by his death, Jesus propitiated the wrath of his Father against sin and thus made it possible for God to be propitious to his people.

But that requires explanation. In the first place, we need to note that the idea of propitiation presupposes the idea of the wrath of God. If God is not wrathful toward sin, there is no need to propitiate him and the meaning of the death of Christ must therefore be expressed in other categories. Right here many modern thinkers would stop, arguing that it is precisely for this reason that the term should not be used or, if it is used, that it should be given another meaning. "We can understand," such a person might say, "how the idea of propitiation would be appropriate in paganism, where God was assumed to be capricious, easily offended, and therefore often angry. But that is not the biblical picture of God. According to the Christian revelation, God is not angry. Rather, he is gracious and loving. It is not God who is separated from us because of sin, but rather we who are separated from God. Thus it is not God who is to be propitiated but we ourselves." Those who have argued this way have either rejected the idea of propitiation entirely, considering its presence in the Bible to be a carryover from paganism's imperfect way of thinking about God—or else they have interpreted the basic Greek word for propitiation to mean not Christ's propitiation of the wrath of God, but rather the covering over or expiation of our guilt by his sacrifice. In other words, they have regarded the work as directed toward humanity rather than toward God. A scholar who has led the way in this is the late C. H. Dodd of Cambridge, England, whose influence led to the translation of the word "propitiation" as "expiation" in the relevant texts in the Revised Standard Version of the Bible (Rom 3:25; Heb 2:17; 1 Jn 2:2; 4:10).[1]

---

[1]Dodd's basic contention is that there is no such thing as wrath in God occasioned by human sin. Therefore, since there is no wrath, the meaning "propitiation" is incorrect in the New Testament, even though the word it translates (*hilasmos, hilastētion*) may well have the idea of propitiation in

At this point, we must be appreciative of the work of those who have distinguished the pagan idea of propitiation from the Christian idea. For it is quite true that God is not capricious or easily angered, a God whom we must therefore propitiate in order to keep in his good graces. That is totally opposite to the Christian position, for God is quite correctly seen as a God of grace and love.

But that is not the whole of the matter, as sympathetic as one may be with the concerns of such scholars. First, we dare not forget what the Bible tells us about God's just wrath against sin, in accordance with which sin will be punished either in Christ or in the person of the sinner. We may feel, because of our particular cultural prejudices, that the wrath of God and the love of God are incompatible. But the Bible teaches that God is wrath and love at the same time. What is more, his wrath is not just a small and insignificant element that somehow is there alongside his far more significant and overwhelming love. Actually, God's wrath is a major element that may be traced all the way from God's judgment against sin in the garden of Eden to the final cataclysmic judgments recorded in the book of Revelation. (That emphasis has already been studied at considerable length in chapter seven.)

Second, although the word *propitiation* is used in biblical writings, it is not used in the same way as in pagan writings. In pagan rituals, the sacrifice was the means by which people placated an offended deity. In Christianity, it is never people who take the initiative or make the sacrifice, but God himself who out of his great love for sinners provides the way by which his wrath against sin may be averted. Moreover, he is himself the way—in Jesus. That is the true explanation of why God is never the explicit object of propitiation in the biblical writings. He is not mentioned as the object because he is also the subject, which is much more important. In other words, God himself placates his own wrath against sin so that his love may go out to embrace and save sinners.

The idea of propitiation is most clearly observed in the Old Testament sacrificial system, for through that system of sacrifices God taught the way by which a sinful man or woman might approach him. Sin means death, as was pointed out earlier. But the sacrifices teach that there is a way of escape and of approaching God. Another may die in a sinner's place. That may seem astounding, even (as some have wrongly suggested) immoral, but it is what the system of sacrifices teaches. Thus, the individual Israelite was instructed to bring an animal for

---

pagan religion. He believes that the Bible deals only with the putting away of sin and thus that "expiation" is the better rendering.

sacrifice whenever he approached God; the family was to kill and consume an animal at the yearly observance of the Passover; the nation was to be thus represented by the high priest annually on the Day of Atonement, when the blood of the offering was sprinkled on the mercy seat of the ark of the covenant within the holy of holies of the Jewish temple. At the end of this process of instruction, Jesus appeared as the offering that was to take away "the sin of the world" (Jn 1:29).

The progression is this: one sacrifice for one individual, one sacrifice for one family, one sacrifice for one nation, one sacrifice for the world. The way to God's presence is now open to anyone who will come, a fact symbolized by the rending of the veil of the temple (which separated the holy of holies from the rest of the temple) at Christ's death.

FOUR NEW TESTAMENT TEXTS

Only four New Testament texts actually use the word *propitiation*, though the idea of sacrifice (to which it is linked) is dominant. The critical passage is Romans 3:23-26.

> For all have sinned and fall short of the glory of God, and are justified by his grace as a gift, through the redemption that is in Christ Jesus, whom God put forward as a propitiation by his blood, to be received by faith. This was to show God's righteousness, because in his divine forbearance he had passed over former sins. It was to show his righteousness at the present time, so that he might be just and the justifier of the one who has faith in Jesus.

How is propitiation to be taken in Paul's statement of the nature of Christ's work of atonement? Does it mean propitiation in the sense of the quieting of God's wrath against sin, or does it mean the covering over of guilt, the meaning reflected in the RSV translation?

If there were nothing but this passage to go on, those questions would perhaps be unanswerable. But we have the entire context of the opening section of Paul's letter. It is quite closely reasoned and has a direct bearing on the nature of Christ's work stated here. We get the beginning of this context in the first chapter at Romans 3:18, where Paul introduces his formal argument by the statement that "the wrath of God is revealed from heaven against . . . men who by their unrighteousness suppress the truth." The passage goes on to state that men and women have been given a knowledge of God in creation, but they have willfully turned away from this knowledge in order to reject God and set up a false and debased form of god in God's place. This is "ungodliness" and "unrighteousness." It is because of this that the wrath of God is directed against them. In the remainder of the chapter Paul shows how this works out. God has decreed that if they will not have him, they must have the result of their own debased thinking and living. Consequently, they are given over to a lie (so that their minds become darkened) and to depraved living, as a result of which envy, murder, strife, deceit, malignity, gossip, slander, hate, and all kinds of other vices proliferate.

In Romans 2, Paul moves from a discussion of the way in which the wrath of God works itself out in history to a discussion of its extent. He knows that women and men are often quite ready to accuse others while nevertheless excusing themselves. So he asks, "Is anyone exempt?" The answer is no. Thus, having shown how the wrath of God affects the pagan world (in Romans 1), he now shows that the so-called moral and religious people are affected too. Moral individuals are affected because, whatever they may imagine their own particular moral attainment to be, they nevertheless fall short of God's standard. What is more, they even boast in their supposed attainment and do not repent. They do not see that the grace and forbearance of God toward them are meant to lead them to repentance (Rom 2:4). Religious persons are also affected, for what they fail to see is that their valued religious practices clean up only the outside of their lives, while leaving untouched the serious corruption within (Rom 2:28-29).

Paul's conclusion in Romans 3 is that all are under the wrath of God, for all have sinned. Nevertheless, at this point the righteousness and grace of God are revealed, for in the person of his Son Jesus Christ, God the Father has provided a way by which those who believe in him might be saved. Though we have sinned, we are nevertheless "justified by his grace as a gift, through the redemption that is in Christ Jesus, whom God put forward as a propitiation by his blood" (Rom 3:24-25).

This means that the wrath of God directed against us because of our sin has now been quenched or turned aside by God's action through the death of Christ.

> The "blood"—that is, the sacrificial death—of Jesus Christ abolished God's anger against us, and ensured that his treatment of us for ever after would be propitious and favorable. Henceforth, instead of showing himself to be against us, he would show himself in our life and experience to be for us. What, then, does the phrase "a propitiation . . . by his blood" express? It expresses, in the context of Paul's

argument, precisely this thought: that *by his sacrificial death for our sins Christ pacified the wrath of God.*"[2]

The passage shows that the wrath of God, far from being the capricious and conceited anger characteristic of the pagan gods, which therefore does not need to be taken seriously today, is actually the unyielding and terrifying opposition of the holy God to all that is opposed to holiness. It is directed against all, for all are unholy. At the same time, the passage shows how God, out of that great love which is also a fundamental part of his nature, has himself acted to propitiate his wrath and thereby save humanity.

The second New Testament passage to use the word *propitiation* is Hebrews 2:17. It does not have the same emphasis as the text in Romans, for in Romans Paul is speaking explicitly of the work of Christ in propitiating the wrath of God, while in Hebrews the author is concerned more with the *how* of propitiation, namely, with the kind of nature Christ needed to have in order to make propitiation. His point is that Jesus became one with humankind in order to represent them as a faithful high priest. "Therefore he had to be made like his brothers in every respect, so that he might become a merciful and faithful high priest in the service of God, to make propitiation for the sins of the people."

This text does not explicitly mention the wrath of God. But it says nothing contrary to the idea of a propitiation of God's wrath against sin and, in fact, may even be said to suggest it, although indirectly. For example, the text speaks of Christ being a "merciful" priest. Mercy means to show favor to one who does not deserve it. So if those for whom Christ is a merciful priest do not deserve mercy, what they clearly deserve is God's wrath, which, however, has been turned away from them by Christ's sacrifice. The verse speaks of Christ being a priest "in the service of God" (literally, "in reference to those things that pertain to God"). So a work directed toward God rather than toward humanity is prominent. Finally, the passage also suggests the ancient sacrificial system. The author's reference to a "faithful high priest" is later explained in the categories of the priesthoods of Aaron and Melchizedek. Jesus is superior to those earlier priests because he offers the perfect and therefore final and all-inclusive sacrifice.

The last two uses of *propitiation* in the New Testament are in the First Epistle of John. "My little children, I am writing these things to you so that you may not sin. But if anyone does sin, we have an advocate with the Father, Jesus Christ the righteous. He is the propitiation for our sins, and not for ours only but also

---

[2]J. I. Packer, *Knowing God* (Downers Grove, IL: InterVarsity Press, 1973), 165.

for the sins of the whole world" (1 Jn 2:1-2); and "In this is love, not that we have loved God but that he loved us and sent his Son to be the propitiation for our sins" (1 Jn 4:10).

What is the central concern of these verses? Again, neither speaks explicitly of God's wrath, but in the first verse the human dilemma is conveyed at least indirectly, just as in the verse from Hebrews. In this case, need is suggested by the reference to Jesus as our "advocate." Why do we need a lawyer or helper if, in fact, we do not stand in a position of difficulty before God? The reason is, of course, that we are in grave trouble. We are sinners, the point that John has been making in the preceding verses (1 Jn 1:5-10), and therefore we stand condemned and need an advocate. In this context, it is understandable that John would choose a word that speaks of the work of a priest in turning away God's wrath, and bring this work forward as the sure ground by which we may approach God and be assured of his favor.

Another indication that this is what John is thinking about is his statement that Jesus' death for sins was "not for ours only but also for the sins of the whole world." It is likely that John is thinking of the fact that in Judaism the propitiatory sacrifice offered by the high priest on the Day of Atonement was for Jews only; now, since the death of Jesus, the sacrifice avails for Gentiles and Jews alike.

The final mention (1 Jn 4:10) does not throw much light on the meaning of *propitiation*, but it does combine it with the idea of the love of God out of which the act of propitiation flows, thereby supplying us with "one of those resounding paradoxes which mean so much for the understanding of the Christian view of sacrifice."[3] Christ's death is a genuine propitiation of God's wrath. But paradoxically it is the love of God that makes the propitiation.

Here, then, we come to the heart of the gospel. In the act of propitiation we have the great good news that the one who is our Creator, but from whom we have turned in sin, is nevertheless at the same time our Redeemer. Packer sums it up in this fashion:

> The basic description of the saving death of Christ in the Bible is as a *propitiation*, that is, as that which quenched God's wrath against us by obliterating our sins from his sight. God's wrath is his righteousness reacting against unrighteousness; it shows itself in retributive justice. But Jesus Christ has shielded us from the nightmare prospect of retributive justice by becoming our representative substitute, in obedience to his Father's will, and receiving the wages of sin in our place. By

---

[3]Leon Morris, *The Apostolic Preaching of the Cross* (Grand Rapids: Eerdmans, 1956), 179.

this means justice has been done, for the sins of all that will ever be pardoned were judged and punished in the person of God the Son, and it is on this basis that pardon is now offered to us offenders. Redeeming love and retributive justice joined hands, so to speak, at Calvary, for there God showed himself to be "just, and the justifier of him that hath faith in Jesus."[4]

LIGHT ON OTHER TRUTHS

The doctrine of Christ's sacrifice, conceived as a true propitiation of God's wrath against sin, throws valuable light on other doctrines. We may close this chapter by looking at some of them.

First, the nature of Christ's sacrifice throws light on *God's attributes*. It is customary in many contemporary theological circles to emphasize the love of God at the expense of his other attributes. We must not minimize the love of God, but we must maintain on the basis of the biblical revelation that love is not the only attribute of God or even, if we are looking at the matter in logical sequence, the first. Looked at in a logical sequence, the first attributes of God must be those that present him as the Creator and sustainer of this world: self-existence, self-sufficiency, eternity, sovereignty, holiness, and omniscience. After them comes that attribute disclosed by the fall and rebellion of the human race: wrath. Only then can we adequately talk about his love. God was love even before the fall or, for that matter, from all eternity, but the full measure of that love is seen only in the offering up of Christ for us "while we were still sinners" (Rom 5:8).

So the fact of propitiation reminds us, first of all, that God is truly wrathful against sin as well as loving toward the sinner. Moreover, it enhances our appreciation of his love. Within this framework, the love of God is not merely some indulgent feeling of good will (which is what human love often is). It is rather an intense, demanding, holy love that is willing to pay the greatest price in order to save the one loved.

Second, the nature of Christ's sacrifice throws light on the nature of *the human dilemma*. If the coming of Christ is only an open declaration of God's favor toward women and men, a demonstration by which God seeks to capture our

---

[4]Packer, *Knowing God*, 170. The meaning of propitiation is discussed by Packer in some detail (161-80). It is also discussed at length by Morris, *Apostolic Preaching of the Cross*, 125-85; B. B. Warfield, *The Person and Work of Christ* (Philadelphia: Presbyterian and Reformed, 1970), 351-426; T. C. Hammond, *In Understanding Be Men* (Downers Grove, IL: InterVarsity Press, 1968), 116-27; H. E. Guillebaud, *Why the Cross?* (Chicago: InterVarsity Christian Fellowship, 1947); and James Denney, *The Death of Christ*, ed. R. V. G. Tasker (Chicago: InterVarsity Press, 1964).

attention and win our love, then our condition as we stand in alienation from God is not serious. God loves us, whatever we may have done, and we may suppose that things will turn out all right in the end, whatever we may choose or not choose concerning Christ now. We do not have wrath to reckon with. However, if Christ's death is a propitiation of God's wrath, then the human situation is quite different. Wrath is real, and we may expect to feel the full force of that wrath unless we too become partakers in Christ's salvation.

The cross of Christ means, among other things, that our state is desperate, so desperate, in fact, that there is no hope for us except there. We are, as Paul says, "dead in . . . trespasses and sins," prisoners of "the prince of the power of the air" and "by nature children of wrath" (Eph 2:1-3). These truths are taught so that men and women might turn, out of a sense of frightful spiritual danger, to the Savior.

Third, light is shed on the *person and work of Jesus Christ*. His nature as the God-man is illumined along the lines developed in chapter eleven. Only as one who is at the same time God and human can he make propitiation. His work is illumined in that this mission alone makes sense of what we find recorded about him in the Gospels.

To give just one example, we notice that in even the most dangerous situations he encountered—the hostility of raging mobs, temptation by Satan, the attempts at entrapment by those leaders of Israel who were antagonistic to him—Jesus was always in total and evident control. Yet as his death drew near, each of the Gospel writers tells us that he began to be greatly distressed and sorrowful (Mt 26:37-38; Mk 14:33-34; Lk 22:44; Jn 12:27), and three of them (Matthew, Mark, and Luke) tell us that he prayed earnestly in the garden of Gethsemane that the cup that he was soon to drink might pass from him. What was that cup? Was it his physical death? If so, Jesus had less courage than did Socrates, who faced his death with self-control and died calmly conversing of immortality. The only explanation other than the view that Jesus was a coward whose faith failed is that his death was quite different from that of the Athenian philosopher or our own. He was to die not only physically but also spiritually, thus being separated from God because of sin and thus bearing the wrath of God against sin on our behalf. The unique quality of his death was that on Calvary he experienced the horror of the wrath of God while making propitiation.

Fourth, the true *nature of the gospel* also emerges in this understanding of the death of Jesus. The gospel is not just a new possibility for achieving joy and fullness in this life, as some seem to suggest. It is not just a solution to what were previously troublesome and frustrating problems. It is rather something much deeper that has been done, something relating to God, on the basis of which and only on the basis of which these other blessings of salvation follow. Packer says, "The gospel does bring us solutions to these problems, but it does so by first solving . . . the deepest of all human problems, the problem of man's relation with his Maker; and unless we make it plain that the solution of these former problems depends on the settling of this latter one, we are misrepresenting the message and becoming false witnesses of God."[5]

Finally, the nature of Christ's death as propitiation also has its bearing on *Christian ethics*. Paul says, "The love of Christ controls us, because we have concluded this: that one has died for all, therefore all have died; and he died for all, that those who live might no longer live for themselves but for him who for their sake died and was raised" (2 Cor 5:14-15). Or again, to refer to a text that more properly introduces the theme of the next chapter, "You are not your own, for you were bought with a price. So glorify God in your body" (1 Cor 6:19-20; compare 1 Cor 7:23). That God loved us so much that he sent his Son to bear his just wrath against sin in our place is the greatest and ultimately only adequate basis for Christian ethics. We love him because of his great love for us, and so we wish to serve him.

---

[5]Packer, *Knowing God*, 171.

CHAPTER 14

PAID IN FULL

Redemption and the work of the Lord as *redeemer* are among the most precious words in the Christian's vocabulary. They are not the terms most frequently used when we speak of Christ's work. We more often speak of him as Savior. We frequently refer to him as Lord. But they speak to us directly of what Jesus Christ did for our salvation and of what it cost him to do it.

In the early part of this century, B. B. Warfield delivered an address to incoming students in which he pointed out that the title *redeemer* conveys an intimate revelation. He wrote,

> It gives expression not merely to our sense that we have received salvation from Him, but also to our appreciation of what it cost Him to procure this salvation for us. It is the name specifically of the Christ of the cross. Whenever we pronounce it, the cross is placarded before our eyes and our hearts are filled with loving remembrance not only that Christ has given us salvation, but that he paid a mighty price for it.[1]

Warfield proved his assertion by a lengthy series of quotations from the hymns of the church in which the word *redeemer* occurs.

> Let our whole soul an offering be
> To our Redeemer's Name.

---

[1] Benjamin Breckinridge Warfield, "Redeemer and Redemption," in *The Person and Work of Christ* (Philadelphia: Presbyterian and Reformed, 1970), 325. This, the opening address for the year, was delivered in Miller Chapel, September 17, 1915, and appeared first in *The Princeton Theological Review* 14 (1916): 177-201.

While we pray for pardoning grace,
Through our Redeemer's Name.
Almighty Son, Incarnate Word,
Our Prophet, Priest, Redeemer, Lord.
O for a thousand tongues to sing
My dear Redeemer's praise.
To our Redeemer's glorious Name
Awake the sacred song.
All hail, Redeemer, hail,
For thou hast died for me.
Guide where our infant Redeemer is laid.
My dear Redeemer and my Lord.
All glory, laud and honor
To thee Redeemer, King.
Our blest Redeemer, ere he breathed
His tender, last farewell.

Warfield cited at least double that number of hymns, and then did the same thing with hymns using the word *ransom*, which, he indicated, is a close synonym of redemption. Today, of course, such words are probably less loved than formerly. But that is because they are less understood and appreciated, not because the idea behind the words is less attractive to Christians. Moreover, even if we admit that they have lost some of their popular appeal, they are more apt than many other words that describe what has been done for us in salvation.

THE SALVATION TRIANGLE

We see this aptness when we consider the three major words relating to what happens in salvation: propitiation, justification, and redemption. Each of these occurs in those key verses introducing the work of Christ in Paul's presentation of the gospel in the book of Romans: "[They] are justified by his grace as a gift, through the redemption that is in Christ Jesus, whom God put forward as a propitiation by his blood, to be received by faith" (Rom 3:24-25).

We can make the comparison easily in a triangle like the one shown in figure 1. Propitiation is represented by the arrow that connects Christ with God the Father. This arrow points upward, for Christ propitiated the Father by his death on our behalf. The line connecting God the Father and Christians is justification. The arrow points downward, for justification refers to something God does to us. We are justified by grace on the basis of Christ's sacrifice. The third and bottom side of the triangle, the arrow connecting Jesus and ourselves, is redemption. It points toward us, for redemption is something Jesus does for his people. He redeems us and sets us free.

In this diagram, God the Father is the initiator of one act: justification. Jesus is the initiator of two acts: propitiation directed toward the Father and redemption directed toward his people. We, who initiate nothing, receive both justification and redemption. But—and this is the point of the illustration—it is redemption alone of the three key words that actually describes what the Savior does for us in salvation. He redeems us! Therefore, it is natural that this word (or the idea it represents) should be most precious.

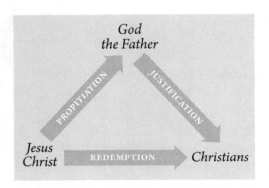

Figure 1

The Greek word at the base of the major word group meaning "redeem," "redeemer" and "redemption" is *luō*, which means "to loose" or "loosen." It was used of loosening clothes or unbinding armor. When applied to human beings, it signified the loosing of bonds so that, for example, a prisoner became free. At times, it was used of procuring the release of a prisoner by means of a ransom; in those cases it meant "to release by payment of a ransom price."

From this last use of the verb the noun *lytron* developed. It referred to the means by which the redemption of the prisoner was accomplished. It meant the "ransom price" itself. From this word a new verb developed, *lytroō*. Unlike the first verb, *luō*, which was merely a general term for "loosing" and would only occasionally mean "to ransom," this verb seems always to have meant "to release by payment of a price." From this, *lytrōsis* ("redemption," "liberation"), *apoluō* ("release," "set free," "divorce," "forgive") and other related terms were derived. Because prisoners were often slaves, and slaves were, in effect, prisoners, these words also had to do with buying a slave with the intention of setting the purchased one free. In English, something of these basic ideas is preserved in redeeming something from a pawnshop; the object is set free again by payment of its redemption price.

Thus far everything seems to be straightforward, for when the word *redemption* is used of Christ's work it obviously means that work by which Jesus freed us from sin. But here problems develop. Just as some scholars have objected to the true meaning of propitiation, thinking that the idea of appeasing God's wrath is unworthy of the Christian God, some have also objected to this basic meaning of redemption. The idea of deliverance is all right to such people, but the idea of a ransom price is all wrong. "How can God extract a price for salvation?" they ask. "If Jesus had to pay the price of his death for our deliverance, doesn't that mean that God is actually selling his favors and that salvation is therefore no longer of grace?" In developing this objection, a serious attempt has been made in recent biblical scholarship to see the word *redemption* differently, generally as a word for "deliverance" but without the overtones of a ransom. Some of this work has been done by German scholars, in whose language the word for redemption (*Erloesung*, but not *Loskaufung*) means deliverance only. English-speaking scholars also point out that the redemption word group does not always strictly involve the idea of a ransom price. For example, the Emmaus disciples speak of their shattered messianic expectations concerning Jesus by saying, "But we had hoped that he was the one to redeem Israel" (Lk 24:21). They note that the disciples are not thinking of a ransom from sin or even of anything spiritual. They mean only that they had hoped that Jesus would have been the one to deliver them from Rome.

Such thinkers also point to verses that speak of a final redemption of our bodies: Luke 21:28—"When these things begin to take place, straighten up and raise your heads, because your redemption is drawing near"; Romans 8:23—"And not only the creation, but we ourselves, who have the firstfruits of the Spirit, groan inwardly as we wait eagerly for adoption as sons, the redemption of our bodies"; Ephesians 4:30—"And do not grieve the Holy Spirit of God, by whom you were sealed for the day of redemption."

What can be said to this objection? An immediate answer is that the Emmaus disciples obviously misunderstood the kind of redemption Jesus came to bring. Another is that, as in the case of propitiation, the price paid is not really a price paid by another to God, but rather a price God pays to himself. It is God paying our bill so that salvation for us might be truly free. A third answer is that there certainly is a sense in which our ultimate redemption is a deliverance from this sinful world. A full answer, however, involves a complete study of the lexical data. There are four areas.

First, the New Testament ideas of redemption are necessarily conditioned by Old Testament forms; in the Old Testament the idea of a ransom or ransom price is prominent. In the Old Testament background, three words are particularly significant. The first is *gaal* ("to set free") or *goel* (usually translated "kinsman redeemer"). It refers to the duty incumbent on a relative to help some member of his family in preserving his family's honor or possessions. For example, if a man should lose his property through debt, as was the case with Naomi's husband as told in the book of Ruth, it was the duty of the kinsman redeemer (in that case, Boaz) to buy the property back—thereby restoring it to the family name. That duty would also extend to buying one of the family out of slavery (Lev 25:47-55).

The second word is *padah*. It means "to ransom by paying a price," as in the redemption of the firstborn, which otherwise would belong to the Lord (Ex 13:11-14; Num 18:15-16). It differs from *gaal* in that the redemption to which it refers is voluntary rather than obligatory as in the case of a kinsman.

The third word is *kopher*, which means a "ransom price." Suppose, for example, that an ox had gored somebody to death. That was a crime as a result of which the ox could be killed, or in certain circumstances (if there was negligence), the owner of the ox could be killed. He would have to forfeit his life for the one whose life had been taken. But he could redeem his life by *kopher*. That means that, if he could fix a price settled on by the relatives of the one who had been killed, the price would stand in place of the forfeiture of his life (Ex 21:28-32).

These three words, each with its connotations and laws, indicate that the idea of redemption by payment of a price was not only common but actually a fundamental principle in the social and religious life of Israel. Unless it can be demonstrated otherwise, redemption rather than the more limited idea of deliverance should be the underlying New Testament conception.

Second, the words for redemption also occur with the idea of the payment of a ransom price in secular Greek of the New Testament period, largely in reference to the redemption of prisoners of war or slaves. In that case, the price is so prominent that it is even stated in standard formulas of manumission. For example, "_____ sold to the Pythian Apollo a male slave named _____ at a price of _____ minae, on the condition that he shall be set free."[2]

---

[2]Leon Morris, *The Apostolic Preaching of the Cross* (Grand Rapids: Eerdmans, 1956), 22. This and other examples are taken from Adolf Deissmann, *Light from the Ancient East: The New Testament Illustrated by Recently Discovered Texts of the Graeco-Roman World* (London: Hodder and Stoughton, 1910).

Third, the most important New Testament passages, those that use the redemption vocabulary of Christ's work, almost always stress the price paid for our deliverance. Matthew 20:28 says, "The Son of Man came not to be served but to serve, and to give his life as a ransom for many." Here the price of redemption is stated by the Lord himself; it is his life. Titus 2:14 speaks of Jesus "who gave himself for us to redeem us from all lawlessness and to purify for himself a people for his own possession who are zealous for good works." The use of sacrificial terminology in this verse ("lawlessness" and "purify") indicates that the author is not thinking of Christ's gift of himself as a living gift merely, as in service, but rather as a gift of himself in death. So again the price of Christ's life is prominent. Finally, in 1 Peter 1:18-19 the clearest language of all is employed. It speaks of "knowing that you were ransomed from the futile ways inherited from your forefathers, not with perishable things such as silver and gold, but with the precious blood of Christ, like that of a lamb without blemish or spot." In each of these (and in other passages), redemption is accomplished by payment of the greatest price that could possibly be imagined, namely, the death or blood of Jesus Christ, the Son of God.

The fourth line of support for the traditional meaning of redemption is that the most common words for redemption, the ones we have been studying, are not the only words for it occurring in the New Testament. On the contrary, there are two others, each of which also involves the idea of deliverance by payment of a price. The idea is inherent in the very meaning of the words themselves. The first is *agorazō*. It means "to buy" and occurs in verses such as 1 Corinthians 6:19-20; 7:22-23; 2 Peter 2:1; Revelation 5:9-10; all speak of the chosen of God being purchased by the death of Christ. The second word is *exagorazō*, which is based on the former word and means "to buy out." Since both are closely related to the word *agora*, which means the marketplace or place of business, these words really mean "to buy out of the marketplace," so that the one who has been purchased might never return there again.

REDEEM: TO BUY OUT OF SLAVERY

A lexical study of the word *redeem* does not really give us its full theological meaning, however, so we now turn to three crucial doctrines basic to it.

The first doctrine is that of humanity's original state, which was sinless. In that state the first man and woman were free, with a freedom proper to created beings. They were in fellowship with God. Redemption implies that one must be bought back to enjoy that state that has been enjoyed previously. Here, of course, Christianity runs counter to the dominant view of humanity in our day: that we are gradually working our way upward from a less perfect or even an impersonal beginning. In the popular contemporary view there is no guilt. That is why it is popular. On the contrary, the human race is to be praised and is in fact its own savior. The biblical view, embodied in the word *redemption* as well as in other terms, is that we are actually fallen from a better state and therefore are guilty and need a Savior. In fact, so great is our guilt and so deep our fall that no one but God can save us.

The second major doctrine related to the biblical idea of redemption is the fall, which has already been suggested. There is a parallel between the ways in which a person could fall into slavery in antiquity and how a person is said to be bound by sin in the Bible. In the ancient world, there were three ways in which a person could become a slave. First, one could be born into slavery. That is, if a person's father and mother were slaves, that person became a slave as well. Second, a person could fall into slavery through conquest. Thus, if one city or state overcame another city or state in warfare, the defeated inhabitants might be led into captivity. Third, a person could become a slave through debt. If he or she owed more than could be paid back, it was possible for that person to be sold into slavery in order to discharge the debt.

These ways of falling into slavery correspond with the various ways in which the Bible speaks of sin having a hold over the individual. One could be born a slave in antiquity. In the same way the Bible speaks of all since Adam being born into sin. David wrote, "Behold, I was brought forth in iniquity, and in sin did my mother conceive me" (Ps 51:5). David does not mean that his mother was living in sin when she conceived him, or that there was something sinful or wrong about the act of conception itself. He means that there was never a moment in his existence that he was free from sin, and that he inherited that sinful nature from his parents as they had from their parents before them. Again, one could become a slave through conquest, and the Bible speaks of sin ruling over a person. David wrote of "presumptuous sins" and prayed that they might not have "dominion" over him (Ps 19:13). The final possibility, that of becoming a slave through debt, is suggested by Romans 6:23, which speaks of "the wages of sin" as death. The expression does not mean that sin is rewarded, except in an ironical sense. It means that sin is indebtedness and that only the death of the sinner can pay the bill.

The ideas of an original or perfect state and a subsequent fall are important to the concept of redemption, but they are still not the central idea. The heart of the matter is in the third key doctrine related to redemption. Although we have fallen into desperate slavery through sin and are held by it as by a cruel tyrant, Christ has nevertheless purchased our freedom from sin by his blood. He paid the price in order that we might be set free.

Perhaps the greatest biblical illustration of salvation (and what is meant by redemption particularly) is the story of Hosea. Hosea was a minor prophet—minor in regard to length, not importance—whose writing is based on the story of his marriage. It was an unfortunate marriage from a human viewpoint, for his wife proved unfaithful to him. But it was a special marriage from God's viewpoint. God had told Hosea that the marriage would work out in that fashion, but he nevertheless told Hosea to go through with it in order to provide an illustration of God's love. God loved the people whom he had taken to himself, even when they proved unfaithful by committing spiritual adultery with the world and its values. The marriage was to be a pageant. Hosea was to play the part of God. His wife would play the part of unfaithful Israel. She would be unfaithful, but the wilder she got, the more Hosea would love her. That is the way God loves us even when we run away from him and dishonor him.

Hosea describes his commission by saying, "When the LORD first spoke through Hosea, the LORD said to Hosea, 'Go, take to yourself a wife of whoredom and have children of whoredom, for the land commits great whoredom by forsaking the LORD.' So he went and took Gomer, the daughter of Diblaim, and she conceived and bore him a son" (Hos 1:2-3).

There are significant lessons in the early stages of this drama—in the naming of the children born to Hosea and Gomer, and in Hosea's care for his wife even after she had left him—but the climax comes at the point at which Gomer fell into slavery, probably because of debt. Hosea was told to buy her back as a demonstration of the way in which the faithful God loves and saves his people. Slaves were always sold naked in the ancient world, and that would have been true of Gomer as she was put up on the auction block in the capital city. She had apparently been a beautiful woman. She was still beautiful even in her fallen state. So when the bidding started the offers were high, as the men of the city bid for the body of the female slave.

"Twelve pieces of silver," said one.

"Thirteen," said Hosea.

"Fourteen."

"Fifteen," said Hosea.

The low bidders dropped out. But someone added, "Fifteen pieces of silver and a bushel of barley."

"Fifteen pieces of silver and a bushel and a half of barley," said Hosea.

The auctioneer must have looked around for a higher bid, and seeing none said, "Sold to Hosea for fifteen pieces of silver and a bushel and a half of barley."

Now Hosea owned his wife. He could have killed her if he wished. He could have made a public spectacle of her in any way he might have chosen. But instead, he put her clothes back on her, led her away into the anonymity of the crowd, and demanded love of her while nevertheless promising the same from himself.

Here is the way he tells it:

> And the LORD said to me, "Go again, love a woman who is loved by another man and is an adulteress, even as the LORD loves the children of Israel, though they turn to other gods and love cakes of raisins." So I bought her for fifteen shekels of silver and a homer and a lethech of barley. And I said to her, "You must dwell as mine for many days. You shall not play the whore, or belong to another man; so will I also be to you." (Hos 3:1-3)

Hosea had a right to demand what she had formerly been unwilling to give, but as he demands it he promises love from himself. The point of the story is that God thus loves all who are his true spiritual children.

This is what redemption means: to buy out of slavery. If we understand Hosea's story, we understand that we are the slave sold on the auction block of sin. We were created for intimate fellowship with God and for freedom, but we have disgraced ourselves by unfaithfulness. First, we have flirted with and then committed adultery with this sinful world and its values. The world has even bid for our soul, offering sex, money, fame, power, and all the other items in which it traffics. But Jesus, our faithful bridegroom and lover, entered the market place to buy us back. He bid his own blood. There is no higher bid than that. And we became his. He reclothed us, not in the wretched rags of our old unrighteousness, but in his new robes of righteousness. He has said to us, "You must dwell as mine . . . ; you shall not . . . belong to another . . . ; so will I also be to you."

FREE TO SERVE

Redemption has two consequences. First, it means we are free. Paradoxical as it may sound, to be purchased by Jesus is to be set free—free from the guilt and tyranny of the law and from sin's power. Paul speaks of this freedom at the high point of the book of Galatians, where he challenges those to whom he is writing.

"For freedom Christ has set us free; stand firm therefore, and do not submit again to a yoke of slavery" (Gal 5:1).

Yet this is a special kind of freedom. It does not mean that we are set free to do anything we might wish, to sin with impunity, or once again fall back into the bondage of rebellion and unfaithfulness. We are released to serve God. We are set free to will the good. We are delivered in order that we might obey and love Jesus. As Paul writes, "You are not your own, for you were bought with a price. So glorify God in your body" (1 Cor 6:19-20). Redemption is a glorious thing. Thoughts of it should warm our hearts and lift us up in praise to that one who gave himself that we might be free. But it is not only that. It also calls on us to make the highest possible level of commitment. Just as Jesus gave himself for us, so also must we give ourselves for him. We must be willing, eager, and determined to serve him. He died for us because of his great love. That love, an amazing love, "demands my soul, my life, my all."

CHAPTER 15

THE GREATNESS
OF GOD'S LOVE

S everal years before his death, the Swiss theologian Karl Barth came to the United States for a series of lectures. At one of these, after a very impressive lecture, a student asked a typically American question. He said, "Dr. Barth, what is the greatest thought that has ever passed through your mind?" The aging professor paused for a long time as he obviously thought about his answer. Then he said with great simplicity,

Jesus loves me! This I know,
For the Bible tells me so.

If the love of God is the greatest thing in the universe, why have we left a discussion of it until now? Why didn't we begin with it, and then place God's other attributes in perspective? Why are we discussing it in book two of this volume, rather than in book one, which more particularly dealt with God's attributes?

The answer is that, although God's love is indeed important and great, we cannot really understand or appreciate it in our fallen state until we know some other things about him and about ourselves. These things must necessarily be in something like a sequence: first, our creation in God's image; second, our sin; third, the revelation of the wrath of God against us because of our sin; and fourth, redemption. If we do not have the sequence firmly in mind, we are unable to appreciate (let alone marvel at) God's love as we should. Instead, it might seem only reasonable that God should love us. "After all, we are really quite lovable," we think. However, when we see ourselves as standing in violation of the just law of God and under God's wrath, then to know that God loves us is truly remarkable. Paul makes this emphasis when he writes, "But God shows his love for us in that while we were still sinners Christ died for us" (Rom 5:8).

That leads us to another reason why we have not been able to look at the love of God earlier. The love of God is seen in its fullness only at the cross of Jesus Christ. The intimations of God's love in creation and providence are somewhat ambiguous. There are earthquakes as well as beautiful sunsets, cancer and other forms of sickness as well as health. Only at the cross does God show his love fully and without ambiguity.

For that reason it is difficult to find a verse in the New Testament that speaks about God's love without also speaking in the same verse or in the immediate context about God's gift of his Son on Calvary. John 3:16—"For God so loved the world that he gave his only Son, that whoever believes in him should not perish but have eternal life." Galatians 2:20—"I have been crucified with Christ. It is no longer I who live, but Christ who lives in me. And the life I now live in the flesh I live by faith in the Son of God, who loved me and gave himself for me." 1 John 4:10—"In this is love, not that we have loved God but that he loved us and sent his Son to be the propitiation for our sins." Revelation 1:5—"To him who loves us and has freed us from our sins by his blood." Such verses hold the love of God and the cross of Christ together. What is more, they are among the most important texts on both subjects.

Only after we have come to appreciate the meaning of the cross can we appreciate the love behind it. Seeing this, Augustine once called the cross "a pulpit" from which Christ preached God's love to the world.

LOVE: GOD'S MOTIVATION

When we say we can appreciate the love of God in its fullness only after we have come to understand the doctrines of creation, sin, wrath, and redemption—that is, only when we stand on the Easter side of the cross—we must be careful. For the love of God does not originate there, but rather is prior to and greater than each of those subsequent matters. If we fail to see that, we are likely to imagine that once God was wrathful toward us but now, since Christ died, his wrath has somehow been changed to love. That is wrong, and it distorts the meaning of the cross.

The love of God stands behind everything: behind creation, behind Christ's death, even (though it is difficult to understand this) behind his wrath toward sin. How can God love us prior to and in greater measure than his wrath toward us and still be wrathful toward us? Augustine said that God hated us "in so far as we were not what he himself had made," while nevertheless loving what he had made and would make of us again.[1] We are reconciled to God, not because Christ's death somehow changed God's attitude toward us, but because God's love sent Christ to make the way by which sin, which bars us from a realization of his love, might be removed forever.

C. S. Lewis captures this idea neatly toward the end of his treatise on *The Four Loves*.

We must not begin with mysticism, with the creature's love for God, or with the wonderful foretastes of the fruition of God vouchsafed to some in their earthly life. We begin at the real beginning, with love as the Divine energy. . . . God, who needs nothing, loves into existence wholly superfluous creatures in order that he may love and perfect them. He creates the universe, already foreseeing—or should we say "seeing"? there are no tenses in God—the buzzing cloud of flies about the cross, the flayed back pressed against the uneven stake, the nails driven through the mesial nerves, the repeated incipient suffocation as the body drops, the repeated torture of back and arms as it is time after time, for breath's sake, hitched up. If I may dare the biological image, God is a "host" who deliberately creates his own parasites, causes us to be that we may exploit and "take advantage of" him.[2]

Wrath has intervened to hide the love of God from us, but when wrath is removed, we see his prior love and are drawn to God by it.

GREAT LOVE

What can we say about the love of God for his creatures, a love out of which they are not only created and redeemed, but also preserved for an eternity of fellowship with him? Obviously, nothing we could say could exhaust the full measure of his love. God's love is always infinitely deeper than our awareness or expression of it.

The Bible is simple when it speaks about God's love, and one of the simple things it says is that God's love is *great*. "But God, being rich in mercy, because

---

[1]Augustine, *The Gospel According to St. John*, cx, 6, in *The Nicene and Post-Nicene Fathers*, ed. by Philip Schaff, first series, vol. 7 (New York: The Christian Literature Company, 1888), 41.
[2]C. S. Lewis, *The Four Loves* (New York: Harcourt, Brace & World, 1960), 175-76.

of the great love with which he loved us . . ." (Eph 2:4). John 3:16 implies as much by the little word *so:* "For God *so* loved the world, that . . ." It means, "God loved the world *so* greatly that . . ." Of course, when God says that his love is great, he is not using the word as we do when we say that some relatively normal thing is great—a great concert, a great dinner, or something similar. God is a master of understatement. So when he says that his love is great, he is really saying that his love is so stupendous that it goes far beyond our own ideas of greatness or our own understanding.

A person once captured the idea on a card on which he had had John 3:16 printed. The verse was arranged in such a way that the greatness of each part of the verse was evident. It looked like this:

God	the greatest Lover
so loved	the greatest degree
the world	the greatest company
that he gave	the greatest act
his only begotten Son,	the greatest gift
that whosoever	the greatest opportunity
believeth	the greatest simplicity
in him	the greatest attraction
should not perish,	the greatest promise
but	the greatest difference
have	the greatest certainty
everlasting life.	the greatest possession

Over it all was the title, "Christ—the Greatest Gift."

An even better way of acknowledging the greatness of the love of God is to notice that the biblical writers probably invented, or at least raised to entirely new levels, a brand new word for love—so real was their need for a superlative to express the unique love they had discovered through the biblical revelation.

The Greek language is rich in words for *love*. The first of the ancient Greek words was *storgē*. It referred to general affection, particularly within the family. The closest English equivalent would be "fondness." The Greek would say, "I love [am fond of] my children."

The second of the Greek words is *philia*, from which we get the English words *philanthropy* and *Philadelphia*. It refers to friendship. Jesus used this word when he said that the person who "loves father or mother more than me is not worthy of me" (Mt 10:37). The third Greek word is *eros*, the word for sensual love. From it we get our English word *erotic*. This type of love had become so debased by New Testament times that the word is never used in the Bible, even though the biblical writers spoke approvingly of sexual love.

Yet when the Hebrew Old Testament was translated into Greek and when the New Testament writers wrote in Greek, they found none of these common words adequate for conveying the true biblical conceptions. They took another word entirely, one without strong associations, and used it almost exclusively. It had been little used previously. So they were able to infuse it with an entirely new character. By doing so they created a word that in time came to convey the type of love they wanted: *agapē*.

It was vague, but it could be and in fact was made to convey the right ideas. Does God love with a righteous, holy love? Yes. That love is *agapē*. Is God's love gracious, sovereign, everlasting? Yes, that too. "I have loved you with an everlasting love," God told Jeremiah (Jer 31:3). That love is *agapē*. Thus *agapē* became the supreme word for speaking about God's love, a new love revealed initially by God through Judaism and then disclosed in its fullness in Jesus Christ through biblical Christianity.

INEXHAUSTIBLE LOVE

Second, the Bible teaches that God's love is infinite. This is not the same as saying that God's love is great; the distinguishing mark is its inexpendability. It cannot be exhausted, nor even fully understood. Paul captures this idea when he prays that those to whom he is writing "may have strength to comprehend with all the saints what is the breadth and length and height and depth, and to know the love of Christ that surpasses knowledge, that you may be filled with all the fullness of God" (Eph 3:18-19). Logically analyzed, his words are contradictory; Paul's prayer is that the Christians might know the unknowable. That is Paul's way of emphasizing that he wants them to enter more deeply into the knowledge of God's infinite love.

How can we comprehend the infinite love of God? We can know it, but only in part. We have been touched by it, yet its fullness lies forever beyond us—just as the infinity of the universe lies beyond the probing human eye.

One hymn puts this aspect of God's love in memorable language. It was written by F. M. Lehman, but the final stanza (perhaps the best) was added to it later, after it was found written on the wall of a room in an asylum by a man said to be insane, but who had obviously come to know God's love.

The love of God is greater far
Than tongue or pen can ever tell;
It goes beyond the highest star,
And reaches to the lowest hell.
The guilty pair, bowed down with care,
God gave his Son to win:
His erring child he reconciled,
And rescued from his sin.
Oh, love of God, how rich and pure!
How measureless and strong!
It shall forevermore endure—
The saints' and angels' song.
Could we with ink the ocean fill,
And were the skies of parchment made;
Were every stalk on earth a quill,
And every man a scribe by trade;
To write the love of God above
Would drain the oceans dry;
Nor could the scroll contain the whole,
Though stretched from sky to sky.

This is the song of everyone who through Jesus Christ has come to know the infinite love of God.

GIVING LOVE

Third, God also tells us that his love is a *giving* love. That is the heart of John 3:16. "For God so loved the world, that he gave his only Son." It is in the nature of God's love to give, and when he gives it is not just a trifle but rather the very best. In *The Four Loves*, C. S. Lewis distinguishes between Gift-love and Need-love, pointing out that it is the former, Gift-love, that characterizes the love of God the Father. "Divine Love is Gift-love. The Father gives all he is and has to the Son. The Son gives himself back to the Father, and gives himself to the world, and for the world to the Father, and thus the world (in himself) back to the Father too."[3] Nowhere is this better seen than in the gift of Jesus for our salvation.

There are two senses in which the Gift-love of the Father is seen in Jesus' death. First, Jesus is the best God had to give, for there is no one to compare

---

[3]Ibid., 11.

with God's Son. Second, in giving Jesus, God gave himself, and there is nothing that anyone can give greater than that.

A minister was once talking to a couple who were having difficulties in their marriage. There was much bitterness and pain, coupled with an acute lack of understanding. At one point in the exchange the husband spoke up in obvious exasperation. "I've given you everything," he said to his wife. "I've given you a new home. I've given you a new car and all the clothes you can wear. I've given you . . ." The list went on.

When he had ended, the wife said sadly, "That much is true, John. You have given me everything . . . but yourself."

The greatest gift that anyone can give is himself or herself, and apart from that gift all other gifts are relatively insignificant. God gave himself in Jesus.

SOVEREIGN LOVE

Fourth, God's love is a *sovereign* love. Because God is God and is therefore under obligation to nobody, he is free to love whom he chooses. Indeed, he declares as much, saying, "Jacob I loved, but Esau I hated" (Rom 9:13). Or again, in reference to Israel, "It was not because you were more in number than any other people that the LORD set his love on you and chose you, for you were the fewest of all peoples, but it is because the LORD loves you and is keeping the oath that he swore to your fathers" (Deut 7:7-8).

If God is sovereign in his love, it means that his love is uninfluenced by anything in the creature. And if that is so, it is the same as saying that the cause of God's love lies only in himself. He loves whom he pleases. That is clear in both texts cited in the preceding paragraph. Thus the point of the reference to Jacob and Esau is not that Jacob was more lovable and that God therefore loved him rather than his brother, but rather that God set his love on Jacob purely as an act of his sovereign will. He made that clear by choosing Jacob over Esau before the twins were born, and thus before they had a chance to do anything either good or evil. Similarly, the verse from Deuteronomy explicitly denies that God loved Israel because of anything in them, such as their strength or size as a nation (they were not large as nations go). Rather, it affirms that God loved them because he loved them.

To most people this is an unpopular teaching, but it is the only way things can be if God is truly to be God. Assume the opposite: God's love is regulated by something other than his sovereignty. In that case, God would be regulated by this other thing (whatever it is) and would thus be brought under its power.

That is impossible if he is still to be God. In Scripture no cause for God's love other than his electing will is ever given. It is always that "he predestined us for adoption to himself as sons through Jesus Christ, *according to the purpose of his will,* to the praise of his glorious grace, with which he has freely blessed us in the Beloved" (Eph 1:5-6).

A second principle related to the sovereign character of God's love is no less important. It is that God's love is extended toward individuals. It is not a general good will directed toward everyone en masse and hence toward no one in particular, but rather a love that singles out individuals and blesses them specifically and abundantly. "God's purpose of love, formed before creation (cf. Eph 1:4), involved, first, the choice and selection of those whom he would bless and, second, the appointment of the benefits to be given them and the means whereby these benefits would be procured and enjoyed. . . . The exercise of God's love towards individual sinners in time is the execution of a purpose to bless those same individual sinners which he formed in eternity."[4] So writes J. I. Packer.

ETERNAL LOVE

A fifth and final point about the love of God is that it is *eternal.* Just as its origins are to be found in eternity past, so is its end to be found in eternity future. In other words, it has no end at all. Paul writes,

> Who shall separate us from the love of Christ? Shall tribulation, or distress, or persecution, or famine, or nakedness, or danger, or sword? As it is written,
>> "For your sake we are being killed all the day long;
>> we are regarded as sheep to be slaughtered."
>
> No, in all these things we are more than conquerors through him who loved us. For I am sure that neither death nor life, nor angels nor rulers, nor things present nor things to come, nor powers, nor height nor depth, nor anything else in all creation, will be able to separate us from the love of God in Christ Jesus our Lord. (Rom 8:35-39)

There are two classes of possible "separators" in Paul's list of the many potential threats to a Christian's relationship to God's love, and he denies the effectiveness of both of them. The first class concerns our natural enemies as persons living in an imperfect and ungodly world: poverty, hunger, natural disasters, and persecutors. These cannot separate. As we read the list and think over Paul's

[4]J. I. Packer, *Knowing God* (Downers Grove, IL: InterVarsity Press, 1973), 112-13.

experiences as a minister of the gospel, we realize that these words of assurance were not said lightly. Paul had himself endured these enemies (2 Cor 6:5-10; 11:24-33). Yet they had not separated him from the love of God, which is eternal. Nor will they separate us if we should have to undergo such suffering.

The second class of enemies is supernatural or, as we might prefer to say, in the very nature of things. Here Paul lists death, life, angels, demonic powers, and anything else that may be assumed to fall within this category. Can they separate us from God's love? Paul answers that these cannot separate us either, for God is greater than any of them.

There is one last point. As Paul gets to the end of his statement of the everlasting and victorious character of God's love, he reaches the high point of this epistle. He speaks of "the love of God [that is] *in Christ Jesus*." This brings us back to the point with which we began, that of God's love being seen at the cross. But there is this additional thought: we must not only look to Christ in the sense of seeing the love of God displayed in him, but must actually be "in him" in the sense of a personal relationship to him by faith, if we would know that love. So the question is this: Do we thus know him? Have we found the great love of God to be a love for us through faith in Christ's sacrifice? Are we his? Is Jesus our own personal Savior and Lord?

There is no other way to know the love of God personally; therefore, there is really no other way to know the love of God at all. It must begin by our commitment to Christ. God has decreed that it is only in Christ that his great, infinite, giving, sovereign, and eternal love for sinners may be known.

CHAPTER 16

THE PIVOTAL DOCTRINE: RESURRECTION

Which is more important to Christian theology: the death of Jesus Christ or his resurrection? The question is unanswerable. Although the death of Christ is what he explicitly came into the world to accomplish, the resurrection is no less important historically as evidence for Christ's claims. It is only because of the resurrection that the gospel of the cross was understood and then was preserved and transmitted across the centuries to us.

The significance of the resurrection is seen from the first moments of the Christian era. To a degree, the disciples had believed in Christ prior to his death and resurrection. An example of their immature but genuine faith is Peter's testimony: "You are the Christ, the Son of the living God" (Mt 16:16). But their faith was profoundly shaken by the crucifixion, so much so that his followers immediately began to scatter back to where they had come from. And Peter, who had given that remarkable testimony, denied the Lord three times on the night of Christ's arrest, even before the crucifixion. These men and women had believed, but the arrest and crucifixion buried their belief. Yet within three days, after the resurrection, their faith had again sprung forth, and they went out to present the gospel of the crucified but risen Savior to the world.

The death and resurrection of Jesus were the core of their message. Jesus had himself shown the way on the evening of his resurrection when he taught his scattering disciples out of the Old Testament. "Then he opened their minds to understand the Scriptures, and said to them, 'Thus it is written, that the Christ should suffer and on the third day rise from the dead, and that repentance for the forgiveness of sins should be proclaimed in his name to all nations, beginning from Jerusalem. You are witnesses of these things'" (Lk 24:45-48). Later Paul described the nature of that very early form of the apostles' preaching, saying that he had delivered to the Corinthians only what he himself had received,

> that Christ died for our sins in accordance with the Scriptures, that he was buried, that he was raised on the third day in accordance with the Scriptures, and that he appeared to Cephas, then to the twelve. Then he appeared to more than five hundred brothers at one time, most of whom are still alive, though some have fallen asleep. Then he appeared to James, then to all the apostles. Last of all, as to one untimely born, he appeared also to me. (1 Cor 15:3-8)

Peter preached that David had written of Christ's resurrection. "For you will not abandon my soul to Hades, or let your Holy One see corruption" (Acts 2:27, from Ps 16:10). The other New Testament preachers did likewise. As many contemporary students of the earliest preaching have noted, the death and resurrection of Christ were always at the heart of the apostles' preaching.[1]

The resurrection proved that Jesus Christ is who he claimed to be and that he accomplished what he claimed to have come to earth to accomplish. Evangelist Reuben A. Torrey called the resurrection of Jesus Christ "the Gibraltar of Christian evidences, the Waterloo of infidelity." The resurrection is the historical base on which all other Christian doctrines are built and before which all honest doubt must falter.

If it can be shown that Jesus of Nazareth actually rose from the dead, as the early Christians believed and as the Scriptures claim, then the Christian faith rests on an impregnable foundation. If it stands, the other doctrines stand. On the other hand, if the resurrection falls, the other truths fall also. Thus the apostle Paul wrote,

> If Christ has not been raised, then our preaching is in vain and your faith is in vain. We are even found to be misrepresenting God, because we testified about God that he raised Christ, whom he did not raise if it is true that the dead are not raised. For if the dead are not raised, then Christ has not been raised. If Christ has not been raised, your faith is futile and you are still in your sins. Then those also who have fallen asleep in Christ have perished. (1 Cor 15:14-18)

---

[1]See C. H. Dodd, *The Apostolic Preaching and Its Developments* (New York: Harper & Bros., n.d.).

THE SEAL ON THE EXISTENCE OF GOD

What doctrines stand with the resurrection? The first is that there is a God and that the God of the Bible is the true God. Is there a God? If so, what kind of God is he? These are the first and most important questions that any religion or religious teacher must answer. But very different answers have been given to such questions by religious teachers. How can we be sure which of those answers are right, if any? The resurrection of Jesus Christ alone gives certainty.

> Every effect must have an adequate cause . . . and the only cause adequate to account for the Resurrection of Christ is God, the God of the Bible. While here on earth, as everyone who has carefully read the story of His life knows, our Lord Jesus went up and down the land proclaiming God, the God of the Bible, the God of Abraham, Isaac and Jacob as He loved to call Him, the God of the Old Testament as well as the New. He said that men would put Him to death, that they would put Him to death by crucifixion, and He gave many details as to what the manner of His death would be. He further said that after His body had been in the grave three days and three nights, God, the God of Abraham, the God of Isaac and the God of Jacob, the God of the Bible, the God of the Old Testament as well as the God of the New Testament, would raise Him from the dead. This was a great claim to make. It was an apparently impossible claim. For centuries men had come and men had gone, men had lived and men had died and as far as human knowledge founded upon definite observation and experience was concerned, that was the end of them. But this man Jesus does not hesitate to claim that His experience will be directly contrary to the uniform experience of long, long centuries. . . .
>
> That was certainly an acid test of the existence of the God He preached, and His God stood the test. He did exactly the apparently impossible thing that our Lord Jesus said he would do. . . . The fact that Jesus was thus miraculously raised makes it certain that the God who did it really exists and that the God He preached is the true God.[2]

THE SEAL ON THE DEITY OF CHRIST

Second, the resurrection of Jesus Christ establishes the doctrine of our Lord's deity. When he lived on earth, Jesus claimed to be equal with God and that God would raise him from the dead three days after his execution by the Jewish and

---

[2]R. A. Torrey, *The Uplifted Christ* (Grand Rapids: Zondervan, 1965), 70-71.

Roman authorities. If he was wrong in that, his claim was either the raving of a deranged man or blasphemy. If he was right, the resurrection would be God's way of substantiating that claim. Did he substantiate it? Did Jesus rise from the dead? Yes, he did. The resurrection is God's seal on Christ's claim to divinity.

Paul, who knew that Jesus had been raised, writes that Jesus was "declared to be the Son of God in power according to the Spirit of holiness by his resurrection from the dead" (Rom 1:4). Paul is writing in an abbreviated fashion here, leaving out many points that he would include in his argument if the verse were intended as a completely reasoned statement of the truth. We remember from high school algebra that for one familiar with solving equations, it was not always necessary to work out every individual step to get the answer. For instance, if one has the equation 2a - 10 = 10, it is possible to work out the answer laboriously like this: 2a - 10 = 10; 2a = 10 + 10; 2a = 20; a = 10. But only a beginner in algebra does that. A student familiar with the terms can see at a glance that if 2a - 10 = 10, then a = 10. It is not necessary to work out the intermediate steps.

That is similar to what Paul does in the opening verses of Romans. He argues that since Jesus has been raised from the dead, Jesus is God. But if he were to spell out his logic, in detail, it would go like this.

1. Jesus claimed to be God's Son in a special sense. He argued that God was his Father (Jn 5:18). He said that he had come into this world from the Father, and that when he left the world, he would return to him (Jn 16:28). He claimed that whoever had seen him had seen the Father (Jn 14:9). Those statements were all claims to divinity, and because of them the religious leaders killed him.

2. Those claims are either true or false. Jesus cannot be partly God and partly not. Either he is who he said he is, or he is a liar.

3. If those claims are false, they are deceitful and blasphemous.

4. If they are blasphemous, it is inconceivable that God could honor the one who made them.

5. But God did honor Jesus by raising him from the dead. God vindicated his claims.

6. Hence, Jesus is the unique Son of God.

Such an analysis is not just reading into Romans 1:4 what we want to find there. The Bible uses that proof at other points, and Paul is merely echoing that teaching. Jesus used the proof when he appealed to the "sign of the prophet Jonah." He had demonstrated unique authority in his teaching and miracles, but many who heard disbelieved. The rulers asked for a sign. Jesus replied that the only sign given would be that of the prophet Jonah, "For just as Jonah was three days and three nights in the belly of the great fish, so will the Son of Man be three days and three nights in the heart of the earth" (Mt 12:40). After that there would be a resurrection, and Christ's unique authority would be vindicated. Similarly, at Pentecost and in the other sermons recorded in Acts, the early disciples used the resurrection to prove Christ's divinity.

THE SEAL ON JUSTIFICATION

Third, the resurrection of Jesus establishes the doctrine that all who believe in Christ are justified from all sin. Paul also teaches that in Romans. "Jesus . . . was delivered up for our trespasses and raised for our justification" (Rom 4:24-25). It might better be translated, "Jesus was put to death because we had transgressed, and he was raised because we were justified." The resurrection is God's declaration that he has accepted the sacrifice of Jesus Christ for human sin.

When Jesus was on earth, he claimed that he would atone for our sin. "The Son of Man came not to be served but to serve, and to give his life as a ransom for many" (Mt 20:28). In time, the hour of his crucifixion came and Jesus died. The sacrifice was offered, the atonement made. But how were human beings to know that it was acceptable? Suppose that Jesus himself had sinned, even while hanging on the cross. In that case the Lamb would not have been without spot or blemish, and the atonement would not have been perfect. Will God accept the sacrifice? For three days the question remains unanswered. Then the moment of the resurrection comes. The hand of God reaches down into the cold Judean tomb, and the body of Christ is quickened. He rises. The stone is rolled away. Jesus is exalted to the right hand of the Father. By these acts we know that God has accepted the perfect sacrifice of his Son for sin.

> When Jesus died, He died as my representative, and I died in Him; when He arose, He rose as my representative, and I arose in Him; when He ascended up on high and took His place at the right hand of the Father in the glory, He ascended as my representative and I ascended in Him, and today I am seated in Christ with God in the heavenlies. I look at the cross of Christ, and I know that atonement has been made for my sins; I look at the open sepulcher and the risen and ascended Lord, and I know the atonement has been accepted. There no

longer remains a single sin on me, no matter how many or how great my sins may have been.[3]

THE SEAL ON SANCTIFICATION

Fourth, the resurrection of Jesus is also proof that the Christian can live a life that is pleasing to God. The Bible's teaching that by God's standards there is no good in people is true of Christians as much as of unbelievers. Human beings can do good things if we measure them by human standards. There have been outstanding humanitarians and philanthropists among unbelievers. But no one can do good when measured by God's standard, for all that we do is corrupted by our touch. There can be no human victory over sin. But if Jesus is living, then his life can be lived out in us and genuine holiness is possible. This happens by "the immeasurable greatness of his power toward us who believe, according to the working of his great might that he worked in Christ when he raised him from the dead" (Eph 1:19-20).

Paul also writes, "We were buried therefore with him by baptism into death, in order that, just as Christ was raised from the dead by the glory of the Father, we too might walk in newness of life" (Rom 6:4). This means that all who believe in Christ are united to him so that his life becomes available to them. We may be weak and utterly helpless, unable to resist temptation for a single minute. But he is strong, and he lives to give help and deliverance at every moment. Victory, therefore, is no longer a question of our strength but of his power. His power is what we need.

Torrey tells a story that illustrates the point. Four men were once climbing the most difficult face of the Matterhorn. A guide, a tourist, a second guide, and a second tourist were all roped together. As they went over a particularly difficult place, the lower tourist lost his footing and went over the side. The sudden pull on the rope carried the lower guide with him, and he carried the other tourist along also. Three men were now dangling over the dizzying cliff. But the guide who was in the lead, feeling the first pull on the rope, drove his ax into the ice, braced his feet, and held fast. The first tourist then regained his footing, the guide regained his, and the lower tourist followed. They then went on and up in safety.

So it is in this life. As the human race ascended the icy cliffs of life, the first Adam lost his footing and tumbled headlong over the abyss. He pulled the

---

[3]R. A. Torrey, *The Bible and Its Christ* (Old Tappan, NJ: Fleming H. Revell, n.d.), 107-8.

next person after him, and the next and the next until the whole race hung in deadly peril. But the last Adam, the Lord Jesus Christ, kept his footing. He stood fast. Thus, all who are united to him by a living faith are secure and can regain the path.

THE SEAL ON ETERNAL LIFE

Fifth, the resurrection of Jesus is proof that death is not the end of this life. Death is, in fact, defeated for all who by faith are united to him. When Jesus was here on earth he said to his disciples, "And if I go and prepare a place for you, I will come again and will take you to myself, that where I am you may be also" (Jn 14:3). These verses presuppose the disciples' own resurrection. Similarly, the apostle Paul wrote, "For since we believe that Jesus died and rose again, even so, through Jesus, God will bring with him those who have fallen asleep" (1 Thess 4:14). The believer in Christ is united to Christ by faith in such a manner that if Jesus rose from the dead, the believer must be raised also. We were united to him in death. So also will we be in the resurrection.

At this point two truths must stand out. First, apart from the resurrection of Jesus Christ there is no certainty of life beyond the grave for anyone. And second, on the basis of the resurrection of Jesus Christ, the believer can have perfect confidence. The writings of philosophers have many arguments for immortality, but at best they offer only speculation that such things may be. One philosopher has called the doctrine of immortality "a candle flickering at the end of a dark tunnel." Another has called it "a star shining dimly on the blackest of nights." That is the philosophical hope of immortality, but it does not give confidence. It is a probability but not a certainty. The only sure evidence of our resurrection is the resurrection of Jesus himself, who said, "Because I live, you also will live" (Jn 14:19). His resurrection makes all the difference.

In the year 1899, two famous men died in America. One was a nonbeliever who had made a career of debunking the Bible and arguing against Christian doctrines. The other was a Christian. Colonel Robert G. Ingersoll, after whom the famous Ingersoll lectures on immortality at Harvard University are named, was the nonbeliever. He died suddenly, his death coming as an unmitigated shock to his family. The body was kept in the home for several days because Ingersoll's wife could not bear to part with it; it was finally removed because the corpse was decaying and the health of the family required it. At length the remains were cremated, and the display at the crematorium was so dismal that some of the scene was even picked up by the newspapers and communicated to the nation at large. Ingersoll had used his great intellect to deny the resurrection, but when death came there was no hope. His departure was received by his relatives and friends as an uncompensated tragedy.

In the same year, the great evangelist Dwight L. Moody died, but his death was triumphant both for himself and for his family. Moody had been declining for some time, and the family had taken turns being with him. On the morning of his death, his son, who was standing by the bedside, heard him exclaim, "Earth is receding; heaven is opening; God is calling."

"You are dreaming, Father," the son said.

Moody answered, "No, Will, this is no dream. I have been within the gates. I have seen the children's faces." For a while it seemed as if Moody were reviving, but he began to slip away again. He said, "Is this death? This is not bad; there is no valley. This is bliss. This is glorious." By this time his daughter was present, and she began to pray for his recovery. He said, "No, no, Emma, don't pray for that. God is calling. This is my coronation day. I have been looking forward to it." Shortly after that Moody was received into heaven. At the funeral, the family and friends joined in a joyful service. They spoke. They sang hymns. They heard these words proclaimed: "O death, where is thy sting? O grave, where is thy victory? The sting of death is sin; and the strength of sin is the law. But thanks be to God, who giveth us the victory through our Lord Jesus Christ" (1 Cor 15:55-57 KJV).[4] Moody's death was a part of that victory.

I do not mean to imply that the death of every Christian is equally glorious. Not all feel the force of these doctrines in the moment of their homegoing. But many do. Death can be victorious for a Christian. There is no hope apart from our Lord's resurrection.

THE SEAL ON JUDGMENT

Finally, the resurrection of Jesus Christ is also the pledge of a final judgment on all who reject the gospel. On Mars Hill, Paul proclaimed that God "has fixed a day on which he will judge the world in righteousness by a man whom he has appointed; and of this he has given assurance to all by raising him from the dead" (Acts 17:31). Christ spoke of a final judgment when he was on earth, claiming that he would be the judge. The fact that God raised him from the dead is proof of his claims. It is a pledge that the judgment day is coming.

---

[4]I have told the story of the death of Ingersoll and Moody in *Philippians: An Expositional Commentary* (Grand Rapids: Zondervan, 1971), 256-57.

Men and women imagine that death is the end of all things, particularly when it strikes their enemies. A mosquito bites us; we are annoyed; we swat it and congratulate ourselves that we have seen the end of that mosquito. A fox breaks into the chicken coop and we shoot it. So much for the fox. We have an enemy, but when he is dead we dismiss him from our minds.

So it was with Christ. Jesus came into the world doing good and people resented his holiness. They resented it so much that they tried to find something of which to accuse him. He claimed to be God's Son; they called it blasphemy. He spoke of their sin and of a coming day in which he would judge all humankind; they hated him for it. Eventually they killed him. We can imagine the jubilation in Jerusalem on the high feast day following the crucifixion. Those who had disposed of Christ congratulated themselves. At last they were done with him. They were secure; they would never need to endure his arrogance again. Then came the resurrection, and by that act God declared that death would never be the end of Christ. It could never be the end for him, for he is himself the life. Evil is in the world, but nothing opposed to God will finally conquer. Sin triumphed at the cross, but God triumphed at the resurrection. Christ "appeared once for all at the end of the ages to put away sin by the sacrifice of himself . . . and after that comes judgment" (Heb 9:26-27).

CHAPTER 17

VERIFYING THE RESURRECTION

*I*f the resurrection of Jesus Christ demonstrates the points covered in the preceding chapter, it is obviously the best news the world has ever heard. But we ask, "Can any news that good be believed?" That question leads to an investigation of the evidences for the resurrection.

Some modern theologians maintain that we have no need for historical evidences for the resurrection of Jesus Christ, or evidences of any other point of Christian belief for that matter. Such things are supposed to be authenticated by the logic of faith alone. There is, of course, a sense in which that is true. Christians know that their faith rests not on their ability to demonstrate the truthfulness of the biblical narratives but rather on supernatural activity of the Holy Spirit within their hearts leading them to faith. Yet many come to faith through the various evidences for the resurrection, and the substance and form of the Christian faith rests on those evidences. Apart from them, our experiences of Christ could be mystical and even quite wrong.

We have every right to investigate the evidences, for the Bible itself speaks of "many infallible proofs" of the resurrection (Acts 1:3 KJV). We want to look at six of them in this chapter.

THE RESURRECTION NARRATIVES

A first important evidence for the resurrection of Jesus Christ is that of the resurrection narratives themselves. There are four of them, one in each Gospel; they are more or less independent. Yet they are also harmonious, and that suggests their reliability as historical documents.

That the accounts are basically independent is evident from the considerable variations of detail. Of course, there might be some overlap simply because reports of a given incident would have been circulating throughout the Christian church when these books were being written. An account could have been told by different people at times in nearly identical language. But the four writers obviously did not sit down together and conspire to make up the story of Christ's resurrection. If four people had sat down together and said, "Let's invent an account of a resurrection of Jesus Christ" and had then worked out the details of their stories, there would be far more agreement than we find. We would not find the many small apparent contradictions. Yet if the story were not true and they had somehow separately made it up, it is impossible that we should have the essential agreement we find. In other words, the nature of the narratives is what we would expect from four separate accounts prepared by eyewitnesses.

Here are two examples. First, there is the variety of statements about the moment at which the women first arrived at the tomb. Matthew says that it was "toward the dawn of the first day of the week" (Mt 28:1). Mark says that it was "very early on the first day of the week, when the sun had risen" (Mk 16:2). Luke says that it was "at early dawn" (Lk 24:1). John says that "it was still dark" (Jn 20:1). These phrases are the kind of thing the authors would have standardized if they had been working on their accounts together. But they are in no real contradiction. For one thing, although John says that it was "still dark," he obviously does not mean that it was pitch black; the next phrase says that Mary Magdalene "saw that the stone had been taken away from the tomb." Presumably, the women started out while it was yet dark but arrived at the garden as day was breaking.

A second example of variation in detail in the midst of essential harmony is the listing of the women who made the first visit to the garden. Matthew says there were two Marys, "Mary Magdalene and the other Mary" (Mt 28:1). Mark writes, "Mary Magdalene, Mary the mother of James, and Salome" (Mk 16:1). Luke refers to "Mary Magdalene and Joanna and Mary the mother of James and the other women with them" (Lk 24:10). John mentions only "Mary Magdalene" (Jn 20:1). Actually, one reference throws light on the others. Mark and Luke, for example, explain who Matthew's "other Mary" was. When we put them together, we find that on that first Easter morning, when it was still dark, at least five women set out for the tomb: Mary Magdalene (who is mentioned by each of the writers), Mary the mother of James, Salome, Joanna, and at least one other unnamed woman (who fits into Luke's reference to "other women," which includes Salome). The purpose of their trip is to anoint Christ's body. They already know of the difficulty they face, for the tomb had been sealed by a large stone and they have no idea how they can move it. It begins to lighten a bit as they travel, so when they finally draw close to the tomb, they see that the stone has been moved. That is something they were not expecting; so, although it suits their purpose, they are nevertheless upset and uncertain what to do. Apparently, they send Mary Magdalene back to tell Peter and John about the new development, which John himself records, although he does not mention the presence of the other women (Jn 20:2). As the women wait for her to return, the morning grows lighter; eventually, emboldened by daybreak, the women go forward. Now they see the angels and are sent back into the city by them to tell the other disciples (Mt 28:5-7; Mk 16:5-7; Lk 24:4-7).

In the meantime, Mary Magdalene has found Peter and John, who immediately leave her behind them and run to the tomb. John records their view of the graveclothes and points out that it was at this moment that he personally believed (Jn 20:3-9). Finally, Mary Magdalene arrives back at the tomb again and is the first to see Jesus (Jn 20:11-18; compare Mk 16:9). On the same day, Jesus also appears to the other women as they are returning from the tomb, to Peter, to the Emmaus disciples, and to the others as they are gathered together that evening in Jerusalem.

Two other factors also strongly suggest that these are accurate historical accounts. The first is that they leave problems for the reader that would have been eliminated were they fictitious. For example, there is the problem, repeated several times over, that the disciples did not always recognize Jesus when he appeared to them. Mary did not recognize him in the garden (Jn 20:14). The Emmaus disciples did not know who he was (Lk 24:16). Even much later, when he appeared to many of the disciples in Galilee, we are told that "some doubted" (Mt 28:17). From the point of view of persuasion, the inclusion of such details is foolish. The skeptic who reads them will say, "It is obvious that the reason why the disciples did not immediately recognize Jesus is that he was actually someone else. Only the gullible believed, and that was because they wanted to believe. They were self-deluded." Whatever can be said for that argument, the point is that the reason why such problems were allowed to remain in the narrative is that they are, in fact, the way the appearances happened. Consequently, they at least provide strong evidence that these are honest reports of what the writers believed to have transpired.

Another example of a problem is Christ's statement to Mary that she was not to touch him because he was "not yet ascended to the Father" (Jn 20:17). Yet Matthew tells us that, when Jesus appeared to the other women, presumably within minutes of his appearance to Mary, they "took hold of his feet and worshiped him" (Mt 28:9). In the whole history of the Christian church, no one has given a thoroughly convincing explanation of that anomaly. But it is allowed to stand because, whatever the reason, that is what happened.

Finally, the accounts evidence a fundamental honesty and accuracy through what we can only call their natural simplicity. If we were setting out to write an account of Christ's resurrection and resurrection appearances, could we have resisted the urge to describe the resurrection itself—the descent of the angel, the moving of the stone, the appearance of the Lord from within the recesses of the tomb? Could we have resisted the urge to recount how he appeared to Pilate and confounded him? Or how he appeared to Caiaphas and the other members of the Jewish Sanhedrin? The various apocryphal Gospels (the Gospel according to the Hebrews, the Gospel of Peter, the Acts of Pilate, and others) contain these elements. Yet the Gospel writers include none, because either they did not happen or else the writers themselves did not witness them. The Gospels do not describe the resurrection because no one actually witnessed it. It would have made good copy, but the disciples all arrived at the tomb after Jesus had been raised.

THE EMPTY TOMB

A second major evidence for the resurrection of Jesus Christ is the empty tomb. We might deny that an actual resurrection took place, but we can hardly deny that the tomb was empty. The disciples began soon after the crucifixion and burial to preach about the resurrection, at a time when those to whom they preached could simply walk to the tomb to see if the body of the supposedly resurrected Lord still lay there.

The empty tomb has been so formidable an argument for the resurrection throughout history that unbelievers have invented a number of theories to account for it. One theory is that the women and later the disciples went to the wrong place. It is conceivable that in the dark the women might have made such an error. But, as we have seen, it was not entirely dark, and besides they had been there earlier and thus were acquainted with its location. Again, we cannot suppose that John and Peter and then all the others would make an identical error.

Another theory is the so-called swoon theory. According to that view, Jesus did not die on the cross but rather swooned—as a result of which he was taken for dead and then buried alive. In the cool of the tomb he revived, moved the stone, and went forth to appear as resurrected. But that explanation has numerous problems. There are the difficulties in believing that a Roman guard entrusted with an execution could be fooled in such a manner; or that the spear thrust into Christ's side would not have killed him even if he had been swooning; or that a weak, barely surviving Christ could have had the strength to move the large stone and overcome Roman guards. Further, one would have to suppose that a Christ in such a condition could convince his disciples that he had overcome death triumphantly.

Finally, there are the views that someone either stole or simply moved the body. But who? Certainly not the disciples, for if they had removed the body, they would later hardly have been willing to die for what they knew to be a fabrication. Nor would the Jewish or Roman authorities have taken the body. We might imagine that they could have moved it initially in order better to guard it—for the same reasons they sealed the tomb and posted a watch: "We remember how that impostor said, while he was still alive, 'After three days I will rise.' Therefore order the tomb to be made secure until the third day, lest his disciples go and steal him away and tell the people, 'He has risen from the dead'" (Mt 27:63-64). If that had happened, they would certainly have produced the body later when the disciples began their preaching. The authorities hated the gospel and did everything in their power to stop its spread. They arrested the apostles, threatened them, and eventually killed some of them. None of that would have been necessary if they could have produced the body. The obvious reason why they did not is that they could not. The tomb was empty. The body was gone.[1]

A NOT QUITE EMPTY TOMB

According to John, the tomb was not quite empty. The body of Jesus was gone, but the graveclothes remained behind. The narrative suggests that there was

---

[1]The evidence of the empty tomb is discussed by John R. W. Stott, *Basic Christianity* (Grand Rapids: Eerdmans, 1958), 46-50; Merrill C. Tenney, *The Reality of the Resurrection* (Chicago: Moody Press, 1963), 113-16; James Orr, *The Resurrection of Jesus* (London: Hodder and Stoughton, n.d.), 111-39; and others.

something about them so striking that at least John saw them and believed in Jesus' resurrection.

Every society has its distinct modes of burial, and that was true in ancient cultures as today. In Egypt bodies were embalmed. In Italy and Greece they were often cremated. In Palestine they were wrapped in linen bands that enclosed dry spices and were placed face up without a coffin in tombs generally cut from the rock in the Judean and Galilean hills. Many such tombs still exist and can be seen by any visitor to Palestine.

Another aspect of Jewish burial in ancient times is of special interest for understanding John's account of Jesus' resurrection. In a book called *The Risen Master* (1901), Henry Latham calls attention to a unique feature of Eastern burials that he noticed when in Constantinople during the last century. He says that the funerals he witnessed there varied in many respects, depending on whether the funeral was for a poor or rich person. But in one respect all the arrangements were identical. Latham noticed that the bodies were wrapped in linen cloths in such a manner as to leave the face, neck, and upper part of the shoulders bare. The upper part of the head was covered by a cloth that had been twirled about it like a turban. Latham concluded that since burial styles change slowly, particularly in the East, that mode of burial may well have been practiced in Jesus' time.

Luke tells us that when Jesus was approaching the village of Nain earlier in his ministry, he met a funeral procession leaving the city. The only son of a widow had died. Luke says that when Jesus raised him from death, two things happened. First, the young man sat up; that is, he was lying on his back on the bier without a coffin. And second, he at once began to speak. Hence, the grave-clothes did not cover his face. Separate coverings for the head and body were also used in the burial of Lazarus (Jn 11:44).

It must have been in a similar manner that Joseph of Arimathea and Nicodemus buried Jesus Christ. The body of Jesus was removed from the cross before the beginning of the Jewish Sabbath, was washed, and then was wrapped in linen bands. One hundred pounds of dry spices were carefully inserted into the folds of the linen. One of them, aloes, was a powdered wood like fine sawdust with an aromatic fragrance; another, myrrh, was a fragrant gum that would be carefully mixed with the powder. Jesus' body was thus encased. His head, neck, and upper shoulders were left bare. A linen cloth was wrapped about the upper part of his head like a turban. The body was then placed within the tomb, where it lay until sometime on Saturday night or Sunday morning.

What would we have seen had we been there at the moment at which Jesus was raised from the dead? Would we have seen him stir, open his eyes, sit up, and begin to struggle out of the bandages? We must remember that it would have been difficult to escape from the bandages. Is that what we would have seen? Not at all. That would have been a resuscitation, not a resurrection. It would have been the same as if he had recovered from a swoon. Jesus would have been raised in a natural body rather than a spiritual body, and that was not what happened.

If we had been present in the tomb at the moment of the resurrection, we would have noticed that all at once the body of Jesus seemed to disappear. John Stott says that the body was "'vaporized,' being transmuted into something new and different and wonderful."[2] Latham says that the body had been "exhaled," passing "into a phase of being like that of Moses and Elias on the Mount."[3] We would have seen only that it was gone.

What would have happened then? The linen cloths would have collapsed once the body was removed, because of the weight of the spices, and would have been lying undisturbed where the body of Jesus had been. The cloth that surrounded the head, without the weight of spices, might well have retained its concave shape and have lain by itself, separated from the other cloths by the space where the neck and shoulders of the Lord had been.

That is exactly what John and Peter saw when they entered the sepulcher, and the eyewitness account reveals it perfectly. John was the first at the tomb, and as he reached the open sepulcher in the murky light of early dawn, he saw the graveclothes lying there. Something about them attracted his attention. First, it was significant that they were lying there at all. John places the word for "lying" at an emphatic position in the Greek sentence. We might translate it, "He saw, lying there, the graveclothes" (Jn 20:5). Further, the cloths were undisturbed. The word that John uses (keimena) is used in the Greek papyri of things that have been carefully placed in order. (One document speaks of legal papers saying, "I have not yet obtained the documents, but they are lying collated." Another speaks of clothes that are "lying [in order] until you send me word.") Certainly John noticed that there had been no disturbance at the tomb.

At that point Peter arrived and went into the sepulcher. Undoubtedly Peter saw what John saw, but in addition he was struck by something else. The cloth

[2]Stott, *Basic Christianity*, 52.
[3]Henry Latham, *The Risen Master* (Cambridge: Deighton Bell and Company, 1901), 36, 54.

that had been around the head was not with the other cloths. It was lying in a place by itself (Jn 20:7). And what was more striking, it had retained a circular shape. John says that it was "wrapped together" (KJV). We might say that it was "twirled about itself." And there was a space between it and the cloths that had enveloped the body. The narrative says, "Then Simon Peter came, following him, and went into the tomb. He saw the linen cloths lying there, and the face cloth, which had been on Jesus' head, not lying with the linen cloths but folded up in a place by itself" (Jn 20:6-7). Finally John too entered the sepulcher and saw what Peter saw. When he saw it he believed.

What did John believe? He might have explained it to Peter like this. "Don't you see, Peter, that no one has moved the body or disturbed the graveclothes? They are lying exactly as Nicodemus and Joseph of Arimathea left them on the eve of the Sabbath. Yet the body is gone. It has not been stolen. It has not been moved. Clearly it must have passed through the clothes, leaving them as we see them now. Jesus must be risen." Stott says, "A glance at these graveclothes proved the reality, and indicated the nature, of the resurrection."[4]

THE POSTRESURRECTION APPEARANCES

A fourth evidence for the resurrection is the obvious fact that Jesus was seen by the disciples. According to the various accounts, he appeared to Mary Magdalene first of all, then to the other women who were returning from the tomb, afterward to Peter, to the Emmaus disciples, to the ten gathered in the upper room, then (a week later) to the eleven disciples including Thomas, to James, to five hundred brethren at once (1 Cor 15:6, perhaps on a mountainside in Galilee), to a band of disciples who had been fishing on the lake of Galilee, to those who witnessed the ascension from the Mount of Olives near Jerusalem, and last of all to Paul, who claimed to have seen Christ in his vision on the road to Damascus. During the days following the resurrection, all these persons moved from blank, enervating despair to firm conviction and joy. Nothing accounts for that but the fact that they had indeed seen Jesus.

During the last century, a well-known critic of the Gospels, Ernest Renan, wrote that belief in Christ's resurrection arose from the passion of a hallucinating woman, meaning that Mary Magdalene was in love with Jesus and deluded herself into thinking that she had seen him alive when she had actually only seen the gardener. That is preposterous. The last person in the world that Mary

---

[4]Stott, *Basic Christianity*, 53.

(or any of the others) expected to see was Jesus. The only reason she was in the garden was to anoint his body. Moreover, even if Mary had believed in some sort of resurrection through the power of love, there is no evidence that the disciples could have been so deluded or that they anticipated anything of the kind. Many despaired; some, like the Emmaus disciples, were scattering. Thomas, for one, was adamant in his disbelief. Yet we find that within a matter of days after the Lord's alleged resurrection, all of them were convinced of what beforehand they would have judged impossible. And they went forth to tell about it, persisting in their conviction even in the face of threats, persecution, and death.

One clear example of unbelieving disciples being convinced of the resurrection solely by the appearance of Jesus is that of the Emmaus disciples. One of them is identified. He is Cleopas (Lk 24:18). If he is to be identified with the Clopas (slight variation in spelling) mentioned in John 19:25, then we know that his wife's name was Mary, that she was in Jerusalem, had witnessed the crucifixion along with the other women, and was therefore probably the one returning to Emmaus with him on the first Easter morning.

The importance of this identification lies in the fact that Mary, and perhaps Cleopas too, had witnessed the crucifixion and therefore had not the slightest doubt that Jesus was dead. Mary had seen the nails driven into Christ's hands. She had seen the cross erected. She saw the blood. Finally, she saw the spear driven into his side. Afterward, Mary undoubtedly went back to where she was staying. The Passover came, and Mary and Cleopas observed it like good Jews. They waited in sadness over the holidays—from the day of the crucifixion until the day of the resurrection—for the same Sabbath restraints on travel that had kept the women from going to the sepulcher to anoint the body would also have kept Cleopas and Mary from returning home to Emmaus. The morning after the Saturday Sabbath finally came. It is possible that Mary is one who went to the tomb to anoint the body. If that is the case, she saw the angels, returned to tell Cleopas about it, and then—look how remarkable this is—joined him in preparing to leave. So far from their thinking was any idea of the literal truth of Christ's bodily resurrection!

What is more, during the time that Cleopas and Mary were getting ready to leave, Peter and John set out for the sepulcher. They entered the tomb. Right then, John believed in some sense, although he may not have understood all that the resurrection meant. Peter and John returned, told Cleopas, Mary, and the others what they had seen. And then—again this is most remarkable—Cleopas and Mary went right on packing. As soon as they were ready, they left Jerusalem. Did that Palestinian peasant couple believe in Christ's resurrection? Certainly not. Did they come to believe, as they eventually did, because of their own or someone else's wishful thinking or a hallucination? No. They were so sad at the loss of Jesus, so miserable, so preoccupied with the reality of his death, that they would not even take twenty or thirty minutes personally to investigate the reports of his resurrection.

If someone should say, "But surely they must not have heard the reports; you are making that part of the story up," the objection is answered by the words of Cleopas. When Jesus appeared to them on the road and asked why they were so sad, Cleopas answered by telling him first about the crucifixion and then adding, "Moreover, some women of our company amazed us. They were at the tomb early in the morning, and when they did not find his body, they came back saying that they had even seen a vision of angels, who said that he was alive. Some of those who were with us [Peter and John] went to the tomb and found it just as the women had said, but him they did not see" (Lk 24:22-24).

What accounts for a belief in the resurrection on the part of Christ's disciples? Nothing but the resurrection itself. If we cannot account for the belief of the disciples in that way, we are faced with the greatest enigma in history. If we account for it by a real resurrection and real appearances of the risen Lord, then Christianity is understandable and offers a sure hope to all.

THE TRANSFORMED DISCIPLES

A fifth evidence for the resurrection flows from what has just been said: the transformed character of the disciples.

Take Peter as an example. Before the resurrection Peter is in Jerusalem tagging along quietly behind the arresting party. That night he denies Jesus three times. Later he is in Jerusalem, fearful, shut up behind closed doors along with the other disciples. Yet all is changed following the resurrection. Then Peter is preaching boldly. He says in his first sermon on the day of Pentecost,

> Men of Israel, hear these words: Jesus of Nazareth, a man attested to you by God with mighty works and wonders and signs that God did through him in your midst, as you yourselves know—this Jesus, delivered up according to the definite plan and foreknowledge of God, you crucified and killed by the hands of lawless men. God raised him up, loosing the pangs of death, because it was not possible for him to be held by it. (Acts 2:22-24)

A few chapters further on in Acts, we find him before the Jewish Sanhedrin (the body that condemned Jesus to death), saying, "Whether it is right in the sight of God to listen to you rather than to God, you must judge, for we cannot but speak of what we have seen and heard" (Acts 4:19-20).

"Something tremendous must have happened to account for such a radical and astounding moral transformation as this. Nothing short of the fact of the resurrection, of their having seen the risen Lord, will explain it."[5]

Another example is James, Jesus' brother. At one point none of Jesus' brothers believed in him (Jn 7:5). Jesus once declared, "A prophet is not without honor except in his hometown and in his own household" (Mt 13:57). But later James does believe (compare Acts 1:14). What made the difference? Obviously, only the appearance of Jesus to him, which is recorded in 1 Corinthians 15:7.

THE NEW DAY OF CHRISTIAN WORSHIP

The final, though often overlooked, evidence for the resurrection of Jesus Christ is the change of the day of regular Christian worship from the Jewish Sabbath (Saturday) to Sunday, the first day of the week. Could anything be more fixed in religious tradition than the setting aside of the seventh day for worship as practiced in Judaism? Hardly. The sanctification of the seventh day was embodied in the law of Moses and had been practiced for centuries. Yet from the very beginning we see Christians, though Jews, disregarding the Sabbath as their day of worship and instead worshiping on Sunday. What can account for that? There is no prophecy to that effect, no declaration of an early church council. The only adequate cause is the resurrection of Jesus Christ, an event so significant that it immediately produced the most profound changes, not only in the moral character of the early believers, but in their habits of life and forms of worship as well.

I was once speaking to another minister about his spiritual experience when the conversation turned to the resurrection. The minister said that when he came out of seminary he possessed no real convictions concerning the gospel of Christ. He probably believed some things intellectually, but they had not gripped his heart. He said that he began to reflect on the resurrection. I asked, "What did you find?" First of all, he replied, he discovered a strange happiness and internal rest as he struggled with the accounts and the questions that they forced to his mind. That indicated to him that, although he did not have the answers yet, at

[5]R. A. Torrey, *The Bible and Its Christ* (Old Tappan, NJ: Fleming H. Revell, n.d.), 92.

least he was on the right track. As he studied he came to see the importance of the issue. He saw that if Jesus really rose from the dead, everything else recorded about him in the New Testament is true—at least there is no sound reason for rejecting it. And he concluded that if Jesus was not raised from the dead, he should leave the ministry.

So he read books. He visited the seminary where he had studied. He talked with his professors. He said that he became convinced that Jesus is indeed risen, as the Bible declares, and that all the other doctrines of the faith stand with it. Interestingly enough, he came to that conclusion several weeks before Easter that particular year, and on Easter he therefore stood up in church to proclaim his personal faith in these things. Afterward members of his congregation said that they had never heard preaching like that before, and several believed in Christ as a result of his preaching.

That has happened to many: to jurists like Frank Morison, Gilbert West, Edward Clark, and J. N. D. Anderson; to scholars like James Orr, Michael Ramsey, Arnold H. M. Lunn, Wolfhart Pannenburg, and Michael Green. Green says that "the evidence in favor of this astonishing fact is overwhelming."[6] Ramsey wrote, "So utterly new and foreign to the expectations of men was this doctrine, that it seems hard to doubt that only historical events could have created it."[7]

Did Jesus rise from the dead? If he did, then he is the Son of God and our Savior. It is for us to believe and follow him.

---

[6]Michael Green, *Runaway World* (Downers Grove, IL: InterVarsity Press, 1968), 109.
[7]A. M. Ramsey, *The Resurrection of Christ* (London: Geoffrey Bles, 1945), 19.

CHAPTER 18

HE ASCENDED
INTO HEAVEN

*I*t is always difficult to measure one's own spiritual maturity. But there is a
sense in which one can assess it generally by the dominant image one has of
Jesus Christ. For example, some persons think of Jesus in terms of his incarnation,
with the result that their mental picture is basically that of a baby lying in a
manger. That is not wrong, of course. The Lord did become a baby in his incarnation, and the incarnation itself is an important concept. But it is at best an
introductory image of Christ. A more mature image is that of Christ on the cross,
which is what other people think of. That is better, because the cross explains
the incarnation. Jesus came to earth to die. "The Son of Man came not to be
served but to serve, and to give his life as a ransom for many" (Mt 20:28). Still,
good as that image is, it is not good enough. Jesus is no longer dead. An image
of the resurrected Christ is necessary to round out the picture. It is the resurrected Christ, not Christ on the cross, who speaks peace to his disciples and
commissions them to the task of world evangelization.

The Bible, having spoken of the resurrection, goes on to Christ's ascension
to heaven—where he is now seated at the right hand of the Father, ruling his
church and awaiting the day in which he shall come forth in power to judge the
living and the dead.

The New Testament refers to Christ's ascension in many places. In the Gospel
of John it is twice referred to in an anticipatory manner. Jesus asked those disciples who were offended by him, "What if you were to see the Son of Man

ascending to where he was before?" (Jn 6:62). To Mary Magdalene he said, "Do not cling to me, for I have not yet ascended to the Father; but go to my brothers and say to them, I am ascending to my Father and your Father, to my God and your God" (Jn 20:17). In Acts his ascension is recounted with circumstantial details: "And when he had said these things, as they were looking on, he was lifted up, and a cloud took him out of their sight" (Acts 1:9). The same account is found in the longer ending of Mark (Mk 16:19) and in Luke 24:51. Later, in the Epistles, the ascension is referred to in speaking of the fullness of Christ's work. "Who is to condemn? Christ Jesus is the one who died—more than that, who was raised—who is at the right hand of God, who indeed is interceding for us" (Rom 8:34). "If then you have been raised with Christ, seek the things that are above, where Christ is, seated at the right hand of God" (Col 3:1). The letter to the Hebrews makes repeated references to Christ's ascension and present position in heaven (Heb 1:3; 6:20; 8:1; 9:12, 24; 10:12; 12:2; 13:20). In 1 Timothy the ascension is placed within the full perspective of Christ's work:

Great indeed, we confess, is the mystery of godliness:
He was manifested in the flesh,
vindicated by the Spirit,
seen by angels,
proclaimed among the nations,
believed on in the world,
taken up in glory. (1 Tim 3:16)

That the ascension of Christ is mentioned so often in the New Testament is a clear indication of its importance. But that does not tell us why it is important or how it relates to us. However, the verses also give us an explanation of the meaning of the ascension, in three main areas. These are framed succinctly in the well-known words of the Apostles' Creed: "He ascended into heaven, and sitteth on the right hand of God the Father Almighty; from thence he shall come to judge the quick and the dead."

ASCENDED INTO HEAVEN

The first thing suggested by the ascension of Jesus to heaven is the idea that heaven is a real place. To say that it is a real place does not mean that we can therefore describe it adequately, even with the help of various biblical symbols. The book of Revelation, for example, speaks of it as a city whose streets are paved with gold, whose foundations are massive, where the light never ceases to shine. But heaven is not necessarily an actual city; such language is symbolic. A city speaks of a place to belong, a home. Foundations convey the idea of permanence. Gold suggests that which is precious. Light speaks of the eternal presence and unhindered enjoyment of God by his people.

Yet in recognizing the symbolism, we do not want to make the error of supposing that heaven is therefore anything less than a real place, perhaps even as localized as New York or London, for example. The explicit teachings of Christ as well as the ascension itself are meant to teach such a reality.

Some have observed that because God is described as being pure spirit—that is, as having no bodily form—heaven should therefore be described as the state of being spirit. But the idea that heaven is a state and therefore everywhere and nowhere is not what the Bible suggests. We recognize the limitations of talking about something entirely beyond our present experience. But at the same time, we notice that although God the Father does not have a concrete, visible form, the second person of the Trinity does. Jesus became man and remains the God-man for eternity. We also will have bodies in the resurrection. Our bodies will be different from what we know now. They will be like Christ's resurrection body, which could move through closed doors, for example. Still they will be real bodies, whatever their mysterious characteristics, and as bodies they must be somewhere. Heaven is the place where our bodies will be. Of course, we will presumably be able to move freely about the universe.

Second, the ascension of Christ speaks to us of his present work, as he himself taught. One aspect of that work is the *sending of the Holy Spirit,* which we should understand not merely as a past sending of the Holy Spirit at Pentecost but also as a present continuous sending of the Holy Spirit to do his work in this world. Jesus said, "It is to your advantage that I go away, for if I do not go away, the Helper will not come to you. But if I go, I will send him to you" (Jn 16:7). A second aspect is his intercession on behalf of his people. The book of Hebrews makes much of this, pointing out that Jesus exercises an intercessory role for us as our heavenly high priest.

Third, in speaking of Christ's present work in heaven, we recall his promise to the disciples that he was going to *prepare a place* for them (Jn 14:2-3). We cannot really know what Jesus is doing in this regard, since we cannot adequately visualize heaven. Nevertheless, we know that in some way he is preparing heaven for us. That assures us of the Lord's present interest in us and of his activity on our behalf.

SITS ON THE RIGHT HAND

The words of the Creed tell us not only that Jesus "ascended into heaven." They also tell us that having ascended into heaven, he now "sitteth on the right hand of God the Father Almighty." That image is drawn from the ancient practice of having a person who was particularly favored by a king seated next to him on the right. It speaks of the honor given to that person and of his role in the king's dominion.

That Jesus has been so *honored* is made clear in many places in Scripture. Hebrews 1:3 is an example: "He is the radiance of the glory of God and the exact imprint of his nature, and he upholds the universe by the word of his power. After making purification for sins, he sat down at the right hand of the Majesty on high." Here, as Charles Hodge points out, "The ground of Christ's exaltation is twofold: the possession of divine attributes by which he was entitled to divine honor and was qualified to exercise absolute and universal dominion; and secondly, his mediatorial work."[1] Again, although specific reference to Christ's being seated at God's right hand is omitted, Philippians 2:5-11 gives a similar basis for Christ being honored. It is because he possessed "equality with God" but nevertheless "emptied himself" and became "obedient to the point of death" for our salvation. "Therefore God has highly exalted him and bestowed on him the name that is above every name, so that at the name of Jesus every knee should bow, in heaven and on earth and under the earth, and every tongue confess that Jesus Christ is Lord, to the glory of God the Father" (Phil 2:9-11).

Christ's position at the Father's right hand also speaks of the Lord's present *authority* over the world and the church. It is the authority he spoke of prior to his ascension but following his resurrection. "All authority in heaven and on earth has been given to me. Go therefore and make disciples of all nations, baptizing them in the name of the Father and of the Son and of the Holy Spirit, teaching them to observe all that I have commanded you. And behold, I am with you always, to the end of the age" (Mt 28:18-20). It is impossible to overestimate the scope of Christ's authority. The announcement is not merely that authority has been given to him but that *all* authority has been given to him. Then, lest we still misunderstand or minimize his authority, he goes on to declare that it is an authority exercised both in heaven and on earth.

That all authority in heaven has been given to Jesus could mean merely that the authority he was to exercise on earth would be recognized in heaven also. If

---

[1] Charles Hodge, *Systematic Theology*, vol. 2 (London: James Clarke & Co., 1960), 635.

so, it would be a good statement of Christ's full divinity—for that authority is God's authority. Yet there is probably more to Christ's statement than that. For one thing, we remember that when the Bible talks about "powers" or "authorities" in heaven it is usually talking about spiritual or demonic powers. When it talks about Christ's victory through his death and resurrection it usually has those powers in mind as well. "For we do not wrestle against flesh and blood, but against the rulers, against the authorities, against the cosmic powers over this present darkness, against the spiritual forces of evil in the heavenly places" (Eph 6:12). Or again, we think of those verses early in the same letter that speak of the greatness of God's power "that he worked in Christ when he raised him from the dead and seated him at his right hand in the heavenly places, far above all rule and authority and power and dominion, and above every name that is named, not only in this age but also in the one that is to come" (Eph 1:20-21).

When we put Christ's announcement into that context we sense that what the Lord is talking about is not so much an acknowledgment of his earthly authority in heaven as a declaration that his authority is over all other authorities, whether spiritual, demonic, or otherwise. His resurrection demonstrates his authority over any power that can possibly be imagined. Consequently, we do not fear Satan or anyone else while we are engaged in Christ's service.

Second, Jesus announces that he has authority over everything on earth. This has several dimensions. It means that he has authority over us, his people. If we are truly his people, it means that we have come to him confessing that we are sinners, that he is the divine Savior, and that we have accepted his sacrifice on our behalf and have pledged ourselves to follow him as Lord. That is hypocrisy if it does not contain a recognition of his authority over us in every area. To be sure, there are other legitimate though lesser authorities over us as well: the authority of parents over children, of officers within the church, of state authorities. But he is the King of kings and Lord of lords.

The declaration of Christ's authority on earth also means that he has authority over those who are not yet believers. That is, his authority extends to the "nations" to whom he sends us with the gospel (Mt 28:19). This means, on the one hand, that the religion of our Lord is to be a world religion. No one is outside the sphere of his authority or to be exempt from his call. On the other hand, it is also a statement of his ability to bring fruit from our efforts, for it is through the exercise of his authority that men and women actually come to believe in him and follow him.

The fundamental basis of all Christian missionary enterprise is the universal authority of Jesus Christ, "in heaven and on earth." If the authority of Jesus were circumscribed on earth, if he were but one of many religious teachers, one of many Jewish prophets, one of many divine incarnations, we would have no mandate to present him to the nations as the Lord and Savior of the world. If the authority of Jesus were limited in heaven, if he had not decisively overthrown the principalities and powers, we might still proclaim him to the nations, but we would never be able to "turn from darkness to light and from the power of Satan to God" (Acts 26:18). Only because all authority on earth belongs to Christ dare we go to all nations. And only because all authority in heaven as well is his have we any hope of success.[2]

To Judge the Living and the Dead

Finally, we have the last picture of which the Apostles' Creed speaks, the picture of Christ coming from heaven "to judge the quick [living] and the dead." There is a reluctance today to talk about judgment, as we pointed out when speaking of God's wrath. Judgment is thought to be ignoble. We can talk about God's love, grace, mercy, care, compassion, strength. We can say he is the answer to whatever problem we have, that he is adequate for every emergency. But to talk about God as a God of judgment and of Jesus Christ as a judge is so offensive to our culture that many let this doctrine pass.

How can we possibly overlook the fact that the great and holy God of the universe will one day judge sin? If it were not true that God will judge sin, it would be a blot on the name of God. We could not talk about a holy God, a just God, a sovereign God, if he were to let sin go on unchecked indefinitely, as he obviously seems to let it do for a time in this world. We may object that sometimes sin *is* punished in this world. Sin has its built-in, self-destructing mechanisms. But to be honest, we must admit that sometimes good people suffer also, and sometimes evildoers go free. Although the evildoer is sometimes punished, no one would seriously maintain that all evil is properly punished and all good properly rewarded *in this world*. So if there is not a final judgment in which the inequities of this life are made right, there is no righteousness in God. There is no ultimate justice anywhere.

[2]John R. W. Stott, "The Great Commission," in *One Race, One Gospel, One Task*, ed. Carl F. H. Henry and W. Stanley Mooneyham, World Congress on Evangelism, Berlin 1966, Official Reference Volumes, vol. 1 (Minneapolis: World Wide Publications, 1967), 46.

But according to the teaching of the Bible, there is justice and there will be a judgment. Whenever we begin to talk of justice before God, there is a sense in which we should rightly draw back in horror. It is not just a matter of this particular good deed, which we imagine ourselves to have done, being rewarded, and that particular bad deed being judged. It is rather that by God's standards

> None is righteous, no, not one;
>> no one understands;
>> no one seeks for God.
> All have turned aside; together they have become worthless;
>> no one does good,
>> not even one. (Rom 3:10-12)

To speak of the judgment of God is to speak of judgment that rightly falls on all of us. What shall we do then? How shall we stand before Christ in that judgment?

There is a beautiful picture in the book of Acts of how the Christian can stand before God. It is a picture of how the one who has believed in Christ will find him—miracle of miracles—not as judge but redeemer. The picture comes to us from the account of the death of Stephen, a common person who had preached in Jerusalem with such power that the authorities hated him and had him stoned to death. Before he died, however, God granted him a vision of the heavenly Christ. He saw Jesus, not seated on the throne of judgment at the right hand of God, but rather standing at God's side to welcome him to glory. His testimony was, "Behold, I see the heavens opened, and the Son of Man standing at the right hand of God" (Acts 7:56). As he died he repeated his Lord's own statements: "Lord Jesus, receive my spirit," and "Lord, do not hold this sin against them" (Acts 7:59, 60).

I summarize this section by saying that Jesus is the source in which all spiritual good may be found. It is as Calvin wrote:

> If we seek strength, it lies in his dominion; if purity, in his conception; if gentleness, it appears in his birth. For by his birth he was made like us in all respects (Heb 2:17) that he might learn to feel our pain (cf. Heb 5:2). If we seek redemption, it lies in his passion; if acquittal, in his condemnation; if remission of the curse, in his cross (Gal 3:13); if satisfaction, in his sacrifice; if purification, in his blood; if reconciliation, in his descent into hell; if mortification of the flesh, in his tomb; if newness of life, in his resurrection; if immortality, in the same; if inheritance of the Heavenly kingdom, in his entrance into heaven; if protection, if security, if

abundant supply of all blessings, in his Kingdom; if untroubled expectation of judgment, in the power given to him to judge.[3]

In view of Christ's person and work it is foolish to seek for spiritual blessing elsewhere. It is wise to trust him only.

---

[3]John Calvin, *Institutes of the Christian Religion*, ed. John T. McNeill, trans. Ford Lewis Battles, 2 vols. (Philadelphia: Westminster, 1960), 527-28.

BOOK 3

AWAKENING *to* GOD

PART I

THE SPIRIT OF GOD

You believe that God is one; you do well.

Even the demons believe—and shudder!

JAMES 2:19

When the Spirit of truth comes, he will guide you into all the truth, for he will not speak on his own authority, but whatever he hears he will speak, and he will declare to you the things that are to come. He will glorify me, for he will take what is mine and declare it to you. All that the Father has is mine; therefore I said that he will take what is mine and declare it to you.

JOHN 16:13-15

I have been crucified with Christ. It is no longer I who live, but Christ who lives in me. And the life I now live in the flesh I live by faith in the Son of God, who loved me and gave himself for me.

GALATIANS 2:19-20

CHAPTER 1

PERSONAL CHRISTIANITY

*E*very religion has a certain amount of intellectual content that the follower of the religion presumably wants to get to know. But Christians face two specific dangers as they grapple with Christianity's doctrines.

On the one hand, they often become unduly subjective. Christian teaching concerns the nature of God and what he has done for our salvation through the death of Jesus Christ. But because this is both mind expanding and emotionally moving, these believers retreat from the hard work of understanding their faith intellectually and instead try to emphasize feeling and experience, sometimes to the point of detaching these from the work of God in history and even from the clear propositions of the Bible. When the experiences they seek are absent or at a low ebb, they try to work up spiritual feelings for God and fall prey to autosuggestion, circumstances, or even the machinations of the devil, who, we are told, at times appears to us as "an angel of light" (2 Cor 11:14).

This emphasis is not always so extreme. Sometimes it is merely the assumption, often not entirely thought through, that a certain intensity of religious experience is necessary if one is to be saved. Certain kinds of revival meetings suggest this. Or, on a more sophisticated level, one might gain that impression from a book such as *The Varieties of Religious Experience* by William James.[1] This classic study of the psychology of religion attempts to reflect a wide breadth of

---

[1]William James, *The Varieties of Religious Experience* (New York: The New American Library, n.d.).

experience and provide an impartial analysis. People may read this or another book like it and sense, perhaps wrongly, that they are not Christians simply because nothing of comparable intensity has occurred in their lives.

The other danger is equally bad: an overly objective Christian faith. Someone may have vast amounts of biblical knowledge and even a certain intellectual assent and commitment to these truths, but still fail to be changed. There is faith. But it may be the kind of faith James speaks of when he says, "You believe that God is one; you do well. Even the demons believe—and shudder!" (Jas 2:19).

This danger is particularly present among conservative Christians. Harold O. J. Brown says,

> Insisting as we rightly do upon the objective nature of the atonement and the effective nature of its application to individual human beings in salvation, we sometimes appear in danger of having a doctrine that is purely historical and judicial, without any believable, human dimensions in the time and space in which we live. . . . [We forget that] we are also in process, and sanctification, the continuing work of the Holy Spirit in our lives, is process and must exist among us.[2]

How may we avoid these dangers? How shall we solve the problem of having both an objective revelation of God in history and a vital appropriation of that salvation? Left to ourselves there probably is no answer. But the Bible tells us that God has a solution. Just as the Father sent his Son to perform the objective, historical work of the atonement as the ground of our salvation, so also he sends the Holy Spirit to apply that manifold salvation to us personally. This is not one simple and indivisible act. Rather, it involves a series of acts and processes: God's calling, regeneration, justification, adoption, sanctification, and glorification. In each case, the Holy Spirit applies the work of Christ to us personally.

This third section of the book deals with these processes and thus with the work of God's Holy Spirit. As Calvin puts it in the title to the third major section of his *Institutes of the Christian Religion*, it means "the way in which we receive the grace of Christ, what benefits come to us from it, and what effects follow."[3]

---

[2]Harold O. J. Brown, "The Conservative Option," in *Tensions in Contemporary Theology*, ed. Stanley N. Gundry and Alan F. Johnson (Chicago: Moody, 1976), 356.

[3]John Calvin, *Institutes of the Christian Religion*, ed. John T. McNeill, trans. Ford Lewis Battles, 2 vols. (Philadelphia: Westminster, 1960), 537.

PERSON OR POWER?

The place to begin in such a discussion is with the nature of the Holy Spirit himself. And the first question is, should we even use the pronoun *himself*? Is the Holy Spirit a real person whose work it is to save and sanctify us, or is he a power that we are to use for our own benefit? If we think of the Holy Spirit as a mysterious power, our thoughts will be, "How can I get more of the Holy Spirit?" If we think of the Holy Spirit as a person, we will ask, "How can the Holy Spirit have more of me?" The first thought is nonbiblical, pagan. The second is New Testament Christianity.

Reuben A. Torrey states clearly,

> The conception of the Holy Spirit as a divine influence or power that we are somehow to get hold of and use, leads to self-exaltation and self-sufficiency. One who so thinks of the Holy Spirit and who at the same time imagines that he has received the Holy Spirit will almost inevitably be full of spiritual pride and strut about as if he belonged to some superior order of Christians. One frequently hears such persons say, "I am a Holy Ghost man," or "I am a Holy Ghost woman." But if we once grasp the thought that the Holy Spirit is a divine person of infinite majesty and glory and holiness and power, who in marvellous condescension has come into our hearts to make his abode there and take possession of our lives and make use of them, it will put us in the dust and keep us in the dust. I can think of no thought more humbling or more overwhelming than the thought that a person of divine majesty and glory dwells in my heart and is ready to use even me.[4]

This distinction in outlook is illustrated in the pages of the New Testament. On the one hand, there is the case of Simon the magician, whose story is told in Acts 8:9-24. Simon was a citizen of Samaria to which Philip, one of the first deacons, had come preaching the gospel. Apparently Simon believed in Christ and was saved, for the account tells us, "Even Simon himself believed, and after being baptized he continued with Philip" (Acts 8:13). Simon knew very little about Christianity, however. So when he saw the miracles that were performed and was amazed by them, he fell into the error of thinking that the Holy Spirit was a power that could be purchased. Later, when Peter and John had come to inspect the work in Samaria and had been used by God to impart the Spirit to others, Simon offered the disciples money so that they would give him "this

---

[4]Reuben A. Torrey, *The Person and Work of the Holy Spirit* (1910; reprint ed., Grand Rapids: Zondervan, 1970), 8-9.

power" (Acts 8:19). Peter replied, "May your silver perish with you, because you thought you could obtain the gift of God with money! You have neither part nor lot in this matter, for your heart is not right before God. Repent, therefore, of this wickedness of yours, and pray to the Lord that, if possible, the intent of your heart may be forgiven you" (Acts 8:20-22).

The contrasting example comes from the beginning of the missionary work involving Paul and Barnabas. In this case we are told, "While they were worshiping the Lord and fasting, the Holy Spirit said, 'Set apart for me Barnabas and Saul for the work to which I have called them'" (Acts 13:2). In the first example, an individual wanted to get and use God. In the second example, God got and used two individuals.

But, some may ask, aren't there passages and even whole sections of the Bible in which the distinct personality of the Holy Spirit is not evident? The Old Testament often speaks of the Spirit of God, as does the second verse of Genesis, "And the Spirit of God was hovering over the face of the waters" (Gen 1:2), or the Old Testament refers to certain individuals of whom it is said that "the Spirit of the LORD [God] clothed" them (Judg 6:34; 2 Chron 24:20). These verses may be said to give intimations of the doctrine of the distinct personality of the Holy Spirit and therefore also of the Trinity. But it must be admitted that in the Old Testament there is very little in the way of a clear presentation of the personal distinctness of the second person of the Trinity, and even less of the personal distinctness of the Spirit of God.

It is entirely different when we come to the New Testament, however. Here the Holy Spirit is shown to be one member of the Trinity, equal in all ways to both the Father and Son and yet distinct from them. This does not mean that there are three gods, as indicated in the first book in this volume.[5] There are three persons. But in a way that is beyond our full understanding, these three are also one.

A person is defined as one who has knowledge, feelings, and a will, and this is just what is stated of the Spirit. In John 14:16-18 Jesus says regarding the Holy Spirit, "And I will ask the Father, and he will give you another Helper, to be with you forever, even the Spirit of truth, whom the world cannot receive, because it neither sees him nor knows him. You know him, for he dwells with you and will be in you." If the Spirit were only a power, this promise would actually be more like compensation: "I am going to be taken from you, but I will give you

---

[5]See book 1, chapter 10, "Three Persons."

some*thing* to make up for my departure." But he is not merely a power. He is not a thing that is being given but another divine personality, a personality who has knowledge, for he will know of the disciples' needs; feelings, for he will identify with them in their distress; and will, for he will determine to comfort them in fulfillment of the Lord's commission.

The New Testament evidence for the distinct personality of the Holy Spirit may be grouped in the following six categories:

1. **The personal actions of the Holy Spirit.** One example is the text just cited. There he is said to comfort Christians. Another is John 16:8-11, which speaks of the Spirit's work of convicting unbelievers. "And when he comes, he will convict the world concerning sin and righteousness and judgment" (John 16:8).

2. **The Holy Spirit's mission, distinct from the Father's and the Son's.** Jesus indicates this clearly in his final discourse: "But when the Helper comes, whom I will send to you from the Father, the Spirit of truth, who proceeds from the Father, he will bear witness about me" (Jn 15:26).

3. **The Holy Spirit's rank and power, equal to those of the Father and the Son.** The various trinitarian formulas of the New Testament express this clearly. In Matthew 28:19, the disciples are told to baptize "in the name of the Father and of the Son and of the Holy Spirit." In 2 Corinthians 13:14, Paul prays that "the grace of the Lord Jesus Christ and the love of God and the fellowship of the Holy Spirit be with" all his readers. Peter speaks of those who are "elect . . . according to the foreknowledge of God the Father, in the sanctification of the Spirit, for obedience to Jesus Christ" (1 Pet 1:2). Jude speaks of our being built up in the Christian faith as we are "praying in the Holy Spirit," keeping ourselves "in the love of God," and "waiting for the mercy of our Lord Jesus Christ that leads to eternal life" (Jude 20-21).

4. **The appearances of the Holy Spirit in a visible form.** At the baptism of Jesus, "the Holy Spirit descended on him in bodily form, like a dove; and a voice came from heaven, 'You are my beloved Son; with you I am well pleased'" (Lk 3:22). On the day of Pentecost "divided tongues as of fire appeared to them and rested on each one of them" (Acts 2:3).

5. **The sin against the Holy Spirit.** This implies offense against a personality (Mt 12:31-32).

6. *The gifts of the Holy Spirit.* In 1 Corinthians 12:11, after having enumerated the gifts of wisdom, knowledge, faith, healing, miracles, prophecy, the discerning of spirits, tongues, and the interpretation of tongues, Paul writes, "All these are empowered by one and the same Spirit, who apportions to each one individually as he wills."[6] The gifts of the Holy Spirit are distinguished from the Spirit himself, indicating that he is no mere force behind these remarkable displays.

Here are six separate lines of argument showing that the Holy Spirit is a person. Yet the problem for many of us may not be so much with the doctrine of the Holy Spirit as with our attitude toward him. Theoretically many of us do believe that the Holy Spirit is a person, the third person of the Godhead. But do we actually think about him in this way? Do we think about him at all? Perhaps we do what a woman did who had attended a series of messages on the Holy Spirit at a Bible conference years ago. She listened carefully and then came up to the speaker to thank him for his teaching. She said, "Before your messages I never thought of it as a person." Apparently she was not thinking of *him* as a person even yet.

IS HE GOD?

There is one other preliminary matter to be studied. We have insisted that the Holy Spirit is a distinct person, but we have also called him a divine person. Is he divine? Or is he some lesser being, perhaps an angel? Is the Holy Spirit God?

One of the clearest indications of the full divinity of the Holy Spirit is found on the lips of Jesus when he promised to send the Spirit to the disciples to be "another Helper" (Jn 14:16). Here the important word is *another*. In Greek there are two different words for *another*. There is *allos*, the word used here (meaning "another just like the first one"), and there is *heteros* (meaning "totally different"), from which we get our word *heterodox*. Since the word *allos* rather than *heteros* occurs in this text, Jesus is saying that he will send the disciples a person just like himself, that is, one who is fully divine. Who is the first Helper? Jesus. He had been the disciples' strength and counsel during the years of his ministry among them. Now he is going away, and in his place he will be sending a second Helper who is just like him. He is to be another divine person living with them and (in this case) in them.

---

[6]The points are suggested by George Smeaton, *The Doctrine of the Holy Spirit* (1882; repr., London: Banner of Truth Trust, 1974), 109.

This is not the only evidence for this important doctrine, of course. We may gather the evidence for the divinity of the Holy Spirit in the following categories:

1. **The divine qualities of the Holy Spirit.** The phrase *Holy Spirit* is itself a striking example, for the word *holy* designates the innermost essence of God's nature. He is the "Holy Father" (Jn 17:11), and Jesus is the "Holy One of God" (Jn 6:69; compare Mk 1:24). The Spirit of God is also said to be omniscient (Jn 16:12-13; 1 Cor 2:10-11), omnipotent (Lk 1:35), and omnipresent (Ps 139:7-10).

2. **The works of God attributed to the Holy Spirit.** The Spirit was active in the work of creation (see Job 33:4). He imparted the Scriptures (see 2 Pet 1:21). He is the agent of the new birth, as we will see more fully in a later chapter (see Jn 3:6). He is the agent of resurrection (see Rom 8:11).

3. **The equality of the Holy Spirit with God the Father and God the Son.** The benedictions and trinitarian formulas cited earlier are examples of this.

4. **The name of God indirectly given to him.** The clearest example is in Acts 5:3-4, where Peter says to Ananias, "Ananias, why has Satan filled your heart to lie to the Holy Spirit and to keep back for yourself part of the proceeds of the land? . . . You have not lied to man but to God." Other examples are those passages from the Old Testament quoted in the New in which, on the one hand, God is said to be the speaker and in which, on the other hand, the Holy Spirit is said to be speaking. Isaiah 6:8 begins, "And I heard the voice of the Lord saying, 'Whom shall I send, and who will go for us?'" In Acts 28:25-27, the Isaiah passage is quoted, beginning, "The Holy Spirit was right in saying to your fathers through Isaiah the prophet . . ."

Earlier I attempted to show how it matters practically that we know that the Holy Spirit is a person. I now ask, does it matter that we know that he is God? Yes, it does. If we know and constantly recognize his deity, we will recognize and rely on his work. J. I. Packer asks,

Do we honor the Holy Spirit by recognizing and relying on his work? Or do we slight him by ignoring it, and thereby dishonor, not merely the Spirit, but the Lord who sent him? In our faith: do we acknowledge the authority of the Bible, the prophetic Old Testament and the apostolic New Testament which he inspired?

Do we read and hear it with the reverence and receptiveness that are due to the Word of God? If not, we dishonor the Holy Spirit. In our life: do we apply the authority of the Bible, and live by the Bible, whatever men may say against it, recognizing that God's Word cannot but be true, and that what God has said he certainly means, and will stand to? If not, we dishonor the Holy Spirit, who gave us the Bible. In our witness: do we remember that the Holy Spirit alone, by his witness, can authenticate our witness, and look to him to do so, and trust him to do so, and show the reality of our trust, as Paul did, by eschewing the gimmicks of human cleverness? If not, we dishonor the Holy Spirit. Can we doubt that the present barrenness of the Church's life is God's judgment on us for the way in which we have dishonored the Holy Spirit? And in that case, what hope have we of its removal till we learn in our thinking and our praying and our practice to honor the Holy Spirit?[7]

The personality and deity of the Holy Spirit are practical teachings, for it is by the activity of this divine being that the gospel of salvation in Jesus Christ is made clear to us and changes our lives. He is the key to a vital and truly personal religion.

---

[7]J. I. Packer, *Knowing God* (Downers Grove, IL: InterVarsity Press, 1973), 63.

CHAPTER 2

THE WORK OF THE HOLY SPIRIT

W̲hen we are first getting to know a person, in most cases we ask, "Who are you?" and, "What do you do?" The person who answers might say, "I'm Diana Black; I work for the school board" or "I'm Leon Hall; I'm a sales representative with the airline." In each case the first part of the reply contains a name, perhaps coupled with the area from which the individual comes. The second part is about his or her occupation. We can ask the same questions in studying the Holy Spirit. In the last chapter we asked, "Who are you?" We saw that the Holy Spirit is a personal, divine being, equal to God the Father and God the Son in all respects. In this chapter we need to ask what this divine being does.

TO GLORIFY CHRIST

In asking what the Holy Spirit does, we sense almost instinctively that our question is nearly unanswerable. For if the Holy Spirit is God, as he is, then all that the Father and Son do, the Holy Spirit also does. Thus, as I suggested in dealing with the doctrine of the Trinity in book one, it is proper to say that the Holy Spirit was active in the creation of the universe (Gen 1:2), inspired the written Scriptures (2 Pet 1:21), governed the earthly ministry of the Lord Jesus Christ (Lk 4:18), gives spiritual life to God's people (Jn 3:6), and calls forth and directs the church (Acts 13:2; 16:6-7; 20:28). All that the other members of the Godhead do, the Holy Spirit does. On the other hand, we may note that the Bible gives certain emphases to the work of the various members of the Trinity. For example, the Father is principally active in the work of creation, and the Son is principally active in the redemption of the human race.

What is the Holy Spirit's primary work? Some would answer by saying that the Holy Spirit is active most in the sanctification of individual believers or in the inspiration of the Bible or in the giving of specific gifts to those serving within the church or in moving unbelievers to accept Christ. But while these items are each examples of things the Spirit does, they are not the best answer to the question. The best answer is found in John 16:13-14 (and related verses), in which Christ himself says of the Spirit's work, "When the Spirit of truth comes, he will guide you into all the truth, for he will not speak on his own authority, but whatever he hears he will speak, and he will declare to you the things that are to come. *He will glorify me*, for he will take what is mine and declare it to you" (my emphasis). In John 15:26, the Lord declares, "He will bear witness about me."

The work of the Holy Spirit is primarily to glorify Christ. Indeed, when they are correctly understood, all the other works that might be mentioned are included within this one overriding purpose.

If we are told that the Holy Spirit will not speak of himself but of Jesus, then we may conclude that any emphasis on the person and work of the Spirit that detracts from the person and work of Jesus Christ is not the Spirit's doing. In fact, it is the work of another spirit, the spirit of antichrist, whose work it is to minimize Christ's person (1 Jn 4:2-3). Important as the Holy Spirit is, he is never to preempt the place of Christ in our thinking. On the other hand, wherever the Lord Jesus Christ is exalted—in whatever way—there the third person of the Trinity is at work. We may recognize his presence and be thankful for it.

By Teaching About Christ

We can now ask, how specifically does the Holy Spirit glorify the Lord Jesus Christ? He does so in four areas.

First, the Holy Spirit glorifies Jesus by teaching about him in the Scriptures. The New Testament tells us that the Holy Spirit was doing this before Christ's incarnation through the inspiration of the Old Testament. But the work did not stop there. The New Testament records what Christ did and explains its meaning. This was to have such bearing on the work of the disciples that it is emphasized in Christ's final conversations with them. He says, "When the Helper comes, . . . he will bear witness about me" (Jn 15:26). And "I still have many things to say to you, but you cannot bear them now. When the Spirit of truth comes, he will guide you into all the truth" (Jn 16:12-13).

The disciples knew, no doubt, that in the Old Testament period the Holy Spirit had come on certain prophets, kings, and other leaders in order to speak through them. They might even have understood that the central message of the Old Testament was the promise of God to send a Redeemer. But now they are told that the same Holy Spirit is going to come on them—indeed, be in them—so that nothing about Christ's work or teachings necessary for our salvation and for the growth of the church might be lost.

How could these people, for the most part unlearned fishermen, be the agents through whom we should receive the New Testament? How can their record of the life and teachings of Jesus be trusted? Perhaps they recorded it incorrectly. Perhaps they mixed truth with error. The answer to these speculations is that they did not make errors because the Holy Spirit guided them and kept them from making mistakes. Some of the events and teachings they recorded were things they had heard and seen and that were brought to their remembrance. Other points were revealed to them later for the first time. In both cases they were led by the Holy Spirit. In fact, it was as true of them as of the Old Testament authors. As Peter said, "No prophecy was ever produced by the will of man, but men spoke from God as they were carried along by the Holy Spirit" (2 Pet 1:21).

In this work the Holy Spirit amply glorified Jesus. The Spirit prepared for Christ's coming through the inspiration of the Old Testament (the Old Testament told people what to expect and when to expect it). Then he preserved the story of his coming and gave the only infallible interpretation of it through the inspiration of the New Testament books.

These verses not only tell us that a new revelation is coming; they also suggest the threefold nature of this revelation. First, the revelation is *historical*. In John 16:13 Jesus says the Holy Spirit "will guide you [the disciples] into all the truth." That is, he would guide them into the truth concerning Jesus. In John 14:26 the historical element is made even clearer: "He will teach you all things and bring to your remembrance all that I have said to you." The disciples were likely to forget certain things that happened, but the Holy Spirit would bring to their minds the historical events connected with the life, death, and resurrection of Jesus Christ. We have the record of this in the Gospels—Matthew, Mark, Luke, John—and also the book of Acts.

The historical nature of Christianity sets it off dramatically from all other religions, mythologies, or philosophies. These conceive of religion largely as a pattern of ideas and of salvation as learning certain things or perhaps doing certain things. Christianity has ideas, that is true; but the ideas are based on what God has actually done, and that is determinative.

This historical basis also cuts Christianity off from the evolutionary view of religion, the view that thousands of years ago men and women had primitive ideas of God that grew as their knowledge grew, and that their writings about God showed this development. Since this has continued to the present, today we can drop what we consider to be unworthy concepts of God and add others we believe to be more valuable. Jesus, on the other hand, taught that far from being disposable, God's own action in history is the very basis of his revelation to men and women. This is seen most clearly in the cross of Christ, where God did not just teach an idea, he did something. He atoned for sin, revealed his love, and showed judgment.

Second, God's revelation is *doctrinal.* Jesus taught that the Holy Spirit "will take what is mine and declare it to you [the disciples]" (Jn 16:14). "He will teach you all things" (Jn 14:26). We have the results of this in the Epistles, beginning with the great letter to the Romans, which unfolds Christian doctrine in its fullest form. The other Epistles deal with particular problems in the church and theology, and conclude with those that are pastoral in nature—1 and 2 Timothy; Titus; 1, 2, and 3 John; 1 and 2 Peter; and Jude.

While God has acted in history, we are not left with that alone. He tells us what the action means. Thus, God came in Christ, but the significance of that is that God is revealed to us. We know that God is love because of Christ. We know he is just because of Christ. We know he is compassionately merciful and so much more because of Christ. Again, we say that Christ died. But everyone dies. Why he died is the issue. The Epistles give us the full implications of why Jesus Christ died.

Finally, God's revelation is *prophetic.* Jesus tells us that the Holy Spirit "will declare to you [the disciples] the things that are to come" (Jn 16:13). We have the results of this scattered throughout the New Testament: Matthew 24–25; Mark 13; Romans 11; 1 Corinthians 15; and particularly the book of Revelation. Prophecy indicates that God is still at work in history. God does not work in some static way, so that our period of history is absolutely identical to earlier periods and to those to come. Rather, God is doing unique things in history— working with people, unfolding a plan—so that what each of us does is important. Moreover, these workings are leading to the day of the Lord's return, at which time God will gather his own out of the world and demonstrate to all that the Lord's way is the only true way. The Holy Spirit has given us the Bible so that in history, in doctrine, and in prophecy the Lord Jesus Christ might be glorified.

BY DRAWING PEOPLE TO CHRIST

The second way the Holy Spirit glorifies Jesus is by drawing men and women to him in saving faith. I discuss this in detail in the section of this book titled "How God Saves Sinners," so it does not need to be fully expounded now. But I should point out that apart from this activity of the Holy Spirit, no one would ever come to Jesus.

After Jesus said that he would send the Holy Spirit to the disciples to be with them forever, he added, "even the Spirit of truth, whom the world cannot receive, because it neither sees him nor knows him" (Jn 14:17). By *the world* John means the world of men and women who are separate from Christ. Apart from the work of the Holy Spirit in leading people to Christ, no one can either see, know, or receive spiritual things. They cannot *see* because they are spiritually blind. As Jesus said, "Unless one is born again, he cannot see the kingdom of God" (Jn 3:3). They cannot *know* because the things of the Spirit "are spiritually discerned" (1 Cor 2:14). They cannot *receive* the Holy Spirit or Christ because, as Jesus said, "No one can come to me unless the Father who sent me draws him" (Jn 6:44).

So what happens? The Holy Spirit opens blind eyes so that the unregenerate may see the truth, unfogs their minds so that they may understand what they see, and then gently woos their wills until they come to place their faith in the Savior. Without this work there would not be even a single Christian in the world. By means of it, the Holy Spirit saves us and glorifies the Lord Jesus.

BY REPRODUCING CHRIST'S CHARACTER

Third, the Holy Spirit glorifies Jesus by reproducing his character in believers. He does this in three ways: first, by leading Christians to greater victory over themselves and over sin; second, by interceding for them in prayer and by teaching them to pray; and third, by revealing God's will for their lives and by enabling them to walk in it. These ministries combine to produce the "fruit of the Spirit," which is the life of Christ within us.

Paul speaks of this fruit in Galatians 5:22-23, saying, "But the fruit of the Spirit is love, joy, peace, patience, kindness, goodness, faithfulness, gentleness, self-control." These virtues were clearly in Christ to the highest degree and are also to be in all Christians, according to Paul's teaching. Commentators have noted the importance of the fruit being one fruit (singular) instead of fruits (plural). The "fruit of the Spirit" in its entirety is to be present in all. This is not true of the "gifts" of the Spirit, which I will discuss in detail in the fourth and final part of this volume. We are told that the Holy Spirit gives the gifts to one Christian or another as he wills (1 Cor 12:11). Thus, one may be a teacher, another a pastor, another an evangelist, and still another an administrator. By contrast, each and every Christian is to possess all the Spirit's fruit.

Love leads the list, and this is entirely appropriate. "God is love" (1 Jn 4:8) and, therefore, the greatest of all Christian virtues is love (1 Cor 13:13). Divine love gives this virtue its character; for God's love is unmerited (Rom 5:8), great (Eph 2:4), transforming (Rom 5:3-5), and unchangeable (Rom 8:35-39). God's love sent Christ to die for our sin. Now, because the Spirit of Christ is implanted within Christians, we are to show great, transforming, sacrificial, and unmerited love both to other Christians and to the world. It is by this that the world is to know that Christians are indeed Christ's followers (Jn 13:35).

Joy is the virtue that corresponds in the Christian life to happiness in the world. On the surface they seem related. But happiness is dependent on circumstances—when fortunate circumstances are removed, happiness is removed with them—while joy is not. Joy is based on the knowledge of who God is and what he has done for us in Christ. When Jesus was speaking to his disciples about joy just before his arrest and crucifixion, he said, "These things I have spoken to you, that my joy may be in you, and that your joy may be full" (Jn 15:11). "These things" involve the teachings of John 14–15, and perhaps of John 16 as well, since Jesus repeats this saying about joy later (Jn 17:13). Because of our knowledge of God's acts on our behalf, Christians can be joyful even in the midst of physical suffering, imprisonment, or other calamities.

Peace is God's gift to the human race, achieved by him at the cross of Christ. Before the cross we were at war with God. Now, because God has made peace with us, we are to show the effects of that peace in all circumstances through what we would call "peace of mind" (compare Phil 4:6-7). Peace is to reign in the home (1 Cor 7:12-16), between Jews and Gentiles (Eph 2:14-17), within the church (Eph 4:3; Col. 3:15), and in the relationships of the believer with everyone else (Heb 12:14).

Patience is putting up with others even when severely tried. God is the supreme example of patience in his dealings with rebellious people. This fact is held out to us as a reason why we should turn to him from our sin (Joel 2:13; 2 Pet 3:9).

Kindness is the attitude God has when he interacts with people. God has a right to insist on our immediate and total conformity to his will, and he could be quite harsh with us in getting us to conform. But he is not harsh. He treats us as a good father might treat a learning child (Hos 11:1-4). This is our pattern. If Christians are to show kindness, they must act toward others as God has acted toward them (Gal 6:1-2).

Goodness is similar to kindness, but it is most often reserved for situations in which the recipient merits nothing. It is linked to generosity.

Faithfulness means trustworthiness or reliability. Truth, a part of the very character of God, is at issue here. Faithful servants of Christ will die rather than renounce him or, to put it on a less exalted plane, will suffer great inconvenience rather than go back on their word. Those who are faithful do what they say they will do. They will not quit. This is also descriptive of the character of Christ, the faithful witness (Rev 1:5), and of God the Father who always acts this way toward his people (1 Cor 1:9; 10:13; 1 Thess 5:24; 2 Thess 3:3).

Gentleness or *meekness* (KJV) is seen most clearly in those who are so much in control of themselves that they are always angry at the right time (as against sin) and never angry at the wrong time. It was the preeminent virtue of Moses, who is praised for being the gentlest or meekest man then living (Num 12:3).

The final manifestation of the Spirit's fruit is *self-control*, which gives victory over fleshly desires and which is therefore closely related to chastity both of mind and conduct. Barclay notes that it "is that great quality which comes to a man when Christ is in his heart, that quality which makes him able to live and to walk in the world, and yet to keep his garments unspotted from the world."[1]

We must not think, however, that just because these nine virtues are aspects of the Spirit's work and because the Spirit is at work in believers that, therefore, every Christian will automatically possess them. It is not automatic. That is why we are urged to "walk by the Spirit" rather than according to "the flesh" (Gal 5:16). What makes the difference between a fruitful Christian and a nonfruitful one is closeness to Christ and conscious dependence on him. Jesus taught this in the illustration of the vine and branches:

> I am the true vine, and my Father is the vinedresser. Every branch of mine that
> does not bear fruit he takes away, and every branch that does bear fruit he prunes,
> that it may bear more fruit. . . . Abide in me, and I in you. As the branch cannot

---

[1]William Barclay, *Flesh and Spirit: An Examination of Galatians 5:19-23* (Nashville: Abingdon, 1962), 127.

bear fruit by itself, unless it abides in the vine, neither can you, unless you abide in me. I am the vine; you are the branches. Whoever abides in me and I in him, he it is that bears much fruit, for apart from me you can do nothing. (Jn 15:1-2, 4-5)

To be fruitful, the branch that bears the fruit must be attached to the vine. It must be alive and not merely a dead piece of wood. In spiritual terms, this means that the individual must first be a Christian. Without the life of Christ within, only the works of the flesh are possible: "sexual immorality, impurity, sensuality, idolatry, sorcery, enmity, strife, jealousy, fits of anger, rivalries, dissensions, divisions, envy, drunkenness, orgies, and things like these" (Gal 5:19-21). The fruit of the Spirit becomes possible when the life of Christ, conveyed by the Spirit of Christ, flows through the Christian.

There must also be cultivation. This is the point of the opening verse of John 15, in which God is called "the vinedresser." This means that God cares for us, exposing us to the sunshine of his presence, enriching the soil in which we are planted, and seeing to it that we are protected from spiritual drought. If we would be fruitful, we must stay close to God through prayer, feed on his Word, and keep close company with other Christians.

Finally, there must be pruning. This can be unpleasant at times, for it means that things we treasure will be removed from our lives. Sometimes it may involve suffering. There is a purpose in the pruning, however, and that makes all the difference. The purpose is to bring forth more fruit.

BY DIRECTING CHRISTIANS TO SERVE

The fourth way in which the Holy Spirit glorifies Jesus is by directing Christ's followers into Christian service and by sustaining them in it. This was to be true of the disciples, as most of the verses about the Holy Spirit in the previous pages indicate; he was to direct them in the future in precisely the way Jesus had directed them in the past. This is also true for today's followers of our Lord.

One example is in the passage mentioned for another reason in the last chapter—Acts 13:2-4. "While they were worshiping the Lord and fasting, the Holy Spirit said, 'Set apart for me Barnabas and Saul for the work to which I have called them.' Then after fasting and praying they laid their hands on them and sent them off. So, being sent out by the Holy Spirit, they went down to Seleucia, and from there they sailed to Cyprus." The Holy Spirit calls men and women into specific lines of work and goes with them as they do it.

Of course, he does not always call in precisely the same way. That is probably why we are not told how the disciples at Antioch came to know that the Holy Spirit had designated Barnabas and Saul for missionary work. Again, the fact that he calls does not mean that we should not consciously look for the Holy Spirit's leading. As those in Antioch worshiped the Lord and fasted—that is, as they were taking the work of the Lord seriously and were engaged in it to the best of their ability and knowledge—the Holy Spirit spoke. The same is true for us.

But I am running ahead of myself. Before looking at the Christian life, let us consider how one can become a Christian in the first place. And before that, we should consider the major but difficult biblical doctrine of the union of the Christian with Christ through the Spirit's activity.

CHAPTER 3

UNION WITH CHRIST

*U*nion with Christ by means of the Holy Spirit is not a peripheral matter in biblical theology, although it is widely neglected. It is a key thought in the Lord's teaching, as this chapter will show, and it is so important to Pauline theology that one commentator rightly calls it "the heart of Paul's religion."[1] John Murray has written, "Union with Christ is the central truth of the whole doctrine of salvation."[2] Calvin explains the point, saying, "This union alone ensures that, as far as we are concerned, he [Jesus] has not unprofitably come with the name Savior."[3]

Most emphatic of all perhaps is A. W. Pink.

> The subject of spiritual union is the most important, the most profound, and yet the most blessed of any that is set forth in the sacred Scriptures; and yet, sad to say, there is hardly any which is now more generally neglected. The very expression "spiritual union" is unknown in most professing Christian circles, and even where it is employed it is given such a protracted meaning as to take in only a fragment of this precious truth.[4]

This biblical theme is indispensable for understanding the work of the Holy Spirit in applying the benefits of Christ's atonement to the Christian.

---

[1]James S. Stewart, *A Man in Christ: The Vital Elements of St. Paul's Religion* (New York: Harper and Brothers, n.d.), 147.

[2]John Murray, *Redemption Accomplished and Applied* (Grand Rapids: Eerdmans, 1955), 170.

[3]John Calvin, *Institutes of the Christian Religion*, ed. John T. McNeill, trans. Ford Lewis Battles, 2 vols. (Philadelphia: Westminster, 1960), 541.

[4]Arthur W. Pink, *Spiritual Union and Communion* (Grand Rapids: Baker, 1971), 7.

UNION PAST, PRESENT, AND FUTURE

As with most New Testament teachings, the seeds of this doctrine are in the recorded words of Jesus, in this case conveyed under various metaphors and pictures. One key metaphor is that of the vine and its branches: "Abide in me, and I in you. As the branch cannot bear fruit by itself, unless it abides in the vine, neither can you, unless you abide in me. I am the vine; you are the branches. Whoever abides in me and I in him, he it is that bears much fruit, for apart from me you can do nothing" (Jn 15:4-5). Another metaphor is contained in those expressions that refer to eating Christ as one would eat bread (Jn 6:35) or drinking him as one would drink water (Jn 4:10-14; compare Mt 26:26-28). How Christ's followers will be received or rejected by the world suggests the same idea, for this is tantamount to a reception or rejection of himself: "The one who hears you hears me, and the one who rejects you rejects me, and the one who rejects me rejects him who sent me" (Lk 10:16).

In the high priestly prayer of the Lord recorded in John 17 this union is discussed explicitly:

> I do not ask for these only, but also for those who believe in me through their word, that they may all be one, just as you, Father, are in me, and I in you, that they also may be in us, so that the world may believe that you have sent me. . . . I in them and you in me, that they may become perfectly one, so that the world may know that you have sent me and have loved them even as you have loved me. (Jn 17:20-21, 23)

In the writings of Paul, this doctrine receives its greatest development and emphasis. We think of the important Pauline formulas, "in him," "in Christ," "in Christ Jesus," which occur 164 times in his writings. By use of these phrases, Paul teaches that we are *chosen* "in him before the foundation of the world" (Eph 1:4), *called* (1 Cor 7:22), *made alive* (Eph 2:5), *justified* (Gal 2:17), *created* "for good works" (Eph 2:10), *sanctified* (1 Cor 1:2), *enriched* "in all speech and all knowledge" (1 Cor 1:5), and *assured of the resurrection* (Rom 6:5). The apostle says that in Christ alone we have *redemption* (Rom 3:24), *eternal life* (Rom 6:23), *righteousness* (1 Cor 1:30), *wisdom* (1 Cor 4:10), *freedom* from the law (Gal 2:4), and every *spiritual blessing* (Eph 1:3). He gives testimony to his own experience by saying, "I have been crucified with Christ. It is no longer I who live, but Christ who lives in me. And the life I now live in the flesh I live by faith in the Son of God, who loved me and gave himself for me" (Gal 2:20).

We can tell from these many expressions that the believer's union with Christ is an extremely broad concept, dealing not only with our present experience of Jesus, but also reaching back into the eternal past and extending forward into the limitless future.

First, looking back, the fountain of salvation lies in the eternal election of the individual by God the Father in Christ. This is the meaning of the full text from Ephesians 1, parts of which were cited above: "Blessed be the God and Father of our Lord Jesus Christ, who has blessed us in Christ with every spiritual blessing in the heavenly places, even as he chose us in him before the foundation of the world" (Eph 1:3-4). We may not understand the full meaning of this eternal election in Christ, but at least we can understand that as far back as we can go, we find that God's purposes for us involved our salvation. Salvation is not an afterthought. It was there from the beginning.

One commentator has written,

> The first work performed by the Holy Spirit in our behalf was to elect us members of Christ's body. In his eternal decrees God determined that he should not be solitary forever, that out of the multitude of sons of Adam a vast host would become sons of God, partakers of the divine nature and conformed to the image of the Lord Jesus Christ. This company, the fulness of him who fills all in all, would become sons by the new birth, but members of the body by the baptism of the Holy Spirit.[5]

Second, in the present we are united with Christ in our regeneration or new birth. Jesus spoke of this to Nicodemus, saying, "Unless one is born of water and the Spirit, he cannot enter the kingdom of God" (Jn 3:5). Paul amplified it, noting, "If anyone is in Christ, he is a new creation" (2 Cor 5:17).

We have a picture of our new birth in the physical birth of Jesus Christ. In his birth the sinless and divine life of God the Son was placed within the sinful and quite human body of the virgin Mary. For a time it appeared as if the divine life had been swallowed up. But it eventually revealed itself through the birth of the infant Jesus.

In an analogous way, we experience the implantation of the divine life within us as the Spirit of Christ comes to reside within our hearts. We may say, as did Mary, "But how can this be, seeing that I have no power to beget the divine life myself?" But the answer is in the words of the angel: "The Holy Spirit will come

---

[5]Donald Grey Barnhouse, *The Epistle to the Romans*, part 6, *God's Freedom* (Grand Rapids: Eerdmans, 1958), 35.

upon you, and the power of the Most High will overshadow you; therefore the child to be born will be called holy—the Son of God" (Lk 1:35). We do not become divine, as some of the Asian religions believe. But in some sense the very life of God comes to live within us so that we are rightly called sons and daughters of God.

Because we were united to Christ in the moment of his death on the cross, redemption from sin has also been secured for us, and we are justified from all sin. Paul writes, "Do you not know that all of us who have been baptized into Christ Jesus were baptized into his death?" (Rom 6:3). And again, "In him we have redemption through his blood" (Eph 1:7). When Jesus died on the cross, those of us who are united to him by saving faith also died with him so far as the punishment of our sin is concerned. God the Father put God the Son to death. Since we are united to him, there is a sense in which we have been put to death too. In this, our sin is punished, and we need not fear that it will ever rise up to haunt us. As Henry G. Spafford expressed it in his well-known hymn,

> My sin—oh, the bliss of this glorious thought!—
> My sin, not in part, but the whole,
> Is nailed to his cross, and I bear it no more;
> Praise the Lord, praise the Lord, O my soul!

While we are united in Christ's death, we are also united in his life. Paul develops this in Romans 6.

> We were buried therefore with him by baptism into death, in order that, just as Christ was raised from the dead by the glory of the Father, we too might walk in newness of life.
>
> For if we have been united with him in a death like his, we shall certainly be united with him in a resurrection like his. We know that our old self was crucified with him in order that the body of sin might be brought to nothing, so that we would no longer be enslaved to sin. For one who has died has been set free from sin. Now if we have died with Christ, we believe that we will also live with him. We know that Christ, being raised from the dead, will never die again; death no longer has dominion over him. For the death he died he died to sin, once for all, but the life he lives he lives to God. So you also must consider yourselves dead to sin and alive to God in Christ Jesus. (Rom 6:4-11)

Through our identification with Christ in his death, the power of sin over us is broken and we are set free to obey God and grow in holiness.

Finally, looking forward, our identification with Christ in this spiritual union assures our final resurrection (Rom 6:5; 1 Cor 15:22) and glorification (Rom 8:17). Since we are united to Christ, we must eventually be like him. Since we can never be separated from him, we will always be with him (1 Jn 3:2).

In one sense "union with Christ" is salvation. Murray writes,

> We thus see that union with Christ has its source in the election of God the Father before the foundation of the world and it has its fruition in the glorification of the sons of God. The perspective of God's people is not narrow; it is broad and it is long. It is not confined to space and time; it has the expanse of eternity. Its orbit has two foci, one the electing love of God the Father in the counsels of eternity, the other glorification with Christ in the manifestation of his glory. The former has no beginning, the latter has no end.[6]

Apart from Christ, we cannot view our state with anything but dread. United to him, all is changed, and dread is turned into indescribable peace and great joy.

THE MYSTERY OF UNION

At this point some may be asking, "But *how* am I united to Christ? In what sense have I actually died with him? It all just seems like theological word games." The questions are certainly understandable in view of the real difficulty of this subject. Yet we should seek understanding, as Anselm suggested in his phrase *Fides quaerens intellectum*, "Faith in search of understanding." When we do, we find, as is generally the case, that the Bible has already provided much to assist our inquiry, especially in illustrations.

The first illustration is the union of a husband and a wife in marriage. In Ephesians 5, Paul portrays Christ in the role of the husband and the church in the role of the wife. He concludes, "This mystery is profound, and I am saying that it refers to Christ and the church" (Eph 5:32).

What kind of union exists within a good marriage? Obviously, it is a union of love involving a harmony of minds, souls and wills. On the human level, we do not always realize this as we should. Yet this is the ideal; and it points quite naturally to our relationship with Christ in which we are enabled increasingly to obey Christ's great commandment: "You shall love the Lord your God with

---

[6]Murray, *Redemption Accomplished and Applied*, 164.

all your heart and with all your soul and with all your mind" (Mt 22:37, a reference to Deut 6:5). We do not always succeed on this level either, but it is the ideal the Holy Spirit moves us toward.

It is possible, however, to conceive of a union of minds, hearts, and souls apart from marriage. What makes marriage unique is the new set of legal and social relationships it creates.

Marriage often changes the woman's name. She comes into the church as Maria Tower, let us say. She is married to Jim Schultz and leaves the church as Mrs. Schultz. Maria has been identified with her husband by means of the marriage ceremony. In the same way, the name of the believer is changed from Miss Sinner to Mrs. Christian as she is identified with the Lord Jesus.

Accompanying the change of name there are also legal changes. If Maria owned property before the marriage ceremony, she could have sold it as late as that morning with no signature but her own on the document. After the marriage ceremony she can no longer do that, for the legal affairs of her husband and herself are bound up together. This single fact throws penetrating light on the necessity of our union with Christ as the basis of our salvation. For through our union with him, he, our faithful husband and bridegroom, is able to pay the penalty that we have incurred because of our sin.

Finally, there are psychological and social changes. Maria knows that she is a married woman and no longer single. She expects to make adjustments to her new husband and will certainly regard other men quite differently from now on, just as he will make adjustments to her and regard other women differently. She may even find herself in new company with new friends and new life goals because of her new relationship. In a similar way, when we are united to Christ, our old relationships change and Christ becomes the center of our life and existence.

The second illustration of union with Christ is that of the head and the body. In Ephesians 1:22-23 we read, "And he [that is, God the Father] put all things under his [that is, Christ's] feet and gave him as head over all things to the church, which is his body, the fullness of him who fills all in all." Again, in Colossians 1:18, Paul writes, "He is the head of the body, the church." The fullest development is in 1 Corinthians 12:12-27, which says in part, "For just as the body is one and has many members, and all the members of the body, though many, are one body, so it is with Christ. For by one Spirit we were all baptized into one body—Jews or Greeks, slaves or free—and all were made to drink of one Spirit. . . . Now you are the body of Christ and individually members of it."

This illustration indicates first that our union with Christ is a union with one another as well. As we see in Paul's first letter to the Corinthians, the Christians there were divided, and Paul was striving to impress them with the need to realize their true unity. Second, the "headship" of Christ stresses his lordship. We are all members of the body, but it is *his* body. He is the head. The body functions properly only when it responds as he bids it. Third and most important, the illustration shows the union of head and body as a living and therefore growing union. This means that the union is not established by the act of joining some external organization, even a true church. Rather it is established only when Christ himself takes up residence within the individual.

The next illustration, that of the vine and the branches (Jn 15:1-17), highlights that the union of the believer with Christ is for a purpose: that we might be fruitful, that we might be useful to God in this world. Note that this fruitfulness is achieved by Christ's power and not by anything in us. Indeed, "apart from [him we] can do nothing" (Jn 15:5). Christ also prunes us, streamlines us for his work so we will be fruitful in the ways he desires.

The final illustration of the union of the believer with Christ is the portrait of a spiritual temple composed of many blocks, but with Christ as the foundation: "built on the foundation of the apostles and prophets, Christ Jesus himself being the cornerstone, in whom the whole structure, being joined together, grows into a holy temple in the Lord. In him you also are being built together into a dwelling place for God by the Spirit" (Eph 2:20-22). There are parallels to this in Christ's illustration of the "wise man who built his house on the rock" (Mt 7:24) and Paul's other scattered references to ourselves as "God's building" (1 Cor 3:9, 11-15). In each of these cases the central idea is the same: permanence. Because Jesus is the foundation and is without change, all that is built on him will be permanent also. Those who are Christ's will not perish but will endure to the end.

THE BAPTISM OF THE SPIRIT

How does this come about? We have seen that union with Christ is a legal change. It is a living relationship. It is the source of divine power within Christians. It is permanent. How does it happen that we who have had one legal relationship (condemnation) should enter into another in which we become sons and daughters of God? How does it happen that we who were spiritually dead should be made alive, that we who were powerless and without strength should be made strong, that we who are made of dust should live forever? The answer is by the

Holy Spirit. Only as the Spirit of Christ unites us to Christ do these truths become realities in our individual experiences.

This is the meaning of the important biblical phrase "the baptism of the Holy Spirit." In our day, this phrase is often used to denote experiences linked to the gift of speaking in tongues, which may or may not be from the Holy Spirit. I will discuss these gifts, including the gift of speaking in tongues, in detail in the fourth and final book in this volume. But this use of the phrase is inaccurate. It is also inaccurate to regard the baptism of the Spirit as a second work of grace, as some have done. Certainly the Christian life should be permeated by many works of grace and many fillings by the Spirit (Gal 5:16; Eph 5:18). My point is simply that "the baptism of the Spirit" does not refer to these. Rather it describes how all true believers become identified with Christ as members of his mystical body. To understand this phrase best, we should examine the seven passages in the New Testament in which it occurs.

Five of these passages are prophetic in nature. They look forward to the pouring out of God's Spirit on his people in accordance with the Old Testament prophecies, such as Isaiah 32:15; 44:3; and Joel 2:28. The distinctive feature about them is that they are all related to the ministry of Jesus. Thus, on four occasions John the Baptist is quoted as saying, "I baptize you with water for repentance, but he who is coming after me is mightier than I, whose sandals I am not worthy to carry. He will baptize you with the Holy Spirit and with fire" (Mt 3:11; parallels in Mk 1:7-8; Lk 3:16; and Jn 1:33). In the fifth instance, Jesus is himself quoted as telling the disciples to wait in Jerusalem for the coming of the Holy Spirit at Pentecost, saying, "John baptized with water, but you will be baptized with the Holy Spirit not many days from now" (Acts 1:5). In the original Greek Jesus is called "the Baptist" or "the Baptizer" because he baptizes with the Holy Spirit, just as John is called "the Baptist" because he baptizes with water.

The sixth reference to the baptism of the Holy Spirit is historic (Acts 11:16). It refers to the simultaneous gift of the Holy Spirit to the household of Cornelius and of the belief of these people in Jesus as a result of Peter's preaching. The reference is significant because it shows that the Holy Spirit was to be given to Gentiles just as he had previously been given to Jews; in other words, that there were not to be two levels or ranks of Christians within the church.

The seventh reference is the most important of all because it is didactic; that is, it is a teaching passage (rather than just a descriptive one). It therefore gives us the doctrine from which the other passages are to be interpreted. In

1 Corinthians 12:13 Paul writes, "For by one Spirit we were all baptized into one body—Jews or Greeks, slaves or free—and all were made to drink of one Spirit." First, we note how the unity of Christians is emphasized here. The Christians at Corinth had allowed their desire for various spiritual gifts to divide them, but Paul writes that they are actually one. His key argument is that they have all been baptized by one Spirit into the one body of Christ. This is an immediate warning to anyone who would allow an emphasis on a "baptism of the Holy Spirit" defined as a distinctive work of grace to divide Christians and destroy fellowship.

Second, we see that this experience is universal for all believers. Here the word *all* is decisive, for Paul writes that "we were *all* baptized" and that "*all* were made to drink of one Spirit." In other words, the baptism of the Holy Spirit is not a secondary and special experience for some Christians, but rather the initial experience of all by which, indeed, they became Christians in the first place. Baptism signifies identification with Christ. It is the Holy Spirit's role to identify us with Christ and, therefore, with his spiritual body, the church. This he does by engendering faith in our hearts while, at the same time, engrafting us into God's family.

John R. W. Stott, in a valuable study of these verses, summarizes the evidence like this:

> The "gift" or "baptism" of the Spirit, one of the *distinctive* blessings of the new covenant, is a *universal* blessing for members of the new covenant, because it is an *initial* blessing. It is part and parcel of belonging to the new age. The Lord Jesus, the mediator of the new covenant and the bestower of its blessings, gives both the forgiveness of sins and the gift of the Spirit to all who enter his covenant. Further, baptism with water is the sign and seal of baptism with the Spirit, as much as it is of the forgiveness of sins. Water-baptism is the initiatory Christian rite, because Spirit-baptism is the initiatory Christian experience.[7]

But what of the description of the coming of the Holy Spirit at Pentecost and the accompanying gift of tongues? Doesn't this suggest that speaking in tongues (or some other spectacular gift) should be the normative and desired experience of Christians, whatever the technical meaning of the phrase "baptism of the Spirit" might mean?

---

[7]John R. W. Stott, *The Baptism and Fullness of the Holy Spirit* (Downers Grove, IL: InterVarsity Press, 1964), 28.

We must think it through clearly. First, if the baptism of the Holy Spirit is the "initiatory Christian experience," as Stott says, and if speaking in tongues or some other spectacular gift is the necessary evidence of that baptism, then none who have not had this experience are saved. This is a drastic conclusion, which few would make, since salvation is based solely on faith in the Lord Jesus Christ as Savior, and many who have not had the gift of tongues or some other spectacular gift clearly make such profession. But the conclusion does follow from linking the experience of Pentecost to the baptism. Most who advocate the necessity of the Pentecostal experience avoid this by speaking of a second work of grace, but without biblical warrant.

When we turn to passages that deal explicitly with gifts and baptism, we find that they are quite balanced. The exercise of the gift of tongues is not forbidden (1 Cor 14:39). It is a valid spiritual gift (1 Cor 12:4-11). But while every Christian has at least one gift, not all have *this* one (1 Cor 12:29-30), and we are not encouraged to seek it more than others (1 Cor 14:1-5). The various listings of the gifts in 1 Corinthians might be read as suggesting that tongues—which always comes last—is relatively low in any listing of gifts by importance.

Why then does Luke emphasize the gift of tongues in his account of Pentecost? It would be enough to say that he does so simply because this is what happened in fulfillment of the prophecy in Joel. But if a theological meaning is sought—which we have every right to do since Luke was a theologically oriented historian and no mere chronicler of dates and facts—this is to be found in the ultimate effect of Pentecost: the proclamation of the gospel and a widespread response to it—not merely the tongues experience. Charles E. Hummel has written a book in which one chapter attempts to bridge the unnecessary gaps between Pentecostal and non-Pentecostal theologies. He denies the distinction, which I have made, between descriptive and didactic passages. Even so, when he comes to speak of Luke's unique theological emphasis, he focuses not on the experience of tongues but on the expansion of the gospel. "According to Luke's teaching, the baptism in the Spirit for the disciples was an empowering for prophetic witness."[8]

We conclude that the baptism of the Holy Spirit is for all Christians and is the equivalent of our being united to Christ in salvation. Christians are also to be filled with the Holy Spirit, an experience of grace that will express itself in

---

[8]Charles E. Hummel, *Fire in the Fireplace: Contemporary Charismatic Renewal* (Downers Grove, IL: InterVarsity Press, 1978), 182.

witness to Christ, but there is not a single instance in the New Testament in which any believer is urged to be baptized with the Holy Spirit or even commanded to be, for the simple reason that one cannot be urged to seek something that has already taken place in one's life. This baptism of the Holy Spirit, or union with Christ, is the foundation and basis from which all other personalized spiritual blessings flow.

PART II

HOW GOD SAVES SINNERS

*Jesus answered him, "Truly, truly, I say to you, unless one is born
again he cannot see the kingdom of God."*

JOHN 3:3

*For by grace you have been saved through faith.
And this is not your own doing, it is the gift of God,
not a result of works, so that no one may boast.*

EPHESIANS 2:8-9

*And to one who does not work but believes in him who justifies
the ungodly, his faith is counted as righteousness.*

ROMANS 4:5

*Everyone who believes that Jesus is the Christ has been born of God, and
everyone who loves the Father loves whoever has been born of him. By
this we know that we love the children of God, when we love God and
obey his commandments.*

1 JOHN 5:1-2

*For all who are led by the Spirit of God are sons of God. For you did not
receive the spirit of slavery to fall back into fear, but you have received
the spirit of adoption as sons.*

ROMANS 8:14-15

*"I do not ask that you take them out of the world, but that you keep
them from the evil one. They are not of the world, just as I am not of
the world. Sanctify them in the truth; your word is truth."*

JOHN 17:15-17

CHAPTER 4

THE NEW BIRTH

*T*he birth of a baby is a wonderful thing. It is wonderful to the mother and father. But it is also wonderful to the doctors and nurses who often continue to speak in awe of the "miracle" of birth, even though they have witnessed the entry of hundreds or even thousands of children into this world. On some occasions, as in the birth of a child to well-known parents, the news is reported by the newspapers, radio, and television.

None of these human births, however, can compare to the supernatural birth of a child of God through God's Spirit. The world around may take little interest in the occurrence. Few of the world's people took notice of the birth of Christ, though the angels celebrated the nativity with their nighttime song in the sky over the fields of Bethlehem. In the same way, few note the birth of a child of God today. Yet as Jesus said, "There is joy before the angels of God over one sinner who repents" (Lk 15:10).

The birth of a child of God is a spiritual resurrection, the passage of one into new life who formerly was dead in trespasses and sins. A child of wrath becomes a child of the Father who is in heaven. The theological term for this new birth is regeneration.

THE SEQUENCE OF SALVATION

Important as regeneration is, it is not the whole of salvation and should not be seen as an end in itself. John Murray notes in *Redemption Accomplished and Applied* that just as God made the earth teem with good things to satisfy men and women, so he showered us with an abundance of good in our salvation. "This superabundance appears in the eternal counsel of God respecting salvation; it appears in the historic accomplishment of redemption by the work of Christ once for all; and it appears in the application of redemption continuously and progressively till it reaches its consummation in the liberty of the glory of the children of God."[1] The words *continuously* and *progressively* indicate that the new birth, though of maximum importance, is but one step in an eternal process. While the accomplishment of our salvation by the death of Jesus was a single event, its application comprises a series of acts and processes that are called the *ordo salutis* or "steps [of God's] salvation."

What are they? One obvious act is the determining choice of God that comes before the new birth. Verses like John 1:12-13 point to this. Those who become "children of God" become so "not of blood nor of the will of the flesh nor of the will of man, but of God." Similarly, James 1:18 declares, "Of his own will he brought us forth by the word of truth, that we should be a kind of firstfruits of his creatures."

Other acts and processes follow the new birth. John 3:3 tells us that "unless one is born again he cannot see the kingdom of God," and John 3:5 adds, "Unless one is born of water and the Spirit, he cannot enter the kingdom of God." The new birth must come before we see the kingdom of God and enter.

Another helpful statement is 1 John 3:9. "No one born of God makes a practice of sinning, for God's seed abides in him; and he cannot keep on sinning, because he has been born of God." John is not talking about perfection in this verse, for earlier he has insisted that Christians do sin. If they claim differently, they are either deceived or lying—"If we say we have no sin, we deceive ourselves, and the truth is not in us" (1 Jn 1:8). He is talking about sanctification, which follows regeneration and is the progressive growth in holiness of one who has become God's child.

Romans 8:28-30 adds justification and glorification:

> We know that for those who love God all things work together for good, for those who are called according to his purpose. For those whom he foreknew he also predestined to be conformed to the image of his Son, in order that he might be the firstborn among many brothers. And those whom he predestined he also called, and those whom he called he also justified, and those whom he justified he also glorified.

---

[1]John Murray, *Redemption Accomplished and Applied* (Grand Rapids: Eerdmans, 1955), 79.

In these verses, foreknowledge and predestination deal with the prior determination by God. Calling, justification, and glorification deal with the application of redemption directly to us. We know from Paul's teaching elsewhere that justification presupposes faith (Rom 5:1), so we can insert faith before justification, but after regeneration. Sanctification follows justification and comes before glorification. In the final pattern we have God's foreknowledge, predestination, then his effectual call of us, regeneration, faith and repentance, justification, sanctification, and glorification.[2]

These steps could be subdivided, and in some cases perhaps even combined with no great loss. But this is the general sequence presented in Scripture and therefore a most helpful one in coming to see how God actually saves us. Before everything there stands God's eternal election. Where our personal experience is concerned, the first step is our spiritual regeneration.

DIVINE INITIATIVE

Rebirth is a metaphor of the initial step in salvation. Its use goes back to Jesus himself. He did not mean to teach the need for a literal, physical rebirth. That would be nonsense, as Nicodemus recognized. "How can a man be born when he is old? . . . How can these things be?" (Jn 3:4, 9). Rather Jesus wished to show the need for a new beginning. We had a beginning once in Adam. It was a good beginning. But we have ruined that through our sin. What we need now is a new start in which "the old has passed away" and "the new has come" (2 Cor 5:17).

The metaphor of rebirth also points out that regeneration is God's work and not the work of sinful human beings. One cannot be born physically by his or her own doing. It is only as a human egg and sperm join, grow, and finally enter this world that birth occurs—a process initiated and nurtured by the parents. Likewise, spiritual rebirth is initiated and nurtured by our heavenly parent and is outside our own doing.

The very first reference to the new birth in John's Gospel, John 1:12-13, tells us more. "But to all who did receive him, who believed in his name, he gave the right to become children of God, who were born, not of blood nor of the will of the flesh nor of the will of man, but of God." Each of these three negatives—not of blood, nor of the will of the flesh, nor of the will of man—is important.

---

[2]For a fuller discussion of the relationship between these various acts and processes, see ibid., 79-87.

"Not of blood" means that regeneration is not by virtue of *physical birth*. To some people, having a certain bloodline is quite important. In Jesus' day there were thousands of Jews who thought that they were right with God simply because they were descendants of Abraham (Jn 8:33). They were like Paul, who boasted that he was "circumcised on the eighth day, of the people of Israel, of the tribe of Benjamin, a Hebrew of Hebrews" (Phil 3:5). Abraham had received promises from God that he would be with him and his spiritual descendants forever. So the Jews thought they had it made just because they were descended from Abraham physically. Jesus pointed out that God was interested in a spiritual relationship and that their actions indicated that they were actually children of the devil (Jn 8:44). In the same way, many people today think that they are right with God simply because they have been born of Christian parents or in a so-called Christian country. But physical birth saves no one.

"Nor of the will of the flesh" is more difficult to interpret. St. Augustine, who took the phrase "not of blood" to refer to human birth (as I have also done), took "nor of the will of the flesh" to be the woman's part in reproduction, and the phrase "nor of the will of man" to be the man's part. Luther referred to "the will of the flesh" as an act of adoption, Frederick Godet to the sensual imagination, Calvin to willpower. Can these differences be resolved? Perhaps, if we consider that in the New Testament the word *flesh* signifies our natural appetites, our sensual or emotional desires. We may therefore come closest to John's meaning by saying that a people cannot become children of God by exercising their *feelings or emotions*.

Some today believe that they are Christians simply because they get an emotional kick out of attending a certain kind of church service or because they were once moved to tears at an evangelistic rally. Emotion may well accompany a genuine experience of the new birth, but the new birth is not produced by that emotion.

The third phrase, "nor of the will of man," is easier to understand. No one can become a child of God by sheer *volition*. In this life we can get ahead through determination, but we cannot be born again this way. You may have little of this world's goods, basic values, education, or ability. Nevertheless, you might work doggedly, go to night school, get a better job, and eventually become quite rich. You might enter politics and perhaps rise to be a congressional representative or even president. Others will praise you and call your effort a story of determination combined with a bit of good fortune. But nothing will make you the natural son or daughter of one set of parents if you have been born to another. Nothing will make you a child of God unless God himself brings about a new birth.

Becoming a child of God requires God's grace. While we must believe on Jesus as the divine Savior to become Christians, we believe because God himself has taken the initiative to plant his divine life within us.

WIND AND WATER

The image of rebirth also helps us understand what happens when God takes the initiative in salvation. Nicodemus came to Christ to talk about spiritual reality, but Jesus replied to Nicodemus's remarks by saying that no one can understand, much less enter into spiritual realities, unless he or she is born again. The word translated "again" is *anōthen*, which means not merely "again" but "from above." Jesus was telling Nicodemus that he must first be the recipient of this free grace from God. Nicodemus did not understand. "'How can a man be born when he is old? Can he enter a second time into his mother's womb and be born?' Jesus answered, 'Truly, truly, I say to you, unless one is born of water and the Spirit, he cannot enter the kingdom of God. . . . The wind blows where it wishes, and you hear its sound, but you do not know where it comes from or where it goes. So it is with everyone who is born of the Spirit'" (Jn 3:4-5, 8). Having identified the source of the new birth, Jesus then spoke of how regeneration occurs.

But what does it mean to be "born of water and the Spirit"? And why does Jesus mention "wind"? There are a number of explanations. The first takes *water* to mean physical birth (in which the appearance of the baby is accompanied by the release of the amniotic fluid from the mother) and *wind* (*spiritus*) to mean the Holy Spirit. According to this view, Jesus is saying that for a person to be saved he or she must first be born physically and then spiritually.

No one can fault the conclusion itself. Indeed, to be saved one must certainly first be physically alive and then also be born again spiritually. But that does not seem to be Christ's meaning. For one thing, the word *water* is never used in this way elsewhere in Scripture. Our thoughts along those lines are modern. Second, a reference to the necessity of physical birth is so self-evident that one wonders if Jesus would have wasted his words in this fashion. Third, *water* cannot refer to physical birth because, as we saw in John 1:13, physical birth has no bearing on regeneration.

A second interpretation of this phrase would take *water* to mean the water of Christian baptism. But baptism is simply not in view in this chapter. Indeed, the Bible teaches that no one can be saved by any external rite of religion (1 Sam 16:7;

Rom 2:28-29; Gal 2:15-16; 5:1-6). Baptism is an important sign of what has already taken place, but it is not the means by which we are regenerated.

The third interpretation takes both *water* and *wind* symbolically. Water, so the argument goes, refers to cleansing; wind refers to power. So one must be both cleansed and filled with power.[3] While sinners must be cleansed from their sin and while it is our privilege as Christians to be given power from on high, it is hard to think that this is the meaning of the passage. For one thing, in the rest of the New Testament, cleansing and power accompany the new birth or are said to follow it, while these verses deal with the way in which the new birth itself comes about. Moreover, neither cleansing nor power are at all related to the birth metaphor, as seems to be required.

Kenneth S. Wuest has proposed a fourth explanation based on the use of *water* as a metaphor in other New Testament texts. *Water* is often used in Scripture to refer to the Holy Spirit. In John 4, for instance, Jesus tells the woman of Samaria that he will give her "a spring of water welling up to eternal life" (Jn 4:14). The language of John 7:37-38 is almost identical to that of John 4:14. John himself adds, "Now this he said about the Spirit, whom those who believed in him were to receive" (John 7:39). Wuest also refers to Isaiah 44:3 and 55:1, both of which should have been known to Nicodemus. If this is the correct interpretation, "of water and the Spirit" is a repetition of ideas. The word *and* should be taken in its emphatic sense. In English this is generally indicated by using the word *even*. Jesus would be saying, "Truly, truly, I say to you, unless one is born of water, even of the Spirit, he cannot enter God's kingdom."[4]

The explanation given by Wuest is good, but I have always felt that more can be said. Besides being a metaphor for the Spirit, water is also used in the Bible to refer to the Word of God. Ephesians 5:26 says that Christ loved the church and gave himself up for her "that he might sanctify her, having cleansed her by the washing of water with the word." In 1 John 5:8, the same author who composed the fourth Gospel writes of three witnesses, "the Spirit and the water and the blood." Since he then goes on to speak of God's written witness to the fact that salvation is in Christ, the Spirit must refer to God's witness within the individual, the blood to the historical witness of Christ's death, and the water to the Scriptures. The same imagery lies behind John 15:3: "Already you are clean

---

[3]William Barclay is one who holds this view. See his *Gospel of John* (Philadelphia: Westminster, 1956), 1:119.
[4]Kenneth S. Wuest, "Great Truths to Live By," in *Wuest's Word Studies from the Greek New Testament*, vol. 3, part 3 (Grand Rapids: Eerdmans, 1966), 55-57.

because of the word that I have spoken to you." Another important text actually cites the Scriptures as the channel through which the new birth comes about, although without using water as a metaphor. James 1:18 reads, "Of his own will he brought us forth by the word of truth, that we should be a kind of firstfruits of his creatures."

When we consider Christ's words to Nicodemus in the light of these passages, we are able to think of God as the divine begetter, the Father of his spiritual children, and of the Word of God employed by the Holy Spirit as the means by which new spiritual life is engendered. That is, in John 3:5 Jesus is using two images: water and wind. The first stands for the Word of God, the second for the Holy Spirit. He is teaching that as the Word is shared, taught, preached, or otherwise made known, the Holy Spirit uses it to bring forth new spiritual life in those whom God is saving. That is why the Bible tells us that it pleased God to save us by the foolishness of preaching (1 Cor 1:21; Rom 10:14-15).

SPIRITUAL CONCEPTION

One more verse dealing with the new birth makes what I have been saying clearer. 1 Peter 1:23 says, "You have been born again, not of perishable seed but of imperishable, through the living and abiding word of God."

In this chapter of 1 Peter, the apostle has said that a person enters the family of God because of Christ's death (1 Pet 1:18-19) and through faith (1 Pet 1:21). Peter then goes on to emphasize that God is the Father of his children by likening the Word of God to human sperm. The Latin Vulgate makes this clearer than our English versions, for the word used there is *semen*.

Let's put the teachings and images of these passages together. God first plants within our heart what we might call the ovum of saving faith, for we are told that even faith is not of ourselves, it is the "gift of God" (Eph 2:8). Second, he sends forth the seed of his Word, which contains the divine life within it, to pierce the ovum of faith. The result is conception. Thus, a new spiritual life comes into being, a life that has its origin in God and no connection to the sinful life that surrounds it. That is why we can now say, "Therefore, if anyone is in Christ, he is a new creation. The old has passed away; behold, the new has come" (2 Cor 5:17). No one is ever the same after the Holy Spirit of God has entered to implant the life of God within him or her.

CHAPTER 5

FAITH AND REPENTANCE

Rebirth is the first point at which the saving activity of God touches us as individuals. But in God's economy regeneration is inseparable from what follows. Next in the sequence are faith and its accompanying grace, repentance.

Faith is the indispensable channel of salvation. In Hebrews 11:6 we are told that *"without faith* it is impossible to please [God]." Ephesians 2:8-9 declares, "For by grace you have been saved *through faith.* And this is not your own doing; it is the gift of God, not a result of works, so that no one may boast." Even John 3:16, which uses the verbal form of the word "faith" ("believe") rather than the noun, says, "For God so loved the world, that he gave his only Son, that *whoever believes* in him should not perish but have eternal life."

WHAT FAITH IS NOT

Let us begin by considering what faith is not. A great deal of confusion exists about faith simply because we inevitably apply the word to people who are untrustworthy. For example, we speak about doing something in "good faith." But in anything important we do not accept the mere word of the individual. We require deeds, contracts, and other written guarantees. In money matters we require collateral. Why? Because, although each side wants to believe in the good faith of the other, each also knows that people cannot always be trusted and must therefore be bound by formal agreements. It is easy to see why faith has often taken on overtones of wishful thinking.

Most commonly, faith is misunderstood as being *subjective*. This is the faith of religious feeling divorced from the objective truth of God's revelation. A number of years ago in a rather extended discussion about religion, a young man told me that he was a Christian. As our conversation developed, I discovered that he did not believe that Jesus Christ was fully divine. He said that Jesus was God's Son, but only in the sense that we are all God's sons. He did not believe in the resurrection. He did not believe that Jesus died for our sin or that the New Testament contains an accurate record of his life and ministry. He did not acknowledge Christ as Lord of his life. When I pointed out that these beliefs are involved in any true definition of a Christian, he answered that nevertheless he believed deep in his heart that he was a Christian. The thing he called faith turned out to be a certain variable outlook on life grounded in his feelings.

Another common substitute for faith is *credulity*. Credulity is the attitude of people who will accept something as true apart from evidence, simply because they earnestly wish it to be true. Rumors of miraculous cures for some incurable disease sometimes encourage this attitude. This is faith of a sort, but it is not what the Bible means by faith.

A third substitute for true faith is *optimism*, a positive mental attitude that is to cause the thing believed in to happen. An example would be sales representatives who so intensely believe in their ability to sell that they actually become successful.

Norman Vincent Peale popularized this outlook in a best-selling book called *The Power of Positive Thinking*. He suggests that we collect a number of the strongest statements about faith in the New Testament, memorize them, allow them to sink down into our subconscious minds and transform us, and thus become believers in God and in ourselves. If we memorize verses like "All things are possible for one who believes" (Mk 9:23) and "If you have faith like a grain of mustard seed, you will say to this mountain, 'Move from here to there,' and it will move, and nothing will be impossible for you" (Mt 17:20), we will be able to do what we previously thought impossible. Peale concludes, "According to your faith in yourself, according to your faith in your job, according to your faith in God, this far will you get and no further."[1]

Apparently in Peale's mind, faith in oneself, faith in one's job, and faith in God are linked together, and what this really means is that the object of faith is irrelevant. John R. W. Stott writes,

---

[1]Norman Vincent Peale, *The Power of Positive Thinking* (New York: Prentice-Hall, 1952), 99.

He [Peale] recommends as part of his "worry-breaking formula" that the first thing every morning before we get up we should say out loud "I believe" three times, but he does not tell us in what we are so confidently and repeatedly to affirm our belief. The last words of his book are simply "so believe and live successfully." But believe *what*? Believe *whom*? To Dr. Peale faith is really another word for self-confidence, for a largely ungrounded optimism.[2]

Of course, there is some value in a positive mental attitude. It can help you do your work better. But this is not faith in the biblical sense.

Against these distortions we must reply that real faith is not at all based on a person's individual attitudes and feelings. In the context of these human definitions faith is unstable. In the context of biblical teaching faith is reliable, for it is faith in the trustworthy God, who reveals himself reliably.

FAITH: THE TITLE DEED

This is why faith can be called "the assurance of things hoped for, the conviction of things not seen" (Heb 11:1). Some have used this verse as if it were suggesting a "pie-in-the-sky-by-and-by" type of religion. But this sole definition of faith in the entire Bible actually teaches the reverse. The word *assurance* does not mean "substitute for evidence," which is what the word *substance* (used in the King James Bible) suggests to many people. It actually means a "title deed to a piece of property." Although none of us has entered into the fullness of the inheritance that is ours through faith in Christ, faith is our title deed to it. Faith is itself the evidence of things not yet fully seen.

If this were a human title deed, there would still be room for doubt. But in dealing with God, doubt is unwarranted because of God's nature. He is the God of truth, so whatever he declares can be trusted. He is infallible, so whatever he declares can be trusted completely. He is faithful. If he promises something, we know that he will stand by that promise. He is omnipotent, all-powerful. Nothing can possibly rise up to frustrate the fulfillment of his desires.

When God calls us to believe in Christ, he is calling us to do the most sensible thing we can ever do. He is asking us to believe the word of the only being in the universe who is entirely reliable.

This is what John is getting at when he writes, "If we receive the testimony of men, the testimony of God is greater" (1 Jn 5:9). John is drawing a contrast between the way in which we trust others, even though they are untrustworthy,

---

[2]John R. W. Stott, *Your Mind Matters* (Downers Grove, IL: InterVarsity Press, 1972), 35-36.

and the way we ought to trust God. We trust other human beings every day of our lives. When we drive our car across a bridge, we have faith that the bridge will hold us up. We have faith in the engineer who designed it, in the people who built and maintain it, and in the inspectors who guarantee its safety—even though we have probably never met any of them. If we get on a bus to go home from a party some night, we have faith that the bus is safe, that the driver is an employee of the transportation company, that the sign on the bus is a true indication of where the bus is going. If we buy a ticket to a sports event, we have faith that the show will be held as advertised and that the ticket will gain us admission. John argues that if we can do this with other human beings who are often untrustworthy, we can do it with God. Indeed, we must. For God commands faith, and the salvation of our souls must express itself through responses to his offer.

THE KNOWLEDGE OF FAITH

True biblical faith has intellectual content, the point that Calvin emphasizes in the chapter on faith in his *Institutes of the Christian Religion*.[3] He stresses that faith's object is Christ, that faith rests on knowledge rather than pious ignorance, that this necessary knowledge comes from God's Word, that faith involves certainty, that the Bible is its shield and so on. He declares, "We shall possess a right definition of faith if we call it a firm and certain knowledge of God's benevolence toward us, founded upon the truth of the freely given promise in Christ, both revealed to our minds and sealed upon our hearts through the Holy Spirit."[4]

This knowledge involves who Jesus is (the second person of the Godhead, born of the virgin Mary, clothed in our nature, offered up for our transgressions, and raised again for our justification), who we are (sinners who need a Savior), and much besides. The Holy Spirit is the one who brings this knowledge of the gospel to us. In John 16 Jesus tells us, "And when he [the Holy Spirit] comes, he will convict the world concerning sin and righteousness and judgment: concerning sin, because they do not believe in me; concerning righteousness, because I go to the Father, and you will see me no longer; concerning judgment, because the ruler of this world is judged" (Jn 16:8-11).

---

[3]John Calvin, *Institutes of the Christian Religion*, ed. John T. McNeill, trans. Ford Lewis Battles, 2 vols. (Philadelphia: Westminster, 1960), 542-92.
[4]Ibid., 551.

The Holy Spirit convicts the world of sin because, as Jesus immediately explains, "They do not believe in me." This may mean, "He will convict the world of wrong ideas of sin that they have because they do not believe," "He will convict the world of its sin because, without this conviction, they do not believe," or "He will convict the world of the sin of unbelief."[5] Any of these translations is possible, and John may even be suggesting more than one, as is his manner. But if conviction with a view to salvation is the major thought of this passage, as it seems to be, then the second interpretation is primary. The primal sin is putting self at the center of life and so spurning belief. Understanding this is essential for salvation.

The third interpretation includes the truth that the Holy Spirit is like a prosecuting attorney who secures a verdict of "guilty" against the world. The second interpretation adds that he brings this guilt home to the human consciousness, so that men and women are disturbed by sin and seek freedom from it.

For example, on the day of Pentecost the disciples gathered together to await the coming of the Holy Spirit. When he came, they went into the streets of Jerusalem and Peter preached that the coming of the Holy Spirit was the fulfillment of the prophecy of Joel, given to call men and women to Christ and salvation. Peter then preached Jesus, concluding his sermon by saying, "Let all the house of Israel therefore know for certain that God has made him both Lord and Christ, this Jesus whom you crucified." We are told that immediately, "when they heard this they were cut to the heart, and said to Peter and the rest of the apostles, 'Brothers, what shall we do?'" (Acts 2:36-37). When Peter answered their question, three thousand believed and were baptized.

This was a remarkable response, but it was not due to Peter's brilliant analysis of the gospel or to his eloquence. If he had preached this sermon the day before, nothing would have happened. No one would have believed. He and the others would have been laughed at. But the Holy Spirit on Pentecost came and convicted the people of their sin. This is why they were "cut to the heart" and asked, "What shall we do?" As faith was born in their hearts, repentance followed. They wanted freedom from the sin they suddenly saw in their lives.

Not everyone has believed that we are unable to convict ourselves or others of sin. This lay at the heart of the controversy between Pelagius and Augustine and later between Arminius and the followers of Calvin. Neither Pelagius nor Arminius denied that salvation was by grace. But they did deny that it was *all*

---

[5]Leon Morris, *The Gospel According to John* (Grand Rapids: Eerdmans, 1971), 698.

of grace, that we make no move toward God unless God first convicts and then draws us. Pelagius said that our will is always free and that it can therefore always choose or reject anything offered to it. As to the gospel, grace makes the offer. But the ultimate criterion by which we are either saved or lost is our will. Pelagius did not understand that it is impossible for us either to become aware of our sin or to understand and respond to the gospel without the Holy Spirit's activity in our lives.[6]

Second, the Holy Spirit convinces people "concerning righteousness," says Jesus, "because I go to the Father, and you will see me no more." This can mean that the Holy Spirit will show the world what true righteousness is, since Jesus is no longer here to demonstrate the meaning of righteousness in his own person. Or Jesus' words could mean that the Holy Spirit will show the world where divine righteousness may be found. It cannot be found here. We cannot save ourselves by any human righteousness. What is needed is in Christ, who was once here but is now at the Father's right hand.

Last, the Spirit convicts the world "concerning judgment, because the ruler of this world is judged." The best understanding of these words seems to be that the Holy Spirit will convince the world that there is such a thing as judgment, which is proved by the judgment of Satan and the breaking of his power at the cross.

Nobody wants to believe in judgment. We want to think that we can do what we wish with impunity and that no day of reckoning will come. We are even encouraged in this thought because God does not always judge immediately, and evil often seems to go unpunished. This, of course, is false thinking. God does not always judge sinners immediately because he is long-suffering. Still, the judgments will come eventually. God's judgment on Satan is proof. Peter makes the same point. After showing that God judged the fallen angels, the world of Noah's time, and the cities of Sodom and Gomorrah, he concludes, "The Lord knows how to rescue the godly from trials, and to keep the unrighteous under punishment until the day of judgment" (2 Pet 2:9).

LOVE AND COMMITMENT

While a rational concept of Christianity is needed for faith, we cannot forget that the devil also understands these things and is probably more orthodox than

---

[6]The controversy between Augustine and Pelagius is discussed more fully in book two, chapter three, "The History of the Debate."

we are. True biblical faith therefore also requires a moving of the heart, much like that described by John Wesley in telling how his heart was "strangely warmed" as a result of the little meeting in Aldersgate.

Calvin was no less concerned to stress the heart as well as the intellect in faith. At one point he says,

> It now remains to pour into the heart itself what the mind has absorbed. For the Word of God is not received by faith if it flits about in the top of the brain, but when it takes root in the depth of the heart that it may be an invincible defense to withstand and drive off all the stratagems of temptation. . . . The Spirit accordingly serves as a seal, to seal up in our hearts those very promises the certainty of which it has previously impressed upon our minds; and takes the place of a guarantee to confirm and establish them.[7]

In another place he concludes, "It follows that faith can in no wise be separated from a devout disposition."[8]

Finally, faith is also trust or commitment. We turn from trusting in ourselves and instead trust God fully. We see the infinite worth and love of the Son of God, who gave himself for our salvation, and commit ourselves to him.

Marriage is a good illustration. It is the culmination of a rather extended process of learning, response, and commitment. The first stages of a courtship may be compared to the first element in faith: content. Here each is getting to know the other, each is learning whether or not the person possesses what is needed for a good marriage. It is a very important step. If the other person cannot be trusted, for example, there will be trouble later. The second stage is comparable to the second element in faith: the movement of the heart. This corresponds to falling in love, which is quite obviously an important step beyond mere knowledge. Finally, the couple says, "I do," and promises to live together and love each other regardless of what their future circumstances might be. So also we commit ourselves to Christ for this life and for eternity.

THE FAITH OF ABRAHAM

Faith does not stop here. As a product of the new birth, it does not disappear into the past, but rather continues throughout life as a present reality. Not only does it continue, it actually grows stronger as it comes increasingly to know the nature of the one in whom it trusts.

---

[7]Calvin, *Institutes*, 583-84.
[8]Ibid., 553.

When God called Abraham to leave Ur of the Chaldees and go into a land that he would afterward inherit, the book of Hebrews says, "Abraham obeyed. . . . And he went out, not knowing where he was going" (Heb 11:8). This was faith, but it did not need to be strong. It was only belief in the ability of God to lead the patriarch into the land. However, Hebrews goes on to say, "By faith he went to live in the land of promise, as in a foreign land, living in tents with Isaac and Jacob, heirs with him of the same promise" (Heb 11:9). Faith was stronger here, for it was trust in God exercised in the face of famine, danger, and the delayed fulfillment of the promise. Two verses farther on, the chapter speaks of the faith through which Sarah received strength to bear a son when she was past the age of childbearing. By this point the faith of both Abraham and Sarah was very strong. It had come to know the God of the promise as the God of miracles. In reference to this event God says of Abraham in Romans, "No distrust made him waver concerning the promise of God, but he grew strong in his faith as he gave glory to God, fully convinced that God was able to do what he had promised" (Rom 4:20-21).

We read finally that Abraham's faith conquered doubt in the midst of great emotional suffering and the seeming contradiction of all that he had previously believed. "By faith Abraham, when he was tested, offered up Isaac, and he who had received the promises was in the act of offering up his only son, of whom it was said, 'Through Isaac shall your offspring be named.' He considered that God was able even to raise him from the dead, from which, figuratively speaking, he did receive him back" (Heb 11:17-19). Abraham believed that God was able to perform a resurrection.

Such is the normal growth of faith. Your faith may be weak. Your faith may be strong. But the essential fact is that your faith is in God the Father and in his Son, our Lord Jesus Christ. God cannot fail. If you grow in your knowledge of God, you will find that your faith will also grow from strength to strength as did the faith of Abraham.

CHAPTER 6

JUSTIFICATION BY FAITH: THE HINGE OF SALVATION

*M*artin Luther, whose rediscovery of the truths about justification launched the Reformation in the sixteenth century, wrote, "When the article of justification has fallen, everything has fallen." He declared, "This is the chief article from which all other doctrines have flowed." He argued, "It alone begets, nourishes, builds, preserves, and defends the church of God; and without it the church of God cannot exist for one hour." He said that it is "the master and prince, the lord, the ruler, and the judge over all kinds of doctrines."[1]

John Calvin, who followed Luther in the early development of the Reformation, said the same. He called it "the main hinge on which religion turns."[2]

Thomas Watson observed, "Justification is the very hinge and pillar of Christianity. An error about justification is dangerous, like a defect in a foundation. Justification by Christ is a spring of the water of life. To have the poison of corrupt doctrine cast into this spring is damnable."[3]

---

[1]Luther, *What Luther Says: An Anthology*, ed. Ewald M. Plass, vol. 2 (St. Louis: Concordia, 1959), 702-4, 715.

[2]John Calvin, *Institutes of the Christian Religion*, ed. John T. McNeill, trans. Ford Lewis Battles, 2 vols. (Philadelphia: Westminster, 1960), 726.

[3]Thomas Watson, *A Body of Divinity: Contained in Sermons upon the Westminster Assembly's Catechism* (1692; reprint ed., London: The Banner of Truth Trust, 1970), 226.

These statements are not hyperbole. They are simple truth, because justification by faith is God's answer to the most basic of all religious questions: How can a man or woman become right with God? We are not right with him in ourselves; this is the doctrine of sin. We are in rebellion against God. If we are against God, we cannot be right with God. Moreover, we are *all* transgressors, as Paul so clearly says: "For all have sinned and fall short of the glory of God" (Rom 3:23). The doctrine of justification by faith says that we may become right with God by the work of Christ alone received by faith.

Paul puts it like this: "All who believe . . . are justified by his [God's] grace as a gift" (Rom 3:22, 24); "one is justified by faith apart from works of the law" (Rom 3:28); "To the one who does not work but believes in him who justifies the ungodly, his faith is counted as righteousness" (Rom 4:5). Justification is God's work. As Paul says, "It is *God* who justifies. Who is to condemn?" (Rom 8:33-34).

THE VERDICT ON WHAT GOD HAS DONE

Two points deserve emphasis. First, it is God who justifies and not we ourselves, as the quotations from Romans show. John Murray writes,

> Justification is not our apology nor is it the effect in us of a process of self-excusation. It is not even our confession nor the good feeling that may be induced in us by confession. Justification is not any religious exercise in which we engage however noble and good that religious exercise may be. If we are to understand justification and appropriate its grace we must turn our thought to the action of God in justifying the ungodly.[4]

Here we are helped by the image of the salvation triangle introduced in book two in a discussion of propitiation and redemption.[5] *Propitiation, redemption,* and *justification,* three key words for understanding the death of Christ, may be used to connect Christ, the Father, and Christians, thus forming a triangle. We are the recipients of two acts: redemption and justification. We contribute nothing to our salvation. Christ is the initiator of two acts: propitiation and redemption, for it is he who achieves salvation for us. God the Father is the recipient of one act: propitiation, Jesus satisfying God's wrath. On the basis of this, the Father initiates the last act: justification, in which he reaches out in grace to reckon the ungodly to be right with himself.

---

[4]John Murray, *Redemption Accomplished and Applied* (Grand Rapids: Eerdmans, 1955), 118.
[5]As seen in book two, chapter fourteen, "The Salvation Triangle."

The second point needing emphasis is that justification is given as a legal pronouncement, and not as a reference to people actually becoming more holy. It is true that they will become increasingly upright if God is actually at work in their lives. But justification does not itself refer to this transformation. When a judge justifies someone, the judge does not make that person upright or blameless. No changes are made in the person whatsoever. Rather the judge declares that in his or her judgment the person is not guilty of the accusation that has been made and is instead in right standing before the law that the judge was appointed to administer. The judge is not saying anything about the accused person's character.

There is some controversy over whether or not *justification* is used in Scripture as a legal term. But there are many reasons for thinking that it is.

1. The Old Testament speaks strongly of God as a God of law. To the Hebrew mind this set him off from the gods of the nations round about. Moreover, because he was a God of law, he was also a God of judgment, for in a universe governed by a sovereign and moral God, evil must be punished. Abraham voiced this outlook when God told him of the pending destruction of Sodom: "Shall not the Judge of all the earth do what is just?" (Gen 18:25). Here, in the early history of Israel, God is designated by the powerful term *Judge*. In later writings these thoughts are elaborated.

> The LORD has taken his place to contend;
>> he stands to judge peoples.
> The LORD will enter into judgment
>> with the elders and princes of his people. (Is 3:13-14)
> But the LORD sits enthroned forever;
>> he has established his throne for justice;
> and he judges the world with righteousness;
>> he judges the peoples with uprightness. (Ps 9:7-8)

Justification is often linked to judgment.

> Enter not into judgment with your servant,
>> for no one living is righteous [justified] before you. (Ps 143:2)
> He who vindicates [justifies] me is near.
> Who will contend with me? (Is 50:8)

The same idea occurs in reference to human judgment in Deuteronomy 25:1: "If there is a dispute between men and they come into court and the judges decide between them, acquitting [justifying] the innocent and condemning the guilty . . ."

2. Justification is contrasted with condemnation. "He who justifies the wicked and he who condemns the righteous are both alike an abomination to the LORD" (Prov 17:15). Since condemnation does not mean to make wicked, neither can justification mean to make righteous. Both rather refer to an official decree or declaration.

3. Several passages use the word *justify* in reference to God being justified. For example, in Romans 3:4 Paul quotes Psalm 51:4 in saying, "Let God be true though every one were a liar, as it is written, 'That you may be justified in thy words, and prevail when you are judged.'" Paul does not mean that God was to be made righteous, for God is and always has been righteous. He means that in the process of judgment God's words would show that he is righteous. Similar verses are Luke 7:29 and 1 Timothy 3:16.

4. Similarly, there are passages in which people are said to justify themselves. This could mean that they were making themselves better, but the passages do not allow this reading. In Luke 16:15 Jesus says, "You are those who justify yourselves before men, but God knows your hearts." He means that they tried to declare themselves upright when actually they were not. In Luke 10:29 it is written of a young lawyer, "But he, desiring to justify himself . . ." He tried to demonstrate that he was right in his conduct.

It would be saying too much to argue that each of these passages clearly refers to a courtroom scene. But some of them do, and the others use the word in a way that is entirely in line with this metaphorical association. There is always the idea of a judgment given and of a favorable verdict received in that judgment. Leon Morris has written,

> The case is not unlike that of English verbs like "to judge," "to acquit," which are capable of being used in connection with matters far remote from law-courts, but which nevertheless are undeniably derived from legal practice and retain the essential part of their legal significance. So is it with *dikaioō* [justify]. It may be used, it is used, in connection with matters where there is no formal giving of sentence in a law-court; but that does not alter the fact that the verb is essentially a forensic one in its biblical usage, and it denotes basically a sentence of acquittal.[6]

---

[6]Leon Morris, *The Apostolic Preaching of the Cross* (Grand Rapids: Eerdmans, 1956), 260. Morris has an extended discussion of the justification terminology in the Old and New Testaments (224-74).

GOD VINDICATED

God's judgment is always according to truth and equity. We are ungodly. How then can God justify us? If we were to declare a person who is guilty to be innocent, our act would be an outrage before both God and humankind. Yet this is what God does. How can he do it?

The Christian doctrine, strictly speaking, is justification *by faith* and not merely justification. Alone, justification means to declare righteous, as we have indicated. But justification by faith is God's declaring believers to be righteous not on the basis of their own works but on the basis of Christ's sacrifice. God declares that he has accepted the sacrifice of Christ as the payment of our debt to the divine justice, and in place of the sin he imputes Christ's righteousness to us.

This is the argument that Paul develops in the latter half of Romans 3:21-26.

> But now the righteousness of God has been manifested apart from law, although the Law and the Prophets bear witness to it—the righteousness of God through faith in Jesus Christ for all who believe. For there is no distinction: for all have sinned and fall short of the glory of God, and are justified by his grace as a gift, through the redemption that is in Christ Jesus, whom God put forward as a propitiation by his blood, to be received by faith. This was to show God's righteousness, because in his divine forbearance he had passed over former sins. *It was to show his righteousness at the present time, so that he might be just and the justifier of the one who has faith in Jesus* [my emphasis].

Quite a few years ago, a society for the spread of atheism prepared a tract containing half a dozen sketches of Old Testament characters combined with a lurid description of their misdeeds. No efforts were spared in describing their sin. One figure was Abraham. The leaflet pointed out that he was willing to sacrifice his wife's honor to save his own life. Yet he was called "the friend of God." The atheists asked what kind of God this is who would have a friend like Abraham. Another figure was Jacob. He was described as a cheat and a liar. Yet God called himself "the God of Jacob." Moses was portrayed as a murderer and a fugitive from justice, which he was. David was shown to be an adulterer who compounded the crime of adultery with the murder of the woman's husband. Yet David was called "a man after God's own heart." The atheists asked what kind of a God he must be who could be pleased with David.

Remarkably, this tract had hit on something that even God acknowledges. God calls himself just and holy. Yet for centuries he had been refusing to condemn and instead had actually been justifying men and women such as these. We might say that for these long centuries there had been a blot on God's name. As Paul says, he had indeed been passing over former sins. Is God unjust? No. In the death of Christ, God's name and purposes are vindicated. It is now seen that on the basis of that death, God had justified and continues to justify the ungodly.

No Other Salvation

The tragedy is that people will not accept this salvation freely offered in Christ and instead attempt to earn their own salvation.

As I suggested in the earlier discussion of propitiation (book two, chapter thirteen), in the two chapters preceding these key verses in Romans 3, Paul puts everyone in one of three categories to show that all people need what is available only through Christ. The first category, described in Romans 1:18-32, contains people we call hedonists, those who would say, "The only standards of conduct I recognize are those I devise for myself. I therefore determine to live for myself and for whatever pleasure I find." Paul says that these people need the gospel because their way of life is leading them from God to condemnation. They may be justified in their own eyes, but this is not the justification that counts. There is still a moral law established by God, and there is still a moral God who will judge them. They must either be justified by faith in Jesus Christ or be lost.

The second category, considered in Romans 2:1-16, contains those who lead ethically superior lives. They are the moral people. They might say, "All you have said about hedonists is true. They certainly are on a path leading away from God, and they will be justly judged for it. But I am not like that. I do not live only for myself or set my own ethical standards. On the contrary, I pursue the highest moral standards I know. Therefore, your proposed solution and your call to repentance do not apply to me." Paul responds, however, that they do, for two reasons.

First, the standards of moralists, however high, still fall short of God's standards. God demands a perfection we cannot even dream of. We all understandably fall short. Second, moralists fall short even of their own standards, regardless of what they may be. Paul says, "Therefore you have no excuse, O man, every one of you who judges. For in passing judgment on another you condemn yourself, because you, the judge, practice the very same things" (Rom 2:1).

What is your ethical standard? You may say, "My standard is the Sermon on the Mount." Well, do you live up to that standard? You do not, and neither does anyone else. In that sermon Jesus said, "You therefore must be perfect, as your heavenly Father is perfect" (Mt 5:48), and no one is perfect. Perhaps you would answer the question by saying that your standard is the Ten Commandments. But you do not keep those either. You do not worship God wholly. You break the Sabbath. You covet things that other people have. Is your standard the Golden Rule? If so, you break that, for you do not always do to others what you would like them to do to you (Mt 7:12). Perhaps your standard is merely the lowest common denominator of human relationships: the standard of fair play. Do you achieve that? Not always! So you stand condemned by that lowest of ethical standards. Clearly, moral people must disabuse themselves of the thought that they can earn heaven. They must admit that they too need God's righteousness.

The third category, spoken of in Romans 2:17-29, is that of religious people. In the context of Paul's experience these were Jews, the recipients of the law of God. They would boast of their heritage. In our day the equivalent person might say, "Yes, all the things you have said of the hedonist and the moral person are true. They are true of me. I also fall short of God's standards. But I do not put my trust there. I am religious, and so I trust God. I have been baptized and confirmed. I take communion. I give toward the church's support." Paul answers that such people need the gospel also, for all these things—though good in themselves—are inadequate. They do not affect one's standing before God. What is needed is the application of a righteousness that is not one's own but that comes from God, followed by a progressive internal transformation.

What does God see when he looks at you? Does he see deeds, even religious deeds, which are not backed up by the divine life within? Or does he see his own righteousness imparted by his own sovereign act now beginning to work its way out in your conduct?

Consider Paul's own conversion. He was not a hedonist. Far from it. He was religious and moral. He trusted in what he could achieve in these areas for his salvation. He tells about it in Philippians 3:4-8: "If anyone else thinks he has reason for confidence in the flesh, I have more: circumcised on the eighth day, of the people of Israel, of the tribe of Benjamin, a Hebrew of Hebrews; as to the law, a Pharisee; as to zeal, a persecutor of the church; as to righteousness under the law, blameless. But whatever gain I had, I counted as loss for the sake of Christ."

In the days before he met Christ, his life was something like a balance sheet with assets and liabilities. He thought that being saved consisted in having more in the column of assets than in the column of liabilities. And he had considerable assets! Some he had inherited and some he had earned. Among the inherited assets was the fact that Paul had been born into a Jewish family and had been circumcised according to Jewish law on the eighth day of life. He was no proselyte, who had been circumcised in later life, nor an Ishmaelite, who was circumcised when he was thirteen years old. He was a pure-blooded Jew, born of Jewish parents ("a Hebrew of Hebrews"). He was also an Israelite, a member of God's covenant people. Moreover, he was of the tribe of Benjamin. When civil war divided Judah from Israel after the death of Solomon, Benjamin was the one tribe that remained with Judah in the south. The northern tribes apostatized from God's revealed religion and set up schismatic altars where blood sacrifices were performed in violation of Leviticus 17. But Benjamin had remained loyal, and Paul was of that tribe.

Paul had also won advantages for himself. In regard to the law he was a Pharisee, the most faithful of all Jewish sects in their adherence to the law. He had been a zealous Pharisee, proven by his persecution of the infant church.

These were real assets from a human point of view. But the day came when Paul saw what these were in the sight of the righteous God. It was the day Jesus appeared to him on the road to Damascus. He understood that these acts of righteousness were actually like filthy rags. Before, he had said, "As to righteousness under the law, [I am] blameless." Now he said, "I am the foremost [of sinners]" (1 Tim 1:15). All that he had accumulated as assets were in reality not assets at all. These were liabilities that kept him from Christ. Under assets he now entered "Jesus Christ alone."

This magnificent truth has been embodied in many hymns, including one by Augustus M. Toplady.

> Nothing in my hands I bring,
> Simply to Thy cross I cling;
> Naked, come to Thee for dress;
> Helpless, look to Thee for grace;
> Foul, I to the fountain fly;
> Wash me, Savior, or I die.
> Rock of Ages, cleft for me,
> Let me hide myself in Thee.

The gospel says that when those who have been made alive by God turn from their own works, which can only condemn them, and instead by faith embrace the Lord Jesus Christ as their Savior, God declares their sins to have been punished at Calvary and imputes the righteousness of Christ to their account.

CHAPTER 7

JUSTIFICATION BY FAITH: THE PLACE OF WORKS

*T*he last chapter pointed out that justification is God's act and that it is entirely apart from any internal change in the individual. That is, justification does not depend on good works or on any other form of human improvement or endeavor. The argument of that chapter was from the perspective of someone who is not yet a Christian. However, now we must think of the matter from the perspective of one who has already believed on Christ and been justified. That person's justification has been by the grace of God through faith, not by works. But does this mean that works no longer have any place in Christianity? If not, Christianity would seem to promote immoral conduct. On the other hand, if we must have works, then isn't it the case that we are not saved solely by the work of Christ after all?

Here is where Roman Catholic theology and Protestant theology part company most radically. Although many Roman Catholics would heartily join with Protestants in affirming that justification is certainly by the grace of God through faith, they would say that works enter into justification in the sense that God justifies us in part by producing good works in us, so that we are justified by faith plus those works. Protestants reply that we are justified by faith in Christ alone. No works enter in; not even faith is a work. But they add (or should add—there is much deficient Protestant theology) that good works must necessarily follow if we are truly justified, though they do not enter at all into justification itself.

This difference may be expressed in two formulas. Catholic theology says,

Faith + Works = Justification

Protestants reply,

Faith = Justification + Works

Calvin states the Protestant view of the proper relationship between faith, justification, and works in these words:

> Why, then, are we justified by faith? Because by faith we grasp Christ's righteousness, by which alone we are reconciled to God. Yet you could not grasp this without at the same time grasping sanctification also. For he "is given unto us for righteousness, wisdom, sanctification, and redemption" (1 Cor 1:30). Therefore Christ justifies no one whom he does not at the same time sanctify. These benefits are joined together by an everlasting and indissoluble bond, so that those whom he illumines by his wisdom, he redeems; those whom he redeems, he justifies; those whom he justifies, he sanctifies. . . . Thus it is clear how true it is that we are justified not without works yet not through works, since in our sharing in Christ, which justifies us, sanctification is just as much included as righteousness.[1]

THE PLACE OF WORKS

This is the teaching of Paul, the great defender of justification by faith alone, in Ephesians 2:8-10. "For by grace you have been saved through faith. And this is not your own doing; it is the gift of God, not a result of works, so that no one may boast. For we are his workmanship, created in Christ Jesus for good works, which God prepared beforehand, that we should walk in them."

It has been pointed out by more than one commentator that there is a striking repetition of the word *works* in Eph 2:9-10. The first mention of works is negative. It tells us that because we have been saved by grace through faith, therefore we are not saved "as a result of works," otherwise it would be possible for a saved person to boast over another person who did not do these works and therefore was not saved. This verse utterly repudiates works as contributing in any measure to our justification. If we think works have a part to play in our justification, we

---

[1]John Calvin, *Institutes of the Christian Religion*, ed. John T. McNeill, trans. Ford Lewis Battles, 2 vols. (Philadelphia: Westminster, 1960), 798.

are trusting in those works rather than in the fully sufficient work of Christ and are not justified. We are not saved. We cannot be saved by grace and grace plus works all at the same time.

On the other hand, no sooner has Paul rejected the role of works in justification than he immediately brings works in again, saying that God has created us precisely "for good works." This is stated in such strong language—"works, which God prepared beforehand, that we should walk in them"—that if there are no works, the person involved is not justified.

Is this a contradiction? Not at all. It is merely a vivid way of saying that although justification aptly describes one important aspect of what it means to be saved, it is not the whole of salvation. God justifies, but that is not the only thing he does. He also regenerates. There is no justification without regeneration, just as there is no regeneration without justification.

Regeneration is the theological term for what Jesus was talking about when he told Nicodemus, "You must be born again" (Jn 3:7). He was telling him that he needed to have a new start as the result of the new life of God being placed within him. It is what Paul was talking about a bit earlier in this same chapter of Ephesians, as he described how "God . . . even when we were dead in our trespasses, made us alive together with Christ" (Eph 2:4-5). It is even what Paul is indicating in Ephesians 2:10. For that verse does not merely say that God commands us to do good works or even urges us to do them, although that is also true, but rather that he "created" us for good works, even adding that those works have been "prepared beforehand" by God. Clearly, if a person has been created by God specifically to do good works, he or she will certainly do those good works—even though they have nothing to do with how that person was saved in the first place.

In my opinion, this is one of the most neglected (but nevertheless most essential) teachings for the evangelical church in America today. At the beginning of this chapter, I contrasted sound Protestant theology with traditional Roman Catholic theology, showing how Protestants teach "Faith = Justification + Works"— the view I am expounding—while Catholics teach "Faith + Works = Justification." I disagree with Catholic theology at this point. But what are we to say of a theology, such as that dominant in today's evangelicalism, that does not have *any* place for good works? What are we to say of a teaching that extols justification apart from sanctification, forgiveness without a corresponding change in life? What would Jesus himself think of such theology?

When we study Christ's teachings, it does not take long to discover that he was not slow to insist on changed behavior. He taught that salvation would be by his work on the cross. He said, "The Son of Man came not to be served but to serve, and to give his life as a ransom for many" (Mk 10:45).

But Jesus also said, "If anyone would come after me, let him deny himself and take up his cross daily and follow me" (Lk 9:23).

He said,

> Why do you call me "Lord, Lord," and not do what I tell you? Everyone who comes to me and hears my words and does them, I will show you what he is like: he is like a man building a house, who dug deep and laid the foundation on the rock. And when a flood arose, the stream broke against that house and could not shake it, because it had been well built. But the one who hears and does not do them is like a man who built a house on the ground without a foundation. When the stream broke against it, immediately it fell, and the ruin of that house was great. (Lk 6:46-49)

He told the disciples, "The one who endures to the end will be saved" (Mt 10:22).

He told the Jews of his day, "Unless your righteousness exceeds that of the scribes and Pharisees, you will never enter the kingdom of heaven" (Mt 5:20). These verses teach that a saved person must do good works and continue in them to the end of life.

Moreover, as is evident even from this short selection of Christ's sayings, it is not only a matter of our demonstrating a genuinely changed behavior and doing good works if we are justified. It must also be true that our good works exceed the good works of others, which is obvious once we consider that the Christian's good works flow from the character of God within the Christian. "Unless your righteousness exceeds that of the scribes and Pharisees, you will never enter the kingdom of heaven" means "Unless you who call yourselves Christians, who profess to be justified by faith alone and therefore confess that you have nothing whatever to contribute to your own justification—unless you nevertheless conduct yourselves in a way that is utterly superior to the conduct of the very best people, who are hoping to save themselves by their works, you will not enter God's kingdom. You are not really Christians."

John H. Gerstner has called this rightly, I think, "a built-in apologetic." It is because no one but God could think up a religion like this.

Whenever you find a person who puts a premium on morality and really specializes in conduct and expects to make it on his or her record, you invariably find that person supposing that he or she can be justified by works. On the other hand, if you find a person who revels in grace, who knows the futility of trying to make it on one's own and simply cannot say enough about the blood of Jesus and salvation full and free, that person has a built-in tendency to have nothing to do with works in any form. When you get a person who really puts a premium on morality, he or she almost inevitably falls into the pit of self-salvation. And, on the other hand, when a person sees the principle of grace, there is a built-in temptation to go antinomian. But the Christian religion, while it preaches pure grace, unadulterated grace with no meritorious contribution from us whatever, at the same time requires of us the loftiest conceivable conduct.

> You cannot for one solitary moment say anything other than "Nothing in my hand
> I bring, simply to thy cross I cling." We are justified by faith alone. But we are not
> justified by a faith that is alone. Therefore, if you really cling to that cross, if you
> really do what you say you do, you will be abounding in the works of the Lord
> and will be living out an exceptional pattern of behavior.[2]

GOD WHO WORKS

I know this sounds confusing and even contradictory. But the problem vanishes as soon as we realize that the good works Christians are called on to do (and must do) are themselves the result of God's prior working in them. It is why in Ephesians 2:10 Paul prefaces his demand for good works by the statement, "For we are his workmanship." It is why, in a similar vein in the very next book in the Bible, he says, "Therefore, my beloved, as you have always obeyed, so now, not only as in my presence but much more in my absence, work out your own salvation with fear and trembling, for it is God who works in you, both to will and to work for his good pleasure" (Phil 2:12-13). It is because God is at work in us that we both will and do those works that please him.

In Ephesians 2:10 Paul calls this work of God a new creation, saying that "we are . . . *created* in Christ Jesus for good works." Beyond any doubt, Paul here has a contrast in mind between our new creation in Christ and our old creation in Adam, just as he does in Romans 5:12-21. When God made the first man, he made him perfectly furnished to do all good works. But Adam fell, as we know. Since that time, from God's perspective the best of the good works of Adam

---

[2]John H. Gerstner, "Man the Saint" in *Tenth: An Evangelical Quarterly*, July 1977, 43-44.

and his posterity have been bad "good works." They are contaminated by sin, because they do not flow from a pure love of God but rather from a desire to enhance our own reputation or position.

But now God re-creates those men and women whom he is joining to the Lord Jesus Christ. He brings into existence something that did not exist before and that therefore now has new and exciting possibilities. Before, the one who was without Christ was, to use Saint Augustine's phrasing, *non posse non peccare* ("not able not to sin"). Now he is *posse non peccare* ("able not to sin") and able to do good works.

In this spiritual *re*-creation God gives a new set of senses. Before, we saw with our eyes physically, but we were spiritually blind. Now we see with spiritual eyes, and everything seems new.

Before, we were spiritually deaf. The Word of God was spoken, but it made no sense to us. Or if it did, we resented that word and resisted it. Now we have been given ears to hear what the Spirit of God says, and so we do hear and re-spond to biblical teaching.

Before, our thinking was darkened. We called the good, bad; we called the bad, good. Indeed, we reveled in the bad, and we could not understand what was wrong when the supposed "good times" turned out to be bad times and we were left feeling miserable. The things of God's Spirit were "folly" to us (1 Cor 2:14). Now our thinking has been changed; we evaluate things differently, and our minds are being renewed day by day (Rom 12:1-2).

Before, our heart was hard. We hated God, and we did not even care very much for others. Now our hearts are softened. God appears altogether lovely, and what he loves we love. "We love because he first loved us" (1 Jn 4:19). Because our hearts have been remade, we now give food to the hungry, water to those who are thirsty, homes to strangers, clothes to the naked, care to the sick, and comfort to those who are in prison—as Jesus said we must do if we are to sit with him in glory.

A PRACTICAL DOCTRINE

Teaching about the place and necessity of good works in Christians' lives has a number of practical consequences.

First, it makes sense of those many biblical passages, particularly those re-porting the Lord's own teaching, that stress works and thus seem to suggest a works salvation. These verses I just referred to (from Mt 25) about feeding the hungry, giving water to the thirsty, homes to strangers, and so on are one example.

So are the other two parables in the same chapter. In the first parable the five foolish virgins are locked out of the marriage feast because they had neglected such a seemingly insignificant thing as providing enough oil for their lamps. The fact that they ran out was not even entirely their own fault, for the bridegroom was delayed (Mt 25:5). They knew him and were waiting for him. Yet they were not saved.

Similarly, the third servant in the second parable was barred from his master's favor because he had failed to use the one talent he had been given. He had not stolen it. On the contrary, he had kept it carefully and safely hidden in the ground and returned it to the master when the master returned from his journey. Yet the servant is rejected. Indeed, he was cast "into the outer darkness" where there will be "weeping and gnashing of teeth" (Mt 25:30).

In the third story, the sheep are separated from the goats on the basis of their good works. These stories and other sayings of Jesus seem to teach that people are saved on the basis of their perseverance, foresight, enterprise or charity. But this problem vanishes when we realize that Jesus is not contradicting but rather is showing the consequences of what it means genuinely to believe on him as Savior. Elsewhere he said, "This is eternal life, that they know you, the only true God, and Jesus Christ, whom you have sent" (Jn 17:3). That remains true. But the ones who know God and Jesus savingly, and thus truly possesses eternal life, will be waiting for the Lord when he returns; that is, they will persevere to the end of life. They will be using the talents given by God to the best of their ability. They will be a source of blessing to the hungry, thirsty, homeless, naked, sick, and imprisoned. These teachings hold together.

Second, an understanding of what God does in producing good works through the changed lives of Christians gives a wonderful basis for praising God for his matchless grace and wisdom. Dr. Paul Brand, chief of the Rehabilitation Branch of the United States Public Health Service Hospital, Carville, Louisiana, has written a book called *Fearfully and Wonderfully Made*. In it, Dr. Brand examines the intricate mechanisms of the human body and marvels at the greatness of a God who can create such wonders. He talks about the body's cells, bones, skin, and complexities of motion. This description leads one to marvel with the doctor. But wonderful as God's creation of the human body is, it is greatly surpassed by the marvels of God's *re*-creation of a man or woman who before was spiritually dead and therefore utterly incapable of doing anything that could possibly satisfy God, but who now, as the result of God's working, is able to be good and to do truly good "good works."

Third, an understanding of God's work in those whom he brings to faith in Christ to cause them to do good works gives a basis for judging whether we have in fact really been born again. The human mind is exceedingly subtle and, in its fallen state, is perverse. If the foolish virgins thought that the bridegroom would admit them to the feast when they knocked on the shut door, if the third servant thought his master would find his zero-growth performance acceptable, if the goats were utterly unaware of their failure to care for those who were in need—how can we be certain that we really are saved people, even if (so far as we know) we believe the right things?

The answer is that there must be a difference in our lives. We must actually become "new creatures" intellectually, morally, and in terms of our relationships to others. But this is where the next chapter begins.

CHAPTER 8

THE TESTS OF FAITH

*A*nyone who has worked with young Christians knows that often doubts set in shortly after a person has believed in Christ. The initial experience of the Christian is one of great joy. Lost in the darkness of sin and ignorance, the person has now come into God's light. Formerly alienated from God, the person is now found by him. But then, as time goes by, it is also frequently the case that the new Christian begins to wonder if, in fact, anything has really changed. The person thought they were a new creature in Christ; but, to speak frankly, they are really much as they were. The same temptations are present; they may even be worse. There are the same flaws of character. Even the joy they once knew seems to be evaporating. At such a time, the Christian often asks how it is possible to know that they are saved by God. They may ask, "How can I be certain I am justified?"

This problem can also affect older Christians. It may arise as a perfectly normal stage in their growth in Christianity or as the result of some severe setback in life—sickness, losing a job, losing someone close through death or falling into sin. Out of a depression born of these events, Christians may ask whether they are truly God's children or whether they were merely mistaken in thinking so.

Such questions are more than a source of great concern. They can greatly affect one's Christian life. As Christians, we are called to serve others as well as God. But how effective in helping others can we be if we are unsure of our own salvation? When Martin Luther was wrestling through these questions, prior to the Reformation, he was a monk shut up in a monastery. Afterward, when he knew that he had been saved by Christ's death and that God had justified him, he left the monastery to launch the Reformation. How can we launch out for God if we are shut up in a monastery of doubts?

CHRISTIAN ASSURANCE

The entire book of 1 John was written to answer this question. The churches to which John was writing had received apostolic teaching, but sometime before the composition of 1 John, some members of the congregations had withdrawn to found a new fellowship (1 Jn 2:19), no doubt claiming that their beliefs represented an improvement on what had been known before. Little is known about this defection, certainly no more than John himself tells us incidentally in this letter. But it was probably an early form of what came to be known as gnosticism.

The gnostics put themselves forward as "the knowing ones," the essential meaning of the word *gnostic*, while at the same time insisting that salvation was primarily by knowledge, that is, by initiation into the mystical and allegedly superior knowledge which they possessed. In most forms of gnosticism, this meant that the importance of moral conduct was denied. Gnostics might say that they had no sin, that what they did was not sin, or that they could have fellowship with God even though they continued sinning.

Gnostics also believed that matter was inherently evil, that spirit alone was good, and that there was no way to bring the two together. This accounted for the denial of the importance of the moral life, for salvation was in the realm of the spirit or mind, which alone was good. It also produced a philosophical religion divorced from concrete history. For the gnostics a real incarnation of the Son of God was impossible. If matter is evil, God could never have taken a human body unto himself. The incarnation must have been in appearance only.

Apparently many of the Christians were confused by this teaching. The new teachers seemed brilliant. Were the gnostics right? Were the old teachings to be abandoned? Had the believers been Christians all along or were their former beliefs only a preparation for this higher and more authentic form of Christianity? John answers their questions, first, by a categorical statement that Christians can and should know that they have eternal life and, second, by a presentation of three practical tests to settle the matter.

THE CHRISTIAN WAY OF KNOWLEDGE

In the letter, John says clearly that his purpose is to write to Christians to show them how they can be sure they are regenerate. "I write these things to you who believe in the name of the Son of God that you may know that you have eternal life" (1 Jn 5:13). Other statements say, "By this we may know that we are in him" (1 Jn 2:5); "I write to you, children, because you know the Father" (1 Jn 2:13); "You have been anointed by the Holy One, and you all have knowledge" (1 Jn 2:20); "I write to you, not because you do not know the truth, but because you know it" (1 Jn 2:21); "Beloved, we are God's children now" (1 Jn 3:2); "We know that we have passed out of death into life" (1 Jn 3:14); "We are of the truth" (1 Jn 3:19); "We know that he abides in us" (1 Jn 3:24); "Little children, you are from God" (1 Jn 4:4); "By this we know that we abide in him and he in us" (1 Jn 4:13); "We know that we love the children of God" (1 Jn 5:2); "We know . . . we know . . . we know" (1 Jn 5:18-20).

Today's world puts a high premium on knowledge and the confidence it is supposed to bring. But knowledge has outstripped the ability of most persons to absorb it, except in highly specialized areas. Can a person really know anything in such circumstances? Can there be certainty? John's answer is that there can be certainty in spiritual matters. This is possible in two ways. One way, developed just preceding John's statement of purpose, is to show that God has promised justification and eternal life to any who believe on his Son. We can have assurance simply because God can be trusted.

John makes this point by contrasting divine and human testimony.

> If we receive the testimony of men, the testimony of God is greater, for this is the testimony of God that he has borne concerning his Son. Whoever believes in the Son of God has the testimony in himself. Whoever does not believe God has made him a liar, because he has not believed in the testimony that God has borne concerning his Son. And this is the testimony, that God gave us eternal life, and this life is in his Son. Whoever has the Son has life; whoever does not have the Son of God does not have life. (1 Jn 5:9-12)

Obviously, John is trying to make the matter as clear as he possibly can. We all accept human testimony. Otherwise we would not be able to sign a contract, write a check, buy a ticket, ride a bus, or do any of the thousands of other things that constitute daily living. "Well then," says John, "why should we not believe God, whose Word alone is entirely trustworthy? God says that if we believe on Jesus as our Savior we are justified."

Certainty also comes in a second way. Those who believe God have an internal assurance that what they have believed is trustworthy. The Reformers termed this work of God's Spirit the *testimonium Spiritus Sancti internum*. On the other hand, those who do not believe God make him out to be a liar. They are saying that God cannot be trusted. Here the heinous nature of unbelief is evident. "Unbelief is not a misfortune to be pitied; it is a sin to be deplored. Its sinfulness lies in the fact that it contradicts the word of the one true God and thus attributes falsehood to him."[1]

In all fairness to those who doubt their salvation, it must be said that not all failures of assurance are sin in precisely this sense. To believe in Christ and yet think that God might go back on his word and not save us *is* sin. But some know that saving faith is not mere intellectual assent to certain doctrines, that it involves commitment and trust, and they know that they have believed in Christ in some sense. But they are not sure if they have believed adequately. "Have I really trusted Christ? Have I really turned from attempts to achieve my own salvation through my own righteousness to receive Christ's righteousness instead? Have I truly been justified?"

In response to such questions, John offers the three tests mentioned earlier. They are repeated in various forms throughout the letter: the *doctrinal* test (the test of belief in Jesus Christ), the *moral* test (the test of righteousness or obedience), and the *social* test (the test of love).

THE DOCTRINAL TEST

A characteristic of our time, often pointed out by contemporary Christian apologists, is that people no longer strictly believe in truth. They use the term in a certain colloquial sense, referring to that which is the opposite of false. But most in the twentieth century do not mean that when a thing is said to be true it is therefore true absolutely and forever. They usually mean that it is true for some people, though perhaps not for others, or that it is true now, but not necessarily for tomorrow or the day after. This results in a great deal of uncertainty and a sense of lostness.

Christianity moves within an entirely different set of presuppositions. In this first test of the presence of new life, the doctrinal test, people begin to see things differently. Before, they doubted whether there even was such a thing as truth.

---

[1]John R. W. Stott, *The Epistles of John*, Tyndale New Testament Commentary (Grand Rapids: Eerdmans, 1964), 182.

Now they see that God is "true," that Christ is "the truth," and that the Bible contains "true" propositions. They do not understand it all, of course. But they do see it differently. One writer on the normal patterns of religious experience puts it like this:

> Every man on whom this divine operation has passed experiences *new views of divine truth*. The soul sees in these things that which it never saw before. It discerns in the truth of God a beauty and excellence of which it had no conception until now. Whatever may be the diversity in the clearness of the views of different persons, or in the particular truths brought before the mind, they all agree in this, that there is a new perception of truth. . . . It is a blessed reality, and there are many witnesses of sound mind and unquestionable veracity who are ready to attest to it.[2]

John develops the doctrinal test at great length in 1 John 2:18-27 and then returns to it in 1 John 4:1-6. He quite naturally emphasizes the Gnostics' errors, primarily their denial that Jesus is the Christ. But as he states it, he shows that it is an error that can be made by anyone. John calls it *the* lie, and the one who embraces it the liar: "Who is the liar but he who denies that Jesus is the Christ? This is the antichrist, he who denies the Father and the Son" (1 Jn 2:22).

When John says, "Jesus is the Christ," he does not mean merely that Jesus is the Messiah of Old Testament expectation. If he did, it would be hard to see why the Gnostics would be opposed to it. In context, John goes on to speak of Jesus as the Son, that is, as the Son of God, and of knowing the Son in the Father and the Father in the Son. In other words, John is giving a confession that includes Christ's full divinity: God became incarnate in Jesus as the Christ. The Gnostics, on the other hand, believed that the divine Christ, conceived as an emanation from the highest and superior God, came on the man Jesus at the time of his baptism and left him before his crucifixion. This type of thinking is not foreign to some forms of modern biblical criticism that drive a wedge between what is called the historical Jesus and the Christ of faith.

This basic confession of the apostle John also includes all that the Father has said about Jesus in the Bible. Calvin writes,

> I readily agree with the ancients, who thought that Cerinthus and Carpocrates are here referred to. But the denial of Christ extends much further; for it is not

---

[2]Archibald Alexander, *Thoughts on Religious Experience* (1844; reprint ed., London: Banner of Truth Trust, 1967), 64.

enough to confess in one word that Jesus is the Christ, but he must be acknowl-edged to be such as the Father offers him to us in the Gospel. The two I mentioned gave the title of Christ to the Son of God, but imagined he was a mere man. Others followed, like Arius, who adorned him with the name of God but despoiled him of his eternal divinity. Marcion dreamed that he was a mere phantom. Sabellius imagined that he differed in nothing from the Father. All these denied the Son of God, for none of them really acknowledged the whole Christ, but adulterated the truth about him so far as they were able and made for themselves an idol instead of Christ. . . .

We now see that Christ is denied whenever the things that belong to him are taken from him. And as Christ is the end of the Law and the Gospel and has within himself all the treasures of wisdom and understanding, so also is he the mark at which all heretics aim and direct their arrows. Therefore, the apostle has good reason to make those who fight against Christ the leading liars, since the full truth is exhibited to us in him.[3]

To confess that Jesus is the Christ is to confess the Christ of the Scriptures. To deny *that* Christ, by whatever means, is heresy—a heresy with terrible consequences.

For one thing, to deny the Son is to deny the Father. No doubt the false teachers would have pretended to be worshiping the same God as the Christians. "We only differ from you in your views about Jesus," they might have said. But John says that this is impossible. If Jesus is God, to deny Jesus as God is to deny God. Second, to deny the Son is to forfeit the presence of God in one's life or, as we could also say, to have no part of him or he of us. John uses the phrase "has the Father" (1 Jn 2:23). In biblical language this is equivalent to saying that such people remain unregenerate and under God's just condem-nation. Those who confess Christ have found the Father and have been justified by him.

THE MORAL TEST

The moral test is cited in 1 John 2:3-6 and 3:4-10 and alluded to at other points in the letter. Simply put, those who know God will increasingly lead righteous lives. It does not mean that they will be sinless. But they will be moving in a direction marked out by the righteousness of God. If this does not happen, if they are not increasingly dissatisfied with and distressed by sin, they are not God's

---

[3]John Calvin, *The Gospel According to St. John 11—21 and the First Epistle of John*, trans. T. H. L. Parker (Grand Rapids: Eerdmans, 1961), 259-60.

children. "Whoever says 'I know him' but does not keep his commandments is a liar, and the truth is not in him, but whoever keeps his word, in him truly the love of God is perfected. By this we may know that we are in him" (1 Jn 2:4-5).

In these verses, John introduces two types of people, those who claim to know God but who do not keep his commandments, and those who obey God out of a genuine love of him. John has harsh words for the first group. He calls them liars, for they are neither deceived by others nor confused by facts. Rather, they openly profess something which they know is not true. When John goes on to say, "The truth is not in him," he may be adding advice that others should not seek truth in such people but should go to another source. If so, the phrase applies to the false teachers (whom true seekers after God should avoid) of John's day and in our time. Truth should be sought not from those who only have intellectual qualifications but from those whose claim to spiritual knowledge is backed by godlike conduct.

The second group, those who obey God, have love for God perfected in them. Though they may make no great claims to know God, as the Gnostics did, John says they still know God.

Some years ago, when the so-called New Morality was at its peak, a number of theologians met at Princeton Theological Seminary to discuss it. Most were in favor. So the discussion centered on the value of being free of all rules and regulation. "But there must be some guidelines," someone said. This was discussed. At length it was decided that the only acceptable guideline was love. Anything that flowed from love was permissible, so long as it did not hurt anybody. While the discussion was proceeding along these lines, a Roman Catholic priest became very quiet. At length it was noticeable. The others turned to him and asked what he thought. "Don't you agree that the only limiting factor in any ethical decision is love?" The priest replied, "If you love me, you will keep my commandments" (Jn 14:15).

Do we say we are Christians? Then, "Whoever says he abides in him ought to walk in the same way in which he walked" (1 Jn 2:6). The call is to emulate the Lord Jesus Christ in our conduct. To walk as Christ walked is to live not by rules but by example. It is to follow him, to be his disciple. A disciple like this is personal, active, and costly.

It is personal because it cannot be passed off on another. Indeed, we are to find ourselves with Christ, as Peter did following the resurrection. Jesus asked Peter, "Do you love me?" When Peter replied "Yes," he was told, "Feed my sheep." This was repeated twice more, and the repetition began to irritate Peter. So, to escape Christ's careful probing, he pointed to the beloved disciple, who was apparently standing some distance away, and asked, "Lord, what about this man?" Jesus replied, "If it is my will that he remain until I come, what is that to you? You follow me!" (Jn 21:15-22). There was no escaping the call to personal discipleship for Peter. To walk as Christ walked is also active because the Lord himself is active. To be inactive is to be left behind. Finally, it is costly because the path that Jesus walked, though it leads to glory, is the path to crucifixion first. Such a path can only be walked by those who have died to self and have deliberately taken up the cross of Christ to follow him.

Such people, whether in John's day or our own, will always have confidence before God and will be sure that they know him. Here C. H. Dodd, former professor of New Testament at the University of Cambridge, concludes,

> In this passage our author is not only rebutting dangerous tendencies in the church of his time, but discussing a problem of perennial importance, that of the validity of religious experience. We may have the feeling of awareness of God, of union with him, but how shall we know that such experience corresponds to reality? It is clear that no amount of clearness or strength in the experience itself can guarantee its validity, any more than the extreme vividness of a dream leads us to suppose that it is anything but a dream. If, however, we accept the revelation of God in Christ, then we must believe that any experience of God which is valid has an ethical quality defined by what we know of Christ. It will carry with it a renewed fidelity to his teaching and example. The writer does not mean that only those who perfectly obey Christ and follow his example can be said to have experience of God. That would be to affirm the sinlessness of Christians in a sense which he has repudiated. But unless the experience includes a setting of the affections and will in the direction of the moral principles of the Gospel, it is no true experience of God, in any Christian sense.[4]

There is more to be said, of course, but thus far the test of one's experience holds. By the test of righteousness we may know that we know God and may assure our hearts before him.

THE SOCIAL TEST

In the midst of his final discourses before his crucifixion, Jesus imparted a new commandment, the command to love. "A new commandment I give to you,

---

[4]C. H. Dodd, *The Johannine Epistles* (London: Hodder and Stoughton, 1946), 32.

that you love one another: just as I have loved you, you also are to love one another. By this all people will know that you are my disciples, if you have love for one another" (Jn 13:34-35). Love is the mark by which the world may know that Christians truly are Christians. In 1 John the command is repeated, but with this difference: it is by love that *Christians* (as well as the world) may know that they are Christians. That is, when Christians find themselves beginning to love and actually loving those others for whom Christ died, they can be assured that they know God. John develops this test in 1 John 2:7-11 and repeats it both in 1 John 3:11-18 and 4:7-21. John's clearest statement of this test is in 1 John 2:9-10: "Whoever says he is in the light and hates his brother is still in darkness. Whoever loves his brother abides in the light, and in him there is no cause for stumbling."

As in the moral test, these verses also contain two specific groups to make the test concrete. The first group is typified by the person who "says he is in the light and hates his brother." Such people are in darkness. Clearly John is thinking of his Gnostic opponents who claimed to be the "enlightened" ones. But the same is true of any who profess regeneration without this change. Paul said essentially the same thing: "If I have prophetic powers, and understand all mysteries and all knowledge, and if I have all faith, so as to move mountains, but have not love, I am nothing" (1 Cor 13:2).

John's second group are those who show that they abide in the light by loving fellow Christians. John says that there is "no cause for stumbling" in them. The idea of stumbling may be applied to those who not only walk in the light themselves but who also do not cause others to trip in the dark. Again, stumbling can apply to those who walk in the light and therefore do not stumble. The context almost demands this second explanation, for the point of the verses is not what happens to others but the effect of love and hate on individuals themselves. The negative equivalent of this statement occurs just one verse later. "But whoever hates his brother is in the darkness and walks in the darkness, and does not know where he is going, because the darkness has blinded his eyes" (1 Jn 2:11).

This last verse introduces the term *walk*, which may be applied to the life of love. It suggests practical steps. Love is not a certain benign feeling nor a smile. It is an attitude that determines what we do. It is impossible to speak meaningfully of love in the Christian sense without speaking of the actions that flow from it, just as it is impossible to speak meaningfully of God's love without mentioning such things as the creation, the giving of the Old Testament revelation, the coming of Christ, the cross, and the outpouring of the Holy Spirit.

What will happen if those who profess the life of Christ actually love one another? Francis Schaeffer has several suggestions. First, when a Christian has failed to love another Christian and has acted wrongly toward that person, the believer will go and apologize. This expresses love and restores that oneness that Jesus said should flow from Christians loving one another. It verifies their Christianity before the world.

Second, when someone else hurts us, we are to show our love by forgiveness. This is hard, particularly when the other person does not say "I am sorry." Schaeffer writes,

> We must all continually acknowledge that we do not practice the forgiving heart as we should. And yet the prayer is, "Forgive us our debts, our trespasses, as we forgive our debtors." We are to have a forgiving spirit even before the other person expresses regret for his wrong. The Lord's prayer does not suggest that when the other man is sorry, then we are to show a oneness by having a forgiving spirit. Rather, we are called upon to have a forgiving spirit without the other man having made the first step. We may still say that he is wrong, but in the midst of saying that he is wrong, we must be forgiving.[5]

Early in John's own life he was known as one of the "sons of thunder." He once wanted to call down fire from heaven on those who rejected Jesus (Lk 9:54). But as he came to know more about God, he called for love among the brethren.

Third, we must show love even when it is costly. Love cost the Samaritan in Christ's parable. It cost him time and money. Love cost the shepherd who endured hardship to hunt for his sheep. Love cost Mary of Bethany, who, out of her love, broke the box of valuable ointment over the feet of Jesus. Love will be costly to all who practice it. But what is purchased by such love will be of great value. It will be proof of the presence of the life of God both to the individual Christian and to the watching world.

---

[5]Francis A. Schaeffer, *The Church at the End of the 20th Century* (Downers Grove, IL: InterVarsity Press, 1970), 145.

CHAPTER 9

A NEW FAMILY

*I*n the opening pages of *A Place for You*, the noted Swiss psychologist Paul Tournier tells of a young man he once counseled. He grew up in a religious home, but it was unhappy. Eventually there was a divorce. This produced unfortunate psychological symptoms in the young man's life. He developed an acute sense of failure, first in not reconciling his parents, then in his studies, then in an inability to settle down and achieve in any area of life. At last he came to see Tournier. They talked, and on one occasion, as if summing up his thought, the young man explained, "Basically, I'm always looking for a place—for somewhere to be."[1]

The need for a place is universal. On the human level the principle is easy to discern. "The child who has been able to grow up harmoniously in a healthy home finds a welcome everywhere. In infancy all he needs is a stick placed across two chairs to make himself a house, in which he feels quite at home. Later on, wherever he goes, he will be able to make any place his own, without any effort on his part. For him it will not be a matter of seeking, but of choosing." On the other hand, "when the family is such that the child cannot fit himself into it properly, he looks everywhere for some other place, leading a wandering existence, incapable of settling down anywhere. His tragedy is that he carries about within himself this fundamental incapacity for any real attachment."[2] On

---

[1] Paul Tournier, *A Place for You* (New York: Harper and Row, 1968), 9. The story is told in full on the following pages.
[2] Ibid., 12.

the spiritual level, the problem is detected in the alienation from God we feel
as a result of the fall and of our own deliberate sins. Saint Augustine once wrote,
"Thou hast formed us for thyself. . . ." That is our true place. But he added in
frank recognition of our dilemma and sin, "And our hearts are restless till they
find rest in Thee."[3]

God has dealt with this great problem of alienation through adoption, taking
a person from one family (or no family) and placing him or her in a new family—
the family of God. Sometimes adoption has been thought of merely as one
aspect of justification, or as only another way of stating what happens in regeneration. But adoption is nevertheless much more than either of these other acts
of grace. John Murray distinguishes adoption from justification and regeneration
like this:

> Justification means our acceptance with God as righteous and the bestowal of the
> title to everlasting life. Regeneration is the renewing of our hearts after the image
> of God. But these blessings in themselves, however precious they are, do not
> indicate what is conferred by the act of adoption. By adoption the redeemed
> become sons and daughters of the Lord God Almighty; they are introduced into
> and given the privileges of God's family.[4]

Only adoption suggests the new family relationship that is ours in Christ and
points to the privileges of that relationship.

> For all who are led by the Spirit of God are sons of God. For you did not receive
> the spirit of slavery to fall back into fear, but you have received the Spirit of
> adoption as sons, by whom we cry, "Abba! Father!" The Spirit himself bears witness
> with our spirit that we are children of God, and if children, then heirs—heirs of
> God and fellow heirs with Christ, provided we suffer with him in order that we
> may also be glorified with him. (Rom 8:14-17)

These verses speak of adoption as a separate work of God's Spirit through which
(1) we are delivered from bondage to the law and from fear; (2) we are assured
of our new relationship to God; and (3) we become God's heirs with Christ.
Murray also writes,

> 1. Though adoption is distinct it is never separable from justification and regen-
> eration. The person who is justified is always the recipient of son-ship. And those

---

[3]Augustine, *The Confessions*, I, 1 in *Basic Writings of Saint Augustine*, ed. Whitney J. Oates, vol. 1 (New
York: Random House, 1948), 3.
[4]John Murray, *Redemption Accomplished and Applied* (Grand Rapids: Eerdmans, 1955), 132.

who are given the right to become sons of God are those who, as John 1:13 indicates, "were born not of blood nor of the will of the flesh nor of the will of man but of God." 2. Adoption is, like justification, a judicial act. In other words, it is the bestowal of a status, or standing, not the generating within us of a new nature or character. It concerns a relationship and not the attitude or disposition which enables us to recognize and cultivate that relationship. 3. Those adopted into God's family are also given the Spirit of adoption whereby they are able to recognize their sonship and exercise the privileges which go with it. "And because ye are sons, God hath sent forth the Spirit of his Son into your hearts, crying Abba, Father" (Gal 4:6; cf. Rom 8:15,16). The Spirit of adoption is the consequence but this does not itself constitute adoption. 4. There is a close relationship between adoption and regeneration.[5]

The relationship is explained by the way a father in ancient times would officially adopt his own son as his legal representative and heir. This was an important moment in the coming of age of a Jewish, Greek, or Roman child. Before, he was a son by birth. Now he became a son legally and passed from the care of his guardian or trustee into manhood. Although in Christian experience regeneration and adoption take place simultaneously, adoption nevertheless emphasizes the Christian's new status, while regeneration emphasizes the newness of life.

New Relationships

Perhaps the words *new status* are not the best. What is really involved in adoption is *new relationships:* a new relationship to God and a new relationship to other people within the household of faith.

The new relationship to God need not have been automatic. Having justified us, God could still have left us on a much inferior level of status and privilege. Instead, he took us into his own family, giving us the status and privilege of daughters and sons. So great is God's condescension in this act of adoption that we would be inclined to dismiss it, thinking it presumption, were it not that God has made a special effort to seal these truths to our hearts. As Paul wrote,

"What no eye has seen, nor ear heard,
    nor the heart of man imagined,
  what God has prepared for those who love him,"
these things God has revealed to us through the Spirit. For the Spirit searches everything, even the depths of God. (1 Cor 2:9-10)

---

[5]Ibid., 132-33.

There is a certain sense in which God may be said to be the Father of all. God is the Creator of all. He sustains our lives moment by moment, for "in him we live and move and have our being" (Acts 17:28; compare Acts 17:24-28). On account of this we may be said to be "God's offspring" (Acts 17:29). But there are no privileges attached to this more general "fatherhood." The relationship that the word properly describes is missing.

Jesus taught quite pointedly that some who thought they were God's children were, according to his teaching, actually children of the devil. After saying, "And you will know the truth, and the truth will set you free," the Jews answered him, "We are offspring of Abraham and have never been enslaved to anyone. How is it that you say, 'You will become free'?" Jesus responded, "I know that you are offspring of Abraham; yet you seek to kill me. . . . If you were Abraham's children, you would be doing the works Abraham did." At this point the people grew angry and accused him of being illegitimate. Then in righteous anger the Lord replied, "If God were your Father, you would love me, for I came from God and I am here. I came not of my own accord, but he sent me. Why do you not understand what I say? It is because you cannot bear to hear my word. You are of your father the devil, and your will is to do your father's desires" (Jn 8:32-33, 37, 39, 42-44). In this exchange Jesus put to an end the misleading doctrine that God is the Father of all and all are his children.

But it is not only that Christians have a new relationship to God as a result of his act of adoption. We also have a new relationship with one another that requires us to love each other and work together, as befits brothers and sisters. Before, we were outside the family of God, each going our own way in opposition to and sometimes in only thinly veiled hostility toward each other. Now we are different: "So then you are no longer strangers and aliens, but you are fellow citizens with the saints and members of the household of God" (Eph 2:19).

The attitudes that should flow from these new relationships do not always follow naturally or easily. But that is all the more reason to grasp this truth forcefully and work at the relationships. John White has put the task in these terms:

> You were cleansed by the same blood, regenerated by the same Spirit. You are a citizen of the same city, a slave of the same master, a reader of the same Scriptures, a worshiper of the same God. The same presence dwells silently in you as in them. Therefore you are committed to them and they to you. They are your brothers, sisters, your fathers, mothers and children in God. Whether you like or dislike

them, you belong to them. You have responsibilities toward them that must be discharged in love. As long as you live on this earth, you are in their debt. Whether they have done much or little for you, Christ has done all. He demands that your indebtedness to him be transferred to your new family.[6]

Membership in God's family does not mean that we will be insensitive to its human faults. Indeed, we must be sensitive to them if we are to have any hope of eliminating them and improving the quality of our family relationships. But neither should we be overly sensitive to the faults of our brothers and sisters in Christ. Even less should we be openly critical. We should be intensely committed to each other with a proper family loyalty and work to help each other in living the Christian life. We should pray for each other and serve one another.

FAMILY PRIVILEGES

Our new relationships give us new privileges. Some we have now. Some pertain more fully to the life we will enjoy in heaven. These latter privileges are described in Scripture as our inheritance. We are not told specifically what they are, though they obviously involve the possession of the life of heaven and other blessings. Our inheritance is described as spiritual "riches" (Eph 1:18) and as a "reward" for faithful service (Col 3:24). It is said to be "eternal" (Heb 9:15). Peter declares that by the mercy of God, "he has caused us to be born again to a living hope through the resurrection of Jesus Christ from the dead, to an inheritance that is imperishable, undefiled, and unfading, kept in heaven for you" (1 Pet 1:3-4). Paul describes the Holy Spirit as a present "guarantee" of what awaits us (Eph 1:14).

Prayer is the key privilege of adoption that we enjoy now. On the one hand, this is described as a consequence of our justification. "Therefore, since we have been justified by faith, we have peace with God through our Lord Jesus Christ. Through him we have also obtained access by faith into this grace in which we stand" (Rom 5:1-2). Access means access to God. On the other hand, access is based on our adoption. Because of it we can approach God as "Father." And only through the Spirit of adoption can we be assured that God is our Father and that he indeed hears our prayers. This is what Paul is speaking of in the verse quoted earlier. "The Spirit himself bears witness with our spirit that we are children of God" (Rom 8:16).

Our authority to call God "Father" goes back to Jesus Christ himself, and to no less important a statement than the opening phrases of the Lord's Prayer. "Pray then like this: Our Father in heaven . . ." (Mt 6:9). No Old Testament Jew

---

[6]John White, *The Fight* (Downers Grove, IL: InterVarsity Press, 1976), 129-30.

ever addressed God directly as "my Father." The invocation of the Lord's Prayer was something new and startlingly original to Christ's contemporaries. This has been documented by the late German scholar, Ernst Lohmeyer, in a book called "*Our Father*" and by the contemporary biblical scholar Joachim Jeremias in an essay entitled "Abba" and a booklet called *The Lord's Prayer*.[7] According to these scholars, three things are indisputable: (1) the title was new with Jesus; (2) Jesus always used this form of address in praying; and (3) Jesus authorized his disciples to use the same word after him.

It is true, of course, that in one sense the title *father* for God is as old as religion. Homer wrote of "Father Zeus, who rules over the gods and mortal men." Aristotle explained that Homer was right because "paternal rule over children is like that of a king over his subjects" and "Zeus is king of us all." In this case the word *father* means "Lord." The point to notice, however, is that the address was always impersonal. In Greek thought, God was called father in the same sense that a king is called a father of his country.

The Old Testament uses the word *father* as a designation of God's relationship to Israel, but even this is not personal. Nor is it frequent. In fact, it occurs only fourteen times in the whole of the Old Testament. Israel is called the "firstborn son" of God (Ex 4:22). David says, "As a father shows compassion to his children, so the LORD shows compassion to those who fear him" (Ps 103:13). Isaiah writes, "But now, O LORD, you are our Father" (Is 64:8). But in none of these passages does any individual Israelite address God directly as "my Father." In most of them, the point is that Israel has not lived up to the family relationship. Thus, Jeremiah reports the Lord as saying,

> I said,
>> How I would set you among my sons,
> and give you a pleasant land,
>> a heritage most beautiful of all nations.
> And I thought you would call me, My Father,
>> and would not turn from following me.
> Surely, as a treacherous wife leaves her husband,
>> so have you been treacherous to me, O house of Israel,
> declares the LORD. (Jer 3:19-20)

---

[7]Ernst Lohmeyer, "*Our Father*," trans. John Bowden (New York: Harper and Row, 1965); Joachim Jeremias, "Abba," in *The Central Message of the New Testament* (London: SCM Press, 1965), 9-30; and Jeremias, *The Lord's Prayer*, trans. John Reumann (Philadelphia: Fortress, 1964).

In the time of Jesus, the distance between people and God seemed to be widening. The names of God were increasingly withheld from public speech and prayers. This trend was completely overturned by Jesus. He always called God Father, and this fact must have impressed itself in an extraordinary way on the disciples. Not only do all four of the Gospels record that Jesus used this address, but they report that he did so in all his prayers (Mt 11:25; 26:39, 42; Mk 14:36; Lk 23:34; Jn 11:41; 12:27; 17:1, 5, 11, 21, 24-25). The only exception enforces its own significance, the cry from the cross: "My God, my God, why have you forsaken me?" (Mt 27:46; Mk 15:34). That prayer was wrung from Christ's lips at the moment in which he was made sin for humankind and in which the relationship he had with his Father was temporarily broken. At all other times, Jesus boldly assumed a relationship to God that was thought to be highly irreverent or blasphemous by most of his contemporaries.

This is of great significance for our prayers. Jesus was the Son of God in a unique sense, and God was uniquely his Father. He came to God in prayer as God's unique Son. Now he reveals that this same relationship can be true for those who believe in him, whose sins are removed by his suffering. They can come to God as God's children. God can be their own individual Father.

But this is not all. When Jesus addressed God as Father, he did not use the normal word for father. He used the Aramaic word *abba*. Obviously this was so striking to the disciples that they remembered it in its Aramaic form and repeated it in Aramaic, even in their Greek Gospels and other writings. Mark uses it in his account of Christ's prayer in Gethsemane, "Abba, Father, all things are possible for you" (Mk 14:36). Paul also makes note of it in the verses to which we referred earlier (Rom 8:15; Gal 4:6).

What does *abba* specifically mean? The early church fathers—Chrysostom, Theodore of Mopsuestia, and Theodoret of Cyrrhus, who came from Antioch (where Aramaic was spoken and who probably had Aramaic-speaking nurses)— unanimously testify that *abba* was the address of small children to their fathers.[8] The Talmud confirms this when it says that when a child is weaned, "it learns to say *abba* and *imma*" (that is, "daddy" and "mommy").[9] That is what *abba* means: daddy. To a Jewish mind, a prayer addressing God as daddy would not only have been improper, it would have been irreverent to the highest degree.

---

[8]Jeremias, *The Lord's Prayer*, 19.
[9]*Berakoth* 40a; *Sanhedrin* 70b.

Yet this was what Jesus said, and this quite naturally stuck in the minds of the disciples, as I have indicated. It was something quite new and unique when Jesus instructed his disciples to call God daddy.

CONFIDENCE IN OUR FATHER

This gives us assurance as we stand before God. When we approach God as Father, being taught and led to do so by God's own Spirit, we know that we stand in a secure relationship.

Is God our Father? If he is, then he will help us in the days of our infancy, teaching us to walk spiritually and picking us up when we fall down. This is why Hosea could report God as saying,

> Yet it was I who taught Ephraim to walk;
> I took them up by their arms. . . .
> I led them with cords of kindness,
> with the bands of love. . . .
> How can I give you up, O Ephraim?
> How can I hand you over, O Israel? (Hos 11:3-4, 8)

A God like this will keep us from falling and will present us "blameless before the presence of his glory" (Jude 24).

Is God our Father? Then he will care for us through the days of this life and will bless us abundantly. The laws of the United States recognize that parents must care for their children. So does God. He has set down the rule that "children are not obligated to save up for their parents, but parents for their children" (2 Cor 12:14). If this is true on the human level, it is also true of the relationship of a person to God. The Lord Jesus said,

> Do not be anxious about your life, what you will eat or what you will drink, nor about your body, what you will put on. . . . Do not be anxious, saying, "What shall we eat?" or "What shall we drink?" or "What shall we wear?" For the Gentiles seek after all these things, and your heavenly Father knows that you need them all. But seek first the kingdom of God and his righteousness, and all these things will be added to you. (Mt 6:25, 31-33)

Is God our Father? Then he will go before us to show the way through this life. Paul alludes to this when he writes, "Therefore be imitators [followers] of God, as beloved children" (Eph 5:1).

Is God our Father? Then we shall know that we belong to him forever. We shall know that while we are being led, taught, and educated for life's tasks, nothing shall interfere with his purpose for us in Christ. We shall look forward to the time when we shall see him and be like him, for we shall see him as he is.

CHAPTER 10

THE UPWARD WAY

One of the early signs of the saving work of God in the life of an individual is dissatisfaction with sin and a striving for holiness. But neither dissatisfaction on the one hand nor striving on the other is the same as holiness itself. Holiness is a goal toward which we move.

If we do not think of holiness in the strongest biblical terms, but rather in our own, we may imagine that we have attained perfection and may even become complacent in the Christian life. If we understand it biblically, we instead find ourselves being thrown back on the power of the Holy Spirit to work in us. Sanctification, which is the proper word for this aspect of the Spirit's work in believers, describes two basic areas of growth. The first is separation to God and his purposes. For the root meaning of holiness suggests that which has been "set apart" to God. The second is God-pleasing conduct or morality, becoming more like Jesus. We will increasingly think as he would think and act as he would act.

This goal of holiness then has an outward standard of morality coupled with an internal conformity to the will and mind of God. Though there are negative implications, sanctification is a positive desire for and actual growth in Christian character.

PERFECT, YET BEING PERFECTED

We are still sinners, even though we are regenerated and justified in God's sight. Although we are perfect in terms of our present standing before God, we are far from perfect in our actual thoughts and conduct. Sanctification aims to close this gap. Paul was aware of this when he wrote to the Philippians, "Not that I have already obtained this or am already *perfect*, but I press on to make it my own, because Christ Jesus has made me his own" (Phil 3:12). Then, just three verses later, he continues, "Let those of us who are mature [the Greek word is the same—*perfect*] think this way" (Phil 3:15). Clearly, although Paul knew that his record had already been cleared before God on the basis of Christ's work and although he had attained maturity in the Christian life, he was also aware of the necessary growth in holiness that lay before him.

All Christians have this experience. When we first believe in Jesus as Savior, most of us have a great sense of joy and gratitude to God for salvation. In this grateful state of mind, we often feel that everything has changed. We are liberated from sin. We are new creatures in Christ. But actually, we are not much different in natural inclinations, character, and conduct. Before, we had bad habits. Now we are saved, but many of these bad habits and wrong actions remain. Should we doubt the reality of salvation? Not at all. The very fact that we are now aware of these imperfections in a new way is proof that God's work of transformation has begun. Instead of discouragement or doubt, we should realize that we have entered on a new way of life in which many former patterns must change. As God works there will be an increasing distaste for sin and a growing hunger for righteousness.

Because sanctification is a process that is never completed in this world does not mean it is of secondary importance or (even worse) dispensable. It is as important and necessary in the application of salvation as regeneration, justification, and adoption. John Murray stresses the gravity of sanctification by three statements: (1) all sin in believers is the contradiction of God's holiness; (2) the presence of sin in believers involves conflict in their hearts and lives; and (3) though sin still remains, it does not have the mastery.[1]

The first statement is drawn from such passages as 1 Peter 1:15-16 ("But as he who called you is holy, you also be holy in all your conduct, since it is written, 'You shall be holy, for I am holy'"), 1 John 2:16 ("The desires of the flesh and the desires of the eyes and the pride in possessions—is not from the Father but is from the world"), and 1 John 3:2-3 ("Beloved, we are God's children now, and what will be has not yet appeared; but we know that when he appears we shall be like him, because we shall see him as he is. And everyone who thus hopes in

---

[1]John Murray, *Redemption Accomplished and Applied* (Grand Rapids: Eerdmans, 1955), 144-45.

him purifies himself as he is pure"). If we are God's children, we should be like him in holiness as well as in other aspects of his character.

Romans 7 is a classic example of the conflict that exists in the believer's life when sin is present—the second of Murray's statements. "I do not understand my own actions. For I do not do what I want, but I do the very thing I hate. . . . When I want to do right, evil lies close at hand. For I delight in the law of God, in my inner being, but I see in my members another law waging war against the law of my mind and making me captive to the law of sin that dwells in my members" (Rom 7:15, 21-23).

It is futile to argue that this conflict is not normal. If there is still sin to any degree in one who is indwelt by the Holy Spirit, then there is tension, yes, contradiction, within the heart of that person. Indeed, the more sanctified the person is, the more conformed that person is to the image of the Savior, the more that person must recoil against every lack of conformity to the holiness of God. The deeper one's apprehension of the majesty of God, the greater the intensity of one's love to God, the more persistent one's yearning for the attainment of the prize of the high calling of God in Christ Jesus, the more conscious will one be of the gravity of the sin that remains, and the more poignant will be one's detestation of it. The more closely one comes to the holiest of all, the more one apprehends the sinfulness that is one's own, and one must cry out, "Wretched man that I am!" (Rom 7:24). Was this not the effect in all the people of God as they came into closer proximity to the revelation of God's holiness? "Woe is me! For I am lost; for I am a man of unclean lips, and I dwell in the midst of a people of unclean lips; for my eyes have seen the King, the LORD of hosts" (Is 6:5).

> I had heard of you by the hearing of the ear,
>   but now my eye sees you;
> therefore I despise myself,
>   and repent in dust and ashes. (Job 42:5-6)[2]

The third of Murray's points, that although sin remains it is not the master, is taught in the very next verses of Romans:

> For the law of the Spirit of life has set you free in Christ Jesus from the law of sin and death. For God has done what the law, weakened by the flesh, could not do. By sending his own Son in the likeness of sinful flesh and for sin, he condemned

---

[2]Ibid., 145.

sin in the flesh, in order that the righteous requirement of the law might be fulfilled in us, who walk not according to the flesh but according to the Spirit. (Rom 8:2-4)

While sanctification is important from the perspective of our own fulfillment as Christians, its importance is seen even more when measured against these three statements. If we were to say that becoming more holy is unnecessary, that we will simply remain in known sin, then we are effectively saying that God is not holy, that sin does not involve a contradiction and conflict in us, and that God has not made provision for victory. In each case we are denying Scripture and calling God a liar.

We should, of course, turn from sin and seek God's help, strength, and encouragement to live the holy life we desperately need.

This way of speaking raises a difficult question, however. Who accomplishes sanctification? This would seem to be the work of God's Spirit. We read in 1 Thessalonians 5:23, "May the God of peace himself sanctify you completely." Again, in 2 Corinthians 3:18-19, "And we all, with unveiled face, beholding the glory of the Lord, are being transformed into the same image from one degree of glory to another. For this comes from the Lord who is the Spirit." There are scores of such references. People who emphasize these Scriptures speak of "letting go" of ourselves and "letting God" do the work of sanctification in us.

But there are other verses that speak of *our* role in sanctification. We are told, "Walk by the Spirit, and you will not gratify the desires of the flesh" (Gal 5:16). "Be imitators of God, as beloved children" (Eph 5:1). "Put on the whole armor of God, that you may be able to stand against the schemes of the devil" (Eph 6:11). People who emphasize these verses speak of our obligation to use these "means of grace" available to us.

Which of these is right and which is wrong? If we mean by "letting go" that we may therefore abandon Bible study, prayer, Christian fellowship, and the worship of God and still expect to grow in the Christian life just because we have "let go," we are greatly mistaken. We will stagnate in the Christian life and drift away from Christian circles. But we are also wrong if we think that by making use of these means we can automatically achieve our own sanctification. The correct understanding is a combination of the two, working as fully and consistently as possible: God working in us and we being as diligent and obedient as possible in these areas.

If there was ever a point to stop and merely rejoice in the wonders of what God is doing in Christ, to sit back and let God work, it is certainly after the hymn of praise to Christ found in Philippians 2:5-11. But Paul does not allow us to do this. Instead he immediately applies the doctrine saying, "Therefore, my beloved, as you have always obeyed, so now, not only as in my presence but much more in my absence, work out your own salvation with fear and trembling, for it is God who works in you, both to will and to work for his good pleasure" (Phil 2:12-13). He does not mean, "Work for your salvation." He means, "Since you are saved, since God has already entered your life in the person and power of his Holy Spirit and is at work within you conforming you to the image of the Lord Jesus Christ—because of these things you are now to work as hard as you can to express the fullness of this great reality in your conduct. Nevertheless, as you do this, it is God who does the working."

Peter said the same thing. "[God's] divine power has granted to us all things that pertain to life and godliness." It is all of God. Nevertheless, Peter continues, "For this very reason, make every effort to supplement your faith with virtue, and virtue with knowledge, and knowledge with self-control, and self-control with steadfastness, and steadfastness with godliness, and godliness with brotherly affection, and brotherly affection with love" (2 Pet 1:3, 5-7).

John White concludes correctly, "Let there be no misunderstanding. Without God's Spirit within, our efforts are futile. No good thing could spring from our corrupt and sinful hearts. But we have been redeemed and we have been sanctified. We have been set apart for God's use. Let us then agree with God in the matter. . . . Let us assume the whole armor of God and by miraculous strength declare war on all that is evil within and without."[3] This is not optional. We are commanded to do this, and there is no point in our Christian lives when we are more conscious of the power of God's Spirit within than when we obey. We can hardly expect to grow spiritually if we will not use that spiritual food and drink which God puts at our disposal.

THE MEANS OF GRACE

The next part of this book will discuss the primary means of grace: prayer, Bible study, and Christian service. But there are others as well, and it is worth considering them together. There are at least seven.

1. Assurance. We have already touched on this matter in the chapter on how we may know we are justified. But assurance is important here also, for

---

[3]John White, *The Fight* (Downers Grove, IL: InterVarsity Press, 1976), 194.

it can also help us grow toward Christlike character. Luther once put the matter graphically:

> A wavering heart that does not firmly believe and hold that it will receive something
> will certainly get nothing, because God cannot give it anything, much as he would
> like to. Such a heart is like a vessel which a man holds in his hands but, instead
> of holding it, constantly moves it to and fro. It will be impossible to pour anything
> into it, and though you would want to do so, you would miss the vessel and waste
> whatever you are pouring. So it is with a wavering, unbelieving heart. God would
> like to give what we need. But there we stand, like a foolish beggar, holding out
> our hat for gifts and yet not holding it still.[4]

Assurance is the first necessary item in sanctification because it is a matter of taking God at his word and of knowing that he has truly begun a work of salvation in us. If we have believed God here, we can believe him in other matters. If we are sure that we have really begun our journey, we can then get on with it as quickly and efficiently as possible.

2. Knowledge. Knowing everything is not essential for sanctification, but knowing the basics will certainly help. One writer has said, "As assurance is the practical foundation . . . so knowledge of our position in Christ is the practical road that leads to experimental holiness."[5]

What truths should Christians know to grow in the Christian life? Some key ones are set forth in the earlier chapters of this book: the person of the Holy Spirit and his work; God's initiative in bringing us to faith in Christ; the Spirit's ministry in uniting us to Christ, from which comes our new status before God; our access to God through prayer; our security in Christ. If we know what our new status is, we can take advantage of its privileges. If we know God hears us, we can depend on the Holy Spirit to help us pray and interpret our stammering prayers. If we are secure in Christ, although we may stumble and fall, we know that nothing will ever pluck us out of Christ's hand.

3. Bible study. The Bible as a source of growth in the Christian life is linked to assurance and knowledge, for from the Bible we gain both. But the Bible as a means of grace is more than either. In Bible study we seek to know God personally. Here God consistently and faithfully reveals himself and his will to us. As Jesus prayed, "Sanctify them in the truth; your word is truth" (Jn 17:17).

---

[4]Luther, *What Luther Says: An Anthology*, ed. Ewald M. Plass, vol. 2 (St. Louis: Concordia, 1959), 429.
[5]Donald Grey Barnhouse, *God's Methods for Holy Living* (Grand Rapids: Eerdmans, 1951), 37.

David wrote,

> Blessed is the man
>> who walks not in the counsel of the wicked,
> nor stands in the way of sinners,
>> nor sits in the seat of scoffers;
> but his delight is in the law of the LORD,
>> and on his law he meditates day and night. (Ps 1:1-2)

Did David meditate on the law of God day and night? He had to. He had immense responsibilities for the security of the nation, administration of government, judgment in legal cases, and other matters. Out of this he was driven to meditate on the law of God constantly. And what happened? The one who feeds on the law

> is like a tree
>> planted by streams of water
> that yields its fruit in its season,
>> and its leaf does not wither.
> In all that he does, he prospers. (Ps 1:3)

If a person really wants to know God and God's will for his or her life, the primary means is Bible study.

4. *Prayer and worship.* Bible study is communication that goes one way. God speaks to us. To round this out, we also need to speak to God. For that we need prayer and worship.

While not necessarily the same thing, worship and prayer are closely related. Prayer is talking to God through praise, confession, thanksgiving, or intercession. Worship is meeting with God to praise him, to sing hymns, and to expound God's Word. Thus worship will include prayer and meditation. Both prayer and worship are based on our knowledge of God through Scripture. Worship, if it is to be "in spirit and truth," as Jesus said, must be based on the truths concerning God which are revealed in the Bible.

Both prayer and worship are essentially a meeting with God and not merely the performance of some religious exercise. Reuben A. Torrey tells of the difficulty he had in the matter of prayer and of how this changed.

> The day came when I realized what real prayer meant, realized that prayer was having an audience with God, actually coming into the presence of God and asking and getting things from him. And the realization of that fact transformed

my prayer life. Before that, prayer had been a mere duty, and sometimes a very irksome duty, but from that time on, prayer has been not merely a duty but a privilege, one of the most highly esteemed privileges of life. Before that the thought I had was, "How much time must I spend in prayer?" The thought that now possesses me is, "How much time may I spend in prayer without neglecting the other privileges and duties of life?"[6]

The same may be said of worship. How much time may I spend in worship and still get on with the other tasks that God has given me?

5. Fellowship. In fellowship we actively express the new relationship with other Christians discussed in chapter nine. Sometimes Christians fall into thinking that because their relationship to God is so personal and wonderful they can do without others. Sometimes they even look down on others as having failed to achieve the high standard of godliness they imagine themselves to possess. They are self-deluded. We should all recognize our need for others and the specific gifts they possess, and be thankful for their fellowship within the company of God's church. When the early Christian community met in Jerusalem, "they devoted themselves to the apostles' teaching and the fellowship, to the breaking of bread and the prayers" (Acts 2:42). Fellowship is on a par with other means of grace.

6. Service. If the Christian life is not to be selfish and introverted, there must be service, service to God and to others through evangelism, generosity, and other acts of compassion. The book of Acts speaks of this explicitly: "And all who believed were together and had all things in common. And they were selling their possessions and belongings and distributing the proceeds to all, as any had need" (Acts 2:44-45). This does not mean that they all sold everything, still less that all Christians in every place should sell everything. The context speaks of them meeting in "their homes," so some at least retained those. But it does mean that they were generous with their possessions, so concerned were they to meet the needs of others.

Today our service should be in the sharing of our material goods, particularly since we in the West have so many. It should also be in the giving of our time to encourage or teach others, to evangelize or to contribute whatever talent or training we have been given to the growth of Christ's church.

7. The return of Christ. A final source of encouragement and growth in the Christian life is the return of Christ, our "blessed hope" (Titus 2:13). It is linked

[6]R. A. Torrey, *The Power of Prayer* (Grand Rapids: Eerdmans, 1955), 77.

to sanctification in 1 John: "Beloved, we are God's children now, and what we will be has not yet appeared, but we know that when he appears we shall be like him, because we shall see him as he is. And everyone who thus hopes in him purifies himself as he is pure" (1 Jn 3:2-3).

If we are Christians, we know that God is going to continue his work with us until that day when we are made like Jesus. It may be through death. It may be at Christ's second coming. But whenever it is, we know that we will be made like Jesus. We will be pure as he is pure. We will be perfected in love as he is love. We will be virtuous as he is virtuous. John says that if we really believe this, we will try to be as much like him now as possible. This should affect every aspect of our personal lives: prayer, our choices in occupations, in ethics, in use of spare time, even our social concerns. Lord Shaftesbury, the great English social reformer and a mature Christian, said near the end of his life, "I do not think that in the last forty years I have ever lived one conscious hour that was not influenced by the thought of our Lord's return." In this case, the expectation of meeting the Lord face to face was one of the strongest motivations behind his social programs.

How can we purify ourselves? We cannot, but God will do it if we use these means of grace. Robert Herrick, the English poet, once wrote of purification,

> Lord, I confess that Thou alone art able
> To purify this my Augean stable,
> Be the seas water and the land all soap,
> Yet if Thy blood not wash me, there's no hope.

Apart from the grace of God there is no hope for anyone. But God has provided the ways for us to grow in grace and in the love and knowledge of our Lord and Savior Jesus Christ.

PART III

THE LIFE OF THE CHRISTIAN

*Then Jesus told his disciples, "If anyone would come after me,
let him deny himself and take up his cross and follow me."*

Matthew 16:24

*For freedom Christ has set us free; stand firm therefore,
and do not submit again to a yoke of slavery.*

Galatians 5:1

*Do not be conformed to this world, but be transformed by the renewal
of your mind, that you may prove what is the will of God,
what is good and acceptable and perfect.*

Romans 12:2

*Do not be anxious about anything, but in everything by prayer and
supplication with thanksgiving let your requests be made known to God.
And the peace of God, which surpasses all understanding, will guard your
hearts and your minds in Christ Jesus.*

Philippians 4:6-7

*Blessed is the man who walks not in the counsel of the wicked, nor stands
in the way of sinners, nor sits in the seat of scoffers; but his delight is in
the law of the Lord, and on his law he meditates day and night.*

Psalm 1:1-2

*For we are his workmanship, created in Christ Jesus for good works, which God
prepared beforehand, that we should walk in them.*

Ephesians 2:10

CHAPTER 11

EMBRACE
THE NEGATIVE

*I*f Madison Avenue executives were trying to attract people to the Christian life, they would stress its positive and fulfilling aspects. They would speak of Christianity as a way to wholeness of life and all happiness. Unfortunately, we who live in the West are so conditioned to this way of thinking (and to precisely this type of Christian evangelism or salesmanship) that we are almost shocked when we learn that the first great principle of Christianity is negative. It is not, as some say, "Come to Christ, and all your troubles will melt away." It is as the Lord himself declared, "If anyone would come after me, let him deny himself and take up his cross and follow me. For whoever would save his life will lose it, but whoever loses his life for my sake will find it. For what will it profit a man if he gains the whole world and forfeits his life?" (Mt 16:24-26).

If I were writing of Christianity the way our culture writes, I might produce a poem such as this one, found on the wall of a guest room on a Christian college campus:

> May the years of your life be pleasant;
> May your beautiful dreams come true,
> And in all that you plan and practice
> May blessings descend upon you.
> May the trail of your life beat onward
> With many surprises in store,

And the days that are happy with memories
Prove merely the promise of more.

If we are true to the Word of God, we will speak as Jesus did: "If anyone comes to me and does not hate his own father and mother and wife and children and brothers and sisters, yes, and even his own life, he cannot be my disciple. Whoever does not bear his own cross and come after me cannot be my disciple. . . . So therefore, any one of you who does not renounce all that he has cannot be my disciple" (Lk 14:26-27, 33); "Unless a grain of wheat falls into the earth and dies, it remains alone; but if it dies, it bears much fruit. Whoever loves his life loses it, and whoever hates his life in this world will keep it for eternal life" (Jn 12:24-25); "Blessed are the poor in spirit. . . . Blessed are those who mourn. . . . Blessed are the meek. . . . Blessed are those who are persecuted for righteousness' sake. . . . Blessed are you when others revile you and persecute you and utter all kinds of evil against you falsely on my account" (Mt 5:3-5, 10-11).

We recognize that there is a certain amount of Semitic hyperbole in these statements. The One who told us to love each other is not advocating that we cultivate a literal animosity toward the members of our own family. Moreover, this is only one side of the story. Jesus also said, "There is no one who has left house or brothers or sisters or mother or father or children or lands, for my sake and for the gospel, who will not receive a hundredfold now in this time, houses and brothers and sisters and mothers and children and lands, with persecutions, and in the age to come eternal life" (Mk 10:29-30). But even this is to be *with persecutions*, and it does not eliminate the element of death and denial.

We do not work ourselves up to death and denial, however. Rather, we need them before we can start out at all. Paul shows this by introducing self-sacrifice as the initial principle of the Christian life in his most formal treatment of that life. "I appeal to you therefore, brothers, by the mercies of God, to present your bodies as a living sacrifice, holy and acceptable to God, which is your spiritual worship" (Rom 12:1).

Calvin understood this theme well. In his comments on Romans 12:1-2, he provides us with some of the most moving appeals in the *Institutes of the Christian Religion*:

> If we, then, are not our own (cf. 1 Cor 6:19) but the Lord's, it is clear what error we must flee, and whither we must direct all the acts of our life. We are not our own: let not our reason nor our will, therefore, sway our plans and deeds. We are not our own: let us therefore not set it as our goal to seek what is expedient for

us according to the flesh. We are not our own: in so far as we can, let us therefore forget ourselves and all that is ours.

Conversely, we are God's: let us therefore live for him and die for him. We are God's: let his wisdom and will therefore rule all our actions. We are God's: let all the parts of our life accordingly strive toward him as our only lawful goal (Rom 14:8; cf. 1 Cor 6:19). O, how much has that man profited who, having been taught that he is not his own, has taken away dominion and rule from his own reason that he may yield it to God! For, as consulting our self-interest is the pestilence that most effectively leads to our destruction, so the sole haven of salvation is to be wise in nothing and to will nothing through ourselves but to follow the leading of the Lord alone.[1]

This idea of death in Christ is repeated with slight variations in other places in the Gospels.[2] So it is worthwhile to consider its three parts: (1) we are to deny ourselves, (2) we are to take up Christ's cross, and (3) we are to follow Jesus.

DENYING OURSELVES

Self-denial should not be difficult for any Christian to understand, for this is what it means to become a Christian. It means to have turned your back on any attempt to please God through your own human abilities and efforts, and instead to have accepted by faith what God has done in Christ for your salvation. No one can save himself or herself. So we stop trying. We die to our efforts. We must say no to them. When we have done this, we receive God's salvation as a free gift. Living the Christian life is, therefore, only a matter of continuing in the way we have started. Yet this is difficult to apply. This principle is so uncongenial that even Christians quickly forget it and try to live by other standards.

It can hardly be otherwise, given our own natural dispositions and the culture in which we live. "We are surrounded by a world that says No to nothing. When we are surrounded with this sort of mentality, in which everything is judged by bigness and by success, then suddenly to be told that in the Christian life there is to be this strong negative aspect of saying No to things and No to self, must seem hard. And if it does not feel hard to us, we are not really letting it speak to us."[3]

---

[1]John Calvin, *Institutes of the Christian Religion*, ed. John T. McNeill, trans. Ford Lewis Battles, 2 vols. (Philadelphia: Westminster, 1960), 690.

[2]Compare Mt 10:34-39; Mk 8:34-38; 10:21, 29-31; Lk 9:23-25; 14:26-27, 33; Jn 12:24-26. Other New Testament writers also make the same point: Paul in Rom 6:3-11; Gal 2:20; 6:14 and the author of Hebrews in Heb 12:1-2.

[3]Francis A. Schaeffer, *True Spirituality* (Wheaton, IL: Tyndale, 1971), 19.

To experience death and denial means we must be willing to say no and then actually say no to anything that is contrary to God's will for us. This includes *anything contrary to the Bible*. We are free from law in the sense of being under a list of rules and regulations. But we are to obey the law in the sense that it reveals the nature of God and shows us those areas of life that by the power of God we are to say no to in order that we might go on with Christ.

The first of the Ten Commandments is an example: "You shall have no other gods before me." Here is a negative, an obvious one. It tells us that we are to say no to anything that would take God's rightful place in our lives. Is it an actual idol? We must say no to the idol; we must burn it or destroy it, as many primitive people have done when they have responded to the gospel. Is it money? We must get rid of the money, for it is better to be poor and yet close to Christ than rich and far from him. Money is not something that necessarily takes the place of God in a life. It is possible to be a devoted and deeply spiritual Christian and rich at the same time. But if money has become a god, then we must say no to it. Has another person taken the place of God? Has a business? An ambition? Your children? Fame? Achievement? Whatever it is, we must say no to it if it is keeping us from Christ.

If you want to test yourself on this, you may do so with each of the other commandments. "You shall not kill." We are to say no to any desire to take another's life or slander his or her reputation. "You shall not commit adultery." We are to say no to any desire to take another man's wife or another woman's husband. "You shall not steal." We should say no to the desire to take another person's property. If we have not said no at these points, we can hardly pretend that we are living in the newness of Christ's resurrection life. Indeed, we are not living the life of Christ at all.

To experience death and denial we must also say no to *anything that is not the will of God for us*. This goes beyond the previous point about the law. Not everything permitted in the Word of God is God's will for us. For instance, there is nothing wrong with marriage. In fact, the contrary is true. Marriage has been established by God and has his blessing. Still, marriage may not be the will of God for you; and if it is not, then you must say no to marriage, consciously and deliberately. The same thing holds for a profession, our own conception of ourselves and other things.

Is this hard? Yes, it is hard. It is hard for the strongest saint as well as for the weakest sinner. Here is Augustine's description of the struggle that went on in him:

The new will that had begun in me—and made me want to be free to worship and to enjoy you, God, the only certain joy—was not yet strong enough to over-power the old will that had become tough with age. So there were now two wills battling it out inside me, one old, one new; one carnal, one spiritual; and in the conflict they ripped my soul to pieces.

From my own experience I know, therefore, what Paul meant when he said, "The flesh lusts against the Spirit, and the Spirit against the flesh." I was on both sides, but mostly I was on the side that I approved in myself, rather than the side I disapproved. When I did things that I knew were wrong I did not act willingly, but just endured them; but habit had been reinforced by that part of my will that had deserted to the enemy, so it was by my own will that I found myself in a spot I didn't want to be in. And what point is there in complaining when a sinner gets what is coming to him? I used to excuse myself by saying I had no clear concept of truth, and that was why I still followed the ways of the world rather than serve you. Now, however, I was quite certain about the truth; and still I kept myself grounded and refused to enlist in your service. I was more afraid of getting rid of my frustrations than I was of being frustrated.

Thus I was put under pressure by the oppressions of the world, but I took it all with a light heart, like a man sound asleep. When I did think about you, my meditations were like the feeble struggles of a man who is trying to wake up but is overcome with drowsiness and falls back to sleep. I had no answer when you said, "Awake, O sleeper, and arise from the dead, and Christ shall give you light." You used every possible means to communicate to me the truth of your words. You had me under conviction so that I could give no reply except a lazy and drowsy, "Yes, Lord, yes, I'll get to it right away, just don't bother me for a little while." But "right away" didn't happen right away; and "a little while" turned out to be a very long while. In my inmost self I delighted in the law of God, but I perceived that there was in my bodily members a different law fighting against the law that my reason approved and making me a prisoner under the law that was in my members, the law of sin. For the law of sin is the force of habit, by which the mind is carried along and held prisoner against its will, deservedly, of course, because it slid into the habit by its own choice. Messed-up creature that I was, who was there to rescue this doomed body? God alone through Jesus Christ our Lord![4]

Augustine's words are a classic statement of the divided will and of the dif-ficulty of surrendering that will to God. On the other hand, here is a classic

---

[4]Sherwood Eliot Wirt, *Love Song: Augustine's Confessions for Modern Man* (New York: Harper and Row, 1971), 108-9.

statement of the blessing of having denied oneself for Christ—from the *Imitation of Christ* by Thomas à Kempis:

> O Lord, thou knowest what is the better way; let this or that be done as thou shalt please. Give what thou wilt, and how much thou wilt, and when thou wilt. Do with me as thou knowest, and as best pleaseth thee, and is most for thy honor. Set me where thou wilt, and deal with me in all things just as thou wilt. . . . When could it be ill with me, when thou wert present? I had rather be poor for thee, than rich without thee. I rather choose to be a pilgrim on earth with thee, than without thee to possess heaven. Where thou art, there is heaven; and where thou art not, there is death and hell.[5]

How can you know when you have said no? When you have stopped complaining. If you are murmuring, as the Israelites murmured in the wilderness, you have not really turned your back on Egypt. If you have stopped murmuring, you are ready to press on.

TAKING UP CHRIST'S CROSS

The second expression of the principle of death and denial is death itself, which Jesus points to by saying that we are to take up our cross in his service. To understand this image, we must first leave behind the meaning usually given to it. Today when people speak of bearing their cross or taking up their cross, what they usually have in mind is stoic endurance of some inescapable hardship: sickness, an alcoholic spouse, blindness, an uncongenial place of work, or similar limitations. This is not what Christ meant. In Jesus' day, the cross was a symbol of death, a means of execution. So Jesus really referred to our dying, dying to self—a step beyond mere self-denial. Moreover, in saying that we were to "take up" our cross, he was indicating that our act is to be a voluntary and continuous activity.

Taking up our cross is beyond mere self-denial because it is possible to deny ourselves many things and yet not utterly give ourselves. It is possible to stop somewhere between the indecision of Augustine and that total surrender we find in à Kempis. We often do what Jacob did (in Gen 32) when he was returning to the land of promise after twenty years of working for his uncle Laban. Jacob had cheated his brother and had to run away and live with his uncle Laban on the other side of the desert. His brother had said he was going to kill him, and

---

[5]Thomas à Kempis, *Imitation of Christ*, III, 15, 59 (ca 1427; reprint ed., Chicago: Moody, 1958), 125, 213.

he was afraid then. But twenty years had passed, and he had forgotten the force of the threat.

Yet as Jacob got closer and closer to the land from which he had fled and in which Esau was still living, he became frightened again. He began to remember what he had done. He began to remember the threats Esau had made. Every step he took became more and more difficult. Finally, he came to the brook Jabbok and looked across to where he knew Esau lived. I believe that if he could have gone back, he would have. But things were so difficult with Laban that retreat was cut off. Jacob had nowhere to go but forward. Finally he told his servants to go over ahead of him and find out what Esau was doing.

The servants went. But they had not gone very far when they met Esau coming with a band of four hundred men. This was an army. So the servants went back and said to Jacob, "Your brother knows you're coming, all right. He's coming to meet you. The only difficulty is that he has his army with him." Now Jacob was truly afraid. What was he to do? Resourcefully, he looked around at his possessions and decided that he would begin to give them up. He would give the things he did not care too much about.

First he took a flock of two hundred goats. He sent them over the Jabbok with his servants. He said to the servants, "When Esau sees you and asks, 'Whose servants are you? And where are you going? And who owns these animals?' you must say, 'They belong to your servant Jacob; they are a present sent to my lord, Esau; and Jacob himself is behind us.'" Jacob thought this would soften Esau up.

But he thought, "Suppose Esau isn't satisfied with the goats? I'd better send some ewes." And so he sent two hundred of them. Then he sent thirty camels, followed by forty cows, followed by ten bulls, followed by twenty female donkeys and ten foals. As you read about it in Genesis 32, it is hilarious. All Jacob's possessions were stretched out in bands across the country going toward Esau. In every case the servants were to say, "These are a present for my lord, Esau."

Finally, all the possessions were gone. Jacob did not have any more camels or sheep or goats or bulls or cows to give up. But he still had his wives and children. So he said, "I'd better give them up too." He took Leah, who was the least favorite wife, and he sent her first with her children. Then he took Rachel, who was the favorite wife, and he sent her with her children. And there at last, all alone and trembling, was Jacob. He still had not given himself.

That is what we do. God gets close to us, and we are a little afraid of him. So we say, "I'll placate him; I'll give him my money." But God does not seem to be satisfied with that, and we do not quite understand why. We say, "I'll give him my time. I'll serve on the church board. I'll teach a Sunday school class." At last we give him our family. But we do not give ourselves. And the time comes when we are standing alone, naked in his sight, and God sends his angel to wrestle us to the point of personal submission.

The only trouble with this illustration is that it suggests that achieving death to self and taking up our cross is a once-for-all surrender, when actually it is the continuous business of daily obedience and discipline. There can be moments of important personal crisis and decision; there probably have to be. But the battle is not won even then, for these decisions must be followed by continuous daily decisions to say no to ourselves in order to say yes to God. The Greek text indicates this by the use of the present (continuative) sense: "Let him take up his cross (repeatedly and continuously) and keep on following me."

Daily Discipleship

This leads to the next point: discipleship. For when Jesus said that we are to deny ourselves and take up our cross, he obviously did not mean that we are literally to die or to cease to function. We are to enter by that gate into a path of lifelong discipleship. In that discipleship, the principles with which we started out, self-denial and death to self, are determinative.

How do we learn such denial, such death to our own plans and interests? There is only one way. We must follow Jesus and constantly keep our eyes on him. He is the supreme example of self-denial. He said no even to the glories of heaven in order to become human and die for our salvation (Phil 2:5-11). The author of Hebrews captures this solution when, in the verses immediately following his great chapter on the heroes of the faith, he writes,

> Therefore, since we are surrounded by so great a cloud of witnesses, let us also lay aside every weight, and sin which clings so closely, and let us run with endurance the race that is set before us, looking to Jesus, the founder and perfecter of our faith, who for the joy that was set before him endured the cross, despising the shame, and is seated at the right hand of the throne of God. (Heb 12:1-2)

Jesus taught this also. We notice when we study the verses on death and denial carefully that in nearly every case they are set in the context of Jesus' teaching concerning his own suffering and death by crucifixion. Mark 10 is the clearest example. In that chapter Jesus is teaching about discipleship, showing that his disciples must all be bound by the revealed Word of God (Mk 10:1-12), that they must come to God with the simple faith of children (Mk 10:13-16), and that possessions are often a hindrance and deterrent to discipleship (Mk 10:17-31). In this last section he introduces the matter of loss of family and lands for his sake and for the gospel.

Then we read,

> And they were on the road, going up to Jerusalem, and Jesus was walking ahead of them. And they were amazed, and those who followed were afraid. And taking the twelve again, he began to tell them what was to happen to him, saying, "See, we are going up to Jerusalem, and the Son of Man will be delivered over to the chief priests and the scribes, and they will condemn him to death and deliver him over to the Gentiles. And they will mock him and spit on him, and flog him and kill him. And after three days he will rise." (Mk 10:32-34)

Jesus was asking the fullest possible measure of devotion from those who followed him. They were to give up everything. But he was not asking them to do something he was not willing to do himself. He was providing them with a perfect example.

He also spoke of his resurrection and thus taught that the way of denial and death, though it involves a true and sometimes painful death to our own desires, is nevertheless the way to the fullness of living. Paul writes in Romans, "If we have been united with him in a death like his, we shall certainly be united with him in a resurrection like his" (Rom 6:5). It is the same in Galatians. "I have been crucified with Christ. It is no longer I who live, but Christ who lives in me. And the life I now live in the flesh I live by faith in the Son of God, who loved me and gave himself for me" (Gal 2:19-20). In the biblical scheme of things, death is always followed by life, crucifixion by resurrection. It is this that is truly exciting and for which we are willing to die.

When we give up trying to run our own life or when we give up what seems so precious and so utterly indispensable to us, it is then (and only then) that we suddenly find the true joy of being a Christian and enter into a life so freed from obsession that we can hardly understand how it could have had such a hold on us.

This is the primary difference between a joyless and a joyful Christian, a defeated and a victorious one. Death and resurrection! Joyless Christians may have died and risen with Christ in some abstract sense, so they can in the same sense be termed new creatures in Christ. But they have certainly never known it in practice. Joyful Christians have found satisfaction in whatever God gives them and are truly satisfied. They have said no to anything that might keep them from the richness of God's own blessing and presence and have risen to new life.

CHAPTER 12

FREEDOM, FREEDOM

*I*n the last chapter we saw the seeming paradox at the heart of the Christian life: we must die to self in order to live to God. There is another as well: we must become Christ's slave before we can be truly free. These are only apparent paradoxes, however. In the ultimate sense there are no paradoxes in Scripture. The doctrine of the Trinity might be thought to be a paradox, but it is not really. When we say that God is both a Trinity and a unity, we mean only that he is three in one sense and one in another. Similarly, when we speak of Christians being slaves to Christ and yet free, we mean that they become servants in one sense so they can become all that God intends them to be.

Christian freedom is like that of a man or woman in marriage. In one sense they are bound to each other; they are not free to love and relate to others in the way that they are obliged to love and relate to their spouse. But in another sense they really are free. They are free to be themselves within the marriage, acting as what they really are—a married man and woman. They are free from the fear of rejection because of their mutual commitment. They are even free to love others with a love that complements their love in marriage.

PURSUIT OF FREEDOM

The key to discovering freedom is to be what one has been created to be—an obedient and grateful servant of the Most High. The difficulty for many people is that they wish to be what they are not or can never be; thus, they are doomed to a life of frustration. Freedom has been defined as "the ability to fulfill one's destiny, to function in terms of one's ultimate goal."[1] In modern culture, freedom has more often been conceived as autonomy. But because this is a universe created and maintained by a sovereign God, no creature is or can be autonomous.

The pursuit of wealth is one attempt to achieve freedom apart from God or even from God himself. It is probably the dominant goal of most in the West and increasingly of the rest of the world as well. If asked, most who pursue this goal would deny that their interest is in money itself. "We are not materialists," they would say. "Money is freedom. Our pursuit of affluence is merely that we might have liberty to go where we wish and do what we want. We do not want to be tied to a particular job or place because of inadequate finances."

Christians have no quarrel with anyone striving to attain a good standard of living. Poverty has truly binding effects in life. But it is not true that money is freedom. Freedom is a matter of the soul or mind. At best, affluence deals only with the lifestyle or mobility of people. Besides, at times the wealthy are even imprisoned by their wealth, as some testify. Others are afraid of theft and barricade themselves as a protection against it.

Refusal to make commitments is a second way some try to find freedom apart from God. Some couples live together without being married because they "want to be free," meaning they want the option of ending the relationship if they grow tired of it. A bumper sticker proclaims, "Happiness is being single." In job interviews many will not promise a prospective employer to remain with the company for more than a test period, because they "want to be free to move on."

But the flaw is that freedom is only freedom if you use it. To make no commitments is really to do (or be) nothing at all. A commitment to things or persons actually *brings* freedom. In Christianity a commitment to Christ brings freedom from sin, alienation, guilt, aimlessness, and eventually death through the resurrection. True, Christians are not free to sin, but they are free to serve. They are not free to hate, but they are set free to love. They are free to follow the path God sets before them.

A rejection of the past is another false attempt to find freedom. Not only are yesterday's standards of morality rejected, but even yesterday's standards for doing anything. Anything new is better than anything old simply because it is new. This view is based on an unwillingness to be bound by anything others may have done or required, particularly in the realm of ethics.

---

[1] Roger R. Nicole, "Freedom and Law," *Tenth: An Evangelical Quarterly*, July 1976, 23.

Yet the law does not go away simply because we reject it, nor is conscience so easily shouted down. This might be possible were we our own makers and therefore truly autonomous, being responsible to no one but ourselves. But we are not our own creators. We are not autonomous. And we are responsible to many: parents, employers, spiritual leaders, the state, God. What is needed is not a rejection of the past and its standards, but rather a freedom of mind and purpose that enables us to choose from the past, retaining what is best and adding to it on the basis of right conduct both before God and others.

Rejection of all authority is the last of the major contemporary attempts to achieve freedom apart from God. Ultimately, this is the rejection of God, for the various human authorities that we know come from him (Rom 13:1-2). What takes their place? The individual. We each become our own authority. Friedrich Wilhelm Nietzsche, the philosopher, held out for the absolute autonomy of the individual, but his own later insanity is a testimony to the futility of this determination.

Any attempt to establish freedom apart from the presuppositions of Christianity is doomed because it makes freedom hang on the individual's own ability, which is not enough to sustain it. Reinhold Niebuhr analyzes this failure in an essay on "Individuality in Modern Culture."[2] He traces the destruction of individual freedom (which, he maintains, has been given to the world by Christianity) through three philosophies: naturalism, idealism, and romanticism. Naturalism failed to maintain individual freedom because it reduced humans to machines. Idealism failed because, although it stressed the higher, spiritual, or rational capacities of the individual, it found these only in a universal Self or Spirit in which the individual is lost. In romanticism the self became everything, but in the end all except a few like Nietzsche were forced to recoil from the pretensions of this individual self-glorification.

Niebuhr sums up these abortive attempts to establish freedom without the presuppositions of Christianity:

> The simple fact is that both the obviously partial and unique and the supposedly universal values of history can be both appreciated and judged only in terms of a religious faith which has discovered the centre and source of life to be beyond and yet within historical existence. This is the God who is both Creator and Judge revealed in Biblical faith. . . . Without the presuppositions of the Christian faith

---

[2]Reinhold Niebuhr, *The Nature and Destiny of Man*, vol. 1, *Human Nature* (New York: Charles Scribner's Sons, 1941), 54-92.

the individual is either nothing or becomes everything. In the Christian faith man's insignificance as a creature, involved in the process of nature and time, is lifted into significance by the mercy and power of God in which his life is sustained. But his significance as a free spirit is understood as subordinate to the freedom of God. His inclination to abuse his freedom, to overestimate his power and significance and to become everything is understood as the primal sin. It is because man is inevitably involved in this primal sin that he is bound to meet God first of all as a judge, who humbles his pride and brings his vain imagination to naught.[3]

THREE FREEDOMS

What does God say about freedom? Apart from the grace of God in Jesus Christ we are not free. Jesus himself said, "Everyone who commits sin is a slave to sin" (Jn 8:34). Freedom is found in obeying the laws of God, but we disobey those laws. In fact, we have lost our ability to obey and so have lost our ability to be free.

> Ever since Adam and Eve fell in paradise, the whole of mankind by natural gen-
> eration is encompassed in a terrible rebellion, corruption, and slavery in which,
> even in spite of some desires that we may have from time to time to do what is
> right, we are constantly carried along. So we sigh deeply in our heart, "What a
> wretched man I am! Who will rescue me?" (Rom 7:24). "How shall I get that
> emancipation? How shall I get freedom?" We say, "Give me liberty, because I am
> already encompassed in death."[4]

The gospel of God's grace in Jesus Christ says that we can be free to fulfill that destiny for which God has created us.

First, the gospel provides us with freedom from condemnation by God's law and thus *freedom of conscience*.[5] Freedom must begin here. Other freedoms will be shallow unless we are liberated from this condemnation. We gain this freedom through faith in Jesus Christ, who died in our place, taking our condemnation on himself. When we look to ourselves, we must admit, as does the 1848 Confession of the Evangelical Free Church of Geneva, Switzerland, "All men are born sinners, unable to do good before God, inclined to evil, bringing condemnation and death on themselves by a just judgment" (Article IV). But when we look to Christ, we find one who has freed us from that condemnation by dying for our sins. He has

---

[3]Ibid., 91-92.
[4]Nicole, "Freedom and Law," 27-28.
[5]Calvin stresses this in his *Institutes of the Christian Religion*, ed. John T. McNeill, trans. Ford Lewis Battles, 2 vols. (Philadelphia: Westminster, 1960), 834-36.

paid the full penalty required by the law for our transgressions, and has given us a standing before God that is the same as if we had never sinned at all.

The law of God is now no longer a threat to us. It is true that we have disobeyed it, but it has been dealt with. We now stand before the almighty God with clean records and liberated consciences.

It was this freedom that impressed the apostle Paul so deeply. He had given himself to obedience to the law. But the law was a stern taskmaster, and he had been burdened by it. He may have claimed to have kept the law perfectly, according to human interpretations (Phil 3:6). But he still was not righteous as God counts righteousness, and he sensed it (Acts 26:14). What was he to do? Through the gospel of Christ he discovered a righteousness apart from the law, which met the requirements of God perfectly. At this point he cried,

> There is therefore now no condemnation for those who are in Christ Jesus. For the law of the Spirit of life has set you free in Christ Jesus from the law of sin and death. For God has done what the law, weakened by the flesh, could not do. By sending his own Son in the likeness of sinful flesh and for sin, he condemned sin in the flesh, in order that the righteous requirement of the law might be fulfilled in us, who walk not according to the flesh but according to the Spirit. (Rom 8:1-4)

Similarly, in Galatians, after a spirited defense of justification by faith alone, Paul rhapsodizes, "For freedom Christ has set us free; stand firm therefore, and do not submit again to a yoke of slavery" (Gal 5:1).

Each of these passages leads immediately to *freedom of obedience*. Each is part of an argument dealing, not merely with freedom from the law's condemnation, but also with a very practical freedom. The Romans passage comes immediately after a chapter detailing Paul's personal struggle between the desires of his new nature and the sinful desires of his old nature. The passage in Galatians leads into a discussion of the life of the Spirit that is a result of justification. Being freed from the condemnation of the law and being given a new nature, believers are now set free from their old desires and rebellion and can obey God.

Once, Jesus had been speaking to the Jews of his day about the source and nature of his teachings, and many had believed on him in a rudimentary sense. But recognizing this, Jesus encouraged them to stay with him and continue to learn from him. He said, "If you abide in my word, you are truly my disciples, and you will know the truth, and the truth will set you free."

This infuriated some who were there, perhaps some unbelievers, though the text does not say so explicitly. They replied, "We are offspring of Abraham and have never been enslaved to any one. How is it that you say, 'You will become free'?" This was ridiculous, of course. For years the Jews had been slaves in Egypt. During the period of the Judges, there were at least seven occasions when the nation came under the domination of foreigners. There was the seventy-year Babylonian captivity. Even as they were talking to Jesus they were watched over by Roman soldiers and carried coins in their purses that showed Rome's rule over Palestine. This very fact made them quite sensitive to the issue of freedom.

But Jesus did not try to show how deluded they were in their thoughts about political freedom. Instead, he answered, "Truly, truly, I say to you, everyone who commits sin is a slave to sin. . . . If the Son sets you free, you will be free indeed" (Jn 8:34-36).

Freedom comes from the new nature of Christ within. Consequently, desiring now to please God, we do what pleases him not because we are forced to do so by the strictures of the law, but simply because we desire to please God. Is the law of no value then? On the contrary, it is of great value. It shows us what pleases God.

This is particularly important in questionable matters. What may I do on Sunday? What occupations are open to me as a Christian? May I smoke? Drink? Play cards? Go to movies? In some of these cases there are obvious limits placed on our conduct. But the Bible does not answer all such questions specifically; and if we are trying to find an answer in this way, we will only be bound up by it and lose the freedom we should have.

Calvin put it well.

When consciences once ensnare themselves, they enter a long and inextricable maze, not easy to get out of. If a man begins to doubt whether he may use linen for sheets, shirts, handkerchiefs and napkins, he will afterward be uncertain also about hemp; finally, doubt will even arise over tow. For he will turn over in his mind whether he can sup without napkins, or go without a handkerchief. If any man should consider daintier food unlawful, in the end he will not be at peace before God, when he eats either black bread or common victuals, while it occurs to him that he could sustain his body on even coarser foods. If he boggles at sweet wine, he will not with clear conscience drink even flat wine, and finally he will come to the point of considering it wrong to step upon a straw across his path, as the saying goes.[6]

[6]Ibid., 839.

The third area of Christian freedom is linked to the other two: *freedom of knowledge*. Through knowledge of who we are as sinners, and of who God is and what he has done in Christ for our salvation, we are saved from the law's condemnation and launched on the Christian life. Having come to know God as he is revealed in Christ, we find that we want to go on learning about him. We also find ourselves growing in the genuine freedom that knowledge of God brings. "You will know the truth, and the truth will set you free."

If a person has no education, the professions are closed to him. He can do manual work, but not white-collar work. If someone is illiterate, even more doors are closed. A person like this will have difficulty finding anything other than menial forms of employment. The fullest enjoyment of the arts—music, drama, sculpture—will probably be excluded as well. Likewise, those who do not know the teachings of the Word of God cannot thrive spiritually. They will be bound by misconceptions of God's nature, superstition, and the prejudices of others. Only those who are increasingly coming to know and love God's Word can grow in freedom.

Once some Christians in Hong Kong talked with an eighty-two-year-old woman who had shortly before been released from China. She was a Christian, but her vocabulary was filled with much of the terminology of communism.

"When you were back in China, were you free to gather together with other Christians to worship?" they asked her.

"Oh, no," she answered. "Since the liberation no one is permitted to gather together for Christian services."

"But surely you were able to get together in small groups and discuss the Christian faith?"

"No, we are not," was the woman's reply. "Since the liberation all such meetings are forbidden."

"Were you free to read your Bible?"

"Since the liberation no one is free to read the Bible."

Freedom does not consist in the words *liberation* or *freedom* alone, but in the reality that Christianity brings.

CHAPTER 13

KNOWING
THE WILL OF GOD

There are not many questions that Christians ask more often than, "What is God's plan for my life? How can I know it? And how can I be sure that I know it?" These questions come naturally to Christian people. But even if they did not, they would be forced on us by the Bible's teaching that God wants us to know his will and embrace it gratefully. This is the implication of Romans 12:1-2, verses that we have looked at several times already in other contexts: "I appeal to you therefore, brothers, by the mercies of God, to present your bodies as a living sacrifice, holy and acceptable to God, which is your spiritual worship. Do not be conformed to this world, but be transformed by the renewal of your mind, that by testing you may discern what is the will of God, what is good and acceptable and perfect." We are to deny ourselves and mature in Christian character by means of an inward transformation so we can understand the perfect will of God for our lives.

In Philippians, after Paul has spoken of the goal of the Christian life and of his own desire to press on toward it, he also writes, "Let those of us who are mature think this way, and if in anything you think otherwise, God will reveal that also to you" (Phil 3:15).

The Psalms are filled with this theme, particularly those of David, who possessed a strong sense of need for God's guidance. In Psalm 25 he asks, "Make me to know your ways, O LORD; teach me your paths. Lead me in your truth and teach me" (Ps 25:4-5). Then he declares,

Good and upright is the LORD;

    therefore he instructs sinners in the way.

He leads the humble in what is right,

    and teaches the humble his way. (Ps 25:8-9)

Psalm 16:7 declares, "I bless the LORD who gives me counsel." A psalm of Asaph says, "I am continually with you; you hold my right hand. You guide me with your counsel" (Ps 73:23-24).

These verses do not mean that we will always be able to see more than one step ahead in the Christian life. They do not even mean that we shall be able always to see ahead at all. But they do mean that God has a plan for us and that he promises to lead us in it, revealing the steps that are necessary for us to know as we go forward.

THE WILLS OF GOD

I need to clarify something before we go on. When we speak of knowing the will of God we commonly think of that which God does not promise to reveal and usually does not reveal. God does not reveal his secret or hidden purposes (Deut 29:29). What he does reveal is that kind of life or character that pleases him.

Thus we see already that there are different meanings attached to the word *will*. In the Bible, one is that of the *sovereign* or *efficacious* will of God. This will is beyond anything we can fully know on earth. Indeed, it provides the origin of all things and orders them. God's will is absolute. It is unlimited. It is determined only by God himself. God does not need to consult anyone in formulating his plans, and he does not need help from anyone in carrying them out. God's will is independent. It is fixed. It does not need to adapt to changing circumstances. It is omnipotent. This is the sense in John 6:40, in which Jesus says, "This is the will of my Father, that every one who looks on the Son and believes in him should have eternal life."

Another meaning of *will* in Scripture is the *disposition* of God or what pleases him. In the Lord's Prayer is the petition that says, "Thy will be done." This does not refer to the sovereign or efficacious will of God, for if that were the case, there would be no need to pray for it. God's will in that sense will be done whether we pray for it or not. In the Lord's Prayer the request is rather that what pleases God might be increasingly realized in our lives and in the lives of others.

So when we speak of wanting to know God's will, are we asking to know God's hidden councils, those that are the expression of his sovereign will, or are we seeking to know what pleases him? If it is the former, we are doomed to frustration. We will not learn God's hidden councils for the simple reason that they are hidden. If we are seeking to know what pleases God, much can be said, for God has revealed that to us. "God wills our righteousness. God wills our obedience. And the law of God clearly reflects something of his will in the perceptive sense, the sense of his disposition."[1]

OUR WILL AND GOD'S

But how do I know what pleases God in the specific circumstances of my life? How do I know whether I should go into an academic or business career? Whom should I marry? What church should I join? How should I spend my time? For work? For Christian activities? For recreation and relaxation? In what ways shall I spend the money that I earn? There are countless similar questions that confront us, and while some of these may concern God's hidden purposes, not all of them do. Barring supernatural disclosures of God's will, which God sometimes gives but does not encourage us to count on, there are three principles we are to follow.

The first is a precondition that can often solve a problem instantly: *we must be willing to do the will of God even before we know what it is.* John 7:17 states clearly, "If anyone's will is to do God's will, he will know whether the teaching is from God or whether I am speaking on my own authority." Jesus is referring to the truth or falsity of his doctrine that had been challenged by the Jewish leaders. But in answering this, he taught the broader principle that knowing the will of God consists largely in being willing to do it. The difficulty with most of us is that, in spite of what we profess, we actually most want to do what we want to do—and in seeking guidance we are actually hoping that God will come around to our way of thinking.

Here is an example about a man who was a prominent leader in church. He told me that he had been deeply concerned about his line of work. He felt secure in doing what he was doing, but he was uncertain about the location. He felt he should work in another state. Unfortunately, he had no job offers from that state, though he had been praying for this. On one occasion he prayed very specifically. He got down beside his desk, on his knees, and spoke to God along

---

[1]R. C. Sproul, "Discerning the Will of God," in *Our Sovereign God*, ed. James M. Boice (Grand Rapids: Baker, 1977), 106-7.

these lines: "Dear God, I am so uncertain about this thing. I do not know what to do. What I really need is a sign from you. I need somebody from the state I am interested in to call me up and offer me a position." While he was still on his knees the phone beside him rang. It was long distance, and the person on the other end offered him a job in precisely the area of the country he had been praying about. A clear sign? Perhaps. But he did not accept the position. He stayed where he was and to this day says, "Maybe I should have said yes when that telephone rang."

I am not quite ready to say that my friend should have taken the new job. Perhaps he should have. But this may have been God's way of showing him that his basic problem in knowing God's will was that he did not really want to do it, regardless of what he was praying or what answers he received. In most cases, our difficulties with knowing God's will are in this area.

When I counsel others on knowing God's will, similar problems often arise. After we have talked and I have led them to consider relevant passages of Scripture, they raise objections. Either the verses do not apply to their situation, they are unreasonable, they cannot be obeyed, or some such thing. This usually tells me that the difficulty is not in knowing what God desires but in wanting to do it.

How are we to become willing to do God's will? We must first recognize our unwillingness. Then, we must submit to those Christian disciplines by which we are "transformed" from within by the renewal of our minds that we might "discern what is the will of God" (Rom 12:2). Prayer is one of these disciplines. It is by prayer that we stop in the rush of our daily routine, think about God and his ways, review our lives in that light, and then ask God's forgiveness for past failures and his guidance for the future. Christian fellowship is another discipline. We need the support, interest, and loving correction of others. Most important is a regular program of Bible study.

The second principle for knowing the will of God is substantive: *God has revealed his will in Scripture.* God's hidden will—involving elements of our future lives and occupations—is not revealed anywhere, even in Scripture. So we do not approach the Bible in a magical way to see whether we should marry John or Bill or Mary or Carol. But what God desires is made abundantly clear in Scripture.

The Bible limits our options. It may not tell us whether we are to marry Bill or Carol, but it does tell us that we are not to live with either one before we are married. It condemns fornication. Similarly, it may not tell us whether we are to be a doctor or a lawyer, but it tells us that we are not to be a thief or a prostitute or enter any line of work that may damage others. The Bible also gives us guidelines on which we may operate. One is stated in the verses we have referred to twice earlier: Romans 12:1-2. It tells us that God wills our sanctification. Anything that contributes to our growth in holiness is an aspect of God's will for us. Anything that hinders that growth is not his will. Above everything, God is interested in having us become like Jesus Christ. "For this is the will of God, your sanctification" (1 Thess 4:3).

Colossians 3:23 is an expression of God's will for our work. "Whatever you do, work heartily, as for the Lord and not for men." This principle applies particularly to students or to those just starting out in a career. A member of my congregation once remarked that all too often young Christians interpret a difficulty in their work or schooling as an indication that what they are doing is not God's will for them when, actually, it is probably God's indication that they should work harder at it. This verse tells us that God wants us to do well in everything we are given to do.

A guideline that is closely related to this is found in Ephesians 6:5-6: "Slaves, obey your earthly masters with fear and trembling, with a sincere heart, as you would Christ, not by the way of eye-service, as people-pleasers, but as servants of Christ, doing the will of God from the heart." This guideline is especially for those who have a difficult boss or a difficult teacher. The Bible says it is God's will that you should avoid gossiping about him or her and instead work as well as you are able. You should do it not only when the boss is watching but also when he or she is not watching—as unto the Lord and not unto people.

Other verses tell us that we are to make a sober analysis of our gifts to see where we might be most useful, and also to seek the guidance of our brothers and sisters in the church. The church is often the one that gives a call for a vocation (see Acts 13:1-3).

DOUBTFUL SITUATIONS

But we must admit that there are situations where matters are not so clear. Can I work for a company that produces war materials? Can I drink alcoholic beverages? Can I enter politics? The theater?

To answer these questions we begin with grace. Romans 6:14 states, "Sin will have no dominion over you, since you are not under law but under grace." This verse is set in a context of godly living. The way to godliness, then, will never be found by organizing a body of Christians to declare whether or not movies, alcohol, cards, the Masons, going to war, or whatever is proper. "You are not under law but under grace."

Does being free of law mean that we are at liberty to do as we please? Should we sin that grace may abound? On the contrary, "Now that you have been set free from sin and have become slaves of God, the fruit you get leads to sanctification and its end, eternal life" (Rom 6:22). Living by grace actually leads to holiness, for our desire is to please the one who has saved us by that grace.

To determine God's will in doubtful matters, we should next realize that although all things are permissible for Christians—because we are not under law but under grace—still all things are not helpful. This is true first because the thing may gain a harmful control over us. "'All things are lawful for me,' but not all things are helpful. 'All things are lawful for me,' but I will not be enslaved by anything" (1 Cor 6:12). Paul knew that God had not set him free from sin simply to be captured by mere things.

The question to ask is, "Am I using things or are things using me?" Take food, the first of Paul's examples (1 Cor 6:13-14). Nothing can be as obviously good for a person as food; it is necessary for bodily strength as well as mental health. But it is possible for a person to become so addicted to overeating that the good end is thwarted and the person's health endangered. Hence, certain eating habits should be avoided. The second of Paul's examples is sex (1 Cor 7:5-20). This, too, is good. It is a gift from God. Within the bonds of marriage it is a force for strength in the home as well as an expression of close union. But it too can be destructive. It can control the person instead of the person controlling it. In this form, sex can destroy the very values it was created to maintain. The Bible teaches that Christians must never use things—food, sex, drugs, alcohol, cars, homes, stocks, or whatever—in such a way that we actually fall under their power. In some of these cases, 1 Corinthians 6:12 is an unequivocal warning to avoid them.

Later on in 1 Corinthians, Paul gives a second reason why all things are not helpful: the freedom of one believer may hurt the spiritual growth of another. "'All things are lawful,' but not all things are helpful. 'All things are lawful,' but not all things build up" (1 Cor 10:23). The verses that follow show that he is thinking of the well-being and growth of fellow Christians.

Taking this verse to its extreme would mean to derive your standards of conduct entirely from what other Christians say or think. If you do that, you are either going to become hypocritical, schizophrenic, or mad. But the verse does mean that there are going to be situations in which you will have to avoid certain things, even though they are right in themselves, because you won't want to harm others. Suppose you have been witnessing to Sharon, a friend of yours. She has been having a hard time overcoming a disposition to sexual sins. She has become a Christian. Still the lure of the flesh is with her. This verse means that you had better not take her to see sex-dominated movies. What is more, you had best not go yourself, for she may be harmed by your freedom. In the same way, you are not to serve alcohol to Christians for whom it is a serious problem; for their sake, if necessary, you are to avoid it also.

Moreover, we should be consistent in our abstinence over a long period of time so as not to appear two-faced or hypocritical. Paul wrote, "Therefore, if food makes my brother stumble, I will never eat meat, lest I make my brother stumble" (1 Cor 8:13). Never! And this from the same apostle who defended the cause of Christian liberty from law successfully before the Jerusalem apostles (Acts 15:1-29; Gal 2:1-10). Clearly, it will sometimes be costly if we are to watch the effect our conduct may have on other Christians.

Last, in deciding how to handle doubtful matters, we should seek to choose the best. It is stated well in Philippians 4:8. "Finally, brothers, whatever is true, whatever is honorable, whatever is just, whatever is pure, whatever is lovely, whatever is commendable, if there is any excellence, if there is anything worthy of praise, think about these things."

This does not exclude the best things in our society, whether explicitly Christian or not. The heart of the verse lies in the fact (not always noticed by commentators and Bible teachers) that the virtues mentioned here are pagan virtues. These words do not occur in the great lists of Christian virtues, which include love, joy, peace, long-suffering, and so on. On the whole they are taken from the writings of Greek philosophers and moralists. In using these words Paul is actually sanctifying, as it were, the generally accepted virtues of pagan morality. He is saying that although the pursuit of the best by Christians will obviously include spiritual things, it will not mean the exclusion of the best values that the world has to offer. The things that are acknowledged to be honorable by the best people everywhere are also worthy to be cultivated by Christians. Consequently, Christians can love all that is true, honest, just, pure, lovely, and of good report, wherever we find it. We can rejoice in the best of art and good literature. We can thrill to great music. We can thrive on beautiful architecture. We can also thank God for giving people, even in their fallen state, the ability to create such beauty.

Take confidence from the promise of God's presence that accompanies Paul's words. He often wrote parenthetically in his letters, and he does so here. The result is that the first half of Philippians 4:9 partially distorts the meaning of the sentence. The first half says, "What you have learned and received and heard and seen in me, practice these things." As the verse stands, you would tend to think that the promise of God's presence is attached to it. Actually, as the Greek syntax, which repeats the word "whatever" throughout Philippians 4:8 and into Philippians 4:9, makes clear, it is attached to Philippians 4:8, and the promise is this: "Whatever is true, whatever is honorable, whatever is just, whatever is pure, whatever is lovely, whatever is commendable . . . think about these things . . . and the God of peace will be with you." When you pursue the highest things in life, both spiritually and secularly, then the God of peace will be with you. You shall have the confidence that he will bless and guide as you seek to please him.

LOOKING TO JESUS

This brings us to the third of the three principles mentioned earlier in this chapter. The first principle was that we must be willing to do the will of God even before we know what it is; the second, that we must get our guidelines from Scripture. The third is the principle of *daily and even hourly fellowship with the Lord.* Psalm 32:8 states it by saying, "I will instruct you and teach you in the way you should go; I will counsel you with my eye upon you." If the Lord is to guide us with *his* eye, he must first catch *our* eye. And this means that we must look to him regularly throughout the day.[2]

Of course, this is what we really need and desire—fellowship with one who knows what we should do and how we should do it. We need more than a mere instruction manual. John White says, "You may seek guidance, but God desires to give something better: himself."[3] What God has really provided is a Guide. We are to stay close to him and follow his leading.

---

[2]Some of the material in this chapter has been borrowed from "How to Know the Will of God" and "How to Know the Will of God in Doubtful Situations" in my *How to Live the Christian Life* (Chicago: Moody, 1982), 33-50.
[3]John White, *The Fight* (Downers Grove, IL: InterVarsity Press, 1976), 154.

CHAPTER 14

TALKING TO GOD

*T*hrough Bible study God speaks to us. By prayer we speak to God. both are as necessary in developing a personal relationship as genuine two-way conversation.

But prayer is even more than conversation. It is a privilege. We place ourselves in the will of God as best we know how. Then, as children approaching our mother or father, we request what we need, knowing that we shall receive it. Prayer is our response to Christ's promise: "Whatever you ask in my name, this I will do, that the Father may be glorified in the Son. If you ask anything in my name, I will do it" (Jn 14:13-14).

Reuben A. Torrey, in one of his books on prayer, has listed eleven reasons why prayer is important: (1) because there is a devil and because prayer is the God-appointed means of resisting him; (2) because prayer is God's way for us to obtain what we need from him; (3) because the apostles, whom God gave as a pattern for us, considered prayer to be the most important business of their lives; (4) because prayer occupied a very prominent place and played a very important part in the earthly life of our Lord; (5) because prayer is the most important part of the present ministry of our Lord, since he is now interceding for us (Heb 7:25); (6) because prayer is the means God has appointed for our receiving mercy from him and of obtaining grace to help in time of need; (7) because prayer is the means of obtaining the fullness of God's joy; (8) because prayer with thanksgiving is the means of obtaining freedom from anxiety and, in anxiety's place, the peace that passes understanding; (9) because prayer is the method appointed for obtaining the fullness of God's Holy Spirit; (10) because prayer is the means by which we are to keep watchful and alert at Christ's return; and (11) because prayer is used by God to promote our spiritual growth, bring power into our work, lead others to faith in Christ, and bring all other blessings to Christ's church.[1]

THE PROBLEM OF PRAYER

In spite of the obvious importance of prayer, most people misunderstand it and find it confusing. The problem may be traced to the fact that so few Christians know God well. Since none of us knows him fully, prayer is at least partially confusing to all of us. Does prayer change things? Or does prayer change people? Does God change his mind as the result of believing prayer? Do we move God? Or does God move us to pray? What does it mean to pray without ceasing? Who can pray? How should one pray? In any gathering of God's people, many of these questions will receive different and sometimes even contradictory answers.

Not only do normal people have difficulty with prayer. So do theologians. At one point in the course of their long and very influential ministries, George Whitefield, the Calvinistic evangelist, and John Wesley, the Arminian evangelist, were preaching together. They conducted several services during the day and returned exhausted to their room together in a boarding house each night. One evening after a particularly strenuous day, the two of them returned to prepare for bed. When they were ready, each knelt beside his bed to pray. Whitefield, the Calvinist, prayed like this: "Lord, we thank Thee for all those with whom we spoke this day, and we rejoice that their lives and destinies are entirely in thy hand. Honor our efforts according to thy perfect will. Amen." He then climbed in bed.

Wesley, who had hardly gotten past the invocation of his prayer in this length of time, looked up and said, "Mr. Whitefield, is this where your Calvinism leads you?" Then he put his head down again and went on praying.

---

[1]R. A. Torrey, *How to Pray* (Westwood, NJ: Revell, 1900), 7-31. A more comprehensive book by Torrey is *The Power of Prayer* (Grand Rapids: Eerdmans, 1955). Those who wish to pursue a study of prayer further than this chapter permits may consult Jacques Ellul, *Prayer and Modern Man*, trans. C. Edward Hopkin (New York: Seabury, 1973); O. Hallesby, *Prayer*, trans. Clarence J. Carlsen (Minneapolis: Augsburg, 1960); Andrew Murray, *With Christ in the School of Prayer* (Westwood, NJ: Revell, 1967); and John Calvin, *Institutes of the Christian Religion*, ed. John T. McNeill, trans. Ford Lewis Battles, 2 vols. (Philadelphia: Westminster, 1960), 2: 850-920.

Whitefield stayed in bed and went to sleep. About two hours later he woke up, and there was Wesley still on his knees beside the bed. Whitefield got up, went around to where Wesley was kneeling and touched him. Wesley was asleep. Whitefield said, "Mr. Wesley, is this where your Arminianism leads you?"

This is not meant to imply that Calvinists inevitably fail to pray simply by virtue of their being Calvinists or that Arminians inevitably fail to pray through human weakness. But it is clear that even the most zealous Christians have difficulties. Calvin believed in God's providence; but in his chapter on prayer, which immediately precedes his chapter on election, he explicitly refutes those who say that God is "vainly importuned with our entreaties."[2] Instead, he speaks of the need to "dig up by prayer" those treasures God has for us.[3]

> After we have been instructed by faith to recognize that whatever we need and whatever we lack is in God, and in our Lord Jesus Christ, in whom the Father willed all the fullness of his bounty to abide (cf. Col. 1:19; Jn 1:16) so that we may all draw from it as from an overflowing spring, it remains for us to seek in him, and in prayers to ask of him, what we have learned to be in him. Otherwise, to know God as the master and bestower of all good things, who invites us to request them of him, and still not go to him and not ask of him—this would be of as little profit as for a man to neglect a treasure, buried and hidden in the earth, after it had been pointed out to him.[4]

Prayer is "digging up" God's treasures. But it is not a way primarily of getting *things* from God, for the treasure about which Calvin speaks includes those riches of grace and glory that are in Christ Jesus.

PRAYER IS TO GOD

Many of our difficulties in prayer may be removed by getting clear about to whom we are praying and what he has done to make prayer possible. This was the point at which our Lord started in his teaching about prayer. In the Sermon on the Mount, he began by stressing that the only prayer that can truly be called prayer is that which is directed consciously and explicitly to God the Father. He said,

> And when you pray, you must not be like the hypocrites. For they love to stand and pray in the synagogues and at the street corners, that they may be seen by others. Truly, I say to you, they have received their reward. But when you pray,

---

[2]Ibid., 853.
[3]Ibid., 851.
[4]Ibid., 850.

go into your room and shut the door and pray to your Father who is in secret.
And your Father who sees in secret will reward you. (Mt 6:5-6)

Jesus is not speaking against the value and practice of public prayer, for the Lord
himself prayed publicly (see Jn 11:41-42). Rather, he is concerned with the
tendency we all have to pray to ourselves or others instead of to God. Prayer
must always be made to God. It must be made in the knowledge that he is always
more ready to answer than we are to pray to him.

Many think that all prayers are offered to God, but that is not the case. It
could be argued that not one prayer in a thousand is really offered to the Father
of the Lord Jesus Christ. In the world at large, millions of prayers are offered to
idols, false gods. In Catholicism many are offered to the saints. In Protestantism
many are like the one once uttered in a fashionable Boston church and described
afterward as "the most eloquent prayer ever offered to a Boston audience." Obviously the one praying was more concerned with impressing others than with
approaching God.

Do my prayers bring me into the presence of God? When I pray, am I really
thinking far more of my friends, my busy schedule, or what I am asking for
than I am of the great God I am approaching? Torrey says that "we should never
utter one syllable of prayer either in public or in private until we are definitely
conscious that we have come into the presence of God and are actually praying
to Him."[5]

Prayer is connected with personal spiritual growth. As the soul grows, the
prayer life deepens and vice versa. When children begin praying, for example,
there is often nothing more than petition. "Now I lay me down to sleep; I pray
thee, Lord, my soul to keep," or, "God, bless mommy and daddy and make me
a good girl. Amen." Somewhat later, as they grow, they are taught to thank
God for things. "Father, I thank you for this food, for rest and play and all
good things. . . ." If growth continues, the child is led to consider the needs
of others and to think of God and praise him. What happens in the growth
of the prayer life of a child should happen in the life of every child of God:
from focusing on self to others and then to God. This should reflect and foster
spiritual growth.

There is a hymn by Frederick W. Faber, itself a great prayer, which looks
ahead (in the last stanza) to that fuller spiritual capacity that will only be possible
in heaven.

---

[5]Torrey, Power of Prayer, 76.

My God, how wonderful Thou art,

Thy majesty how bright!

How beautiful Thy mercy seat,

In depths of burning light!

O how I fear Thee, living God,

With deepest, tend'rest fears;

And worship Thee with trembling hope,

And penitential tears.

Yet I may love Thee too, O Lord,

Almighty as Thou art;

For Thou hast stooped to ask of me

The love of my poor heart.

Father of Jesus, love's reward!

What rapture will it be,

Prostrate before Thy throne to lie,

And gaze and gaze on Thee.

In those final words Faber has come to a place that is the spiritual parallel to having fallen in love, when one wants only to be with and gaze on the beloved.

This movement of prayer—from ourselves to others to God himself—does not stop with God, but necessarily returns from him to our own needs and those of others. It is brought about by a new recognition of our sin and weakness, which we always experience when we look on the holy and omnipotent God. This leads to confession of sin. Our concern for others is nourished by the discovery that in his grace God cares for them even as for us. This leads to intercession.

This movement is suggested in the wording of the Lord's Prayer. The prayer begins with God and his interests, as it should. We are instructed to pray,

Our Father in heaven,

hallowed be *your* name.

Your kingdom come,

your will be done,

on earth as it is in heaven. (Mt 6:9-10)

This is a prayer for God's honor. But then, no sooner are these petitions outlined, than the prayer goes on,

Give us this day our daily bread;

and forgive us our debts,

    as we also have forgiven our debtors;

and lead us not into temptation,

    but deliver us from evil. (Mt 6:11-13)

By contrast with the first part of the prayer, these are human or earthly concerns. Moreover, the pronouns are not in the singular ("I," "me," or "mine") but in the plural ("we," "us," and "our"). Having seen God in our worship, we will inevitably turn back to pray for others.

There is a simple acronym for prayer, which many have found helpful: ACTS. A stands for adoration, C for confession, T for thanksgiving, and S for supplication. Really meeting God means we will inevitably confess our sin, thank him for his forgiveness and all other blessings, and intercede for others.

THROUGH JESUS CHRIST

I pray. But how is this possible? God is holy. How can I, a sinful human being, approach a holy God? The answer is that true prayer is prayer offered to God the Father on the basis of the death of Jesus Christ. The author of the book of Hebrews puts it like this: "Therefore, brothers, since we have confidence to enter the holy places by the blood of Jesus, . . . let us draw near with a true heart in full assurance of faith" (Heb 10:19, 22). Jesus taught the same thing when he said, "I am the way, and the truth, and the life. No one comes to the Father except through me" (Jn 14:6). If we were to approach God on our own merit, God would have to turn from us. If it were not for Jesus Christ, God would never hear any prayer offered by any human being. However, we can be purified in his sight through faith in Jesus and in this state we may come.

This means, of course, that prayer is for believers only. It is not for the heathen. It is not for the atheist. It is not for the good person who, nevertheless, regards Jesus as nothing more than a man, worth little more than an example.[6]

---

[6]Calvin writes, "Since he [Christ] is the only way, and the one access, by which it is granted us to come to God (cf. John 14:6), to those who turn aside from this way and forsake this access, no way and no access to God remain; nothing is left in this throne but wrath, judgment, and terror. Moreover, since the Father has sealed him (cf. John 6:27) as our Head (Matt. 2:6) and Leader (1 Cor 11:3; Eph 1:22; 4:15; 5:23; Col. 1:18), those who in any way turn aside or incline away from him are trying their level best to destroy and disfigure the mark imprinted by God. Thus Christ is constituted the only Mediator, by whose intercession the Father is for us rendered gracious and easily entreated" (*Institutes*, 876).

While God does not hear the prayer of non-Christians, it is also true that he does not hear the prayers offered by many Christians when they cling to some sin. David said, "If I had cherished iniquity in my heart, the Lord would not have listened" (Ps 66:18). Isaiah wrote,

> Behold, the LORD's hand is not shortened, that it cannot save,
>   or his ear dull, that it cannot hear;
> but your iniquities have made a separation
>   between you and your God,
> and your sins have hidden his face from you
>   so that he does not hear. (Is 59:1-2)

Do these verses describe your prayer life? If so, you must confess your sin openly and frankly, knowing that God "is faithful and just to forgive our sins and to cleanse us from all unrighteousness" (1 Jn 1:9).

If I have been dishonest with a friend, it is not very easy for me to talk about anything with him or her. I may be able to force my way through a conversation about the weather, my work, or our families. But I do not bring up more personal things. It is only after the air has been cleared between us, after forgiveness has been asked and received, that I am once again able to open up with my friend. It is the same in my relationship with God. If sin keeps me from him, then he is like a stranger and my prayer flows slowly, even though I have believed in Jesus. Instead, I must confess my sin and learn to spend time alone with my heavenly Father. When I do that, my prayer will become the kind of communion that I have in conversation with a close friend.

IN THE HOLY SPIRIT

Prayer is communion with God the Father through the Lord Jesus Christ. But it is also in the Holy Spirit. Ephesians 2:18 says, "For through him [Jesus] we both have access in one Spirit to the Father." Prayer is coming to God the Father through the Lord Jesus Christ in the Holy Spirit. What does this mean? It is the work of the Holy Spirit to lead us into God's presence, to point God out to us and to make God real when we pray. This is suggested by the Greek word *prosagōgē*, which is translated "access" in the above verse. Literally it means "an introduction." The Holy Spirit introduces us to God. The Holy Spirit makes God real to us while instructing us how we should pray (Rom 8:26-27).

Have you ever begun to pray and had the experience that God seems to be far away? If you have, it may be that sin or disobedience to God is hindering you. But it may simply be that things are filling your mind or that worries are obscuring the sense you should have of God's presence. What are you to do in that case? Should you stop and pray again another time? Certainly not, for it is then that you probably need it most. Instead you should be still and, looking to God, ask him to work through his Holy Spirit to make himself real to you and to lead you into his presence. Many Christians find that their most wonderful times of prayer are those in which they start without a clear sense of God's presence but come to it by praying.

If It Be Thy Will

When we approach God as he has told us to approach him, we can have great boldness in prayer, as Wesley, Whitefield, Calvin, Torrey, and other great prayer warriors have had. This is what the Lord encouraged in that verse quoted at the beginning of this chapter. "Whatever you ask in my name, this I will do" (Jn 14:13). This does not mean that we can ask for any foolish or sinful thing and get it. To ask in Christ's name means to ask in accordance with his will. But it does mean that when we ask in accordance with that will we can be confident.

To be faithful to this text, however, we must also say that there are Christians who use the idea of God's will in a way that was never intended and that is not intended here. They use it to save face. Many pray with so little confidence that God will ever answer their prayers that they are constantly adding "if it be thy will" to each of them, as if to say to each other and to themselves that they already know in advance that the thing they are asking for will not happen. Many of these people are deeply astonished when God actually does answer some prayer.

When Herod Antipas was the reigning king in Palestine, the apostle Peter was imprisoned in Jerusalem. The Christians were worried. Peter had been arrested before and released, but Herod had just killed James, the brother of John, and there was every reason to think that he would execute Peter also. The Christians began to pray. They were praying in one part of Jerusalem—at the house of Mary, the mother of John Mark—while God was already at work in another part of the city releasing Peter from prison. The gates were flung open, and an angel led Peter out into the streets of the sleeping city.

We do not know what the Christians at Mary's home were saying. They may have been praying that God would comfort Peter or that God would stay the hand of Herod or, which is more likely, that God would deliver the apostle from prison. But I am sure they were praying "if it be thy will," for they were not expecting God's answer. As they prayed Peter came to the door and knocked. A maid went to see who was there. She was astonished—so much so that she returned to the group who were praying without letting Peter in. But they were worse off than she was, for when they were told that it was Peter, they said, "You are out of your mind." The story continues, "But she kept insisting that it was so, and they kept saying, 'It is his angel!' But Peter continued knocking, and when they opened, they saw him and were amazed. But motioning to them with his hand to be silent, he described to them how the Lord had brought him out of the prison" (Acts 12:15-17).

Many of our prayers are like the prayers of those Christians. In many of our churches prayer has become a duty, and Christians pray without any sure expectation of God's answer. What a pity this is! By contrast, Jesus taught that we can live and pray so much in the sphere of God's will that we can be bold in saying, "Thy will be done." We may ask in confidence, knowing that God's will shall be done in our lives and churches.

It was a sense of being in the center of God's will that gave Luther his great boldness in prayer. In 1540, Luther's great friend and assistant, Frederick Myconius, became sick and was expected to die within a short time. On his deathbed he took the effort to write a farewell note to Luther. Luther received the letter and instantly sent back a reply. "I command thee in the name of God to live because I still have need of thee in the work of reforming the church. . . . The Lord will never let me hear that thou art dead, but will permit thee to survive me. For this I am praying, this is my will, and may my will be done, because I seek only to glorify the name of God." The words are almost shocking to us, for we live in a more sensitive and cautious day, but they were certainly from God. For although Myconius had already lost the ability to speak when Luther's letter came, in a short time he revived. He recovered completely, and he lived six more years to survive Luther himself by two months.[7]

We are never so bold in prayer as when we can look in the face of God and say, "My Father, I do not pray for myself in this thing, and I do not want my will done. I want thy name to be glorified. Glorify it now in my situation, in my life, and do it in such a way that all will know it is of thee."[8]

---

[7]Hallesby, *Prayer*, 131-32.

[8]I have written on prayer at greater length in a number of my other books, and sections of the preceding chapter are based upon them. See *Philippians: An Expositional Commentary* (Grand Rapids: Zondervan, 1971), 273-79; "Is Prayer a Problem?" (Philadelphia: Evangelical Foundation, 1974); *The Sermon on the Mount* (Grand Rapids: Zondervan, 1972), 183-237; and *How to Live the Christian Life* (Chicago: Moody, 1982), 17-24.

CHAPTER 15

GOD TALKING TO US

D wight L. Moody once said, "In prayer we talk to God. In Bible study, God talks to us, and we had better let God do most of the talking."[1] The Bible stresses the importance of Bible study too. In the first psalm, David speaks of Bible study as the essential source of blessing in the religious life:

Blessed is the man
who walks not in the counsel of the wicked,
nor stands in the way of sinners,
nor sits in the seat of scoffers;
but his delight is in the law of the LORD,
and on his law he meditates day and night.
He is like a tree
planted by streams of water
that yields its fruit in its season,
and its leaf does not wither.
In all that he does, he prospers. (Ps 1:1-3)

In Psalm 119, the author speaks of Bible study as the secret of holy living:

How can a young man keep his way pure?
By guarding it according to your word. . . .
I have stored up your word in my heart,
that I might not sin against you. (Ps. 119:9, 11)

---

[1]Quoted by Reuben A. Torrey, who knew Moody personally, in *How to Succeed in the Christian Life* (Westwood, NJ: Revell, 1975), 49.

In the New Testament Paul speaks of Bible study as the key to becoming equipped for Christian service: "All Scripture is breathed out by God and profitable for teaching, for reproof, for correction, and for training in righteousness, that the man of God may be complete, equipped for every good work" (2 Tim 3:16-17).

MISUSE OF THE BIBLE

Unfortunately, human beings have a knack for abusing the gifts of God. Bishop John C. Ryle of Liverpool says that Christendom as a whole has neglected and abused the Bible. He observed that in his day there were more Bibles, and there had been more Bible selling and distribution, than at any previous period of Christian history. Yet many if not most who possessed the Bible simply did not read it.[2] That is not something uniquely characteristic of England in the latter half of the nineteenth century, however. It is a characteristic of our day also. We have billions of Bibles in many scores of translations. Yet millions scarcely read God's Word. Instead, they allow activities to surfeit their lives and stunt their souls.

The Bible is sometimes misused in other ways as well. One way in which it is misused is to consider it an end in itself and thus fail to allow it to accomplish its primary purpose—to lead us to a knowledge of God through faith in Jesus Christ. Sometimes this happens in biblical scholarship. The nineteenth-century "historical Jesus" movement is an example. This movement was a century-long attempt to get behind the Jesus of the New Testament, who was regarded as the faith product of the early church, to the actual historical Jesus, who was to be stripped of all "unhistorical" supernatural elements. This effort was prodigious, but it produced nothing lasting. In failing to be led by the Bible to the true, New Testament Jesus, scholars succeeded only in producing a Jesus made in their own image. Rationalists discovered him to be a great teacher of ethics. Socialists viewed him as a revolutionary. Radicals, such as Bruno Bauer, denied that he even existed. At length Albert Schweitzer put an end to the search with his devastating critique in *The Quest of the Historical Jesus*.[3] Scholarship had made the Gospels an end in themselves. The Bible had become a book to be weighed and manipulated rather than to be believed and obeyed.

---

[2]John Charles Ryle, *Practical Religion* (1879; repr., Cambridge: James Clarke & Co., 1959), 70.

[3]This movement is discussed at greater length in book 1, chapter 7, "The Jesus of History." In recent years there has been a revival of the historical Jesus quest, but along much sounder lines. See Boice, "New Vistas in Historical Jesus Research," *Christianity Today*, March 15, 1968, 3-6.

We may have something similar in the evangelicals' use of translations. Clearly, translations are necessary (for few Christians know Greek and Hebrew, the original languages of the Bible), and a good, accurate, contemporary translation is invaluable in any serious program of Bible study. But at times there is an unfortunate and unhealthy preoccupation with the "best" or "latest" or "most contemporary" translation that titillates our interest but does little to actually get us into the principles of God's Word and produce obedience to them. The small variations between different texts prove more interesting than the teaching itself. In this way obedience to Christ and a desire to know him better are sidelined.

I believe that there is no need for another English translation in our day. We have all varieties. Any taste can be satisfied. I even believe that much of our current interest in translations is traceable to the publishers who encourage it for commercial purposes. The immense amounts of effort expended on producing such translations would be far better spent in getting the Bible into the languages of men and women who have not yet seen even one version of the Scriptures.

In light of these problems, Jesus' warning to the Jews of his day is quite relevant. He said, "You search the Scriptures because you think that in them you have eternal life; and it is they that bear witness to me, yet you refuse to come to me that you may have life" (Jn 5:39-40).

No one could fault the Jews for their meticulous study of the Scriptures. The scribes, whose work it was to copy the scrolls, subjected the pages of the Bible to the closest scrutiny. They gave attention to every syllable. They even counted the words and letters so that they knew which came in the middle of the page and how many of each a given page should have. We can be thankful for this care in one sense, for the accuracy of our present Old Testament texts is a result. Nevertheless, in most cases the reaction of the scribe to the Word of God stopped with the copying. And those who used their texts, being possessed of the same mentality, looked at the finest points but missed the Bible's message. The words were accurate, but what is the value of these without meanings? What is the value of letters if these are not inscribed on an obedient heart?

Many who are reading this book have a high degree of biblical knowledge. You can name the twelve apostles, the cities Paul visited, and perhaps even the Hebrew kings. But have you missed what the Scriptures have to teach about sin (your sin), justification (your justification), the Christian life (your Christian life), and obedience (your obedience)?

STUDYING THE BIBLE

The importance of the Bible and the proper approach to Bible study arise from what the Bible is: the very Word of God. That the Bible is "breathed out by God" (2 Tim 3:16) makes it utterly unlike any other book ever written by any man or woman. While the Bible is also a human product, God taught the writers what to say and guided them in their writing. The result? Precisely what God desired to be written.

When we read the Bible, we are not reading the thoughts of men and women like ourselves, which may or may not be true. Rather, we are reading the Word of God to us. And just because it is the Word of *God*, we cannot read it and be indifferent or unchanged. Ryle writes,

> When you read [the Bible], you are not reading the self-taught compositions of poor imperfect men like yourself, but the words of the eternal God. When you hear it, you are not listening to the erring opinions of short-lived mortals, but to the unchanging mind of the King of kings. The men who were employed to indite the Bible spoke not of themselves. They "spake as they were moved by the Holy Ghost" (2 Pet 1:21). All other books in the world, however good and useful in their way, are more or less defective. The more you look at them the more you see their defects and blemishes. The Bible alone is absolutely perfect. From beginning to end it is "the Word of God."[4]

But the Bible is not remote, impersonal information that dropped in from outer space. The living God continues to speak to his people through it. So we approach the Bible devotionally, as though it were a holy place where we meet and have fellowship with God.

God speaks in Scripture through the Holy Spirit. That is why the subject of Bible study recurs here, in book three of this volume, rather than being exhausted in book one. In book one, I considered the role of the Spirit primarily in the inspiration of the Bible. Here I discuss his role in teaching us from what he inspired. Paul writes in 1 Corinthians that in ourselves we are unable to understand spiritual truth, even when it is recorded in the pages of the Word of God. But the Spirit of truth speaks to us from its pages to bring understanding.

---

[4]Ryle, *Practical Religion*, 71. I have discussed the nature of the Bible, its claims about itself, and its effects on those who read it, as well as the evidence for its being the Word of God, in book 1, chapter 3, "The Bible." Subsequent chapters discuss inerrancy, modern biblical criticism, and the basic principles according to which the Bible should be studied.

As it is written,

> "What no eye has seen, nor ear heard,
>   nor the heart of man imagined,
> what God has prepared for those who love him"—

these things God has revealed to us through the Spirit. For the Spirit searches everything, even the depths of God. For who knows a person's thoughts except the spirit of that person, which is in him? So also no one comprehends the thoughts of God except the Spirit of God. Now we have received not the spirit of the world, but the Spirit who is from God, that we might understand the things freely given us by God. And we impart this in words not taught by human wisdom but taught by the Spirit, interpreting spiritual truths to those who are spiritual. (1 Cor 2:9-13)

"What is the right way to study the Bible?" There are those who confess that the Bible is the Word of God and who want to meet the living God in its pages but who perhaps are not quite sure how to go about it. Here are five answers to their important question.

1. Study the Bible daily (Acts 17:11). Certainly we can turn to the Bible more than once each day or, equally, there may be occasions when legitimate concerns consume the daily time we would normally spend studying. But we should discipline our lives to include a daily period of Bible study, just as we discipline ourselves to have regular periods for sleep, for brushing our teeth, for meals, and so on. In fact, the comparison with regular mealtimes is a good one, for these are necessary if the body is to be healthy and if good work is to be done. On occasion we may miss a meal, but normally we should not. In the same way, we must feed regularly on God's Word if we are to become and remain spiritually strong.

What happens if we neglect such daily Bible reading? We grow indifferent to God and lax in spiritual things. We throw ourselves open to temptation and the sin which can easily follow.

The regular time we set aside for Bible study may be long—for those who are mature in the faith and who have time for such study, perhaps an hour or two. It may be shorter—for those who are new in the faith or who lead tight schedules, perhaps only ten or fifteen minutes. Whatever the length of time, it should be fixed and at a set period of the day.

When should this be? Again, this may vary from person to person. Many have found that the best time is at the very beginning of the day. Torrey writes,

Wherever it is possible, the best time for this study is immediately after arising in the morning. The worst time of all is the last thing at night. Of course, it is well to spend a little while Bible reading just before we retire, in order that God's voice may be the last to which we listen, but the bulk of our Bible study should be done at an hour when our minds are clearest and strongest. Whatever time is set apart for Bible study should be kept sacredly for that purpose.[5]

2. Study the Bible systematically. Some people read the Bible at random, dipping here or there. This may be characteristic of the way they do most things in life, but it is a mistake in Bible study (as well as in most other things). It inevitably leads to a lack of proportion and depth, which is so often characteristic of Christians today. A far better system is a regular, disciplined study of certain books of the Bible or even of the Bible as a whole.

New Christians could begin with one of the Gospels, perhaps the Gospel of John or Mark. After this they could go on to Acts, Ephesians, Galatians, Romans, or an Old Testament book such as Genesis. It is always valuable to read and meditate on the Psalms.

Certain procedures should be followed during study. First, the book itself should be read through carefully as many as four or five times, perhaps one of these times aloud. Each time something new will strike you.

Second, divide the book into its chief sections, just as we divide modern books into chapters (not necessarily the same chapters as in our Bibles), subsections, and paragraphs. At this stage, the object should be to see which verses belong together, what subjects are covered, and what the sequence of subjects is.

Third, these sections should be related to one another: Which are the main sections or subjects? Which are introductory? Which are excursuses? Applications? At this stage one should be developing an outline of the book, and should be able to answer such questions as, what does this book say? To whom was it written? Why was it written? If you were studying Romans, for example, you should be able to say, "This book was written to the church at Rome, but also to churches in all places and at all times. It says that the human race is lost in sin and that the answer to that sin is the righteousness of God revealed in Jesus Christ. Its purpose is to explain this gospel. A minor purpose was to alert the Romans to Paul's desire to visit them on his way to a future ministry in Spain."

---

[5]Torrey, *How to Succeed*, 50.

You can now proceed to a more detailed study of the individual sections. What is the main subject of each section? What is said about it? Why is it said? To whom? What are the conclusions that follow from it? It is helpful in this study to watch the small connecting words like *but, because, then, and, since,* and *therefore.*

Last, you can study key words. How do you go about it? Begin by looking at other passages in the same book in which the word occurs. You can find these by your own reading or by using a concordance in which important verses containing such words are listed. Simple concordances are in the back of many Bibles.

Suppose you were studying Romans 3:21-26 and wanted to learn more about the important word *righteousness,* with which the section begins. One key verse is Romans 10:3, in which the righteousness of God is distinguished from our righteousness. Also, Romans 1:17 says that the righteousness of God is made known in the gospel. In all, *righteousness* is used thirty-five times in this one letter alone, and most of these uses throw light on one another. At this point you may also observe the use of the word in other books of the Bible, perhaps using the chain-reference system that some Bibles provide. You can also use the dictionary. Some large dictionaries contain the derivations of words, which also throw light on their meanings.

Normally it is only at the end of a personal, inductive system of Bible study such as this that the comments of others on the text should be considered. Where these are used, good commentaries on individual books of the Bible will generally be found more helpful than skimpier one-volume commentaries on the whole of the Old and New Testaments.

3. Study the Bible comprehensively. Alongside serious, in-depth study of one book or section of the Bible, there should also be an attempt to become acquainted with the whole Bible. This means reading it comprehensively. True, many parts of the Bible will not appeal to us at first. This is natural. But if we never make an attempt to become acquainted with them, we limit our growth and may even warp our understanding. Paul told Timothy, "*All* Scripture is breathed out by God and profitable for teaching, for reproof, for correction, and for training in righteousness" (2 Tim 3:16, my emphasis).

Ryle's testimony on this point is that "it is by far the best plan to begin the Old and New Testaments at the same time—to read each straight through to the end, and then begin again." He acknowledges that this is a matter of individual preference, but he says, "I can only say it has been my own plan for nearly forty years, and I have never seen cause to alter it."[6]

4. Study the Bible prayerfully. Doing this provides the remedy for studying the Bible for its own sake, discussed earlier in this chapter. By prayer we can avoid the mere formalism of the scribes. In true Bible study we first ask the Holy Spirit to open our minds to understand his truth, and then obey it as he applies it to our lives.

The author of Psalm 119 indicates the proper attitude when he writes,

> Deal bountifully with your servant,
>   that I may live and keep your word.
> Open my eyes, that I may behold
>   wondrous things out of your law. (Ps 119:17-18)

What will a prayer like this accomplish? It makes us conscious that we are actually meeting with God in our reading and not merely going through some prescribed religious ritual. After we pray we must say to ourselves, "God is now going to speak to me," and then we must read to hear what he will say. There is probably nothing that will make Bible study more exciting than this—to know that as we read, God is actually speaking to us personally and is teaching us. This makes Bible study and the prayer that accompanies it a time of personal communion with him.

5. Finally, study the Bible obediently. Earlier I suggested a number of questions that should be asked if we want to understand a given passage of Scripture. But in that list some of the most important questions were left out. How does this passage and its teachings apply to me? Does this instruct me in something I should do? In something I should not do? What does it tell me about the will of God and how I can please God and serve him better? James had this in mind when he instructed those to whom he was writing, "But be doers of the word, and not hearers only, deceiving yourselves" (Jas 1:22).

God requires obedience. If he instructs us, it is so we will obey him and grow. What should we do? "Cultivate prompt, exact, unquestioning, joyous obedience to every command that it is evident from its context applies to you. Be on the lookout for new orders from your King. Blessing lies in the direction of obedience to them. God's commands are but signboards that mark the road to present success and blessedness and to eternal glory."[7] If we are not willing to obey

---

[6]Ryle, *Practical Religion*, 96.
[7]Torrey, *How to Succeed*, 60.

God, we will not even understand what we read (Jn 7:17) and Bible study will become dull, oppressive, and meaningless. We will even drift away from God and find ourselves criticizing his Word. We will find ourselves susceptible to critical theories that demean it. But if we are willing to obey, God will help us understand his truths and lead us to others as well.

One writer has observed, "Serious Bible study does not consist merely in digging into the Word, but it demands a translation of that Word through our lives to the world. We are to be God's epistles read of all men. . . . If we take our Bible study seriously, to the extent that we will obey him, then we shall discover the way of real spiritual blessing, and we shall be successful men of God for our Lord Jesus Christ."[8]

---

[8]Ralph L. Keiper, "The Rewards of Bible Study," in *Why and How to Study the Scriptures*, by James Montgomery Boice and Ralph L. Keiper (Philadelphia: Evangelical Ministries, 1977), 29.

CHAPTER 16

SERVING

A young man once wrote me to ask advice on how to remain a strong Christian during his years in college. He was in his first year at Harvard University, to which he had come from the Midwest. He was worried that pressures of study and the dominant secular viewpoint in many fields might undermine his faith. As I thought, three things came to mind. So I wrote that he should arrange his schedule to provide for these elements: (1) a period of daily Bible study and prayer; (2) regular fellowship and worship with other Christians, both with his peers (perhaps in a dorm Bible study or in some other student meeting of Christians) and in a weekly church service; and (3) some form of regular service to others. I suggested that this last point could take many forms: an outreach to non-Christians, a tutoring project for the disadvantaged, or social service work, for example. Only in such activity do we get our minds off ourselves and onto others and their problems, as Christ indicated we should do if we are to be his disciples (Phil 2:4).

If we neglect such works, we will inevitably be impoverished. Reuben A. Torrey once put it, "If you wish to be a happy Christian, if you wish to be a strong Christian, if you wish to be a Christian who is mighty in prayer, begin at once to work for the Master and never let a day pass without doing some definite work for him."[1]

---

[1] Reuben A. Torrey, *How to Succeed in the Christian Life* (Westwood, NJ: Revell, 1975), 83.

AVOIDING AN OBLIGATION

Ephesians 2:10 occurs at the end of a series of well-known verses explaining how we are saved by the grace of God through faith, not works. But this passage immediately goes on to say quite practically, "For we are his workmanship, created in Christ Jesus for good works, which God prepared beforehand [the KJV says 'ordained'], that we should walk in them." God has a plan for every individual Christian's life, and good works are in that plan. Yet our insensitivity to God's plan or our laziness is so great that we constantly try to evade this obligation.

Some try to evade it theologically. They stress justification by grace through faith, apart from works, to such an extent that our obligation to do good works evaporates. For example, one of the most thorough treatments of Ephesians 2 in print today is a four-hundred-page analysis in which twenty-four pages are given to an examination of Ephesians 2:8-10. But this key phrase dealing with our ordination to good works receives only one paragraph of exposition.

While justification by faith, apart from works, is certainly biblical teaching, as we saw in chapter seven, this does not mean that there is no place for good works if one is justified. Ephesians 2:8-10 itself makes this strikingly clear because the word *works* occurs twice—once as that which God curses and once as that which God blesses. In Ephesians 2:9 we are told that salvation is "not a result of works, so that no one may boast." These are works that arise out of our own nature and that we might trust for salvation. But immediately after this Paul speaks of those "works" that God has appointed to be done by those who are justified.

Another attempt to evade our obligation to do good works is spiritual. Some take it to mean the good, spiritual things we know we should do as Christians—pray, read the Bible, witness. While these aspects of the Christian life are indeed valuable, they are not really "good works" in the sense that Paul is speaking. If Paul was thinking of witnessing, for example, he would have said that God has ordained us to be witnesses.

The third way in which the implication of Ephesians 2:10 is avoided is organizational. How often we stress our immense social programs and plans for social action! It seems strange to say that an emphasis on evangelical social action, which is greatly needed and long overdue in our generation, can actually stifle good works. But it happens quite simply. People hear of these problems, are impressed with their scope, conclude that the only way they can ever adequately be dealt with is by massive organizational effort, and then wrongly neglect the good they can do as individuals.

We need good theology. We need prayer, Bible study, and other elements of a healthy Christian life and ministry. We must establish and support effective social action programs. But these do not replace being doers of good works individually. Apart from the life and ministry of Jesus himself, Christians are to be the best thing that ever happened to this world. We are to be sources of constant good, sharing, love, and service so that the world might be blessed and some (we do not forget this) might come to faith in our Savior.

The Lord pointed to this need in the Sermon on the Mount when he called his followers "the salt of the earth" and "the light of the world." Salt is good and light is valued. So let your saltiness be tasted and your light seen, he argued. And do this that the world "may see your good works and give glory to your Father who is in heaven" (Mt 5:13-16).

THE COMPASSION OF CHRIST

What Jesus prescribed for others he did no less himself. Today we tend to focus on his teaching and marvel at it, as people also did in his own day (Mt 7:28-29). But when we read the Gospels with the subject of good works in mind, we are immediately impressed with how major a part of Christ's ministry doing good was.

This was the note on which Jesus began his ministry when reading from the scroll of Isaiah in the synagogue at Nazareth. He had been asked to take part in the service by reading a lesson for the day. So he turned to that part of Isaiah's prophecy concerning the coming of the Messiah that says,

> The Spirit of the Lord is upon me,
>> because he has anointed me
>> to proclaim good news to the poor.
> He has sent me to proclaim liberty to the captives
>> and recovering of sight to the blind,
>> to set at liberty those who are oppressed,
> to proclaim the year of the Lord's favor. (Lk 4:18-19; quoting Is 61:1-2)

This has overtones of a spiritual ministry, of course, for eyes were opened to truth and captives to sin were set free. But that is not the whole of the matter, as the remainder of the chapter shows. The second half of Luke 4 records the beginning of Christ's miracles: the casting out of demons and the healing of

Peter's mother-in-law. It then says, "Now when the sun was setting, all those who had any who were sick with various diseases brought them to him, and he laid his hands on every one of them and healed them" (Lk 4:40).

Again, when John the Baptist was in prison and began to have doubts about Jesus being the Messiah, he sent disciples to ask Jesus about it. Jesus referred to this same passage and directed John to consider the healing of the blind, lame, deaf, and lepers that Jesus had done as the prophecy's fulfillment.

These works were not just done to get people to believe in him. He simply had compassion for those who were sick, hungry, or needy. Not all he healed believed, at least we are not told that they did. Not all were even friends. He healed the ear of the servant of the high priest who had come to arrest him in the garden of Gethsemane and who had been attacked by Peter in a misguided attempt to save Jesus (Lk 22:50-51). He taught that good should be done even to our enemies by reminding us that God "makes his sun rise on the evil and on the good, and sends rain on the just and on the unjust" (Mt 5:45). In the parable of the good Samaritan, he taught that good should be done even to those who are culturally despised (Lk 10:30-37).

It was not just miraculous works that Jesus performed either. If that were true, we might conclude that true good works are beyond us. Apparently, the Lord and his disciples kept a fund out of which they gave to those who were needy (Jn 13:29).

Jesus also encouraged others to do good works. He noticed a poor widow putting two small copper coins, which together only added up to a penny, in the temple poor box. "This poor widow," he said, "has put in more than all those who are contributing to the offering box. For they all contributed out of their abundance, but she out of her poverty has put in everything she had, all she had to live on" (Mk 12:43-44). On the other hand, Mary of Bethany broke a box of costly ointment to anoint his feet just before his arrest and crucifixion. Judas and perhaps others objected, but he replied, "Leave her alone. Why do you trouble her? She has done a beautiful thing to me. For you always have the poor with you, and whenever you will, you can do good for them. But you will not always have me" (Mk 14:6-7). And when Zacchaeus was converted and promised to give half of his goods to the poor and repay fourfold any he had cheated, Jesus responded, "Today salvation has come to this house" (Lk 19:9).

THE SALT OF THE EARTH

The early Christian communities were noted for being generous and caring for one another and for the poor. After about three thousand were saved following Peter's great speech at Pentecost, we are told that "all who believed were together and had all things in common. And they were selling their possessions and belongings and distributing the proceeds to all, as any had need" (Acts 2:44-45). After the church had increased even further, it is recorded that "there was not a needy person among them, for as many as were owners of lands or houses sold them and brought the proceeds of what was sold and laid it at the apostles' feet, and it was distributed to each as any had need" (Acts 4:34-35).

This selling of goods and holding of all things in common does not overturn the right of private property. This right is recognized in Acts 5:4. But this was a generous church all the same. Other churches were also generous in other ways.

In Acts 6 we are told of the choice of the first church officers (apart from the apostles who were picked and commissioned by Christ). The duties of these deacons, as they were called, were to care for the sick and poor, and to distribute goods to them as they had need (Acts 6:1-6). Among these was Stephen, the first martyr.

In a later chapter of Acts we are told of Dorcas who "was full of good works and acts of charity" (Acts 9:36). When she died, there was great mourning and all the widows whom she had helped came "weeping, and showing tunics and other garments that Dorcas made while she was with them" (Acts 9:39). Peter raised Dorcas from the dead. Another person noted for good works in Acts 9 was Simon the tanner who was a resident of Joppa (Acts 9:43). He made his house available to Peter when Peter was in the city. In the next chapter, Cornelius, the Roman centurion, is praised as one who "gave alms generously to the people, and prayed continually to God," even before his conversion (Acts 10:2). In Acts 12:12 we are introduced to Mary, the mother of John Mark, who made her house available for Christian meetings, in this case an all-night prayer meeting.

Several times in Acts we read of collections being taken to aid the poor. On one occasion this was done in response to a famine in Jerusalem (Acts 11:27-30). On another, it was an offering from the Gentile churches to the Jerusalem poor (Acts 24:17; compare 1 Cor 16:1-4; 2 Cor 8:1–9:5).

Apparently, the charitable instincts of the early church carried over into the period of the apologists, for they often pointed to the goodness of Christians as part of their defense of the faith. The Athenian philosopher Aristides wrote this about Christians to Hadrian:

> They do not commit adultery or immorality; they do not bear false witness, or embezzle, nor do they covet what is not theirs. They honor father and mother, and do good to those who are their neighbors. Whenever they are judges, they judge uprightly. They do not worship idols made in the image of man. Whatever they do not wish that others should do to them, they in turn do not do; and they do not eat the food sacrificed to idols. Those who oppress them they exhort and make them their friends. They do good to their enemies. Their wives, O king, are pure as virgins, and their daughters are modest. Their men abstain from all unlawful sexual contact and from impurity, in the hope of recompense that is to come in another world. . . . They love one another; the widow's needs are not ignored, and they rescue the orphan from the person who does him violence. He who has gives to him who has not, ungrudgingly and without boasting. When the Christians find a stranger, they bring him to their homes and rejoice over him as a true brother. They do not call brothers those who are bound by blood ties alone, but those who are brethren after the Spirit and in God. When one of their poor passes away from the world, each provides for his burial according to his ability. If they hear of any of their number who are imprisoned or oppressed for the name of the Messiah, they all provide for his needs, and if it is possible to redeem him, they set him free. If they find poverty in their midst, and they do not have spare food, they fast two or three days in order that the needy might be supplied with the necessities.[2]

As Christianity made its way in the Roman world, the impact of its compassion was felt. The cruel sports of the arena were checked. Laws were passed to protect slaves, prisoners, and women. The exposure of infants was outlawed. Hospitals and orphanages were founded. The status of underprivileged people was upgraded. The progress was not always constant. But this was the general direction.

The same concerns were particularly evident during the Reformation and in the modern missionary movement. The missionary movement established hospitals and schools literally around the world. Even today, many leaders in nearly every independent nation of Africa acknowledge receiving their early training and motivation to serve their country in mission schools.

---

[2]Helen H. Harris, *The Newly Recovered Apology of Aristides* (London: Hodder and Stoughton, 1893); cited in Sherwood Eliot Wirt, *The Social Conscience of the Evangelical* (New York: Harper and Row, 1968), 29-30.

What of today? The situation is confused by the proliferation of government services. Social Security, Medicare, unemployment, and various other social programs preempt what many Christians did previously, doing it better in total resources but not necessarily better in compassion or personalized care. Yet there are ample opportunities for those who are alert to the need to do good works. Groups of Christians, such as those meeting weekly in home Bible studies, are particularly effective. I have watched Bible study groups in my own church help people move from one apartment to another or from an apartment to a retirement home. Some have taken turns staying overnight in a home where someone was sick and needed care. They have collected food for those in need, including some inner-city Christian workers. They have collected clothing, given blood, cleaned apartments, transported the sick to hospitals for care or treatment, and done other such things. Many simply work hard in jobs through which others are benefited.

Throughout history Christians have truly been "the salt of the earth" in precisely the way their Lord envisioned when he instructed them to do good works. Yet this has not always been the case. If we are to be ruthlessly truthful, we have probably fallen particularly short in our own generation. Christians are no longer especially known as those who do good to others. Some of us seldom do anything particularly good for anybody.

It is easier to serve ourselves, of course. But we must not. First, the presence of good works in a Christian's life is one evidence of salvation. We now think differently than we did before our conversion and seek to serve others in ways that would never have occurred to us before. Here is evidence that we are new creatures in Christ. In chapter eight I said that a practical expression of love for others is one proof of new life presented by the apostle John. "We know that we have passed out of death into life, because we love the brothers" (1 Jn 3:14).

Second, doing good works is a means of growth in the Christian life. If we desire this, we should serve others faithfully. What happens if we do not? We become introverted, selfish, insensitive, and mean. When we do good to others our horizons are broadened, we grow in soul, and become more and more like Jesus.

Third (and how self-evident), good works are a blessing to those we serve. It is hard to put ourselves in the place of others, particularly when they are needy and we are well off. But it will help us in this regard to remember that service to others is service to our Lord.

Then the King will say to those on his right, "Come, you who are blessed by my Father, inherit the kingdom prepared for you from the foundation of the world. For I was hungry and you gave me food, I was thirsty and you gave me drink, I was a stranger and you welcomed me, I was naked and you clothed me, I was sick and you visited me, I was in prison and you came to me." (Mt 25:34-36)

Jesus is blessed through our service to others; and if he is, so are they.

Finally, God is glorified by our works. Only through his life within and by his grace are we able to do them. Some may ask, "If justification is not by works, what value do they have? And why does the Bible sometimes speak of 'rewards' for good works if these are not meritorious?" Calvin answers:

> There is no doubt that whatever is praiseworthy in works is God's grace; there is not a drop that we ought by rights to ascribe to ourselves. If we truly and earnestly recognize this, not only will all confidence in merit vanish, but the very notion. We are not dividing the credit for good works between God and man, as the Sophists do, but we are preserving it whole, complete, and unimpaired for the Lord. To man we may assign only this: that he pollutes and contaminates by his impurity those very things which are good. For nothing proceeds from a man, however perfect he be, that is not defiled by some spot. Let the Lord, then, call to judgment the best in human works: he will indeed recognize in them his own righteousness but man's dishonor and shame! Good works, then, are pleasing to God and are not unfruitful for their doers. But they receive by way of reward the most ample benefits of God, not because they so deserve but because God's kindness has of itself set this value on them.[3]

If our chief end is "to glorify God, and to enjoy him forever," as the Westminster Shorter Catechism suggests, the doing of good works is an important way to fulfill the first part.

---

[3]John Calvin, *Institutes of the Christian Religion*, ed. John T. McNeill, trans. Ford Lewis Battles, 2 vols. (Philadelphia: Westminster, 1960), 1: 790-91.

PART IV

THE WORK OF GOD

And we know that for those who love God all things work together for good, for those who are called according to his purpose. For those whom he foreknew he also predestined to be conformed to the image of his Son, in order that he might be the firstborn among many brothers. And those whom he predestined he also called, and those whom he called he also justified, and those whom he justified he also glorified.

ROMANS 8:28-30

And I am sure of this, that he who began a good work in you will bring it to completion at the day of Jesus Christ.

PHILIPPIANS 1:6

Salvation belongs to the LORD!

JONAH 2:9

CHAPTER 17

CALLED BY GOD

*I*t is often pointed out that Calvin does not discuss the doctrine of election, for which he is noted, at the beginning of his *Institutes*, but rather toward the end of book three, that is, about three-quarters of the way through. Calvin did not start with some rigid preconception as to how God must have operated in saving the human race. Rather, he began as a biblical theologian, teaching what God actually has done. Only after that did he look back to see the matter in its fullest perspective: on the one hand, salvation begins in eternity past, in God's determination to save a people for himself, and, on the other hand, it continues into the eternal future, in God's final perseverance with his saints. I am going to follow the same procedure in this chapter and the next.

GOD OF BEGINNINGS

In the book of Jonah, at the end of the prophet's great prayer of deliverance there is the sentence: "Salvation is of the LORD" (Jon 2:9 KJV). This sentence is simple and profound. The origin, the end, and, indeed, the only possible source of salvation is God. Salvation begins with God's choice of us, rather than our choice of him, and continues to a successful conclusion, because God perseveres with us. Jonah's case is a perfect example. God elected him to do a work that he did not want to do: the evangelization of Nineveh. God persevered with Jonah in spite of the rebellious prophet's attempts to run away.

Though Jonah's call was to a particular ministry and not to salvation, the principle is the same. For nothing can take place spiritually in a person's life until God on the basis of his own determination calls that person to him. It would be foolish for a preacher to enter a funeral home to encourage the corpses to lead an upright life. The corpses are dead. If the words are to have any purpose, the corpses must first be made alive. After that they can respond. In the same way, the call to discipleship must begin with the act of God in making a spiritually dead person alive. The choice to do that is not with the one who is spiritually dead, but with God who alone is able to give life.

This is what new birth means. Before conversion, God says we are dead in trespasses and sins. We are alive physically and intellectually, but not spiritually. We cannot respond to spiritual stimuli. The Word of God is a hidden book; the gospel is nonsense. But then God touches us. He brings life out of death. We then believe in Jesus Christ and begin to understand the Bible. This is what it means to be called by God, and this must happen before there can be any true discipleship. Jesus said, "You did not choose me, but I chose you and appointed you that you should go and bear fruit and that your fruit should abide" (Jn 15:16).

Abraham was called. He did not choose God. He was apparently perfectly satisfied being where he was in the Mesopotamian river valley in a pagan culture. But God called him and sent him on his way to Palestine.

Moses was called even before he was a baby floating in the Nile in a basket. God said, "I am going to deliver my people from Egypt, and I am going to do it by means of this baby. I am going to protect him from Pharaoh. I am going to give him the best of the world's training and education, and then I am going to send him to Pharaoh to say, 'Let my people go.'"

It was the same with David. God put his stamp on the future king while David was still out protecting some sheep. God sent the prophet Samuel to David's home to anoint one of the sons in the family as the future king, but when Samuel arrived, David was missing. The father brought out all his sons except David. They were there in order. Samuel looked at the boys and thought how good a king the oldest son would make. His name was Eliab. But before Samuel could anoint him, God indicated that he was not the one. Next came Abinadab, who was not the future king either. Then there was Shammah, and so on until seven of Jesse's sons were presented.

Samuel said, "The LORD has not chosen these." Then he asked, "Are all your sons here?"

Jesse replied, "There remains yet the youngest, but behold, he is keeping the sheep."

Samuel said, "Send and get him, for we will not sit down till he comes here."
When David had come, the Lord said, "Arise, anoint him, for this is he."
The Bible continues the account by saying, "Then Samuel took the horn of oil
and anointed him in the midst of his brothers. And the Spirit of the LORD
rushed upon David from that day forward" (1 Sam 16:10-13). It was God who
called David.

In the New Testament God chose John the Baptist—even before he was born.
Jesus called his disciples while they were still fishermen. God called Paul when
he was in the process of persecuting Christians. In every case the call of God
was primary, and this in turn was based on God's own determination to save
and use that one.

GOD'S PURPOSE

Not only do examples help us understand this doctrine. There is also the specific
teaching of Scripture. One key passage, indeed one of the most important passages of all, is Romans 8:28-30, in which the election and calling of God are put
in a carefully expressed sequence of acts.

> And we know for those who love God all things work together for good, for those
> who are called according to his purpose. For those whom he foreknew he also
> predestined to be conformed to the image of his Son, in order that he might be
> the firstborn among many brothers. And those whom he predestined he also
> called, and those whom he called he also justified, and those whom he justified
> he also glorified.

These verses do not contain every step that might possibly be listed in God's
dealings with an individual. Nothing is said of regeneration, adoption, or sanctification. Yet although this is a truncated list, it is an orderly list that gives a
proper sequence to God's actions.

In part two of this book, I considered the application of salvation by the Holy
Spirit. But this is only the second half of God's work. A prior determination of
God precedes our awakening and spiritual growth. This is expressed in the words
his purpose, foreknew, and *predestined.* The next term in the sequence, *called,* is
the point at which this eternal determination passes over into the experience of
the individual. The overall term is *purpose,* an eternal purpose expressed first in
foreknowledge and predestination (Rom 8:29) and then, as a follow-up to that,
in calling, justification, and glorification. The remainder of the passage shows

that this work of God is certain of completion. For nothing "will be able to separate us from the love of God in Christ Jesus our Lord" (Rom 8:39).

Use of the word *foreknow* has led some to argue that election is based on foreknowledge, in the sense that God foresaw that certain people would be more responsive to the gospel than others and would therefore yield to the Holy Spirit, where others would not. As a consequence, he predestined those who would yield to salvation. These thoughts are wrong if for no other reason than because the passage does not start with the idea of foreknowledge, but rather with a statement of God's purpose to save. Arthur W. Pink writes that this wrong thinking also

> repudiates the truth of total depravity, for it argues that there is something good in some men. It takes away the independency of God, for it makes his decrees rest upon what he discovered in the creature. It completely turns things upside down, for in saying that God foresaw certain sinners would believe in Christ, and that because of this, he predestinated them unto salvation, it is the very reverse of the truth. Scripture affirms that God, in his high sovereignty, singled out certain ones to be recipients of his distinguishing favors (Acts 13:48), and therefore he determined to bestow upon them the gift of faith.[1]

The debate can be ended by answering, What does the word *foreknowledge* mean in Scripture? If I said I had foreknowledge, I would mean I had advance information of something that was going to happen. Having this I could take some particular action. But God is not a creature of time as we are. He sees the end from the beginning, and the reason he sees things as they are is that he determined them. All history is eternally present to God.

We should also note that the word *know* is characteristically used in the Old and New Testaments to mean "to look upon with favor" or even "to love." "And the LORD said to Moses, 'This very thing that you have spoken I will do, for you have found favor in my sight, and I know you by name'" (Ex 33:17).

> You only have I known
> > of all the families of the earth;
> therefore I will punish you
> > for all your iniquities. (Amos 3:2)

"Then will I declare to them, 'I never knew you; depart from me, you workers of lawlessness'" (Mt 7:23). "I am the good shepherd. I know my own and my own know me" (Jn 10:14). "But if anyone loves God, he is known by God" (1 Cor 8:3).

---

[1] Arthur W. Pink, *The Attributes of God* (Grand Rapids: Baker Book House, n.d.), 20.

"God's firm foundation stands, bearing this seal: 'The Lord knows those who are his'" (2 Tim 2:19).

The word *foreknowledge* itself is never used in reference to events or actions— that is, as advance knowledge of what one would or might do—but always of persons, whose lives are affected by that foreknowledge, rather than the other way around.

Aside from Romans, there are only three passages in Scripture where the word *foreknowledge* is used, and they all involve the idea of election. The first is Acts 2:23. "This Jesus, delivered up according to the definite plan and foreknowledge of God, you crucified and killed by the hands of lawless men." In this verse it is not the crucifixion that was foreknown by God (though, of course, he did foreknow it in our sense of the word as well), but rather Jesus himself. The verse teaches that God had fixed a plan as a result of which we would be saved, and that Jesus was elected to implement that plan.

Romans 11:2 is the second passage. "God has not rejected his people whom he foreknew." Again, it is a people and not their actions that are said to be the object of God's foreknowledge. In spite of what appears to be the case in some instances, none of those who are the elect of God will be lost.

The third text is 1 Peter 1:2. "Chosen and destined [elect according to the foreknowledge of God, KJV] by God the Father and sanctified by the Spirit" (RSV). Those chosen are the "exiles of the Dispersion" mentioned in the previous verse. God has elected these to salvation.

It is the same in Romans 8:28-30. Persons are foreknown, and the result is their predestination to an effectual calling, justification and glorification. Pink asks,

> In view of these passages (and there are no more) what scriptural ground is there for anyone saying God "foreknew" the acts of certain ones, viz., their "repenting and believing," and that because of those acts he elected them unto salvation? The answer is, None whatever. Scripture never speaks of repentance and faith as being foreseen or foreknown by God. Truly, he did know from all eternity that certain ones would repent and believe, yet this is not what Scripture refers to as the object of God's "foreknowledge." . . . God foreknows what will be because he has decreed what shall be. It is therefore a reversing of the order of Scripture, a putting of the cart before the horse, to affirm that God elects because he foreknows people. The truth is, he "foreknows" because he has elected.[2]

---

[2]Ibid., 24.

GOD'S CALL

God's eternal, electing purpose to save to himself a people chosen out of all nations does not remain in eternity past. It also has a present expression as described in Romans 8:30: "And those whom he predestined he also called." In theology, the call of God is usually termed an "effectual call" to distinguish it from a human call that might or might not be effective. The situation here is quite parallel to that involving the word *foreknow*. On the human level *foreknow* means advance knowledge, while in God's case, where time references do not enter in, it means elective favor or choice. Similarly, *to call* on the human level may make something possible, but it does not actually bring it about. By contrast, in God's case it does.

Take, as an example, a summons to appear in court. A summons is a form of call, a serious one at that. It has the authority of the law and the power of the state behind it. Yet even this extremely serious call does not actually have the power to bring the person summoned to court. The person may hide from the law, jump bail, skip the country, or otherwise thwart the court's intention. Not so with God. In God's case, the call actually brings about the response of the one summoned.

Many verses show this meaning of the word, but none more clearly than those in Romans 8. John Murray writes,

> Nothing clinches the argument for this feature of the call more clearly than the teaching of Romans 8:28-30 where the call is stated to be according to God's purpose and finds its place in the center of that unbreakable chain of events which has its beginning in the divine foreknowledge and its consummation in glorification. This is just saying that the effectual call insures perseverance because it is grounded in the security of God's purpose and grace.[3]

Those who have been chosen by God and brought to faith in Christ by the power of this summons are those "called to belong to Jesus Christ" (Rom 1:6). They are "called to be saints" (Rom 1:7), that is, to be set apart to God by his call. They are to live holy lives. This is the point of Paul's admonition to the believers in Ephesus, "I therefore, a prisoner for the Lord, urge you to walk in a manner worthy of the calling to which you have been called" (Eph 4:1).

Lazarus was dead before Christ called him from the tomb. He was impervious to any call. If you or I were present, we could have called loudly, persuasively,

---

[3]John Murray, *Redemption Accomplished and Applied* (Grand Rapids: Eerdmans, 1955), 91.

and eloquently, but Lazarus would still not have responded. When Jesus called, it was different. His call had power to bring the dead to life. In the same way his call quickens those who have been chosen by God to be his people. And none fail to be quickened! As Jesus said, "My sheep hear my voice, and I know them, and they follow me" (Jn 10:27).

THE BENEFITS OF THE DOCTRINE

Some people believe that election is a useless doctrine and perhaps even pernicious. They say it encourages irresponsibility or even sin. Actually it does nothing of the sort. People are responsible before God for what they do, regardless of whether God elects them to salvation or not. They are not judged by God for failing to do what they cannot do, but for failing to do the good they can do and for committing evil that they do not need to do. God forbids such conduct and has established laws of cause and effect to hinder it (Rom 1:24-32). Election does not affect these facts one way or the other.

On the positive side, there are great benefits for Christians.

First, election eliminates boasting within Christian ranks. Non-Christians or those who do not understand election often suppose the opposite, and those who believe in election do sometimes appear smug. But this is a travesty. God tells us explicitly that he has chosen to save a people to himself by grace entirely apart from any merit or receptivity in them, precisely so that pride will be eliminated: "For by grace you have been saved through faith. And this is not your own doing; it is the gift of God, not a result of works, so that no one may boast" (Eph 2:8-9). Salvation is of grace so that the glory might be God's.

Second, this doctrine encourages love for God. If we have a part in salvation, then our love for God is diminished by just that amount. If it is all of God, then our love for him must be boundless. We did not seek him; he sought us. When he sought us, we ran from him. When he came to us in the person of his Son, we killed him. Yet still he came; still he elected a great number of recalcitrant rebels to salvation. "God shows his love for us in that while we were still sinners, Christ died for us" (Rom 5:8).

Finally, the doctrine of election has this benefit also: it encourages us in evangelism. It is often thought to do the opposite. If God is going to save certain individuals, then he will save them, and there is no point in having anything to do with it. But it does not work that way. God's election does not exclude the use of means through which he calls, and the Bible explicitly tells us that the proclamation of the gospel by believers is that means (1 Cor 1:21; see Rom 1:16-17).

Moreover, it is only this that gives us hope of success as we proclaim the gospel. If the heart of a sinner is as hard and as opposed to God and his ways as the Bible declares it to be, and if God does not elect the individual, then what hope could we possibly have in witnessing? If God cannot call effectively, then certainly we cannot. But if he is doing such a work in the world, then we can go boldly knowing that all whom God has determined to save will come to him. We do not know who they are. The only way we know the elect is through their response to the gospel and their living of the Christian life that follows that call. But we can call them boldly, knowing that those who are called by God will surely come.

CHAPTER 18

THE KEEPING
POWER OF GOD

> There are two points in religion on which the teaching of the Bible is very plain
> and distinct. One of these points is the fearful danger of the ungodly; the other
> is the perfect safety of the righteous. One is the happiness of those who are con-
> verted; the other is the misery of those who are unconverted. One is the blessedness
> of being in the way to heaven; the other is the wretchedness of being in the way
> to hell.[1]

These words by England's Bishop Ryle introduce the subject of God's perseverance
with his saints and tie this chapter to the last. The doctrine of perseverance
means that God, who has begun a good work in electing and then calling an
individual to salvation, according to his own good purpose, will certainly keep
on in that purpose until the person elected and called is brought home to the
blessedness that has been prepared for him or her. If a person could be saved
and then lost, there would be no blessedness in salvation, only anxiety. There
could be no safety or happiness. But because God is doing the work and because
it is God's nature to finish what he starts, there can be perfect joy for the one
who trusts him.

Perseverance is the fifth of the five distinguishing points of Calvinism. It is
linked to the other points and gets its strength from them. These have sometimes
been expressed by an acrostic, TULIP, though the words suggested by those
letters are not necessarily the best expressions of the doctrines. *T* stands for *total
depravity*, the doctrine that the unregenerate can never do anything to satisfy

---

[1] J. C. Ryle, *Old Paths* (1877; reprint ed., Cambridge: James Clarke & Co., 1977), 476.

God's standards of righteousness and, in fact, do not even try. *U* stands for *unconditional election*, the doctrine considered in the last chapter. It means that salvation begins with God's choice of us and not our choice of God. *L* stands for *limited atonement*, the doctrine that Christ's death was a real atonement for the specific sins of his people, as a result of which they are truly saved. It was not merely a general atonement that makes salvation possible but actually saves no one. *I* stands for *irresistible grace*, the doctrine that we have referred to in the preceding chapter as effectual calling. Finally, *P* stands for the *perseverance of the saints*. None of those called by God and redeemed by the Lord Jesus Christ will be lost. As God stands at the beginning and middle of this plan of salvation, so does he stand at the end.

These doctrines were not invented by Calvin, nor were they characteristic of his thought alone during the Reformation period. These are biblical truths taught by Jesus and confirmed by Paul, Peter, and all the other Old and New Testament writers. Augustine defended these doctrines against the denials of Pelagius. Luther believed them. So did Zwingli. That is, they believed what Calvin believed and later systematized in his influential *Institutes of the Christian Religion*. The Puritans were Calvinists; it was through them and their teaching that both England and Scotland experienced the greatest and most pervasive national revivals the world has ever seen. In that number were the heirs of John Knox: Thomas Cartwright, Richard Sibbes, Richard Baxter, Matthew Henry, John Owen, and others. In America, others were influenced by men such as Jonathan Edwards, Cotton Mather, and, later, George Whitefield.

In more recent times, the modern missionary movement received nearly all its initial impetus and direction from those in the Calvinistic tradition. The list includes William Carey, John Ryland, Henry Martyn, Robert Moffat, David Livingstone, John G. Paton, John R. Mott, and others. For all these the doctrines of grace were not an appendage to Christian thought but were, rather, central, firing and forming their preaching and missionary efforts.

WHAT PERSEVERANCE IS NOT

Before looking at the biblical teaching regarding perseverance, let us consider what the doctrine is not. First, perseverance does not mean that Christians are free of all spiritual danger just because they are Christians. On the contrary, their danger is even greater, for the world and devil will be active opponents for them.

Consider Christ's prayer for his disciples before his crucifixion.

> And now I am no longer in the world, but they are in the world, and I am coming
> to you. Holy Father, keep them in your name, which you have given me, that they
> may be one, even as we are one. . . . I have given them your word, and the world
> has hated them because they are not of the world, just as I am not of the world.
> I do not ask that you take them out of the world, but that you keep them from
> the evil one. (Jn 17:11, 14-15)

These words are ominous in the context of John's Gospel, for "the evil one" was
even then entering into Judas, and "the world" was to condemn Christ to death
before morning. This was the deadly environment in which the disciples were
to be left. Left to themselves they would surely perish. But Christ prays for them.
Although their danger is great, they are to be kept by God's power.

Second, perseverance does not mean that Christians are free from falling into
sin just because they are Christians. We might reason this way on the basis of
Christ's prayer in John 17, but this would be wrong; for those for whom Christ
prays do sin, though they do not sin so as to fall away from Christ forever. The
Lord told Peter, as an example, that he would sin even to the point of denying
Christ and that he would do so repeatedly (Jn 13:38). "Simon, Simon, behold,
Satan demanded to have you, that he might sift you like wheat." But Christ added,
"I have prayed for you that your faith may not fail. And when you have turned
again, strengthen your brothers" (Lk 22:31-32). In this incident Jesus foretold
Peter's denial, but he also foretold his recovery. He assured Peter of his inter-
cession that Peter's faith might not fail.

Noah fell into drunkenness. Abraham lied twice about his wife Sarah, saying
she was his sister, and thus risking her honor to save his own skin. Lot chose
Sodom. Jacob cheated his brother Esau and deceived his father Isaac. David
committed adultery with Bathsheba, and then tried to cover it up by having her
husband, Uriah, killed. In Gethsemane, the disciples abandoned Jesus to protect
their own lives. Paul and Barnabas fought over John Mark and had to part
company. Paul persisted in returning to Jerusalem with the offering from the
Gentiles when even the Lord himself appeared to him and forbade him to do
it. All these sinned. Yet they were not lost. In fact, there is not a single story in
the whole Bible of one who was truly a child of God who was lost. Many were
overtaken by sin, but none perished.

Third, perseverance does not mean that those who merely profess Christ without
being born again are secure. Specific warnings are given to those who heard the
gospel and appeared to trust in Christ, and yet were not truly saved. For example,

Jesus said, "If you abide in my word, you are truly my disciples" (Jn 8:31). This seems to say that perseverance on the part of the believer is the final proof of whether he or she is truly born again. Again, our Lord said, "The one who endures to the end will be saved" (Mt 10:22). Peter wrote, "Therefore, brothers, be all the more diligent to confirm your calling and election" (2 Pet 1:10). It is possible to be quite close to Christian things and yet not truly be regenerate.

THE KEEPER OF ISRAEL

Perseverance in grace means rather, as Thomas Watson puts it, that "the heavenly inheritance is kept for the saints, and they are kept for the inheritance. . . . Though the saints may come to that pass that they have but little faith, yet not to have no faith. Though their grace may be drawn low, yet it is not drawn dry; though grace may be abated, it is not abolished; though the wise virgins slumbered, yet their lamps were not quite gone out."[2] Perseverance means that once one is in the family of God, he or she is always in that family.

The Bible is clear that those who are justified from sin cannot be lost. David wrote in Psalm 138:8, "The LORD will fulfill his purpose for me; your steadfast love, O LORD, endures forever." The author of Hebrews declares, "For by a single offering he [Jesus] has perfected for all time those who are being sanctified" (Heb 10:14). Paul wrote, "We are afflicted in every way, but not crushed; perplexed, but not driven to despair; persecuted, but not forsaken; struck down, but not destroyed; . . . knowing that he who raised the Lord Jesus will raise us also with Jesus and bring us with you into his presence" (2 Cor 4:8-9, 14). Perseverance is suggested by the images that the Bible applies to believers: trees that do not wither (Ps 1:3); the cedars of Lebanon that flourish from year to year like California redwoods (Ps 92:12); a house built on a rock (Mt 7:24); Mount Zion that cannot be moved (Ps 125:1).

The Old Testament often speaks specifically of the keeping power of God. In Psalm 121 the Lord is compared to a divine watchman whose concern is to keep watch over his people during their earthly lives. The words *keep* or *keeper* are used six times.

> He will not let your foot be moved;
>> he who keeps you will not slumber.
> Behold, he who keeps Israel

---

[2]Thomas Watson, *A Body of Divinity: Contained in Sermons upon the Westminster Assembly's Catechism* (1692; repr., London: The Banner of Truth Trust, 1970), 279-80.

will neither slumber nor sleep.
The LORD is your keeper;
    the LORD is your shade on your right hand.
The sun shall not strike you by day,
    nor the moon by night.
The LORD will keep you from all evil;
    he will keep your life.
The LORD will keep
    your going out and your coming in
    from this time forth and forevermore. (Ps 121:3-8)

Another important passage is Ezekiel 34:11-16. God has been speaking against those who had been the shepherds of Israel who, he says, had not done their work. They were to watch over the sheep, but they had forsaken them. Now, says God, he will do what these faithless leaders had failed to do.

Behold, I, I myself will search for my sheep and will seek them out. As a shepherd seeks out his flock when he is among his sheep that have been scattered, so will I seek out my sheep, and I will rescue them from all places where they have been scattered on a day of clouds and thick darkness. And I will bring them out from the peoples and gather them from the countries, and will bring them into their own land. And I will feed them on the mountains of Israel, by the ravines, and in all the inhabited places of the country. I will feed them with good pasture, and on the mountain heights of Israel shall be their grazing land. There they shall lie down in good grazing land, and on rich pasture they shall feed on the mountains of Israel. I myself will be the shepherd of my sheep, and I will make them lie down, declares the Lord GOD. I will seek the lost, and I will bring back the strayed, and I will bind up the injured, and I will strengthen the weak, and the fat and the strong I will destroy. I will feed them in justice.

In Isaiah 27:2-3 God is compared to a keeper of vineyards.

A pleasant vineyard, sing of it!
    I, the LORD, am its keeper;
    every moment I water it.
    Lest any one punish it,
I keep it night and day.

Christ drew on these images in his teaching. He compared both himself and the Father to a watchman, shepherd, and husbandman to encourage the disciples.

The danger was great without and great within. The disciples possessed an old nature that would surely drag them down into sin again and again. But he proclaimed that there was One who was even greater than the danger and who would certainly preserve them as he had kept and preserved Israel.

FOUR KEY TEXTS ON THE BELIEVER'S SECURITY

In the New Testament there are four great texts that, more than any others, teach the security of the believer. Two are from the lips of Jesus. Two are from Paul. The first is John 6:37-40.

> All that the Father gives me will come to me, and whoever comes to me I will never cast out. For I have come down from heaven, not to do my own will but the will of him who sent me. And this is the will of him who sent me, that I should lose nothing of all that he has given me, but raise it up on the last day. For this is the will of my Father, that everyone who looks on the Son and believes in him should have eternal life, and I will raise him up on the last day.

Having declared that all who have been given to him by the Father will in fact come to him, the Lord goes on to stress that he will certainly keep the ones who do come. In Greek, this sentence contains a double negative that might be translated "and him who comes to me I will never, never cast out."

If the passage stopped at this point, it might be argued that the double negative refers only to Christ's receiving the one who comes to him initially—that he will never, never reject anyone who comes to him—but that such a person may nevertheless decide to leave Christ on his own initiative. But that is not possible. As Christ makes clear in the following verses, all who have been given to him by the Father and who therefore come to him and are received by him will be raised up at the last day. He will lose nothing of all that God has given to him.

The second great text on perseverance is John 10:27-30, which follows the same outline as the verses in John 6. But in this case the Lord is responding to a request from his listeners to speak "plainly" (Jn 10:24). Of course, the difficulty was not in his speech but in their hearing. Nevertheless, he replied, "My sheep hear my voice, and I know them, and they follow me. I give them eternal life, and they will never perish, and no one will snatch them out of my hand. My Father, who has given them to me, is greater than all, and no one is able to snatch them out of the Father's hand" (Jn 10:27-29). Election, the effectual call, and perseverance!

"I know that no one shall ever pluck us out of Christ's hand," says one. "But suppose they choose to jump out of their own accord?"

"They shall never perish," says Jesus.

"Never?"

"Never," says Jesus. "They shall never perish, and no one shall snatch them out of my hand."

I have sometimes thought that what Jesus did in uttering these words was like something a carpenter often does. Sometimes in rough carpentry a worker will drive a long nail through thinner boards so that the point sticks out the back. Then, with a blow of his hammer, he will drive the point of the nail sideways, embedding it in the wood. This is called clinching the nail. It makes the joint just a bit more firm because the nail cannot work itself out from this position.

This is what Jesus did in these verses. He was so interested in getting the doctrine to stick in his disciples' minds that he not only drove one nail, he drove two and clinched them both.

First, he taught that those who are his have been given eternal life. "I give them eternal life"—that is the nail. This alone makes the truth fast; for eternal life is life that can never be lost. If it could be lost after a few years or even after many years, it would not be eternal. Nevertheless, Jesus knew that many would attempt to explain it away. So he said, "They shall never perish"—that is the clinch by which the doctrine of perseverance is made fast.

One nail, however well fastened, does not always make a good joint, though. So Jesus went on to drive a second nail and clinch that as well. His second nail, "No one shall snatch them out of my hand." The clincher, "My Father, who has given them to me, is greater than all, and no one is able to snatch them out of the Father's hand."

We can imagine ourselves to be a coin folded in his fingers. That is a secure position for any object, but especially for us, considering whose hand holds us. But Jesus adds that the hand of God is over his hand. We are enclosed in two hands. We are doubly secure. If we feel insecure, we can remember that even when we are held in that manner, the Father and Son still have two hands free to defend us.

The third important text on perseverance is from Paul, Romans 8:33-39. It is a sequel to the verses studied in the last chapter and is part of the same sequence of God's acts in salvation which they introduce.

Who shall bring any charge against God's elect? It is God who justifies. Who is to condemn? Christ Jesus is the one who died—more than that, who was raised—who is at the right hand of God, who indeed is interceding for us. Who shall separate us from the love of Christ? Shall tribulation, or distress, or persecution, or famine, or nakedness, or danger, or sword? As it is written,

"For your sake we are being killed all the day long;

we are regarded as sheep to be slaughtered."

No, in all these things we are more than conquerors through him who loved us. For I am sure that neither death nor life, nor angels nor rulers, nor things present nor things to come, nor powers, nor height nor depth, nor anything else in all creation, will be able to separate us from the love of God in Christ Jesus our Lord.

Paul lists three possible causes of separation from God's love in these verses but then dismisses them all. First, sin (Rom 8:33-34). Christians know that although they are justified by God, they are still sinners and sin daily in thought, word, and deed. "Well, what of it?" asks Paul. "Christ has died for sin [past tense]; therefore, in God's sight our sin is gone forever." Suppose someone should accuse us? "God is the judge," Paul answers. Christians have been acquitted before the bench of the highest court of all, and no one is authorized to reopen their case.

Second, in Romans 8:35-37 Paul speaks of suffering, external suffering (tribulation, famine, nakedness, peril), and internal suffering (the anguish of soul known by those who face persecution for the sake of their testimony). This suffering is real. It should be expected, as Paul indicates by his quotation of Psalm 44:22 in Romans 8:36. But suffering will not triumph. It cannot separate us from God's love.

The third potential cause of separation from Christ's love is the existence of supernatural powers (Rom 8:38-39), but Paul says that even these cannot triumph. Paul knew the extent of spiritual wickedness in this world and had wrestled against it himself. He had written to the Ephesians, "For we do not wrestle against flesh and blood, but against the rulers, against the authorities, against the cosmic powers of this present darkness, against the spiritual forces of evil in the heavenly places" (Eph 6:12). But frightening as these may be, they cannot triumph for the simple reason that Jesus has been victorious over them. To the Colossians Paul wrote, "He disarmed the rulers and authorities and put them to open shame, by triumphing over them in [Christ]" (Col 2:15).

The final text is Philippians 1:6, which says, "And I am sure of this, that he who began a good work in you will bring it to completion at the day of Jesus Christ." This is a condensed statement of the principle stated at greater length in other places—God finishes what he starts—but it suggests another thought too. Literally, the Greek says that God will "keep on perfecting his work until the day of Christ." To put it in stark language, he will do so whether we want him to or not.

The verse speaks of "a good work" that God will bring to completion. What is that good work? It is not spelled out very clearly in Philippians 1:6 but is in Romans 8:29. "For those whom he foreknew he also predestined to be conformed to the image of his Son." Is this something that is to happen in heaven only? Not at all! It is also God's plan for us now. Philippians 1:6 is saying that God will not give up in his efforts to make us like Christ even now, though we may want him to. Christ is the holy One of God, so this plan involves our growth in holiness. We know that we sin as Christians. What happens when we sin? Does God ignore it? We might like him to, for we sometimes enjoy sin—at least for the moment. But God does not permit us to continue on our way unhindered. He disciplines us for it. He prods us, woos us, sometimes even makes our lives miserable so that we will get out of the path of destruction and back onto the road that he has mapped out for us. Sometimes God will break a Christian's life in pieces, if that is what is necessary to get him or her out of sin and back into fellowship.

That is why the doctrine of perseverance is not the dangerous doctrine some have imagined it to be. "Perseverance may be true," says one, "but surely to teach it is dangerous. If people believe that nothing can ever snatch us from God's hand, then surely they will feel free to sin. The doctrine will encourage loose living." The knowledge of the greatness of the love of God that perseveres with us actually tends to keep us faithful. To know such love is to wish, above everything else, not to do anything against it.

Beyond this, knowledge of God's perseverance teaches us to persevere. Our work is often discouraging. We often see few results. But we will keep at it because God has given it to us, and we must be like him in faithfully fulfilling this responsibility. We often find witnessing disheartening. People do not want the gospel. They hate the God who gave it. Still, we will keep at it, knowing that the same God who is able to keep us in the world is able as well to save others out of it. Our families are a special area of responsibility. We are often depressed when a son or daughter or brother or sister or spouse will not walk in God's way. Sometimes the situation seems hopeless. But God does not allow it to be hopeless for us. We will not give up. We will not quit. God is faithful. He is our keeper. With God all things are possible.

We live in a day that is so weak in its proclamation of Christian doctrine that even many Christians cannot see why such truths should be preached or how they can be used of the Lord to save sinners. This was not always so. God used the doctrine of perseverance to save Charles Spurgeon, one of the greatest preachers who ever lived. When he was only fifteen he had noticed how friends of his, who had begun life well, made a wreck of their lives by falling into gross vices. Spurgeon feared that he himself might fall into them. "Whatever good resolutions I might make," he thought, "the probabilities are that they will be good for nothing when temptation actually assails me. I will be like those of whom it is said, 'They see the devil's hook and yet cannot help nibbling at his bait.' I will disgrace myself, and I will be lost." It was then that he heard that Christ will keep his saints from falling. It had a particular charm for him and he found himself saying, "I will turn to Jesus and receive from him a new heart and a right spirit; and so I shall be secured against those temptations into which others have fallen. I shall be preserved by him." It was this truth along with others that brought Spurgeon to the Savior.

Christianity does not have a shaky foundation. It is not a gospel of percentages and possibilities. It is a certain gospel. It is the message of our complete ruin in sin but of God's perfect and certain remedy in Christ.

BOOK 4

GOD *and* HISTORY

PART I

TIME AND HISTORY

That which we have seen and heard we proclaim also to you,

so that you too may have fellowship with us; and indeed our

fellowship is with the Father and with his Son Jesus Christ.

1 JOHN 1:3

Our Father in heaven, hallowed be your name.

Your kingdom come, your will be done, on earth as it is in heaven.

MATTHEW 6:9-10

But when the fullness of time had come, God sent forth his Son,

born of woman, born under the law, to redeem those who were

under the law, so that we might receive adoption as sons.

GALATIANS 4:4-5

CHAPTER 1

WHAT'S WRONG WITH *ME?*

Margaret Halsey is an author whose work has appeared in *Newsweek* magazine. I mention her because an article she wrote, "What's Wrong With Me, Me, Me?" is an excellent reference point with which to begin this fourth and final book of *Foundations of the Christian Faith*. As Halsey pointed out, ours has rightly been termed the "me" generation and our recent past the decade of the new narcissism. The outlook on life to which those designations point is based on the idea that "inside every human being, however unprepossessing, there is a glorious, talented and overwhelmingly attractive personality [which] will be revealed in all its splendor if the individual just forgets about courtesy, cooperativeness and consideration for others and proceeds to do exactly what he or she feels like doing."[1]

With such a philosophy, however narrow or even wrong it may be, one would expect that people would at least have the best of all chances for fulfilling themselves. But it does not work that way. In spite of almost unlimited indulgence and uninhibited expression, the cult of *self* has left thousands dissatisfied.

There are many disadvantages to the self-absorbed worldview. One is the tendency of the individual to manipulate others for his or her own gratification—a disadvantage to the other person as well as to the manipulator. The typical male egoist lauded by the *Playboy* philosophy is an example. He uses women much

---

[1]Margaret Halsey, "What's Wrong With Me, Me, Me?," *Newsweek*, April 17, 1978, 25.

as he uses cars, stereo sets, or clothes: to enhance his self-image and increase his pleasure. A tendency to manipulation can also be seen in some segments of the women's liberation movement, even though in theory it rejects the *Playboy* attitude. Writing in *Harper's*, contributing editor Sally Helgesen speaks of the view that a woman's goal should be to "eat, sleep, make love, watch television, listen to music, go out, come in, read, use the telephone, write, type, talk, work, sing—when you want to," noting that such a goal is in reality no different from the *Playboy* worldview and therefore is equally subject to commercial exploitation. "This imaginative creed, wherein the tenets of a timeless hedonism are harnessed to serve the ends of a consumer culture, is attended by all kinds of clever justifications, which assure the adherent that, by thinking of his own needs first, he will somehow benefit mankind in the long run."[2]

Frustration is a second disadvantage to the cult of self. Fulfillment does not come from unlimited self-expression or indulgence. If people think it should, they are inevitably frustrated or even angered when things do not work out as they anticipate. A warping of the personality or an unreasonable tendency to blame others—husband or wife, politics, the state, the environment, or God—is the result.

THE SEARCH FOR IDENTITY

In her article, Halsey suggests a number of flaws in the self-absorbed worldview. She argues first that the basic theory "that inside every human being . . . there is a glorious, talented and overwhelmingly attractive personality" is false. Although there may be attractive elements in everyone, the reality of human nature is that "a mess of unruly primitive impulses" spoils our "self-discovery." When people say, "I don't know who I am," what they actually mean is that they are not satisfied with what they know themselves to be. Since they do not know how to be delivered from themselves or change themselves, they turn their backs on the unpleasant facets of their being. Second, Halsey argues that "a search for identity is predestined to fail" for the simple reason that identity is not something *found* but rather something *made* through choices, hard work, and commitments to others.

Here Christianity is in hearty support of Halsey's thesis, although it would state it in even stronger terms. It would agree that within the heart of the individual there is "a mess of unruly primitive impulses." But the situation is worse.

---

[2]Sally Helgesen, "Virtue Rewarded," *Harper's*, May 1978, 23-24.

The heart is "dull" (Mt 13:15), "proud" (Lk 1:51), "hard and impenitent" (Rom 2:5), and filled with "lusts" (Rom 1:24). Above all, it is set rebelliously against God (Mt 15:8). Jesus taught that the largest part of the world's evil comes out of such a heart (Mt 15:18-19). The individual needs a new heart through the work of God's Son.

Christianity also stresses that identity is something to be developed. True, it speaks of an identity that is given to us by revelation and redemption. We are creatures of God who are brought into the family of God by Christ's work. But Christianity also speaks of a developing sense of identity—as those who have been saved by Christ enter increasingly into an experiential knowledge of Jesus and his character through the work of the Spirit of God in their hearts. That is what Christian theology calls sanctification.[3]

Yet Christianity shines out against any merely secular analysis. It goes on to speak of the church and history as a further and fuller answer to the human dilemma. Human beings have many needs: to know God, for salvation, of a power able to overcome the sinful and debilitating tendencies of their nature. But in addition there is a need for relationships on the highest level and a sense of purpose and belonging within history.

The contemporary pursuit of the self erupts in two main agonies: isolation (with its accompanying sense of cosmic loneliness) and meaninglessness. According to the Bible, God has dealt with the first through creation of the church, to which a believer in Christ automatically belongs, and with the second by the incorporation of the Christian into the meaningful flow of biblical history.

FELLOWSHIP

Roman Catholics have an expression—"No one has God for his Father who does not also have the Church for his Mother"—which, although it is sometimes used wrongly to maintain that there is no salvation outside the Roman Catholic Church, nevertheless has an element of truth. Fellowship with God inevitably brings fellowship with other Christians within the body of the church. The apostle John indicated this in the opening verses of his first letter: "That which we have seen and heard we proclaim also to you, so that you too may have

---

[3]These steps correspond to the doctrines developed in the first three books of this volume: (1) the knowledge of God and the corresponding knowledge of ourselves as rebels in need of a Savior; (2) the knowledge of Christ as Savior; and (3) the knowledge of the Holy Spirit and his work of applying the salvation provided by Christ to us in the initial moment of our belief in Christ and throughout our lives as Christians.

fellowship with us; and indeed our fellowship is with the Father and with his Son Jesus Christ" (1 Jn 1:3). Here are two fellowships: with God and with other Christians. Yet nothing in this verse indicates that either one of them can be had without the other. Rather, they are one fellowship. To have fellowship with other Christians is to enter into fellowship with the Father. To have fellowship with the Father is to have fellowship with those for whom Christ also died. It is to be a part of God's family.

People today and in every age need to understand this. When God created a companion for Adam he explained his action by saying, "It is not good that the man should be alone" (Gen 2:18). That expresses God's reasons for marriage, but also refers to the whole of life. Isolation is not good. People need fellowship, and it is God's will that they should have it.

Lacking the true and fulfilling fellowship that God means for them to have, many people go about establishing an empty kind of "fellowship" based more on proximity than on true relationships. The camaraderie of the social club is one example. So is the frenzied interaction of the discotheque. These groupings of people have been popular because they substitute proximity for true community and thereby help people to forget the fundamental and tragic loss of personal identity that drives them there.

Four kinds of loss of identity are common today: loss of family identity, national identity, religious identity, and personal identity. Each is supplied in the church, even though the other supportive institutions that we should ideally enjoy—an understanding and stable family and a country of which one can be proud—may be lacking.

The church was established on earth for several purposes: worship, service, organized dissemination of the gospel. In addition to these obvious purposes, another chief end of the church is the union of Christ's followers into one visible fellowship and the substitution of a social for a "privatized" Christianity. Nothing that rightly pertains to the relationship of an individual to God is set aside by that fact. On the contrary, one's relationship to God is actually to be developed and expanded by relationships with other believers.

James Bannerman, who wrote a study of the church as an outgrowth of his lectures to theological students in Scotland in the nineteenth century, declared,

> There is something in the very nature of man that makes union and fellowship
> with other men essentially necessary to develop the whole faculties and powers
> of his being; and this characteristic of man's nature has been taken advantage of

in the economy of grace; so that, under the power of association, believers are not merely or only units in the dispensation of God, but brethren also in the enjoyment of communion with each other collectively, as well as in the enjoyment of communion individually, each one with his Savior. According to the arrangement of God, the Christian is more of a Christian in society than alone, and more in the enjoyment of privileges of a spiritual kind when he shares them with others, than when he possesses them apart. . . . Such, for example, is the blessing promised to "two or three" when "gathered together in the name of Christ," over and above what is promised to the solitary worshipper; and such is the more abundant and gracious answer that will be returned to prayer, when men, even a few, "shall agree together to ask anything of God," rather than when they ask separately and alone. . . .

The Christian Church was established in the world, to realize the superior advantages of a social over an individual Christianity, and to set up and maintain the communion of saints. In his union to Christ the Head, the individual believer becomes ingrafted into the same body, and partakes of the same privileges with other believers. He is one with them in the same Spirit, in the same faith, in the same baptism, in the same hopes, in the same grace, in the same salvation. The bonds of that spiritual union go to strengthen his own individual Christianity, the sympathy of it to call forth his own individual affections, and the incitement of it to enlarge his own personal faith and hope; so that, in the fellowship of the Church, and within the magic circle of its influences, the believer is in a more eminent sense a believer, than apart from them.[4]

A HISTORICAL IDENTITY

God's answer to human isolation and meaninglessness is not only the church, through which the individual enters into fellowship with others of like mind. Entering into the church also brings the Christian into the flow of biblical history, which makes one's own life meaningful. The church locates believers spatially. They belong to the church of God at Jerusalem or Rome or New York or London, to use the New Testament method of referring to churches. History locates believers in time—in the twentieth century, for example, rather than in the period of the early church or the age of the Reformation.

---

[4]James Bannerman, *The Church of Christ: A Treatise on the Nature, Powers, Ordinances, Discipline and Government of the Christian Church*, vol. 1 (1869; repr., London: Banner of Truth Trust, 1974), 91-92.

Biblical religion is historical and the God of the Bible is preeminently the God of history. That factor more than any other sets Judaism and Christianity off from the religions among which they flourished. In Old Testament times, virtually all the religions of the peoples surrounding the Hebrews were nature religions. They identified the most high god or gods with the sun, winds, rains, seasons. In some cases, as in the religion of Baal, which was a constant threat to Israel through much of its history, those identifications produced a fertility religion. At particularly low periods, even the human reproductive organs were worshiped. The same was true in Egypt. In all cases, the flow of the religion was cyclical—from one moon to the next or from one harvest to the next—and history as such had no meaning.

The religion of the Old and New Testaments is different. Note how God called Abraham:

> Go from your country and your kindred and your father's house to the land that
> I will show you. And I will make of you a great nation, and I will bless you and
> make your name great, so that you will be a blessing. I will bless those who bless
> you, and him who dishonors you I will curse, and in you all the families of the
> earth shall be blessed. (Gen 12:1-3)

Two features of this call stand out. First, the call was in the nature of a promise or covenant made by God to Abraham—it was unsolicited by Abraham. Second, it was made in and is to be fulfilled in history. As we read the biblical history that follows, we realize that this historical fulfillment unfolded over a considerable period of time. Abraham did leave his own land, and God did bring him to a new land. But the nation that was to descend from him did not come into existence during Abraham's lifetime, in fact not until several generations later. Nor did the full measure of the blessing come until the appearance of the Messiah at the start of the Christian era.

Another milestone in the historical religion of the Old Testament was the deliverance of the descendants of Abraham, by then a large nation, from Egypt. In that deliverance, God altered the normal behavior of the elements, animal life, and heavenly bodies to bring judgments on Pharaoh and force him to let the people go (Ex 5:1). Because of that deliverance, Israel was to worship the Lord and obey the ethical commandments he gave them (Ex 20:1-17). The covenant made with Abraham was reiterated, but this time with a balance of blessings and curses depending on the people's obedience or disobedience (Deut 11, 27–28).

During David's reign a promise was given of One who would govern Israel forever (2 Sam 7:12-16).

In each of these milestones in God's dealings with his people, the historical element is dominant. God intervenes and guides in history so that the promises he has made to his people might be fulfilled. History is going someplace, according to this system of thought, and because it is going someplace it has meaning to the individuals who by God's grace are caught up in it.

The appearance of Jesus of Nazareth brought this period of promise and expectation to a climax, but it also launched a new period of history that flows from his work of redemption. The appearance of Jesus was the *decisive* intervention of God in history. It gave the conclusive meaning to history as well as the basis for judgment on it.

The Greek language has many words for time: *hēmera* (day), *hōra* (hour), *kairos* (season), *chronos* (time), *aiōn* (age), and others. The most important word is *kairos*, which is used repeatedly of the coming of Christ and of his death and resurrection as the key moments or events in that coming. The impact of this word is best seen by contrasting it with *chronos*. Both *kairos* and *chronos* refer to time and are frequently translated *time* in our Bibles. But *chronos* refers only to the flow of time, the following of one event on another. We have this idea in our word *chronology*. *Kairos* refers to a moment in time that is especially significant or favorable. It can be used secularly as in the words of King Felix to Paul, "When I get an *opportunity* I will summon you" (Acts 24:25). But *kairos* is especially appropriate in referring to the appearance of Christ. Thus, Peter wrote of the Old Testament prophets' inquiry about "what person or *time* the Spirit of Christ in them was indicating when he predicted the sufferings of Christ and the subsequent glories" (1 Pet 1:11). Jesus referred to his passion as his *kairos:* "My *time* is at hand" (Mt 26:18). In John's Gospel, the same effect is achieved by Christ's reference to the *hour* of his death and glorification (Jn 2:4; 7:30; 8:20; 12:23; 13:1; 16:32; 17:1).

Jesus was a figure of history whose life and teachings may be investigated by normal academic techniques. Whenever that truth is lost, Christianity itself is lost, for it is and must be historical. Yet the life of Christ is even more than this—it is *historic*. The meaning of all history is disclosed in the history of the Lord Jesus Christ, and a choice between commitment to him or rejection of him and his history determines our destinies.

That line of thought brings us back sharply to the dilemma of contemporary men and women. We have seen that the two felt needs of our age, a need for identity and a need for significance or meaning, are met by incorporation into the church and into biblical history. But here we must say that only through faith in Christ and commitment to Christ does that incorporation take place. True, the church is the answer to loneliness on the deepest level. But it is Christ's church. It is his body (1 Cor 12:27; Eph 1:23; Col 1:18), and he is the door through whom alone we are enabled to enter into its fellowship (Jn 10:7-10).

The answer to meaninglessness is to enter into the flow of meaningful history. It is Christ's history, and the way into it is through him.

THE IMPORTANCE OF THE PRESENT

Without the church we are left with a religion of pure individualism in which each person does what is right in his or her own eyes. Without a biblical view of history we are left with a religion of nebulous love and sentimental fellowship. Both are needed. Only then are we part of a company on the move, a company seeking to carry out the directives of God for our time and place—knowing that the results will be significant.

Some years after the end of World War II, an English historian, Herbert Butterfield, wrote a book on the Christian view of history. In it he tried to set the events of the recent past in perspective and to rally believers to significant and ethical behavior. He wrote,

> It has always been realized in the main tradition of Christianity that if the Word was made flesh, matter can never be regarded as evil in itself. In a similar way, if one moment of time could hold so much as this, then you cannot brush time away and say that any moment of it is mere vanity. Every instant of time becomes more momentous than ever—every instant is "eschatological," or, as one person has put it, like the point in the fairy-story where the clock is just about to strike twelve. On this view there can be no case of an absentee God leaving mankind at the mercy of chance in a universe blind, stark and bleak. And a real drama—not a madman's nightmare or a tissue of flimsy dreams—is being enacted on the stage of human history. A real conflict between good and evil is taking place, events do matter, and something is being achieved irrespective of our apparent success or failure.[5]

That insight is one that every Christian, and not just a Christian historian, should share.

---

[5]Herbert Butterfield, *Christianity and History* (New York: Charles Scribner's Sons, 1950), 121.

I conclude this chapter with one more biblical word for time, the word *now* (*nun*). It shows us that the *kairos* in which we live is of eternal importance: "Once you were not a people, but *now* you are God's people; once you had not received mercy, but *now* you have received mercy" (1 Pet 2:10); "Blessed are you who are hungry *now*, for you shall be satisfied. Blessed are you who weep *now*, for you shall laugh" (Lk 6:21); "Behold, *now* is the favorable time; behold, *now* is the day of salvation" (2 Cor 6:2).

If Christ's life counted in the flow of history, then by God's grace and by union with Christ our lives can count too. Our *now* matters.

CHAPTER 2

THE MARCH OF TIME

During World War II and for a number of years before and after, a series of popular newsreels was shown weekly in most American movie theaters. The series, produced by the Time-Life corporation, was called *The March of Time*. Stirring march music, the voice of an enthusiastic and assured announcer, and a sequence of scenes from around the world impressed the viewer with all that seemed to be happening in this "modern," fast-paced age. The title of the series said it all. Time really did seem to be marching along, perhaps even racing. It was an age of progress. So, although there was often bad news—about military reverses, for example—few doubted that time would eventually take care of things and that progress was inevitable.

How times have changed! Today people are not at all sure that progress is inevitable (though they often speak as if that were the case). Progress requires planned or directed motion, and that requires both a Planner and a plan. Today people are not so sure that either a Planner or a plan exists. The optimistic, progressive view of history of an earlier age has given way to a view that sees history as just possibly a series of unrelated and uncontrolled motions. And that is frightening.

Does history march? If it does, to what drummer? The only way to answer these questions is to go back to the beginning and ask where the modern view of historical progress came from and on what grounds it was believed. We have to begin with the ancient view of history that the modern view replaced.

A CIRCULAR VIEW OF HISTORY

Although the Greeks epitomize the ancient view of history, it is sometimes said that they were not interested in history. That is not an entirely fair comment on a race that produced such historians as Herodotus, who chronicled the rise of Greece, and Thucydides, who recorded its decline. But there is more than an element of truth in that negative statement, despite those two eminent figures.

The Greeks' interest in history, insofar as it existed (and it was not universal), was directed to where their own race and its unique outlook on life had come from. But while they undoubtedly considered themselves to be a giant step beyond and above the barbarism that preceded them, they did not think of that as a stage in some unending upward movement of the race. Rather it was a peak that would inevitably give way to poorer times again. The Greek view of time was circular. That is, there was undoubtedly change in history, but it was change that constantly returned on itself, just as the planets or seasons do. Nations had risen to power in the past and had then declined. They would do so again. But the citizens of those nations did not "get anywhere" by their rise, nor did others "advance" by their fall. The only meaning was in the circle itself, and the only salvation for a person caught up in such a circle was to escape from it. As far as history was concerned, the Greeks would have had no trouble applying the carnival barker's description of his wheel of fortune: "Round and round and round she goes, and where she stops nobody knows."

The classical view of the Greeks involved five propositions:

1. The Greeks had no interest in the past, in the sense of studying it to seek reasons for why things are as they are. It may be true, R. G. Collingwood maintains, that Herodotus was an exception at this point, but the dominant view was that if the past had interest at all, it was only as an illustration of those characteristics of human thought and behavior that were also observable in the present.[1]

2. They had no real interest in the future.

---

[1] R. G. Collingwood, *The Idea of History* (London: Oxford Univ. Press, 1976), 28-31. "The Greek mind tended to harden and narrow itself in its anti-historical tendency. The genius of Herodotus triumphed over that tendency, but after him the search for unchangeable and eternal objects of knowledge gradually stifled the historical consciousness" (29).

3. Nothing new was to be expected in history. Epicurus said, "Nothing new happens in the universe, if you consider the infinite time past."[2] Marcus Aurelius, a later Roman Stoic philosopher, said the same thing:

> The rational soul . . . traverses the whole universe, and the surrounding vacuum, and surveys its form, and it extends itself into the infinity of time, and embraces and comprehends the periodical renovation of all things, and it comprehends that those who come after us will see nothing new, nor have those before us seen more, but in a manner he who is forty years old, if he has any understanding at all, has seen by virtue of the uniformity that prevails all things that have been and all that will be.[3]

4. Human bondage to time through bodily existence is a curse.

5. Salvation is deliverance from that eternal circular course and therefore from time itself. Plato gave a classic expression to that thought:

> The soul . . . is . . . dragged by the body into the region of the changeable, and wanders and is confused; the world spins round her, and she is like a drunkard when under their influence. . . . But when returning into herself she reflects; then she passes into the realm of purity, and eternity, and immortality, and unchangeableness, which are her kindred, and with them she ever lives . . . and being in communion with the unchanging is unchanging.[4]

We may summarize by saying that for the Greeks, the events of history were cyclical, and that salvation consisted in being freed from history through rational thought.

HISTORY AS PROGRESS

It would be difficult to show, even in a very long essay, how and at what point the classical view of history passed over into the modern notion of historical progress. It is enough to say that Christianity had a major if not exclusive role in that transformation.

Christianity brought to the picture its doctrine of a God who revealed himself in history, the point made in the last chapter. God was neither one of the futile, half-human, half-divine gods and goddesses of the Greek pantheon,

---

[2]Epicurus, *Fragments*, 55, in *The Stoic and Epicurean Philosophers*, ed. Whitney J. Oates (New York: Random House, 1940), 50.

[3]Marcus Aurelius, *Meditations*, xi, 1, in Oates, *The Stoic and Epicurean Philosophers*, 571.

[4]Plato, *Phaedo*, *The Works of Plato*, trans. B. Jowett, vol. 3 (New York: Tudor Pub. Co., n.d.), 217-18.

nor the unchanging and unchangeable First Mover of the Greek philosophers. This God loved his people, grieved for his people, and moved heaven and earth, as it were, for their deliverance. Another element that Christianity brought into the picture was its view of the human being, not as a divine soul imprisoned in a perishable and evil body (as the Greeks thought), but as a union of body, soul, and spirit, all created in God's image. Each part of the human being was important and valuable. Salvation was to be conceived, therefore, not as salvation of the soul or spirit alone but of the body as well, through a final historical resurrection. Finally, Christianity introduced a heightened moral consciousness that required a final balancing out of rewards and punishments at the last judgment.

Those doctrines slowly worked their way into history. During the Middle Ages, Christianity mingled with Platonism and Aristotelianism to produce an otherworldliness that often obscured Christianity's historical interests. But in the late sixteenth and seventeenth centuries—first through the budding scientism of Francis Bacon (1561–1626) and then through the philosophy of such thinkers as René Descartes (1596–1650) and Baruch Spinoza (1632–1677)—the value of knowledge, perceived by the Greeks, and the idea of a flow of history, derived from Christianity, were combined into a faith in inevitable scientific and social progress. That view flowered in the eighteenth-century rise of science and the nineteenth-century rise of industry—the Industrial Revolution. At the end of that period, when Charles Darwin (1809–1882) introduced the idea of an evolutionary progression among living things, the victory of the new outlook seemed complete.

Gordon H. Clark summarizes the matter by showing that this final, mature view of history as progress involved three cardinal doctrines.

1. Progress is a natural process and must always have been in operation.

2. Progress must occur in all spheres. There must be social, moral, and philosophical improvement as well as scientific advance.

3. If progress is conceived of as a natural law, then it must be necessary and inevitable.

These points gave the nineteenth and early twentieth centuries their optimism. It was believed that, although there are sometimes setbacks in history through mistakes in judgment, it is nevertheless the nature of the human will to seek progress, and that innate desire, like any other "natural" law, will win out ultimately. The causes of such progress are the accumulation of *knowledge*, political and social *planning*, and biological *evolution*.[5]

Each of these three causes is today increasingly seen to be inadequate to sustain such optimism. The advance of scientific knowledge is obviously inadequate, for the reason that nothing in the scientific enterprise in itself determines how the discoveries of science are to be used. Science can produce atomic energy, but the energy can then be used to produce nuclear weapons as well as to provide for peacetime nuclear power stations—and even those stations are not unambiguously a step forward. Science can produce a seemingly infinite variety of things for the hyped-up consumer market. But it is questionable whether such multiplication is progress, or whether it is not rather a case of the soul being suffocated beneath its possessions.

Again, there is faith in social planning, but what does that amount to? It is questionable whether political and social planning really work, to begin with. In our day, most major problems seem to be beyond the solutions proposed for dealing with them—inflation, international unrest, crime, irrational violence, to name just a few. But even if it were true that such planning could be effective, there is still no guarantee that the planning would be put to truly "progressive" ends. In the hands of evil rulers, for example, such planning could be used to debase and enslave a people.

Finally, as far as evolution is concerned, the arrogance of those who assume the human race to be the epitome of biological advance seems ludicrous in view of our ability to blow ourselves off the face of the planet.

In his treatment of these themes, Clark makes one other sly observation, asking if a philosophy of progress does not itself ultimately require its own rejection. He asks,

> If progress is the law of history; if our moral and intellectual baggage is superior to that of antiquity; and if our society and our ideas are to grow into something better and vastly different; if our imagination is to evolve to a degree not now imaginable; if all the old concepts which served their time well are to be replaced by new and better concepts, does it not follow that the theory of progress will be discarded as an eighteenth and nineteenth century notion, which no doubt served its age well, but which will then be antiquated and untrue? Could it be that the best contemporary evidence of progress is a growing disbelief in "progress"?[6]

---

[5]Gordon H. Clark, *A Christian View of Men and Things* (Grand Rapids: Eerdmans, 1967), 46-49.
[6]Ibid., 53.

No doubt the values of these arguments vary, but their accumulated weight is such that the optimistic view of history as progress that dominated the nineteenth century can now be said to be shattered. It has been shattered by two world wars, numerous small wars, and their accompanying atrocities. One war might be termed an aberration, a war "to make the world safe for . . . whatever." But a sequence of wars and other horrors demands a more rigorous explanation.

Are we to say that the modern view of historical progress is entirely mistaken? Shall we conclude that history contains no meaning after all? Must we return to the historical escapism of the Greeks and other ancient peoples? That is not necessary. What is necessary is a return to the biblical view of history in which God, not human beings, is in control. His will, rather than human will or some abstract historical principle, is done. Christians express confidence in this and desire for it when they pray, "Your kingdom come, your will be done, on earth as it is in heaven" (Mt 6:9-10).

A CHRISTIAN VIEW OF HISTORY

Those sentences from the Lord's Prayer illustrate several components of a Christian view of history: a goal (God's kingdom), a struggle (the recognition that God's kingdom does not naturally come, nor is his will naturally done, without opposition), and human responsibility (to pray for and work toward the realization of that kingdom). But a better way of tracing a Christian view of history is inherent in the unique biblical doctrines that bear on it: creation, providence, revelation, redemption, and judgment. When applied to history, those doctrines teach that there is a comprehensive and universal history of the human race; that God controls history; that because of this, history has a pattern or goal; that God acts redemptively in history; and that men and women are responsible for what they do or do not do within history's flow.

The doctrine of creation. The first teaching is the biblical *doctrine of creation:* the world is not eternal but came into being as an expression of God's will and through his explicit acts. The natural world is viewed as the backdrop for the world of men and women (Gen 1). That is, the human race is not one minor or accidental part of an eternal order of things, but rather a specific and valuable part of creation, for which the other parts were brought into existence. The entire human race descended from one original pair, Adam and Eve, and is therefore one, despite subsequent division into national or ethnic groups. The purpose of history must involve all these groups and not merely Western or other "favored" ones.

The ancient world had no philosophy like this anywhere, nor is any like it today except through borrowings from Christianity. The Greeks had no concept of creation; for them matter was eternal. Nor did they have anything like a universal outlook in which all human beings from all races were part of one grand picture or design.

The need for a universal scope for history has been stressed only recently by secular historians. One thinks of the histories of Oswald Spengler and Arnold J. Toynbee. What is unique about these authors is their explicit desire to write a universal history of the race. Spengler, in his two-volume *Decline of the West*, is critical of his predecessors at this point.[7] He says they have been provincial in thinking that Europe is the all-important center of history simply because they happened to live there. They have neglected other people and areas. More serious than their provincialism, however, is the error of interpretation to which such provincialism leads. By restricting one's concern to Europe, it may be possible to devise the kind of progressive view of history the historians of recent centuries have provided. But when one looks beyond Europe to Asia and other previously neglected areas of the world, one sees at once that history is not an upward linear process but rather a phenomenon in which cultures are born, grow strong, deteriorate, and die. On the basis of that analogy Spengler predicted the West's decline (hence the title of his book). That prediction gained him instant recognition.

Toynbee is more optimistic than Spengler and also less pretentious. His work is called *A Study of History*; that is, he regarded it as merely one interpretation among many and not as *the* interpretation of history for all time.[8] Although different in approach, Toynbee's object is the same as Spengler's, namely, to bring all history within one overall framework. In doing that, he has isolated thirty-four civilizations, including thirteen "independent" civilizations, fifteen "satellite" civilizations, and six "abortive" civilizations. Each is characterized by a dominant motif.

Here is the interesting thing. Although both Spengler and Toynbee seem alert to the fact that the human race is one and that the history of the race should therefore be a universal history, their histories are remarkably different. It is

---

[7]Oswald Spengler, *The Decline of the West*, trans. Charles Francis Atkinson, 2 vols. (New York: Alfred A. Knopf, 1926, 1928).

[8]Arnold J. Toynbee, *A Study of History*, 12 vols. (London: Oxford University Press, 1934–1961).

striking how little overlap there is between them. What is wrong? Does this mean that desire for a universal history is misplaced, that no one history exists after all? Not necessarily. But significant divergence between such great historians as Spengler and Toynbee does point out how difficult it is for one human mind to grasp a subject of such proportions. That point can be put even more strongly. Since the writing of history involves a selection and interpretation of facts, and since selection is always made at least in part on the basis of the subjective experience and judgment of the interpreter, it is impossible to write a purely objective history. Historical interpretations of this scope, or even of a more limited scope, will always differ. The only way out of the problem is for us to receive an interpretation of history from outside history, as it were, from a Being who perfectly understands history but who is above and beyond it and is therefore not affected by the distortions and prejudices that living and working in history introduce. The only way to have an objective and universal view of history is for God, the God of history, to provide it.

Christianity maintains that God has done that. When we talk of a doctrine of creation and its implications for a universal view of history, we do so only because God has first revealed these things to us through the Holy Scriptures.

The doctrine of providence. Such reasoning leads naturally into the Christian doctrine of revelation, but before considering that point, it is necessary to look at the *doctrine of providence*, which also follows naturally the doctrine of creation. The Bible reveals that having created the world, God did not then abandon it, as if it were a large mechanical clock that he had wound up and was then allowing to run down. On the contrary, God guides the development of history through his eternal decrees and sometimes intervenes supernaturally both in nature and history to accomplish them.

The doctrine of divine providence puts a Christian view of history into categories entirely different from those of naturalism. The naturalist believes that there are certain unalterable laws to history according to which it is possible to predict what is coming. Spengler is an example of that view; he has used laws of birth, growth, decline, and death to predict the fall of Western civilization. An even better example is Karl Marx (1818–1883), who reduced the laws of history to materialistic or economic factors. Marx was influenced by Hegel's dialectic, but he boasted that he had stood the dialectic on its head. What he meant was that Hegel had made the spirit of rationality the determining factor in the eternal flow from thesis to antithesis to synthesis, whereas he, by contrast, had based even those rational forces on nature. Marx's view was that of Ludwig

Feuerbach (1804–1872), who taught by use of a pun in the German language that *der Mensch ist was er isst* (man is what he eats). According to his view, materialistic or economic factors are everything—with the result that class struggle, revolutionary action, and eventually the classless society are the inevitable products of them.

Christians are not locked into such determinism. According to the Bible, God does have a plan in history and history is following out that plan. But that does not mean that the outworking of this plan is mechanical. Here, of course, we get into one of the great mysteries of the Christian faith: the relationship between the eternal decrees or will of God and contrary human wills. We cannot always say precisely how that relationship works, but we can say that each is real and that the flow of history is therefore wrapped up at least partially in human obedience to or rebellion against God. The most important consequences of that human factor in regard to God's plan in history is that his plan therefore does not unfold with what we would regard as mathematical regularity. By contrast, it comes in fits and starts. There are periods of fast-moving spiritual events. There are periods in which God's promises seem delayed. The deliverance of Israel under Moses contrasted with the previous four hundred years of captivity, for example. As individuals, God seems at times to be moving quickly in our lives. At other times we see little progress.

With our modern penchant for tight schedules and regular progress, that kind of ambiguity usually seems frustrating. But it makes sense when we realize that God's purpose in history is not to build buildings (even churches) faster than anyone else or run the trains or planes according to a tighter schedule, but rather to develop godly character and conduct in his people. This must have happened with Abraham during the twenty-five years he waited in the Promised Land for the birth of Isaac, the son of promise. He was seventy-five years old when God first appeared to him and gave him the promise, but he was one hundred years old when the child was born. Likewise, Joseph spent many years in slavery and later in prison before he was raised to the position of second-in-command in Egypt. Moses was forty years old when he made his choice to identify with his people rather than with Egypt's elite. But he had to flee Egypt, and it was another forty years before he was finally called by God to return with God's command to Pharaoh: "Let my people go." In each case, God used the difficult years to develop the kind of character he needed in one later to be called to great responsibility.

Moreover, since such conduct and character can come only from association with himself, God has arranged things so that we will inevitably be drawn to him in prayer and other forms of fellowship. Thus, we pray for the coming of God's kingdom, and we ask for a revelation of his will where our individual lives are concerned.

The doctrine of revelation. Another teaching that has major bearing on a Christian view of history is the *doctrine of revelation.* This doctrine has relation to the first two. We know that this world has been created by God and is guided by God according to his own perfect plan only by the revelation of these things to us.

Revelation has both a general or objective character and a personal or subjective one. That is, there is a revelation of God's overall plan in Scripture beginning with the creation of the race and continuing through the fall, the calling out of a special people through whom a Redeemer would come, the appearance and work of Christ, the establishing of the church, and the promise of Christ's eventual return. All that is the objective framework for a Christian view of history. But the revelation also has a subjective character. As we read the Bible, God also speaks to us to call us personally into that framework through faith in and obedience to Christ. Christ is the focal point of history. We become a part of God's work in history and serve his plan for history only as we come into a relationship to that One who stands at the center of his workings.

The most important biblical idea at this point is the kingdom of God, which was discussed at some length in book two.[9] The kingdom of God has three dimensions, each of which bears on a Christian view of what is happening in history. One dimension is what we would call God's general or sovereign rule. "The Most High God rules the kingdom of mankind and sets over it whom he will" (Dan 5:21).

> For his dominion is an everlasting dominion,
>> and his kingdom endures from generation to generation;
> all the inhabitants of the earth are accounted as nothing,
>> and he does according to his will among the host of heaven
>> and among the inhabitants of the earth;
> and none can stay his hand
>> or say to him, "What have you done?" (Dan 4:34-35)

---

[9]See book 2, part IV, chapter 12, "Prophet, Priest, and King," in this volume.

The LORD brings the counsel of the nations to nothing;
> he frustrates the plans of the peoples.

The counsel of the LORD stands forever,
> the thoughts of his heart to all generations. (Ps 33:10-11)

I form light and create darkness;
> I make well-being and create calamity,
> I am the LORD, who does all these things. (Is 45:7)

"And we know that for those who love God all things work together for good, for those who are called according to his purpose" (Rom 8:28). God's rule in history is true whether men and women acknowledge it or not. They cannot break God's rule. They can only break themselves on it like weak iron on an anvil.

The personal dimension of God's kingdom is seen in God's drawing a person out of a state of rebellion and opposition to his rule to a state of glad participation in it. God does this by the new birth. The kingdom is then seen in God's work within that individual to conform him or her increasingly to the standards of that kingdom and to use the person's witness to bring that kingdom to others. When we pray "Thy kingdom come," we are praying for this present realization of God's rule in willing individuals (and not merely a future coming of Christ).

Finally, there will be a future coming of God's kingdom, when Jesus will return to judge the living and the dead.

So the Bible is a revelation of (1) God's overall guidance and rule of history, (2) a present reality in which the Spirit of God is bringing many individuals into willing conformity to the goals of God's kingdom, and (3) a promise that the kingdom will one day be consummated in the judgment of sinners and the eternal and glorious reign of Christ. Within that framework those who believe in Christ have a twofold responsibility: to live for Christ and to be his witnesses throughout the world.

The doctrine of redemption. The doctrine of redemption introduces two ideas that have already been alluded to but not adequately discussed: sin and God's unique act in Christ to save the sinner.

The first theme explains why no naturalistic or nonethical explanation of history can ever be adequate. Those who are committed to the modern, progressive understanding of history are particularly vulnerable at this point, since the progress they have envisioned is not pure progress, and in some cases it is questionable whether what they point to is progress at all. The problem is not that so-called progressive elements are not present. They are. But a tragic human flaw—what Christian theology calls original sin—mars those elements of progress and at times perverts them for destructive rather than constructive ends.

Sometimes, particularly in the self-righteous climate of modern times, it is assumed that this destructive element resides in institutions and can therefore be eliminated by social restructuring or revolution. But the problem is deeper than that. It is in the deep nature of men and women and therefore cannot be dealt with except by God for whom all things, even a restructuring of human nature, are possible.

Today, some secular thinkers are willing to recognize what *Time* magazine once called "a dark underside" to human nature. In the essay "On Evil: The Inescapable Fact," written just after the My Lai massacre at one of the worst periods of the Vietnam war, *Time* sought to get beyond the immediate tragedy to the underlying evil in human nature. The writers said,

> Today's young radicals, in particular, are almost painfully sensitive to these and other wrongs of their society, and denounce them violently. But at the same time they are typically American in that they fail to place evil in its historic perspective. To them, evil is not an irreducible component of man, an inescapable fact of life but something committed by the older generation, attributable to a particular class or the "Establishment," and eradicable through love and revolution. . . .
>
> My Lai is a token of the violence that trembles beneath the surface of American life; where else, and in what ways will it explode? How much injustice and corruption distort the reality of democracy that the U.S. offers to the world?[10]

A few years later, a campus magazine made the same observation in reaction to a book by Harvard Divinity School theologian Harvey Cox, in which he had optimistically called for faith in the "inner world" of human imagination. The magazine objected, "Three generations of American literary artists, however, have testified that the cruelty, the viciousness, and indeed the insanity rampant in our society are things which came exactly out of our own 'inferiority'; that our institutions were not flown in from the moon but are in fact projections of structures envisioned deep in the pits of our imagination."[11]

Christians concur with that analysis. It is the problem of history, from the original fall in Eden up to and including modern times. But what is the solution? If God did not act in history, there would be no solution. There would only be

---

[10]"On Evil: The Inescapable Fact," *Time*, December 5, 1969, 27.
[11]Robert F. Lucid, "People's Religion," *Pennsylvania Gazette*, March 1974, 7.

a continuing struggle with evil in which pessimism (the destruction of the race) or escapism (the Greek view of history) would have to win out. But God does act. He acts decisively, not merely to guide history or to provide a moral framework in which the worst sins are inevitably judged, but to redeem those who are responsible for the evil. He redeems them through the work of Jesus Christ. The Bible tells us that "in Christ God was reconciling the world to himself, not counting their trespasses against them, and entrusting to us the message of reconciliation" (2 Cor 5:19). As long as Christ stands in history there can be no pessimism for the person who believes in him and the value of his sacrifice.

The doctrine of God's final judgment. But all are not to be redeemed. That is a hard saying, yet it is the clear teaching of the Word of God. Therefore, to make the Christian view of history complete there must be added to the doctrines already considered—creation, providence, revelation, and redemption—the *doctrine of God's final judgment* at the end of history. Christians express belief in this doctrine in the Apostles' Creed: "From thence [that is, from heaven] he [Christ] shall come to judge the quick and the dead."

In saying that Christ is to judge the dead as well as the living (the quick), the creed is saying that in the ultimate analysis, the meaning of history is not found only at the end of history—as if everything had been building up to one final peak of accomplishment that shall then be judged fit or not fit for glory. The meaning of history is rather found in any given moment in the choice or choices made by any given individual, no matter who that person is, where he or she has come from, or how important he or she may seem to be.

Here we come back to the idea made toward the end of the last chapter, that the important moment in history is always *now*. I quote Butterfield again, who makes this point by an intriguing analogy:

> History is not like a train, the sole purpose of which is to get to its destination; nor like the conception that my youngest son has of it when he counts 360 days prior to his next birthday and reckons them all a wearisome and meaningless interim, only to be suffered for the sake of what they are leading up to. If we want an analogy with history we must think of something like a Beethoven symphony— the point of it is not saved up until the end, the whole of it is not a mere preparation for a beauty that is only to be achieved in the last bar. And though in a sense the end may lie in the architecture of the whole, still in another sense each moment of it is its own self-justification, each note in its particular context as valuable as any other note, each stage of the development having its immediate significance,

apart from the mere fact of any development that does take place. . . . We envisage
our history in the proper light, therefore, if we say that each generation—indeed
each individual—exists for the glory of God.[12]

GOD'S GLORY

There is no better example for us at this point than the example of our Lord.
Christ came to earth not to do his own will but the will of the Father who sent
him (Jn 5:30; 6:38).

"I glorified you on earth, having accomplished the work that you gave me to
do" (Jn 17:4). How did Christ's work bring glory to God? It did so by revealing
God himself clearly. Glorifying God means "to acknowledge God's attributes"
or "to make God's attributes known." God's attributes are best seen at the cross
of Christ. There above all other places God's sovereignty, justice, righteousness,
wisdom, and love are abundantly and unmistakably displayed. We see God's
sovereignty in the way in which the death of Christ was planned, promised, and
then took place, without the slightest deviation from the prophecies of the Old
Testament concerning it or adjustment to meet some unforeseen circumstance.
We see God's justice in sin's actually being punished. Without the cross, God
could have forgiven our sin gratuitously (to speak from a human perspective),
but it would not have been just. Only in Christ is that justice satisfied. We see
God's righteousness in recognition of the fact that only Jesus, the righteous One,
could pay sin's penalty. We see God's wisdom in the planning and ordering of
such a great salvation. We see his love. Only at the cross do we know beyond
doubt that God loves us even as he loves Jesus. "For God so loved the world,
that he gave his only Son, that whoever believes in him should not perish but
have eternal life" (Jn 3:16).

Jesus fully revealed these attributes of the Father by his death. Hence, his
obedience to the Father's will in dying fully glorified him. We cannot glorify
the Father as Jesus did, perfectly or by a substitutionary atonement, but we
can honor God by the way we attempt to accomplish his purposes for us—
through obedience.

---

[12]Butterfield, *Christianity and History*, 67.

CHAPTER 3

CHRIST, THE FOCAL POINT OF HISTORY

*A*t the beginning of his influential book *Christ and Time*, University of Basel professor of New Testament and early Christianity Oscar Cullmann calls attention to the fact that we in the Western world do not reckon time in a continuous forward-moving series that begins at a fixed initial point, but from a center from which time is reckoned both forward and backward. The Jewish calendar begins from what it regards as the date of the creation of the world and moves on from that point. We, by contrast, begin with the birth of Jesus of Nazareth—fixed within the space of a few years—and then number in two directions: forward, in an increasing succession of years that we identify as AD *(anno Domini,* "in the year of [our] Lord"), and backward, in a regression of years that we identify as BC ("before Christ").

That system did not come into being all at once. The custom of numbering forward from the birth of Christ was introduced in AD 525 by a Roman abbot, Dionysius Exiguus, and came into widespread use during the Middle Ages. The custom of numbering backward from the birth of Christ originated only in the eighteenth century. The interesting point is not so much the time at which those customs originated, but rather the testimony they give to the conviction in Christian hearts that Jesus is the focal point of history.

A secular historian might judge that the coming of Jesus was a pivotal event because of his obvious influence on later history. But the Christian conviction, symbolized by the division of time, goes beyond that recognition. As Cullmann says,

The modern historian may when pressed find a historically confirmed meaning in the fact that the appearance of Jesus of Nazareth is regarded as a decisive turning point of history. But the *theological* affirmation which lies at the basis of the Christian chronology goes far beyond the confirmation that Christianity brought with it weighty historical changes. It asserts rather that from this mid-point all history is to be understood and judged.[1]

Christianity affirms that apart from Christ there is no way of determining what history as a whole is all about, nor can we legitimately weigh historical events so that one may be pronounced better or more significant than another. With Christ, however, both those essentials for a true historical outlook are provided. We affirm this by our division of time into two great halves of history.

FULLNESS OF TIME

Such a division of time is not stated in the Bible explicitly. But it is pointed to by the fact that our Bible has two Testaments: the Old Testament leading up to the time of Christ, and the New Testament telling of his life and the events that flowed from it. The book of Galatians points to the significance of the specific time in history at which Christ came. It uses a phrase ("the fullness of time") that occurs nowhere else in the Bible. "But when the fullness of time had come, God sent forth his Son, born of woman, born under the law, to redeem those who were under the law, so that we might receive adoption as sons" (Gal 4:4-5).

That phrase refers primarily to historical events, so its significance in regard to Christ must first be viewed historically. What is it that made the particular time in which he came, the first century of our era, significant? A number of answers are usually given. First, it would be impossible to imagine the rapid expansion of Christianity in the world as it was prior to the time of Alexander the Great and the subsequent Roman Empire. Before Christ's birth, the world was divided into nations and religions that were separate from and hostile to one another. These were insuperable barriers to missionary work, but they had been broken down by the time of Christ's coming. Then the world was truly one world, and the missionaries of the gospel found the doors of the nations wide open as they traveled about to proclaim Christ's message.

A second factor was also important: the heritage of the Greek and Roman civilizations. The Greeks had left their language as the common, trade language

---

[1]Oscar Cullmann, *Christ and Time: The Primitive Christian Conception of Time and History*, trans. Floyd V. Filson (Philadelphia: Westminster Press, 1950), 19.

of the world. It was spoken everywhere and was therefore the language in which the Christian faith was communicated. The New Testament is written in Greek, for example, rather than in Hebrew, Aramaic, or Latin. Rome had brought peace to the world (the *pax Romana*) and had linked the world by a magnificent system of roads, some of which still exist in parts of Italy, France, Switzerland, Britain, and elsewhere. On these roads (and at sea), under the general protection of the Roman legions, the apostle Paul and his companions brought the good news of the gospel to Asia Minor, Greece, and even to Rome.

Third, the expansion of the gospel was prepared for by the dispersion of Jews throughout the Empire. The Jews had special privileges for the conduct of their religion as a result of their timely help of Julius Caesar during a particularly tense moment in the Egyptian campaign, and they were present everywhere with their synagogues, Scriptures, and general God-consciousness. The early church flourished under the wing of Judaism in its early days, and it was within the synagogues that the first converts to Christianity were made.

A fourth factor in this historical preparation for the coming of Christ was the failure of philosophy to provide sure answers to life's great questions, along with the uncertainty that had crept into the various religious systems of the times. It was a time of such moral decline and depravity that even the pagans cried out against it.

What this means, when we take it together, is that Christ's time was the focal point of history. The earlier centuries of the human race, both sacred and secular, were a preparation for him. They may have had meaning on other levels too; undoubtedly they did. But the biblical perspective is that all this was leading to Christ. Emil Brunner has written of this preparation:

> Plato and Alexander, Cicero and Julius Caesar must serve God, in order to prepare the way for Christ. It is significant that the Gospel of Luke begins with the incident of the census taken by order of Augustus, and the Gospel of Matthew begins with the story of the Magi from the East who prepare to leave their homes to follow the Star which leads to Palestine and the Court of Herod. . . . Long ago, from the very earliest beginnings, God had prepared that which he then willed to give as the salvation of the world "in the fullness of the times," as something which on the one hand—according to its human nature—grows out of this history, as well as something which came into history, as something which could not be explained from itself.[2]

---

[2]Emil Brunner, *The Christian Doctrine of Creation and Redemption: Dogmatics*, trans. Olive Wyon, vol. 2 (Philadelphia: Westminster, 1952), 237-38.

In the same way, the biblical history now unfolds from Christ through a development of his work and an outpouring of his Spirit, as the New Testament shows.

TIME MADE FULL

To speak of the fullness of time as the preparation in history for the coming of Christ is only one part of the meaning of that phrase, however, and it is not even necessarily the most important part. True, the events of history under the guidance of the sovereign God did prepare for Christ, and in that sense the time of his coming was propitious. But the time was also full in the sense that God made it full through what he did in Christ. The time of Christ bears a relationship to history as has no other time before or since.

We should focus on three key moments in Christ's life: the initial moment of the incarnation, the central moment of the crucifixion, and the climactic moment of the resurrection. Each is an unparalleled part of that total life of Christ by which history is to be understood and judged.

The essence of the *incarnation* is that by it God became man in order to achieve salvation and establish the rule of God in history and over history. The means by which that was accomplished historically was the virgin birth. The conception of Christ without benefit of a human father has always staggered the unbelieving mind, both within and outside the church, and it has been denied, thereby reducing Jesus to the level of a mere man with certain not-too-well-defined spiritual sensibilities. But the incarnation is more than this. It is the invasion by God of history through One who is uniquely both God and man. It is a supernatural or miraculous event, and it is this character of the event that the doctrine of the virgin birth both defines and preserves.

Whether or not there was a virgin birth is a historical question that has been definitively handled by J. Gresham Machen in *The Virgin Birth of Christ*, a book that no one has ever refuted or even attempted to answer.[3] Machen defends the virgin birth by an exhaustive study of the original documents (in which he demonstrates their consistency and inherent credibility) and by a devastating critique of all rival theories of the doctrine's origin. The person who wishes to investigate this side of the issue can do no better than to begin with Machen's work. What Machen does not discuss, but is of great significance for a Christian view of history, is the importance of the doctrine for history itself. The biblical narratives themselves do this.

---

[3] J. Gresham Machen, *The Virgin Birth of Christ* (New York: Harper, 1932).

Let us take Mary's hymn after the annunciation of Christ's birth and her subsequent visit to Elizabeth, who was then awaiting the birth of John the Baptist (Lk 1:46-55). It is known as the *Magnificat*, from the opening word of the hymn in Latin.

> My soul magnifies the Lord,
>> and my spirit rejoices in God my Savior,
> for he has looked on the humble estate of his servant.
>> For behold, from now on all generations will call me blessed;
> for he who is mighty has done great things for me,
>> and holy is his name.
> And his mercy is for those who fear him
>> from generation to generation.
> He has shown strength with his arm;
>> he has scattered the proud in the thoughts of their hearts;
> he has brought down the mighty from their thrones,
>> and exalted those of humble estate;
> he has filled the hungry with good things,
>> and the rich he has sent empty away.
> He has helped his servant Israel,
>> in remembrance of his mercy,
> as he spoke to our fathers,
>> to Abraham and to his offspring forever.

The power of that hymn comes from the view of God's definitive invasion of human history that its author held. Mary was describing nothing less than the total overturning of the entire state of history as we know it, a state in which the mighty usually triumph and the poor starve. The mighty are to be brought down and the poor exalted. The rich will be sent away empty and the hungry will be fed. This is to be done in accordance with God's promises to Abraham and the other fathers of the Jewish nation. It is an event from outside history, but it is also now within history. It is decisive.

We find the same thing further on in the same chapter in the *Benedictus* of the aged Zechariah (Lk 1:68-79).

> Blessed be the Lord God of Israel,
>> for he has visited and redeemed his people
> and has raised up a horn of salvation for us
>> in the house of his servant David,

as he spoke by the mouth of his holy prophets from of old,

that we should be saved from our enemies

and from the hand of all who hate us;

to show the mercy promised to our fathers,

and to remember his holy covenant,

the oath that he swore to our father Abraham, to grant us

that we, being delivered from the hand of our enemies,

might serve him without fear,

in holiness and righteousness before him all our days.

And you, child, will be called the prophet of the Most High;

for you will go before the Lord to prepare his ways,

to give knowledge of salvation to his people

in the forgiveness of their sins,

because of the tender mercy of our God,

whereby the sunrise shall visit us from on high

to give light to those who sit in darkness and in the shadow of death,

to guide our feet into the way of peace.

This hymn is referring in the first instance to the birth of John the Baptist, the "prophet of the Most High" who should "go before" him. Yet it looks beyond the work of the forerunner to the fulfillment of God's promises to Israel in the coming of Christ. In this hymn, as in the *Magnificat*, the focus is on God's intervention in history with inevitable historical results.

Rousas J. Rushdoony, who has looked at the historical aspects of the incarnation in an essay on "The Virgin Birth and History," writes,

> Prior to Jesus Christ, the movement of history was meager, and in the dark. The pilgrims of history were afraid to move; they could not move, having no direction in the dark. . . . Now, with the fullness of the revelation, God's people move with him in the light of Christ. According to the *Benedictus*, the great forward movement of man in history began in Christ and with Christ. . . . Every aspect of the nativity narrative is not only historical but directed towards the fulfillment of the historical process.[4]

The second important moment in Christ's life is the *crucifixion*, which, as a part of this central time in history, is the most central of all. It is that for which the incarnation took place, and to which the resurrection attests.

---

[4]Rousas J. Rushdoony, *The Biblical Philosophy of History* (Nutley, NJ: Presbyterian and Reformed Publishing Co., 1969), 110.

The cross is the central feature of the New Testament. Each of the Gospels devotes an unusually large proportion of its narrative to the events of Christ's final week in Jerusalem, culminating in his crucifixion and resurrection, and it is no exaggeration to say that the cross overshadows the life and ministry of Christ even before this time. The very name *Jesus*, given to the child by Joseph at the direction of the angel, looks forward to his death on Calvary. The angel explained the choice of the name, saying, "You shall call his name Jesus, for he will save his people from their sins" (Mt 1:21). Jesus, too, spoke of the suffering that was to come. "And he began to teach them that the Son of Man must suffer many things and be rejected by the elders and the chief priests and the scribes and be killed, and after three days rise again" (Mk 8:31). "The Son of Man is going to be delivered into the hands of men, and they will kill him. And when he is killed, after three days he will rise" (Mk 9:31). Jesus linked the success of his mission to his crucifixion. "And I, when I am lifted up from the earth, will draw all people to myself" (Jn 12:32). He spoke of the crucifixion as that vital "hour" for which he came (Jn 2:4; 12:23, 27; 17:1; compare Jn 7:30; 8:20; 13:1). In narrating these events, Matthew gives two-fifths of his Gospel to the final week in Jerusalem; Mark, three-fifths; Luke, one-third; and John, nearly one-half.

Again the crucifixion is a theme of the Old Testament: the Old Testament sacrifices, given to Israel by God for pedagogical purposes, prefigured Christ's suffering. The prophets explicitly foretold it. Jesus probably referred to both those lines of witness when he taught the downcast Emmaus disciples that the Old Testament had foretold his death. "And he said to them, 'O foolish ones, and slow of heart to believe all that the prophets have spoken! Was it not necessary that the Christ should suffer these things and enter into his glory?' And beginning with Moses and all the Prophets, he interpreted to them in all the Scriptures the things concerning himself" (Lk 24:25-27).

It is not surprising in view of this biblical emphasis that the centrality of Christ's cross has been recognized by Christians in all ages, even before Constantine made the cross the universal badge of Christendom. "The cross stands as the focal point of the Christian faith. Without the cross the Bible is an enigma, and the Gospel of salvation is an empty hope."[5]

Anyone who knows anything at all about the Bible should know why the crucifixion of Christ is central to it. The Bible is a story of man's hopeless fall

---

[5]James Montgomery Boice, *Philippians: An Expositional Commentary* (Grand Rapids: Zondervan, 1971), 144. For a full discussion of the nature of Christ's work on the cross, see book two.

into sin and of God's perfect remedy for that sin through Christ. The cross is God's solution to the sin problem. But there is even more to the centrality of the cross than this. If the cross is the solution to the sin problem and the *only* solution, then the cross confronts each individual as a crisis to which he or she must respond, and in accordance with which decision he or she will either live or die. People in Old Testament times either looked forward to Christ as the Savior whom God had promised, or did not look forward to him. We either look back in simple faith to what he has done for our salvation, or we do not look back. In that difference hangs our destiny.

The third key moment in the life of Christ is the *resurrection*. It is important in two ways. First, it is important historically. Only because of the resurrection did the church of Christ (and with it Christianity) come into existence. Apart from a true resurrection within history, the early disciples would simply have scattered to their homes, their dreams shattered. They would have said, as did the Emmaus disciples, "But we had hoped [past tense] that he was the one to redeem Israel" (Lk 24:21). Only because Jesus appeared to them again after the resurrection did the disciples regather as a community, convinced of their message and empowered to go out with their testimony, even in the face of persecution and death. In this historical about-face the resurrection was both climactic and pivotal.

Second, the resurrection is important for each individual. It is part of God's solution to the human problem. What is our problem? It is sin. Sin has three chief areas of expression: it causes us to be ignorant of God; it alienates us from God; and it makes us powerless to live for God—even if we could somehow come to know him and be reconciled to him. The incarnation is God's answer to the first problem: although God has also revealed himself in Scripture, it is in Christ above all that we see and know him. God's answer to the second problem is the crucifixion: in it God has made an atonement for sin by which the guilt of sin is removed, and we, who once were far off, are now brought near by the blood of Christ (Eph 2:13). God's answer to the third problem is the resurrection. It is not only proof of Christ's divinity and of the value of his death for sinners. It is also the promise and proof of new life and power for all who believe in Jesus. It may be said of the resurrection, as well as of the incarnation, that with it a new thing came into the world and that the world can never be the same because of it.

The importance of the resurrection was detailed in book two, where it was argued that it proves the following:

1. There is a God, and the God of the Bible is the true God.

2. Jesus of Nazareth is the unique Son of God.

3. All who believe in Christ are justified from all sin.

4. The Christian can live a life that is pleasing to God.

5. Death is not the end of this life.

6. There will be a final judgment on all who reject the gospel.[6]

So at the middle of history, symbolized by the division into BC and AD, stands the central event, the life and work of Christ. History prepared for it and was changed by it. History is understood by it and is judged by it. The greatest of all human decisions is how we, each one, will respond to Jesus.

LORD OF HISTORY

One more thing must be said before leaving this subject. Although we speak of Christ as the focal point of history, that statement is not to be understood as if we are saying that Christ appeared only there—and that, apart from that brief interval in time, he and history are separate. On the contrary, we say that the One who appeared in history is also the Lord of history. He is to be seen at its very beginning; he is currently ruling history to accomplish his own wise ends, and he will also appear at the end of history as its judge. In other words, he is the One through whom the Father exercises his relationship to history (as we saw in the last chapter).

Cullmann summarizes the biblical evidence like this:

> Even the time before the Creation is regarded entirely from the position of Christ; it is the time in which, in the counsel of God, Christ is already foreordained as Mediator before the foundation of the world (Jn 17:24; 1 Pet 1:20). He is then the Mediator in the Creation itself (Jn 1:1; Heb 1:2; and especially vv. 10ff.; 1 Cor 8:6; Col. 1:16). . . . The election of the people of Israel takes place with reference to Christ and reaches its fulfillment in the work of the Incarnate One. . . . Christ's role as Mediator continues in his Church, which indeed constitutes his earthly body. From it he exercises over heaven and earth the Lordship committed to him by God, though now it is invisible and can be apprehended only by faith (Mt 28:18; Phil. 2:9ff.). Thus Christ is further the Mediator of the completion of the entire redemptive plan at the end. That is why he returns to the earth; the

---

[6]See book 2, part IV, chapter 16 of this volume.

new creation at the end, like the entire redemptive process, is linked to that re-demption of men whose Mediator is Christ. Upon the basis of his work the resur-rection power of the Holy Spirit will transform all created things, including our mortal bodies; there will come into being a new heaven and a new earth in which sin and death no longer exist. Only then will Christ's role as Mediator be fulfilled. Only then will Christ "subject himself to him who subjected all things to him, in order that God may be all in all" (1 Cor 15:28). At that point only has the line which began with the Creation reached its end.[7]

Although Christ is the focal point of history, he is also and at the same time over and in control of history. Thus, it is his history and contains his meaning. We may enter that history consciously through faith in him.

---

[7]Cullmann, *Christ and Time*, 108-9.

PART II

THE CHURCH OF GOD

To me . . . this grace was given, to preach to the Gentiles the unsearchable riches of Christ, and to bring to light for everyone what is the plan of the mystery hidden for ages in God, who created all things, so that through the church the manifold wisdom of God might now be made known to the rulers and authorities in the heavenly places.

EPHESIANS 3:8-10

God is spirit, and those who worship him must worship in spirit and truth.

JOHN 4:24

Do this in remembrance of me.

1 CORINTHIANS 11:24

And he gave the apostles, the prophets, the evangelists, the pastors and teachers, to equip the saints for the work of ministry, for building up the body of Christ, until we all attain to the unity of the faith and of the knowledge of the Son of God, to mature manhood, to the measure of the stature of the fullness of Christ.

EPHESIANS 4:11-13

CHAPTER 4

CHRIST'S CHURCH

*I*f the life, death, and resurrection of Jesus Christ is the focal point of history, then the church of Christ, his body, is a focal point too. It cannot be a focal point in the same sense. Christ's work is the church's foundation; he, not the church, is the point at which history is to be understood and judged. Yet Christ's work continues in the church; the fullness of the mystery of God in redemption is disclosed among his people. A text from Paul's writings says,

> To me, though I am the very least of all the saints, this grace was given, to preach to the Gentiles the unsearchable riches of Christ, and to bring to light for everyone what is the plan of the mystery hidden for ages in God, who created all things, so that *through the church* the manifold wisdom of God might now be made known to the rulers and authorities in the heavenly places. (Eph 3:8-10)

Any reader of the New Testament will understand that the church is important in this age, just as God's dealings with Israel were important in the Old Testament period. But the text from Ephesians says more. The fullness of God's wisdom is being revealed in the church even now, and the principalities and powers—the phrase refers to spiritual powers such as angels and demons—are scrutinizing the church to learn of the wisdom and plan of God revealed there.

It is as though the church is a stage on which God has been presenting the great drama of redemption, a true-life pageant in which it is shown how those who have rebelled against God and wrecked his universe are now being brought back into harmony with him, becoming agents of renewal and healing instead.

Those who have become members of the body of Christ are given the privilege of becoming what Ralph Keiper calls "the verifying data of God's grace."

> God's will for you and me is to be agents of his wisdom, to show that truly we are the capstone of his creation, that men may behold us as the masterpiece of God. . . . We have been redeemed with such a salvation that in the midst of a sinful and crooked world we can become the sons of God without rebuke, demonstrating the marvelous salvation of which we speak, that we might become, as it were, the picture book leading people to the written Book that they by the Holy Spirit might come to know the living Book, even Jesus.[1]

Because of the church's critical importance for disclosing the redemptive plan of God, our attention in this section must therefore be on this reality. We will study the church's nature, marks, life, organization, and responsibilities.

OLD TESTAMENT BACKGROUND

Strictly speaking, the church is the creation of the historical Christ and therefore dates from the time of Christ. But the church has roots in the Old Testament and cannot be understood well without that background. This is true theologically because the idea of a called-out "people of God" obviously existed in the Old Testament period, just as in the New. It is also true linguistically since the Greek word for *church* (*ekklēsia*) occurs frequently in relation to Israel in the Greek translation of the Old Testament (the Septuagint) and was therefore known to the New Testament writers. The passages in which *ekklēsia* occurs may therefore be supposed to have exerted an influence on the thinking of the New Testament writers.

In the Septuagint *ekklēsia* generally translates the Hebrew term *qhl*, which, like the Greek term, refers to those who are "called out" or "assembled" by God as his special possession. That is the case in regard to the earliest appearances of this term—in the phrase "the day of the assembly" (Deut 9:10; 10:4; 18:16); it refers to the nation of Israel assembled at Mount Sinai. This is also its meaning in Psalm 22:22, 25, where the term is translated "congregation." It is the idea behind Stephen's reference to the assembly in his sermon in Acts: "This is the one who was in the congregation in the wilderness with the angel who spoke to him at Mount Sinai, and with our fathers" (Acts 7:38). In these passages and others the key element is the call of God, followed by the response of the ones

---

[1] Ralph L. Keiper, "The Problem of Knowledge in the World of Men," *Tenth: An Evangelical Quarterly*, July 1975, 10.

called and God's solemn covenant with them to bless them—to be their God and they his people.

We see an illustration of these elements in the call of Abraham, with whom the Old Testament "assembly" begins. We are told that God appeared to Abraham saying, "Go from your country and your kindred and your father's house to the land that I will show you. And I will make of you a great nation, and I will bless you and make your name great, so that you will be a blessing" (Gen 12:1-2). In this narrative the initiative was entirely with God. He was the one who sought and called Abraham; it was not Abraham who sought him.

Again, we see the beginning of the promise or covenant: "I will make of you a great nation . . . I will bless you." That covenant is elaborated in God's subsequent revelations to Abraham. "Know for certain that your offspring will be sojourners in a land that is not theirs and will be slaves there, and they will be afflicted for four hundred years. But I will bring judgment on the nation that they serve, and afterward they shall come out with great possessions. . . . To your offspring I give this land" (Gen 15:13-14, 18).

> Behold, my covenant is with you, and you shall be the father of a multitude of nations. . . . And I will establish my covenant between me and you and your offspring after you throughout their generations for an everlasting covenant, to be God to you and to your offspring after you. And I will give to you and to your offspring after you the land of your sojournings, all the land of Canaan, for an everlasting possession, and I will be their God. (Gen 17:4, 7-8)

Abraham's response was to believe God (Gen 15:6) and worship him (Gen 12:8).

We see the same pattern in God's dealings with Isaac, Abraham's son, and with Jacob, his grandson. Later there was a special call to Abraham's descendants when they had become slaves in Egypt. On that occasion God told Moses, "I have surely seen the affliction of my people who are in Egypt and have heard their cry because of their taskmasters. I know their sufferings, and I have come down to deliver them out of the hand of the Egyptians and to bring them up out of that land to a good and broad land, a land flowing with milk and honey" (Ex 3:7-8).

Finally, a call and promise to Israel followed the Babylonian captivity:

> Therefore, behold, the days are coming, declares the LORD, when it shall no longer be said, "As the LORD lives who brought up the people of Israel out of the land of Egypt," but "as the LORD lives who brought up the people of Israel out of the

north country and out of all the countries where he had driven them." For I will bring them back to their own land that I gave to their fathers. (Jer 16:14-15)

In each of these passages there is the creation of an *ekklēsia*, an assembly of those who are called out of a normal relationship to the world in order to be a special people of God. That call is accompanied by special promises and is met by faith, worship, love, and obedience from those to whom the call comes.

FOUNDED ON CHRIST

Each of these Old Testament elements is present in the New Testament understanding of the church, but the church has characteristics that cannot rightly be applied to the Old Testament assembly and that therefore set it off as something new. The church (1) is founded on the Lord Jesus Christ, (2) is called into being by the Holy Spirit, and (3) is to contain people of all races who thereby become one new people in the sight of God.

The first reference to the church in the New Testament makes the first of these points clearly: the sole foundation on which the church can stand is its master, Jesus Christ. Matthew 16:18 is probably the Bible's best-known text dealing with the church. Jesus had left the dangerous area of Galilee for Caesarea Philippi, where he had begun to question his disciples about people's opinion of him. "Who do people say that the Son of Man is?" he asked them.

They answered, "Some say John the Baptist, others say Elijah, and others Jeremiah or one of the prophets."

"But who do you say that I am?" he continued.

Peter answered for the rest, "You are the Christ, the Son of the living God." At that point Jesus began to speak of the church and of the sufferings that would precede its founding. "Blessed are you, Simon Bar-Jonah! For flesh and blood has not revealed this to you, but my Father who is in heaven. And I tell you, you are Peter, and on this rock I will build my church, and the gates of hell shall not prevail against it." He then "began to show his disciples that he must go to Jerusalem and suffer many things from the elders and chief priests and scribes, and be killed, and on the third day be raised" (Mt 16:13-21).

That passage makes several important points. First, the emphasis is on Peter's confession, which focused on *the person of Christ* and not on Peter himself. Jesus announced that this insight had been given to him by special revelation.

The Roman Catholic Church has built its doctrine of the supremacy of the pope on this passage, claiming that Christ founded the church on Peter and his successors. Actually, the Greek underlying this passage contains a play on words between the masculine and feminine forms of the word *petros*, meaning stone or rock, which shows that the church's true foundation must be Jesus. Peter's name (*petros*, the masculine form) meant "stone." But it could be a big stone or a little one; it could even mean what we might call a pebble. *Petra*, the feminine form, meant "bedrock," such as the living rock of a mountain. So the passage really means, "You, Peter, are a little quarried stone, solid (in this confession at least) but easily moved. I, by contrast, am the living rock of ages, and on that solid foundation, which your confession points to, I will build my church." Nowhere in his later New Testament writings did Peter ever suggest that he was the foundation of the church. Yet he spoke of Jesus as the foundation, using Christ's image, which had undoubtedly impressed itself on his imagination.

Not long after the resurrection, Peter and John were preaching and were arrested by the Sanhedrin, the same body that had tried and condemned Jesus, and were asked to give an account of themselves. Peter used the occasion to testify clearly to the Lord. He spoke of Christ's power, through which a crippled man had just been healed. Then he continued on in clear reference to Christ. "*This Jesus is the stone* that was rejected by you, the builders, which has become the cornerstone. And there is salvation in no one else, for there is no other name under heaven given among men by which we must be saved" (Acts 4:11-12).

We have the same thing in Peter's first epistle, in which he compared Christ to a foundation stone on which we, as quarried stones, may be fastened. His words are,

> Come to him, a living stone rejected by men but in the sight of God chosen and precious, you yourselves like living stones are being built up as a spiritual house, to be a holy priesthood, to offer spiritual sacrifices acceptable to God through Jesus Christ. For it stands in Scripture:
>
> "Behold, I am laying in Zion a stone,
>> a cornerstone chosen and precious,
> and whoever believes in him will not be put to shame." (1 Pet 2:4-6)

A second important point of this first mention of the church in the New Testament is its stress on the *work of Christ*. Peter had pointed to Christ's person, confessing that he was "the Christ, the Son of the living God." But after acknowledging that this was correct, Jesus said that his initial work as Messiah (Christ) would not be what the disciples expected of him. Rather it would be a work of suffering and death. "From that time Jesus began to show his disciples that he must go to Jerusalem and suffer many things from the elders and chief priests and scribes, and be killed, and on the third day be raised" (Mt 16:21). Peter did not understand that. He thought it unnecessary and rebuked Christ for it. "Far be it from you, Lord!" he said. "This shall never happen to you."

But Jesus considered his suffering so necessary that he regarded Peter's words as a satanic temptation. He answered Peter, "Get behind me, Satan! You are a hindrance to me. For you are not setting your mind on the things of God, but on the things of man" (Mt 16:23).

So the first thing that must be said about the church is that the person and work of the Lord Jesus Christ is its foundation. It is based on him. It is the assembled body of those for whose sins he, the eternal Son of God, died to make atonement. Any assembly of people founded on any other foundation is not the church, no matter what it calls itself. On the other hand, all who are united to the crucified but risen Christ by faith are part of his church, regardless of their background or denominational labeling.

This concept has an important application, namely, that the church of Christ is one church and must be seen to be one church by the world. Jesus taught this to the Jews of his day by an image drawn from rural life. He compared himself to a shepherd and his church to sheep. He would die for them, he said, and then he would call forth his sheep from many different sheepfolds to follow him. "I have other sheep that are not of this fold. I must bring them also, and they will listen to my voice. So there will be one flock, one shepherd" (Jn 10:16).

We must understand what Christ said in that verse, since it has been badly misused. The initial problem can be traced to Jerome and the Latin Vulgate. In that translation of the Bible, Jerome failed to distinguish between a *fold* (mentioned in the first part of the verse) and a *flock* (mentioned later). They are two entirely different words in Greek. Yet Jerome treated them the same, and many of our translations have followed him. The error is corrected in the RSV and other versions. In Jerome's translation, Jesus seemed to be saying that there is only one organization, and the obvious deduction was that there could therefore be no salvation outside the formal organization of the then-existing church. That interpretation became official Roman Catholic teaching, but it is based on that wrong translation.

The church about which Christ was speaking is not an organization (though it obviously has organized parts) but rather the entire company of those who have the Lord Jesus Christ as their shepherd. Thus, the unity comes not from forcing all the sheep into one great organization, but in the fact that all have heard Jesus and have left lesser loyalties to follow him. Moreover, to the degree that they do follow him, a visible (though not necessarily structural) unity follows.

The question is, do we truly have or acknowledge such unity? We often do not. The error of the older Roman Catholic Church is in supposing that the Holy Spirit must work along ecclesiastical lines. It is a real error. But although it expresses itself differently, the same error often exists within Protestantism. The problem is not so much that there are different denominations within Protestantism. People are different, and there is no reason why there ought not to be different organizations with different forms of service and church government to express those differences. To insist that there must be one Protestant denomination (which some in the ecumenical movement insist on) is a similar error.

The real problem is that believers in one denomination refuse to cooperate with believers in another denomination, justifying their noncooperation on grounds that other Christians are somehow contaminated by their associations or are disobeying the Lord by remaining in their church or are not actually Christians. That attitude is a great hindrance to the advance of the gospel in the world today. Moreover, it is sin, and we will not have great revival until believers repent of that sin and ask God to cleanse them of it.

What are we to conclude about the church on the basis of these and other biblical passages? We can say the following:

1. There is one church to which all who confess Jesus as Lord and Savior belong. All who are Christians are one with all other Christians and should acknowledge that to be true, even though the other believer is wrong about or denies what we consider to be important doctrines.

2. Nothing in the Bible tells us that there should be or even that we should desire to have one all-encompassing organization. Instead we may expect God to call people to faith within various organizations and lead believers into Christian service within those or other organizations. We dare not say that another believer is out of God's will because he or she is serving somewhere else.

3. God's people need one another and must learn from one another, whether Baptists, Presbyterians, Episcopalians, Roman Catholics, Pentecostals, Methodists, independents, or members of any other denomination. It does not mean that each of us will therefore think those other believers are completely right in church matters or even in doctrine—we do not

dare say that we are totally right—but it does mean that we need to learn something about the body of Christ and receive help for the body of Christ from many Christians.

4. Because of the love that is to bind the true church together, we also have an obligation to demonstrate that love-unity tangibly, over and above denominational programs and concerns. To do so is the indispensable basis for our mission. "By this [your love for one another] all people will know that you are my disciples," said Jesus (Jn 13:35).[2]

EMPOWERED BY THE SPIRIT

A second unique characteristic of the New Testament church is that it is brought into being and is empowered by the Holy Spirit. Although the Lord Jesus Christ is the church's foundation, the church did not come into being immediately following his death, resurrection, and ascension, but at Pentecost when the Holy Spirit came on the disciples in power and caused many to respond to the first preaching about Jesus. The Lord prepared the disciples for this coming of the Holy Spirit by commanding them to stay in Jerusalem until that moment. Then they were to go forth as his witnesses. "But you shall receive power when the Holy Spirit has come upon you, and you shall be my witnesses in Jerusalem and in all Judea and Samaria, and to the end of the earth" (Acts 1:8).

The Holy Spirit does three things for the church in all times and places. First, as the verse just quoted says, he *empowers the church* to do Christ's bidding and to be effective in doing it. That is the thrust of Christ's command. He was telling the disciples that they were to be his witnesses throughout the whole world, beginning in Jerusalem. But they would not be able to do that until the Holy Spirit came on them to fill their words with power.

When Peter preached on Pentecost, three thousand people responded to the gospel. They then entered into the church's fellowship, devoting themselves to "the apostles' teaching and fellowship, to the breaking of bread and the prayers" (Acts 2:42). When Peter next preached five thousand believed (Acts 4:4). It was a phenomenal response for any age or place, but particularly so for a city and people who had earlier rejected Jesus. Two months earlier they had hounded Jesus to his death. Now they were responding in massive numbers. What made

---

[2]I have borrowed a portion of the material on Christ as Shepherd and the church as his flock from my own lengthier study of this passage in *The Gospel of John*, vol. 4 (Grand Rapids: Zondervan, 1978). See "One Flock, One Shepherd," 113-20. The full treatment of the passage is on 76-120.

the difference? Not the preaching of Peter certainly, or we would have to conclude that he was a more effective communicator than the Lord. It was rather that the Holy Spirit spoke through Peter's message and changed the hearts of his hearers. So it is today. We preach Christ and witness to him, but we cannot change people's hearts. Only the Holy Spirit can do that, and he does.

Second, the Holy Spirit has been sent to develop the *character of the Lord Jesus Christ* in his people. We are not like him naturally, but we are to become like him as the Spirit of Christ increasingly transforms us into his image. "And we all, with unveiled face, beholding the glory of the Lord, are being transformed into the same image from one degree of glory to another. For this comes from the Lord who is the Spirit" (2 Cor 3:18).

Finally, by means of the Holy Spirit the risen *Christ is with his people* to comfort and direct them during this age. The Lord spoke of this even before his crucifixion. "I will ask the Father, and he will give you another Helper, to be with you forever, even the Spirit of truth, whom the world cannot receive, because it neither sees him nor knows him. You know him, for he dwells with you and will be in you" (Jn 14:16-17). It was because of the Holy Spirit's coming that Christ could say, "Behold, I am with you always, to the end of the age" (Mt 28:20), and "Let not your hearts be troubled, neither let them be afraid" (Jn 14:27).

The church of Christ is to be a spiritual reality in which the distinct endowments of the Spirit of Christ are seen. That reality should be true of the organized or visible church. The organized church is not identical with the church of God, and it often fails to show these characteristics. Yet these characteristics should be seen wherever true believers gather together in Christ's name; the world should be able to recognize that there is something spiritual about them. Francis Schaeffer writes,

> These are the things that the world should see when they look upon the church— something that they cannot possibly explain away. . . . The church of the Lord Jesus Christ should be functioning moment by moment on a supernatural plane. This is the church living by faith, and not in unfaith. This is the church living practically under Christ's leadership, rather than thinking of Christ being far off and building the invisible Church, while we build that which is at hand with our own wisdom and power.[3]

---

[3]Francis A. Schaeffer, *True Spirituality* (Wheaton, IL: Tyndale, 1971), 172, 174.

Including All People

A third special characteristic of the church was suggested in discussing the church's foundation, but was not adequately developed there. It is the universal nature of the church, in which people of all cultures are brought together into its fellowship and all national, racial and other barriers are broken down.

Bannerman writes,

> The invisible Church of Christ made up of the whole number of true believers throughout the world, is *catholic*, or, in other words, not confined to any place or people. In this respect, it stands contrasted with the limited and local economy of the church under the Jewish dispensation. In so far as the Jewish church constituted a society of the worshipers of God, it was local, not catholic. It had its center at Jerusalem, and its circumference at the geographical limits of Judea. . . . There is a striking contrast between all this and the Christian church under the Gospel. There is now no local center for the religious service of Christ's people—no holy place to which they must repair personally for their worship, or towards which, when at a distance, they must turn their face in prayer. Neither at Jerusalem, nor in the temple, are men now to worship the Father. Wherever on the wide earth there is a true worshipper, *there* is a true temple of Jehovah, and *there* he may be worshipped in spirit and in truth. . . . The narrow barriers of a former economy have been thrown down; and in the gift of the Spirit to all believers, and in the fellowship of the Spirit coextensive with all, there is laid the foundation of a Church, no longer confined to one nation as before under the law, but worldwide and universal.[4]

That union of peoples within the church is *given* to the church by God, but it is something that must be achieved historically. The church must actually develop brotherhood, a sense of family oneness, among those to whom the gospel spreads. Many barriers to such a union existed in the early church. There were barriers of race—the Greek despising the Roman, the Roman contemptuous of the Greek. There were barriers of nationhood—most captive people chafing under the yoke of Rome. There were barriers of sex, language, and culture—the same barriers that exist among people today. But they were broken down as those who were called to faith in Christ increasingly came to see their oneness in him. "For he himself is our peace, who has made us both [Jews and Gentiles] one

---

[4]James Bannerman, *The Church of Christ: A Treatise on the Nature, Powers, Ordinances, Discipline and Government of the Christian Church*, vol. 1 (1869; reprint ed., London: Banner of Truth Trust, 1974), 42-43.

and has broken in his flesh down the dividing wall of hostility" (Eph 2:14). To the Corinthians Paul wrote, "God . . . through Christ reconciled us to himself and gave us the ministry of reconciliation" (2 Cor 5:18).

In his commentary on the Gospel of John, William Barclay tells of an incident from the life of Egerton Young, the first missionary to the Indians of Saskatchewan, Canada. Young had gone to them with the message of the love of God the Father, and they had received it like a new revelation. When he told his message an old chief said, "When you spoke of the great Spirit just now, did I hear you say, 'Our Father'?"

"Yes, I did," said the missionary. "We know him as Father because he is revealed to us as Father by Jesus Christ."

"That is very new and sweet to me," said the chief. "We never thought of the great Spirit as Father. We heard him in the thunder; we saw him in the lightning, the tempest and the blizzard, and we were afraid. So when you tell us that the great Spirit is *our Father*, that is very beautiful to us." The chief paused, and then asked, "Missionary, did you say that the great Spirit is *your* Father?"

"I did," said Young.

"And," said the chief, "did you say that he is the Father of *the Indians*?"

"Yes," said the missionary.

"Then," said the old chief, "*you and I are brothers*."[5]

Nothing will abolish distinctions between nations. There will always be nations. Nothing (so far as I can see) will ever abolish denominations. But in spite of that—in spite of race, nations, and denominations—there can be a real and visible unity among those who acknowledge the Lord Jesus Christ as their shepherd. As Dr. D. Martyn Lloyd-Jones says in his study of the second chapter of Ephesians, "We are all equally sinners. . . . We are all equally helpless. . . . We have all come to one and the same Savior. . . . We have the same salvation. . . . We have the same Holy Spirit. . . . We have the same Father. . . . We even have the same trials. . . . And finally, we are all marching and going together to the same eternal home."[6] Only a knowledge of the love of the Lord Jesus Christ will draw us together.

---

[5]William Barclay, *The Gospel of John*, vol. 2 (Philadelphia: Westminster Press, 1956), 74-75.

[6]D. Martyn Lloyd-Jones, *God's Way of Reconciliation* (Grand Rapids: Baker Book House, 1972), 282-88.

CHAPTER 5

THE MARKS OF THE CHURCH

The church is founded on the Lord Jesus Christ and is called into being by the Spirit of Christ. The church must therefore be like Christ, possessing at least some of his characteristics. That statement is not only the result of a process of reasoning. It is clearly taught in the Bible. We find the apostle John saying, "As he is so also are we in this world" (1 Jn 4:17).

What does that mean? What should characterize the church? The most comprehensive answer is seen in Jesus' prayer for the church recorded in John 17. He prayed that the church might be characterized by six things: joy (Jn 17:13), holiness (Jn 17:14-16), truth (Jn 17:17), mission (Jn 17:18), unity (Jn 17:21-23), and love (Jn 17:26). His life was marked by each of those qualities. These marks of the church are so important that we should study each of them carefully before going on to other items that are also part of the church's life and ministry.

A JOYOUS PEOPLE

It is interesting that the characteristic mentioned first by Jesus is joy. Many of us would not naturally mention it, let alone put it first. We would point to love or holiness or true doctrine. But Jesus said, "I am coming to you [the Father], and these things I speak in the world, that they may have my joy fulfilled in themselves" (Jn 17:13). That most of us do not think of joy as a primary characteristic of the church probably indicates how little we regard it and how far we have moved from the spirit of the early church. The early church was a joyous assembly.

We see their joy immediately when we begin to study the subject in the New Testament. In the Greek language, the verb meaning "to rejoice" or "be joyful" is *chairein;* it is found seventy-two times. The noun, meaning "joy," is *chara;* it occurs sixty times. As we study these usages, we find that joy is not a technical concept, found only in highly theological passages. Rather it most often occurs simply as a greeting, meaning "Joy be with you!" To be sure, *chairein* is not always restricted to the speech of Christians. It is used, for example, in the letter to Felix about Paul by the Roman officer Claudius Lysias, where it means "greetings" (Acts 23:26). But in Christian hands it obviously meant much more than it did with pagans and is used more frequently.

We notice, for example, that the angel who announced the birth of Jesus to the shepherds said, "Behold, I bring you good news of great joy that will be for all the people. For unto you is born this day in the city of David a Savior, who is Christ the Lord" (Lk 2:10-11). The word here obviously meant more than "greetings!" Later Jesus said, "These things I have spoken to you, that my joy may be in you, and that your joy may be full" (Jn 15:11). The things he had spoken were great promises.

Paul's writings contain many uses of the word. In Philippians, the apostle, wishing to give a final admonition to his friends, wrote, "Rejoice in the Lord always; again I will say, Rejoice" (Phil 4:4). As Barclay says in his discussion of this term, "This last greeting, 'Joy be with you!' rings triumphantly through the pages of the New Testament. . . . There is no virtue in the Christian life which is not made radiant with joy; there is no circumstance and no occasion which is not illumined with joy. A joyless life is not a Christian life, for joy is one constant in the recipe for Christian living."[1]

Is the church today joyful? Are Christians? We need not doubt that we are all far more joyful than we would be if we were not Christians, or that there are places where joy is particularly evident. Joy is often very evident in new believers, for example. But in most churches, if one were to observe them impartially week after week, I wonder whether joy would be visible. We think of joy as something that should characterize the church ideally and will doubtless characterize it in that day when we are gathered together around the throne of grace to sing God's

---

[1]William Barclay, *Flesh and Spirit: An Examination of Galatians 5:19-23* (Nashville: Abingdon, 1962), 77-78.

glory. But here? Here it is often the case that there are sour looks, griping, long faces, and other manifestations of an inner misery.

A SEPARATED PEOPLE

A second characteristic of the church is holiness, the characteristic of God most mentioned in the pages of the Word of God. Holiness therefore should characterize God's church. We are to be a "holy" people (1 Pet 2:9). We are to "strive" for holiness "without which no one will see the Lord" (Heb 12:14). Jesus spoke of this mark of the church when he prayed that God would keep it from the evil one. "I do not ask that you take them out of the world, but that you keep them from the evil one. They are not of the world, just as I am not of the world. Sanctify them in the truth; your word is truth" (Jn 17:15-17).

Some people have identified holiness with a culturally determined behavioral pattern, and so have identified as holy those who do not gamble or smoke or drink or play cards or go to movies or do any of a large number of such things. Their approach betrays a basic misconception. It may be that holiness in a particular Christian may result in abstinence from one or more of these things, but the essence of holiness is not found there. Consequently, to insist on such things for those in the church is not to promote holiness but rather to promote legalism and hypocrisy. In some extreme forms, it may even promote a false Christianity according to which men and women feel they are justified before God on the basis of some supposedly ethical behavior.

The apostle Paul found that to be true of the Israel of his day, as Jesus had also found it before him. So Paul distinguished clearly between that kind of holiness (the term he used is *righteousness*) and true holiness, which comes from God and is always God-oriented. He said of Israel, "For, being ignorant of the righteousness that comes from God, and seeking to establish their own, they did not submit to God's righteousness" (Rom 10:3).

Israel had imagined that holiness was something that could be graded. That is, as we look around we see some whom we consider low on the scale of human goodness: criminals, perverts, habitual liars, and other base characters. We might give them a score in the low teens, for although they are not very good by our standards they are nevertheless not entirely without any redeeming qualities. A little higher up are the average people of society. They score between thirty and sixty. Then there are the very good people. They may score in the seventies. Beyond that, if you push the score up to one hundred (or higher if that is possible), you get to God. His holiness is perfect holiness. According to that way of looking at holiness, God's holiness is only a perfection of the holiness that lies to a greater or lesser degree in all of us. We are to please him (some would say "earn heaven") by trying harder.

That is what Israel had done, and it is what nearly everybody naturally does. But it does not reflect the biblical idea of holiness. According to the Bible, holiness actually deals (on God's level) with transcendence, and (on our level) with a fundamental response to him that we would call commitment or dedication.

The biblical idea of holiness is made somewhat clearer when we consider words that are related to it, namely, *saint* and *sanctify*. Christ used the second one in John 17. A saint is not a person who has achieved a certain level of goodness (although that is what most people think) but rather one who has been "set apart" for God. Therefore, in the Bible the word is not restricted to a special class of Christians, still less a class that is established by the official action of an ecclesiastical body. Rather it is used of all Christians (Rom 1:7; 1 Cor 1:2; 2 Cor 1:1; Eph 1:1; Phil 1:1; and so on). The saints are the "called-out ones" who make up God's church.

The same idea is present when the Bible refers to the sanctification of objects (as in Ex 40). Moses was instructed to sanctify the altar and laver in the midst of the tabernacle. That is, he was to "make saints" of them. The chapter does not refer to any intrinsic change in the nature of the stones—they are not made righteous. It merely indicates that they were to be set apart for a special use by God.

In John 17:19 Jesus prayed, "I consecrate [the word is *sanctify*] myself, that they also may be sanctified in truth." The verse does not mean that Jesus made himself more righteous, for he already was righteous. Instead it means that he separated himself for a special task, the task of providing salvation for people by his death. If holiness is to be understood at all, it must be understood in that framework.

But if holiness has to do with separation or consecration, and if believers are already holy by virtue of their being set apart for himself by God, why did Christ pray for our sanctification? Why pray for what we already have? The answer is that although we have been set apart for God, we often fail to live up to that calling. To paraphrase Wordsworth, it is "trailing clouds of old commitments, sins and loyalties that we come."

A TRUTH-ROOTED PEOPLE

What is the cure? That question brings us to the third mark of the church: truth. We are led to truth because both Christian joy and holiness depend almost entirely on how well we know God's Word—that is, how well we know and practice the principles of God's written revelation. Jesus said, "*These things* I have spoken to you, that my joy may be in you, and that your joy may be full" (Jn 15:11), and "*These things* I speak in the world, that they may have my joy fulfilled in themselves" (Jn 17:13). Again, "Sanctify them in the *truth*; your word is *truth*" (Jn 17:17).

A striking thing that we realize more and more as we grow in the Christian life is that nearly all that God does in the world today he does by the Holy Spirit through the instrumentality of his written revelation. That is true of sanctification. Since sanctification means to be set apart for God's use, our text is saying that the only way this will ever happen to us is by appropriating God's truth recorded in the Bible.

As far as truth goes, the world lives by an illusion. Its views are an inevitable problem for us unless we have a sure way of countering and actually overturning its influence. Ray Stedman writes of this problem when he says,

> The world lives by what it thinks is truth, by values and standards which are worthless, but which the world esteems highly. Jesus said, "What is exalted among men is an abomination in the sight of God" (Lk 16:15). . . . How can we live in that kind of a world—touch it and hear it, having it pouring into our ears and exposed to our eyes day and night, and not be conformed to its image and squeezed into its mold? The answer is, we must know the truth. We must know the world and life the way God sees it, the way it really is. We must know it so clearly and strongly that even while we're listening to these alluring lies we can brand them as lies and know that they are wrong.[2]

Stedman is saying that Christians should be the greatest of realists, because their realism is that of the truth of God. That by its very nature should lead to greater joy and sanctification.

A MISSIONARY PEOPLE

Up to this point Christ's prayer (Jn 17) has been dealing with things that concern the church itself or that concern individual Christians personally. We have looked at joy, holiness, and truth. But while those characteristics are important and undoubtedly attainable to some degree in this life, it does not take much thinking to figure out that all three would be more quickly attained if we could only be transported to heaven. We have joy here. But what is it compared to that abundant joy we will have when we eventually see the source of our joy face to face? The

---

[2]Ray C. Stedman, *Secrets of the Spirit* (Old Tappan, NJ: Revell, 1975), 147-48.

Bible acknowledges this when it speaks of the blessedness of the redeemed saints, from whose eyes all tears shall be wiped away (Rev 7:17; 21:4). In this life we undoubtedly know some sanctification. But someday we shall be made completely like Jesus (1 Jn 3:2). In this life we are able to assimilate some aspects of God's truth. "Now we see in a mirror dimly, but then face to face. Now I know in part; then I shall know fully, even as I have been fully known" (1 Cor 13:12). If that is true, why should we not go to heaven immediately?

The answer is in a fourth mark of the church. The church is not only to look inward and find joy, Christward and find sanctification, to the Scriptures and find truth. It is also to look outward to the world and find there the object of its mission. Jesus said, "As you [the Father] sent me into the world, so *I have sent them* into the world. And for their sake I consecrate myself, that they also may be sanctified in truth" (Jn 17:18-19).

The first thing these verses tell us is where our mission is to be conducted. The word *mission* comes from the Latin verb meaning "to send" or "dispatch." But when we ask, "To whom (or where) are we sent?" the answer is, "Into the world." That answer is probably the explanation of why the evangelical church in America is not the missionary church it claims to be. It is not that the evangelical church does not support foreign missions. It does. The problem does not lie there. Rather it lies at the point of the evangelicals' personal withdrawal from the culture. Many seem afraid of the culture. They try to keep as far from the world as possible, lest they be contaminated by it. They have developed their own subculture. It is possible, for example, to be born of Christian parents, grow up in that Christian family, have Christian friends, go to Christian schools and colleges, read Christian books, attend a Christian country club (known as a church), watch Christian movies, get Christian employment, be attended by a Christian doctor, and finally die and be buried by a Christian undertaker in hallowed ground. A Christian subculture? That is certainly not what Jesus meant when he spoke of his followers being "in the world."

What does it mean to be in the world as a Christian? It does not mean to be like the world; the marks of the church are to make the church different. It does not mean that we are to abandon Christian fellowship or our other basic Christian orientations. It means that we are to know non-Christians, befriend them, and enter into their lives in such a way that we begin to infect them with the gospel, rather than their infecting us with their outlook.

A young pastor in Guatemala went from seminary to a remote area known as Cabrican. Cabrican was unpopular; it was located at an altitude of about nine thousand feet and was nearly always damp and cold. The church he went to was small, having only twenty-eight members, including two elders and two deacons. These believers met together on most nights of the week, but they were not growing as a congregation. There was no outreach. In one of his first messages to them the young pastor, Bernardo Calderón, said, "I know God cannot be satisfied with what we are doing." Then he challenged them to this program.

First, they abandoned the many dull meetings at the church, retaining only the Bible-school hour on Sunday. In their place home meetings were established. On Monday night they would meet in a home in one area of Cabrican, and everyone would attend. As they made their way to that home they were to invite everyone they encountered, even passers-by on the streets. Since the Christians came from different areas of the city and took different paths to get there, this meant that quite a bit of the city was covered. On Tuesday the church met somewhere else. This time different paths were used as the twenty-eight members converged, and different villagers were invited. So it was on Wednesday and Thursday and the other days of the week, as the church literally left its four small walls to go out into the world with the gospel. The result? Within four years the church had eight hundred members. The next year a branch church was started, and today there are six churches in that area of Guatemala, two of which have nearly one thousand members. There is even an agricultural cooperative in which the church members buy land for their own poor and then buy and sell the produce their own people supply. The entire area has been revitalized.

The second thing these verses talk about is the character of the ones who are to conduct this mission, which means our character as Christian people. We are to be *as Christ* in the world. Jesus compared the disciples to himself, both in having been sent into the world by the Father and being sanctified or set apart to that work. He said, "As you sent me into the world, so I have sent them into the world. And for their sake I consecrate myself, that they also may be sanctified in truth" (Jn 17:18-19). We are to be in our mission as Jesus was in his mission. We are to be like the One we are presenting.

A UNIFIED PEOPLE

A fifth mark of the church is unity. Christ said,

> I do not pray for these only, but also for those who will believe in me through their word, that they may all be one, just as you, Father, are in me, and I in you, that they also may be in us, so that the world may believe that you have sent me.

The glory that you have given me I have given to them, that they may be one even as we are one, I in them and you in me, that they may become perfectly one, so that the world may know that you have sent me and loved them even as you loved me. (Jn 17:20-23)

What kind of unity is this to be? If the unity is to be organizational, our efforts to achieve and express it will be in one direction while, if it is to be a more subjective unity, our efforts will be expended differently.

One thing the church does not need to be is a great *organizational unity*. Whatever advantages or disadvantages may be found in massive organizational unity, that in itself obviously does not produce the results Christ prayed for. Nor does it solve the church's other problems. It has been tried and found wanting. In the early days of the church there was much growth but little organizational unity. Later, as the church came into governmental favor under Constantine and his successors, the visible church increasingly centralized, until during the Middle Ages there was literally one united ecclesiastical body covering all Europe. Wherever one went—north, south, east, or west—there was one united, interlacing church with the pope at its head. Was it a great age? Was there deep unity of faith? Was the church strong? Was its morality high? Did men and women find themselves increasingly drawn to that faith and come to confess Jesus Christ as their own Savior and Lord? On the contrary, the world believed the opposite. Spurgeon wrote, "The world was persuaded that God had nothing to do with that great crushing, tyrannous, superstitious, ignorant thing which called itself Christianity; and thinking men became infidels, and it was the hardest possible thing to find a genuine intelligent believer north, south, east or west."[3]

Certainly there is something to be said for some form of outward, visible unity in some situations. But it is equally certain that this type of unity is not what we most need, nor is it that for which the Lord prayed.

Another type of unity that we do not need is *conformity*—that is, an approach to the church that would make everyone alike. Here we probably come closest to the error of the evangelical church. If the liberal church for the most part strives for organizational unity—through the various councils of churches and denominational mergers—the evangelical church seems to strive for an identical pattern of appearance and behavior for its members. Jesus was not looking for that either. On the contrary, there should be diversity among Christians, diversity

---

[3]Charles Haddon Spurgeon, "Unity in Christ," *Metropolitan Tabernacle Pulpit*, vol. 12 (Pasadena, TX: Pilgrim Publishing, 1970), 2.

of personality, interests, lifestyle, and even methods of Christian work and evangelism. Uniformity is dull, like rows of Wheaties boxes. Variety is exciting. We see it in the variety of nature and the actions of God.

But if the unity for which Jesus prayed is not an organizational unity or a unity achieved by conformity, what kind of unity is it? It is a unity analogous to the unity that exists in the Godhead. Jesus spoke of it like this: "That they may all be one, just as you, Father, are in me, and I in you, that they also may be in us . . . I in them and you in me, that they may become perfectly one" (Jn 17:21, 23). The church is to have a spiritual unity involving the basic orientation, desires, and will of those participating. "Now there are varieties of gifts, but the same Spirit; and there are varieties of service, but the same Lord; and there are varieties of activities, but it is the same God who empowers them all in everyone" (1 Cor 12:4-6).

This is not to say that all true believers actually enter into this unity as they should. Otherwise, why would Christ have prayed for it? Like the other marks of the church, unity is something given to the church but also something for which the body of true believers should strive.

A LOVING PEOPLE

At last we come to love, the greatest mark of all. Love is the mark that gives meaning to the others, and without which the church cannot be what God intends it to be. Having written about love and having placed it in the context of faith, hope and love, the apostle Paul concluded, "But the greatest of these is love" (1 Cor 13:13).

With the same thought in mind, the Lord Jesus Christ, having spoken of joy, holiness, truth, mission, and unity as essential marks of the church in his high priestly prayer (Jn 17), concluded with an emphasis on love. Here we see the "new commandment" of John 13:34-35 again: "that you love one another; just as I have loved you, you also are to love one another. By this all people will know that you are my disciples, if you have love for one another." Jesus said that he declared the name of God to the disciples in order that "the love with which you [the Father] have loved me may be in them, and I in them" (Jn 17:26).

We understand the preeminence of love if we see it in reference to the other marks of the church. What happens when you take love away from them? Suppose you subtract love from joy? What do you have? You have hedonism, an exuberance in life and its pleasures, but without the sanctifying joy found in relationship to the Lord Jesus Christ.

Subtract love from holiness. What do you find then? You find self-righteousness, the kind of self-contentment that characterized the Pharisees of Christ's day. By the standards of the day the Pharisees lived very holy lives, but they did not love others and thus were quite ready to kill Christ when he challenged their standards.

Take love from truth and you have a bitter orthodoxy, the kind of teaching that is right but that does not win anybody.

Take love from mission and you have imperialism, colonialism in ecclesiastical garb.

Take love from unity and you soon have tyranny. Tyranny develops in a hierarchical church where there is no compassion for people or desire to involve them in the decision-making process.

Now express love and what do you find? All the other marks of the church follow. What does love for God the Father lead to? Joy. Because we rejoice in God and in what he has done for us. What does love for the Lord Jesus Christ lead to? Holiness. Because we know that we will see him one day and will be like him: "Everyone who thus hopes in him purifies himself as he is pure" (1 Jn 3:3). What does love for the Word of God lead to? Truth. If we love the Word, we will study it and therefore inevitably grow into a fuller appreciation of God's truth. What does love for the world lead to? Mission. We have a message to take to the world. Where does love for our Christian brothers and sisters lead us? Unity. Because by love, we discern that we are bound together in that bundle of life that God himself has created within the Christian community.

Like all divine things, love comes to us by revelation only. God has revealed himself to be a God of love in the pages of the Old Testament. We are told there that he set his love on Israel even though nothing in the people merited it. God is revealed to be a God of love in Christ's teaching. He called him Father, indicating that his was a father's love. The best and fullest revelation of love is at the cross of Jesus Christ. "For God so loved the world, that he gave his only Son, that whoever believes in him should not perish but have eternal life" (Jn 3:16).

There has never been, there never will be, a greater demonstration of the love of God. So, if you will not have the cross, if you will not see God speaking in love in Jesus Christ, you will never find a loving God anywhere. The God of the Bible is going to be a silent God for you. The universe is going to be an empty universe. History is going to be meaningless. Only at the cross do we find God in his true nature and learn that these other things have meaning.[4]

---

[4]For a fuller treatment of these six marks of the church see the author's *The Gospel of John*, vol. 4 (Grand Rapids: Zondervan, 1978), 395-445, 463-71, from which the material in this chapter has been condensed.

CHAPTER 6

HOW TO WORSHIP GOD

*C*hristians believe that true worship is the highest and noblest activity of
which man, by the grace of God, is capable."[1] Those words by John R. W.
Stott find an echo in the hearts of all who know God and desire to serve him.
Yet much that passes for worship today is not worship at all.

"What is worship?" some ask. "Who can worship? Where can one worship?
How does one worship?" ask others. Many who sincerely desire to worship do
not know how to go about it. A. W. Tozer, a pastor and Bible student of the last
generation, wrote about the problems he saw in his churches:

> Thanks to our splendid Bible societies and to other effective agencies for the dis-
> semination of the Word, there are today many millions of people who hold "right
> opinions," probably more than ever before in the history of the church. Yet I
> wonder if there was ever a time when true spiritual worship was at a lower ebb.
> To great sections of the church the art of worship has been lost entirely, and in
> its place has come that strange and foreign thing called the "program." This word
> has been borrowed from the stage and applied with sad wisdom to the type of
> public service which now passes for worship among us.[2]

A person might argue that program nevertheless has a place in the church's activity and that right opinions about God are essential. Tozer would agree with
the second point (and perhaps even with the first). But having said that, we

---

[1]John R. W. Stott, *Christ the Controversialist: A Study in Some Essentials of Evangelical Religion* (London:
Tyndale Press, 1970), 160.
[2]A. W. Tozer, *The Pursuit of God* (Harrisburg, PA: Christian Publishing, 1948), 9.

cannot avoid the problem. Is the "worship" we often see in the churches really what God would have? Is it genuine worship? The only way to answer those questions is to study what the Bible has to say about the subject.

BIBLICAL PRINCIPLES OF WORSHIP

Let us begin by setting down some of the Bible's basic teachings about worship, and then go on to discuss its essential nature and forms.

1. God desires worship—in fact, he commands it. We see that in Christ's words to the woman of Samaria. The woman had asked Jesus a question about the proper place to worship, but he had directed her thoughts away from the place of worship to the nature of worship itself, saying that God desires such worship. "The hour is coming, and is now here, when the true worshipers will worship the Father in spirit and truth, for the Father *is seeking* such people to worship him" (Jn 4:23). Similarly, when our Lord was tempted by Satan with the gift of the kingdoms of this world if only he would fall down and worship Satan, Jesus replied by quoting Deuteronomy 6:13. "Be gone, Satan! For it is written, 'You shall worship the Lord your God and him only shall you serve'" (Mt 4:10). In Revelation 19:10 an angel says simply, "Worship God."

2. God alone is to be worshiped. That truth is explicit in Christ's reply to Satan. It is also the essence of the first and second commandments in the Decalogue: "You shall have no other gods before me. You shall not make for yourself a carved image, or any likeness of anything that is in heaven above, or that is in the earth beneath, or that is in the water under the earth. You shall not bow down to them or serve them" (Ex 20:3-5). The God who makes these commands is the triune God who has revealed himself in Jesus Christ, his Son. Therefore, the only true and acceptable worship is worship directed to him. If it is not directed to him, it is not true worship, no matter how decorous or impressive the ceremony.

3. The worship of God is a mark of saving faith. Paul wrote about this in Philippians: "For we are the real circumcision [that is, the true people of God], who worship by the Spirit of God and glory in Christ Jesus and put no confidence in the flesh" (Phil 3:3). That verse speaks of three marks of faith. The last, putting "no confidence in the flesh," is obviously important, for it is a matter of adhering to the true gospel. The second, "glory" in Christ or "joy," is also a mark of faith and of the church, as indicated in John 17 (studied in the last chapter) and in Galatians 5. But who would naturally think of worship as being a mark of saving faith? Not many. Yet Paul included it here along with other essentials.

4. Worship is a corporate activity. This does not mean that we are not to worship privately. Indeed, the Lord commanded privacy in regard to prayer ("When you pray, go into your room and shut the door and pray to your Father who is in secret"—Mt 6:6). But worship in its fullest expression is to involve the entire people of God. This is noticeable in Scripture from the earliest chapters of Genesis ("At that time people began to call upon the name of the LORD"— Gen 4:26) to the book of Revelation ("And I heard every creature in heaven and on earth and under the earth and in the sea, and all that is in them, saying, 'To him who sits on the throne and to the Lamb be blessing and honor and glory and might forever and ever!' And the four living creatures said, 'Amen!' and the elders fell down and worshiped" [Rev 5:13-14]).

5. God is not pleased with all worship. Jesus made that point to the Pharisees of his day. "Well did Isaiah prophesy of you hypocrites, as it is written, 'This people honors me with their lips, but their heart is far from me; in vain do they worship me'" (Mk 7:6-7). Jesus taught that God desires worship, but not all that passes for worship is acceptable to him. True worship must be of the heart and not a ceremony only.

It is sobering to note that in the pages of the Bible God says more about unacceptable worship than he does about acceptable or pleasing worship. The prophet Amos quoted him as saying,

> I hate, I despise your feasts,
> > and I take no delight in your solemn assemblies.
> Even though you offer me your burnt offerings and grain offerings,
> > I will not accept them;
> and the peace offerings of your fattened animals,
> > I will not look upon them.
> Take away from me the noise of your songs;
> > to the melody of your harps I will not listen.
> But let justice roll down like waters,
> > and righteousness like an ever-flowing stream. (Amos 5:21-24)

The prophet Isaiah wrote,

> What to me is the multitude of your sacrifices?
> > says the LORD;
> I have had enough of burnt offerings of rams
> > and the fat of well-fed beasts;
> I do not delight in the blood of bulls,
> > or of lambs, or of goats.

When you come to appear before me,
> who has required of you
> this trampling of my courts?
Bring no more vain offerings;
> incense is an abomination to me.
New moon and Sabbath and the calling of convocations—
> I cannot endure iniquity and solemn assembly.
Your new moons and your appointed feasts
> my soul hates;
they have become a burden to me;
> I am weary of bearing them.
When you spread out your hands,
> I will hide my eyes from you;
even though you make many prayers,
> I will not listen;
> your hands are full of blood.
Wash yourselves; make yourselves clean;
> remove the evil of your deeds from before my eyes;
cease to do evil,
> learn to do good;
seek justice,
> correct oppression;
bring justice to the fatherless,
> plead the widow's cause. (Is 1:11-17)

David said,
> You will not delight in sacrifice, or I would give it;
> you will not be pleased with a burnt offering.
> The sacrifices of God are a broken spirit;
> a broken and contrite heart, O God, you will not despise. (Ps 51:16-17)

God desires and commands worship, but although worship is an important and essential mark of the corporate people of God, not all that goes by the name of worship is pleasing to him.

GOD'S "WORTH-SHIP"

"What is true worship?" "How can we know that what we are doing in our worship of God is pleasing to him?" Part of the answer is in the root meaning of the word *worship*. If we had been living in England during the days of the formation of modern English, between the period of Geoffrey Chaucer and William Shake-speare, we would not have used the word *worship* at all. Instead we would have said *worth-ship*, meaning that in worshiping God we were assigning to him his true worth. Linguistically speaking, worship of God is the same thing as praising God or glorifying his name.

Here let us ask what it means to "glorify" God. In the early years of the Greek language, when Homer and Herodotus were writing, there was a Greek verb, *dokeō*, from which the Greek noun *doxa* (meaning "glory") came. The verb originally meant "to appear" or "to seem." Consequently, the noun that derived from it meant "an opinion," which is the way something appears or seems to the observer. From that meaning we have acquired the English words *orthodox*, *heterodox*, and *paradox*, meaning "straight (or correct) opinion," "other (or in-correct) opinion," and "contrary (or conflicting) opinion." The theological dic-tionary edited by Gerhard Kittel gives several pages to this early history of the words. In time, the verb *dokeō* was used only for having a good opinion about some person, and the noun, which kept pace with the verb in development, came to mean the "praise" or "honor" due to one of whom that good opinion was held. Kings possessed glory because they merited the praise of their subjects. Psalm 24 speaks of the King of glory:

Who is this King of glory?
 The LORD, strong and mighty,
 the LORD, mighty in battle! . . .
 The LORD of hosts,
 he is the King of glory! (Ps 24:8, 10)

At this point, we can see the effect of taking the word over into the Bible and applying it to God, for if a person had a right opinion about God, it meant that she or he was able to form a correct opinion of God's attributes. God is sovereign, holy, omniscient, just, faithful, loving, immutable. God is glorified when he is acknowledged to be so.

The good Anglo-Saxon word *worth* might well have been used to express the essence of "glory" in the English language had not the French word *gloire* predominated. Since the French word did, we normally speak of glorifying God rather than of worth-ifying him. Nevertheless the idea remains in our word *worship*, as we have indicated. To glorify God is to acknowledge his worth-ship. We worship God, just as we glorify God, when we acknowledge his perfections.

IN SPIRIT AND TRUTH

Such a definition of the word *worship* must not lead us to think only in terms of orthodox persuasions, however. Those are important—we must worship the true God and not another—but they are not the whole of what is involved. An element that must also be present is our personal response to the one we are worshiping, which means that we must worship "in spirit and truth," as Jesus indicated (Jn 4:24). True worshipers must worship "in truth" because truth has to do with what God's nature is. They must worship in "spirit" because they can respond to this only spiritually.

Some Bible readers have been misled in understanding this verse by their assumption that when Jesus spoke of "spirit" he was thinking of the Holy Spirit, meaning that it is only by means of the Holy Spirit that worship is made possible. That is true, of course. Nothing spiritual is possible except by the Spirit's work. Nevertheless, that is not the meaning of the verse. Here Jesus is speaking of "spirit" generally (without the definite article), not *the* Holy Spirit. He is teaching that, in the age he was then inaugurating, the place of worship would not matter. A man or woman would not worship merely by being in the right place and doing certain things. Believers would worship in their spirit, which could take place anywhere.

Many people worship with the body. They consider themselves to have worshiped if they have been in the right place doing the right things at the right time. In Christ's day, the woman of Samaria thought this meant being in Jerusalem at the Jewish temple, or on Mount Gerizim at the Samaritans' temple. In our day, this would refer to people who think they have worshiped God because they have occupied a seat in a church on Sunday morning, sung a hymn, lit a candle, crossed themselves, or knelt in the aisle. Jesus says that those customs are not worship. They may be a vehicle for real worship; in some cases they may also hinder it. But they are not worship in themselves. We must not confuse worship with the particular things we do on Sunday morning.

In addition, we must not confuse worship with feeling. It may be the case, and often is, that emotions are stirred in real worship. At times tears fill the eyes or joy floods the heart. But it is possible for these things to happen and still not to have worship. It is possible to be moved by a song or by oratory and yet not come to a genuine awareness of God and praise him.

True worship occurs only when that part of human beings, their spirit, which is akin to the divine nature (God is spirit), actually meets with God and finds itself praising him for his love, wisdom, beauty, truth, holiness, compassion, mercy, grace, power, and other attributes. On this point, William Barclay wrote, "The true, the genuine worship is when man, through his spirit, attains to friendship and intimacy with God. True and genuine worship is not to come to a certain place; it is not to go through a certain ritual or liturgy; it is not even to bring certain gifts. True worship is when the spirit, the immortal and invisible part of man, speaks to and meets with God, who is immortal and invisible."[3]

To worship God in spirit also has bearing on the question of the various types of liturgy used in Christian churches. It means that, with the exception of liturgical elements that suggest wrong doctrine, no liturgy in itself is either inherently better or worse than another. For any given congregation, one type of service will presumably be more valuable than another. But decisions about the most valuable type of service should be arrived at, not by asking whether one likes emotional or nonemotional hymns, extemporaneous or read prayers, congregational responses or silence—in short, whether one prefers Anglican, Lutheran, Presbyterian, Methodist, Baptist, Congregational, or Quaker liturgies—but by asking how effective the service is in turning the worshipers' attention away from the service itself to God.

In thinking through this particular issue, I have been greatly helped by C. S. Lewis. Lewis was a member of the Church of England and was accustomed to various forms of what we generally call a "liturgical" service. Nevertheless, Lewis did not plead for liturgy. He asked merely for what he called *uniformity*, on the grounds that "novelty" in the worship service at best turns our attention to the novelty and at worst turns it to the one who is enacting the liturgy.

Lewis wrote, "As long as you notice, and have to count, the steps, you are not yet dancing but only learning to dance. A good shoe is a shoe you don't notice. Good reading becomes possible when you need not consciously think about eyes, or light, or print, or spelling. The perfect church service would be one we were almost unaware of; our attention would have been on God."[4] We should pray that God will use any form of church service in which we happen to be participating to that end.

But that does not mean that "anything goes" in Christian worship, or that some elements are not necessary and that others are not detrimental. In defining worship as "in truth," Christ meant at least three things.

---

[3]William Barclay is one who holds this view. See his *Gospel of John*, vol. 1 (Philadelphia: Westminster, 1956), 154.
[4]C. S. Lewis, *Letters to Malcolm: Chiefly on Prayer* (New York: Harcourt, Brace & World, 1964), 4.

First, we must approach God *truthfully*, that is, honestly or wholeheartedly. Jesus said of the people of his day, "This people honors me with their lips, but their heart is far from me; in vain do they worship me" (Mk 7:6-7). According to Jesus, nothing is worship unless honesty of heart characterizes the worshiper. We must not pretend to worship. We must worship truthfully, knowing that our hearts are open books before him.

Second, we must worship on the basis of *biblical revelation*. The above verse goes on to condemn those who have substituted "the precepts of men" for the doctrines of Scripture. "Your word is truth," says the Scripture (Jn 17:17). If we are to worship in truth, our worship must be in accord with the principles and admonitions of the Bible.

A true sermon is an exposition of Scripture. Its purpose is to direct the worshipers' attention to the truth of God and invite them to order their lives in accordance with it. The Westminster Confession of Faith speaks of "the reading of the Scriptures with godly fear; the sound preaching and conscionable hearing of the Word, in obedience unto God, with understanding, faith, and reverence" as being "ordinary" parts of our worship (chap. XXI, 5).

When the Protestant Reformation first took place under Martin Luther in the early sixteenth century, there was an immediate elevation of the Word of God in Protestant services. Doctrines and principles of the Word of God, long covered over by the traditions and ceremonial encrustations of the medieval church, again came into prominence. John Calvin particularly carried this out with thoroughness, ordering that the altars (the center of the Latin Mass) be removed from the churches and that a pulpit with a Bible on it be placed in the center of the building. Every line of the architecture would carry the worshipers' gaze to the Book that alone contains the way of salvation, and outlines the principles on which the church of the living God is to be governed.

Third, to approach God in truth means that we must approach him *christo-centrically*. Jesus said to his disciples, "I am the way, and the truth, and the life. No one comes to the Father except through me" (Jn 14:6). That is a difficult point for many to accept. Because of the difficulty, God has taken pains to teach throughout Scripture that this is the way of approach to him.

In the Old Testament, God gave Moses clear instructions for the design of the Jewish temple. What was the temple? It was not a thing of great beauty or permanence. It had no stained-glass windows, no arches. It was made of pieces of wood and animal skins. But each part was significant. It taught the way to God. Take that temple with its altar for sacrifice, its laver for cleansing, its holy place, and its holy of holies. The altar is the cross of Christ. It teaches that without the shedding of blood there is no remission of sins. It directs attention to the Lamb of God who was to come to take away the sins of the world. The laver is a picture of cleansing, which Christ provides when we confess our sins and enter into fellowship with him. The table of showbread, which was within the holy place, speaks of Christ as the bread of life. The seven-branched candlestick reveals him as the light of the world. The altar of incense is a picture of prayer. Behind the altar of incense was the great veil, dividing the holy place from the holy of holies. The veil was torn in two at the moment of Christ's death in order to demonstrate that his death was the fulfillment of all those figures. His death is the basis of our approach to the Almighty. Finally, within the Holy of Holies was the Ark of the Covenant with its mercy seat, on which once a year on the Day of Atonement the high priest placed the blood of a lamb. There, symbolized by the space above the mercy seat, was the presence of God to whom we can now come because of Christ's death on our behalf.

There is no other way to come to God. To come through Christ is to come in truth. He is the truth. We must come in God's way and not in any way of human devising.[5]

---

[5]Parts of this chapter have already appeared in print as part of the author's commentary on *The Gospel of John*, vol. 1 (Grand Rapids: Zondervan), 363-69.

CHAPTER 7

SALVATION'S SIGNS
AND SEALS

*T*he last chapter contained a section of the Westminster Confession of Faith
that spoke of "the reading of the Scriptures" and "sound preaching" as being
ordinary parts of Christian worship. The Confession goes on to speak of other
parts of worship, among which are "the due administration and worthy receiving
of the sacraments" (chap. XXI, 5).

There has been much debate in the church about the sacraments—their
number, for example, or whether a particular form of administration of the sacraments is necessary for the existence of a true church. To a greater or lesser degree,
however, nearly all Christians have acknowledged that there are sacraments instituted by Christ and that these are to have a place in the normal or "ordinary"
worship of God's people. The word *sacrament* (like the word *Trinity*) is an ex-
trabiblical term. It entered theology by means of the Latin Vulgate, where it is
customarily used to render the Greek word *mysterion*. It designates those "ordinances" (practices) to which the Lord himself gave special significance.

In most Protestant churches the sacraments are two: baptism and the Lord's
Supper. In the Roman Catholic Church there are seven: the two sacraments
already referred to plus the ceremonies of penance, confirmation, marriage, holy
orders, and final unction.

Peter Lombard (1100–1160) called a sacrament "a sign of a sacred thing."[1]
John Calvin wrote that a sacrament is "an outward sign by which the Lord seals

---

[1]Peter Lombard, *The Four Books of Sentences*, book 4, 1, 2, in *A Scholastic Miscellany: Anselm to Ockham*,
ed. Eugene R. Fairweather, The Library of Christian Classics, vol. 10 (Philadelphia: Westminster
Press, 1956), 338.

on our consciences the promises of his good will toward us in order to sustain
the weakness of our faith; and we in turn attest our piety toward him in the
presence of the Lord and of his angels and before men."[2]

FOUR ELEMENTS OF A SACRAMENT

In what way do the Scriptures represent the sacraments of the church as being
different from other practices, such as the reading of Scripture or prayers, which
are not sacramental? What constitutes a sacrament? There are four elements.

1. The sacraments are *divine ordinances instituted by Christ himself*. In that
respect, the sacraments are similar to other necessary ordinances that also form
part of the church's worship—prayer, for example. Christ told us to pray. But
they differ from things that we may do but that are not commanded. We sing
when we assemble, and we have biblical warrant for it, including the example
of Jesus and his disciples (Mk 14:26). But the singing of hymns is not specifically
commanded by the Lord, and consequently falls in the category of those things
that are permissible and even good, but not mandatory. The sacraments are
mandatory. The Lord's Supper was instituted by Jesus on the night in which he
was betrayed. Baptism was instituted shortly before his ascension into heaven.

2. The sacraments are ordinances in which *material elements are used as visible
signs of God's blessing*. In baptism the sign is water. In the Lord's Supper two
signs are used: bread, which signifies the broken body of the Lord Jesus Christ,
and wine, which signifies his shed blood.

This feature is important in understanding the nature of a sacrament. It sets
baptism and the Lord's Supper off from other proper but nonsacramental things,
which do not use a material element as a sign. The material element distinguishes
the sacrament from the reality that it signifies. A sign is a visible object that
points to a reality different from and more significant than itself. A sign saying
"New York" points to New York. A sign reading "Drink Coca-Cola" directs our
attention to Coca-Cola. The sacrament of baptism points to our identification
with Christ by faith. The Lord's Supper points to the reality of our communion
with him. In the case of the sacraments, the sign is secondary, outward, and
visible. The reality is primary, inward, and invisible.

An important consequence of this is that neither baptism nor the Lord's
Supper make or keep one a Christian. That is, we do not become a Christian

---

[2]John Calvin, *Institutes of the Christian Religion*, ed. John T. McNeill, trans. Ford Lewis Battles, 2 vols.
(Philadelphia: Westminster, 1960), 1172.

by being baptized, nor do we remain a Christian by "taking communion" periodically. Those signs merely point to something that has taken place or is taking place internally and invisibly.

Again, a sign frequently indicates ownership, and the sacraments do that too, particularly baptism. Baptism indicates to the world and to ourselves that we are not our own but that we have been bought with a price and are now identified with Jesus. That truth was a great comfort to Martin Luther, who had times when he was confused about everything, no doubt because of the strain of being in the forefront of the Reformation for twenty-eight years. In those bleak periods he questioned the Reformation itself; he questioned his faith; he even questioned the value of the work of the Lord Jesus Christ on his behalf. At such times, we are told, he would write on his table in chalk the two words *Baptizatus sum!* (I have been baptized!). That would reassure him that he really was Christ's and had been identified with him in his death and resurrection.

3. The sacraments are *means of grace* to the one who rightly partakes of them. In saying this, we must be careful to point out that we are not therefore assigning some magical property to baptism or the observance of the Lord's Supper, as if grace, like medicine, is automatically dispensed along with the material elements. That error, in regard both to the sacraments and grace, led to the abuse of the sacraments in the early Roman Catholic Church and then later in some of the groups that emerged from the Reformation. In each case the sacrament rather than faith became the means of salvation. The custom arose even of delaying baptism (in particular) until the last possible moment before death, in order that the greatest number of sins might be washed away by it.

To say that the sacraments are not magical or mechanical, however, does not mean that they do not have value. God has chosen to use them to encourage and strengthen faith in believers. Thus, they presuppose the acknowledgment of God's grace by the one who partakes of them, but they also strengthen faith by reminding the believer of what they signify and of the faithfulness of the One who has given them. John Murray writes,

> Baptism is a means of grace and conveys blessing, because it is the certification to us of God's grace and in the acceptance of that certification we rely upon God's faithfulness, bear witness to his grace, and thereby strengthen our faith. . . . In the Lord's Supper that significance is increased and cultivated, namely, communion with Christ and participation of the virtue accruing from his body and blood. The Lord's Supper represents that which is continuously being wrought. We partake

of Christ's body and blood through the means of the ordinance. We thus see that the accent falls on the faithfulness of God, and the efficacy resides in the response we yield to that faithfulness.[3]

4. The sacraments are *seals, certifications,* or *confirmations* to us of the grace they signify. In our day the use of seals is infrequent, but the examples we have suggest the idea. The seal of the United States of America appears on a passport, for example. It is stamped into the paper so that the document cannot be altered, thus validating the passport and showing that the one possessing it is a United States citizen. Other documents are validated by a notary public. The notary's seal is confirmation of the oath taken. The sacraments are God's seal on the attestation that we are his children and are in fellowship with him.

BAPTISM

The first of the two Protestant sacraments is baptism. "All authority in heaven and on earth has been given to me. Go therefore and make disciples of all nations, baptizing them in the name of the Father and of the Son and of the Holy Spirit, teaching them to observe all that I have commanded you. And behold, I am with you always, to the end of the age" (Mt 28:18-20). It is evident from those verses that baptism is an initiatory sacrament belonging to the task of making disciples; the text speaks of the authority or lordship of Christ and of the baptized person as one who recognizes and professes.

Major difficulties have arisen in dealing with this subject, as the controversy surrounding it would indicate.[4]

---

[3]John Murray, *Collected Writings*, vol. 2, *Select Lectures in Systematic Theology* (Edinburgh: Banner of Truth Trust, 1977), 367-68.

[4]Not all these difficulties are dealt with in this chapter. Many of them concern other areas of theology: for example, the validity of infant baptism, which is actually a question of covenant theology rather than of the significance of baptism itself. Those who wish to pursue the subject further can refer to the substantial literature available. One of the most influential works on baptism is a book by Karl Barth titled *The Teaching of the Church Regarding Baptism*, trans. E. A. Payne (London: SCM Press, 1948). It restates many of the Reformed doctrines about baptism but opposes infant baptism. Shortly after Barth's book appeared, Oscar Cullmann, Barth's colleague at the University of Basel, wrote a book disagreeing with Barth. It is called *Baptism in the New Testament*, trans. J. K. S. Reid (London: SCM Press, 1950). Joachim Jeremias wrote a masterful volume entitled *Infant Baptism in the First Four Centuries* (London: SCM Press, 1960). He was contradicted by Kurt Aland in *Did the Early Church Baptize Infants?*, trans. G. R. Beasley-Murray (London: SCM Press, 1962). Jeremias's reply to Aland is *The Origins of Infant Baptism*, trans. G. M. Barton (London: SCM Press, 1963). Two other works are Dwight Hervey Small, *The Biblical Basis for Infant Baptism* (Westwood, NJ: Revell, 1959); and G. R. Beasley-Murray, *Baptism in the New Testament* (London: Macmillan, 1963). The last volume has a bibliography of 234 items.

A good beginning for our present purposes may be made by recognizing that there are two closely related words for *baptism* in the New Testament, and that they do not necessarily have the same meaning. The first word, *baptō*, means "dip" or "immerse." The second word, *baptizō*, may mean "immerse," but it also occurs with a variety of other meanings that in turn lead to a proper understanding of what the passages using this word signify. In the English Bible *baptizō* has generally been transliterated to give us the word *baptize*. When a word is transliterated into English from another language, it is quite often an indication of a multiplicity of meanings. Thus, if the word *baptizō* had lent itself to easy translation, an obvious English word would have been used to translate it. If *baptizō* had meant only "immerse," then *immerse* would be the word used. We would speak of "John the Immerser." Or we would recite, "Go therefore and make disciples of all nations, immersing them in the name of the Father and of the Son and of the Holy Spirit." That is not the case. We therefore must look beyond the purely literal meaning of the word *baptize*, "to immerse," to the more important metaphorical meanings of the word.

Here we gain help from classical Greek literature. The Greeks used the word *baptizō* from about 400 BC to the second century after Christ. In their writings, *baptizō* always points to a change having taken place or, as we might properly say, to a change of identity by any means. Thus, to give a few examples, it can refer to a change having taken place by immersing an object in a liquid, as in dyeing cloth, by drinking too much wine and thus getting drunk, by overexertion, and by other causes.

Of all the texts that might be cited from antiquity, the one that gives greatest clarity to this issue is a text from a Greek poet and physician, Nicander, who lived about 200 BC. In a recipe for making pickles he used both words. Nicander said that the vegetable should first be dipped (*baptō*) in boiling water and then baptized (*baptizō*) in the vinegar solution. Both had to do with immersing the vegetable in the solution. But the first was temporary, while the other, the operation of baptizing the vegetable, produced a permanent change. We could say that the baptizing had identified the vegetable with the brine.[5]

This meaning of the word is obvious in many Old Testament and New Testament texts. Thus, in Isaiah 21:4, we read, "My heart misleads me, lawlessness

---

[5]See the article on "*Baptō, Baptizō*" by A. Oepke in *Theological Dictionary of the New Testament*, ed. Gerhard Kittel, trans. Geoffrey W. Bromiley, vol. 1 (Grand Rapids: Eerdmans, 1964), 529, for the early history of these words.

baptizes me" (literal translation of the Septuagint). The writer was changed from a state of quiet trust in God to fearfulness as a result of seeing great wickedness and knowing that terrible judgments would follow. Similarly, Galatians 3:27 says, "For as many of you as were baptized into Christ have put on Christ." That is, the Christians in Galatia had been identified with him.

That the word *baptizō* may be used metaphorically does not mean that it must be used in that way in passages dealing with the sacrament of baptism. But in point of fact, those passages above all require a metaphorical meaning. They require it because only an understanding of baptism as identification with Christ makes sense of them.

An example of such verses is Mark 16:16. "Whoever believes and is baptized [*baptizō*] will be saved." People have read that verse and have drawn the false conclusion that unless a person is baptized (or immersed) in water he or she cannot be saved. We should know that such a conclusion is wrong because of the teaching of the rest of Scripture about the way in which a person is to be saved: by grace through faith in the death of Jesus Christ alone. If baptism is required for salvation, then the believing thief who was crucified with Christ is lost. Once we get away from the idea that the verse is talking about water, and instead think of the believer's identification with Christ, then the statement becomes clear. We recognize that Jesus was calling for an intellectual belief in himself plus personal commitment. "He who believes in me and is identified with me shall be saved." In that form the verse is a theological parallel to John 1:12: "But to all who *did receive* him, who *believed* in his name, he gave the right to become children of God," and Revelation 3:20: "Behold, I stand at the door and knock. If anyone *hears* my voice and *opens* the door, I will come in to him and eat with him, and he with me." All three verses teach that there must be a personal identification with Jesus by the person believing.

A second verse illuminated by the metaphorical meaning of the word *baptizō* is 1 Corinthians 10:1-2. "I want you to know, brothers, that our fathers were all under the cloud, and all passed through the sea, and all were baptized into Moses in the cloud and in the sea." That passage is especially significant in understanding baptism, since the people of Israel were obviously not immersed either in the sea or the cloud. The cloud was behind them, separating them from the pursuing Egyptians. The Egyptians were immersed in the sea, and they drowned in it.

The meaning here is a change of identity. Before the crossing of the Red Sea the people were in rebellion against Moses. Their original attitude changed into an attitude of obedience and rejoicing after the Red Sea crossing.[6]

BAPTIZED INTO CHRIST

Study of the word *baptize* points to the primary meaning of baptism as a sign of our union with Christ through the work of the Holy Spirit. Hence, we find many references to being baptized with or by the Spirit, or being baptized "into" Christ or "in the name of" Christ.

In what ways are we identified with Christ in our baptism? The answer is, in all ways—in his birth, life, death, and resurrection—but chiefly in his death and resurrection. Paul spoke of our identification with Christ in his death when he wrote, "Do you not know that all of us who have been baptized into Christ Jesus were baptized into his death? We were buried therefore with him by baptism into death, in order that, just as Christ was raised from the dead by the glory of the Father, we too might walk in newness of life" (Rom 6:3-4). We are baptized into Christ's death in two ways. First, when Jesus died on the cross God regarded us as having died with him as far as our sin is concerned. God the Father put God the Son to death, and since all who believe were united to him by the Holy Spirit from before the foundation of the world, they too were put to death. Their sin was punished, and they may now stand boldly in God's presence as his justified people.

Second, there is a sense in which our union with Christ in his death refers to our life here and now. Paul says that believers are to count themselves as dead to sin but alive to God through Jesus (Rom 6:11). Through our identification with Christ in his death, the power of sin over us is broken and we are set free to serve God.

We are also identified with Christ in his resurrection. Paul says, "For if we have been united with him in a death like his, we shall certainly be united with him in a resurrection like his" (Rom 6:5). As in the case of our union with Christ in his death, that identification means two things—first, our future resurrection. "For as in Adam all die, so also in Christ shall all be made alive" (1 Cor 15:22). It also means newness of life now (the main point of Romans 6). In Philippians Paul wrote about his desire to "know him [Christ] and the power

---

[6]For a similar discussion of these and other passages see Jay E. Adams, *Meaning & Mode of Baptism* (Nutley, NJ: Presbyterian and Reformed Publishing Co., 1975).

of his resurrection" (Phil. 3:10). He wanted to experience the holy "resurrection power" of Christ as he went about his life of service for him.

Baptism is our sign and seal of that identification with Christ and hence a proof of our true security as God's people (Eph 4:30). The book of Ezekiel contains a prophecy that has to do with God's dealing with Israel at the end of history. Six men enter Jerusalem to pronounce judgment on the inhabitants; but before they go in, one man clothed in linen and carrying a writer's case enters to "put a mark on the foreheads of the men who sigh and groan over all the abominations that are committed in" Israel (Ezek 9:4). Afterward the others are told, "Kill old men outright, young men and maidens, little children and women, but touch no one on whom is the mark" (Ezek 9:6).

All who believe in the Lord Jesus are identified by the Holy Spirit of God as "Christ's ones," Christians, and are made secure in that identification. The Bible says, "God's firm foundation stands, bearing this seal: 'The Lord knows those who are his,' and, 'Let everyone who names the name of the Lord depart from iniquity'" (2 Tim 2:19).

THE LORD'S SUPPER

The second of the two Protestant sacraments is the Lord's Supper, which Jesus instituted on the night before his crucifixion. That event is recorded in each of the Synoptic Gospels (Mt 26:17-30; Mk 14:12-26; Lk 22:7-23), but the best and fullest account is in 1 Corinthians, in a passage in which Paul was attempting to correct certain abuses of the supper prevailing in the Corinthian church. This passage reads,

> For I received from the Lord what I also delivered to you, that the Lord Jesus on the night when he was betrayed took bread, and when he had given thanks, he broke it, and said, "This is my body, which is for you. Do this in remembrance of me." In the same way also he took the cup, after supper, saying, "This cup is the new covenant in my blood. Do this, as often as you drink it, in remembrance of me." For as often as you eat this bread and drink the cup, you proclaim the Lord's death until he comes.
>
> Whoever, therefore, eats the bread or drinks the cup of the Lord in an unworthy manner will be guilty of profaning the body and blood of the Lord. Let a person examine himself, then, and so eat of the bread and drink of the cup. (1 Cor 11:23-28)

The Lord's Supper is like baptism in possessing all the elements of a sacrament. But it is unlike baptism in that baptism is an initiatory sacrament (it testifies to a primary identification with Christ without which one is not a Christian at all), while the Lord's Supper is a continuing sacrament meant to be observed again and again ("as often as you drink it") throughout the Christian life. This character of the Lord's Supper is seen in its past, present, and future significance.

The *past significance* of the Lord's Supper is made clear by the word *remembrance*. In the Lord's Supper we look back to the Lord's death. We remember his substitutionary atonement, first of all; it is this that the broken bread, representing the Lord's broken body, and the wine, representing his shed blood, most clearly signify. Atonement has to do with our being made right with God. Substitutionary means that this was achieved by the death of another in our place.

Why did Jesus die? The Bible teaches that all who have ever lived are sinners, having broken God's law, and that the penalty for sin is death. The Bible says,

None is righteous, no, not one;
> no one understands;
> no one seeks for God.
All have turned aside; together they have become worthless;
> no one does good,
> not even one. (Rom 3:10-12)

It says, "The soul who sins shall die" (Ezek 18:4), and "the wages of sin is death" (Rom 6:23). This death is not merely physical, though it is that. It is spiritual as well. Death is separation. Physical death is the separation of the soul and spirit from the body. Spiritual death is the separation of the soul and spirit from God. We deserve that separation as a consequence of our sin. But Jesus became our substitute by experiencing both physical and spiritual death in our place.

A vivid illustration of this principle is seen in the early chapters of Genesis. Adam and Eve had sinned and were in terror of the consequences. God had warned them. He had said, "You may surely eat of every tree of the garden, but of the tree of the knowledge of good and evil you shall not eat, for in the day that you eat of it you shall surely die" (Gen 2:16-17). At that point they probably did not have a very clear idea of what death was, but they knew it was serious. Consequently, when they sinned through disobedience and then later heard God walking toward them in the garden, they tried to hide.

But no one can hide from God. God found them, called them out of hiding, and began to deal with their transgression. What should we expect to happen as a result of that confrontation? Here is God, who told our first parents that in the day they sinned they would die. Here are Adam and Eve, who have sinned. In that situation we should expect the immediate execution of the sentence. If God had put them to death in that moment, both physically and spiritually, banishing them from his presence forever, it would have been just.

But that is not what happened. Instead, we have God first rebuking the sin and then performing a sacrifice. As a result, Adam and Eve were clothed with the skins of the slain animals. It was the first death that anyone had ever witnessed. It was enacted by God. As Adam and Eve looked on, they must have been horrified. Yet even as they recoiled from the sacrifice, they must have marveled as well. For what God was showing was that although they deserved to die it was possible for another, in this case two animals, to die in their place. The animals paid the price of their sin, and they were clothed in the skins of the animals as a reminder of that fact.

That is the meaning of substitution. It is the death of one on behalf of another. Yet we must also say, as the Bible teaches, that the death of animals could never take away the penalty of sin (Heb 10:4). That event was only a symbol of how sin was to be taken away. The real sacrifice was performed by Jesus Christ, and we look back to it in the communion service.

We also look back to something that Jesus suggested when he spoke of the wine as the "blood of the covenant" (Mk 14:24) and as "the new covenant in my blood" (1 Cor 11:25). We look back to that victory on the basis of which God has established a new covenant of salvation with his redeemed people. A covenant is a solemn promise confirmed by an oath or sign. So when Christ spoke of the cup as commemorating a new covenant, he was pointing to the promises of salvation that God made to us on the basis of Christ's death. It comes to us by grace alone.

The Lord's Supper has a *present significance*. First, the sacrament is something in which we repeatedly take part, thereby remembering the death of the Lord again and again until he comes. Second, it is an occasion for examining our lives in the light of our profession of faith in his death. Paul says, "Let a person examine himself, then, and so eat of the bread and drink of the cup. For anyone who eats and drinks without discerning the body eats and drinks judgment on himself" (1 Cor 11:28-29).

At the heart of the present significance of the Lord's Supper is our communion or fellowship with Christ, hence the term *communion service*. In coming to this service, the believer comes to meet with Christ and have fellowship with him at his invitation. The examination takes place because it would be hypocrisy for us to pretend that we are in communion with the Holy One while actually cherishing known sin in our hearts.

The manner in which Jesus is present in the communion service is a matter that has divided the Christian church. There are three theories. The first is that Jesus is not present at all, at least no more than he is present all the time and in everything. To those who hold that view, the Lord's Supper takes on an exclusively memorial character. It is only a remembrance of Christ's death. The second view is that of the Roman Catholic Church. In it, the body and blood of Christ are supposed to be literally present under the appearance of the bread and wine. Before the Mass the elements are merely bread and wine. But in the Mass, through the ministrations of the priest, they are changed so that, although worshipers perceive only the bread and wine, they nevertheless actually eat and drink the body and blood of Jesus. That process is called transubstantiation. The third view, the view of John Calvin particularly, but also of other Reformers, is that Christ is present in the communion service, but spiritually rather than physically. Calvin called this "the real presence" to indicate that a spiritual presence is every bit as real as a physical one.

What are we to think of these theories? To begin with, we must say that there can be no quarrel with the memorial theory, since it is certainly true as far as it goes. The only question is whether more than remembrance is involved. The real division is between the view of the majority of the Reformers and the doctrine of the Roman Catholic Church. Those who favor a literal, physical presence (and Luther was one, though he did not accept the theory of transubstantiation) argue from a literal interpretation of Christ's words, "This is my body" (Mk 14:22). But that hardly decides the matter, because such expressions occur frequently in the Bible with obviously figurative or representational meanings. For example:

"The seven good cows are seven years."
"You are the head of gold."
"The field is the world."
"The Rock was Christ."
"The seven lampstands are the seven churches."
"I am the door of the sheep."
"I am the true vine."[7]

---

[7]Gen 41:26; Dan 2:38; Mt 13:38; 1 Cor 10:4; Rev 1:20; Jn 10:7; 15:1. For a discussion of these and other texts, see James Bannerman, *The Church of Christ: A Treatise on the Nature, Powers,*

That Jesus was using figurative language and not performing a miracle of transubstantiation should be evident from the fact that his body was right there with the disciples as he spoke. Today his resurrected body is in heaven.

A reason for taking the presence of Christ in the sacrament to be spiritual is that this is the sense in which every other promise of the presence of Christ with us in this age must be taken. Bannerman writes,

> Such promises as these—"Lo, I am with you alway, even unto the end of the world"; "Where two or three are met together in my name, there am I in the midst of you"; "Behold, I stand at the door and knock: if any man hear my voice, and open the door, I will come in to him, and will sup with him, and he with me"; and such like—plainly give us ground to affirm that Christ, through his Spirit, is *present* in his ordinances to the faith of the believer, imparting spiritual blessing and grace. But there is nothing that would lead us to make a difference or distinction between the presence of Christ in the Supper and the presence of Christ in his other ordinances, in so far as the manner of that presence is concerned. The efficacy of the Savior's presence may be different in the way of imparting more or less of saving grace, according to the nature of the ordinance, and the degree of the believer's faith. But the manner of that presence is the same, being realized through the Spirit of Christ, and to the faith of the believer.[8]

Some well-known verses in John 6 also speak of faith in Christ and of a spiritual feeding on him, though they do not speak literally of the Lord's Supper, since that sacrament had not yet been instituted. "Truly, truly, I say to you, unless you eat the flesh of the Son of Man and drink his blood, you have no life in you. Whoever feeds on my flesh and drinks my blood has eternal life, and I will raise him up on the last day. For my flesh is true food, and my blood is true drink" (Jn 6:53-55).

If we want synonyms for "eat" and "drink," we find them in John 6 in such concepts as believe (Jn 6:29, 35, 47), come (Jn 6:35), see (Jn 6:40), hear and learn of (Jn 6:45). All indicate a response to Jesus. The terms *eat* and *drink* stress that this feeding by faith is to be as real as literal eating.

The third significance of the Lord's Supper is *future*. Paul said, "As often as you eat this bread and drink the cup, you proclaim the Lord's death *until he comes*" (1 Cor 11:26). The Lord suggested the same when he told the disciples

---

Ordinances, Discipline and Government of the Christian Church, vol. 2 (1869; reprint ed., London: Banner of Truth Trust, 1974), 147-52.
[8]Ibid., 158-59. The texts are Mt 28:20; 18:20; Rev 3:20.

who were eating the last meal with him, "Truly, I say to you, I will not drink again of the fruit of the vine until that day when I drink it new in the kingdom of God" (Mk 14:25).

We speak of the real presence of the Lord Jesus Christ in the service as we know it now, and we seek to respond to him and serve him. We readily admit that there are times when this is difficult and the Lord does not seem to be present. Whether because of sin, fatigue, or simply lack of faith, Jesus often seems to be far away. Though we continue on in Christian life and in service, we long for that day when we will see him face to face and be like him (1 Jn 3:2). The communion service is a reminder of that day. It is a foreshadowing of the great marriage supper of the Lamb. It is an encouragement to faith and an impulse to a higher level of holiness.

CHAPTER 8

SPIRITUAL GIFTS

*O*ne of the marks of the church is unity. This mark is inherent in the very definition of the church. The church is (1) founded on the Lord Jesus Christ, (2) called into being by the Holy Spirit, and (3) made up of people of all races who thereby become one new people in the sight of God. If the church is founded on Jesus Christ, it has one foundation, meaning one Lord and one theology centered in him. If it is called into being by the Holy Spirit, the fundamental experience of the people of God is identical. They come from various backgrounds, but they are called into a relationship to God by a work of regeneration, justification, and adoption. If they have become one new people, they are obviously set off from the world as a separate and holy entity.

A person who becomes a Christian notices this unity. Before, the person was to a greater or lesser extent on his or her own. Now that has changed. As Paul said in writing to the Ephesians, "So then you are no longer strangers and aliens, but you are fellow citizens with the saints and members of the household of God" (Eph 2:19).

One is not a member of the church for long, however, before the many diversities within it are also evident. Some are the results of sin and are entirely unjustified. Others are actually the gift of God to the church and are of great importance for the church's proper functioning in the world.

This twofold emphasis, on unity and diversity, appears at important points in the New Testament writings. For example, in Ephesians 4 a number of phrases speak eloquently of our unity. "There is one body and one Spirit—just as you were called to the one hope that belongs to your call—one Lord, one faith, one baptism, one God and Father of all, who is over all and through all and in all" (Eph 4:4-6). But no sooner had Paul articulated that truth than he went on to speak of diversity in the area of gifts. "But grace was given to each one of us according to the measure of Christ's gift. . . . And he gave the apostles, the prophets, the evangelists, the shepherds and teachers, to equip the saints for the work of ministry, for building up the body of Christ" (Eph 4:7, 11-12). In the next verses he illustrated his point by speaking of a body that, although it is one body, nevertheless has many differently functioning parts.

In 1 Corinthians the examples of unity and diversity are mixed. "Now there are varieties of gifts, but the same Spirit; and there are varieties of service, but the same Lord; and there are varieties of activities, but it is the same God who empowers them all in everyone" (1 Cor 12:4-6). After listing nine of these gifts, the apostle concluded, "All these are empowered by one and the same Spirit, who apportions to each one individually as he wills" (1 Cor 12:11).

The book of Romans has a similar emphasis. "For as in one body we have many members, and the members do not all have the same function, so we, though many, are one body in Christ, and individually members one of another" (Rom 12:4-5).

These verses teach that a certain kind of unity and a certain kind of diversity are necessary for the health of the church. Without the unity, a unity of relationship to Christ through the work of God's Spirit, there is no church at all. We are still in our sins. On the other hand, without diversity the church cannot be healthy and will certainly not function properly, any more than a body without arms or legs.

Up to now, everything said about the church may be looked at as being in the area of unity: the definition of the church, its marks, the nature of its worship, the sacraments. These things are the experience of all who are God's people. Now we must look at the areas of diversity. First, we want to look at spiritual gifts, including the role of leaders in helping others to discover and develop those gifts. Second, we will look at church offices and how they fit into the larger picture.

TO EACH A GIFT

Spiritual gifts have been widely discussed in the church recently. Others in earlier years were poorer for the absence of such discussion. Ray C. Stedman of the Peninsula Bible Church of Palo Alto, California, defines a spiritual gift as "a capacity for service which is given to every true Christian without exception and which was something each did not possess before he became a Christian."[1]

That definition is worth looking at in detail. First, it defines a spiritual gift as being given to the believer by God, as the words *spiritual gift* imply. In the New Testament, the word for that kind of gift (the word that is almost always used in speaking of them) is *charisma* or *charismata* (plural). We get our word *charismatic* from it, though the word is far more restricted in its English meaning. The most important thing about the word *charisma* is that it is based on the Greek noun *charis*, meaning "grace." Since grace is God's unmerited favor, the emphasis is that spiritual gifts are dispensed by God according to his good pleasure. One Christian will receive one gift, another Christian another. Some will receive more than one gift. Paul emphasized this in the verse already quoted. "All these are empowered by one and the same Spirit, who apportions to each one individually *as he wills*" (1 Cor 12:11).

In saying that a spiritual gift is something the Christian did not possess before becoming a Christian, Stedman distinguishes a spiritual gift from what we would call a natural talent. Natural talents are also gifts of God. We are told that "every good gift and every perfect gift is from above," which is true of talents and for Christians and non-Christians alike (Jas 1:17).

It is also true that a Christian may exercise a spiritual gift through a natural talent. Examples would be one who fulfills the gift of "helping" through a talent for carpentry, baking, financial management, or similar things, or one who fulfills the gift of "exhortation" through a natural ability to get close to people. Still, spiritual gifts are not talents for the simple reason that they are given for spiritual ends only, and only to Christians. They are "to equip the saints for the work of ministry, for building up the body of Christ" (Eph 4:12).

An example of the relationship between a spiritual gift and talent is found in the Old Testament in the case of Bezalel, one of the craftsmen who worked on the art objects of the Jewish tabernacle. The Lord said of this man, "I have filled him with the Spirit of God, with ability and intelligence, with knowledge and all craftsmanship, to devise artistic designs, to work in gold, silver, and bronze, in cutting stones for setting, and in carving wood, to work in every craft" (Ex 31:3-5). Bezalel had been given the natural talent of craftsmanship, but he had also been given the spiritual gift of knowledge or intelligence that directed

---

[1]Ray C. Stedman, *Body Life* (Glendale, CA: Regal Books, G/L Publications, 1972), 39.

him in the way his natural talents were to be used. Because of the spiritual gift, he was able to produce objects for Israel's worship.

A third point of Stedman's definition of spiritual gifts is that every Christian has been given at least one. Paul said, "To *each* is given the manifestation of the Spirit for the common good" (1 Cor 12:7). Peter wrote, "*Each* has received a gift" (1 Pet 4:10).

Failure to see that truth has led in church history to what John R. W. Stott has termed "the clerical domination of the laity." There has developed within the church (for a variety of reasons) a kind of division between clergy and laity in which the clergy are supposed to lead and do the work of Christian ministry, while the people (which is what the word *laity* means) are to follow docilely— and, of course, give money to support the clergy and their work. As an example of that outlook, Stott quotes from a 1906 papal encyclical titled *Vehementer Nos*: "As for the masses, they have no other right than of letting themselves be led, and of following their pastors as a docile flock."[2]

That is not what the church as the people of God is to be. Where such a view prevails, the church and its ministry suffer by the loss of the exercise of gifts given to the laity. Gifts are for use in serving others. The laity serve the church and the world. The clergy serve the laity, particularly in helping them to develop and use their gifts. As Stott says, "Clergy are not hyphenated to the laity as if they were a separate class; they are 'ministers of the people' because they themselves belong to the people they are called to serve."[3]

Those three points about the nature of spiritual gifts show how important they are. They are important theologically, because they lead us to a fuller understanding of the grace of God. They are important personally and experientially, because they have direct bearing on the individual believer's service to Christ and others within the church. They are important organizationally, because they show how clergy and laity should relate to one another.

WHAT ARE THE GIFTS?

The gifts of the Spirit are listed in four separate chapters of the New Testament and in one of those chapters in two places. That makes five lists in all (Rom 12:6-8; 1 Cor 12:8-10; 1 Cor 12:28-30; Eph 4:11; 1 Pet 4:11). These lists vary in regard to the gifts listed. The shortest is 1 Peter 4:11, which contains only two gifts,

---

[2]Quoted in John R. W. Stott, *One People* (London: Falcon Books, 1969), 9.
[3]Ibid., 47.

speaking and service. The lists in 1 Corinthians 12 each contain nine, though those nine are not identical. In all, there may be nineteen gifts mentioned, but that is not an absolute figure: different words can conceivably be used to describe the same or nearly identical gifts, and there may be gifts not mentioned.

Table 1. Spiritual gifts in the New Testament

	Ephesians 4:11	1 Corinthians 12:8-10	1 Corinthians 12:28-30	Romans 12:6-8	1 Peter 4:11
1.	Apostles		Apostles		
2.	Prophets		Prophets	Prophecy	
3.				Service	Service
4.	Evangelists				
5.		Wisdom			
6.		Knowledge			
7.	Pastors				
8.	Teachers		Teachers	Teaching	Speaking
9.				Exhortation	
10.		Faith			
11.		Healing	Healing*		
12.		Working miracles [Prophecy]	Working miracles		
13.		Ability to distinguish spirits			
14.				Contributing	
15.			Helpers	Giving aid	
16.				Mercy	
17.			Administrators		
18.		Tongues	Tongues		
19.		Interpretation of tongues	Interpretation of tongues		

In 1 Corinthians 12:28-30, working miracles is actually listed before healing.

Apostles and prophets. First in the lists found in Ephesians 4:11 and 1 Corinthians 12:28-30 is the gift of apostles and prophets. Some who have written about the gifts have tried to show that apostles and prophets are present today. They point out that the word *apostle* does not mean only the original band of authoritative spokesmen commissioned by Christ; it can also refer to anyone who is sent forth as a witness, particularly to establish churches. Similarly, *prophet* does not always mean one who receives a special inspired word from God; it also refers to anyone who speaks boldly in his name (as in 1 Cor 14). Those points are well taken. But they do not really apply to the use of the words in the two lists mentioned. In these lists both *apostle* and *prophet* must be taken in their most technical sense. Therefore, *apostles* refers to those witnesses who were specifically commissioned by Christ to establish the church on a proper base, and *prophets* refers to those who received God's message (like prophets of old) and recorded it in the pages of what we call the New Testament.

Neither one of these gifts exists today. We no longer have apostles or prophets in that sense. But we are not deprived of the benefits of those first gifts of God to the Christian community. The apostles did establish the first churches and taught them authoritatively, and those who spoke from God have left us the New Testament.

Evangelists. The second category of gifts contains just one item. Obviously the gift of evangelism has not ceased. An evangelist is one who possesses a special ability in communicating the gospel of salvation from sin through Jesus Christ. The existence of such a spiritual gift does not mean that others who are not evangelists are excused from the obligation to tell others about Jesus. On the contrary, that is a task we all share. The Great Commission declares it. But it does mean that some are especially gifted in this area.

The evangelist does not necessarily have to be a well-educated or highly intelligent person. True, evangelists must know their message. They must be able to answer questions about it. But their primary gift is in being able to communicate the basic gospel clearly and well. The gift of evangelism is not limited to those who are "professionals," like Billy Graham. It is more often the gift of laypersons. In his study of spiritual gifts in *The Holy Spirit*, Graham points out that the only person in the entire Bible who was actually called an evangelist is Philip, and he was a deacon. Speaking personally, I can say that I have known quite a few men and women who have had this gift, and none of them was ordained. Rather, they were people who enjoyed and were particularly effective in speaking about Christ to others.

Pastors, teachers, and the gift of exhortation. I put the three gifts of pastoring, teaching, and exhorting in one category because they often go together and may in fact actually be one gift. In Ephesians 4:11 the words *pastors* and *teachers* may be joined together due to the nature of the Greek phrasing in that sentence, so that we could speak of the gift of pastor-teacher.

Pastor refers to one who has a pastoral oversight of others. It is based on the idea of shepherding and looks back to the pattern of Jesus, who described himself as "the good shepherd" (Jn 10:11), and who is referred to as "the great shepherd" (Heb 13:20) and "chief Shepherd" of the sheep (1 Pet 5:4). As in the case of evangelists, many have this gift who are not ordained. For example, pastoring should be the gift of elders, and also of deacons if they have duties involving spiritual oversight. It should also be a gift of Sunday school teachers.

The word *teacher* is self-explanatory. It is always an important gift and may be one of the gifts most needed at the present time. We see the importance of the gift of teaching when we recognize that this is a key idea in Matthew's version of the Great Commission. There Jesus says, "Go . . . and make disciples of all nations, baptizing them in the name of the Father and of the Son and of the Holy Spirit [and then, in order to explain how that specifically is to be done], *teaching* them to observe all that I have commanded you" (Mt 28:19-20). Those who are brought to faith in Christ are to be discipled primarily through teaching.

In Romans 12:8 "exhortation" follows immediately after teaching. Having been taught in the Word, disciples next need to be encouraged to press on in the things they have learned. Again, this is a pastoral responsibility. In fact, when Paul used this word in Romans, he may have had pastors in mind particularly, since the word *pastor* does not occur elsewhere in the passage.

Another listing of the gifts should be considered at this point, since it throws light on the gifts in this category. In 1 Corinthians 12:8-9, Paul did not mention any of the gifts already considered that, however, occur first in each of the other Pauline passages: apostles, prophets, evangelists, pastors, and teachers in Ephesians 4:11; apostles, prophets, and teachers in 1 Corinthians 12:28-30; prophecy, service, teaching, and exhortation in Romans 12:6-8. Instead he mentions "wisdom" and "knowledge." Perhaps in this passage the apostle is substituting those two items for his customarily longer list. Wisdom and knowledge are gifts particularly associated with the evangelistic, pastoral, and teaching ministries. This fact is helpful in trying to determine whether God has given an individual the gift of being an evangelist, pastor, or teacher, a matter we will come to more fully later. We may ask, does that person have spiritual wisdom? Does he or she have the gift of knowledge? The point is also a helpful indication of areas in which believers can profitably pray for their pastors. We can pray that God will give them true spiritual knowledge, based on careful study of the Bible and wisdom to apply it properly.

Faith. The word *faith* is one of the most important terms in the Christian vocabulary. It has several uses. It can refer to "saving faith" (Eph 2:8 RSV). It can refer to the content of the gospel (Acts 6:7; 13:8; 14:22; Rom 10:8). It can mean faithfulness (Gal 5:22). It can refer to trust in God in adversity (Eph 6:16). In the list of gifts in 1 Corinthians 12:8-10, faith probably refers to the ability to look ahead to something God has promised and act as if it were already present. Stedman says that faith in this sense is what we today would probably call vision. "It is the ability to see something that needs to be done and to believe that God will do it even though it looks impossible."[4]

The heroes of faith listed in Hebrews 11 had this gift. In each case their lives demonstrated the "assurance of things hoped for, the conviction of things not seen" (Heb 11:1). Abel, who had been promised salvation through the seed of the woman who would crush Satan's head, testified to his faith in that future reality through obedience in the matter of the blood sacrifice. Enoch believed God and lived a righteous life. Noah accepted God's word about a future destruction of the ungodly, and acted on that conviction by building an ark in which he and his family were saved. Abraham exhibited faith throughout his lifetime. He left his homeland for a land not yet seen, endured hardship in the land of promise, changed his name as a symbol of his faith in God's ability to provide him with a son when both he and Sarah were past the age of childbearing, was willing to offer Isaac as a sacrifice on an altar on Mount Moriah—all because he believed God was able to do what he had promised (compare Rom 4:21).

After noting these persons and in anticipation of other examples of outstanding faith to follow—Isaac, Jacob, Joseph, Moses, Rahab, Gideon, Barak, Samson, Jephtha, David, Samuel—the author of Hebrews declared, "These all died in faith, not having received the things promised, but having seen them and greeted them from afar" (Heb 11:13). Isaac Watts referred to such persons in a stanza of his hymn "Am I a Soldier of the Cross?"

> Thy saints, in all this glorious war,
> Shall conquer, though they die;
> They view the triumph from afar,
> And seize it with their eye.

Healings and miracles. The gifts of healings and miracles occur at two separate places in 1 Corinthians 12 and are therefore obviously related. This conjunction of gifts is important in interpreting the nature of the gift of healing. Although it is true that the word *healing* (actually, *healings*—plural) can refer to various types of cures—emotional as well as bodily ailments, and healing by natural as

---

[4]Stedman, *Body Life*, 43.

well as miraculous means—the use of the word in these verses must refer to the miraculous.

The question arises as to whether such gifts exist today, a matter on which Christians are divided. We may note, on the one hand, that some gifts (such as the gifts of apostleship and prophecy) no longer occur in their biblical sense. The gifts of healings and miracles could be like them.

Yet gifts like evangelism, teaching, and faith continue to exist and clearly must continue to the end of church history. Healings and miracles could be like them.

A third possibility exists. Healings and miracles could exist but could occur infrequently. There are several reasons for preferring this interpretation. Miracles and healings are bracketed by other gifts that continue: in the case of 1 Corinthians 12:8-10, by wisdom, knowledge, and faith before, and by the discerning of spirits afterward; in the case of 1 Corinthians 12:28-30, by teaching before and the gift of helping after. The working of miracles is similar to the case of speaking in tongues, which is treated at great length two chapters later and in regard to which we receive an explicit warning: "Do not forbid speaking in tongues" (1 Cor 14:39). Paul is not encouraging tongues-speaking, but he recognizes that God may continue to give this gift and it should therefore not be discouraged. Nowhere does Paul indicate that either healings, miracles, or tongues will cease. Further, accounts of healings and other miracles exist from every period of church history. (Although it may be true that many of them are myths, mistakes, or even deliberate deceptions, it would be brash indeed to declare that they all are.)

We dare not put God in a box on this matter, saying that he cannot give the gifts of healings or miracles today. He can. On the other hand, to say that is not the same thing as saying we have a right to expect healings or that what passes for the miraculous today is authentic.

A man whose opinion in this area should be highly valued is Dr. C. Everett Koop, surgeon general of the United States and former surgeon-in-chief of Children's Hospital in Philadelphia, Pennsylvania, and professor of pediatric surgery at the University of Pennsylvania School of Medicine. Koop is a strong Bible-believing Christian whose testimony has been used to lead many persons to faith in Christ. He has solid technical understanding of the development of disease and the process of healing. He is an expert in the area of surgery for birth defects and childhood cancers, a field of medicine where the question of supernatural healing quite often arises. Koop believes in miracles. But—and this is the point—in spite of believing in miracles, and in spite of a lifetime of work with many families who have undoubtedly prayed in faith that God would heal their deformed or suffering children, in nearly forty years of active practice he has never seen one. He writes, "I believe in miracles. I understand that all healing comes from God. I would love to see a miracle of healing where God supervenes his natural law and heals by miracle. If I were to see such a miracle, I would be overjoyed. I would give God the praise. But now, in spite of believing that all healing comes from God and in spite of believing in miracles, I have never seen one."[5] His experience has led him to conclude that truly supernatural healings are not occurring in our time. Whether one would fully agree with him in that conclusion or not, his experience and opinion should be a warning to those who talk loosely about this matter and even claim miracles in questionable cases.

Ability to distinguish spirits. The gift of discernment is mentioned at only one place in the various lists of gifts, but it is nevertheless important. The gift of discernment relates to a prophet's or a teacher's teaching. In 1 Corinthians 12:10, discernment occurs immediately after the reference to prophecy, which makes one think that Paul was referring to the ability to discern whether a person who is speaking in the name of God is actually inspired by the Holy Spirit or is speaking in his or her own strength or by means of a demonic spirit. On the other hand, discernment can refer merely to discerning the truth or error of a religious teacher's instruction (compare 1 Jn 4:1-6). Peter exercised this gift when he saw through the deception being perpetrated by Ananias and Sapphira. "Ananias, why has Satan filled your heart to lie to the Holy Spirit? . . . How is it that you have agreed together to test the Spirit of the Lord?" (Acts 5:3, 9).

Some people today are easily taken in by any new "Christian" fad. Others are not. The latter may have the gift of discernment. The church should recognize such persons and seek their judgment in areas where true discernment is needed.

Helpers. The reference to helpers in 1 Corinthians 12:28 is amplified in Romans 12:7-8 by the gifts of contributing (financially), giving aid, showing mercy, and perhaps also rendering service (which occurs earlier). We could add many more things. Some individuals exhibit this gift in doing the work necessary to keep a home, business, or church running smoothly. They see what needs to be done and do it. Some care for older people, buying groceries for them when they are unable to go out, cleaning, shoveling snow, taking them back and forth to medical appointments or to visit friends or to church. Some help the poor.

---

[5]C. Everett Koop, "Faith Healing and the Sovereignty of God," *Tenth: An Evangelical Quarterly*, July 1976, 61.

Some assist the sick by sending in food or doing the necessary errands until the sick person recovers. What distinguishes their service from the similar service that non-Christians may give is that it is done in the name of Jesus Christ and for his glory. Peter encourages those who render service to do it "by the strength that God supplies—in order that in everything God may be glorified through Jesus Christ" (1 Pet 4:11).

Administrators. Some versions of the Bible call this gift "governments," but it really refers to administrative rule or leadership. Most of us know situations when there was obviously work to be done and many people available to do it. But the job did not get done because there was no one around to take charge, make assignments, and then see that the various responsibilities were carried out. On the other hand, there have been times when the necessary gifts and people did not seem to be present. Then someone came along who saw how the work could be done and did it through those who were available.

Here we must avoid two errors. One is the error of being superspiritual, distrusting strong administration on the ground that it is of the flesh and that God must therefore work in other ways. People who feel that way, or are intimidated by others who do, frequently fail to exert the leadership God has given them. The other error is in thinking that what is done in the area of strong leadership is always of God or that God is working only when such leadership is present. That is not true either. People need to recognize the difference between the gift of administration and mere force of personality, willfulness, or an aggressive success-oriented mentality.

The Lord obviously had all the spiritual gifts. But he did not boss people about, trample on feelings or press on obstinately like a steamroller in order to accomplish some goal.

Tongues and the interpretation of tongues. None of the gifts mentioned anywhere in the New Testament has been so controversial as the gift of tongues and the accompanying gift, interpretation. Some people have insisted that the gift of tongues means being able to speak so that other people hear in their own but different languages. That kind of miracle took place at Pentecost (Acts 2:1-11); but it does not seem to be identical with the gift of tongues as it was practiced at Corinth. At Corinth interpreters were necessary because the listeners were not hearing in their own language.

Other people speak of the exercise of tongues as being the ability to speak in "heavenly tongues," that is, in no known human language. Others deny that either possibility exists today; they say that what passes for tongues is either a self-induced psychological phenomenon or the work of demons.[6] The only way to proceed is to limit oneself to what is said in the one portion of Scripture that deals with the phenomenon.

That section of Scripture is 1 Corinthians 12 and 14, in which Paul made the following points. First, *the gift of tongues can be counterfeited.* That is, there is a genuine gift; but there is also a duplication of that gift by other spirits, whether the spirit of Satan or merely the spirit of the individual. Paul was talking about this when he reminded the Corinthians that before their conversions they were "led astray to dumb idols" and warned them that it was necessary to test the spirits on the basis of their confession or lack of confession of Christ. "No one speaking in the Spirit of God ever says 'Jesus is accursed!' and no one can say 'Jesus is Lord' except in the Holy Spirit" (1 Cor 12:3). Apparently before their conversion to Christ the Christians at Corinth had been fooled by the ecstatic utterances of pagan priests. Now they were being fooled by some who professed to speak in the power of the Holy Spirit but were not actually empowered by him.

It is worth noting that in many parts of the world glossolalia (the technical term for speaking in tongues) is well known in non-Christian circles even today. Unitarian groups sometimes speak in tongues. Buddhist and Shintoist priests often speak in tongues when in a trance. The phenomenon exists in much of South America, India, and Australia in a variety of environments. So speaking in tongues is itself no proof of the Holy Spirit's presence.

A second principle that Paul laid down is that *there are many different and valuable gifts of the Holy Spirit, and the gift of tongues is just one.* He said this in 1 Corinthians 12:4-11, stressing that there were different needs in the church and that it was the Holy Spirit's prerogative to meet those needs by giving the necessary gifts to those people he had called to work in those areas. Paul's emphasis was on the fact that it was by one and the same Spirit that the gifts were given (1 Cor 12:8-11). If the Holy Spirit gives a gift to each Christian and for his own purposes, then obviously we are unable to take pride in our particular gift. The

---

[6]A supposed textual basis for the ceasing of tongues is 1 Corinthians 13:8. "Love never ends. As for prophecies, they will pass away; as for tongues, they will cease; as for knowledge, it will pass away." But to read this verse as saying that tongues are to cease after the apostolic age is to misuse it. If the verse means that, then knowledge must cease too, which is not the case. Actually, the verse is looking ahead to the time of Christ's return and is warning that the limited experiences of this present day shall pass when we are made like Jesus. "When the perfect comes, the partial will pass away" (1 Cor 13:10).

fact that Paul later minimized the gift of tongues indicates that pride was a particular danger for those at Corinth who possessed that gift.

The third of Paul's points is that *the gifts of the Spirit are for a purpose: the edification and unity of the church* (1 Cor 12:12-27). In one sense these are two separate purposes. But Paul treated both through the image of the body to which each part contributes. He stressed that (1) there are "many members" of the body (1 Cor 12:12); (2) all "are indispensable" (1 Cor 12:22); and (3) there should be "no division" (1 Cor 12:25). If a particular exercise of the gift of tongues does not promote growth or, worse yet, leads to schism, then either the gift is not of God, or it is being exercised in a way contrary to God's purposes for it.

Fourth, Paul indicated (perhaps in this case to humble those who were boasting of their gift of tongues) that *if the gifts were to be listed in the order of importance, tongues would always come relatively low on the list* (1 Cor 12:28–14:12). We see this in several ways. Whenever he listed the gifts, tongues and the interpretation of tongues always came last. This is most marked in 1 Corinthians 12:28, where Paul actually numbered the gifts: "And God has appointed in the church first apostles, second prophets, third teachers, then miracles, then gifts of healing, helping, administrating, and various kinds of tongues." Another way Paul made that point was by emphasis on the importance of love. His concern for love was so great that he interrupted his discussion of the problems of gifts to talk about it (1 Cor 13). Finally, he concluded that if any gift was to be sought after, it was the gift of prophecy, by which in this passage he meant the ability to preach and teach the Word clearly (1 Cor 14:1). Although he too spoke in tongues, he would rather speak five words in an intelligible language than ten thousand in an unknown tongue (1 Cor 14:19).

Paul's fifth principle is that *the gift of tongues is fraught with particular dangers and must therefore be exercised with safeguards* (1 Cor 14:13-38).

The first danger is disorder. Paul regarded disorder as a disgrace; God's work should not be done in a disruptive way. Here he laid down guidelines. First, do not allow anyone to speak in church at the same time another person is speaking; people should speak one at a time. Second, do not allow everyone to speak, but at the most two or three. Third, do not permit even those two or three to speak in tongues unless someone can interpret. In these verses Paul was exercising concern lest he quench the voice of the Spirit (which he had no desire to do) while, at the same time and for the same reasons, guaranteeing that the voice of the Spirit would be heard in the assembly. The Holy Spirit obviously could not be heard if everyone was shouting and crying out at the same time under his supposed influence.

A second danger is the danger of a contentless Christianity, which Paul countered by insisting on interpretation. Then, as now, Christianity was threatened by an outlook that made experience central. Content was secondary. The emotional "high" was everything. But Paul would not allow it. True, he did not want to suppress any valid emotional response to the truth of Christianity (and neither must we). There is and should be emotion within Christianity. But it cannot be allowed to become the basis of faith. The objective revelation of God in history and in the Scriptures is the basis of Christianity. If experience is trusted above revelation, it will lead to a distortion of true Christianity and to excesses.

We see this today and not just in the tongues movement. We see a kind of emotional, almost contentless Christianity in which experience is everything. Following Paul's example, we must stress content. Francis Schaeffer writes, "We must stress that the basis for our faith is neither experience nor emotion but the truth as God has given it in verbalized, propositional form in the Scripture and which we first of all apprehend with our minds—though, of course, the whole man must act upon it."[7] John Stott makes this same point in arguing against what he terms "mindless Christianity."[8]

One last point should be noted in Paul's presentation of the tongues question. It is simply that, notwithstanding the dangers of this gift, *no Christian should forbid its exercise.* Specifically he said, "So, my brothers, earnestly desire to prophesy, and do not forbid speaking in tongues" (1 Cor 14:39). If tongues is not your gift, you are not to desire it—at least not more than any other gift. (You are to desire the gift of prophecy.) But, on the other hand, if another has been given the gift, you are not to forbid its exercise. To forbid it would be to the church's impoverishment.[9]

FINDING YOUR GIFT

At this point someone may be saying, "I recognize the importance of the spiritual gifts and am aware now of what they are. But I am still puzzled because I don't know where I fit into the picture. How can I discover what my own gifts are?" A good question.

---

[7]Francis A. Schaeffer, *The New Super-Spirituality* (Downers Grove, IL: InterVarsity Press, 1972), 24.
[8]John R. W. Stott, *Your Mind Matters* (Downers Grove, IL: InterVarsity Press, 1972), 10.
[9]Some of the material on tongues has been adapted from Boice, *The Gospel of John*, vol. 4 (Grand Rapids: Zondervan, 1978), 195-200.

First, *we can begin by studying what the Bible has to say about spiritual gifts.* The Bible is God's primary provision for spiritual growth and sanctification. God speaks to us in the Bible. Without a knowledge of what God's Word explicitly teaches in this area, we can easily be led to desire experiences that are not his will for us. We can even begin to think of spiritual gifts in secular terms. As we study the Bible's teaching we must be careful to discern what God's purpose in giving spiritual gifts is. It is for the growth of the body and not merely for personal growth or satisfaction.

Second, *we must pray.* This is not a matter to be taken lightly or one in which we may feel free to trust our own judgment. We do not know our hearts. We may find ourselves wanting a gift that exalts our sense of self-importance but that God does not have in mind for us. We may find ourselves resisting the gift he actually has in mind. The only way we will get past this hurdle is to lay the entire matter before the Lord in serious, soul-searching prayer and ask him, as he speaks through his Word, to show us the gift he actually has given us.

Third, *we will be helped by making a sober assessment of our own spiritual strengths and abilities.* If we do not do this on the basis of a careful study of the Word of God and through prayer, we will be misled. But if we have first sought the wisdom and mind of God, we can then go back and look at ourselves through spiritual eyes. We can ask, what do I like to do? That is not a sure guide to what our gift or gifts are, but it is one indication. God's leading is always toward that for which he has prepared us and which we therefore naturally find enjoyable and satisfying. Stedman writes,

> Somewhere the idea has found deep entrenchment in Christian circles that doing what God wants you to do is always unpleasant; that Christians must always make choices between doing what they want to do and being happy, and doing what God wants them to do and being completely miserable. Nothing could be more removed from truth. The exercise of a spiritual gift is always a satisfying, enjoyable experience though sometimes the occasion on which it is exercised may be an unhappy one.[10]

Another question we can ask is, what am I good at? If you are seeking to fulfill a certain ministry in the church but are constantly failing and feel frustrated, it is quite likely that you are working in the wrong area and have assessed your gifts improperly. If God is blessing your work, if you see spiritual fruit from your

---

[10]Stedman, *Body Life*, 54.

efforts, you are probably on the right track and should pursue it even more vigorously. As skill in exercising this gift develops, you will find that the results are even better.

You can ask, what are my talents? Spiritual gifts are not talents, but they are often related. We are seldom wrong if we try to exercise our talents spiritually and for spiritual ends.

A fourth thing you can do is *seek the wisdom of other Christians.* The church does not always function as it should, but where it functions properly, one of the things that should happen is that others with the gift of insight or wisdom should be able to sense what your gifts are and point them out in terms of the needs of your particular Christian congregation. Others are almost always more objective about ourselves than we are. We must cultivate the ability to listen to these other members of the family of God and follow their guidance.

CHAPTER 9

EQUIPPING THE SAINTS

*A*t the beginning of the last chapter, I pointed out that within the overall unity of the church, there are nevertheless two areas of difference or distinction: spiritual gifts and church office. We come to the second of these now. I want to approach it indirectly, first seeing not what those offices are and who qualifies for them—that will come in the next chapter—but rather what the purpose of the various offices, particularly the office of elder, teacher, or pastor, is.

The reason for an indirect approach is that we must get over a common misunderstanding of how the church is to function: the idea that the work of the church is to be done by ministers or clergy. In that view, the role of laymen and laywomen is, at best, merely to follow where the ordained persons lead. Nothing could be further from the biblical pattern. The New Testament makes clear that the work of ministry is to be done by all Christians. The job of the clergy or other church officers is to equip other Christians for that task. That is the meaning of those verses quoted earlier: "And he [the Spirit] gave the apostles, the prophets, the evangelists, the pastors and teachers, to equip the saints for the work of ministry, for building up the body of Christ, until we all attain to the unity of the faith and of the knowledge of the Son of God, to mature manhood, to the measure of the stature of the fullness of Christ" (Eph 4:11-13).

Those verses are so basic to understanding the nature of the ministry of all Christians that the simplest questions must be asked of them: Whom are they about? What are the persons involved to do? Why are they to do it? How are they to do it? When or how long must the work in question be done?

TWO FUNCTIONS

The first two questions go together. The verses mention both those whom we would call clergy (apostles, prophets, evangelists, pastors, teachers—elders are also included, though we will come to that later) and all other Christians (the saints). The former are to equip the latter to do the church's work. All Christians are to be active in the church's work in some way—either equipping others, doing the work of ministry or building up the body of Christ. Each has a gift and is to use it. None is to be inactive. The difference between professional clergy and lay Christians is to be one of function only, not a difference of status, holiness, domination, or prestige.

Recent years have seen a new readiness in many evangelical circles to see and welcome this truth, just as many have also recognized the importance of spiritual gifts. That was not always the case. Earlier ages of the church were often characterized by false patterns of ministry rather than biblical ones, though, of course, there have always been properly functioning churches and ministries.

John R. W. Stott points out that three false answers have been given to the question of the relationship of clergy to other Christians.[1] The first he calls *clericalism*, the view that the work of the church is to be done by those paid to do it; the role of laypeople is at best to support those endeavors financially. How did that false picture arise? Historically, it resulted from the development of the idea of the priesthood in the early Roman Catholic Church. In those days the professional ministry of the church was patterned after the Old Testament priestly system, with the Mass taking the place of the Old Testament blood sacrifices. Only "priests" were authorized to perform the Mass, and that meant drawing a false and debilitating distinction between clergy and laity. Those who favor this view of the church say that it goes back to the days of the apostles, but that claim is demonstrably false. As reflected in the New Testament, the early church often used the word *minister* or *ministry* to refer to what *all* Christians are and must do. It never used the word *hiereus* (priest) of the clergy. As Robert Barclay pointed out in the seventeenth century and Elton Trueblood has emphasized in modern times, "the conventional modern distinction between the clergy and

---

[1]John R. W. Stott, *One People* (London: Falcon Books, 1969), 28-42. Stott discusses the proper pattern on 42-47.

laity simply does not occur in the New Testament at all."[2] There are pastors, as distinct from other Christians, but the difference is one of spiritual gifts and service, rather than of ministry versus nonministry. Above all, it is not a matter of priests versus those who can serve only a lesser function.

There are historical reasons for the development of clericalism then, but those reasons in themselves are not the whole or even the most significant. We see this when we ask why such developments took place. Was it a matter of biblical interpretation, or did other factors enter in and perhaps even distort the interpretation?

Some causes of clericalism lie deep in the human constitution. Some people always want to run the show, to dominate others. That tendency can lead to outright abuse or tyranny. An example in the New Testament was Diotrephes, who liked "to put himself first" (3 Jn 9-10). A warning against such a pattern is found in a New Testament passage conveying instruction to church elders: "Shepherd the flock of God that is among you, exercising oversight, not under compulsion, but willingly, as God would have you; not for shameful gain, but eagerly; not domineering over those in your charge, but being examples to the flock" (1 Pet 5:2-3). The chief biblical example of the right way is the Lord Jesus Christ, who, though Lord of all creation, nevertheless put on a servant's garment and performed a servant's job in washing his disciples' feet.

A third reason for the rise of clericalism is the tendency of laypeople to sit back and "let the pastor do it." Stott quotes a remark of Sir John Lawrence: "What does the layman really want? He wants a building which looks like a church; clergy dressed in the way he approves; services of the kind he's been used to, *and to be left alone*."[3] Thus laypersons abandon their God-given tasks and responsibilities and the professional clergy pick them up—to the church's impoverishment.

A second false answer to the relationship of clergy to laymen and laywomen is, understandably enough, *anticlericalism*. If the clergy despise the laity or think them dispensable, it is no surprise that the laity sometimes return the compliment by wanting to get rid of the clergy.

That is not always bad. We can imagine situations in which the church has become so dominated by a corrupt or priestly clergy that a general housecleaning is called for. That has happened historically. We can think of areas of the church's work that are best done by laypeople; the clergy are not at all necessary. But

---

[2]Elton Trueblood, *The Incendiary Fellowship* (New York: Harper & Row, 1967), 39.
[3]Stott, *One People*, 30.

that does not give grounds for anticlericalism as the normal stance of Christian people. On the contrary, where the church wishes to be biblical, it must recognize not only that gifts of teaching and leadership are given to some within the church for the church's well-being, but also that there is ample biblical teaching about the need for such leadership. The apostle Paul appointed elders in every church he founded and entrusted to them the responsibility for training the people for ministry (Acts 14:23). In the Pastoral Epistles, the appointment of such leaders is specifically commanded (Titus 1:5), and the qualifications for such leadership are given (1 Tim 3:1-13; Titus 1:5-9).

Some who have understood the idea of ministry as belonging to the whole church have begun to wonder whether there is room for clergy. But that insight about ministry, good as it is, does not lead to such a conclusion. As Trueblood says, "The earliest Christians were far too realistic to fall into this trap, because they saw that, if the ideal of universal ministry is to be approximated at all, there must be some people who are working at the job of bringing this highly desirable result to pass."[4]

A third false model of the relationship between the professional clergy and laity is what Stott calls *dualism*. The idea is that clergy and laypeople are each to be given their sphere, and neither is to trespass on the territory of the other. For example, in the traditional Roman Catholic system a "lay status" and a "clerical status" are very carefully delineated. That dualism also characterizes certain forms of Protestantism. In such a system, the sense of all being part of one body and serving together in one work easily evaporates. The church is partitioned and rivalry is apt to enter in instead.

What then is a proper pattern? The proper relationship of clergy to laypersons is *service*. According to Ephesians, the clergy are to direct their energy to equipping the saints. They are to assist them and train them to be what they should be and to do the work entrusted to them—which is the main or essential work of the church as it relates both to the world and to the body of the church itself. Jesus exemplified that pattern of service. He "came not to be served but to serve, and to give his life as a ransom for many" (Mk 10:45).

TO EQUIP THE SAINTS

We are now ready for the third of the five questions we asked at the start of this chapter. Why are pastors or teachers to serve the body of the Christian

---

[4]Trueblood, *Incendiary Fellowship*, 40.

community in this way? The answer is that the saints might be equipped to do the work of the church in two areas: the work of ministry, and building up the body of Christ.

The contrast between the work of ministry and building up the body of Christ is the contrast between service in the world and service within the Christian community. It is important to stress the first of these, because the church is often in danger of forgetting it. As is the case with families, the church sometimes becomes entirely wrapped up in itself and forgets that it is in the world to be of service to the world. It is to minister to the world as Christ did.

In *Body Life*, Ray Stedman turns to Christ's description of his ministry in the world on the occasion of his reading the Scripture in the synagogue of Nazareth, early in his ministry. He read from the book of Isaiah where it is written,

> The Spirit of the Lord is upon me,
>> because he has anointed me
>> to proclaim good news to the poor.
> He has sent me to proclaim liberty to the captives
>> and recovering of sight to the blind,
>> to set at liberty those who are oppressed,
> to proclaim the year of the Lord's favor. (Lk 4:18-19; compare Is 61:1-2)

Some of those prophesied actions involve natural activities, some supernatural ones in the case of Christ—healing the blind, for example—but, as Stedman points out, there is a sense in which those who are Christ's are nevertheless to do each one. First, there is a work of *evangelism*, described as preaching good news to the poor. Second, there is a *service* ministry in which captives are freed and the blind healed. That service may be literal; our equivalent would be work among prisoners and various forms of medical service, such as Dr. Victor Rambo's work in India among the curably blind. It may also be spiritual service in the sense that those who are captive to sin are set free by the truth of God (Jn 8:32) and those who are spiritually blind are made to see (compare Jn 9). Third, there is a ministry of *mercy* to those who are oppressed, a ministry of liberation. Fourth, there is the proclamation of *hope* to a world that has almost lost sight of hope. It is a ministry of assurance that this is the age of God's grace, and he is accepting those who turn from sin to faith in his Son, the Lord Jesus Christ.

Each of those forms of gospel ministry may be viewed spiritually, but we must not lose sight of the fact that they also involve true physical service in the world. Stedman writes,

We must never forget our Lord's story of the sheep and the goats, and the basis of their judgment. The whole point of the story is that Christians must not evade activities that involve them in the hurt of the world. The hungry must be fed, the naked clothed, the sick visited, and those in prison encouraged. We must put our gifts to work. We dare not hide them in the ground as that unfaithful steward did in one of the Lord's parables, for we must someday meet him for an accounting.[5]

The Christian can perform these forms of ministry in many spheres: in the home, on the job, through voluntary welfare agencies, even through church-directed public service projects. The important point is that Christians perform them as one part of their high calling.

The second end for which Christians are to be equipped is building up the body of Christ. This is the churchward side of ministry. It includes such things as the training of children, the discovery and development of spiritual gifts in all the church's members, the bearing of one another's burdens, praying for one another, encouraging one another, and helping one another to grow in the knowledge and love of Christ. The goal is Christian maturity, not merely for the individual (though that is part of it and is a necessary step to the greater end), but for the whole church. Paul put it like this: "until we all attain to the unity of the faith and of the knowledge of the Son of God, to mature manhood, to the measure of the stature of the fullness of Christ" (Eph 4:13).

The health of the church is related to the first area of service in that an unhealthy church cannot minister to the world properly. What keeps the church from being the good and godly influence that Christ intended it to be? Disunity is one factor. A church expending all its energies fighting within itself can hardly be of much use elsewhere. Ignorance is another cause of failure. If the church does not understand the issues of the day or the solutions provided by the gospel, it cannot help the world even though it is not divided internally and is anxious to help. The church can also be hindered by immaturity. It can be weakened by sin. Each of those faults can ruin the church's effectiveness.

How are we to reach the maturity that Paul described? Each Christian is to help others. It is not the job of the minister alone.

HOW TO EQUIP

The fourth and fifth questions asked at the beginning of this chapter were the following: How are evangelists, pastors, and teachers to equip the saints for this

---

[5]Stedman, *Body Life*, 105. The full discussion of Luke 4:18-19 is on 95-105.

work? When or how long must the work of equipping be done? The answer to the final question is "until we all attain to the unity of the faith and of the knowledge of the Son of God, to mature manhood"—that is, throughout the entire church age until Christ returns for us. The answer to the other question is by teaching and preaching the Word of God—in biblical language often described as "feeding the sheep."

The work of pastor-teacher is similar to the work of a shepherd in caring for sheep. The idea is present in the Old Testament (Ps 77:20), but it is more predominant in New Testament usage. It is based on Christ's special words of instruction to Peter, "Feed my sheep" (Jn 21:17). The sheep are called Christ's sheep. They are his first by creation (he made them) and second by redemption. Earlier, the Lord had said, "I am the good shepherd. The good shepherd lays down his life for the sheep" (Jn 10:11). If the flock were ours, whether as ministers or elders or even as parents (thinking of our children of whom we are overseers), we could do with it as we wished or as we thought best. But if it is Christ's, we must do as he wishes, recognizing our responsibility to him.

Those with the gift of being a pastor-teacher (clergy, elders, Sunday school teachers, youth leaders) are to "feed" those entrusted to their spiritual care. They are to do that by teaching, sharing, and in any other way communicating the Word of God. The job of the equipper is to teach the Bible both by word and example.

Very few of us do not have some degree of responsibility for someone. We are all usually undershepherds in some way. But we need to say a special word to preachers, for the task of teaching the Word of God is particularly theirs. Most preachers have many functions. They must administer, counsel, visit, and do scores of other things. But just as the primary responsibility of a carpenter is to build and a painter to paint, so the primary responsibility of pastors is to teach the Word of God.

This area is in decline today, first in regard to teaching, and then in preaching generally, for several reasons. First, attention has been shifted from preaching to other needed aspects of the pastoral ministry, things like counseling, liturgies, small group dynamics, and similar concerns. Those things are important. They are part of a minister's work. But they must not shift attention away from the primary responsibility, which is to teach the Word of God. Further, the two are not in opposition. When the Word of God is best preached, those other concerns are best cared for. An example is the age of the Puritans. Preachers in that period were noted for their mature expository sermons. Their material was so weighty in some instances that few today are even up to reading it. Yet other aspects of the ministry were not neglected. Worship services were characterized by a powerful sense of God's presence, and those who preached and led such services were intensely concerned with the problems, temptations, and growth of those God had placed under their care.

A second reason for the decline in preaching is the contemporary distrust of oratory. People are sensitive to being manipulated and dislike it. Since preaching is clearly directed to moving people (and not merely instructing them), it may seem to be manipulative and some therefore turn from it.

The trouble with those explanations is that, although they have an element of truth about them, they are based on external matters or external situations, and so miss the internal or fundamental cause of preaching's decline. The current decline in preaching and teaching the Word of God comes from a prior decline in belief in the Bible as the authoritative and inerrant Word of God on the part of many of the church's theologians, seminary professors, and ministers who are trained by them. It is a loss of confidence in the existence of a sure word from God.

Here the matter of inerrancy and authority go together. It is not that those who abandon inerrancy as a premise on which to approach the Scriptures necessarily abandon a belief in scriptural authority. On the contrary, they often speak of the authority of the Bible most loudly precisely when they are abandoning the inerrancy position. Yet, lacking the conviction that the Bible is without error in the whole and in its parts, those scholars and preachers inevitably approach the Bible differently from those who believe in inerrancy, whatever may be said verbally. In their work, the Bible is searched for whatever light it may shed on the world and life as the minister sees them, and not as that binding and overpowering revelation that tells us what to think about the world and life and even formulates the questions we should be asking of them.[6]

Yet the work of equipping is to be done not only by speaking the Word of God but also by living it, by example. In describing his work, Jesus said, "When he [that is, himself] has brought out all his own, he goes before them, and the sheep follow him" (Jn 10:4). Jesus has set the pattern that others are to follow. So should those whose task it is to equip other Christians.

---

[6]I have borrowed a section of this word to preachers from a chapter of my own in *The Foundation of Biblical Authority* (Grand Rapids: Zondervan, 1978).

CHAPTER 10

CHURCH GOVERNMENT

*O*ur first approach to the subject of church offices has shown that the primary reason for these offices is service to the people of God. Everything else relates to that. When that end is not perceived, troubles follow. In *One People*, John Stott reports a saying current in the Roman Catholic Church but (with the exception of its reference to bishops) true of many Protestant churches too: "The bishops are the servants of the clergy, the clergy are the servants of the laity, the laity are kings with a servant problem."[1] Many churches have that problem either through failure to understand and act on biblical principles of church leadership and government, or through a determined effort on the part of some, principally the clergy, to circumvent them. It is strange that it should be so. Basic to Christian life, whether of leaders or other Christians, is service. To be a Christian is to minister, and that means "to serve."

An article on the ministry of deacons by George C. Fuller, although it is about the forms of service peculiar to deacons, begins with an emphasis on the diaconal or service ministry of each believer in Christ. Fuller points out that the world measures greatness by the service a person receives. In business, the "important" people are those at the top of the organizational pyramid. The bigger the organization, the more important the top person is. In personal affairs, the "great" are those who have servants, and the greater the number of servants the greater the great one is. Jesus reversed all that. He "turned the whole thing upside down, making, as it were, the first last and the last first." In God's eyes, greatness consists

---

[1]John R. W. Stott, *One People* (London: Falcon Books, 1969), 43.

not in the number of people who serve us but in the number of people we serve. The greater that number, the better the Christian. Fuller writes, "If Jesus had not taken upon himself the 'form of a servant'; if the Lord of glory had not 'humbled himself and become obedient unto death, even death on a cross,' the world's standard would have remained unchallenged." Having done those things, Jesus changed that standard. Now "he is *the* 'deacon,' our ultimate example, and in fulfilling that charge from God he assured power for his people, his body on earth, to do his ministry."[2]

In the church of God, all are deacons, ministers, or servants for the benefit of the world and the building up of Christ's body.

A MINISTRY OF SERVICE

Although all Christians are to be engaged in service to the world and to each other, special responsibilities for service are given to some specifically equipped for that task. To be specific in terms of the offices outlined in the New Testament, elders (or bishops) are to serve by teaching and encouraging others to serve, and deacons are to lead the way in actual service.

It is important to start with the office of deacon. The word itself means "servant" and the role of the servant is clearly seen in this office. As far as we can judge from the New Testament, it was the first office instituted by the apostles in the church. The "apostles" had been chosen by Jesus himself and were present from the beginning, but the diaconate was the first office instituted. The record of the institution of this office is found in Acts 6:1-6.

> Now in these days when the disciples were increasing in number, a complaint by the Hellenists arose against the Hebrews because their widows were being neglected in the daily distribution. And the twelve summoned the full number of the disciples and said, "It is not right that we should give up preaching the word of God to serve tables. Therefore, brothers, pick out from among you seven men of good repute, full of the Spirit and of wisdom, whom we will appoint to this duty. But we will devote ourselves to prayer and to the ministry of the word." And what they said pleased the whole gathering, and they chose Stephen, a man full of faith and of the Holy Spirit, and Philip, and Prochorus, and Nicanor, and Timon, and Parmenas, and Nicolaus, a proselyte of Antioch. These they set before the apostles, and they prayed and laid their hands on them.

---

[2]George C. Fuller, "Deacons, the Neglected Ministry," *The Presbyterian Journal*, November 8, 1978, 9.

Although brief, that account of the choice of the first deacons teaches essential principles of sound church leadership and contains particular insight into the nature of the deacons' ministry. There are four clear principles.

First, there is to be a *division of responsibility*. It is true that all Christians are to serve one another and the world, but any one person cannot fulfill that responsibility in all ways. In this case, the apostles simply were not able to deal with the heavy responsibility of prayer and teaching *and* the care of needy persons within the church. So, certain men were appointed to that third task in order to give the apostles ample time to pray and teach.

Second, there is to be a *plurality of leadership*. The church did not install merely one person to do this job but several. In fact, there is no reference anywhere in the New Testament to the appointment of only one elder or one deacon to a work. We would tend to appoint one leader, but God's wisdom is greater than our own at this point. In appointing several persons to work together, the church at God's direction provided for mutual encouragement among those who shared in the work as well as lessened the chance for pride or tyranny in office.

Third, there is a concern for *spiritual qualifications*. The apostles did not ask the believers to consider whether those elected to this office had private wealth so that they could minister out of their own pockets should the church's funds run out. They did not ask whether they were in positions of secular power or influence. Such concerns did not enter in at all. They were simply asked to pick out men who were of good repute, and full of the Spirit and of wisdom.

We find that emphasis in every passage dealing with qualifications to church office. Qualifications for elders are listed in 1 Timothy 3:1-7; Titus 1:5-9; and 1 Peter 5:1-4. In regard to deacons, the key passage is 1 Timothy 3:8-13.

> Deacons likewise must be dignified, not double-tongued, not addicted to much wine, not greedy for dishonest gain. They must hold the mystery of the faith with a clear conscience. And let them also be tested first; then let them serve as deacons if they prove themselves blameless. The wives likewise must be dignified, not slanderers, but sober-minded, faithful in all things. Let deacons each be the husband of one wife, managing their children and their households well. For those who serve well as deacons gain a good standing for themselves and also great confidence in the faith that is in Christ Jesus.

Some of those qualifications are the same as those for elder, but others are different. An elder, for example, must be "able to teach" (1 Tim 3:2; Titus 1:9), which is not said of deacons. On the other hand, a deacon must not be "double-tongued," which is not said of elders specifically. Since deacons are to be closely involved in the lives of many people, they must have their tongue under control even more than others. Otherwise, there will be no end of gossip, misunderstandings, hurt feelings, and jealousies.

Fourth, leaders are to be *elected by the people they serve*. In Acts 6 we are not told how the believers chose the first deacons, but we *are* told that *they* chose them. They were not appointed by the apostles. Moreover, the people did a good job in choosing. Note that the complaint about the administration of church funds was brought by Greek Christians, Hellenists, and those who were chosen were apparently Greek, to judge by their names—a shrewd move, which undoubtedly hushed complaints and furthered unity.

A MINISTRY OF MERCY

The Acts passage is important not only for what it teaches about sound principles of church leadership, particularly as those principles apply to deacons. It also contains insight into the nature of the deacons' ministry. We must be careful at this point, however. The passage is a historical one, dealing with a specific problem in the early church; therefore, while it illustrates what is undoubtedly a true diaconal function, it is obviously not intended to limit the deacons' work to that sole responsibility.

What are deacons to do? Starting with this passage but also taking into account the nature of leadership itself and the particular significance of the word *deacon*, we may say that there are at least three key areas of responsibility.

The first is what Fuller calls the *ministry of mercy*[3]—service to those in need, obviously to those within the church (widows), but also to others (if only because this is a universal Christian responsibility). There is a division among deacon boards at this point: whether the deacons' financial responsibility is to members of their own congregation alone, or to other people as well. What are we to say to those who insist that their responsibility is to the household of God alone? Obviously, we must recognize that the concern this view expresses is a valid one: Christians are to care for Christians. Not to do so would be a disgrace. Again, we can agree that if funds are limited, the work of mercy should begin with those who are part of our spiritual family. Paul says as much when he instructs the Galatians, "So then, as we have opportunity, let us do good to everyone, and especially to those who are of the household of faith" (Gal 6:10).

---

[3]Ibid., 10.

But is this all that deacons are to do? How can it be if they are to lead the church in its ministry to the world as well as to those within the Christian community? No doubt, priorities must be set. No body of Christians can meet all the needs that present themselves. But if deacons are to lead the way in the church's service, they must show that our compassion is aroused by need wherever we find it and not merely among ourselves.

Here we have the example of the Lord Jesus Christ, who, although he showed a special concern for Israel, nevertheless also performed acts of mercy among the half-Gentile masses of Galilee (Mt 14:13-21; 15:32-39) and to individuals in such Gentile areas as Tyre and Sidon (Mk 7:24-30) or the Decapolis (Lk 8:26-39).

If deacons minister only to the needy in the local congregation, that is a good thing and will undoubtedly encourage other members of the church to serve widely. But if a board can conceive of its ministry more broadly, it can be even more helpful. Fuller writes,

> A board of deacons, functioning properly, will give creative attention to the neighborhood in which it is called by God to function. It will also work to devise a plan to give every member of the congregation a clear opportunity for ministry to others. As the apostles, even after the appointment of the "seven," continued to minister to people in need, we should not withhold that privilege from many Christians who simply wait for direction. The problems of our cities need study, reflection, prayer. . . . The disfavor that many of us have toward the pronouncements and postures of many Church bodies on varied political matters ought not to prohibit us from seeking wisdom for positive contributions in world affairs when survival is at stake. At the very least the board of deacons might ask for authority to sponsor an annual drive for funds for hunger, in an effort to bring that offering above the level of a collective pittance.[4]

Apart from finances, the deacons might organize a ministry of prison visitation, services to the elderly, or visitation in hospitals and nursing homes. In most large cities, the majority of those in nursing homes never receive a visit from anyone.

Another key area of responsibility is *evangelism*. This naturally follows the ministry of mercy, in that numerous opportunities to share the gospel arise in such situations. Various biblical examples encourage us to think along these lines.

[4]Ibid., 19.

Philip, one of the original deacons, is called "the evangelist" (Acts 21:8). God used him to take the gospel to the Samaritans (Acts 8:5) and later to an Ethiopian nobleman (Acts 8:26-40). He had a gift for crosscultural evangelism. Another of the original deacons, Stephen, preached with great power before the Jewish Sanhedrin, the same body that had condemned Jesus. His preaching brought such conviction that they killed him too. He was the first martyr. It is no small honor to be in a succession going back to such examples.

Third, deacons have an *obligation to train others*. The responsibility of an elder is primarily to teach, as we shall see in the next section; that is not the calling of all Christians. But all are called to acts of mercy and evangelism, and therefore in those areas the deacons have an obligation not only to train but also to lead the *whole* family of God. One way is by example, particularly as a deacon takes along one who is not a deacon as works of mercy and evangelism are done. Another is by more formal training, in adult classes or seminars. Deacons who also have the gift of administration may organize the congregation in more comprehensive efforts: to penetrate a neighborhood, to have a voice in the political affairs of the city, to render service in prisons or nursing homes or hospitals.

Fuller suggests that where this is done (1) Christians will become bound together as never before, (2) they will be responding properly to Christ's service to us, (3) hypocrisy will be removed from Christians' intercessory prayer, and (4) people will be helped. Even more, we will be demonstrating the reality of the presence of God in our lives.

We must not forget that in our Lord's parable of the sheep and goats, told just before his arrest and crucifixion, it was the presence or absence of genuine service to others that marked the corresponding presence or absence of a saving relationship to him. What was done to and for others was regarded as service to himself.

> Then the King will say to those at his right hand, "Come, you who are blessed by my Father, inherit the kingdom prepared for you from the foundation of the world. For I was hungry and you gave me food, I was thirsty and you gave me drink, I was a stranger and you welcomed me, I was naked and you clothed me, I was sick and you visited me, I was in prison and you came to me." Then the righteous will answer him, saying, "Lord, when did we see you hungry and feed you, or thirsty and give you drink? And when did we see you a stranger and welcome you, or naked and clothe you? And when did we see you sick or in prison and visit you?"

And the King will answer them, "Truly, I say to you, as you did it to one of the least of these my brothers, you did it to me." (Mt 25:34-40)

OVERSIGHT AND TEACHING

Deacons are not the only ones who are to serve the people of God in the local church, however. They are to lead the way in practical, outward service. Others, elders or bishops, are to serve by their oversight of the congregation and by a ministry of teaching. Since these persons have the chief responsibility in the church, it is no surprise that greatest attention is given to their qualifications for ministry.

Acts 20:28 is a key verse. It occurs in the middle of the account of the apostle Paul's last meeting with the elders of the church of Ephesus, with whom he had spent several years earlier in his ministry. At that point, Paul was on his return to Jerusalem for what proved to be the last time, and he had called the elders to the nearby city of Miletus for a final meeting. He used the time to instruct these men and warn them of their responsibilities as well as of the dangers to come. He said, "Pay careful attention to yourselves and to all the flock, in which the Holy Spirit has made you overseers, to care for the church of God, which he obtained with his own blood." That verse is important chiefly because of its delineation of the two main areas of responsibility of the eldership: spiritual oversight (or rule) and teaching.

Spiritual *oversight* is the thrust of the word *episkopos* (translated "overseer"), which in other places is sometimes translated "bishop." It occurs in 1 Timothy 3:1, where Paul began to list the qualifications for those to be elected to this office. "If anyone aspires to the office of overseer, he desires a noble task." It occurs in Titus 1:7: "For an overseer, as God's steward, must be above reproach." In each of these passages and others, the word *episkopos* is used as a descriptive term for elder and is therefore to be considered synonymous with that term. That is, *bishop* does not denote another higher office in the church of Jesus Christ that would have authority over local clergy, but rather speaks of a particular function of the elder's office, namely, spiritual oversight.[5]

---

[5]This is not to say that the existence of bishops as a special office within certain branches of the Christian church is necessarily wrong, but only that their existence is not supported by the use of the word in the New Testament. A denomination will want to look very carefully and critically at any aspect of its structure that does not arise out of the specific instructions of the apostles as recorded in the New Testament. It will want to ask whether its practice is a proper extension of what is found there and is compatible with it. But the fact that a church adds structures not found in the New Testament is not in itself wrong, since different situations in different periods

The function of oversight is seen in the meaning of the word *episkopos* itself. *Bishop* is merely an Anglicized pronunciation of the Greek word, but the word itself means "guardian." *Epi*, the prefix, means "over." *Skopos* is "guardian." So *episkopos* refers to one who is a guard over other persons. An elder has a responsibility for oversight. Elders are to be concerned for others' welfare.

The word often occurs in the context of pastoral imagery, as it does here. The function of an elder is comparable to that of a shepherd. In Acts 20:28, Paul referred to the church as a "flock" and reminded the elders of Ephesus that they had a responsibility to feed it. Similarly, Peter instructed the elders of a church to which he was writing,

> So I exhort the elders among you, as a fellow elder and a witness of the sufferings of Christ, as well as a partaker in the glory that is to be revealed: shepherd the flock of God that is among you, exercising oversight, not by compulsion, but willingly, as God would have you; not for shameful gain, but eagerly; not domineering over those in your charge, but being examples to the flock. And when the chief Shepherd appears, you will receive the unfading crown of glory. (1 Pet 5:1-4)

Elders must take Peter's charge seriously, and when they do, it will inevitably involve them deeply in the lives of those in their keeping. They must be concerned for the spiritual health and growth of these people. At times they must be concerned with discipline.

In Presbyterian churches, in which the role of elder is taken seriously, the body of elders is generally called the "session." The word is taken from a word meaning "sit" and means "a sitting together." It has been chosen to highlight the highest duty of this body, which is to sit together as a church court. But the difficulty with so many Presbyterian churches (and perhaps with others also) is that the persons who sit on sessions sometimes think that sitting is all elders have to do. As Lawrence R. Eyres points out in a valuable study of the responsibilities of elders, "They forget that elders, as Christ's undershepherds, must also *stand* to minister to the saints; they must *walk* (and sometimes *run*) to seek Christ's wandering sheep; they must *kneel* daily to lift up the flock before the throne of grace in prayer!"[6]

---

of church history sometimes call for different and even highly innovative programs. It can be argued that the office of bishop fills the administrative role formerly filled by the apostles and thus serves properly to tie the local churches together.

[6]Lawrence R. Eyres, *The Elders of the Church* (Philadelphia: Presbyterian and Reformed Publishing Company, 1975), 14.

656 BOOK 4~PART II

The second responsibility of elders is *teaching*. The structure of Acts 20:28 makes clear that the ministry of oversight is to be exercised chiefly through teaching. In other words, the rule that has been given to them is not some form of autocratic, absolute authority according to which the elders sit back and decide what should be done, who should do it, who is not doing it, and who should be disciplined. Rather, it is an oversight in which authority is established on the basis of the teaching of the Word of God.

This does not mean that every elder must necessarily be able to teach large groups publicly. But all elders must know the Scriptures and have the ability to bring them to bear on any particular problem encountered in the lives of those (perhaps an individual or small group of individuals) in their charge.

During the days of his earthly ministry, Jesus exercised his authority in this way. One author writes,

> He was not limited to a classroom, but rather taught anywhere he saw people in need—on a hillside, in an upper room, in the synagogue, by a well, on a rooftop, in a boat in the middle of a lake, on a mountain top, and even as he hung between two thieves on the cross. Sometimes they came to him; other times he went to them. At times he delivered a discourse and at other times he asked questions. Sometimes he told stories. Frequently he visualized his words by referring to the fowls in the air, the water in the well, the sower on the hillside, or even to people themselves. He was never stereotyped; never rigid; never without the right words. He was always meeting their needs, getting them intellectually and emotionally involved, and always penetrating to the deepest recesses of their personality. He was indeed the *master* Teacher![7]

The teaching patterns of Jesus can be an example to all elders as they seek to fulfill this important area of their responsibility.

SPIRITUAL QUALIFICATIONS

Who is to have this responsibility? What are the spiritual qualifications? Qualifications for elder are given in two sections of Paul's pastoral letters. The first, 1 Timothy 3:1-7, contains fourteen of these requirements. The second passage, Titus 1:5-9, contains most of these plus six more. There are twenty items in all. They may be considered in the following categories.

1. An elder must be *blameless* or *above reproach* (1 Tim 3:2; Titus 1:6-7). This item comes first in both of Paul's lists and clearly deserves to stand by itself,

---

[7]Gene A. Getz, *Sharpening the Focus of the Church* (Chicago: Moody Press, 1974), 124.

inasmuch as it aptly summarizes everything that comes afterward. It has to do with a person's reputation. Because elders have the chief position of responsibility in the church and most clearly represent the church before the world, they must be without blame in order that the cause of Christ might not be slandered.

2. An elder must be the *husband of one wife* (1 Tim 3:2; Titus 1:6) and have his *children in subjection* (1 Tim 3:4; Titus 1:6). It was necessary to stress the first of those qualifications in a culture in which a man frequently had more than one wife or several mistresses. But it is also linked to a proper rule of one's children. Paul was saying that elders must be proper leaders and managers of their own households if they are to be considered as possible leaders and managers of the household of God. Paul said, "If someone does not know how to manage his own household, how will he care for God's church?" (1 Tim 3:5).

In my opinion, it follows from this latter reason especially that elders in the church should be men and not women. That is not necessarily true of deacons, though the qualification "husband of one wife" is also applied to them. The phrase shows that Paul was thinking of deacons being men when he wrote that requirement, but that is not the same thing as saying that a woman cannot be a deacon. (Phoebe, described in Romans 16:1 as *diakonou*, may be an example of a woman deacon.) On the other hand, though Paul does not say that a woman cannot be a deacon, he does seem to say that a woman cannot be an elder. For example, in 1 Timothy 2:12, the two key responsibilities of an elder are mentioned specifically: "I do not permit a woman to teach or to exercise authority over men."

3. An elder must be *temperate* (1 Tim 3:2; Titus 1:8), *sensible* (1 Tim 3:2; Titus 1:8), and *dignified* (1 Tim 3:2). Those words may be taken as expressions of a mature, balanced stance before the world.

4. An elder must be *hospitable* (1 Tim 3:2; Titus 1:8). Hospitality is not often discussed as a necessary qualification for leadership in the church, but for that reason special attention should be paid to it. The need for hospitality is emphasized throughout the New Testament: "Show hospitality" (Rom 12:13); "Do not neglect to show hospitality to strangers" (Heb 13:2); "Show hospitality to one another without grumbling" (1 Pet 4:9). We must note, too, the severity with which a lack of hospitality is judged. Diotrephes, about whom the apostle John wrote, is one example. It was said of him that he "refuses to welcome the brothers, and also stops those who want to and puts them out of the church" (3 Jn 10). John called his conduct "evil" and said that he would rebuke Diotrephes publicly when he came.

Hospitality is not merely opening one's home to those who have need of it. A far more basic matter is the attitude of one's heart. As Eyres says, "The hospitable man is one whose heart is first open to the lonely, the rejected, the alien among men of all kinds and in all conditions. . . . Hospitality is really a matter of faith, the faith without which no man can please God."[8]

5. An elder must be *able to teach* (1 Tim 3:2). That requirement is made of elders but not of deacons; it is essential to the elder's role. It has been discussed in the previous section of this chapter.

6. An elder must also be marked by the absence of the following negative characteristics: *no drunkard, not violent but gentle, not quarrelsome, no lover of money* (1 Tim 3:3), *not arrogant, not quick-tempered* (Titus 1:7). These six items are related, in having to do with how a person gets on with other people. Leaders of the church must not possess flaws of character that will harm their witness or make trouble for the church of God. It might be said that these are the negative characteristics corresponding to those positive traits considered under section 3.

A similar statement of what is required in this area is Paul's list of the fruit of the Spirit in Galatians 5:22-23. "But the fruit of the Spirit is love, joy, peace, patience, kindness, goodness, faithfulness, gentleness, self-control."

7. An elder must *not be a novice* (1 Tim 3:6). This refers to spiritual maturity, not physical age. Anyone who is to lead the church must not be a neophyte or new convert. That is obvious, of course. But strangely enough, hardly a qualification in these lists is more regularly or clearly flouted by the contemporary church. We seem to do the opposite. Instead of waiting for new converts to mature, we tend to push them forward into positions of responsibility or visibility on the theory that it will cause them to grow. Paul said that to do this may cause the novice to be "puffed up with conceit and fall into the condemnation of the devil."

Christians need to grow in the faith and prove themselves. Getz writes, "Paul's concern is that a new convert has not had time to develop the qualities of a mature man of God. He may have lots of experience in business, he may be highly skilled in some profession. Or he may be very talented as a musician, actor or sportsman. But he has not had opportunity nor time to develop a good reputation, to prove himself morally and ethically."[9] It is no favor either to the

---

[8]Eyres, *Elders of the Church*, 30.
[9]Gene A. Getz, *The Measure of a Man* (Glendale, CA: Regal Books, G/L Publications, 1974), 210.

new Christian or to the church to push a novice into a place of visible responsibility.

8. An elder must be *well thought of by outsiders* (1 Tim 3:7). Sometimes Christians look down on non-Christians to such a degree that they consider their opinion unimportant. But non-Christians are certainly able to see when a Christian's profession is contradicted by his or her conduct. Since elders represent the church before the world they must be beyond reproach at this point. Many New Testament passages speak of this goal in regard to Christians generally (1 Cor 10:31-33; Col 4:5-6; 1 Thess 4:11-12; 1 Pet 2:12).

9. An elder must be a *lover of goodness, master of himself, upright, holy*, and *self-controlled* (Titus 1:8). Each of these terms is self-explanatory, and some seem to be speaking of nearly the same thing that 1 Timothy 3:1-7 speaks of. Two terms, *master of himself* and *self-controlled*, have to do with self-discipline. Being upright refers to justice. Holiness refers to personal piety; it may also be translated "devout." These qualities are developed by walking closely with God.

10. Finally, an elder must *hold firm to the sure word*, "so that he may be able to give instruction in sound doctrine and also to rebuke those who contradict it" (Titus 1:9). Ability to hold fast to the truth of God when that truth is under attack is essential. An elder should not be shaken by conflicting secular theories or by deviations from the truth within the church. Such developments characterize every age and will occur increasingly as the return of Christ draws near. Paul wrote,

> But understand this, that in the last days there will come times of difficulty. For people will be lovers of self, lovers of money, proud, arrogant, abusive, disobedient to their parents, ungrateful, unholy, heartless, unappeasable, slanderous, without self-control, brutal, not loving good, treacherous, reckless, swollen with conceit, lovers of pleasure rather than lovers of God, holding the appearance of godliness, but denying its power. (2 Tim 3:1-5)

Paul warned Timothy to avoid such people and to continue instead in his calling in Christ Jesus.

When the elders of Tenth Presbyterian Church in Philadelphia, the church I serve, meet to discuss these qualifications we find the list quite sobering. Yet we find it encouraging as well. We realize that Paul did not provide these qualifications to discourage anyone—rather he encouraged Christians to seek this office (1 Tim 3:1). What makes a good leader after all? Paradoxical as it may sound, a good leader is one who is a good follower, a follower of Christ. When Christ came to earth he said, "I have come down from heaven, not to do my own will but the will of him who sent me" (Jn 6:38). He said of the Father, "I always do the things that are pleasing to him" (Jn 8:29). To be a leader is to be a close follower of the Lord Jesus Christ, who follows the Father.

CHAPTER 11

BODY LIFE

A t the beginning of part two, I listed three characteristics that set the church off from any other institution, either in the Old or New Testament periods. Those are (1) its being founded on the Lord Jesus Christ, (2) its being called into being by the Holy Spirit, and (3) its containing people of all races who thereby become one new people in the sight of God. The first four chapters of this section dealt with the first characteristic. The next three chapters dealt with the second. The last characteristic is to be considered now.

The church from its earliest days consisted of people of many races. That undoubtedly commended it to those who were observing it from outside. The ancient world was divided in hundreds of ways by nation, race, and religion. But in Christianity from the beginning, Parthians, Medes, Elamites and residents of Mesopotamia, Judea, Cappadocia, Pontus, Asia, Phrygia, Pamphylia, Egypt, Libya, Crete, and Arabia entered into the church as equals and experienced a common life together (Acts 2:9-11).

It was not merely an organizational togetherness. It was more. Members of the church were aware of being something new in Christ. Barriers that had previously divided them were broken down. They were a family, or, as Paul put it, they were "one body" in Christ. "For he [Christ] himself is our peace, who has made us both one and has broken down in his flesh the dividing wall of hostility, by abolishing the law of commandments expressed in ordinances, that he might create in himself *one new man* in place of the two, so making peace" (Eph 2:14-15). "So then you are no longer strangers and aliens, but you are *fellow citizens* with the saints and *members of the household* of God" (Eph 2:19). Later on in the book he put this in terms of a goal. "Speaking the truth in love, we are to grow up in every way into him who is the head, into Christ, from whom the whole body, joined and held together by every joint with which it is equipped, when each part is working properly, makes the body grow so that it builds itself up in love" (Eph 4:15-16).

LIFE IN COMMON

Life in common is no less a goal of the church of Christ today, though it is perhaps less often achieved than at the beginning. The Greek word for fellowship is *koinōnia*, which in turn is based on the Greek noun *koinos*, meaning "common." It has reference to the things one shares. A partner is a *koinōnos*. The Greek language of the time of Christ and the apostles is called Koine because it was so widely spoken. So the fellowship or *koinōnia* of the church is based on what we hold in common.

In many churches, it would be hard to recognize that Christians have anything in common except that they tend to worship together at a certain fixed time on Sunday morning. Apart from that, their lives go in different and almost totally unrelated directions. They do not pray for one another or help one another. Sometimes they do not even know one another. As Ray C. Stedman says, "What is terribly missing is the experience of 'body life'; that warm fellowship of Christian with Christian which the New Testament calls *koinōnia*, and which was an essential part of early Christianity."[1]

What is wrong? Possibly a number of things. First, it may be the case—it often is in our day—that those coming together for church services are not in fact Christians. They may have a Christian background. Their parents may have been Christians. But they are not Christians themselves, and since they are not, it is no wonder that true Christian fellowship is lacking. Christian fellowship includes many things, but at its heart is a common experience of God's grace in Jesus Christ. If a person is not a Christian, he or she does not share in that.

A second problem may be sin in the lives of the Christians involved. I mean not merely that we are all sinners. I mean specific, unconfessed sin that first of all destroys the Christian's fellowship with God and then necessarily also destroys fellowship with other believers. The apostle John spoke of a twofold fellowship, with God and with one another. "That which we have seen and heard we proclaim

---

[1]Ray C. Stedman, *Body Life* (Glendale, CA: Regal Books, G/L Publications, 1972), 107.

also to you, so that you too may have fellowship with us; and indeed our fellowship is with the Father and with his Son Jesus Christ" (1 Jn 1:3). Then he went on to show how this fellowship may be disrupted. "If we say we have fellowship with him [that is, God] while we walk in darkness, we lie and do not practice the truth. But if we walk in the light, as he is in the light, we have fellowship with one another, and the blood of Jesus his Son cleanses us from all sin" (1 Jn 1:6-7). Sin erects a barrier between ourselves and God. If that has happened, the solution is confession of the sin, cleansing, and restoration of fellowship, first with God and then also with others.

Lack of fellowship may result from the way the church is organized. It may be stiffly formal. It may be so large that people get lost in the bigness. John Stott recognized this latter difficulty with his own relatively large church in London. He wrote, "There is always something unnatural and subhuman about large crowds. They tend to be aggregations rather than congregations—aggregations of unrelated persons. The larger they become, the less the individuals who compose them know and care about each other. Indeed, crowds can actually perpetuate aloneness, instead of curing it."[2]

The problem of bigness may be countered in several ways. One is to divide the church into two or more churches. That is sometimes done and should probably be done more often. But division is difficult to bring about and is not always desirable. It would certainly be regrettable if all large churches were to divide up into smaller units, since large churches can accomplish things that smaller churches cannot. They can launch pioneer works, for example. Under the umbrella of a large church other smaller works can function.

Another way to establish *koinonia* in a large assembly is to subdivide the church into smaller fellowship groups. That is the solution we have found to be most effective at Tenth Presbyterian Church in Philadelphia. We have tried to do three things at once. First, we have tried to divide the congregation according to age levels. Thus we have a fully graded Sunday school, and on the upper levels we have tried to establish groups for college students, postcollege students, young couples, other adult classes, and meetings for senior citizens. Part of this is an adult elective program. Second, we have tried to divide the congregation geographically. Tenth Church comes from a large and scattered metropolitan area. Some of the members drive twenty, thirty, or more miles to get there. Midweek meetings at the church are impractical for most. Therefore, we have established

---

[2]John R. W. Stott, *One People* (London: Falcon Books, 1969), 70.

over sixty area Bible studies where people can meet weekly with those in their area. They meet to study the Bible, share concerns, and pray together. These area groups are probably the least structured, but also are the most exciting and profitable of the church's activities. Finally, we have begun to divide the church according to professional interests. There are meetings of groups of artists, musicians (we have a choir and chamber orchestra), medical students and nurses, and at times ministerial candidates and young pastors.

The experience of our church is similar to that of All Souls in London. Stott wrote, "The value of the small group is that it can become a community of related persons; and in it the benefit of personal relatedness cannot be missed, nor its challenge evaded. . . . I do not think it is an exaggeration to say, therefore, that small groups, Christian family or fellowship groups, are indispensable for our growth into spiritual maturity."[3]

ONE ANOTHER

To speak of small churches or small fellowship groups does not in itself solve the problem of lack of Christian fellowship, however. What should happen in such gatherings? Here we must turn to the specific biblical teaching about Christian fellowship. The many verses that use the words "one another" tell us what our relationship to others should be.

Love one another. We are to love one another. That demand is emphasized most, and in a sense includes everything else that can be mentioned. We find it in John 13, where Jesus gave his new commandment: "A new commandment I give to you, that you love one another: just as I have loved you, you also are to love one another. By this all people will know that you are my disciples, if you have love for one another" (Jn 13:34-35). It is repeated twice in that Gospel. "This is my commandment, that you love one another as I have loved you" (Jn 15:12). "These things I command you, so that you will love one another" (Jn 15:17). In Romans Paul said, "Owe no one anything, except to love each other, for the one who loves another has fulfilled the law" (Rom 13:8). Paul described how he prayed for the Thessalonians: "May the Lord make you increase and abound in love for one another and for all, as we do for you" (1 Thess 3:12). He wrote, "You yourselves have been taught by God to love one another" (1 Thess 4:9). In 1 John, the command to "love one another" occurs five times (1 Jn 3:11, 23; 4:7, 11-12) and appears again in the second letter (2 Jn 5).

---

[3]Ibid., 70, 73.

This love is not to be mere sentiment, still less a profession in words only. It is to be "in deed and in truth," as John says in 1 John 3:18. It is to be seen in such practical matters as giving money and other material goods to those of our fellowship who lack those necessities (1 Jn 3:17).

Our love is to cross racial and cultural lines. Francis Schaeffer writes,

> In the church at Antioch the Christians included Jews and Gentiles and reached all the way from Herod's foster brother to the slaves; and the naturally proud Greek Christian Gentiles of Macedonia showed a practical concern for the material needs of the Christian Jews in Jerusalem. The observable and practical love among true Christians that the world has a right to be able to observe in our day certainly should cut without reservation across such lines as language, nationalities, national frontiers, younger and older, colors of skin, levels of education and economics, accent, line of birth, the class system in any particular society, dress, short or long hair among whites and African and non-African hairdos among blacks, the wearing of shoes and the non-wearing of shoes, cultural differentiations and the more traditional and less traditional forms of worship.[4]

The expression of fellowship along such lines is so important that Jesus held it out as a sign by which the world will know that we actually are his disciples.

Serve one another. We are to serve one another. Paul said that service is an outgrowth of love. "You were called to freedom, brothers. Only do not use your freedom as an opportunity for the flesh, but through love serve one another" (Gal 5:13). Our example is Jesus, who demonstrated the servant character of love by removing his robes, dressing in the garb of a servant, and stooping before each of his disciples to wash their dusty feet. "I have given you an example, that you also should do just as I have done to you" (Jn 13:15).

Is our fellowship to be expressed in foot washing? It could, but the obvious meaning of the Lord's act was that we are to be servants generally, that is, in all ways. The deacons are to lead in such service. As small groups we may serve together in supporting a Christian work in the area of the city in which we meet, helping in special projects needed by the church, visiting the sick, taking turns caring for the elderly, helping members of the church to move from one dwelling to another, and scores of other such things. After speaking of some of those projects as they have been conducted in his own church, Stott writes, "Certainly

---

[4]Francis A. Schaeffer, *The Church at the End of the 20th Century* (Downers Grove, IL: InterVarsity Press, 1970), 140.

without some such common concern and service, the fellowship of any Christian group is maimed."[5]

Bear one another's burdens. We are to bear one another's burdens. "Bear one another's burdens, and so fulfill the law of Christ" (Gal 6:2). We love by helping shoulder the cares that are wearing down our fellow Christians.

Small groups are important in doing this effectively. How are we to bear another's burdens unless we know what they are? How are we to learn about them unless we have a context in which Christians can share with one another honestly? Many problems can arise at this point, of course, one of which is our natural reluctance to let our hair down and confess what is really bothering us. If we have problems with our schoolwork or at home with our children, we hesitate to say so because admitting to what may be a failure leaves us vulnerable. We worry about what others will think. If we are having marital difficulties, we are afraid to admit it. We keep it in, and the problems build to a point where they sometimes prove unsolvable. How are Christians to learn to share their burdens? The easiest way is through a natural building of acceptance and confidence in the small group setting.

Forgive one another. We are to forgive one another. Quite a few texts talk about this necessary element in true *koinōnia*. The obvious reason is that we frequently wrong one another or are wronged, and so we need to forgive and be forgiven. "Let all bitterness and wrath and anger and clamor and slander be put away from you, along with all malice. Be kind to one another, tenderhearted, forgiving one another, as God in Christ forgave you" (Eph 4:31-32). "Put on then, as God's chosen ones, holy and beloved, compassion, kindness, humility, meekness, and patience, bearing with one another and, if one has a complaint against another, forgiving each other; as the Lord has forgiven you, so you also must forgive" (Col 3:12-13). "I therefore, a prisoner for the Lord, urge you to walk in a manner worthy of the calling to which you have been called, with all humility and gentleness, with patience, bearing with one another in love, eager to maintain the unity of the Spirit in the bond of peace" (Eph 4:1-3).

We learn from these verses that although the early church had a high degree of true fellowship, it also had troubling moments in which bitterness and wrath erupted and the peace of the church was threatened. Christians had to learn to be patient with one another and forgive the slights, whether real or imagined.

---

[5]Stott, *One People*, 87.

Confess our sins to one another. We are to confess our sins to one another. "Therefore, confess your sins to one another and pray for one another, that you may be healed" (Jas 5:16).

In opposition to the traditional Roman Catholic doctrine of confession, in which confession is made to a priest and absolution or remission of sins is received from him, Protestants have stressed that the proper biblical pattern is mutual confession. One Christian may confess to another and be assured by that person that God has pardoned the sin and has forgiven the believer through Christ. This Reformation doctrine of the priesthood of all believers is an important concept. Confession of that type, however, is more theory than practice among us. Perhaps most Protestants go through life without ever confessing anything to anybody. To judge from our speech one would think that we do not sin and never have problems.

How destructive this is of true fellowship! Ray Stedman writes,

> It goes against the grain to give an image of oneself that is anything less than perfect, and many Christians imagine that they will be rejected by others if they admit to any faults. But nothing could be more destructive to Christian *koinōnia* than the common practice today of pretending not to have any problems. It is often true that Christian homes may be filled with bickering, squabbling, angry tantrums, even bodily attacks of one member of the family against another, and yet not one word of this is breathed to anyone else and the impression is carefully cultivated before other Christians that this is an ideal Christian family with no problems of any serious consequence to be worked out.
>
> To make matters even worse, this kind of conspiracy of silence is regarded as the Christian thing to do, and the hypocrisy it presents to others (not to mention how it appears to individual members of the family) is considered to be part of the family's "witness" to the world. How helpful, how wonderfully helpful, it would be if one of the members of this family (preferably the father) would honestly admit in a gathering of fellow Christians that his family was going through difficulties in working out relationships with one another, and needed very much their prayers and counsel through this time of struggle. The family members would immediately discover at least two things: (1) that every other Christian in the meeting identified with his problem and held him in higher esteem than ever because of his honesty and forthrightness; and (2) a wealth of helpful counsel would be opened to him from those who had gone through similar struggles and had learned very valuable lessons thereby. Further, the prayers of other Christians willing to help him bear his burden would release great spiritual power into the

situation so that members of the family would be able to see much more clearly the issues to be resolved and be empowered to bear with patience and love the weaknesses of each other.[6]

James obviously intended this last result. In encouraging us to confess our sins to each other he linked it to prayer and promised power in it: "The prayer of a righteous person has great power as it is working" (Jas 5:16).

Instruct one another. We are to instruct one another. If we do not know the Word of God and do not walk closely with him, we cannot do this. We have no right to teach another. On the contrary, if we do know the Scriptures and are close to God, it should be true of us as Paul said it was of the Christians at Rome: "I myself am satisfied about you, my brothers, that you yourselves are full of goodness, filled with all knowledge and able to instruct one another" (Rom 15:14). In a small group fellowship we learn to learn from other Christians.

Comfort one another. Finally, we are to comfort one another. Paul spoke of this to the Thessalonians, where there had recently been some deaths among the Christians. Confusion had then arisen about the doctrine of Christ's second coming, and Paul wrote to them to explain what Christ's coming again would mean in regard both to them and to all who had died. Christ would return, and those who had died in Christ would be the first to be raised in their new, Christlike bodies. Clothed in their resurrection bodies, they would be united again with believers then still living. "Therefore encourage one another with these words" (1 Thess 4:18).

GOD'S FIRE

One last point. Whenever we talk of fellowship, however hard we try to be practical, our words are always filtered through the rather bland idea of fellowship that most of us have. Fellowship is something like sitting together around a warm fire on a cold day. That concept leaves out something important: the radical nature of true biblical fellowship. Far from being bland and passive, it is actually an active, burning thing.

A wonderful portrayal of this appears in the last chapter of Elton Trueblood's study of the church, *The Incendiary Fellowship*. He shows that in the Old Testament the word *fire* characteristically carried overtones of judgment, but in the New Testament it became a symbol of the contagious, spreading nature of the

---

[6]Stedman, *Body Life*, 110-11.

gospel of Christ and the church's fellowship. John the Baptist said that when Christ came he would baptize with fire (Lk 3:16). Jesus spoke of people being "salted with fire" (Mk 9:49). At Pentecost the disciples experienced "divided tongues as of fire" resting "on each one of them" (Acts 2:3). Trueblood says that, whatever else may be said about the fellowship of the early church, "it was certainly intense." Those who had been set on fire by Christ and who maintained the blaze by their close contact with one another set the world on fire.[7] We will see this even in our day where "body life" becomes a reality.

---

[7]Elton Trueblood, *The Incendiary Fellowship* (New York: Harper & Row, 1967), 105. The full discussion is on 100-121.

CHAPTER 12

THE GREAT COMMISSION

*I*t is impossible to discuss the responsibility of believers within the church fellowship without also emphasizing that part of their activity must be directed outward to the world. Gene Getz notes this in reference to the church's health and vitality: "Believers need . . . three vital experiences to grow into mature Christians. They need good Bible teaching that will give them theological and spiritual stability; they need deep and satisfying relationships both with each other and with Jesus Christ; and they need to experience seeing people come to Jesus Christ as a result of corporate and individual witness to the non-Christian world."[1]

The church does not exist for its members' self-interest. We are in the world to bear witness to the grace of God in Christ. We are "a chosen race, a royal priesthood, a holy nation, a people for his own possession, that you may proclaim the excellencies of him who called you out of darkness into his marvelous light" (1 Pet 2:9).

The most common error that Christians make at this point is to admit the importance of the Great Commission, but then relate it solely to the work of those who are specially appointed to it: missionaries. Some are called to missionary work as a special vocational assignment, but witnessing is not their work alone. It is every Christian's job.

Acceptance of that responsibility was an important factor in the astounding outreach and expansion of the early church. It was not simply that Paul and

---

[1]Gene A. Getz, *Sharpening the Focus of the Church* (Chicago: Moody Press, 1974), 80.

other leaders carried the gospel to the farthest corners of the Roman world. On the contrary, many of the church's leaders were apparently not particularly zealous about missionary effort. Rather, Christians, whoever they were, wherever they were, told others about the Lord. Historian Edward Gibbon, who was by no means sympathetic to Christianity, showed that the gospel had reached the shores of India by AD 49 and even the borders of China by AD 61.

Tertullian, writing around the year 200, declared to his contemporaries, "We are but of yesterday, and we have filled every place among you—cities, islands, fortresses, towns, market-places, the very camp, tribes, companies, palace, senate, forum—we have left nothing to you but the temples of your gods."[2]

How did that phenomenon occur? Gibbon wrote that in the early church "it became the most sacred duty of a new convert to diffuse among his friends and relations the inestimable blessing which he had received."[3] Adolf Harnack, a great church historian, declared,

> The most numerous and successful missionaries of the Christian religion were not the regular teachers but Christians themselves, in virtue of their loyalty and courage. . . . It was characteristic of this religion that everyone who seriously confessed the faith proved of service to its propaganda. . . . We cannot hesitate to believe that the great mission of Christianity was in reality accomplished by means of informal missionaries.[4]

Informal missionaries. That is what all Christians everywhere should be.

THE LORD'S COMMAND

Why should Christians risk their comfort, even their lives, in order to bring the gospel of Christ to people who sometimes hate and often ridicule them and their message? There are several reasons, but chief among them is the fact that followers of Christ are not at liberty to set their own priorities. We have been told to evangelize.

That command, referred to as the Great Commission, is found five times in the New Testament: once in Matthew, Mark, Luke, and John, and once in the

---

[2]Tertullian, *Apology*, chap. 37, in *The Ante-Nicene Fathers*, vol. 3, ed. Alexander Roberts and James Donaldson (Grand Rapids: Eerdmans, 1963), 45.

[3]Edward Gibbon, *The History of the Decline and Fall of the Roman Empire*, vol. 1 (New York: Random House, n.d.), 388.

[4]Adolf Harnack, *The Mission and Expansion of Christianity in the First Three Centuries* (New York: Harper, 1961), 366-68.

opening chapter of Acts. We can hardly miss its importance when it is repeated so often.

In each case of repetition the emphasis of the Great Commission is slightly different, which suggests that we are to study it and reflect on it from different angles. In Mark, emphasis is on final judgment. "And he said to them, 'Go into all the world and proclaim the gospel to the whole creation. Whoever believes and is baptized will be saved, but whoever does not believe will be condemned'" (Mk 16:15-16). In Luke, emphasis is on fulfillment of prophecy. "Then he opened their minds to understand the Scriptures, and said to them, 'Thus it is written, that the Christ should suffer and on the third day rise from the dead, and that repentance and the forgiveness of sins should be preached in his name to all nations, beginning from Jerusalem'" (Lk 24:45-47). In John's account, Christ placed the Great Commission in the context of his own commissioning by the Father: "As the Father has sent me, even so I am sending you" (Jn 20:21). In Acts, the command is linked to a program for world evangelization: "But you will receive power when the Holy Spirit has come upon you, and you will be my witnesses in Jerusalem and in all Judea and Samaria, and to the end of the earth" (Acts 1:8). The best-known statement of the Great Commission is in Matthew, where the emphasis falls on Christ's authority: "All authority in heaven and on earth has been given to me. Go therefore and make disciples of all nations, baptizing them in the name of the Father and of the Son and of the Holy Spirit, teaching them to observe all that I have commanded you. And behold, I am with you always, to the end of the age" (Mt 28:18-20).

Dr. R. C. Sproul, founder and staff theologian of the Ligonier Valley Study Center in western Pennsylvania, was once a student at Pittsburgh Theological Seminary, where he took a course from Dr. John H. Gerstner, professor of church history. The professor had given a lecture on predestination and then, as was his custom, began to ask questions of the students. Sproul was seated on one end of a large semicircle. Gerstner began at the other end. He asked, "Now if predestination is true, why should we be involved in evangelism?"

The first student looked back at the professor and said, "I don't know."

Gerstner moved on to the next student, who replied, "It beats me."

The next seminarian answered, "I am glad you raised that question; I have always wondered about it myself, Dr. Gerstner."

The professor kept going around the semicircle, inquiring of students one by one. Sproul was sitting in the corner feeling like a character in one of Plato's dialogues. Socrates had raised a difficult question. He had heard from the lesser stars. But he still awaited the lofty answer to the impenetrable mystery of the question. Sproul was scared to death. Finally Gerstner came to him and asked, "Well, Mr. Sproul, suppose you tell us. If predestination is true, why should we be involved in evangelism?"

Sproul says that he slid down in his seat and began to apologize. "Well, Dr. Gerstner, I know this isn't what you're looking for, and I know that you must be seeking some profound, intellectual response which I am not prepared to give. But just in passing, one small point that I think we ought to notice here is that God commands us to evangelize."

Gerstner laughed and said, "Yes, Mr. Sproul, God does command us to be involved in evangelism. And, of course, what could be more insignificant than the fact that the Lord of glory, the Saviour of your soul, the Lord God omnipotent, has commanded you to be involved in evangelism?"[5]

Jesus not only commands us to evangelize, he also tells us how to do it. First, we are to *make disciples* of all nations. We are to preach the gospel to them so that through the power of the Scriptures and the Holy Spirit they are converted from sin to Christ and thereafter follow him as their Lord. Evangelism is the primary and obvious task in this commission. On the other hand, without what follows, evangelism is at best one-sided and perhaps even unreal.

Jesus went on to say, second, that those who are his must lead their converts to the point of being publicly *baptized* "in the name of the Father and of the Son and of the Holy Spirit." This does not mean that suddenly empty rites or ceremonies are to take place. Far from it. Rather, it means two things. First, at some point a total heart commitment to Jesus as Savior and Lord must go public. Baptism is a public act. It is a declaration before other believers and the world that the person being baptized intends to follow Jesus. Second, the person is now uniting with the church, Christ's visible body. If we are truly converted, we will want to be identified with other converted people.

Finally, Jesus instructed those carrying out his commission to *teach* others all that he has commanded them. A lifetime of learning follows conversion and church membership. Proper missionary work is to go out with the gospel, win men and women to Christ, bring them into the fellowship of the church and then see that they are taught the truths recorded in the Scriptures.

---

[5]R. C. Sproul, "Prayer and God's Sovereignty", in *Our Sovereign God*, ed. James M. Boice (Grand Rapids: Baker, 1977), 127-28.

As we obey the Lord in this matter, we are encouraged by two things: an announcement that all authority has been committed to Christ (which comes before the specific command to evangelize) and a promise of his continuing presence with us to the end of the age (which comes afterward). The promise reads, "Behold, I am with you always, to the end of the age." This is a very great promise indeed.

We think back to the passage at the beginning of Matthew's Gospel where the newborn Christ was named. "'Behold, the virgin shall conceive and bear a son, and they shall call his name Immanuel' (which means, God with us)" (Mt 1:23). We are told that the great God of the universe has become "God with us" through the incarnation. It is a great thought. But in the closing chapter of the book we are told, not only that God was with us during the thirty-three or so years of Christ's earthly life, but that as a result of his death and resurrection he is now to be with us forever. He is with us always in all places equally. The all-powerful Christ will be with us to bless us as we go forth with his gospel.

GOD'S WRATH

A second motivation for the missionary enterprise is the need of men and women. They are lost without Christ. Their greatest need is to escape the fearsome judgment of the wrath of God which hangs over them. Are men and women really lost? The weight of opinion in our day is against that conclusion. But the Bible clearly teaches it, and Christians must be impelled by God's Word.

Paul wrote to the Ephesians that before their conversion they were "separated from Christ, alienated from the commonwealth of Israel and strangers to the covenants of promise, having no hope and without God in the world" (Eph 2:12). Jeremiah described people as "lost sheep" (Jer 50:6). Jesus told pointed stories about lostness: a sheep, a coin, and a son (Lk 15). John wrote, "Whoever believes in him [Jesus] is not condemned, but whoever does not believe is condemned already, because he has not believed in the name of the only Son of God" (Jn 3:18). Paul's teaching in the book of Romans begins, "For the wrath of God is revealed from heaven against all ungodliness and unrighteousness of men, who by their unrighteousness suppress the truth" (Rom 1:18). In Revelation 20:11-15, we are told about the judgment of the great white throne. At that judgment all will be called to account, and those whose names are not found written in the book of life will be lost.

Nothing is so important to any individual as to escape the wrath of God, whether the person is aware of that need or not. Although persons outside of

Christ may be unaware of their danger, there is no excuse for Christians to be unaware of it. Awareness of that terrible need should impel all of us who have found the grace of God in Christ to speak the gospel as wisely, widely, and relevantly as we can.

CHRIST'S LOVE

Finally, the love of the Lord Jesus Christ should be a strong missionary motivation. Paul wrote, "For the love of Christ controls us, because we have concluded this: that one has died for all, therefore all have died; and he died for all, that those who live might no longer live for themselves but for him who for their sake died and was raised" (2 Cor 5:14-15). Those verses are not referring to our love for Christ, though that may perhaps also be a motivation for mission, but rather to Christ's love working through those who are his people. He loves through us, and his love should cause us to reach out and identify with those who need the gospel.

Do we? Here are two stories by which we can evaluate the presence or absence of the love of Christ for others in our lives.

During the years I spent in Basel, Switzerland, doing graduate study, I met a woman named Sheila. She had come from a bad background in England and had gone to Switzerland when still young in order to make a better life for herself. She was lonely. Having no one to turn to, she fell in with a young man who did not marry her but left her with a child. By the time I met her, the child was about four years old, and Sheila herself was on guard against most people and was very hostile to the church and Christianity.

In time, through the witness of the English-speaking community, she became a Christian, and about the time I left Switzerland to return to America she immigrated to Canada. My wife and I corresponded with her for about six months after she arrived in Canada and had the impression that she was not fitting in with any Christian group in her area. We went to visit her and found that we were right. We began to talk about her with various Christian people we knew in her city. There was interest to a degree, but no real love. They told us, "Oh, there is a very good church in our city." They gave us the name. Sometimes it was a Presbyterian Church, sometimes Baptist, sometimes independent. But in all our conversations no one said, "Give me her name and address. I'll stop by and invite her to go with me on Sunday morning."

Finally, being very unhappy, she left that city for another and (I am afraid) once again fell in with bad company. Eventually, in spite of much effort, we lost touch with her.

The second story is more promising. It was told at the Berlin Congress on Evangelism (1966) by the Rev. Fernando Vangioni, now an assistant evangelist with the Billy Graham Evangelistic Association. He said that he was in South America for a series of meetings, and after one of them a woman came to him and said, "I wonder if you would take time to speak to a young woman I am bringing to the meeting tomorrow night. She went to New York some years ago, full of hope, thinking that America was the land of opportunity. Instead of doing well she went through terrible times in the city. She was used by one man after another. All treated her badly. Now she has returned to this country very bitter and hostile to all forms of Christianity." The evangelist said he would speak to her.

On the next night the young woman was there. Vangioni said he had never looked into such hard eyes or listened to a voice so hostile. At last, seeing he was making no progress in talking with her, he asked, "Do you mind if I pray for you?"

"Pray if you like," she said, "but don't preach to me. And don't expect me to listen."

He began to pray, and as he prayed he was greatly moved. Something in the tragedy of her life caused tears to run down his face. At last he stopped. There was nothing to add. He said, "All right, you can go now."

But the woman did not go. Touched by that manifestation of love for her, she replied, "No, I won't go. You can preach to me now. No man has ever cried for me before."

We need to ask whether we have ever been touched at all for one who is lost and ignorant of Christ's love. Do we say, "We have a wonderful church; they should go there"? Or do we go out of our way to know and communicate? We should be able to say as Paul did, "For if we are beside ourselves, it is for God; if we are in our right mind, it is for you. . . . We are ambassadors for Christ, God making his appeal through us. We implore you on behalf of Christ, be reconciled to God" (2 Cor 5:13, 20).

PART III

A TALE OF
TWO CITIES

The King answered and said, "Is not this great Babylon,
which I have built by my mighty power as a royal residence
and for the glory of my majesty?"

DANIEL 4:30

But understand this, that in the last days there will come times of difficulty.
For people will be lovers of self, lovers of money, proud, arrogant, abusive,
disobedient to their parents, ungrateful, unholy, heartless, unappeasable,
slanderous, without self-control, brutal, not loving good, treacherous, reckless,
swollen with conceit, lovers of pleasure rather than lovers of God, holding
the appearance of godliness, but denying its power. Avoid such people.

2 TIMOTHY 3:1-5

Then I saw a new heaven and a new earth; for the first heaven and the
first earth had passed away, and the sea was no more. And I saw the
holy city, new Jerusalem, coming down out of heaven from God, prepared
as a bride adorned for her husband.

REVELATION 21:1-2

Jesus answered him, "You would have no authority over me at all unless
it had been given you from above. Therefore he who delivered me over
to you has the greater sin."

JOHN 19:11

CHAPTER 13

THE SECULAR CITY

*I*n AD 410 a Visigoth king, Alaric, laid siege to Rome and sacked it. The capital of the Roman Empire had been besieged by barbarians before. Parts of the empire had already been overrun by foreign armies. But the sack of Rome was politically and psychologically devastating in a way those other events had not been. Rome had been master of the world. The empire had stood for more than one thousand years. When Rome fell, the citizens of the empire (who no doubt could hardly assimilate the depths of the tragedy) searched about for someone or something to blame.

It was not long before blame fell on the Christians, as it had nearly four hundred years before for less serious troubles. The pagans charged that the fall of Rome had resulted from neglect of worship of the old gods under whose tutelage Rome had grown great. The cause of that neglect, so they said, was Christianity.

In God's providence there was a man particularly suited for that era of history: Augustine of Hippo (in North Africa).

In AD 412, he began a wise and spirited defense of Christianity called *The City of God*, perhaps the best known of all his writings except the *Confessions*. Augustine was a long time in writing that work, finishing it in AD 426. The result was what scholars have since called the first true philosophy of history. It contains twenty-two books or chapters. The first ten answer the pagans' charge, showing that the worship of the old gods had not protected Rome in earlier times—there had been many military and other disasters—nor had they protected other cities or cultures. Rather, the worship of pagan deities had plunged Rome into increasing vice, for which the gods were notorious. Rome fell as a result of its own corruption. Then, in the next twelve books, Augustine developed his philosophy of history proper, showing that from the first rebellion of the fallen angels against God, "two cities have been formed by two loves: the earthly by the love of self, even to the contempt of God; the heavenly by the love of God, even to the contempt of self."[1]

In his work Augustine used *city* to refer to two societies. One is the church, composed of God's elect. It is destined to rule the world. The other is the earthly society, having as its highest representatives the city cultures of Babylon in ancient times and Rome, in what was for Augustine immediate past history. The earthly city is destined to pass away. In the second part of his work, Augustine traces the origins, history, and final destiny of the two societies.

Not all have agreed with Augustine's interpretation of history, of course. Certainly secular thinkers have not, and even Christians have often dissented from one or more parts of it. Still, the central thesis of *The City of God* is one that needs rehearing. *The City of God* was influential at the time of the Reformation, forming the basis of Martin Luther's and John Calvin's doctrine of the two kingdoms. It needs to be influential again, particularly in our own age in which the line between sacred and secular has been so systematically smudged. Christians need to recapture what it means to be "children of God without blemish in the midst of a crooked and twisted generation" among whom they are to "shine as lights in the world" (Phil 2:15).

Two Cities

There has been so much emphasis on the secular in the twentieth century (even the secularization of Christianity) that one might wonder if the doctrine of the two cities is valid. Is not the church to be in the world in order to minister to the world? Are not the concerns of the world to be the concerns of Christians also? The answer to each of those questions is yes. The church is to minister to the world. It is to share the world's concerns. But that is not the whole story. Although the church is in the world, it is not to be of the world. Although it shares many of the concerns of non-Christian men and women, it has concerns they do not know of.

---

[1] Augustine, *The City of God*, book 14, chapter 28, in *A Select Library of the Nicene and Post-Nicene Fathers of the Christian Church*, vol. 2, ed. Philip Schaff (Grand Rapids: Eerdmans, 1977), 282-83.

The most important thing to be said about the two cities (by whatever name they are known) is that the distinction is found throughout the Bible.

The first appearance is in Genesis 3:15, in the words of God to the serpent following the temptation and fall of Adam and Eve. The serpent, who was himself in rebellion against God, had led the man and woman to rebellion, and God had now appeared to judge each of them. He cursed the serpent. Then he gave this word of decree and prophecy:

> I will put enmity between you and the woman,
>   and between your offspring and her offspring;
> he shall bruise your head,
>   and you shall bruise his heel.

We see three sets of antagonists: the serpent and the woman, the descendants of the serpent and the descendants of the woman, and Satan himself and the ultimate descendant of the woman, Jesus Christ. Here are divisions in conflict with one another. But the victory of the godly seed of the woman is to be assured by the ultimate victory of her specific descendant, Jesus.

If Genesis 3:15 was the only text to go on, we might think its second contrast is between demons (the seed of the serpent) and humanity. But that is not the case, as the next two chapters of Genesis make plain. It is true that there is antagonism between the fallen angels and *believing* men and women. But there is also conflict between the holy angels and the fallen angels and between believing men and women and those who do not believe. Genesis 4–5 show that the antagonism in view in Genesis 3:15 is between godly and ungodly men and women.

The first illustration is the conflict between Abel and Cain. Cain was the first child of Adam and Eve (born after the fall), and the essential meaning of his Hebrew name is "Possession," or colloquially, "Here he is!" Adam and Eve had heard God's promise of a deliverer who would crush the head of Satan. So when Cain was born, they may have assumed that he was this deliverer. As things turned out, instead of a savior, Cain became a murderer. In later years, Cain grew jealous over God's acceptance of his brother Abel's offering rather than his own and killed him.

The cause of Cain's jealousy is very important, because it concerns the means of approaching God. Cain had brought an offering from the field, the result of his own labor. Abel had brought a lamb, which was then killed and offered as the innocent substitute bearing the guilt that Abel recognized as his own. We do not know how much Abel understood about the proper means of approaching God through sacrifice (which anticipated the ultimate and only truly effective sacrifice of Christ). But he is praised in the book of Hebrews as having done what he did through faith. "By faith Abel offered to God a more acceptable sacrifice than Cain, through which he was commended as righteous, God commending him by accepting his gifts" (Heb 11:4). The essential point is that Abel came to God in the right way and Cain did not. When God accepted Abel's offering and not Cain's, Cain grew angry and murdered his brother. In these brothers we see the first examples of the two humanities.

The remainder of Genesis 4 and the next chapter show how the stance of these two individuals gave birth to two different cultures. Cain is driven away to be a wanderer in the earth, and his descendants are listed: Enoch, who built a city; Irad, the son of Enoch; Mehujael; and finally Methushael, the father of Lamech. Lamech received special mention as an illustration of what was happening in the line of these who walked in "the way of Cain" (Jude 11). He had three sons: Jabal, who, we are told, "was the father of those who dwell in tents and have livestock"; Jubal, "the father of all those who play the lyre and pipe"; and Tubal-cain, "forger of all instruments of bronze and iron" (Gen 4:20-22).

Although brief, those descriptions speak of a fairly well-developed culture. But it was a godless and cruel culture:

Lamech said to his wives:
  "Adah and Zillah, hear my voice;
        you wives of Lamech, listen to what I say:
  I have killed a man for wounding me,
        a young man for striking me.
  If Cain's revenge is sevenfold,
        then Lamech's is seventy-sevenfold." (Gen 4:23-24)

It is the story of a man boasting about murder and, since the boast seems to be in poetic form, actually writing a song about it. He is saying, "Look what a neat guy I am. A fellow hurt me, and I killed him. I just killed him. That will teach people not to mess around with Lamech." As Francis Schaeffer says in his discussion of this incident, "Here is humanistic culture without God. It is egotism and pride centered in man; this culture has lost the concept not only of God but of man as one who loves his brother."[2]

---

[2]Francis A. Schaeffer, *Genesis in Space and Time: The Flow of Biblical History* (Downers Grove, IL: InterVarsity Press, 1972), 114.

At that point in Genesis 5, the godly line of Seth is introduced. Seth took the place of the murdered Abel, and his line continued through Noah and his family, the sole survivors of the flood. The names in this line are Seth, Enosh, Kenan, Mahalalel, Jared, Enoch, Methuselah, Lamech, and Noah. Two are mentioned in Hebrews 11: Enoch, who is said to have "pleased God" (Heb 11:5) and Noah, of whom it is written, "By faith Noah, being warned by God concerning events as yet unseen, in reverent fear constructed an ark for the saving of his household. By this he condemned the world and became an heir of the righteousness that comes by faith" (Heb 11:7).

These lines may be traced through history, as Augustine did in *The City of God*. The godless line is traceable in the world's cultures. The godly line is in Abraham and his descendants, the faithful within Israel, and within the church.

BABYLON AND JERUSALEM

The two societies are traceable not only by a succession of godly and godless individuals. The Bible also makes the contrast by a comparison of two literal cities: Babylon, which epitomizes the earthly society and its goals, and Jerusalem, which symbolizes the goals and society of God's people. Babylon was founded in ancient times, grew, eventually besieged and overthrew the earthly Jerusalem, and was in turn overthrown and abandoned. Today it is a desert. Jerusalem was founded, besieged, overthrown by Babylon—but was then refounded. In the book of Revelation these literal cities are raised into significance as symbols of the two cultures. There, as in actual history, Babylon is overthrown ("Fallen, fallen is Babylon the great!" [Rev 18:2]). Jerusalem is reconstituted as a new "holy city . . . coming down out of heaven from God" (Rev 21:2), which is to endure forever.

The chief characteristic of the secular city, illustrated by earthly Babylon, is its radical secular humanism, which may be described as its being *of* humanity, *by* humanity, and *for* humanity exclusively. When we say that it is *of* humanity we mean that it is bounded by human beings and their horizons; it has no place for God. *By* humanity means that human beings are the creators of this city; it has their values. *For* humanity indicates that its goal is human glory.

The Babylon of Nebuchadnezzar in the days of Daniel the prophet is the clearest biblical illustration of these elements. It was the focal point of the struggle between Nebuchadnezzar, who embodied the secular city, and God, who operated through Daniel and his friends. The key to the book is in the opening verses, which say that after Nebuchadnezzar had besieged and conquered

Jerusalem (though it was "the Lord [who] gave Jehoiakim king of Judah into his hand"), he took some of the sacred vessels of the temple treasury to Babylon and there "placed the vessels in the treasury of his god" (Dan 1:2). That was Nebuchadnezzar's way of saying that his gods were stronger than Jehovah. And so it seemed. God had permitted Nebuchadnezzar to triumph over the people of Judah in punishment for their sins. Still, Nebuchadnezzar's rebellion was more than that. It was the rebellion of a humanism that would seek to eliminate God entirely. We might think, because of the disposition of the temple vessels, that this is the story of a struggle between the Lord and Nebuchadnezzar's *gods*. But it is actually a struggle between the Lord and Nebuchadnezzar himself, as the unfolding story shows.

One evening Nebuchadnezzar had a dream that involved a large image of gold, silver, brass, and iron. The head was gold. It represented the kingdom of Nebuchadnezzar and was God's way of acknowledging that Babylon was indeed magnificent. But, as God went on to point out, Babylon would be succeeded by another kingdom, represented by the silver arms and chest of the figure; that second kingdom would be succeeded by another, represented by the figure's brass middle portions; and then that by a kingdom represented by iron legs. Only at the end of this period would the eternal kingdom of God in Christ come and overthrow all others, grow up, and fill the earth. In this vision God was telling Nebuchadnezzar that he was not so important as he thought he was and that God himself rules history.

In the next chapter we are told that Nebuchadnezzar set up a huge golden statue on the plain of Dura. On the surface this seemed to be only the foolish gesture of a vain monarch who insisted that the statue be worshiped as a symbol of the unity of the empire. When the story is read with the vision of the statue of Daniel 2 in view, however, one realizes that the later episode actually shows Nebuchadnezzar's rebellion against God's decree. It is not a question of God struggling against Nebuchadnezzar's gods, but of Nebuchadnezzar defying God's pronouncements. God had said, "Your kingdom will be succeeded by other kingdoms, kingdoms of silver, brass and iron." Nebuchadnezzar replied, "No, my kingdom will endure forever; it will always be glorious. I will create a statue of which not only the head will be of gold, but the shoulders, thighs and legs also. It will represent me and my descendants forever." The king's personal involvement with the statue explains his violent reaction when the three Jewish men refused to bow down to it.

It also explains the violent reaction of the secular mind to Christian claims today. It is not just a question of the Christian God versus other gods, each individual adherent presumably thinking that his or her god is the true one. It is the rebellion of human beings against God. God is the one to whom we are responsible, but fallen men and women do not want to be responsible to anyone. They want to rule themselves. They want to exclude God even from his own universe and limit their horizons to the secular.

SECULAR AND SACRED

In twentieth-century America, secularism is strikingly noticeable in our current doctrine of the separation of church and state. The doctrine of the separation of church and state used to mean that each functioned separately, kings or presidents not being allowed to appoint clerical authorities or run the church, and clerical authorities not being allowed to appoint kings or presidents. Nevertheless, it was always understood that both church and state were responsible to God, in whose wisdom each had been established. They were two independent servants of one master. Although neither was permitted to rule the other, each was to remind the other of its God-appointed duties and recall it to upright, godly conduct if it should stray. Today, however, the doctrine of the separation of church and state is taken, primarily by church people, to mean that the church is irrelevant to the state—though the state increasingly brings its secular philosophy to bear on the church. Thus Christians withdraw from politics, neglect even to inform themselves of national and international issues. And as a result, the articulation of spiritual or moral principles is eliminated from debates on national and international policy. The state becomes its own god, with its chief operating principle being pragmatism.

A second example of current society being humanistic to the point of excluding God is the philosophy of evolution, which is dominant in most contemporary thinking and extends to everything. There are different reasons for evolution's popularity, of course. First, according to evolutionary thought, everything is knowable. Everything is the result of something prior, and the sequence of cause and effect can be traced backward indefinitely. Such an outlook has obvious appeal. Second, reality has *one* explanation: the fittest survive, whether a biological form, a government, or an ideal. Third, and this is undoubtedly the chief reason for evolution's popularity, evolution eliminates God. If all things can be explained as the natural outworking or development of previous causes, then God may be safely banished to an otherworldly kingdom or even be eliminated altogether, as many, even so-called theologians, have done.[3]

That the secular city is also *by* humanity and *for* humanity comes out in the remainder of Nebuchadnezzar's story. One day, a year or more after the earlier incident, Nebuchadnezzar was walking on the roof of his royal palace in Babylon and looked out over the city. He was impressed with its magnificence. Judging himself to be responsible for that magnificence, he then took to himself the glory that should have been given to God. He said, "Is not this great Babylon, which I have built by my mighty power as a royal residence and for the glory of my majesty?" (Dan 4:30). His statement was a claim that the earthly city had been constructed *by* humans and *for* human glory.

In a sense it was true. Nebuchadnezzar had constructed the city, and his conquests had brought it to its present level of architectural splendor. He had constructed it for his glory, as his self-satisfied boasting shows. His mistake was that he had forgotten that ultimately it is God who rules in human affairs and that the achievements of any ruler are made possible only through God's gifts to humanity.

Is the spirit of Nebuchadnezzar present today? Undoubtedly. It has always been present, either overtly or just beneath the surface of the secular city's culture. Algernon Charles Swinburne's "Hymn of Man" is an example.

> But God, if a God there be, is the
> Substance of men which is Man.
> Thou art smitten, thou God, thou art smitten;
> Thy death is upon thee, O Lord.
> And the love-song of earth as thou diest
> Resounds through the wind of her wings—
> Glory to Man in the highest!
> For Man is the master of things.[4]

Human beings are not the master. The presumption of that claim is a sin God will not tolerate. God promises to bring the secular city down.

---

[3]Not all evolutionists are motivated by each of those three desires. Since there are Christian scientists who accept a theistic evolutionary hypothesis, obviously *they* are not. Still, I would maintain that the appeal of the evolutionary outlook and the general hold it has on contemporary life have to do with its elimination of God as a factor in human affairs.

[4]See Philip Edgcumbe Hughes, *Christianity and the Problem of Origins* (Philadelphia: Presbyterian and Reformed Publishing Company, 1974), 11.

He did it in the case of Nebuchadnezzar. Nebuchadnezzar had judged himself superior to those around him because of his political achievements, so superior that he had no need of God. Then God spoke to show how mistaken Nebuchadnezzar was. He said,

> O King Nebuchadnezzar, to you it is spoken: The kingdom has departed from you, and you shall be driven from among men, and your dwelling shall be with the beasts of the field. And you shall be made to eat grass like an ox, and seven periods of time shall pass over you [that is, seven years shall go by], until you know that the Most High rules the kingdom of men and gives it to whom he will. (Dan 4:31-32)

That judgment was immediately put into effect. Nebuchadnezzar's mind went from him, and he was driven out of the city. The text says, "He was driven from among men and ate grass like an ox, and his body was wet with the dew of heaven till his hair grew as long as eagles' feathers, and his nails were like birds' claws" (Dan 4:33). When God caused Nebuchadnezzar to be lowered from the pinnacle of pride to the baseness of insanity and to behave like a beast, God was indicating that this is the result when humans take his glory to themselves and attempt to eliminate him from their lives. Indeed, they become worse than beasts—because beasts, when they are beastlike, are at least behaving the way beasts should behave, while we, by contrast, commit crimes of which they cannot even conceive.

THE CITY OF GOD

Over against the secular city stands the city of God. It is not a visible city, as the kingdoms of this world are visible. The world may call the city of God an illusion. But though invisible it is not illusory. In fact, it alone is substantial, in contrast to the cities of this world, which are in the process of passing away.

God is its life. This is so even now, but it will be so in full measure when the new Jerusalem rises on the ruins of the old. In his description of the holy city, John said that there is no temple in that city because "its temple is the Lord God the Almighty and the Lamb" (Rev 21:22). He wrote, "Behold, the dwelling place of God is with man. He will dwell with them, and they will be his people, and God himself will be with them" (Rev 21:3). This city is brought into being by God and not by humans. It exists for his glory.

All men and women are born into the secular city. No one is born into the heavenly city naturally. But the city of God can be entered by new birth through faith in the Lord Jesus Christ as Savior. Jesus said, "Unless one is born again, he cannot see the kingdom of God" (Jn 3:3). The doors of that city stand open for any who will come. The New Testament says of Abraham, "By faith he went to live in the land of promise, as in a foreign land, living in tents with Isaac and Jacob, heirs with him of the same promise. For he was looking forward to the city that has foundations, whose designer and builder is God" (Heb 11:9-10).

As you seek to come, you can be encouraged by the fact that evidently even Nebuchadnezzar got the message. After the seven years of his punishment had passed and he returned to his senses, he confessed that the God whom he had earlier called Daniel's God (Dan 2:47) was now his God as well.

> At the end of the days I, Nebuchadnezzar, lifted my eyes to heaven, and my reason returned to me, and I blessed the Most High, and praised and honored him who lives forever,
>
> > for his dominion is an everlasting dominion,
> > > and his kingdom endures from generation to generation;
> > all the inhabitants of the earth are accounted as nothing;
> > > and he does according to his will among the host of heaven
> > > and among the inhabitants of the earth;
> > and none can stay his hand
> > > or say to him, "What have you done?" (Dan 4:34-35)

His last words were, "Now I, Nebuchadnezzar, praise and extol and honor the King of heaven, for all his works are right and his ways are just; and those who walk in pride he is able to humble" (Dan 4:37).

As we humble ourselves, we find ourselves exalted in the role God has called us to fill and rejoice as citizens of that heavenly city that shall never pass away.

CHAPTER 14

THE SECULAR CHURCH

*D*iscussion of the secular city leads naturally to the city of God, the direction in which the last chapter was moving. But before we come to further consideration of God's city, we need to deal with a view that emerged into prominence in the 1960s and may be said to characterize much if not most modern theology.

This view denies the distinction between the sacred and secular, saying either that life has no sacred dimension or that the sacred and secular are one. It says that Christians are called, not to be otherworldly, but to be this-worldly. They are to forget God and get on with the business of being human in a world from which God has vanished. What makes this a unique position, and not just another expression of the secular mind, is that it is maintained by a number of so-called Christian theologians as well as the hierarchy of many Christian denominations.

The "death of God" theologians, who received so much publicity in the mid-'60s, were a clear example: Thomas J. J. Altizer, William Hamilton, Gabriel Vahanian, and Paul van Buren. The views of Harvard Divinity School professor Harvey Cox and John A. T. Robinson, England's bishop of Woolwich, were widely quoted. Since then, hosts of church functionaries and lesser-known but more original theologians have arisen, all of whom were trying to be radically secular. They wrote of "man come of age," a phrase drawn from the writings of Dietrich Bonhoeffer. Some referred to their outlook as "worldly Christianity."

Christian Secularization

The best example of "Christian secularization" is Harvey Cox, whose book *The Secular City* hit the religious world as a bombshell in 1965. Although Cox later repudiated some of his ideas, *The Secular City* is still the best example of this view for two reasons: (1) Cox regarded the secular city as a good thing, something to be affirmed and applauded rather than denied; and (2) Cox maintained that the Judeo-Christian tradition itself leads us to regard secularization positively.

Cox finds a biblical base for the second assertion in three areas. First, he believes that the Genesis account of creation teaches the "disenchantment" of nature. Presecular human beings lived in a world where trees, rocks, glens, groves, droughts, and storms were alive with friendly or hostile spirits. Everywhere people looked they were confronted with mysterious forces to be managed, appeased, or warded off. In Genesis that view was radically subverted. There both God and human beings were distinguished from nature, with the result that humans could then regard nature in a matter-of-fact way. Now nature is merely nature, natural. It is there to be used. Cox calls this disenchantment of the natural world "an absolute precondition" for the development of natural science and hence for the emergence of the modern technopolis. He says that in this sense, the Genesis account of creation is really a form of "atheistic propaganda."[1]

A second area in which the Judeo-Christian tradition has led to secularization is politics, which Cox traces to the Jewish exodus from Egypt. In presecular society anyone who ruled, ruled by divine right. Therefore, rebellion against any duly installed ruler was a rebellion against God or a god. The exodus changed all that. Here was an act of civil disobedience or rebellion sanctioned by the Hebrew God. Cox writes, "As such, it symbolized the deliverance of man out of a sacral-political order and into history and social change, out of religiously legitimated monarchs and into a world where political leadership would be based on power gained by the capacity to accomplish specific social objectives."[2] The old, sacred view of politics did not disappear at once, of course. Jewish people were often tempted to return to sacral politics, especially in the time of the monarchy.

The struggle of pope against emperor reenacted the same temptation in the Middle Ages. In contemporary history, the British state church, presided over by

---

[1]Harvey Cox, *The Secular City: Secularization and Urbanization in Theological Perspective* (New York: Macmillan, 1965), 23. The entire discussion is on 21-24.
[2]Ibid., 26.

the archbishop of Canterbury, and the use of the Bible for the taking of the oath of office by the president of the United States are remnants of the earlier view, according to Cox. But these have little substance, and politics can now be seen to be thoroughly secular, except in some Third World countries such as Nepal.

A third area of biblical desacralization is the Sinai covenant, which Cox calls the "deconsecration of values." He means that values or moral norms are made relative. If we ask how anyone can say such a thing—in that Sinai was the place, above all others, in which God gave what has always been regarded as an absolute and binding moral law—the answer, according to Cox, is in the opposition to idolatry seen there (Ex 20:3). It was because the Jews believed in Yahweh rather than the gods of the heathen that their values were relativized.

On this so-called biblical basis, Cox believes that modern people, in their technology, urbanity, and pragmatism, are the product of biblical faith and divinely directed historical forces. These people live in the secular city, from which for all practical purposes God is banished. They enjoy a freedom made possible by technology and undergirded by almost total privacy. Values are private, as each is left free to live as he or she desires. Cox calls on Christians to support this outlook. He writes,

> Clearly, those whose present orientation to reality is shaped by the biblical faith can hardly in good faith enter the lists as adversaries of secularization. Our task should be to nourish the secularization process, to prevent it from hardening into a rigid world view, and to clarify as often as necessary its roots in the Bible. Furthermore, we should be constantly on the lookout for movements which attempt to thwart and reverse the liberating irritant of secularization.[3]

TURNING TO THE WORLD'S WISDOM

How can we explain the tremendous attention and acclaim that Cox's book received on its appearance? The reason for that acclaim was that the secularization of the church that Cox described was already well under way, in fact, even entrenched in some church bureaucracies. Consequently, when *The Secular City* appeared, those persons naturally hailed it as a theoretical justification of a lifestyle and denominational policy they were already following.

One element in this secularization of the church, which clearly preceded Cox, was its exchange of the ancient wisdom of the church (embodied in Scripture) for the world's wisdom. In earlier ages, Christian people stood before the Word

---

[3]Ibid., 36.

of God and confessed their ignorance of spiritual things. They even confessed their inability to understand what was written in the Scriptures except through the grace of God in the ministry of the Holy Spirit. Christian people confessed their natural resistance to God's teaching. In our time, this old wisdom, the strength of the church, has been set aside. The authoritative, reforming voice of God through the Scriptures has been forgotten.

Once I was taking part in a series of Moderator's Conferences in the United Presbyterian Church, USA. In one of these, a professor from a theological seminary disagreed with everything I said. I had expected this from some source, but the words this man used were so forceful they stuck in my mind. I had spoken of the historical Christ, but this professor violently disagreed with my position. He said, "We must understand that each of the Gospels was written to correct the other Gospels. So it is impossible to speak of the historical Christ." Then, since I had also said something about the return of the Lord, he added, "We must get it into our heads that things are always going to continue as they are now and that Jesus Christ is never coming back."

That is not an isolated incident. A pastor, who has been an active leader for the evangelical cause, told me that after he had spoken to a particular issue at a presbytery meeting, another minister demanded, "Why are you always talking about the Bible when you argue a point? Don't you know that nobody believes the Bible anymore?" Then, because my friend had referred to the apostle Paul on this occasion, his critic added, "After all, the apostle Paul was not infallible."

I see four consequences of this capitulation to the world. First, it has produced a pitiful state of uncertainty and insecurity in church leaders. It is often covered up, of course. But at times it is honestly stated, as in these words from the inaugural address of Robin Scroggs, professor of New Testament at the Chicago Theological Seminary:

> We are thus in no secure place. We have found no single authoritative standard from the past of what to say or how to live. Neither have we a secure self-understanding erected on the basis of our immediate experience. We in fact find ourselves in the abyss of a continual uncertainty, but we are kept from falling into chaos by the very tension between past and present. . . . We have no assurance that where we happen to be is the best or final place to stand.[4]

---

[4]Robin Scroggs, "Tradition, Freedom and the Abyss," in *The Chicago Theological Seminary Register* 60, no. 4 (May 1970): 12-13. Quoted by Donald G. Bloesch, *The Invaded Church* (Waco, TX: Word Books, 1975), 75.

A second result is the church's turning to the world and its values. One analyst of the secularizing movement in today's theology is John Macquarrie (variously classified as a secular or process theologian). In his study of the intellectual history of many secular theologians, *God and Secularity*, he describes many of these men as "disillusioned Barthians."[5] Since Karl Barth denied that the Bible was the Word of God, calling it only humanity's witness to the Word of God, and since Barth stressed the transcendence or hiddenness of God, those who followed him wondered if anything could honestly be termed a revelation. And if not, or if one could not be certain of such a revelation, then the secular world with its vacillating but audible words was the only place to which one could turn for direction.

A third result of abandonment of the Scriptures as the wisdom of God given to the church is a pragmatic dependence on the 51 percent vote, the validation of values, goals, objectives, and programs by consensus. If people throw out a transcendent authority, an earthly authority will inevitably take Scripture's place.

A final consequence of the church's abandonment of God's wisdom is that the church becomes irrelevant (as indeed even Cox's *The Secular City* must seem to secular men and women). This is being noted widely, and not just by evangelicals. Speaking in the early 1970s at a meeting of the Consultation on Church Union in Denver, Peter Berger of Rutgers University criticized the lack of authority in the churches, which leads to their irrelevance. He argued,

> If there is going to be a renaissance of religion, its bearers will not be people who have been falling all over each other to be "relevant to modern man." . . . Strong eruptions of religious faith have always been marked by the appearance of people with firm, unapologetic, often uncompromising convictions—that is, by types that are the very opposite from those presently engaged in the various "relevance" operations. Put simply: Ages of faith are not marked by "dialogue" but by proclamation. . . . I would affirm that the concern for the institutional structures of the Church will be vain unless there is also a new conviction and a new authority in the Christian community.[6]

---

[5]John Macquarrie, *God and Secularity*, New Directions in Theology Today 3 (Philadelphia: Westminster Press, 1967), 30, 52.
[6]Peter L. Berger, "Needed: Authority," *The Presbyterian Journal*, October 20, 1971, 10.

TURNING TO THE WORLD'S THEOLOGY, AGENDA, AND METHODS

It is not only in the area of the world's wisdom that the church has fallen into secularism. It has also capitulated in the areas of the world's theology, agenda, and methods. The world's theology is easy to define. It is the view that human beings are basically good, that no one is really lost, that belief in Jesus Christ is not necessary for salvation. Such capitulation is common in some church circles. When I was speaking at those Moderator's Conferences, a section of my paper had to do with human lostness. I discussed it as a motivation for mission: we take the gospel of Jesus Christ to others because they are lost without it. In every consultation, that point in my paper aroused anger on the part of those listening. Some were infuriated. Nearly all were dissatisfied. Each time as I moved into that section of the paper, people began to shift, cough, move. When I finished, it was the part of the paper they brought up for objection.

Thus, the theological terms that we have always used and that the church continues to use (because it is part of its heritage) are being redefined. People still speak of sin, salvation, faith, and many other biblical terms. But having adopted the world's theology, they no longer mean by those terms what evangelicals mean when they use them biblically. Thus, *sin* means, not rebellion against God and his righteous law, for which we are held accountable, but rather ignorance or merely the kind of oppression found in social structures. Since sin is located in the system, the way to overcome it is clearly not by the death of Jesus Christ, but rather by changing the structures either through legislation or revolution.

In that outlook, *Jesus* becomes, not the incarnate God who came to die for our salvation, but rather the pattern for creative living. We are therefore to look to Jesus as an example, but not as Savior. In some forms of this theology, he is even considered to be what we might call the evolutionary peak of the race, a peak we are all supposed to attain.

Salvation is defined, not as the old theology would say, as "getting right with God" or even "God moving to redeem us in Christ," but rather as liberation from the oppression of this world's structures.

Faith is no longer believing God and taking his Word seriously, but rather awareness of the situation as we see it. This approach is closely related to Marxism, because Marxists say that commitment to communism arises from becoming aware of oppression and beginning to do something about it.

Evangelism is also redefined. It no longer means carrying the gospel of Jesus Christ to a perishing world, but rather working to overthrow injustice.

Again, there is the matter of agenda. In mainline church circles the phrase "the world's agenda" is quite popular. It means that in order of priority the church's concerns should be the concerns of the world, even to the exclusion of the gospel. If the world's first concern is hunger, that should be our first concern too. If it is the problems of underdeveloped countries, that should be our primary concern. Racism. Ecology. The energy crises. Aging. Alcoholism. Anything you read about in the evening paper should be uppermost in our thinking. In recognizing this danger, we do not want to go to the opposite extreme and suggest that there are areas of life about which God, and therefore also the church, is unconcerned. That would be a dualism that denies the sovereignty of God over all things. It is simply that these concerns must not be allowed to eclipse the gospel. If that happens, the church loses the framework from which alone she can say something truly unique and actually help with these problems.

Finally, the capitulation to the world of large segments of the organized church is seen in the church's methods. God's methods are prayer and the power of the gospel, through which the Holy Spirit moves to turn God's people from their wicked ways and heal their land. That has always been the strength of the church of Christ. Today that power is despised by the great denominations. It is laughed at, because the methods that those laughing want to use (and do use) are politics and money.

Some time ago I came across a cartoon in *The New Yorker* magazine. Two pilgrims were coming over on the *Mayflower*, and one was saying, "Religious freedom is my immediate goal, but my long-range plan is to go into real estate." In a sense that is what we are seeing today. Prayer and the power of the gospel are being crowded out by commitment to real estate, money, politics, and all those things with which we are so familiar from secular sources.

The nineteenth-century Irish playwright George Bernard Shaw saw it clearly years before these developments actually took place, saying that in his view the religion of the future would be politics. The idea is in several of his plays. It is in *Caesar and Cleopatra*, where Caesar becomes a religious figure in these terms. It is most explicit in *Major Barbara*. Barbara is a major in the Salvation Army, and she is converted in the play from Salvation Army religion to political activism. Politics is the new religion. Politics and money.

Let me illustrate how money is equated with God's work. A little brochure was published by the program agency of one denomination titled "God's Work in

God's World." Looking at that title, one might think that it would be a report on what was being done in evangelism, social services, the mission field, church building, or such things. Opening it, one found in bold type the words "The Good News." At that point we might imagine the report to have something to do with the gospel. What was this "good news"? It was that the results of a special emergency appeal had "provided the first increase" in general mission receipts since 1967. In other words, the "gospel" was that the church had received more money recently. The brochure then went on to show what could be done with the money. "In 1975, these additional dollars for mission have: 1) provided the capacity to increase the overseas missionary force by twenty-four persons." Wonderful. But if one read carefully, it did not say that the missionary force *was* increased by twenty-four persons. All it said was that there was enough money to do that if those in charge would like to. Did they? They did not. In fact, the total missionary force went down that year, just as it had declined before and has since. It is now less than 350 in a church that once had a missionary force in excess of two thousand.

A CHALLENGE

The story does not stop at this point (though the chapter must), because we will go on to show that evangelicals are not exempt from this criticism and must therefore not be self-righteous. What we can say here is that the situation calls for a major effort on the part of God's people. We should not be surprised by ecclesiastical secularism. This is the point of those verses that say that

> in the last days there will come times of difficulty. For men will be lovers of self, lovers of money, proud, arrogant, abusive, disobedient to their parents, ungrateful, unholy, heartless, unappeasable, slanderous, without self-control, brutal, not loving good, treacherous, reckless, swollen with conceit, lovers of pleasure rather than lovers of God, having the appearance of godliness, but denying its power. (2 Tim 3:1-5)

That is the secular church: "having the appearance of godliness [and sometimes not even that], but denying its power." The challenge for God's people is to be the opposite. If the secular church employs the world's wisdom, the world's theology, the world's agenda, and the world's methods, the church of the Lord Jesus Christ must do the opposite. It must employ the wisdom of God, the theology of the Scriptures, the agenda of God's written revelation ,and the methods that have been given to us for our exercise in the church until the Lord comes again. Only as the church does that can it affirm what is actually good in secular culture and be bold enough to challenge what is not.

CHAPTER 15

GOD'S CITY

*T*he vision of the city of God in Revelation 21 is a utopia: "I saw the holy city, new Jerusalem, coming down out of heaven from God, prepared as a bride adorned for her husband" (Rev 21:2). But it is not like the utopias envisioned by human beings. Most human utopias present either what their inventor would like to see happen (Plato's *Republic*, Thoreau's *Walden*), or they warn against what might happen (Huxley's *Brave New World*, Orwell's *1984*). The biblical utopia is something that has already happened but is also to happen more fully when Christ returns.

In theology this unique biblical perspective has been expressed as the "already" and the "not yet." Already the kingdom of God is in our midst (Lk 17:21). Nevertheless we pray, "Your kingdom come" (Mt 6:10).

The Revelation vision of the new Jerusalem has this perspective. As John wrote, he was thinking of the city that would be. It is characterized by God's presence. "And I heard a loud voice from the throne saying, 'Behold, the dwelling place of God is with man. He will dwell with them, and they will be his people, and God himself will be with them'" (Rev 21:3). It is marked by holiness. "Nothing unclean will ever enter it, nor anyone who does what is detestable or false, but only those who are written in the Lamb's book of life" (Rev 21:27). Death, sorrow, and pain will be eliminated. "Death shall be no more, neither shall there be mourning, nor crying, nor pain anymore, for the former things have passed away" (Rev 21:4). It is a place of constant delight and satisfaction.

Yet those things are already present in some measure in the Christian community. God already dwells with his people in the person of his Holy Spirit (Jn 14:16-18). Christians are marked by a discernible measure of holiness (Jn 17:17; 15:3). They sorrow, but not as those who have no hope (1 Thess 4:13). The value for Christians of the portrait of the ideal city of God in Revelation is that it tells us what we already are, what we increasingly can be even in this life, and what we will inevitably be as God brings to completion that work already begun.

EVANGELICAL SECULARISM

However, the place to begin in a discussion of any present realization of the city of God is not with the perfection to come, but with the realization that genuinely believing people are also themselves sometimes quite secular.

When we speak of the secularization of the church, we mean in part that the large denominations have capitulated to the world's system. That is, they have capitulated in the areas of biblical authority, theology, program, and methods, with the result that in place of the old standards of the church there have come new standards marked by the same dependence on politics and money that is characteristic of secular organizations. But there is also an *evangelical* secularism that must be faced and dealt with if true Christians are to be any use in the world. To be sure, the evangelical church has not capitulated in the same ways that the larger denominations have. Nevertheless, the values of the world have increasingly forced themselves on us, so that we have become secular in at least some areas, almost without knowing it. The gospel is present, or we would not be able to speak of "evangelical" churches. To a degree even theology is present. But the world's values have begun to take effect anyway. So we see evangelical secularism in materialism, faddism, Madison Avenue techniques, and indifference to spiritual realities and concerns.

Many persons point to our materialism. *World Vision* magazine, in its issue of January 1976, quoted a number of evangelical leaders who had been asked to write about Western civilization and the mission of the church. Most of them in one way or another criticized our materialism. J. D. Douglas, editor of the *The New International Dictionary of the Christian Church* and editor-at-large for *Christianity Today*, wrote, "Pervading our society is an even more insidious materialism which makes Christians short of breath through prosperity and ill-equipped to run the race that is set before them." Horace L. Fenton Jr., general director of Latin America Mission, wrote, "In the Western Church we ought to cut back immediately on all unnecessary expenditures—including the elaborate building programs which have obsessed us far too long. It is just as much a sin for a church to lay up treasure on earth as it is for an individual Christian." Frank E. Gaebelein, headmaster emeritus of the Stony Brook School and general editor of *The Expositor's Bible Commentary*, wrote, "Negatively the growing materialism in the more affluent western nations is detrimental to the total Christian discipleship essential to the faithful mission of the Church."[1] Each of these men puts his finger on something that is not just a characteristic of our country or of the liberal church but characteristic of evangelicals as well.

This is not a philosophical materialism. A philosophical materialism would be a materialism similar to that of communism. Evangelicals are not adopting materialism in that sense. There is a negative argument that says that, because we are not communists and communists are materialists, we are not materialists. But that does not necessarily follow. True, we do not have a philosophical materialism, but if we are honest we must admit that nevertheless we have a very practical materialism that is detrimental to the advance of the gospel in our age.

Second, we become secularized in that we so easily follow the fads of this world. I once had a conversation with Dr. Hudson Armerding, then president of Wheaton College, in which we talked about the situation on the campuses, particularly Christian ones. I asked Armerding what it was that bothered him most about the culture on our Christian campuses. He said, "It's the fact that the Christian campuses always seem to be following along behind the world; they have the same concerns, but it's always a year or two later." Then he spelled it out, noting that when the Vietnam War became a concern in the secular schools, it became a concern in the Christian schools too, but several years later. When ecology became the burning issue on the secular campuses, it also became a burning issue on the Christian campuses, but a year or two later. When women's liberation became the issue elsewhere, it also became the issue in the Christian world, but again some time later. What he was saying is that we have here a case of the world leading the church rather than the church leading the world. And what is that, if that is not the secularization of the evangelical community?

The third area in which we see secularism in our evangelical churches is our Madison Avenue approach to Christian commitment. We see this in certain stylized forms of evangelism. I want to be very careful here, because obviously the greater problem in evangelism is not doing it at all. If through a method we are able to rally people to the cause of presenting the gospel of Jesus Christ to

---

[1]*World Vision*, January 1976, 8-10.

those who have not heard it, it is not altogether bad to do that, even if the method is faulty. But at the same time we have to recognize that secularism can enter in even here.

For example, sometimes Christians are required to memorize a certain stylized presentation of Christian truth. This is something that in the hands of a person who understands the gospel well can be useful. Certainly it helps to have thought through the kind of questions you might be asked and the answers that seem most helpful to most people. But to present the gospel in a rigid way, where the words are carefully chosen by a kind of popular opinion poll or analysis, is secularism.

We see the same thing in the way in which the gospel and Christian concerns are sold to our constituency; that is, through advertisements in our magazines, direct mail, and so on. It should be said, in defense of this, that it is often the case that this is the only way in which evangelical leaders seem to be able to awaken the concerns of Christian people. But the proper stance from the perspective of the individual is to be ahead of the appeal in your own commitment as to how you are going to use money. In other words, before the appeal comes, when you are before the Lord on your knees, ask how the resources that he has given you should be used and then determine to do that on the basis of the Lord's leading, and not necessarily on the basis of the sentimental pictures that happen to be on the front of the brochure that comes in the mail about three weeks before Christmas.

Finally, we see secularism in the evangelical church in our great indifference. Indifference to what? The answer is to practically anything and everything worthwhile. We are indifferent to the *state of the lost*. Francis R. Steele, home director of the North American Council of the North Africa Mission, has written an article for one of the publications of that mission titled, "Indifference—Involvement."[2] In it, he points to indifference as the number one problem in recruiting missionaries and support for missionaries. He says there are short-term projects that are well received; but the number of those who would commit themselves to a lifetime of missionary endeavor for the sake of Christ and who would support such persons is dwindling. It is due to the indifference of God's people.

There is indifference to the *suffering of the world's poor*. We are often so isolated in North America from the very poor that we seldom really see deep suffering

---

[2] *The Cross*, Fall 1975, 8-9.

face to face. We do not know what it is to see people who are so hungry that they can hardly think of anything but food. So we are indifferent to these things.

There is indifference to the *needs of our fellow believers*. If there is anything you hear in the evangelical church today, it is that evangelicals do not want to listen to the hurts in the hearts and lives of other Christians. They do not want to be bothered. They do not want to hear these things because they are demanding; they require a response, and we are not prepared to make it. Instead we want to rest in our own personal peace and affluence.

There is indifference to the *leadership vacuum in the churches*. There is work to be done, but the hardest thing in Christian work is to find men and women who recognize the need and who will step into it and do what is necessary by the grace of God, faithfully, if necessary year after year and at great personal hardship. We do not have much of this commitment. Somebody once handed me a little poem on the role of the pastor which concluded:

> Ashes to ashes, dust to dust;
> If the people won't do it, the pastor must.

But the pastor cannot do it all. Moreover, if he is trying to do it all, a number of things, including the preaching of the Word of God, will be buried by the wayside. If people in the church are indifferent to obvious need and the pastor responds in their place, then the whole church suffers. Each one has a gift. Each one must be willing to use it to the glory of God.

The following question was asked of a number of officials in church circles: What is the number one problem in the evangelical church today? "Apathy," said an official of the National Association of Evangelicals. "Lack of discipline," said another. "Not caring enough," said somebody who was involved in the Watergate scandal.

The evangelical church must be different. It will be in the world and, in some areas, will identify with the world's interests. But it will not be of the world. Its values will not be the world's values, nor will its priorities be the world's priorities. The true church must always strive to be increasingly what it essentially is, namely, God's city.

DIFFERENT AUTHORITY, THEOLOGY, PRIORITIES

Let me suggest some areas in which our difference must be evident. First, the city of God must be clear as to what its *authority* is. One evidence of the secularism of the large denominations is that biblical authority, the authority of the

Scriptures, has been thrown out, and the authority of consensus has replaced it. Things are done in the denominations today, not because the Bible says they should be done or even because the creeds say so, but because 51 percent of our people say so. If the true church is to be distinct in this area, it must let it be known that it does what it does because the Bible says so. We must be men and women of "the Book." In theory we are. We acknowledge that our standards come from the Bible. But much of the time, in practice, evangelical churches operate exactly the way other churches do.

We have to recover the biblical standard. We cannot say, as evangelicals have often said on important issues, "Well, that particular thing just does not bother me." That kind of response is not good enough. Instead, we have to get to what the Word of God says. We have to study it, do our homework, and then we must ask, on the basis of this Word, what does God want for the church in this age?

We are going to have to do that sooner or later anyway, or else we are going to have to go the world's way entirely. History does not allow us to stand long in an ambiguous position. In the Nazi period in Germany, the church went in one of two ways: either it capitulated to the Nazi point of view (and most of the established church did), or it became increasingly a church of the Book. Those who lived by the Book eventually established a communion of their own. They signed documents identifying themselves as the "Confessing Church." They did that because, when the whole drift of the society and the culture is contrary to biblical standards, it is impossible to appeal to any external norms. You cannot say, "This is backed up in the area of psychology or science or social relations," because it is not. Much of the material being written in those areas is contrary to biblical truth. So the church must increasingly fall back on the divine revelation. Has God spoken in this Book? Does he speak? Those are the important questions. If God does speak, then we must be clear and say, "Let God be true and every person a liar." Evangelical churches are increasingly going to have to re-capture that outlook.

Second, we need to be distinct in our *theology*. When we are, those who hunger for the truth of the Word of God will come to it. We see the evidence in our seminaries. I received a report of a meeting of the Council of Theological Seminaries of the United Presbyterian Church in which the needs of the United Presbyterian seminaries—Dubuque, Louisville, McCormick, Pittsburgh, Princeton, San Francisco, and J. C. Smith—were discussed, and at which representatives from two leading evangelical seminaries, Fuller and Gordon-Conwell, were present. This report showed that enrollment at the denominational seminaries, where there is often no clear theology and most certainly not an evangelical theology, is declining. The lowest of the seven was Dubuque; it had only 111 students. The highest was Princeton. At the time it had 581, though that figure has since risen. But to put those figures in perspective, one must recognize that enrollment at the five leading evangelical seminaries in this country is growing and already exceeds them all, Fuller alone having 1,200 students at that time.

Where are the young men and women from Presbyterian churches going for seminary training? At the time of this report, 38.4 percent of them were being trained outside Presbyterian seminaries, at schools like Trinity, Gordon-Conwell, Fuller, and others. Today it is even higher. Why? Because those seminaries are distinct in their theology. The thesis of Dean Kelley's *Why Conservative Churches Are Growing* is that such churches are growing because they know where they stand and, therefore, people know where they stand and turn to them. The same thesis applies to seminaries. Seminaries grow for that reason too. They are an illustration of what we need in theology.

We need to articulate the great biblical doctrines, not just adopt the theology of our culture. We need to speak of human depravity, of men and women in rebellion against God, so much so that there is no hope for them apart from God's grace. We need to speak of God's electing love, showing that God enters the life of the individual in grace by his Holy Spirit to quicken understanding and draw the rebellious will to himself. We must speak of perseverance, that God is able to keep and does keep those whom he so draws. All those doctrines and all the supporting doctrines that go with them need to be proclaimed. We have to say, "This is where we stand. We do not adopt your theology. We do not agree with what we hear coming from denominational headquarters."

Third, we have to be different in our *priorities*. The denominations set their agenda, the world's agenda. We must say that our priorities are not going to be the world's priorities but the priorities of the Word of God. That determination does not mean that we will neglect social concerns. They are part of the priority of the Christian life. But it does mean that we will not reject the gospel of salvation through faith in the vicarious atonement of Christ either. We will make proclamation of the gospel our number-one priority.

At the end of *The Invaded Church*, Donald G. Bloesch asks what evangelicals must do to change the world. He answers that what is needed is "a new kind of man." He gives examples. When he gets into the area of racism he analyzes the problem like this:

For modern secular humanism, including Marxism, the poison of racism can be removed through social reform and education. Biblical Christianity sees this problem in a different light. The real enemy is racial and cultural pride, not ignorance. And behind this pride is unbelief, hardness of heart, what the Bible calls original sin. . . . Laws are necessary to protect the defenseless, but they can only hold the dike against sin. It is the gospel alone that takes away sin, and this means that the final solution to racism and other social ills is biblical evangelism.[3]

When we set our priorities we must be clear that this is where our emphasis goes—in time, money, and in the choice of what we do and say.

NEW LIFESTYLE

Fourth, we need to be distinctly different in the area of *lifestyle*. Evangelicals have not been too conscious of this need until fairly recent times; we have lived in a culture that, although it is not Christian, nevertheless held on in part to the vestiges of an earlier Christianity. We have laws on our books because Christians of an earlier age said this is what we should do. We follow certain norms of behavior because of the influence of this earlier Christianity. All that is disappearing. Laws are changing, and there is going to be more agitation to change in future days. When those changes take place, Christians must be distinct. They must say that they do not go along with the trends of the times, the increasing secularization.

One of the priorities we must have concerns time. Sports take an enormous amount of time in people's lives, through television as well as our own participation. Sport has almost become the religion of America. It is what many people do on weekends. Even some evangelicals find their time so taken up with sports that Christian activities are crowded out. Isn't this an area in which we have to say that the drift of our day is not in the direction we want to go? Dr. Anthony Campolo, a professor at Eastern College in Pennsylvania, calls a commitment to sports the most serious threat to America today.

Much time is also spent watching television, and most of it is not edifying. At best it is diverting. Statistics say that the average American watches television for over seven hours every day, and those figures are probably true of Christian people also. Is the tube worth that time? The Bible says, "[Make] the best use of the time, because the days are evil" (Eph 5:16). It means, make your life count.

---

[3]Donald G. Bloesch, *The Invaded Church* (Waco, TX: Word Books, 1975), 99.

I wonder if many Christians are not missing out here, and if the challenge of the age is not going to require us to sharpen up in such areas.

How about the use of Sunday? Personally, I do not believe that we should have blue laws. I do not believe in prescribing what is proper and improper Sunday activity for everybody. But how do *we* use Sunday? Do we go to church? Do we want to worship God? Is sixty minutes, seventy or eighty minutes, on Sunday morning the whole of our Sunday commitment? Is it the total time we want to be with Christian people? Is it all the time we can spare to receive religious instruction?

I have noticed recently that public schools are increasingly scheduling school events for Sunday, which is having its effect on our children. Our schools have the rest of the week filled up. So what do they do when they want to establish a new activity? There is a glee club, and they need people to sing. There are sports, and someone wants to get in an extra practice. There is an orchestra, and they need time to rehearse. When do they do it? They set it for Sunday morning. Christian people are going to be confronted with that again and again. Are those activities more important than having our children in church? We must ask that question. We cannot avoid it. Even if it means not getting ahead as much as we would like, even if it means not being as popular as we would like, even if it means that our children are not going to be as popular as we would like them to be—we must say, "But as for me and my house, we will serve the LORD" (Josh 24:15).

When we do that we will have an influence on the world. I know cases where Christian parents have said to their children, "You are not allowed to do that on Sunday morning; we go to church at that hour." The children have gone to their teachers and have said, "We are sorry but we can't participate; our family goes to church at that hour." And the teachers have replied, "Oh, we didn't know anybody did that. All right, we'll change the hour." Victories can be won, but we have to stand by our convictions.

Perhaps the most pressing area in which we have to be distinct is sexual ethics, particularly in our conception of marriage and the way we conduct our marriages. It is not easy to have a Christian marriage today. Everything in the world works against it. The overriding concern of our time is for personal satisfaction, and there are always things in marriage that do not seem personally satisfying. We wish it could be different. But the question is this: What are we in the marriage for? Are we in it for personal satisfaction above all? Or are we there because we believe that God has brought us together with our spouse to establish a Christian

home in which the truth of his Word can be raised high, Christian values demonstrated, and children raised to know the Bible and live a Christian lifestyle?
It must be the latter. Further, in our speaking we must make a distinction between
marriages that are Christian marriages and marriages that are marriages only in
the world's sense.

I recall a fictitious marriage service I once saw on television. I was curious
about how the writers were going to handle the vows. The vows are Christian,
as everyone knows. I wondered, will they use them because they are the traditional vows and they cannot avoid them, or will they doctor them up to make
them more secular? In this particular service the couple promised to "live with
one another and cherish one another, as long as . . ." I thought they were going
to say "as long as life shall last." But they said, " . . . as long as *love* shall last." In
other words, "As long as I love her I'll live with her; but if I stop loving her, that's
the end of the marriage." It could be a year, a month, a week. That is the viewpoint of secular men and women, and it is being openly expressed today. When
Christians stand to take vows, they must make it known that their vows are for
life—"until death us do part"—because that is what God wants. And they must
live as Christians within the marriage bond.

Finally, the city of God must be distinct in its use of money and other resources. How do we use our money? All of us are hit by inflation. But if we
compare our standard of living with that of the rest of the world, we are all
millionaires. All of us have money we could use in the Lord's work. Are we
faithful in that area? Some of us do not even give the Old Testament tithe, let
alone our life and soul and all that we have to be used in the Lord's way.

DEPENDENCE ON GOD

I have listed four areas in which we need to be distinctly different. Those areas
correspond to the areas of secularization delineated in the last chapter. But we
need to add a fifth point. We need to be distinctly different in our *visible dependence on God.* Nothing less will capture the attention of a secular world.

When I was at the Moderator's Conferences I mentioned, something happened that was very revealing. When I spoke about human lostness, I got a
terrible reaction on the part of those present. Nobody wanted to hear that men
and women are lost apart from the grace of God. But everybody seemed to agree
with one doctrine. It startled me. I had stressed the grace of God in calling some
to salvation. I said, "We cannot move people; we cannot change the world. If
the world is to be changed it must be by God's doing, and for that we must pray

and ask him." They agreed with that just as much as they had disagreed with total depravity. I began to analyze this, and after I had done so I began to understand the reaction. It was because the people to whom I was talking were people engaged in the very things I have been talking about. They were working in the social arena—trying to help alcoholics, serving those in the ghetto, looking for improvement. And what had happened? They had looked for improvement, but it had not come. So when I said that change had to be by the grace of God, the echo of their hearts said "Amen." They did not like biblical theology, but they knew that the power of God is necessary if change is to come.

How can Christians change the world? The Lord Jesus Christ gave the answer in the Sermon on the Mount. He did not say that we are to maneuver the world. He did not say, "Get elected to high positions in the Roman Empire. See if you can get an evangelical promoted to emperor." It could happen, of course. He did not forbid it. But that is not the option he gave. He said, "You are the salt of the earth. You are the light of the world."

Salt does no good at all if it has lost its saltiness. Only when it is salty is it effective. So, if we are those in whom the Spirit of God has worked to call us to faith in Jesus Christ, we must really be Christ's people. It must be evident that by his grace we are not what we were previously. Our values must not be the world's values. Our commitments must not be secular commitments. Our theology must not be a decimated theology. Rather, there must be a new element in us and, because of us, in the world.

We are also "light." The purpose of light is to shine, to shine out. So the Lord said, "Look, nobody lights a candle and puts it under a bushel. It is to be set up on a candlestick where everyone will see it." We are to be lighthouses in the midst of a dark world. Being a lighthouse will not change the rocky contours of the coast. Sin is still there. The perils of destruction still threaten men and women. But by God's grace the light can be a beacon to bring ships into a safe harbor.

CHAPTER 16

CHURCH AND STATE

*T*wo major ambiguities exist in the relationship of the city of God to the
secular city. One is the secular church, which we have already considered.
It is an obvious ambiguity because, although it should be sacred in the sense of
being totally devoted to God and his kingdom, it is nevertheless motivated by
the authority, theology, agenda, and methods of the world. It is Christian in
name only. The other ambiguity is the state. It presents a problem because, although it is secular and clearly expresses the mindset of the secular city, it
nevertheless has been established by God for good ends and therefore deserves
the support and prayers of Christian people.

The second ambiguity is founded in Scripture. On the one hand, the state is
described as directed by demonic powers. Paul tells us we are to strive against
them. "For we do not wrestle against flesh and blood, but against the rulers, against
the authorities, against the cosmic powers of this present darkness, against the
spiritual forces of evil in the heavenly places" (Eph 6:12). In its extreme form the
state is portrayed as godless Babylon destined for destruction (Rev 18). It is a beast
from the pit (Rev 17). We are told that Christ triumphed over the powers that
stand behind the state by his victory on the cross (Col 2:15). On the other hand,
the Bible also views the state in a positive light, telling us that "there is no authority
except from God, and those that exist have been instituted by God" (Rom 13:1).
We are to obey such authority and pray for those who exercise it (1 Tim 2:1-2).

The state sometimes functions as it should. At other times it functions in a
demonic way. Under normal circumstances the church is to be thankful for the

state and obey it. It may even regard the state as one of "the external means or aids by which God invites us into the society of Christ and holds us therein," as Calvin did. (That is the title of the fourth book of the *Institutes*, in which the proper role of the state is discussed.) On the other hand, the church must also be ready to challenge the state in the name of God and his righteousness, and even disobey the state whenever its laws conflict with the laws of God.

It is not always easy to determine which of the two situations one is in, however, if only because the dilemmas confronting a Christian citizen are often not clear-cut. That is the case even with the classic text concerning a Christian's responsibility to government: "Therefore render to Caesar the things that are Caesar's, and to God the things that are God's" (Mt 22:21).

The background for that guideline was a question about taxes. "Is it lawful to pay taxes to Caesar, or not?" (Mt 22:17). Christ's answer was affirmative, an answer echoed by Paul. "Pay to all what is owed to them: taxes to whom taxes are owed, revenue to whom revenue is owed, respect to whom respect is owed, honor to whom honor is owed" (Rom 13:7). But suppose the commands of Caesar and the commands of God disagree? Do we obey Caesar, arguing that God has set him over us and that God will take care of the consequences of our act? Or do we obey God? Even the matter of taxes is not entirely clear. What if our taxes are being used for immoral ends: to support a gestapo, an unjust war, oppression of the disenfranchised by the rich and privileged, or other evils? Clearly there are puzzling dimensions to this relationship.

One thing Christ's words about taxes do say is that the state has its legitimate sphere. Christians should be respectful of that legitimacy even more than others because they know that God has established it. Christians can never be entirely pragmatic at this point, still less opportunistic. They can never knowingly try to overthrow a legitimate government simply because they would prefer a different type of government or different people in government, still less because they want to rule themselves. Within a democracy there are legitimate procedures for changing rulers, and these are open to Christians. Revolution for its own sake or the sake of the revolutionaries themselves is excluded.

What is the legitimate sphere of government? Calvin regarded it as "the establishment of civil justice and outward morality."[1] He argued that Christ's spiritual kingdom and the civil jurisdiction are distinct. Yet the distinction does

---

[1]John Calvin, *Institutes of the Christian Religion*, ed. John T. McNeill, trans. Ford Lewis Battles, 2 vols. (Philadelphia: Westminster, 1960), 2:1485.

not mean that the whole of government is polluted; it exists "to cherish and protect the outward worship of God, to defend sound doctrine of piety and the position of the church, to adjust our life to the society of men, to form our social behavior to civil righteousness, to reconcile us to one another, and to promote general peace and tranquility."[2]

John Murray, in a study of "The Relation of Church and State," says that the sphere of civil government "is that of guarding, maintaining, and promoting justice, order, and peace."[3] On the other hand, "to the church is committed the task of proclaiming the whole counsel of God and, therefore, the counsel of God as it bears upon the responsibility of all persons and institutions. . . . When the civil magistrate trespasses the limits of his authority, it is incumbent upon the church to expose and condemn such a violation of his authority."[4]

What those men are saying, and what Scripture also says, is not merely that church and state represent two separate spheres of authority: God's and Caesar's. Rather, they are saying that church and state stand in relationship to one another in that both are established by God, share certain areas of concern and are responsible ultimately to the same divine Sovereign.

Light is thrown on this relationship by the appearance of the Lord Jesus Christ before Pilate at the time of his crucifixion. The situation itself is significant. Jesus, the head of the church, was appearing before the chief representative of human government in Palestine. The issue of the trial was whether Jesus, a "king," stood in a right or wrong relationship to Caesar.

In the early part of the trial the matter of Christ's kingship came up and was quickly dismissed by Pilate. He understood rightly that Christ's kingdom was "not of this world" (Jn 18:36) and therefore was no threat to legitimate government. But the matter did not stop there. The accusers of Christ persisted, arguing that Christ should die because he made himself "the Son of God" (Jn 19:7). Pilate, intrigued and perhaps even slightly alarmed by this new line of accusation, reopened the examination. "Where are you from?" he asked. When Jesus gave no answer (Pilate being unqualified to examine him on what was clearly a spiritual matter), the Roman judge demanded, "You will not speak to me? Do you not know that I have authority to release you and authority to crucify you?" (Jn 19:9-10).

---

[2]Ibid., 1487.
[3]John Murray, "The Relation of Church and State" in *Collected Writings*, vol. 1, *The Claims of Truth* (Edinburgh: Banner of Truth Trust, 1976), 253.
[4]Ibid., 255.

Jesus replied, "You would have no authority over me at all unless it had been given you from above. Therefore he who delivered me over to you has the greater sin" (Jn 19:11). This is an extremely important statement regarding the state's proper role, for it shows that the authority of human government does not come from anything intrinsic to itself but from God. It is a delegated authority. Consequently, there are always the matters of the government's responsibility and sin.

To get the full measure of this we need to combine it with Christ's words about God and Caesar, mentioned earlier. They suggest four possible options regarding legitimate authority: (1) God alone as an authority with the authority of Caesar denied, (2) Caesar alone as an authority with the authority of God denied, (3) the authority of both God and Caesar, but with Caesar in the dominant position, and (4) the authority of God and Caesar but with God in the dominant position.

GOD ALONE

The first position, God alone, is one some Christians have adopted at some periods of history. In the early church, there were persons called anchorites who went off into the desert, separating themselves from all social contacts and living solely for God. From that early movement monasticism was born. In our time we see a somewhat similar response among some evangelical Protestants. They believe that the Christian community should be so separated from the secular sphere that individual Christians should not go into politics or vote in elections, that they should withdraw from the culture, live in distinct communities, have Christian friends exclusively, work for Christian companies, or in general have nothing to do with this world. It is a way of saying that the authority of the state is illegitimate.

But Christ did not so regard it. When he told Pilate that his authority (the word is *exousia*, rather than *dynamis* or *kratos*, meaning "authority") came from God, he legitimated that authority and showed by his conduct at the trial that his disciples should also acknowledge it. Jesus respected Pilate's rule. He answered Pilate courteously and never once suggested that Pilate did not have authority to pronounce a judgment over him. Pilate pronounced wrongly, as we know. But he had authority to make the pronouncement. His authority was from God. Jesus did not suggest that it be wrested from him, even though he was about to make the great error of condemning the Son of God.

Here we must again emphasize that Christians are to be subject to the higher authorities. There are some limits, as we will see. But we must begin with the fact that Christians should be model citizens. Regrettably, it is often the case that Christians disrespect authority—elected officials, police, and others—and this quite naturally leads to a light attitude in regard to obeying them. That ought not to be. Rather we should be scrupulous in obeying the speed limits and other civil laws. John Calvin had a justified fear of anarchy because of the troubles of his own time. Warning against it, he wrote that obedience must be given even to wicked rulers. "We are not only subject to the authority of princes who perform their office toward us uprightly and faithfully as they ought, but also to the authority of all who, by whatever means, have got control of affairs, even though they perform not a whit of the princes' office."[5]

Are there limits? What if the king is a very wicked king, or the president a very wicked president? Yes, there are limits. Therefore, although we must be careful to render every possible measure of obedience to those in authority (usually much more than we wish), we must still do nothing contrary to the express command of God in Scripture or to that standard of morality arising from it, even though a contrary act is commanded.

Here the second part of Christ's statement comes in. After instructing Pilate in regard to the ultimate source of his authority, Jesus went on to speak of sin. "Therefore he who delivered me over to you has the greater sin" (Jn 19:11). If it were only power that Pilate had been given, it would be impossible to speak of sin as intrinsic in the exercise of the power—just as it is impossible to speak of sin in the case of the cat who kills a mouse or the germ that kills another germ. But since it was authority that Pilate was given, that is another matter entirely. Authority, being granted by another, necessarily involves responsibility to that other one; and responsibility, if it is not properly exercised, involves sin against that one. In other words, authority enhances human government, but it also limits it. It is an authority bound by the moral nature of the God from whom it comes.

One biblical limit on obedience to human authority is in regard to the *preaching of the gospel*. This is a Christian duty based on the explicit command of Jesus Christ (Mt 28:18-20). What should happen when authorities demand differently is illustrated in the fourth and fifth chapters of Acts. The disciples had been preaching and doing miracles, which had created such a stir that they were called before a

---

[5]Calvin, *Institutes*, 1512.

council of elders in Jerusalem. The authorities examined the disciples, in this case Peter and John. Then, since the miracle they had done in healing a lame man was so evident and the rulers could not deny it, they settled on the expedient of merely commanding the disciples to keep silence. Peter and John replied, "Whether it is right in the sight of God to listen to you rather than to God, you must judge, for we cannot but speak of what we have seen and heard" (Acts 4:19-20).

The apostles were threatened, but they went back to their preaching and were soon rearrested. The authorities again questioned them and said, "We strictly charged you not to teach in this name, yet here you have filled Jerusalem with your teaching, and you intend to bring this man's blood upon us" (Acts 5:28).

Peter answered, "We must obey God rather than men. The God of our fathers raised Jesus, whom you killed by hanging him on a tree. God exalted him at his right hand as Leader and Savior, to give repentance to Israel and forgiveness of sins. And we are witnesses to these things, and so is the Holy Spirit, whom God has given to those who obey him" (Acts 5:29-32).

The incident indicates that Christians are to give precedence to the preaching of the gospel and are not to cease from it, even though commanded to do so by the civil authorities. A second biblical limit on obedience to human authorities is in *Christian conduct and morals*. No government has the right to command Christians to perform immoral or non-Christian acts. During the Nazi era, Christians in Germany were faced with a devilish state and its openly anti-Christian and even antihuman practices. German citizens were commanded to have no dealings with Jews. They were not to trade with them, help them, have friendships with them, or acknowledge them in any way.

Some stood up against these monstrosities. One who did so was Martin Niemoeller, who, for preaching the truth, was eventually thrown into prison. We are told that another minister then visited him in prison, and argued that if he would only keep silent about certain subjects and respect the government, he would be set free. "And so," he concluded, "why are you in jail?"

"Why aren't *you* in jail?" Niemoeller answered.[6]

Niemoeller's course was the right one. By his silence, the visiting minister was upholding a lie and indirectly encouraging a demonic regime.

In this country Christians must speak out against racism, government and corporate corruption, sex and age discrimination, and other evils. They must

---

[6]Donald Grey Barnhouse, *The Epistle to the Romans*, vol. 9, *God's Discipline* (Grand Rapids: Eerdmans, 1958), 106-7.

staunchly refuse to participate in them in any way, even if they are commanded
to do so by their government or a business superior.

CAESAR ALONE

The second of the four options is the one chosen by most secularists and sometimes even by so-called Christians: the choice of Caesar alone. It is the most
dangerous option. We find an expression of it at the trial of Jesus when the chief
priests told Pilate, "We have no king but Caesar" (Jn 19:15). In this option God,
who is the ultimate check on godless rulers, is forced out of the picture and
therefore cannot be appealed to. Even under the worst of tyrants, if God is in
the picture, he can at least be appealed to for help, and the injustices may be
corrected. But if God is gone, there is nothing left but human whims and cruelty.

Without God in the picture there is no rein on Caesar, and Caesar needs a
rein. In America, we recognize this secularly. We have developed a system of
checks and balances according to which one branch of government has control
on another. Congress makes laws that govern all citizens; but the judicial branch
can declare them unconstitutional. The president appoints Supreme Court judges;
but Congress has authority to impeach the president. The president may initiate
programs; but the Congress must fund them. We recognize the need of checks
and balances on the secular level because we know by experience that persons
in power are untrustworthy. If that is true on the human level, how much truer
it is on the cosmic level. The united voices of rulers cannot be ultimate. God is
ultimate. If we forsake God, we are at the mercy of our governors.

Second, without God in the picture we have no sure means of guiding government properly. We need checks to keep government from becoming a law
unto itself and therefore abusing and tyrannizing the governed. But suppose
the government is not tyrannous. Suppose it operates well. Even then it needs
God. Only from God do we receive a system of morality and a wisdom beyond
our own.

Today in America some persons are attempting to remove every vestige of
religion from national life. It is argued that government is not in business to
legislate morality. But what does the state do if it does not legislate morality?
When the state develops and enforces laws against homicide, what is that but
the legislation of morality? It is the state's way of saying, "We agree that life is
precious and that it is wrong to take it away." In this, the state supports the sixth
of the Ten Commandments. When the state makes laws against larceny and
burglary, it is enforcing the eighth commandment. The same is true in its

requirement of legal marriages, contracts, labor negotiations, and so on for hundreds of different areas. In each of those areas the state is dealing with morality. The only point in dispute is the kind of morality to be followed. Christians must be strong to remind the state that it must seek God's wisdom in this matter.

CAESAR DOMINANT

The third option is one in which God and Caesar both properly exercise authority but Caesar is dominant. It is the option of cowards. If God's authority is recognized at all, it is evident by definition that he must be supreme. Those who favor Caesar do so generally only because they fear him.

That was the case with Pilate. Pilate did not want to condemn Jesus. First, he pronounced him innocent. Next he tried expedients by which he might be freed: sending him to Herod, suggesting his release rather than the release of Barabbas, causing him to be beaten and then suddenly exhibited to evoke sympathy from the mob. Even after Pilate had failed in those expedients, he still tried to get Christ acquitted. "From then on Pilate sought to release him, but the Jews cried out, 'If you release this man, you are not Caesar's friend. Everyone who makes himself a king opposes Caesar'" (Jn 19:12).

If Pilate was unwilling to pass the death sentence on Jesus, why was he eventually prevailed on to do so? The answer is in that verse. The Jewish leaders threatened to denounce him to Caesar with the result that Pilate, who feared such a denunciation more than anything else, capitulated.

Pilate is seen here in his most contemptible stance, yet he is also pitiable. Pilate was the governor. He spoke for Caesar and had the legions of Caesar at his call to enforce his bidding. Yet this individual who should have been above fear was riddled by it and thus was made weak-kneed in the greatest moral encounter of his career. Of what was the governor afraid? He was afraid of three things. He was afraid of *Christ*. We are told that after Pilate had heard that Jesus made himself out to be the Son of God, "he was even more afraid" (Jn 19:8) and determined anew to release him. It was certainly not the kind of holy reverence for Christ that a true follower of the Lord might have. But it was a true fear. Pilate thought that Jesus might actually be more than a man, perhaps one of the half-human, half-divine gods of Greek and Roman antiquity, and so might move fate against him if he judged unfairly.

Pilate was afraid of the *people*. He did not like them, of course. His many dealings with the Jews showed his consummate disdain and even hatred for them. Yet he knew their power and feared to have them united in opposition to him.

If he had not feared the people, he would have released Jesus and have shown no concern to pacify them.

Most significant, Pilate feared *Caesar*. With cause. The suspicious nature of Caesar Tiberius was well known, and Pilate had already had other confrontations with the Jews which had worked to his disfavor. What if Caesar should disapprove of his handling of this matter? What if the Jewish leaders should send a delegation to Caesar saying that Pilate had refused to deal forcefully with one who was guilty of high treason? If Pilate had possessed a clean record, he could perhaps have overlooked a threat based on false charges. But his record was not clean, and it was possible that Pilate could lose his position and even his life if such an accusation was made. (Several years later, Pilate was removed from office by the proconsul of Syria and banished to France.)

Pilate's failure suggests the answer to the questions raised earlier. Pilate feared human beings. Consequently, he was unable to do the just thing, and even fell so low as to pronounce sentence on the Son of God.

GOD DOMINANT

The fourth option is the right one: the authority of God and Caesar but with God in the dominant position. This position is basic to Christ's words: "You would have no power over me unless it had been given you from above; therefore he who delivered me to you has the greater sin." From this position, the Christian can in a sense demythologize the state, reminding it of the obvious limitations of its power and even the absurdity of some of its claims. Jacques Ellul does this in *The Political Illusion*.[7] He regards contemporary appeals to the state to solve our most basic problems as the height of folly, and calls on individuals to resist its ever-expanding encroachment on their lives. Christians can also remind the state of its divinely given responsibilities and of the fact that it is accountable to God.

In short, Christians must fear God more than people and must let it be known that they do. To do this effectively, there must be three requirements. First, individual Christians must have it firmly fixed in their minds that God is truly sovereign in human affairs, including affairs of state. Most Christians know this, of course, because the Bible teaches it. But they must also have it planted in their minds so firmly that they can actually trust God when the crunch comes.

---

[7]Jacques Ellul, *The Political Illusion*, trans. Konrad Kellen (New York: Vintage Books, 1967).

Daniel was one person who was able to exercise that kind of trust. He knew that God was sovereign. When God revealed Nebuchadnezzar's dream of the statue of gold, silver, bronze, and iron to him, he responded by praising God in these terms:

> Blessed be the name of God forever and ever,
>   to whom belong wisdom and might.
> He changes times and seasons;
>   he removes kings and sets up kings;
> he gives wisdom to the wise
>   and knowledge to those who have understanding. (Dan 2:20-21)

But in addition to knowing this intellectually, Daniel also knew it experientially and was not afraid to stand by his convictions. When he was tempted to abandon his worship of God for a period of thirty days under threat of being thrown into a den of lions, he resisted the state in its encroachment on his religious obligations. He spurned its decrees.

We know that God delivered Daniel from the lions, just as he had earlier delivered his three companions from the fiery furnace. But the fact that God would deliver him and the others was not known to Daniel at the time his moral stand was taken. What gave him the ability to do this, particularly when so many plausible arguments might have been raised in favor of compliance, was trust in a sovereign God to whom even the powerful Nebuchadnezzar was responsible. Daniel believed that in the ultimate analysis it was God and not Nebuchadnezzar who would control the outcome.

A second requirement for an effective Christian stance against the state is a comprehensive and perceptive knowledge of Scripture on the part of individual Christians and church bodies. The reason for this is that situations are not always black and white. They may be gray. Awareness of God's sovereignty and willingness to trust him are not always sufficient. A person may be willing to do the right thing and trust God for the outcome but still not know what the right thing is. The only way the right will be known at such times is by the teaching of God's Spirit through Scripture.

Even then some areas may remain ambiguous. The matter of fighting in wartime is one, and Christians have been divided on that issue. Answers in the areas of abortion on demand, artificial prolongation of life, legal defense of criminals, the death penalty, covert government activities, and so on are not always so evident as we might wish. But without the Bible there are no sure answers at all. That is the point. Consequently, no substitute exists (even for the busiest Christian) for studying the Bible and conscientiously striving to submit one's life and thoughts completely to it.

If we do not do this we are in much danger. When Jesus spoke to Pilate, reminding him of his sin, he used the word *greater*. Although Pilate's sin was great—he was sinning against his conscience in that he had already pronounced Jesus to be entirely innocent—the sin of the religious leaders was greater. They were sinning out of hate-filled hearts and against their own laws, which should have protected Jesus. It may even be that the sin of Judas was greatest, since he was closest to Christ and therefore sinned out of a background of the greatest knowledge. The comparison teaches that the greater danger lies, not with the state, but with those who are closest to spiritual things. Others may sin out of ignorance or neglect or cowardice. But religious people are inclined to sin out of arrogance or pride or actual hatred of God and God's truth—even when they think they are most moral.

Christians must look to the truth they affirm. It is not enough to have the name of Christian. That in itself does not give us any superior insight into morality or any point of leverage from which to speak against or disobey the government that God has set up. We can do that only as we respond, painfully at times, to God's voice, which comes to us in Scripture. Then we are gripped, not by a lesser authority than that of the state (that is, our own), but by a greater one, the overriding and only infallible authority of God.

There is a third need if we are to know what is right and actually do it, even when confronted with a contrary claim by some strong social pressure. We need to be willing to surrender everything. It is quite possible to have followed the first two steps suggested—to believe and trust that God is sovereign in human affairs and to study the Bible to such a degree that we know what is right—and yet fail at the crucial moment, simply because the proper course would be too costly.

This is what was wrong with Pilate after all. We cannot say that Pilate really believed in the sovereignty of God, but he believed in something like it—the power of the gods, or some form of ultimate retribution. Otherwise he would not have been afraid when told that Jesus claimed to be God's Son. We cannot say that he knew the moral standards of the true God as revealed in the Bible, because he had undoubtedly never read the Bible. Still, he knew what was right in this situation, but he went against it. Why? If it was not from fear of God and not from failure to know what was right, it can only have been from unwillingness to lose his official position. Clearly, he valued his job above all else. Pilate had to choose between what was right and what the world wanted. And when the issue was clearly defined, he did not hesitate to choose the world and its rewards.

In contrast, I think of Aleksandr Solzhenitsyn, the Russian writer who was unjustly confined in the Soviet Union's notorious prison system for eleven years and lived to tell about it in *The Gulag Archipelago*. He saw suffering such as few free people have ever seen. He saw the dehumanizing practice of the Soviet guards and the equally dehumanizing practices of some of the prisoners. He saw some break down and others grow strong. He asks, "So what is the answer? How can you stand your ground when you are weak and sensitive to pain, when people you love are still alive, when you are unprepared? What do you need to make you stronger than the interrogator and the whole trap?"

Solzhenitsyn answers,

> From the moment you go to prison you must put your cozy past firmly behind you. At the very threshold, you must say to yourself: "My life is over, a little early to be sure, but there's nothing to be done about it. I shall never return to freedom. I am condemned to die—now or a little later. But later on, in truth, it will be even harder, and so the sooner the better. I no longer have any property whatsoever. For me those I love have died, and for them I have died. From today on, my body is useless and alien to me. Only my spirit and my conscience remain precious to me."
>
> Confronted by such a prisoner, the interrogation will tremble.
> Only the man who has renounced everything can win that victory.[8]

Solzhenitsyn has enunciated a great Christian principle. We must be willing to renounce everything if we are Christ's disciples. In the thick of the battle we must be willing to cast all material rewards aside.[9]

---

[8]Aleksandr I. Solzhenitsyn, *The Gulag Archipelago, 1918-1956: An Experiment in Literary Investigation*, I-II (New York: Harper & Row, 1973), 130.

[9]Large portions of this chapter are based on studies of Christ's appearance before Pilate already published in Boice, *The Gospel of John*, vol. 5 (Grand Rapids: Zondervan, 1980).

PART IV

THE END
OF HISTORY

For the Lord himself will descend from heaven with a cry of command, with the voice of an archangel, and with the sound of the trumpet of God. And the dead in Christ will rise first. Then we who are alive, who are left, will be caught up together with them in the clouds to meet the Lord in the air, and so we will always be with the Lord. Therefore encourage one another with these words.

1 THESSALONIANS 4:16-18

And if I go and prepare a place for you, I will come again and will take you to myself, that where I am you may be also.

JOHN 14:3

CHAPTER 17

HOW WILL IT ALL END?

*C*hristianity is a historical religion. That point has been made in earlier pages, but it needs to be reiterated as we draw to the end of this volume on Christian doctrine. Christianity is historical not merely in the sense that as a religion it is a phenomenon of history—that would be true of every other religion as well. Rather, it is historical in the sense that according to its teaching, God has acted decisively in history, revealing himself in specific external events attested in the Old and New Testament Scriptures, and will yet act to bring history to its predestined conclusion.

That teaching sets Christianity off from the modern form of gnosticism known as existentialism. To existentialists, even the so-called existential theologians, historical considerations are irrelevant for faith. It makes no difference whether God actually created the world, or whether the fall of the race actually took place in history. It makes no difference whether Jesus actually died for sin or rose from the dead. Historical disproof of the resurrection of Christ, or even his existence, means nothing to such theologians.

Existential theology has two separate realms of truth, one historical and verifiable, the other above or beyond history and nonverifiable. True Christianity knows nothing of that dichotomy. It insists that the events of its history are as real as any other events and as equally subject to historical verification. They differ from other events only in that God has acted in them in a special way and has thereby filled them with meaning.

There is also a sense in which Christianity gave rise to the very idea of history. The idea of movement in history leading to a meaningful goal simply did not exist before the full impact of the biblical faith. Theologian Carl F. H. Henry has written of this impact:

> The ancient world perceived human events in relation to cosmic or astral processes which it often divinized, or it viewed these events in the context of repetitive cycles or as significant only within a given culture or civilization, if indeed it regarded what happens in time as significant at all. Contemporary extensions of such theories may be seen in current notions of dialectical materialism, cultural relativity, and astrological influence upon human affairs. In contrast to the Greeks to whom the idea of history was fundamentally foreign, and who sought nothing of perpetual and abiding significance in history, the Hebrew prophets knew that history is the realm in which God decisively acts and works out his purposes. The Bible throughout insists that God the Creator holds mankind eternally accountable for every thought, word and deed, and that each successive generation moves toward a final future in which the God not only of creation but also of redemption and judgment will consummate human history in the light of his divine offer of salvation.[1]

God, who has acted *in history* in past events, is also to act *in history* to consummate this age. So when we ask, "How will it all end?" we do not suddenly pass out of the realm of history into a never-never land of utopian speculation. We merely pass to that which has not yet occurred but is nevertheless certain of occurring, for the simple reason that God is behind it and is himself the one who tells us it will.

When we speak of certainty, we must acknowledge that Christians are not in full agreement about the details of these future events. They disagree about the millennium, a period of one thousand years during which Jesus is to reign on earth; some see this as a specific future period, some as symbolic of the age of the church in which we are now living. Even among those who accept the millennium as a specific future period there are differences as to where it fits in with other events. How do the millennium and the return of Christ relate to the period of great tribulation spoken of in Daniel 9:27 and other texts, assuming that these do in fact speak of a specific tribulation period? What about the role of Israel in prophetic events? Armageddon? Antichrist? The diversity among

---

[1]Carl F. H. Henry, *God, Revelation and Authority*, vol. 2, *God Who Speaks and Shows* (Waco, TX: Word Books, 1976), 312.

evangelicals in handling these themes may be readily seen by comparing the final sections of most books of theology.

What tends to be lost in the awareness of such differences, however, is the large *agreement* that exists, plus the fact that the areas in which Christians are agreed (at least all evangelical Christians) are the most important. Regardless of the way the millennium, the great tribulation, and other problems of prophecy are handled, most writers focus on the return of Christ, the resurrection of the body, and the final judgment as the essential and dominant elements of eschatology. Wherever the other events fit in (assuming there are other events), they at least have to fit in around those more important elements.

CHRIST'S RETURN

Agreement is particularly evident about Christ's return. Arnold T. Olson has written,

> Ever since the first days of the Christian church, evangelicals have been "looking for that blessed hope, and the glorious appearing of the great God and our Saviour Jesus Christ." They may have disagreed as to its timing and to the events on the eschatological calendar. They may have differed as to a pre-tribulation or post-tribulation rapture—the pre- or post- or non-millennial coming. They may have been divided as to a literal rebirth of Israel. However, all are agreed that the final solution to the problems of this world is in the hands of the King of kings who will someday make the kingdoms of this world his very own.[2]

The reason for their agreement is the overwhelming evidence in the Bible as to the certainty and importance of Christ's return.

In the New Testament, one verse in twenty-five deals with the Lord's return. It is mentioned 318 times in the 260 chapters. It occupies a prominent place in the Old Testament in that most of the Old Testament prophecies concerning the coming of Christ deal, not with his first advent, in which he died as our sin bearer, but with his second advent, in which he is to rule as king.

The return of Jesus Christ is mentioned in every one of the New Testament books except Galatians (which was written with a particular and quite different problem in view) and the very short books such as 2 John, 3 John, and Philemon.

---

[2]Arnold T. Olson, "The Second Coming of Christ," in *Prophecy in the Making: Messages Prepared for the Jerusalem Conference on Biblical Authority*, ed. Carl F. H. Henry (Carol Stream, IL: Creation House, 1971), 115. The diversity of views among evangelicals and others is well represented in the essays appearing in this volume. My own views can be found in *The Last and Future World* (Grand Rapids: Zondervan, 1974).

Jesus spoke of his return quite often. Mark records him as saying, "Whoever is ashamed of me and of my words in this adulterous and sinful generation, of him will the Son of Man also be ashamed when he comes in the glory of his Father with the holy angels" (Mk 8:38). "Then they will see the Son of Man coming in clouds with great power and glory. And then he will send out the angels, and gather his elect from the four winds, from the ends of the earth to the ends of heaven" (Mk 13:26-27). John tells us that Christ's last words to his disciples included the promise, "If I go and prepare a place for you, I will come again and will take you to myself, that where I am you may be also" (Jn 14:3).

In the last chapter of John, the author records a statement of Jesus to Peter in which a reference to his return is incidental but is, nevertheless, all the more impressive on that account. Jesus had been encouraging Peter to faithfulness in discipleship, but Peter with his usual impetuousness had turned and seen the beloved disciple. He asked, "Lord, what about this man?" (Jn 21:21). Jesus replied, "If it is my will that he remain until I come, what is that to you? You follow me!" (Jn 21:22). John pointed out that although many Christians of his day had interpreted this to mean that John would not die until Christ came back, that was not what Jesus had said. He said only that even if that were the case, it should not affect Peter's call to faithful service.

Paul's letters are also full of the doctrine of Christ's return. To the Christians at Thessalonica he wrote, "For the Lord himself will descend from heaven with a cry of command, with the voice of an archangel, and with the sound of the trumpet of God. And the dead in Christ will rise first. Then we who are alive, who are left, will be caught up together with them in the clouds to meet the Lord in the air, and so we will always be with the Lord" (1 Thess 4:16-17). To the Philippians Paul wrote, "But our citizenship is in heaven, and from it we await a Savior, the Lord Jesus Christ, who will transform our lowly body to be like his glorious body, by the power that enables him even to subject all things to himself" (Phil 3:20-21).

Peter called the return of Jesus Christ our "living hope" (1 Pet 1:3). Paul called it "our blessed hope" (Titus 2:13). John declared with conviction, "Behold, he is coming with the clouds, and every eye will see him, even those who pierced him, and all tribes of the earth will wail on account of him" (Rev 1:7). He ended the Revelation with "He who testifies to these things says, 'Surely I am coming soon.' Amen. Come, Lord Jesus!" (Rev 22:20).

In these verses and many others, the early Christians expressed their belief in Jesus' personal return, a return that was to be closely associated with a period of great wickedness on earth, the resurrection and transformation of their own bodies, an earthly rule of the glorified Jesus, and a final judgment of individuals and nations. They acknowledged that their lives should be lived on a higher plane because of it.

This is the first reason why the return of Christ is a practical doctrine and not merely an escape valve for wishful thoughts. Lord Shaftesbury, a great English social reformer, said near the end of his life, "I do not think that in the last forty years I have lived one conscious hour that was not influenced by the thought of our Lord's return."

If we are expecting the Lord's return, that conviction ought to alter our concern for social issues. At the height of the race crisis in the United States in the early 1960s, two signs hung on the wall of a restaurant in Decatur, Georgia. The first sign was biblical. It read "Jesus is coming again!" The second sign, directly below it, said "We reserve the right to refuse service to anybody!" The signs were humorous because they implied that the owner of the restaurant, who apparently was looking for the return of Jesus, might refuse him service, and because racial or any other form of discrimination is incongruous in the light of Christ's coming. If we are motivated by prejudice, contemplating some sin, tearing down or criticizing other people, wasting our gifts, or in any other way failing to live as Christ's faithful disciples—then the return of Jesus has not made its proper impression on our thinking.

A second reason why the return of Jesus is a practical doctrine is that it comforts those who are suffering. It helped the early Christians. We may imagine that as they lay in prison, suffering and tormented, often near death, they looked for Christ's coming and thought that perhaps in an instant and without warning Jesus would appear and call them home. As they entered the arena to face the lions or looked up in their cell to face their executioner, many would have thought, "Perhaps this is the moment Jesus will return; even now, before the beasts can spring or the ax can fall, I shall be caught up to meet him."

Believers in Christ have lost children, parents, and close friends. Belief in the return of Jesus is comforting to them. The people of Paul's day had lost friends through death, and he wrote to them reminding them of this blessed hope. "Therefore encourage one another with these words" (1 Thess 4:18). Reuben A. Torrey, a former president of the Bible Institute of Los Angeles, once wrote, "Time and again in writing to those who have lost for a time those whom they love, I have obeyed God's commandment and used the truth of our Lord's return to comfort them, and many have told me afterwards how full of comfort this truth has proven when everything else had failed."[3] The return of Jesus is a practical doctrine because it is an encouragement to godly living and, at times, even to go on living—which means that it has bearing on present history as well as on history's end.

RESURRECTION OF THE BODY

The second doctrine of the "end things" on which Christians are widely agreed is the resurrection, specifically the resurrection of the bodies of believers at Christ's second coming. This doctrine is of tremendous importance for several reasons.

First, the Christian doctrine of the resurrection recognizes that death is an enemy (1 Cor 15:26) and is therefore something unnatural, something evil that was not God's original intention for humanity. It is important to stress this because some forms of Christianity encourage a false optimism that denies the reality of the three great evils: sin, suffering, and death. Christian Science (which is not Christianity at all, even though it uses the name *Christian*) carries this outlook to an extreme, but the tendency is often present in Christian circles too.

We sometimes see it in relation to a person who is dying. I read the story of a Christian who was in the last stages of cancer and who described what had been happening. She said, "I can see the people who come to visit me because there is a mirror in the hall and they are reflected there as they come by. Many pause to put on a pleasant expression. Then they come into the room and talk about what is going to be taking place at church next week or the week after that. They speak of the time when I am going to be better and be with them again. But they know I won't be. They know I'm dying. I know I'm dying, but they don't want to talk about it. So they put on a pleasant face and pretend that the evil isn't there." In the case of the person whose testimony I was reading, there was a triumphant faith in Jesus who rose from the dead and gives eternal life to all who believe in him—in addition to an awareness of the evil. Death in that room was transformed. But it is not always so, and frequently, as in the case of the friends, there is denial that death is an enemy.

Do we deny because we think that somehow it is more spiritual to pretend that death is not real? I do not know. But I do know that such attempts are unsuccessful. Try doing that with sin. Say, "Sin is not sin." See if that is more spiritual. Pretend that homosexuality is all right, that pornographic films are not

---

[3]R. A. Torrey, *The Return of the Lord Jesus* (Grand Rapids: Baker Book House, 1966), 15.

bad, that economic injustice and racial oppression do not exist. If you do that, you lose the cutting edge of Christian social concern and reformation, and evil soon becomes tolerable. If you cannot operate that way in the area of social evil, you cannot operate that way in regard to death. Because, although in one sense denial might satisfy *us* if we are not now facing death—at least to the extent that we are not thinking about it—it does not satisfy anybody who is face to face with it. False optimism does no good.

On the other hand, the Christian doctrine of the resurrection speaks of victory over death provided for us by the Lord Jesus. After writing about death as an enemy, Paul went on to speak of the ultimate victory to come. "When the perishable puts on the imperishable, and the mortal puts on immortality, then shall come to pass the saying that is written: 'Death is swallowed up in victory'" (1 Cor 15:54). He concluded, "But thanks be to God, who gives us the victory through our Lord Jesus Christ" (1 Cor 15:57).

What a victory that is! It is an entrance of the soul and spirit into the presence of God, to be followed in God's own time by a physical resurrection.

Death involves every part of our being. When God said to Adam and Eve in the garden, "Of the tree of the knowledge of good and evil you shall not eat, for in the day that you eat of it you shall surely die" (Gen 2:17), they ate of it and died. They died in every part of their being. They had a spirit, soul, and body, and died in each one. They died in spirit and showed it by hiding from God. They died in soul; all the anger, lust, hate, jealousy, pride and other sins we know so well began to enter the experience of the race. Eventually their bodies died also.

When God saves us he saves us in spirit, soul, and body. He gives us a new spirit in the moment of the new birth. He creates a new soul through the process of sanctification. At the resurrection he gives us a new body. The salvation he provides is a *whole* salvation.

Assurance of these things is ours because of Christ's resurrection. Without this, our hope of a resurrection would be no more than wishful thinking. It might be true, but it would not have the certainty that it has for Christian people. Jesus' own resurrection provides powerful assurance of the Christian's resurrection.

We begin by noting that Christ's death was a real death; unless it was a real death we are not talking about a real resurrection. Jesus really died. Unbelievers usually try to deny either that there was a real resurrection or that there was a real death. Elaborate theories have been worked out, particularly in the nineteenth century, to deny Christ's death. Some suggested that Jesus only swooned and then revived in the tomb or that the authorities crucified the wrong person. Theories like that were developed seriously.

Today not even the most liberal scholars would take such an approach. They know that Jesus really died. The death of Jesus Christ under Pontius Pilate is a fact of history. Rather, they "spiritualize" the resurrection.

When Hollywood tries to portray these things in movies, it at best spiritualizes Christ's resurrection. I saw one such movie on television. There was the death. It was real enough. When the Roman soldier took his hammer and drove the nail through the hand, there was no doubt that it was real metal and flesh and wood. The death was real. But when the resurrection came, all you could hear was music. You could not even see the Lord. People rushed about joyfully. But where was Jesus? I looked for him. At last there was a ghostly view of him floating off into the clouds. If the resurrection had been like that, I guarantee that Thomas for one would not have believed in it, and I do not think Peter and John would have either. The resurrection was not like that. It was a real flesh-and-blood resurrection, and those men knew it when they touched Christ's body. Because it had taken place, they were willing to go out from that obscure corner of the Roman Empire into their world proclaiming the Lord's death and resurrection. They were willing to be crucified themselves rather than deny their Lord. That is how real his death and resurrection were.

A mythical resurrection does not give birth to conviction. A real resurrection does.

DAY OF JUDGMENT

Most of what has been said up to this point has been encouraging, particularly for Christians, but there is a sober side too. Christ is coming. His coming will be a joy for Christians, who will be raised to meet him. But it will also mean the beginning of Christ's judgments for those who have spurned the gospel.

Christians acknowledge this truth every time they recite the Apostles' Creed. They say Jesus will come again from heaven "to judge the living and the dead." The Victorian poet Robert Browning wrote, "God's in his heaven; all's right with the world." But although God is in his heaven, all is not right with the world, and a day is coming when God will speak out against the world in judgment. Paul told the Athenians that God "has fixed a day on which he will judge the world in righteousness by a man whom he has appointed, and of this he has given assurance to all by raising him from the dead" (Acts 17:31).

That is a sobering fact. It tells us that history has an end, and its end involves accountability. We shall answer for what we have done, and we shall all be judged either on the basis of our own righteousness (which will condemn us) or on the basis of the perfect righteousness of him who is our Savior. Some people refuse to face this reality and go on ignoring the day of reckoning.

In a sermon given on the Mount of Olives in the middle of his last week in Jerusalem, Jesus used three parables to teach what the final judgment would be like for such people. One parable was about ten maidens who had been invited to a wedding banquet. Five were wise and five were foolish. The five wise maidens prepared for the banquet by buying oil for their lamps. The five foolish maidens did not. As they waited in the long evening hours they all fell asleep. Suddenly a cry went forth, "Here is the bridegroom! Come out to meet him" (Mt 25:6). They arose, but the five foolish maidens had no oil for their lamps. On the advice of the wise they set out to buy some. But while they were getting their oil the bridegroom came and the wedding party followed him into the house and the door was shut. Later the five foolish maidens returned and called at the door, "Lord, lord, open to us" (Mt 25:11).

But he answered, "Truly, . . . I do not know you" (Mt 25:12).

Jesus concluded, "Watch therefore, for you know neither the day nor the hour" (Mt 25:13).

The second parable was about three servants. Their master was to go on a journey. He called the servants to him and gave each money: to the first, five talents; to the second, two talents; to the third, one talent—each according to his ability. Then he departed, and the servants who had received five talents and two talents respectively invested the money, while the third servant hid his talent in the ground. After a long time the master returned and asked for an accounting. The man who had received five talents produced those talents plus five more. The servant who had received two talents produced two talents plus two more. But the one who had been given only one talent returned only that one to the Lord saying, "Master, I knew you to be a hard man, reaping where you did not sow, and gathering where you scattered no seed, so I was afraid, and I went and hid your talent in the ground. Here, you have what is yours." The master condemned that servant, taking away his talent and casting him forth into "the outer darkness" (Mt 25:24-25, 30).

Finally, the Lord told the parable of the separation of the sheep from the goats. The goats are the lost, and they were condemned because they neglected to feed the Lord when he was hungry, give him drink when he was thirsty, welcome him when he was a stranger, clothe him when he was naked, visit him when he was sick, and comfort him when he was cast in prison. They said, "Lord, when did we see thee hungry or thirsty or a stranger or naked or sick or in prison, and did not minister to thee?" He replied, "Truly, I say to you, as you did not do it to one of the least of these, you did not do it to me" (Mt 25:44-45). On the other hand, he welcomed those who did these things.

Each of those parables, though different from the others in detail, contains the same essential features. In each case, there is a sudden return of the Lord. In each case, some are prepared for his coming and others are not. In each case there are rewards and judgments. In each case, those who are lost are no doubt amazed at that outcome.

Thus it will be with our generation. We have more opportunities to learn about Christ in our day than ever before in history. Books and magazines and radio programs and movies and television have all told about him. The call has gone forth, "Behold the man! Look to this one for salvation. He loves you. He died for you. He rose again. Turn from your sin and place your trust in him as your Savior!" But many go blithely on and will be overwhelmed in the day of God's reckoning.

Today is the day of God's grace. Wisdom consists in knowing "Jesus Christ and him crucified" (1 Cor 2:2).

CHAPTER 18

HOME AT LAST

The first few verses of John 14 are among the most popular in the Bible. They speak about heaven, but the reason for their popularity is not that they reveal details about heaven or even about life beyond the grave. They do not. Nor is it that other, more extensive passages on the subject of heaven are lacking. The book of Revelation describes heaven as a glorious city, a country, God's kingdom, paradise. It abounds in walls, thrones, precious jewels, choirs, angels. Why is John 14 so popular? The answer is probably because of the warm image that is found there: heaven is a home. We need a home. We long for a home. Jesus calmly told his troubled disciples that we have one.

"Let not your hearts be troubled. Believe in God; believe also in me. In my Father's house are many rooms. If it were not so, would I have told you that I go to prepare a place for you? And if I go and prepare a place for you, I will come again and will take you to myself, that where I am you may be also" (Jn 14:1-3).

Our need for a home arises from the fact that we have lost one. We had a home once, in Eden. But sin caused the loss of that home and, ever since, the history of the human race has been one of wandering. We think of Cain, who killed his brother and was condemned to a life of drifting. He had no home. In Genesis 11 we find humans trying to create a city in which homes would be established. But the people of Babel were in opposition to God, and God scattered them. They were made homeless.

With the coming of Abraham we find a new, heartening element. To be sure, God's first dealings with Abraham were to take him from his home—it was a sinful place filled with idols and idol worshipers. But in place of the home he lost, God promised Abraham a new place: "the land that I will show you" (Gen 12:1). What is more, God gave the boundaries and indicated the specific territory. It was "from the river of Egypt to the great river, the river Euphrates, the land of the Kenites, the Kenizzites, the Kadmonites, the Hittites, the Perizzites, the Rephaim, the Amorites, the Canaanites, the Girgashites and the Jebusites" (Gen 15:18-21). But even though Abraham was brought into the land and even though his descendants were later settled there in large numbers, even as great a land as the promised land was ultimately inadequate. Abraham is praised in the New Testament not because he fixed his hope on some earthly home (important as that may be), but because he looked for a heavenly home. "He was looking forward to the city that has foundations, whose designer and builder and maker is God" (Heb 11:10).

Although our earthly homes are necessary and significant, they are not permanent. Our basic need for a home is fully met only when the Lord Jesus Christ himself prepares a home for us in heaven. Now we are in a strange land, even in an enemy's country. In that day we shall be in the Father's house and shall be home. That is a Christian's destiny.

WHERE JESUS IS

We do not know much about heaven except that it is where we shall be and where we shall be with Jesus. One day my six-year-old daughter's first-grade science class was discussing the universe—how big it is and what it is composed of. The conversation drifted around to heaven, and the children began to ask where heaven fit in. Was it between the stars? Was it beyond them? The only valid answer (the one we gave our daughter when she came home) was that heaven is where God is and where Jesus has gone to prepare that place which he has promised us.

This is the focal point of Revelation 5. It speaks of the four and twenty elders, the angels, and a vast host of other creatures from everywhere in the universe. These beings were mentioned, not for descriptive purposes, but because each bore testimony to Christ and thus served to show how he is prominent. The four and twenty elders praised him with this song:

> Worthy are you to take the scroll
> and to open its seals,
> for you were slain, and by your blood you ransomed people for God

> from every tribe and language and people and nation,
>> and you have made them a kingdom and priests to our God,
>>> and they shall reign on the earth. (Rev 5:9-10)

Then the angels gave their testimony: "Worthy is the Lamb who was slain, to receive power and wealth and wisdom and might and honor and glory and blessing!" (Rev 5:12). At last the remaining creatures joined in: "To him who sits on the throne and to the Lamb be blessing and honor and glory and might forever and ever!" (Rev 5:13). Heaven is where God is. It is his presence (and not some high concentration of golden streets or jewels) that makes it heaven.

The words of Jesus were a comfort to the disciples and are precious to us. The disciples were going to lose the physical presence of Jesus for a time, but he told them that one day they would be reunited with him in his Father's home. Heaven would be a home for them because they would be with Jesus.

Dwight L. Moody used to illustrate this point by the story of a young child whose mother became very sick. While the mother was sick, one of the neighbors took the child away to stay with her until the mother got well again. But the mother grew worse and died. The neighbors thought they would not take the child home until the funeral was over and would never tell her about her mother being dead. After a while they simply brought the little girl home. At once she went to find her mother. First she went into the sitting room to find her mother; then she went into the parlor. She went from one end of the house to the other, but she could not find her. At last she asked, "Where is my mama?" When they told her that her mother was gone, the little girl wanted to go back to the neighbor's house again. Home had lost its attraction for her, since her mother was not there any longer. Moody says, "No, it is not the jaspar walls and the pearly gates that are going to make heaven attractive. It is the being with God."[1]

REUNION

In heaven we will also be with one another, and that too makes heaven attractive. Many Christian people are anxious about whether they will recognize their friends in heaven. They have no doubt that they will *be* in heaven; "to be absent from the body [is] to be present with the Lord" (2 Cor 5:8 KJV). Still, they are confused about what is to happen in the life to come. "Do you think I will know my Bill?" "Will I recognize Sally?" If we could not recognize our friends and family, then heaven inevitably would lose much of its attractiveness. It is hard

---

[1]*Dwight L. Moody*, Great Pulpit Masters, vol. 1 (New York: Revell, 1949), 210-11.

to see how we could really be happy there in that case, regardless of how dazzling the streets or how beautiful the music of the angels.

But the Word of God is explicit about our mutual recognition. We *will* know each other. Bill will know Sally. Sally will know Bill. We will know parents and children, friends and relatives, and those who have died in the Lord before us.

One very encouraging indication that comes from the Old Testament is a phrase often used in connection with the death of the patriarchs. It is the phrase "and he was gathered to his people." It occurs in texts like these: "Abraham breathed his last and died in a good old age, an old man and full of years, and *was gathered to his people*" (Gen 25:8); "These are the years of the life of Ishmael: 137 years. He breathed his last and died, and *was gathered to his people*" (Gen 25:17); "Isaac breathed his last, and he died and *was gathered to his people*, old and full of days. And his sons Esau and Jacob buried him" (Gen 35:29); "When Jacob finished commanding his sons, he drew up his feet into the bed and breathed his last and *was gathered to his people*" (Gen 49:33); "Let Aaron *be gathered to his people*, for he shall not enter the land that I have given to the people of Israel" (Num 20:24); and "The LORD said to Moses, 'Go up into this mountain of Abarim and see the land that I have given to the people of Israel. When you have seen it, you also *shall be gathered to your people*, as your brother Aaron was'" (Num 27:12-13).

Many Old Testament scholars regard this phrase as being nothing more than a conventional way of saying that he died. It is to be explained, so they say, by the thought that the individual was being placed in the same graveyard as those who had died before him. But that is hardly satisfactory in the case of the Bible stories involved. When Abraham died, he was buried in a cave at Machpelah in the land that was to become Israel; it was not the burial place of his ancestors. They had been buried back in Ur of the Chaldees, and his father had been buried at Haran. Further, in reading the account of his death, it is hard to overlook the fact that Abraham is said to have been gathered to his ancestors in Genesis 25:8, but to have actually been buried only in Genesis 25:9. Consequently, the phrase "gathered to his people" cannot refer to the burial but must refer to the death itself, as a result of which Abraham joined those who had gone before him. The same thing is true of Moses, who died by himself on the mountain. The book of Deuteronomy tells us that "no one knows the place of his burial to this day" (Deut 34:6).

David's comment on being told of the death of Bathsheba's child is also important; it shows that David believed in a personal reunion with departed loved ones in the life to come. God had struck the child so that it became sick and died. While it was languishing, David (who understood that he was to blame) prayed for the child and fasted, lying all night on the earth. His grief and concern were so great that later, after the child had died, those who were close to him were afraid to tell him lest his grief should then know no bounds. But David detected the change in their attitude. He asked, "Is the child dead?" When they told him that the child had died, David surprised them by rising from his place of mourning, washing himself and dressing, and resuming his duties as leader of the nation.

The servants asked about his change of attitude; they could not understand it. David explained, "While the child was still alive, I fasted and wept, for I said, 'Who knows whether the LORD will be gracious to me, that the child may live?' But now he is dead. Why should I fast? Can I bring him back again? I shall go to him, but he will not return to me" (2 Sam 12:22-23). The last comment does not mean merely that David would eventually die himself. The point of the story is that David comforted himself (and Bathsheba) after the child's death, and there would be no comfort unless David believed that, although he could not bring the child back, nevertheless, one day they would see the child again in heaven.

In the New Testament we find additional indication of these truths in the events that took place on the Mount of Transfiguration. On that occasion the Lord took three of his disciples, Peter, James, and John, with him to the mountain and there was transformed to show forth his celestial glory. Moses and Elijah, two other glorified saints, appeared beside him. Luke called them "men" (that is, not disembodied spirits), and reported that Peter and presumably also the others recognized them. Peter said, "Master, it is good that we are here. Let us make three tents, one for you and one for Moses and one for Elijah" (Lk 9:33). Here both Moses and Elijah had retained their identities and were recognized by the three disciples.

Christ's story about the rich man and Lazarus makes a similar point. The Lord told how the rich man went to hell and, being in torment, lifted up his eyes and "saw Abraham far off and Lazarus at his side" (Lk 16:23). Here is a case that involves recognition of the departed, not only as they appear in this life, but as they appear to each other in the life to come.

Finally, there are the words of Jesus in which he speaks of Gentiles joining with believing Jews in a great reunion in heaven. "I tell you, many will come from east and west and recline at table with Abraham, Isaac, and Jacob in the kingdom of heaven" (Mt 8:11). That is a great promise. But it is not possible unless there is to be a full recognition of all who have died when they come together in the life to come. The patriarchs are to know each other at that reunion, and so will all those who have died in Christ and who will be gathered to him from the far corners of the earth. In that day we may well be surprised at who is in heaven, for many will be there whom we do not expect to be there. And we will probably be surprised to find that many whom we thought would be there are not present.

Many have lost loved ones. If we live long enough, we will all lose loved ones. Yet we have not lost them ultimately. They are with Jesus, and we will be reunited with them.

As We Are Meant to Be

We have seen that, first, we will see Jesus and, second, we will see and recognize each other. A third point is that we will see each other not as we are now or have been but as we are meant to be. "Beloved, we are God's children now, and what we will be has not yet appeared; but we know that when he appears we shall be like him, because we shall see him as he is" (1 Jn 3:2).

For many years, every time I read that verse I read the word *we* as if it said *I*. I read "I will be like him," and I took comfort in that. I reasoned that I will be like him in *holiness*, and that was wonderful. Now I am unholy. I constantly sin and must constantly ask for forgiveness. In that day I will no longer have to pray "Father, forgive me. . . ." Then I shall be without sin, like Jesus. I also reasoned that I will be like Christ in *knowledge*, not exhaustive knowledge, to be sure (I will not be omniscient), but accurate knowledge. Now, by contrast, so much of what I know is mixed with error. Finally, I reasoned that I will be like him in *love*. It is true that by his grace I do love now. But that love is imperfect. It vacillates. It is selective. In that day I will be able to love as Jesus loves, perfectly and without wavering.

Those truths were a great comfort to me, and I was right to be comforted. Now I am impressed with something else that is also true. Not only will *I* be made like Jesus. *We* will *all* be like him. As a result, the sin, ignorance, anger, hate, weariness, and perversity that so often mar our relationships with each other will be eliminated.

Moreover, we will see each other rewarded for faithful service in this life, since the Bible speaks of crowns given to those who have been faithful. The Lord said, "Behold, I am coming soon, bringing my recompense, to repay everyone for what he has done" (Rev 22:12). There is a wrong way of thinking of rewards. If we are serving only for what we get out of the arrangement, we are no more than hirelings. If we are working for rewards in this life—for money or the praise others may (or may not) give us—we are not fit to be Christ's servants. Still, there is a right way to think about rewards. They are set before us as one reason why the patriarchs and other biblical characters were faithful. They had much to discourage them. Often they experienced trials, hardships, beatings, pain, ridicule, but they endured because they were "looking to the reward" (Heb 11:26). Rewards can strengthen our perseverance too.

LIKE JESUS NOW

For some people these words are already quite meaningful. They are old or sick, some close to dying. The thought of being with Jesus forever and being like him is a great blessing. On the other hand, others are not in that position, and for them this study does not seem timely. I could point out that we are all dying, some nearer to that point than others. I could point out that no one knows the moment of his or her death. It could be thirty years from now; it could be tomorrow or tonight. Instead, let me make an application in two other areas.

First, if you are a Christian and if it is true that you will eventually be with Jesus, spend time with him now. Do this through your own personal Bible study and prayer. What would we think of a couple who are about to be married but who do not feel the need to spend time together before the marriage? They say, "Oh, we will be together a lot after we are married; we have other things we want to do now." Such a marriage would not seem promising. We should want to get to know Jesus better if we are looking forward to being with him in heaven.

A second application is to our moral conduct. If we are going to be like Jesus one day, we must strive to be like him now. Having said that we will be like him in glory, John added, "And everyone who thus hopes in him purifies himself as he is pure" (1 Jn 3:3).

Many winters, after the pressures of the Christmas and New Year's services at Tenth Presbyterian Church in Philadelphia, my family and I would take a four-day vacation to the Pocono Mountains in eastern Pennsylvania, vacationing at an immense lodge, beautifully situated on a large mountain estate. We looked forward to this greatly as the vacation days approached. When the time eventually would come, we would drive for about three hours and arrive in the evening as dusk was settling over the mountain landscape. We would park and approach the door. The doormen, who have been there in some cases for twenty or thirty years, would come to greet us and take our bags. Then they would say, "Welcome home! Welcome home!" It was not home (regrettably). It was only a clever device on the part of the lodge to make its guests welcome. But one day we are going to glory, where those words will be spoken by our own blessed Lord, the one who has prepared our home for us. "Welcome home!" he will say. And we really will be home. Forever.[2]

---

[2]Parts of this chapter are drawn from a fuller treatment of heaven in chapters 12, 13, and 57 of Boice, *The Gospel of John*, vol. 4 (Grand Rapids: Zondervan, 1978).

PART I
The Knowledge of God

SUMMARY

Knowing the truth about God is possible because he has mercifully chosen to reveal himself to us. If we fulfill our responsibility to respond to that divine revelation with gratefulness and worship, we can have a personal relationship with the one who made us. If we refuse to do that, we move further away from him and justly receive his wrath and judgment.

KEY CONCEPTS

Wrong ideas about knowledge (pp. 5-7). Many people in the world today think that we can gain knowledge by reason alone or by emotional experience. In other words, they say, "I know this is true because it makes sense to me," or "I know this is true because it makes me feel happy." All such human approaches to knowledge are equally flawed, but there is a better way to understand the world, and that is by knowing the one who made it. Only through a relationship with him can we truly understand anything (Prov 1:7; 9:10).

What does it mean to know God? (pp. 7-9). Knowing God is not just knowing about God, nor is it merely an experience we have. It is a personal relationship with him that includes understanding, trust, obedience, and love (J. I. Packer quote, p. 9).

The importance of knowing God (pp. 9-12). Here are some benefits of knowing God, according to the Scriptures: eternal life (Jn 17:3), a true knowledge of ourselves (Is 6:5), a true knowledge of the world around us (Jer 9:23-24), personal holiness (Jer 31:34), and strength and effectiveness for the church (Dan 11:32). (See also the quote by Spurgeon on p. 13.)

General revelation and the universal knowledge of God (pp. 14-18). "Knowing God" in the sense of an intimate relationship with him is something that only true Christians can experience, because it comes through trusting in Jesus Christ and obeying his Word. But the Scriptures speak of a lesser knowledge of God that is possessed by every person who lives in this world, even those who have never heard the name of Jesus Christ. In Romans 1:18-23, God says that he has revealed his existence and his power to everyone, so that we all have an internal awareness that God is real and that we should worship him. This is what theologians call "general revelation," and it is made known primarily through the wonders of creation all around us (Ps 19:1-4).

Romans 1 also says that suppressing the truth in unrighteousness and worshiping false gods is the state of everyone in the world who has not been born again by the Spirit of God through faith in Jesus Christ. And Roman 1:20 says that they are without excuse and under the wrath and judgment of a holy God. So this universal knowledge of God is not enough to save people, because it does not tell them the specific facts about Jesus, but it *is* enough to condemn them, because they do not respond to it in the right way.

In order for us to be saved from our sinful rejection of God and to know him as our Father in a personal relationship, we must be transformed into worshipers of him through an understanding of his Word by the power of the Holy Spirit. In other words, we must receive *special revelation* in addition to general revelation. The next lesson is about God's special revelation, the Bible.

QUESTIONS FOR STUDY AND DISCUSSION

1. Why are reason and experience inadequate and unreliable ways to find out what is true? (pp. 6-7)

2. How do these verses help us to understand what the Bible means when it talks about "knowing" God: Genesis 4:1, Matthew 7:21-23, John 10:14, and John 24–27?

3. How have you experienced the difference between merely knowing about God and actually knowing him? How did that change occur in your life?

4. According to Romans 1:18 and 1:21-23, what do fallen human beings do by nature with the general revelation we receive? (See pp. 15-18.)

5. Based on Romans 1:18-23, how would you answer someone who says to you, "What about the people in parts of the world who have never heard about Jesus? Are they still accountable to God's judgment?" (See also Luke 8:16-18.)

RECOMMENDED READING FOR FURTHER STUDY

Dallas Willard, *Hearing God*

J. I. Packer, *Knowing God*, chapters 1–3

John Calvin, *Institutes of the Christian Religion*, book 1

QUESTIONS FOR PERSONAL DISCIPLESHIP

1. Do you know God? Evaluate your life in light of J. I. Packer's definition of knowing God: Are you learning what God's Word says and how it applies to your life? Are you understanding more about God's character? Are you obeying his commands? Are you worshiping him from a grateful heart?

2. What implications do you think Romans 1:18-23 has for our approach to evangelism? Do you think it is profitable to attempt to prove the existence of God to an agnostic or atheist, or do you think it is better to simply communicate what the Bible says about sin and salvation? How might you use this passage itself in sharing the gospel with someone?

PART II
The Word of God

SUMMARY

Because the general revelation of God in creation and conscience does not inform us about the specific facts regarding Christ, the only way we can know God is if he reveals himself in words. By his grace, he has done this throughout history in various ways, and today he reveals himself in the written words of the Bible.

KEY CONCEPTS

The inspiration of Scripture (chapters 3–5). Following are eight reasons why we believe the Bible is the Word of God:

1. *The testimony of Scripture Itself* (pp. 26-31). Over 3,800 times in the Bible, the writers say something like "The Lord says" (in the KJV it is translated "Thus saith the Lord").

2. *The testimony of Jesus Christ* (pp. 31-34). Jesus Christ believed that every word of the Old Testament was revealed by God. In Matthew 5:18, he says that the law has such a supernatural quality that even the smallest letter (the Hebrew *iota*) and the smallest part of a letter (like a serif) are important. In John 10:35 he says, "Scripture cannot be broken." He also taught that the New Testament writings of the apostles would be from God (Jn 14:25-26; 16:12-14).

3. *The internal witness of the Holy Spirit* (pp. 35-45). A third reason that we know the Bible is the Word of God is that the Holy Spirit, who inspired the Scriptures, convinces all true believers that this is so.

4. *The unity of the Bible* (pp. 46-48). Though it was written over 1,500 years by many different authors from varied backgrounds, the Bible has one common and central theme, which is the person and work of Jesus Christ. This can only be explained by a supernatural design (p. 47).

5. *The amazing accuracy of the Bible* (pp. 48-51). The Bible exhibits an accuracy in recording historical facts that is uncommon among ancient literature. Its accounts have never proven contrary to the corresponding historical and archaeological records, and it never contradicts itself. All the alleged discrepancies have been explained plausibly by Bible scholars for hundreds of years. (Example of resurrection accounts on pp. 50-51.)

6. *Fulfilled prophecy* (pp. 51-52). The Old Testament contains hundreds of predictive prophecies that were fulfilled to the letter later in history. Massive cities like Babylon, Tyre, Sidon, and Nineveh fell exactly as the prophetic writings said they would. Even more impressively, the life and death of one man—Jesus Christ—was predicted in great detail with astonishing accuracy. Only a sovereign Creator knows the end from the beginning, so a book that tells the future can only have come from him.

7. *The preservation of the Bible* (pp. 52-53). The inevitable scarcity of copies that calls into question the content of many ancient works of literature has not even touched the Bible, nor have the many efforts to wipe it out. In fact, there is an "embarrassment of riches" when it comes to the thousands of biblical manuscripts that have endured through time (1 Pet 1:23-25).

8. *Changed lives* (pp. 53-56). The Bible has demonstrated an ability to transform even the worst people, making them a blessing to their families, friends, and community (Ps 19:7-9, Heb 4:12).

The inerrancy of Scripture (chapters 6–7). Since the Bible is the inspired Word of God, it follows by logical necessity that the Bible contains no mistakes or errors, because its Author is perfect.

1. *The history of inerrancy* (pp. 57-63). Prior to the last several centuries, the inerrancy of Scripture was never challenged or debated in the Christian Church (see examples of church leaders on pp. 57-60). The Roman Catholic Church weakened the orthodox view of the Bible around the time of the Reformation, because it officially raised the unwritten traditions of church history to the same level of importance as Scripture itself. And then Protestant liberalism denied inerrancy outright.

2. *The case for inerrancy* (p. 63). We believe in the inerrancy of Scripture because it is the only viewpoint that is logically compatible with the truths about the Bible earlier in this lesson. But the doctrine of inerrancy is also established by some key texts that cannot be adequately interpreted in any other way (Ps 19:7-9; 119:128, 137-44, 151, 160; Prov 30:5; Mt 4:4; 5:17-20; Jn 10:34-36; Gal 3:16; 2 Tim 3:16).

3. *The enemy of inerrancy—modern biblical criticism* (pp. 69-79). Many churches, denominations, and seminaries today practice a kind of biblical "scholarship" that is often called higher criticism (as opposed to lower criticism, which is done by many conservative scholars and involves studying manuscripts of the Bible). This approach denies the traditional understanding of the inspiration and inerrancy of the Scriptures, in favor of a Bible that is full of mistakes and outdated in its morality.

The interpretation of Scripture (chapter 8)

If we do not know how to interpret the Bible, we will be ignorant of God's will or mistaken about it. Thankfully, the Bible itself teaches us how it should be interpreted. As Boice explains, "The answers are found in the four most important truths about the Bible, all of which have been covered in the previous chapters."

1. *One book, one author, one theme* (pp. 81-83). Although God uses human writers in the process of revelation, he is behind all of it, and all Scripture ultimately comes from him (remember 2 Tim 3:16). So there is a grand design to the Bible, and every Scripture must fit together with every other Scripture. There can be no contradictions from a God who never lies or makes mistakes, so if one passage seems to contradict another passage, the interpreter must do some

more work. This principle that "Scripture interprets Scripture" must be applied with any passage you study. (Quote from Westminster Confession on p. 83.)

2. *The human component* (pp. 83-86). Although the Bible ultimately comes from God, it has been given to us through human channels. This means that it is basically written in the same way that other books are (except for errors) and we should use the same fundamental principles in interpreting the Bible that we would use to understand the meaning of other books—principles like grammar, context, genre, author's style, audience, and so on.

3. *Responding to the Word* (pp. 86-87). The Bible is given by God in order to provoke a personal response in us. So if we don't respond with a willingness to believe and obey what it says, we will inevitably misunderstand and misinterpret the Bible (Jn 5:39-44; 7:17).

4. *The internal witness of the Spirit* (pp. 87-88). Not only was the Holy Spirit active in the writing of the biblical books, but he is also active in conveying the truth of the Bible to the minds of those who read it. Only with the illuminating work of the Holy Spirit can we truly understand it (1 Cor 2:12-14).

QUESTIONS FOR STUDY AND DISCUSSION

1. How do these passages indicate that the words of the Bible come from God himself: 2 Timothy 3:16, Galatians 3:8, 2 Peter 1:21, and 1 Thessalonians 2:13?

2. Can you think of some things about Christ's life that were predicted in the Old Testament? Do you know where those prophecies are? (References and quote from R. A. Torrey on p. 47.)

3. How do these verses teach the specific truth that the Bible is without error, even down to its smallest parts: Psalm 19:7-9; 119:128, 137-44, 151, 160; Proverbs 30:5; Matthew 4:4; 5:17-20; John 10:34-36; Galatians 3:16; and 2 Timothy 3:16?

4. What are some of the problems with the "modernist" or "higher critical" approach to the Bible? (pp. 75-79)

5. According to Boice, what are the four main issues for determining the meaning of God and the human author in a particular passage? (pp. 83-86)

6. Does the fact that the Spirit grants us understanding of Scripture mean that we should not work hard at our study? In other words, is it right to just pray

and expect the meaning of a passage to "hit us" all of a sudden without much study? (See Phil 2:12-13; Col 1:29.)

RECOMMENDED RESOURCES FOR FURTHER STUDY

B. B. Warfield, *The Inspiration and Authority of the Bible*

Dan McCartney and Charles Clayton, *Let the Reader Understand*

Donald Bloesch, *Holy Scripture*

Gleason Archer, *Encyclopedia of Bible Difficulties*

John MacArthur, *Is the Bible Reliable?* Sermon Series

Norman Geisler, editor, *Inerrancy*

Peter Jensen, *The Revelation of God*

R. C. Sproul, *Knowing Scripture*

QUESTIONS FOR PERSONAL DISCIPLESHIP

1. How would you answer an unbeliever who asks why you believe the Bible is the Word of God? What would you encourage that person to do to find out for him- or herself?

2. It has been said that all sins are a result of not really believing what God says in his Word. Do you find that to be true in your life? Give some examples.

3. How would you respond to someone who says the Bible is full of contradictions?

4. Are you willing to put into practice whatever command or principle you see in Scripture? Why or why not?

PART III
The Attributes of God

SUMMARY

A proper knowledge of God's character and attributes is essential to an understanding of all truth, because *what he is* determines *what he does* in the world. We must also understand who God is to understand ourselves, because he has created us in his image.

KEY CONCEPTS

The self-existence of God (pp. 91-93). The words of God to Moses in Exodus 3:13-14 ("I AM WHO I AM") indicate that God has no origins. No one created God. He exists because he exists, and he is not dependent on anyone or anything for his existence (Matthew Henry quote, p. 92).

The self-sufficiency of God (pp. 93-95). God has no needs, and therefore he does not depend on anyone or anything in any way. As James Boice says, "Here we run counter to a widespread and popular idea: [that] God cooperates with human beings, each thereby supplying something lacking in the other" (p. 93).

The eternality of God (pp. 95-97). God had no beginning and he will have no end. He always has been and he always will be (Gen 21:33; Ps 90:1-2; Rev 1:8; 4:8; 21:6; 22:13). Our human minds begin to hurt after only moments of dwelling on the concept of God's existence stretching back endlessly through time (and before time)! Our finite minds are simply unable to comprehend the infinite. But it is good to know that God is not like us, and it should produce an awe of him in our hearts.

The triunity of God (pp. 100-108). The mysterious characteristic of God that is most often marveled at, questioned, or denied outright is the fact that he is both one and three, or three persons in one unified Godhead. The term *Trinity* that is used to describe God is not found in the Bible, but the doctrine it represents clearly is. Numerous passages in Scripture say that there is only one God, and numerous other passages indicate that there are three distinct persons who are God: the Father, the Son, and the Holy Spirit. These three are each said to be God, and yet they interact with one another throughout Scripture, which indicates that they cannot just be different manifestations of the same person. So God is one, and God is three. Three in one. This is not contradictory, but it is incomprehensible to our human minds. And again, God reveals this truth about himself so that we will be humbled and marvel at his greatness, because he is so far above us.

The sovereignty of God (chapter 11). God controls all things; nothing happens without his permission and purposes. There are numerous passages that proclaim his sovereignty over all in a general way: (1 Chron 29:11-12; Ps 47:7; Is 46:10; Eph 1:11; 1 Tim 6:15), and there are also numerous passages that speak of God's sovereignty over specific parts of his creation.

The clear biblical affirmations and examples of God's total control of the universe raise numerous questions in our minds. The most prevalent ones relate to human choices and human responsibility to obey God. The Bible clearly teaches that men and women make choices contrary to the revealed commands of God and will be held accountable for those choices. But as Boice says,

> This observation cannot overthrow the teaching of the Bible concerning God's rule over his creation, unless the Bible is allowed to be self-contradictory. The explanation of the seeming contradiction is that human rebellion, while it is in opposition to God's express command, falls within his eternal or hidden purpose. That is, God permits sin for his own reasons, knowing in advance that he will bring sin to judgment in the day of his wrath, and that in the meantime it will not go beyond the bounds that he has fixed for it. (p. 111)

The holiness of God (chapter 12). The Bible uses the word *holy* more than any other adjective when it is describing God. God is so holy, in fact, that sometimes the Scriptures are not content with just one use of the word in referring to him (Is 6:3; Rev 4:8). This attribute of God is often misunderstood, however, as having primary reference to the *sinlessness* or *perfection* of God. He certainly is sinless and perfect, and those are truths that correspond to his holiness, but the primary meaning of holiness is "to be set apart" or "to be different." So when we refer to God as "holy" (Gk *hagios*), we mean that he is so set apart from his creation that "there is no one like the LORD our God" (Ex 8:10).

The omniscience of God (chapter 13). This attribute of God means that he is all-knowing. God has never learned anything from anyone else and cannot learn, for he already knows and has always known everything. God's omniscience should be a cause of great fear to those who don't believe, because it means that everything we seek to hide from other people is clearly known to God. And because God is sovereign and holy, as we have studied, we know that he will judge all the sinful thoughts, desires, and actions he sees in all of us. We cannot hide from his knowledge and therefore we cannot escape his judgment. The wonderful thing about being a Christian, however, is that we can be aware of the fact that God knows all our sins, but still have confidence before him that he loves us and will not judge us for all the sin he sees. This is because of the sacrifice of Jesus Christ, through which he paid the penalty for our sins and clothed us in his perfect righteousness.

The unchangeableness of God (chapter 14). This attribute of God has historically been called his "immutability." It simply means that unlike his fickle creatures, he never changes. Malachi 3:6 and James 1:17 are two of the many verses that teach us about this characteristic of God. This unchangeableness applies to his essential being (for example, he will always exist in a Trinity), to all of his attributes (he will always be sovereign, holy, omniscient, and so on), and to his purposes and plans (Ps 33:11; Prov 19:21; Is 14:24; 46:9-10).

QUESTIONS FOR STUDY AND DISCUSSION

1. What are some implications to the self-existence and self-sufficiency of God? (See pp. 91-95.)

2. Why is it important for you to know that God is eternal? (pp. 95-97)

3. Some attempts have been made to find an analogy to the Trinity in human experience. Have you heard any? How are they helpful, and how are they not? (See pp. 100-104.)

4. What aspect of human experience does each of these passages teach us that God is sovereign: Genesis 50:20; Job 1:12; 2:6; Psalm 139:13-15, 16; Proverbs 16:9; Matthew 5:45; Romans 9:15-18; 13:4-5; and 2 Corinthians 12:7-9?

5. Read Isaiah 6:1-8 and Revelation 1:17-19. What were the effects on Isaiah and John when they encountered the holiness of God? How should our lives change because of this attribute of God?

6. In the following passages, notice the examples of how far God's knowledge extends. What do these verses say that he knows: Job 38:1-7; Psalm 139:1-4; Isaiah 40:13-14?

7. How should it affect our lives to know that God never changes? (See pp. 132-34.)

RECOMMENDED RESOURCES FOR FURTHER STUDY

A. W. Pink, *The Attributes of God*
Clark Pinnock et al., *The Openness of God*
Donald Bloesch, *God the Almighty*
Gerald Bray, *The Doctrine of God*
James Beilby and Paul Eddy, eds., *Divine Foreknowledge: Four Views*
Jerry Bridges, *Trusting God*

R. C. Sproul, *The Holiness of God*

Stephen Charnock, *The Existence and Attributes of God*

QUESTIONS FOR PERSONAL DISCIPLESHIP

1. Are you willing to accept whatever God says about himself, even if it is hard for you to understand or accept? What are some truths about God that are challenging for you, and how do you plan to learn more about them?

2. When you pray, do you take time to praise God for his attributes, or do you tend to rush right into your requests? How can you include more praise in your prayer times?

3. Is there any event or circumstance that has happened in your life that you have not recognized God's sovereignty over, and thanked him for the good he will bring out of it (Rom 8:28)? How have you seen him bring good out of trials?

4. Do you tend to feel afraid when you consider the holiness, omniscience, and unchangeableness of God, or are you assured of his love in Christ? Is there some sense in which we should still fear God, even after we are saved?

PART IV
God's Creation

SUMMARY

This lesson is about what God has made and how he governs and sustains it. It discusses three aspects of God's creation—humanity, nature, and the spirit world—and then the "providence" of God that he exercises over all his creation.

KEY CONCEPTS

Humanity (chapter 15). Human beings are the most important part of God's creation. Genesis 1:26-27 indicates that we are different from the rest of what God made, because we were given dominion over it and we were created "in the image of God." That image was marred and perverted as a result of our fall into sin (Gen 3; Eph 2:1-3), but by God's grace it is being restored by sanctification in this life, and by glorification in the next (Rom 8:29; 2 Cor 3:18; 1 Jn 3:2-3; Rev. 21:1-5; and 22:1-5).

Nature (chapter 16). We need to understand that God has created all of nature, not only humanity, because as Psalm 19:1 says, "The heavens declare the glory of God, and the sky above proclaims his handiwork." The fact of God's existence and his divine attributes are revealed by his handiwork in nature (Rom 1:20), so it is important to know what the Bible says about the rest of his creation as well.

The spirit world (chapter 17). Sometime at or before the creation of our universe, God also made a huge number of spirit beings called "angels." Some are good and others are evil.

1. *The elect angels* (pp. 164-67). That name for the good angels comes from 1 Timothy 5:21, where they are called "elect" in contrast to other similar spirit beings who have fallen into sin (more later about them). These good angels are mentioned over one hundred times in the Old Testament and over 150 times in the New Testament. So God obviously wants us to know about their nature and ministries.

2. *The fallen angels* (pp. 67-69). God's Word says that there are many other spirit beings in the universe who, unlike the holy angels, are opposed to God and his people. Their leader's name is Satan, and we learn about all the fallen angels by the many things the Bible says about him. As Boice writes,

   Although Christians must never ignore or underestimate Satan and his stratagems, neither must they overestimate him. Above all, they must never concentrate on Satan to the point of taking their eyes away from God. God is our strength and our tower. He limits Satan. God will never permit Christians to be tempted above what we are able to bear, and he will always provide the way of escape that we may be able to bear it (1 Cor 10:13). As for Satan, his end is the lake of fire (Mt 25:41) (p. 172).

God didn't reveal all this about angels merely to fascinate us like science fiction or fantasy—it has deep relevance for our lives. Knowing that there is an unseen world helps us to recognize that there is more to this universe than our own needs, desires, and feelings—there is a bigger picture that we need to focus on. We will look forward more to the glories of heaven that await us when we realize that God has created so many wonderful things that we cannot see now. And

God's authority over the angels reminds us that his glory is the ultimate purpose for the existence of all his creatures, including us.

The providence of God (chapter 18). Boice says, "Providence means that God has not abandoned the world that he created, but rather works within that creation to manage all things according to the 'immutable counsel of his own will'" (p. 173). Another way of defining providence is "God's sovereignty exercised for the good of his people," and it is often discussed in relation to God bringing good out of evil. As Romans 8:28 says, "We know that for those who love God all things work together for good, for those who are called according to his purpose." The "all things" in that verse includes the evil done by Satan, other people, and even by ourselves.

QUESTIONS FOR STUDY AND DISCUSSION

1. What responsibilities do human beings have because we have been created "in the image of God"? (See pp. 150-53, main points in italics.)

2. How do you think the truth of God's creation of nature should affect our lives? (See pp. 161-62.)

3. What do each of these passages reveal about the nature of angels: Luke 2:8-14; Jude 9; Revelation 5:11-12? (See p. 164.)

4. What are some ministries of the angels, according to Scripture? (See pp. 165-67.)

5. What are some common misconceptions about Satan? (See pp. 167-69.)

6. In contrast to those wrong ideas about the devil, what does the Scripture actually teach about him? (See pp. 169-72.)

7. Can you think of some examples from Scripture of how God used the evil intents and actions of people for the good of those who love him? (See pp. 177-80.)

RECOMMENDED RESOURCES FOR FURTHER STUDY

Francis Schaeffer, *Genesis in Space and Time*

John Calvin, *Institutes of the Christian Religion*, book 1, chapters 14–16

John MacArthur, *Standing Strong: How to Resist the Enemy of Your Soul*

John Walton, *The Lost World of Genesis One*

Paul Helm, *The Providence of God*

R. C. Sproul, *The Invisible Hand: Do All Things Really Work for Good?*
Roger Ellsworth, *What the Bible Teaches About Angels*

QUESTIONS FOR PERSONAL DISCIPLESHIP

1. How would you respond to a non-Christian who asked you about evolution?

2. Have you been thanking God for his creation in nature and delighting in it? If not, how could you start?

3. Hebrews 13:2 says that strangers that we meet can sometimes be angels of God. In light of that, think back over the last few strangers that you talked to and think about how you treated them.

4. What are some of the "schemes" or "tricks" that Satan uses in your life to tempt you to sin? How do you fight them?

5. Why is worrying a sin and how can God's providence help you with it?

PART I
The Fall of the Race

SUMMARY

In the last lesson, we learned some important things about ourselves when we learned about how God created us. But the story of humanity doesn't end there, and so to understand ourselves and our God rightly, we have to know what happened to us at the tragic event known as the fall of humanity. In a sense, the theme of the whole Bible rests on an understanding of the fall, because the salvation that is revealed on all its pages is necessary because of this event, and a misunderstanding of the fall will inevitably lead to a misunderstanding of other doctrines as well. So in this lesson we'll review what happened at the fall, its results, and how it has been understood and taught throughout church history.

KEY CONCEPTS

What happened at the fall? (chapter 1). God said that everything he made was "good." But not long after humans had been created by God, Satan came to the garden in the form of a serpent and tempted Eve (Gen 3:1-5). In response to the temptation of Satan, Adam and Eve committed the first (and worst) sin in the history of humanity (Gen 3:6). It was also the prototypical sin, in that all disobedience to God takes the same essential form and has the same character-istics. The nature of this first sin tells us a lot about the nature of all sin.

Boice mentions these characteristics on pages 189-94: (1) a lack of faith and trust in God's Word—Adam and Eve followed Satan's suggestion and did not believe that God would do what he said he was going to do; (2) a rebellious selfishness, in which their desire for the fruit was more important to them than God's will for their lives; and (3) a pride and arrogance in thinking that they knew better than God about what was good for them! At least one of these three sins of the heart—unbelief, selfishness, and pride—lies at the root of most, if not all, disobedience to God.

What were the results of the fall? (chapter 2). According to the Bible, Adam and Eve's sin affected all of their descendants, including you and me. They became sinful people, and we are sinful people because we come from them. They came under the judgment of God for their disobedience, and we enter this world under the judgment of God because they were our representatives. So the results of the fall are very bad, to say the least, and some may think this topic is too negative or depressing to study. But Boice explains well why we need to understand the terrible condition of humanity: "When we are sick physically and know that we are sick, we seek out a doctor and follow his or her prescription for a cure. But if we did not know we were sick, we would not seek help and might well perish from the illness. It is the same spiritually. If we think we are well, we will never accept God's cure; we think we do not need it. Instead, if by God's grace we become aware of our sickness—actually, of something worse than sickness, of spiritual death so far as any meaningful response to God is concerned—then we have a basis for understanding the meaning of Christ's work on our behalf, and can embrace him as Savior and be transformed by him" (p. 195).

What has been taught in church history about the fall of humanity? (chapter 3). Ever since the Scriptures were completed, Christians have debated the issue of the effects of the fall on the human will. Some, like Pelagius, Erasmus, and Arminius, taught that everyone still has "free will," meaning the ability to turn to Christ and be saved without God changing our nature first. (In that understanding faith logically precedes regeneration—we must believe of our own free will before we can be born again.) Others, like Augustine, Luther, Calvin, and Jonathan Edwards, taught that being "dead in the trespasses and sins" (Eph 2:1) means that the human will is bound in the sense that we are not able to believe unless God first changes our nature by the Holy Spirit, and grants us faith as a gift of his sovereign grace (Jn 3:3; 6:44, 65; Eph 2:8-9). The latter is commonly called the "Reformed" view, and it is the one Boice advocates in chapter three.

QUESTIONS FOR STUDY AND DISCUSSION

1. In Genesis 3:1-5, what are some things you notice about Satan's approach in tempting the woman?

2. Think further about the sin of Adam and Eve and describe it in more depth. What were the characteristics of their choice to eat of the tree that made it so wrong and so offensive to God? (pp. 191-94)

3. How does spiritual death reveal itself in our human experience? In other words, name some aspects of our nature and our lives that have been adversely affected by the fall. (pp. 197-200)

4. Can you think of any answers to the question of fairness that arises because of the imputation of one man's sin to the rest of the human race (Rom 5:12)? In other words, is God "unfair" in allowing us to be born sinners because of Adam's fall? (See pp. 201-4.)

5. How might an understanding of "the bondage of the will" affect our lives practically? (pp. 208-13)

RECOMMENDED RESOURCES FOR FURTHER STUDY

Charles Sherlock, *The Doctrine of Humanity*
Francis Turretin, *Institutes of Elenctic Theology*, vol. 1, pp. 604-85
Henri Blocher, *Original Sin*
John Calvin, *Institutes of the Christian Religion*, book 2, chapters 1–5
Jonathan Edwards, *Freedom of the Will*
John Walton, *The Lost World of Adam and Eve*
Martin Luther, *The Bondage of the Will*

QUESTIONS FOR PERSONAL DISCIPLESHIP

1. God had given Adam and Eve a perfect environment, yet they still chose to disobey the one restriction he had placed on them. Do you see this same dynamic occurring in your life? Have you sinned against God by grasping at something forbidden when there is so much good he has given you to enjoy?

2. Discuss those sins and others you struggle with, and consider how that sin reflects unbelief, selfishness, or pride in your heart. How can you pray better about those sins when you realize the heart problems causing them?

3. You are "in Adam" because you were born into the human race, so you deserve to be judged by God in hell. But are you "in Christ" through faith, headed to heaven instead? Do you trust in his righteousness to save and forgive you, and do you love him for his kindness to you? If so, are there people you know who are still "in Adam," and how could you share the good news about Christ with them?

PART II

Law and Grace

SUMMARY

In this lesson the term *law* is referring to God's expression of his character to humanity, particularly in the commandments he lays down as the divine standard for our thought and action. In other words, the law is all that God requires of us in his written revelation. This lesson discusses the various purposes of it, the summary of it in the Ten Commandments, the consequence of breaking it, and its relation to contrasting yet complementary principle of God's grace, especially in the salvation of Old Testament believers.

KEY CONCEPTS

The purposes of God's law (chapter 4).

1. *The law restrains evil* (pp. 219-20). The commands of God, whether merely written on the conscience or woven into the civil laws of a society, keep people from carrying out their sinful desires to the fullest extent. This happens even in pagan societies, according to Romans 2:14-15.

2. *The law reveals sin* (pp. 220-22). Romans 3:19-20 says that we cannot be saved by the law, and it goes even further and says that God actually gave us the law so that we would understand how bad we are and that we cannot save ourselves. "For through the law comes the knowledge of sin." Paul says the same thing in his own personal testimony in Romans 7:7-13.

3. *The law points us to Christ* (pp. 222-23). God did not give his law merely to condemn us, but in the lives of his people, he uses it to show us our need for a Redeemer who obeyed the law perfectly on our behalf and paid the penalty we owe for our disobedience. That Redeemer is Jesus Christ, who "redeemed us from the curse of the law by becoming a curse for us" (Gal 3:13).

The Ten Commandments—a summary of the law of God (chapters 5–6). The Ten Commandments do not contain the entire law of God, nor are they necessarily any more important in God's eyes than the rest of his commands, but they are helpful to study for the purpose of instructing and illustrating the nature of God's law. Here are some important principles that should govern our

interpretation of them: (1) the commandments are not restricted to outward actions but apply also to the dispositions of the mind and heart; (2) the commandments always contain more than a minimum interpretation of the words; and (3) a commandment expressed in positive language also involves the negative, and a negative commandment also involves the positive.

1. *The first four commandments—love of God (chapter 5).* In Exodus 20:1-9 we find these commandments: (1) "You shall have no other gods before me"; (2) "You shall not make for yourself a carved image. . . . You shall not bow down to them or serve them"; (3) "You shall not take the name of the LORD your God in vain"; and (4) "Remember the Sabbath day, to keep it holy. Six days you shall labor."

2. *The last six commandments—love of others (chapter 6).* Exodus 20:12-17 adds these: (5) "Honor your father and your mother"; (6) "You shall not murder"; (7) "You shall not commit adultery"; (8) "You shall not steal"; (9) "You shall not bear false witness against your neighbor"; and (10) "You shall not covet."

The law of God, part of which is expressed in the Ten Commandments, shows us all to be unholy sinners before a holy God. This is bad news because of the anger that God has against sin, which demands that sin and the sinner be punished. The good news, however, is that God in his grace has chosen to pour his wrath out on Jesus Christ, who died in the place of all those who will believe in him. Romans 6:23 summarizes both: "For the wages of sin is death, but the free gift of God is eternal life in Christ Jesus our Lord."

The wrath of God—the result of disobedience to the law (chapter 7). God's holy and just anger at sin is taught in both the Old Testament (Ex 22:22-24; Ps 2:5-9) and in the New Testament (Jn 3:36; Rom 1:18; 2:5; 9:22). Many Christians today—even many preachers—don't like to talk about the wrath of God, but God wants us to know about it so we can fully understand our need for salvation and be truly grateful for his redemption. The solution to God's wrath is that it was satisfied by the atoning sacrifice of Jesus Christ for everyone who believes in him.

Salvation in the Old Testament (chapter 8). How were people saved in the Old Testament times? The basic answer is that they were saved *in the same way* that we are saved today, though they possessed less information about the Savior. As Boice says, "The person who lived before Christ's time was saved by grace through faith in a Redeemer who was to come, just as today a person is saved by grace through faith in the Redeemer who has already come" (p. 255). "By *grace* . . . through *faith*," as Ephesians 2:8 says, is the way that all God's people in all times have been saved.

1. *The electing grace of God in the Old Testament* (pp. 256-58). Being saved by grace means that salvation is an unmerited gift bestowed on the undeserving, not as a result of anything they have done, but only because of the love and mercy of God. Romans 9:1-12 makes clear that those who were saved before Christ came were saved on that same basis. In the Old Testament, as in the New, God had to choose to give his mercy to people for them to be saved. Because of the spiritual death that fell on humanity when Adam sinned (Rom 5:12), none of us would reach out to God if he did not first reach out to us (see pp. 255-63).

2. *The faith of God's people in the Old Testament* (pp. 259-63). Romans 3:21-26 says that Abraham and David were saved by *faith*. This saving faith was that antithesis, or opposite, of "works," so it obviously included an understanding that nothing we can do can cause us to be right with God. It is a trust in what Christ has done for us on the cross and an abandonment of all efforts of our own to be right with God. It is relying on God and God alone to declare us righteous, even while we remain ungodly in so many of our thoughts, words, and actions. It is a gratefulness to God for his merciful forgiveness that motivates us to want to obey him with our lives (Jas 2:20; 1 Jn 2:3).

QUESTIONS FOR STUDY AND DISCUSSION

1. Why is it that none of us can be "justified" or declared righteous before God by obeying the law? (See pp. 219-22.)

2. According to Galatians 3:22-24, how does God use the law to bring us salvation?

3. In Matthew 5:21-32, what are the attitudes and actions that Jesus says are violations of the sixth and seventh commandments ("You shall not murder," "You shall not commit adultery")?

4. How would you answer someone who says that the Old Testament God was a God of wrath, but Jesus is not?

5. According to Romans 9:1-12, what would the apostle Paul say about the idea that the Jews were saved because they were born Jewish, or because of something they did, such as keeping the law and offering sacrifices?

RECOMMENDED RESOURCES FOR FURTHER STUDY

Greg Bahsen, Walter Kaiser, et al., *Five Views on Law and Gospel*

Jonathan Edwards, *Sinners in the Hands of an Angry God*

John Calvin, *Institutes of the Christian Religion*, book 2, chapters 8–9

Martin Luther, *Commentary on the Epistle to the Galatians*

Phillip Graham Ryken, *Written in Stone: The Ten Commandments and Today's Moral Crisis*

QUESTIONS FOR PERSONAL DISCIPLESHIP

1. What would you say to someone who claims to be headed for heaven because they keep the Ten Commandments? How could you use the story in Matthew 19:16-22 to show them the truth about the law?

2. Examine yourself in light of each of the first four commandments. In what ways do you fall short of God's standard in these areas, and how can you improve?

3. Examine yourself in the light of each of the last six commandments. In what ways do you fall short of God's standard in these areas, and how can you improve?

4. Is the wrath of God hanging over you now, waiting to be poured out on you in all its fury at the judgment day? Why or why not?

PART III
The Person of Christ

SUMMARY

John 17:3 says that to have eternal life is to know Jesus Christ (cf. Mt 7:23), so we must know who Jesus truly is in order to have eternal life. If we think that we are worshiping Jesus, but we have a wrong conception of who he is, then we are really worshiping a false Jesus, and do not have true biblical faith. First, we need to know and believe that Jesus is God. He could not be our Savior from sin if he was not God, because only a divine being could bear the penalty of sin for so many people. Second, it is also essential to recognize his humanity as well. Jesus was not only God, but he became man also when he entered the world, and he remains both God and man today and forever. As Boice says, "The Bible is never hesitant to put the twin truths of the full deity and the true humanity of Christ together," and it does so in verses like Isaiah 9:6; Romans 1:3-4; and Galatians 4:4-5. Finally, it is important to understand that the primary reason for the incarnation (Christ becoming a man) was so that he could live and die as the representative for God's people.

KEY CONCEPTS

The deity of Jesus Christ (chapter 9). The divinity of Christ is one of the clearest truths in all of Scripture. The apostles obviously believed Jesus was God, because their New Testament epistles are filled with references to that truth. For example, Paul says that Christ existed before the beginning of the world "in the form of God" (Phil 2:5-11), John says that Jesus "was God" from the beginning (Jn 1:1-3), and the writer of Hebrews says he is the "exact imprint" of God's nature (Heb 1:3). The apostles were so utterly convinced that Christ was God because there was no other way to explain his miraculous works and flawless character. But they also believed it so strongly because Jesus himself taught that he was God. He told the Jews, "Before Abraham was, I am" (Jn 8:57-58), using the title God had given to Moses at the burning bush when Moses asked him for his name (Ex 3:13-14). And Jesus said, "I and the Father are one" (Jn 10:30). In both cases the Jews realized that he was claiming to be God—that's why they attempted to stone him for blasphemy (Jn 8:59; 10:31-33).

The fact that Jesus claimed to be God makes it impossible that he was "just a good man," like so many people think he was. Good people do not claim to be God—only madmen and deceivers do. So if Jesus was not God, then he was either a madman or a deceiver, and neither of those descriptions fit the facts of the Gospel records or the historical impact of Christ. So we are left with only one conclusion that has any logical validity—Jesus was God. (For more about this, see pp. 267-78.)

The humanity of Christ (chapters 10–11). Jesus became like us in every respect (except for sin), so that we could become like him one day. Recognizing that

Jesus was truly and fully human is a necessary element of biblical faith. As 1 John 4:2-3 says, "Every spirit that confesses that Jesus Christ has come in the flesh is from God, and every spirit that does not confess Jesus is not from God." Besides the clear statements in Scripture about Christ's humanity (Jn 1:14; Phil 2:7; Heb 2:17), we can see it in the narrative descriptions of his life in the Gospels. He experienced *human emotions*, like grieving to the point of tears (Jn 11:35) and anger at the sin and injustice of others (Mk 10:13-14); *human temptations*, like when he battled with the devil in the wilderness (Mt 4:1-11); and *human suffering*, like the emotional agonies of Gethsemane and the physical horrors of flogging and crucifixion. As Hebrews 4:15 says, "For we do not have a high priest who is unable to sympathize with our weaknesses, but one who in every respect has been tempted as we are, yet without sin."

The reason for the incarnation (chapter 11). The term *incarnation* means "becoming flesh" and refers to the eternal Son of God becoming a human being in the person of Jesus Christ (Jn 1:14). A number of Scripture passages indicate that the primary purpose for the coming of Christ was his death on the cross (Mt 1:20-21; Lk 24:13-27, especially Lk 24:26; Jn 12:23-27; Heb 10:4-14). Jesus became a man so he could pay the penalty owed by other human beings as their substitute and representative. The Bible also says that he came to live a perfect life so that he could impute his righteousness to all who believe (Rom 5:19; 1 Cor 1:30) and so that he could provide an example for us (1 Jn 2:6). But the most fundamental reason for the incarnation is this: God's justice requires him to punish the sins of humanity, so the only way he could save his chosen people was to send his Son to become like them, taking their place on the cross and bearing the wrath of God that was due to them. Because this was the primary reason he came into the world, Jesus cried out "It is finished!" at the end of his offering on the cross. (See quote on pp. 289-91.)

QUESTIONS FOR STUDY AND DISCUSSION

1. How do the following passages support the deity of Christ: John 8:19, 57-58; Philippians 2:5-11; Colossians 1:19; 2:9; Hebrews 1:3, 8?

2. What are some emotions that you see Jesus expressing in the Bible? What provoked those feelings in him, and how are those motivations different from the ones behind many of our emotions? (See Mk 6:34; 8:2-3; 10:13-14; Lk 10:21-24; Jn 2:13-17; 11:32-35.)

3. Besides seeing the humanity of Christ depicted in Matthew 4:1-11, what other lessons can we learn from this story about the temptations we face in our lives?

4. Why is it important for you to know that Jesus suffered so much as a man? (See Heb 2:16-18; 1 Pet 2:21-23; 4:12-16.)

5. Why is it important to recognize that the cross was Christ's primary purpose for coming to the earth? (See pp. 293-95.)

RECOMMENDED RESOURCES FOR FURTHER STUDY

B. B. Warfield, *The Person and Work of Christ*
C. S. Lewis, *Mere Christianity*
Donald Bloesch, *Jesus Christ: Savior & Lord*
Donald Macleod, *The Person of Christ*
John Calvin, *Institutes of the Christian Religion*, book 2, chapters 12–15

QUESTIONS FOR PERSONAL DISCIPLESHIP

1. How would you prove the deity of Christ to a member of one of the cults who deny the doctrine? How would you convince that person that they are lost if they do not believe in the deity of Christ?

2. Read John 20:24-30. Describe some times in your life when you have been like Thomas, doubting Christ but then realizing his truth in repentance and faith. Is there any area of your life in which you are presently doubting the Lord?

3. What temptations have you been facing, and how can you respond to them in the way Jesus did? Be specific and practical.

4. When you talk to unbelievers, and even other Christians, about spiritual matters, how often do you bring the cross into those discussions? How can you do that more often?

PART IV
The Work of Christ

SUMMARY

What Jesus did when he was on the earth has often been summarized by the words: prophet, priest, and king. He was our prophet by revealing the Word of God to us—in fact, he himself is called the "the Word" in John 1. His priestly role as a mediator between us and God includes the atoning sacrifice he made for us and the redemption he accomplished because of the greatness of God's love for sinners. His resurrection from the dead proved that he is worthy to be the king of this universe, and he took his rightful place of authority at the right hand of the Father when he ascended to heaven at the end of his earthly ministry.

KEY CONCEPTS

Propitiation: Quenching God's wrath (chapter 13). God's holy and just anger God against sin creates a barrier that must be overcome if we are to have a personal relationship with him. Fortunately he has chosen to pacify his own wrath, and this act is known as "propitiation" (Rom 3:25; 1 Jn 2:2). The sacrificial system of the Old Testament was a foreshadowing of the real and final atonement (substitutionary sacrifice) that Christ would make when he offered himself up for us on the cross (Is 53; Jn 1:29). This doctrine helps us to better understand other scriptural truths and avoid serious and prevalent errors about them. For example, it reminds us that God's nature includes attributes like wrath and justice, as well as love and mercy, and that the gospel is a remedy for our sin, rather than merely a new possibility for achieving joy and fullness in this life.

Redemption: Paid in full (chapter 14). As a result of Christ's sacrificial atonement, the Bible says we have been *redeemed* from our sins (Rom 3:24, Gal 3:13). The basic idea of redemption in the Scriptures is "to be bought out of slavery," as the story of Hosea and his harlot wife illustrates (Hos 1–3). Like the prophet in that passage, God paid the price that we owed because of our unfaithfulness to him, and freed us from the dominion of sin and death. "For the wages of sin is death, but the free gift of God is eternal life in Jesus Christ our Lord" (Rom 6:23). We are no longer slaves to sin with the threat of hell hanging over us, but adopted children of God who should live for the one who redeemed us. As Paul writes,

"You are not your own, for you were bought with a price. So glorify God in your body" (1 Cor 6:19-20; cf. 2 Cor 5:15).

The greatness of God's love (chapter 15). When we understand the harder truths of the wrath of God against our sin and the terrible price of eternal death that we owed because of it, the love of God for us becomes all the more amazing and inspiring (see Eph 2:1-5). In regard to *agapē*, the Greek word most often used for God's love in the New Testament, Boice says, "The biblical writers probably invented, or at least raised to entirely new levels, a brand new word for love—so real was their need for a superlative to express the unique love they had discovered through the biblical revelation" (p. 339). God's love is inexhaustible, eternal, and life changing, and can only be fully experienced by those who are "in Christ" (Rom 8:39; Eph 1:3-6).

The resurrection and ascension of Christ (chapters 16–18). Our Lord's resurrection from the dead proved that he was the Son of God and heir to the throne of David (Rom 1:3-5), and he ascended to sit at the right hand of the Father and rule all the nations as their rightful King (Dan 7:13-14; Mt 28:18-20; Phil 2:9-11). The resurrection is one of the most well-attested events in ancient history (see the proofs in chapter 17), and the ascension is one of the most overlooked, despite its importance in the biblical record (see chapter 18).

QUESTIONS FOR STUDY AND DISCUSSION

1. How would you respond to someone who criticizes the biblical concept of sacrificial atonement by calling it "divine child abuse"? (See pp. 305-8.)

2. If propitiation means God's wrath is satisfied (chapter 13), redemption means the price has been paid (chapter 14), and saving love is sovereign (pp. 342-43), what implications might that have for the debate between about the extent and purpose of the atonement (i.e., whether it was "limited" or "unlimited")?

3. What are some reasons that a belief in the bodily resurrection of Christ is so important, according to 1 Corinthians 15?

4. What are some arguments you would use to convince a skeptic that Jesus rose from the dead? (See chapter 17.)

5. What are some things that Jesus is doing right now at the right hand of God, and how could each of them affect your life practically?

RECOMMENDED RESOURCES FOR FURTHER STUDY

B. B. Warfield, *The Person and Work of Christ*

D. A. Carson, *Scandalous: The Cross and Resurrection of Jesus*

John Calvin, *Institutes of the Christian Religion*, book 2, chapters 15–17

John Murray, *Redemption Accomplished and Applied*

John Stott, *The Cross of Christ*

Robert Lethem, *The Work of Christ*

QUESTIONS FOR PERSONAL DISCIPLESHIP

1. How is Jesus Christ a prophet to you in your daily life? How is he a priest? How is he a king?

2. What are some specific problems you are facing right now, and how can your understanding of the cross help you with each of them?

3. If you have been placed by faith into union with Christ in his death and resurrection, what experiences can you expect in your life now and in the future, by virtue of that union? (See Rom 6:1-13; 8:17-23.)

PART I
The Spirit of God

SUMMARY

The Holy Spirit may be the person of the Trinity who is the most easily and often misunderstood, so it is very important for us to carefully study who he is and what he does. He is indeed a person, not a mere power or "force." And his work in human hearts is all related to the kingdom of Christ coming to the earth, and all flows from his foundational work of bringing us into spiritual union with Christ.

KEY CONCEPTS

Who the Holy Spirit is (chapter 1). According to the Scriptures, the Holy Spirit is a *divine person*, a member of the eternal Trinity along with God the Father and God the Son. He has his own personality distinct from the Father and the Son, as evidenced by his personal actions (Jn 16:8-11), his unique mission (Jn 15:26), his rank and power (Mt 28:19), his appearances in visible form (Lk 3:22), the ability to be personally offended (Eph 4:30), and the gifts he gives to the church (1 Cor 12:11). But he is also is fully God, equal with the Father and the Son. He has divine qualities like omniscience (Jn 16:12-13; 1 Cor 2:10-11), omnipotence (Lk 1:35), and omnipresence (Ps 139:7-10). He also performs works that only God can do, like creation (Job 33:4), regeneration (Jn 3:6), and resurrection (Rom 8:11).

What the Holy Spirit does (chapter 2). In John 15:26, Jesus said, "When the Helper comes, whom I will send to you from the Father, the Spirit of truth, who proceeds from the Father, he will bear witness about me." All the primary works of the Holy Spirit in the Scriptures are in some way related to Jesus Christ. He brings glory to Christ (Jn 16:14), he teaches us about Christ (Jn 16:12-13), he draws people to Christ (Jn 3:3-7), he reproduces Christ's character in us (2 Cor 3:18-19; Gal 5:22-23), and he directs us to serve Christ (Acts 13:2-4).

Our union with Christ (chapter 3). The greatest work of the Holy Spirit is the one from which all the others flow. He places believers into union with Christ by what the Scripture calls "the baptism of the Holy Spirit." As 1 Corinthians 12:13 says, "For in one Spirit we were all baptized into one body." This spiritual union is a mystery, but it is the basis for all the blessings we receive from God, because if we were still "in Adam" or related to him merely in ourselves, we would have no hope of a love relationship with a God who is holy and wrathful against sin. But because we are "in Christ" (a phrase found 164 times in Paul's epistles), we are forgiven, loved, adopted, gifted, and blessed in every other way the Bible promises.

QUESTIONS FOR STUDY AND DISCUSSION

1. What are some differences between the nature of the Holy Spirit and other spiritual concepts like Eastern mysticism or "the force" in Star Wars? (pp. 381-86)

2. How would you answer someone who believes a "modalist" view of the Trinity (taught by the United Pentecostal Church and Apostolic Churches), which says that there is only one person (not three) who appears in different forms at different times in history? (See Mt 3:16-17; 28:19; Jn 14:26; 15:26.)

3. In what ways does the Holy Spirit reveal the truth about Christ to us? (pp. 388-94)

4. Self-control is a fruit of the Spirit (Gal 5:23). How might that relate to some of the experiences (like being "slain in the Spirit") that people claim are caused by the Spirit?

5. How does the analogy of human marriage help us to understand the nature and implications of our union with Christ? (pp. 400-402)

RECOMMENDED RESOURCES FOR FURTHER STUDY

Donald Bloesch, *The Holy Spirit: Works & Gifts*
John Murray, *Redemption Accomplished and Applied*
Sinclair Ferguson, *The Holy Spirit*

QUESTIONS FOR PERSONAL DISCIPLESHIP

1. Have you been thinking of the Holy Spirit as a person who can be grieved or pleased, and who has a personal relationship with you? How might knowing that affect your life?

2. Review the ways that the Holy Spirit works in us, according to chapter 2. Have you seen him work in you in any of those ways?

3. Besides marriage, what are some other illustrations of union with Christ that Boice discusses on pages 402-6? How do they encourage and challenge you in your spiritual life?

PART II
How God Saves Sinners

SUMMARY

The history of our salvation began before the foundation of the world with the Father's sovereign election (Eph 1:3-5), continued with the Son's sacrifice on our behalf (Eph 1:6-8), and is applied to our lives today when the Holy Spirit places us into union with Christ (Eph 1:13-14). When that happens, we are born again spiritually (Jn 3:3-7), granted faith and repentance by his power (Jn 6:65; Acts 11:18), and declared righteous or "justified" in God's sight (Rom 4:3-8). The Holy Spirit continues to work in us for the rest of our lives (Phil 1:6), producing the good works of obedience and service that prove our faith to be genuine (Eph 2:10; Jaas 2:14-26), connecting us with other believers in the spiritual family called the church (Eph 2:19; 1 Tim 3:16), and progressively sanctifying us to make us more like Christ (2 Cor 3:18-19).

KEY CONCEPTS

Regeneration (chapters 4–5). Jesus used the metaphor of new birth to describe what the initial work of God in the process of Christ's redemption being applied in our lives. John 3:3, 5-7 says, "Unless one is born again, he cannot see the kingdom of God. . . . Truly, truly, I say to you, unless one is born of water and the Spirit, he cannot enter the kingdom of God. That which is born of the flesh is flesh, and that which is born of the Spirit is spirit. Do not marvel that I said to you, 'You must be born again.'" This metaphor emphasizes the divine initiative required for any of us to be saved (Jn 6:44, 65), and the radical change that takes place in our hearts and lives when we are (2 Cor 5:17).

The result of regeneration, and our response to the Holy Spirit's work in our hearts, is faith and repentance (Acts 11:18; Eph 2:8-9). We turn away from living in our sins and look to Christ for forgiveness and change (Rom 10:9-10). A biblical understanding of saving faith is so important, because it has often been misrepresented as mere credulity, optimism, or intellectual assent (see pp. 416-18). Rather, true belief is a confident reliance on the promises of God, and particularly those concerning the person and work of Jesus Christ. Abraham, as the "father of all the faithful," is a wonderful illustration of all the necessary elements of saving faith (pp. 422-23).

Justification (chapters 6–8). When we believe in the gospel, God declares us to be righteous in Christ, even though we are still sinful in ourselves (Rom 4:3-8). As many opponents of Christianity have pointed out, nearly every major figure in the biblical narrative (other than Jesus himself) disobeyed God and hurt others in various ways, yet the Lord repeatedly says they were his beloved children and friends. This is because of our eternal relationship to God is never dependent on our performance, but always on what Christ has done on our behalf (Lk 18:9-14; 2 Cor 5:14). This doctrine of "justification by faith alone," in the words of Martin Luther, "is the chief article from which all other doctrines have flowed" (pp. 424-25).

Although good works are not the basis of our justification (Gal 2:16), they are a necessary *evidence* that we have been justified (Jas 2:14-26). True faith is always accompanied by repentance from sin, and justification is always joined by sanctification (a growth in godliness). According to the Scriptures, those who claim to be saved but live the same way they did before are still lost (Mt 7:21-23; 1 Jn 3:6-10). On the other hand, we can experience real assurance of our justification when we see certain evidences in our lives, such as a belief in the basic doctrines of the faith (pp. 443-45), an obedience to God's commands (pp. 445-47), and a love for our brothers and sisters who have also been adopted into his family (pp. 447-49).

Adoption (chapter 9). The metaphor of the new birth not only implies that we receive a new nature from God, but also that we become part of a new family (Rom 8:14-17). This divine adoption brings us into a new relationship with God as our Father, and with other believers as our brothers and sisters (pp. 453-54). It also is the source of tremendous privileges, like free access to throne of God through our prayers (Heb 4:16), and a heavenly inheritance befitting those who are no longer slaves, but now sons and daughters of the Most High God (1 Pet 1:3-4).

Sanctification (chapter 10). Though our justification gives us a totally pure record before God in a legal sense, we still remain in need of growth and change in our practical lives. As Paul said in Philippians 3:12-13, "Not that I have already obtained this or am already perfect, but I press on to make it my own, because Christ Jesus has made me his own." To help us grow and change, God has provided for us *means of grace* like assurance of salvation, knowledge of his promises, Bible study, prayer and worship, fellowship with other believers, service, and the "blessed hope" we have when we look forward to the return of Christ (pp. 459-63).

QUESTIONS FOR STUDY AND DISCUSSION

1. Some commentators believe that Christ's main point in using the "new birth" metaphor in John 3 was that he wanted to emphasize that as with physical birth, we do not choose or cause ourselves to be born of the Spirit. Why do you think that would be important for us to know?

2. Read the famous "Hall of Faith" passage in Hebrews 11. What are some things you notice about the nature of saving faith from the teaching and examples there?

3. What did Paul say about his own justification in Philippians 3:4-8? (See pp. 430-31.)

4. What is the difference between Roman Catholic and Protestant theology concerning the role of works in salvation? (See pp. 432-36.)

5. How can the analogy of a loving earthly, physical family help us to understand how we should relate to one another in the household of God? (See 1 Cor 12; Col 3:12-17.)

6. How and why does our sanctification (growth in Christ) need to be based on the free grace of God, rather than an attempt to earn his love through our good works?

RECOMMENDED RESOURCES FOR FURTHER STUDY

Donald Alexander, ed., *Christian Spirituality: Five Views of Sanctification*
Jerry Bridges, *The Discipline of Grace*

John Calvin, *Institutes of the Christian Religion*, book 3
John MacArthur, *Saved Without a Doubt*
John Murray, *Redemption Accomplished and Applied*
Kelly Kapic, *Sanctification*
Leon Morris, *The Apostolic Preaching of the Cross*
N. T. Wright, *Justification*

QUESTIONS FOR PERSONAL DISCIPLESHIP

1. Do you think you have been born again? Why or why not?

2. Imagine if you died today and stood before God, and he said to you, "Why should I let you into heaven?" What would you say?

3. What are some Scriptures you would share with a person who claimed to be a Christian but was obviously living in unrepentant sin?

4. Which of the means of grace listed on pp. 463-67 do you have the most of in your life, and which do you have the least? How can you "add to your faith" in those areas, like 2 Peter 1:5 says?

PART III
The Life of the Christian

SUMMARY

The glorious, many-faceted salvation that we receive as a gift of God's free grace (see last lesson) should cause us to live for the one who died for us (2 Cor 5:14-15), and love him because he first loved us (1 Jn 4:19). The fundamental commitment we make as Christians was described by Christ himself when he said, "If anyone would come after me, let him deny himself and take up his cross daily and follow me" (Lk 9:23). He also said, "If you abide in my word, you are truly my disciples, and you will know the truth, and the truth will set you free" (Jn 8:31-32). We should seek to know God's will and be directed by the Holy Spirit in all situations and choices we face in our lives (Eph 5:17), and constantly be growing in our personal relationship with him through prayer, Bible study, and Christian service (2 Pet 3:18).

KEY CONCEPTS

The irony of the kingdom (chapters 11–12). Contrary to our natural human perspective, the path to success in life does not lie in self-fulfillment and freedom from all authority. Rather Jesus said that it starts with self-denial (Lk 9:23), and true freedom comes from obedience to the God who made us and knows what is best for us (Jn 8:31-32).

Knowing the will of God (chapter 13). God's sovereign will includes everything that he has planned to occur (Eph 1:11), which we cannot know until after it happens. But our decisions should be made according to his revealed will in the Scriptures (Deut 29:29), and wisdom, which is the God-given ability to apply the truth practically in our lives (Eph 5:15-17). Romans 14 and 1 Corinthians 8 provide a number of principles that we can follow when it comes to "doubtful situations," or issues outside the law of God on which Christians differ.

A relationship with God (chapters 14–15). We have free access to talk to God at any time, if we come in the name of Jesus Christ (based on his righteousness given to us) and by the power of the Holy Spirit (Eph 2:18). And God talks to us through the truth he has revealed in the Bible, as the Holy Spirit illumines us concerning its meaning as if we study it faithfully, and applies it to our lives if we are willing to obey its commands and principles.

Serving God and others (chapter 16). Ephesians 2:10 says, "For we are his workmanship, created in Christ Jesus for good works, which God prepared beforehand, that we should walk in them." God has given gifts to all his people for the purpose of service (1 Cor 12; 1 Pet 4:10-11), and he is especially concerned that we should care for those less fortunate than ourselves (Mt 25:31-46; Jas 1:27).

QUESTIONS FOR STUDY AND DISCUSSION

1. What are some ways that "the truth will set you free," as Jesus said in John 8:32? (See pp. 484-86.)

2. What are some of the principles in Scripture that apply to our decision making, especially in regard to what Boice calls "doubtful situations"? (See pp. 491-94; Rom 14; 1 Cor 8.)

3. Why is it important to ask God for what we desire, like Jesus did when he prayed, "My Father, if it be possible, let this cup pass from me" (Mt 26:39a)? Why is it important to also say, like Jesus did, "Nevertheless, not as I will, but as you will" (Mt 26:39b)?

4. What are some potential errors we should avoid in our study of the Bible? (See pp. 507-12 for some examples.)

5. How do you think the lives of Christians today compare to the description of the early church by Aristides on pages 517-18?

RECOMMENDED RESOURCES FOR FURTHER STUDY

Dave Swavely, *Decisions, Decisions: How and How Not to Make Them*
J. C. Ryle, *Practical Religion*
Jerry Bridges, *The Discipline of Grace*
John Calvin, *Institutes of the Christian Religion*, book 3, chapters 6–8 and 19–20

QUESTIONS FOR PERSONAL DISCIPLESHIP

1. How have you responded personally to Jesus' call to deny yourself, take up your cross daily, and follow him? (See pp. 471-79.)

2. Are your prayers "according to his will" (1 Jn 5:14)? Why or why not?

3. How does your personal Bible study compare to the suggestions Boice makes on pages 507-12?

PART IV

The Work of God

SUMMARY

Our spiritual relationship with God and others is strengthened by an understanding of the biblical doctrines of election and perseverance. To know that God chose us for salvation before the beginning of the world, and that he will permanently preserve our faith, helps us to rely on him more than ourselves and to be more gracious toward others. "Salvation belongs to the Lord!" (Jon 2:9), from beginning to end.

KEY CONCEPTS

Sovereign election (chapter 17). Ephesians 1:4-5 says that God "chose us in him [Christ] before the foundation of the world. . . . In love he predestined us for adoption to himself as sons through Jesus Christ, according to the purpose of his will." Romans 8:29 says, "Those whom he foreknew he also predestined to be conformed to the image of his Son." The foreknowledge mentioned in that verse is not merely "foresight," but a choice made by God to love us as his own special people (Ex 33:17; Amos 3:2; Jn 10:14; 2 Tim 2:19).

The perseverance of the saints (chapter 18). As the Puritan theologian Thomas Watson explained, "The heavenly inheritance is kept for the saints, and they are kept for the inheritance. . . . Though the saints may come to that pass that they have but little faith, yet not to have no faith. Though their grace may be drawn low, yet it is not drawn dry; though grace may be abated, it is not abolished." Perseverance means that once one is in the family of God, he or she is always in that family. It means we have "eternal security," but also that the Holy Spirit will enable us to continue in the faith. As Paul said in Philippians 1:6, "I am sure of this, that he who began a good work in you will bring it to completion at the day of Jesus Christ."

QUESTIONS FOR STUDY AND DISCUSSION

1. How would you answer someone who said that God chooses us on the basis of our faith, so it's ultimately up to us whether we are saved or not?

2. What are some of the benefits of the doctrine of election? (pp. 529-30)

3. Do you think a strong belief in election will make someone less committed to personal holiness, prayer, and evangelism? Why or why not?

4. What are some passages in Scripture that say believers can never lose their salvation (pp. 536-40)? How should we understand others who seem to say the opposite?

5. Boice mentions the "Five Points of Calvinism." What are they, and what do you think about them?

RECOMMENDED RESOURCES FOR FURTHER STUDY

David Basinger and Randall Basinger, eds., *Predestination and Free Will: Four Views*
John Calvin, *Institutes of the Christian Religion*, book 3, chapters 21–24

John Murray, *Redemption Accomplished and Applied*
R. C. Sproul, *Chosen by God*

Questions for Personal Discipleship

1. What questions does the doctrine of election raise in your mind? How could you get some answers to them?

2. Has the doctrine of election produced any benefits in your life, like the ones Boice mentions on pages 529-30?

3. God has given us warnings that are intended to motivate us to continue in the faith (Heb 3:12-14; 10:19-31). Do you take those warnings seriously, and what are you doing to cultivate perseverance in your own life? (See 2 Pet 1:5-11.)

PART I
Time and History

SUMMARY

Human beings have always wanted to know answers to questions like "Who am I?" and "Why am I here?" "According to the Bible, God has dealt with the first through creation of the church, to which a believer in Christ automatically belongs, and with the second by the incorporation of the Christian into the meaningful flow of biblical history" (p. 547). A Christian view of history is understood by the biblical doctrines of creation, providence, revelation, redemption, and final judgment (pp. 559-67). The ultimate purpose for everything that happens in this universe is the glory of God through the exaltation of Jesus Christ, which is illustrated by the fact that even our dating system begins with and centers on his coming to the earth.

KEY CONCEPTS

Identity and purpose (chapter 1). Unlike what many modern people think, our lives are not all about us and what we want. Such a narcissistic approach to life leads to manipulation of others and disillusionment with ourselves. But God's plan for us is to find fulfillment through fellowshipping and serving others in the body of Christ, and through playing an important role in the building of Christ's kingdom on the earth.

A Christian view of history (chapters 2–3). The biblical doctrine of *creation* tells us that we are here for a purpose; *providence* tells us that God is working everything together for that purpose; *revelation* is how we know what the purpose is; *redemption* is how we are able to participate in it; and the *final judgment* is when it will all become clear to us. Every era and event in human history is ultimately all about Jesus Christ, because the universe has been created, sustained, and governed so that he as the God-man would end up receiving all glory and praise as a result of his incarnation, crucifixion, and resurrection.

QUESTIONS FOR STUDY AND DISCUSSION

1. How does the modern emphasis on self-fulfillment (in the "me" generation) end up hurting us more than helping us? (pp. 545-46)

2. How does the existence of God, and his sovereignty over history, give our lives meaning and purpose that we would not otherwise have? Put another way, if there were no God who had a plan for the universe, what meaning could our lives possibly have?

3. What do these passages say about the purpose for the universe and our lives: Genesis 12:1-3; Isaiah 46:8-13; Matthew 6:10; Romans 8:28-29; 1 Corinthians 15:21-28; Galatians 4:4-5; Ephesians 1:3-11; 3:8-11; and Revelation 4:11?

4. It's been said that history is really HIStory. How would you explain God's plan for the world to an unbeliever?

RECOMMENDED RESOURCES FOR FURTHER STUDY

Gordon Clark, *A Christian View of Men and Things*

Gregory Koukl, *The Story of Reality: How the World Began, How It Ends, and Everything Important That Happens in Between*

John Piper, *Don't Waste Your Life*

Mark Noll, *Turning Points: Decisive Moments in the History of Christianity*

Nancy Pearcey, *Total Truth: Liberating Christianity from Its Cultural Captivity*

Robert Rea, *Why Church History Matters*

QUESTIONS FOR PERSONAL DISCIPLESHIP

1. What are some ways that you can grow in your understanding of history from a Christian perspective?

2. Take some time to review how Jesus Christ has impacted the world, and your own personal life. Praise and thank him for what he has done.

3. Memorize one of the passages mentioned above in question 3.

PART II
The Church of God

SUMMARY

The Greek word for church (*ekklēsia*) refers to those who are "called out" or "assembled" by God as his special possession. We are chosen to reflect the nature of Christ to one another and to the world by our joy, holiness, commitment to truth, compassion for the lost, unity, and love for one another. We worship him "in spirit and truth" (Jn 4:24) and partake together in the sacraments, which are signs and seals of our common salvation in Christ. The church has received spiritual gifts from Christ to enable us to serve others (1 Pet 4:11), and gifted leaders who "equip the saints for the work of the ministry" (Eph 4:12) and "care for the church of God" (Acts 20:28). We fellowship by living out the "one another" commands of the New Testament, and reach out to the world by obeying the Lord's Great Commission in Matthew 28:18-20.

KEY CONCEPTS

What the church is (chapter 4). The New Testament body of Christ is a continuation and expansion of the Old Testament covenant people known as Israel (see the use of *ekklesia* in Ps 22:22, 25 and Acts 7:38). This new covenant people is made up of both Jews and Gentiles, and is spread throughout the whole world (Mt 28:19-20; Jn 12:32). Jesus Christ is the cornerstone on which the church is built (Acts 4:11-12; 1 Pet 2:4-6), and the Holy Spirit empowers us to do his work in the world (Acts 1:8; 1 Thess 1:5).

What the church is called to do (chapters 5–8). According to the Scriptures, the church should reflect the character and will of God by being a joyous people (Phil 4:4), a separated people (Heb 12:14), a truth-rooted people (Jn 17:17), a missionary people (Jn 17:18-19), a unified people (Jn 17:20-23), and a loving people (Jn 17:26). We should regularly worship God together in spirit and in truth (Jn 4:24; Heb 10:24-25), and those gatherings should include the practice of the sacraments of baptism and the Lord's Supper (Mt 28:19; 1 Cor 11:23-28). And as we relate to one another, every member of the church should use the spiritual gifts they have received from God to encourage and strengthen one another (1 Cor 12).

How the church should be led (chapters 9–10). Ephesians 4:11-12 says that God has given leaders to the church "to equip the saints for the work of ministry, for building up the body of Christ." The two offices of church leadership in the New Testament are elders and deacons. Generally speaking, elders are to provide spiritual oversight for the congregation (Acts 20:28), and deacons are to make sure that the physical needs of the church are met (Acts 6:1-6). The leaders must be qualified according to the lists of requirements in 1 Timothy 3:2-13 and Titus 1:6-9.

How the church can change the world (chapters 11–12). Jesus said, "By this all people will know that you are my disciples, if you have love for one another" (Jn 13:35). So in order to be effective in its mission, the church must first have a biblical "body life" that fulfills the many "one another" commands of the New Testament. These include not only loving one another (Jn 15:12, 17), but also serving one another (Jn 13:15), bearing one another's burdens (Gal 6:2), forgiving one another (Eph 4:31-32), confessing our sins to one another (Jas 5:16), instructing one another (Rom 15:14), and comforting one another (1 Thess 4:18). Then when the body is functioning the way it has been designed by God, we can become his hands and feet in reaching out to a needy world with the gospel of Jesus Christ (Mt 28:19-20; Acts 1:8).

QUESTIONS FOR STUDY AND DISCUSSION

1. Why do you think it is important to know that the word *church* in the Bible does not refer to a building, but to *a group of people* who worship and serve the Lord together?

2. Evaluate your church based on the marks in chapter 5. What are its strengths and weaknesses?

3. What does it mean to worship God "in spirit and truth"? (pp. 607-10)

4. Why are baptism and the Lord's Supper important for believers today? How can you use them to draw unbelievers to Christ?

5. How would you advise someone who wanted to know what his or her spiritual gifts are? (pp. 624-39)

6. Based on the discussions of biblical church leadership in chapters 9–10, how would you assess the state of most churches today?

7. What are some motivations that will help Christians to live out the Great Commission?

RECOMMENDED RESOURCES FOR FURTHER STUDY

David Wright, ed., *Baptism: Three Views*

Donald Bloesch, *The Church*

Edmund Clowney, *The Church*

Gordon Smith, ed., *The Lord's Supper: Five Views*

J. I. Packer, *Evangelism and the Sovereignty of God*

John Calvin, *Institutes of the Christian Religion*, book 4

Leonard Vander Zee, *Christ, Baptism and the Lord's Supper*

Ray Stedman, *Body Life*

Simon Chan, *Liturgical Theology*

Veli-Matti Kärkkäinen, *An Introduction to Ecclesiology*

Wayne Mack and Dave Swavely, *Life in the Father's House: A Member's Guide to the Local Church*

QUESTIONS FOR PERSONAL DISCIPLESHIP

1. How can you help your church to be more like the descriptions of a good one in chapter 5?

2. Do you desire to be a leader in the church (see 1 Tim 3:1)? How does your life compare to the qualifications listed in 1 Timothy 3 and Titus 1?

3. What are your spiritual gifts and how are you using them to fulfill the "one anothers" of the New Testament? How could you do better?

4. How are you using them to fulfill the Great Commission, and how could you do better?

PART III

A Tale of Two Cities

SUMMARY

The fifth century theologian Augustine wrote a book in which he referred to the church as the "city of God" and the godless world system as the "city of man." These two cities have been in conflict since the fall of humanity in the garden (Gen 3:15), are often illustrated in Scripture by the earthly cities of Jerusalem and Babylon, and can be seen today in the distinction between the "secular" and the "sacred." There is a "secular church" today (often called the "liberal church") that has largely replaced God's Word with human wisdom, and similar trends have also made inroads into the evangelical churches. In regard to human government, the Bible recognizes its authority but challenges us to remember that it must be subordinated to God's sovereign rule.

KEY CONCEPTS

The world and the church (chapters 13–15). When the Bible uses the term *world*, it is often referring to the realms of human experience and endeavor in which God's presence and authority are not recognized (Jn 17:14; 1 Jn 2:15-17). Unfortunately, many of the churches and schools that are called "Christian" today are a part of the world in that sense, because they reflect the theology, agenda, and methods of the world more than what the Scripture teaches. They constitute what Boice calls the "secular church," "having the appearance of godliness, but denying its power" (2 Tim 3:5). The true church, which Boice refers to as the "evangelical church," is still the city of God on the earth, but is being threatened by worldly influences like materialism, indifference to important matters, and a decline in our commitment to biblical authority and sound theology.

The church and the state (chapter 16). Jesus said, "Render to Caesar [human government, or 'the state'] the things that are Caesar's, and to God the things that are God's" (Mk 12:17). There are four different approaches that people take to the relationship between the two, as Boice explains: "(1) God alone as an authority with the authority of Caesar denied, (2) Caesar alone as an authority with the authority of God denied, (3) the authority of both God and Caesar, but with Caesar in the dominant position, and (4) the authority of God and Caesar but with God in the dominant position" (p. 711). The fourth is the biblical approach to the relationship (Dan 2:20-21; Rom 13:1-7).

QUESTIONS FOR STUDY AND DISCUSSION

1. How does the story of King Nebuchadnezzar illustrate both the city of God and the city of Man? (pp. 686-88)

2. How does 1 John 2:15-17 describe "the world," and what would be some examples of worldly attitudes and actions?

3. How would you respond to someone who says, "Most Christians today don't believe the Bible is all true"?

4. What are some ways that we can stem the tide of secularism that threatens the church today? (pp. 694-96)

5. Read several commentaries on Romans 13:1-7. How does that passage apply to our relationship with the government today?

RECOMMENDED RESOURCES FOR FURTHER STUDY

Augustine, *The City of God*

Chuck Colson, *God and Government*

David F. Wells, *No Place for Truth* and *God in the Wasteland*

Gary Scott Smith, ed., *God and Politics: Four Views*

James Boice and Benjamin Sasse, eds., *Here We Stand! A Call from Confessing Evangelicals for a Modern Reformation*

J. Gresham Machen, *Christianity and Liberalism*

QUESTIONS FOR PERSONAL DISCIPLESHIP

1. Are you a "wordly Christian"? Why or why not?

2. Do you struggle with any of the kinds of indifference discussed on pages 700-701? If so, how do you think you could change?

3. How do you relate to the government that is in authority over you? Is there any way you can be used by God to improve it?

PART IV
The End of History

SUMMARY

Christians have many different views about the details of eschatology (biblical teaching about the future), but there are some things on which almost all believers agree. Christ will return to the earth in bodily form someday (Acts 1:11; 1 Thess 4:16-17), our physical bodies (like his) will be resurrected (1 Cor 15:12-23; Rev. 20:11-15), and "we must all appear before the judgment seat of Christ"

(2 Cor 5:10; Rev 20:11-15). We also look forward to an eternal home in heaven, or more accurately "a new heaven and a new earth" (Rev 21:1), where we will have the joyous experiences of the presence of Jesus (Rev 5), reunion with our loved ones (1 Thess 4:13-18), permanent deliverance from all sin and pain (Rev 21:4), and rewards for the service we have rendered to Christ (Rev 22:12).

KEY CONCEPTS

The return of Christ (chapter 17). All the outcomes mentioned in the summary above will occur at Jesus' second coming, which is a major emphasis in the New Testament. It is mentioned 318 times in the 260 chapters. Examples include John 14:3, where Jesus says, "If I go and prepare a place for you, I will come again and will take you to myself, that where I am you may be also," and Titus 2:13, where Paul says that we are "waiting for our blessed hope, the appearing of the glory of our great God and Savior Jesus Christ."

The new heavens and earth (chapter 18). "Heaven," as we often call it, is the place where all the prophecies of eternal blessing will be fulfilled. Romans 8:18-23 says,

> For I consider that the sufferings of this present time are not worth comparing with the glory that is to be revealed to us. For the creation waits with eager longing for the revealing of the sons of God. . . . The creation itself will be set free from its bondage to corruption and obtain the freedom of the glory of the children of God. For we know that the whole creation has been groaning together in the paints of childbirth until now. And not only the creation, but we ourselves, who have the firstfruits of the Spirit, groan inwardly as we wait for adoption as sons, the redemption of our bodies.

QUESTIONS FOR STUDY AND DISCUSSION

1. What do these passages say about the judgment that will occur when the Lord returns: Matthew 25:31-46; 1 Corinthians 3:10-15; 2 Thessalonians 1:5-10; and Revelation 20:11-15?

2. What do these passages indicate about what our next life will be like: Luke 16:19-31; 2 Corinthians 5:1-8; Revelation 6:9-11; 21–22?

3. How should looking forward to heaven affect your life practically? (pp. 739-40)

RECOMMENDED RESOURCES FOR FURTHER STUDY

Darrell Bock, ed., *Three Views on the Millennium and Beyond*
Donald Bloesch, *The Last Things*
Erwin Lutzer, *One Minute After You Die*
Randy Alcorn, *Heaven*
Robert Clouse, ed., *The Meaning of the Millennium*
Stanley Grenz, *The Millennial Maze*

QUESTIONS FOR PERSONAL DISCIPLESHIP

1. Would you want Christ to return today? Why or why not?

2. What are some things about heaven that you are most looking forward to?

GENERAL INDEX

1984, 697

Aaron, 98, 222-23, 228-29, 257, 736
  priesthood of, 321
  rebuked by Moses, 252-53
Abel and Cain. *See* Cain and Abel
ability to distinguish spirits, 628, 633
Abraham, 28, 31, 43, 50, 67, 167, 230-31, 255, 287, 301, 347, 426, 428, 484, 533
  anticipated Christ, 261-63, 275
  call of, 95, 105, 140, 227, 258, 524, 550, 583
  children of, 94, 259, 453, 562, 572-73, 583, 683
  death of, 736-37
  faith of, 422-23, 631, 688
  looked for a home, 733-34
  sacrifice of Isaac, 261-62
  salvation of, 256-59, 261, 290
accountability, 731
ACTS acrostic, 500
AD (Anno Domini), 568, 576
Adam, 102, 148, 206-7, 217, 332, 350-51, 398, 411, 436-37, 548, 617
Adam and Eve, 43, 147, 189, 256, 260, 483, 559, 619-20, 681, 729
  clothed by God, 43, 131, 260, 620
  fall of, 42, 161, 170, 188-94, 212, 681
Adams, Jay E., 617
administrators, 628, 634
adoption, 161, 254, 270, 280, 329, 343, 380, 412, 451-54, 460, 525, 569, 624
adoration, 269, 500

adultery, 221, 225, 231, 238-40, 244, 252, 262, 333-34, 428, 474, 518, 533, 761
agenda, the world's, 695
agnosticism, 54-55
alaric, 679
alcoholism, 116, 695
Alexander, Archibald, 444
Alexander the Great, 569-70
alienation, 197-200, 324, 451, 481
aloes, 359
Altizer, Thomas J. J., 689
Anabaptists, 44
Ananias
  and Sapphira, 242-43, 633
  tempted by Satan, 170-72, 385
Anchorites, 711
Anderson, J. N. D., 365
angels, 29, 40, 50, 62, 105, 163-65, 170, 172, 175, 286-87, 344, 356, 362-63, 409, 421, 581, 612, 726, 733-36
  fallen the, 167-69, 203, 421, 680-81
  hierarchy of, 151-52, 164, 271
  ministry of, 165-67
anger, 121, 136, 176-77, 244, 246-50, 318, 320-21, 394, 453, 546, 666, 694, 729, 728, 738
  forbidden, 225, 237-28
  of Jesus Christ, 283-85
Anna, 263
Anselm of Canterbury, 289-92, 400, 611
Antichrist, 167, 282, 388, 444, 724
anticlericalism, 642-43
antinomianism, 436
apologetic
  "built-in," 435

apostasy, 192
apostle, 45, 50, 231, 246, 268, 346, 358, 402, 466, 493, 495, 506, 517, 654-55, 662, 713
  qualifications for, 33-34, 625, 628-32, 636, 640-41, 649-52
Apostles' Creed, 367, 371, 566, 730
appearances
  resurrection, 50, 356-57, 361-63
archaeology, 49-50, 67, 76, 311
Arianism, 280
Aristides, 518
Aristotle, 40, 186-87, 455
Aristotelianism, 557
Arius of Alexandria, 105, 280, 445
Ark of the Covenant, 165, 218, 223, 319, 610
Armageddon, 724-25
Armerding, Hudson, 699
Arminians, 208, 211, 496-97
Arminius, Jacob, 208, 420-21
assurance, 36, 175, 270, 344, 352, 441-43, 463-64, 631, 644, 692, 729-30
  of faith, 418-19, 457, 500
Astruc, Jean, 69-70
Athanasian Creed, 282
Athanasius, 282
atheism, 18, 20, 112, 129-30, 428
atonement, 26, 107, 125, 288-89, 300, 305-6, 319, 322, 349, 380, 396, 532, 567, 586, 610, 619, 703
  initiated by God, 289-95, 575
attributes of God, 89-141
Augustine, 41, 58, 62, 114, 147, 206-8, 282, 337-38, 412, 420-21, 437, 451, 474-76, 532, 679-80, 683

center of worship, 584-88
command to evangelize,
 673-74
compassion of, 515-16
deity of, 26, 104-6, 267-78,
 347-49
egocentric character of his
 teachings, 302
emotions of, 283-85
focal point of history,
 563-66
fulfilled Scripture, 32-33,
 41, 51-52
grief of, 284
humanity of, 279-82
imitators of, 314-15
indignation of, 283-85
intercession of, 307-8
judge, 352-53, 371-73
last Adam, 351
like us in suffering and
 temptation, 285-87
looking to, 478, 494
Lord of history, 576-77
mediator, 259, 263, 294,
 305-9, 369, 404,
 576-77
prophet, priest, and king,
 299-315, 316
real death of, 729-30
resurrection of, 345-53
return of, 33, 466-67,
 659, 724-25, 727
sacrifice of, 82, 306, 349
seated at God's right hand,
 306, 366-67, 369-71,
 478
second coming of, 75, 166,
 467, 668, 728
shepherd, 526-27, 586-87,
 591 629-30
teacher, 5, 628-30, 656
teaching about himself,
 388-91
temptation of, 117, 166,
 168-69, 285-87, 586
union with, 396-406
who he is, 270-71, 288
witness to the Bible, 33-34
work of, 252, 297-373, 388,
 566

Christian life, the, xvii, 133,
 217, 285, 294-92, 392-95,
 403, 454, 459-67, 471-73,
 480, 486, 487-88, 506, 514,
 519, 530, 593, 596, 619,
 703
Christian Science, 728
Christianity
 as a world religion, 370
 contentless, 637
 contribution to a view of
  history, 552-53
 is Christ, 288-89
 personal, 379-86
 union with Christ,
  396-406
Chrysostom, John, 206,
 456
church, and state, 112, 685,
 708-19
"Confessing," the, 702
 diversity in, 599-600, 625,
  725-26
 empowered by the Holy
  Spirit, 588-89
 focal point of history,
  581-82
 founded on Christ, 584-88
 government, 587, 648-60
 marks of the, 308, 592-601,
  624
 Old Testament back-
  ground, 582-84
 one, 586-87
 secular, 689-96, 708
 unity of, 600
 universal, 590-91
cities, the two, 680-83
city of God, 687-88, 689,
 697-707
 invisible, 687
City of God, The, 679-80, 683
Clark, Edward, 365
Clark, Gordon H., 557-58
Claudius, Lysias, 593
Cleopas, 40, 362-63. See
 Emmaus disciples
clergy
 role of, 627, 640-43, 648,
  654
clericalism, 641-43
Collingwood, R. G., xvi, 555

comfort, 110, 613, 668, 671,
 727, 732, 735-36
 God's, 96, 115, 128-31,
  137-38, 312, 502
 of the Holy Spirit, 132, 308,
  383, 589
commitment, 188, 380, 546
 love and, 421-22
 to Jesus Christ, 344,
  480-81, 551-52, 673
communion. See Lord's Supper
communism, 6, 188, 486, 694,
 699
conception, spiritual, 415
condemnation, 132, 201-4, 222,
 238, 293, 372, 402, 427,
 429, 445, 483-86, 658
conduct, 8, 44, 126, 393, 427
 Christian, 446, 713
 faith and, 31, 61, 231, 281
 standard of, 195, 244,
  429-30, 432, 435-36,
  441, 739
confession, 240, 269-70, 425,
 444, 635
 prayer and, 465, 500
 Peter's, 584-85
 Roman Catholic doctrine,
  667-68
 of sin, 140, 499, 663
conformity, 96, 147, 393, 459,
 461, 564, 599-600
conscience, 36-37, 82, 185,
 306, 612, 650, 718-19
 ensnared, 485
 freedom of, 483-84
consensus, 693, 702
conversion, 41, 177, 282, 300,
 430, 517, 519, 524, 635, 673
Council of Trent, 60, 208
Counselor, the, 308-9, 431. See
 also Holy Spirit
covenant, 71, 250
 Abraham and, 550, 573,
  583
 God and the human race,
  161, 193, 674
 new, 404, 618, 620
 Sinai, 233, 691
coveting, 252
Cox, Harvey, 239, 565, 689-91,
 693

SCRIPTURE INDEX

Finding the Textbook You Need

The IVP Academic Textbook Selector
is an online tool for instantly finding the IVP books
suitable for over 250 courses across 24 disciplines.

ivpacademic.com